2457

Fifteen leading economists, political scientists, and professors of law contribute their views to this symposium on the politics and economics of high employment without inflation. They focus attention on some of the conflicts involved and show that the means for the creation of employment and the prevention of inflation are not evolved from strictly economic principles but have many of their roots in values outside that field. In their examination of the basic factors in this major problem, they stress the present controversies, the political and historical settings of the economic role, and the interplay of economic policies with cultural conditions.

Contributors to this extensive analysis of a vital present-day problem are: Ralph S. Brown, Jr., associate professor of law, Yale University; Francis W. Coker, Alfred Cowles Professor of Government, Emeritus, Yale University; Gerhard Colm, chief economist, National Planning Association; Robert A. Dahl, associate professor of political science, Yale University; Thomas I. Emerson, professor of law, Yale University; Everett E. Hagen, industrial economist, Knappen, Tibbetts, and Abbett Engineering Company; Albert Gailord Hart, professor of economics, Columbia University; Victor Jones, professor of government, Wesleyan University; Harold D. Lasswell, professor of law, Yale University; Robert F. Lenhart, secretary of the Research and Policy Committee, Committee for Economic Development; Charles E. Lindblom, associate professor of economics, Yale University; Max F. Millikan, professor of economics, Massachusetts Institute of Technology; Eugene V. Rostow, professor of law, Yale University; Paul A. Samuelson, professor of economics, Massachusetts Institute of Technology, and Carl S. Shoup, professor of economics, Columbia University School of Business.

mares. Many of the tools that economists now use were fashioned originally to help us understand this unhappy phenomenon. Recent experience has taught us again what we should have learned many times in the past, that there is another side to the coin—that periods of high employment can be associated with other evils usually grouped under the heading of inflation. Indeed, so violently does the pendulum of intellectual fashion swing that we are now in some danger of forgetting that depressions are still possible and in time even probable.

Most economists are now aware that the analytic apparatus designed to expose the roots of depressions can also be used, if perhaps not quite so successfully, to study inflationary pressures.

These two diseases of the economic system, superficially so different in their symptoms, can be described in terms of the extremes of fluctuations of a single magnitude, the national money income. It does not take an economist to persuade one that a depression is a time when incomes are too low. This is, for almost everyone, a direct fact of experience. The average man may be somewhat more reluctant to accept the notion that an inflation is a period when incomes are *too* high. The trouble with inflation as he sees it is usually that he never has enough money income to keep up with the price increases which continually face him. Nonetheless it is true that the main reason prices rise is because somebody somewhere has the money to pay the higher prices. The deceptive thing about it is that it always seems to be somebody else. But if national money income did not rise sharply there would probably be few serious inflationary pressures. There might be some, which is why what has come to be called *income analysis*, which was developed to explain depressions, cannot always provide us with a completely satisfactory explanation of inflations; but the two phenomena are sufficiently symmetrical so that as a first approximation we may describe the problem of avoiding both depressions and inflations as the problem of income stabilization.

The word stabilization is an unfortunate one because it implies that the object of policy is to hold real incomes strictly constant, which we do not intend to suggest. There is every hope and expectation that the gradual increase in standards of living which has characterized the last century can be continued if we follow the right policies. Economists enjoy arguing about whether it is better for this slow increase in physical output to be accompanied by a corresponding increase in money incomes so that prices can be held constant or even slightly rising, or for prices to fall very gradually so that constant money incomes will buy ever more and more goods. This is, for our purposes in this study, an unimportant problem. We are concerned not with annual changes in money incomes of 2 or 3 per cent, such as are involved in this controversy, but with the much wider swings which reflect mass unemployment at one extreme and rapid general price increases at the other. If the fluctuations of national money income could be kept within 5 per cent per year we could regard incomes as effectively stabilized within our meaning of the term.

We should, of course, be concerned with whether or not measures taken to stabilize money incomes are likely to interfere with the growth of productivity. This study takes it for granted that we all want an economy in which there will be continued development of new products, the use of new and ever more efficient processes, a continual increase in the level of knowledge and competence of the labor force, and an ever growing stock of capital goods to lighten the manual load. In other words we want a dynamic and growing society, not a static and secure one. It was to reflect our assumption that the community would not wish income stabilization to be achieved at the expense of progressive change that the word "developing" was inserted in the title of the study. Indeed this is one of the most important of the potential conflicts of basic objectives that we have set out to examine.

The term income stabilization is intended to refer only to aggregate national income and not to the incomes of individuals or groups in the community. Whether and to what extent the stabilization of individual incomes by such devices as social security, wage control, tax policy, and the like is desirable is an important policy problem. It is considered in this study, however, only insofar as it is related to the stabilization of over-all employment and the price level.

What is meant by democracy will have to emerge from the discussion which follows, especially in Part I which is devoted to establishing a framework of social, political, and economic ideas within which the problem of income stabilization can be analyzed. It has been the aim of this study to see how far we could get on the basis of a minimum set of propositions about the Good Society to which the overwhelming majority of informed Americans could agree. Such a set of propositions takes as its starting point the Western liberal notion that the individual counts, that society should be so organized as first, to preserve for the individual the negative values of freedom from compulsion to do, say, or consume anything he does not choose except insofar as such compulsion is required to preserve the freedom of others; second, to encourage such positive values as maximum opportunity for each individual to share in decision-making, to develop his own particular capacities to their fullest, to secure the recognition and respect of his fellows, to acquire a fuller understanding of the world around him, and to provide himself

Studies in National Policy

This series is designed to present the result of studies made in the course of an interdepartmental program of research in national policy, organized at Yale University in 1946, by members of the Departments of Economics and Political Science, and the School of Law.

BOOKS IN THE SERIES

INCOME STABILIZATION
for a DEVELOPING DEMOCRACY

A STUDY OF THE POLITICS AND

ECONOMICS OF HIGH EMPLOYMENT

WITHOUT INFLATION

edited by MAX F. MILLIKAN

New Haven: YALE UNIVERSITY PRESS 1953

LONDON: GEOFFREY CUMBERLEGE, OXFORD UNIVERSITY PRESS

Preface

This book was not intended as a tract for the times. It was conceived in 1946 at a time when it appeared that all the instruments of policy might have to be mobilized to meet the problem of a major postwar depression. Later, when first drafts of some of the chapters became available for the seminar discussion to which all of them were subjected, it seemed inconceivable that there could be a threat to stability from any cause but inflation. As later drafts came under review we moved through the mild recession of 1949 and the post-Korean inflation into the period of relative stability of prices, employment, and the money market in which we have found ourselves for over a year and a half. At this writing, as a new administration is about to take over its duties in Washington, opinion is divided as to whether stability is menaced more in the immediate future by an insufficiency of demand growing out of the tapering off of the defense program or by a further burst of inflationary forces.

The authors were given two contradictory instructions. They were to avoid topical comment on the current scene, but they were to make sure that their analysis was highly relevant to the practical problems faced in all their complexity by administrators. As the reader will observe, they have solved this dilemma with varying degrees of success. Some have retreated into fundamental principle and been spared the necessity of frequent revision to catch up with the news. They have avoided obsolescence by leaving to the reader the sometimes difficult task of relating what they say to current policy issues.

Others, with a misplaced trust in the successive deadlines announced by the editor, have struggled manfully in revision after revision to retain in their contributions the sense of current relevance, only to be thwarted in the end by a delay (for which I am wholly responsible) of over a year between the receipt of the last revision and submission of the manuscript to the printer. My apologies to these authors are tempered only by my conviction that in every case it is merely their illustrations and not their underlying analysis which has been rendered out of date by the passage of time.

In one case delay was fatal. The book was to have included an essay on the vital topic of the relation between defense expenditure and income stabilization. Such an essay was attempted, but the march of events was so swift and violent that the author despaired of generalizations broad enough to cover the range of recent and possible future history, and withdrew from the race.

Two other omissions will be noted. There is no chapter on the problems posed for stabilizers by developments in international trade and finance, and there is no treatment of the impact on stabilization policy of the peculiar place of agriculture in American economic and political life. The editor has no excuse for these omissions other than his inability to find qualified contributors on these topics willing to undertake them.

A major effort was made, in the course of assembling this book, to avoid the universal defect of symposia that the various contributions do not relate to one another. The mechanics employed were the circulation of drafts to all authors and the holding of a number of seminar meetings on each chapter, participated in by several of the authors, by a continuing group of Yale faculty members, and by guest experts invited in for particular meetings. In the judgment of the editor this effort had only limited success. Genuinely cooperative thinking requires more sustained and continuous contact and perhaps more determination to submerge the sharpness of one's own insight in a common conceptual scheme than our procedure could produce.

But cooperative thinking is not always, or perhaps even usually, better than the individual kind. If these essays suffer from inadequate integration it is partly because the different perspectives of the various authors contribute something that would be lost if a more dictatorial imposition of uniformity had been attempted. In any case the differences are mainly in emphasis and in ways of saying things. We are all talking about essentially the same problem, and it is my belief based on long discussions with all the authors that we share a very nearly common value system as a point of departure. We hope it is shared by many Americans, and that they will find this analysis of a series of conflicts of objectives helpful in straightening out their thinking on a complex policy issue.

ACKNOWLEDGMENTS

Our thanks are due first to the Carnegie Corporation whose generous grant to the National Policy Committee made possible a degree of communication among the authors and their critics which could otherwise not have been achieved. The members of the National Policy Committee itself, both in their collective and their individual capacities, added critical guidance to extraordinary patience with the time-consuming procedure we chose to adopt. Special mention should go to those of this group who, in terms of time and effort, deserve a place among the authors but whose names do not appear in the table of contents, namely Kent Healy, John Miller, and Percy Corbett (a member of the committee until his departure from Yale). Ralph Brown deserves listing as more than one of the authors since he shared some of the duties of editorship, especially in the time-consuming early days of planning.

The volume is permeated throughout by the influence of the loyal band of Yale faculty members who met repeatedly over nearly four years for discussion of the project as a whole and of drafts of individual chapters. In addition to the authors this group included G. D. Braden, R. T. Bittker, F. F. Kessler, and M. S. MacDougal from the Law School; E. Wight Bakke, Ralph C. Jones, Challis Hall, Dean Morse, Lloyd Reynolds, Richard Ruggles, and Richard Tennant from the Economics Department; V. O. Key, Robert Lane, and Howard Penniman from the Government Department; and Bernard Brodie, F. S. Dunn, W. T. R. Fox, and Klaus Knorr from the Institute of International Studies.

A large group of economists, businessmen, lawyers, and government officials came to New Haven to participate in seminars or commented at length by mail on drafts prior to their revision. It would be impossible to try to identify the nature or extent of the contribution of each, but since the ideas of all are reflected in one way or another at some point in the book it seems appropriate to list them: Moses Abramovitz, George L. Bach, Kingman Brewster, E. Cary Brown, MacGeorge Bundy, John Buttrick, J. Keith Butters, Edmond Cahn, Neil Chamberlain, J. M. Clark, Ernest Dale, John Dunlop, Carl Freese, Milton Friedman, Benjamin Graham, Bertram Gross, Lowell Harriss, J. R. Hicks, Benjamin Higgins, Roy Jorgensen, E. R. Livernash, Ruth Mack, Arthur MacMahon, Gardner Means, Arthur S. Meyer, Geoffrey Moore, Jacob Mosak, David Riesman, Robert Rosa, Dan T. Smith, Harold Stein, J. C. Sweeten, Lazare Teper, William Vickrey, Henry Wallich, C. R. Whittlesey, D. M. Wright, and various members of the staff of the Council of Economic Advisors.

I am much indebted to Miss Beatrice Rogers for the preparation of the index.

Max F. Millikan

Cambridge, Massachusetts
January 19, 1953

About the Authors

BROWN, RALPH S., JR., Associate Professor of Law, Yale University

COKER, FRANCIS W., Alfred Cowles Professor Emeritus, Government, Lecturer in Political Science, Yale University; author, *Recent Political Thought, Democracy, Liberty and Property*, etc.

COLM, GERHARD, chief economist, National Planning Association, formerly economist, President's Council of Economic Advisers; author, *Economics of Government Expenditures, Who Pays the Taxes?*

DAHL, ROBERT A., Associate Professor of Political Science, Yale University; author, *Congress and Foreign Policy*

EMERSON, THOMAS I., Professor of Law, Yale University; formerly general counsel, Office of Economic Stabilization and Office of War Mobilization and Reconversion

HAGEN, EVERETT E., industrial economist for Knappen, Tibbetts, and Abbett Engineering Company; formerly economist, Division of Fiscal Analysis, U.S. Bureau of the Budget

HART, ALBERT GAILORD, Professor of Economics, Columbia University; author, *Money, Debt and Economic Activity, Defense Without Inflation*, joint author, *Jobs and Markets*

JONES, VICTOR, Professor of Government, Wesleyan University; author, *Metropolitan Government*

LASSWELL, HAROLD D., Professor of Law and Political Science, Yale University; director of War Communications Research, Library of Congress; author, *World Politics Faces Economics, National Security and Individual Freedom, Power and Society*, etc.

LENHART, ROBERT F., Secretary, Research and Policy Committee, Committee for Economic Development

LINDBLOM, CHARLES E., Associate Professor of Economics, Yale University; author, *Unions and Capitalism*

MILLIKAN, MAX F., Director, Center for International Studies and Professor of Economics, Massachusetts Institute of Technology; formerly research associate, Yale University

ROSTOW, EUGENE V., Professor of Law, Yale University; author, *A National Policy for the Oil Industry*

SAMUELSON, PAUL A., Professor of Economics, Massachusetts Institute of Technology; author, *The Foundations of Economic Analysis, Economics, an Introductory Analysis*

SHOUP, CARL S., Professor of Economics, Columbia University School of Business, tax consultant to U.S. Treasury and Council of Economic Advisers; author, *Principles of National Income Analysis, The Sales Tax in American States*

Summary Table of Contents

Part Four: The Political Process

Analytical Table of Contents

Part Three: Correlative Goals

Part Four: The Political Process

INTRODUCTION: *The Problem and the Issues*

BY MAX F. MILLIKAN

1. The notion that it is a responsibility of government to help prevent excessive fluctuations in the level of national money income and expenditure is now quite generally accepted in America by people of all political persuasions. When money income grows too rapidly we have inflation, a widespread but unbalanced rise in prices which, as we have recently learned, benefits almost nobody. The responsibility of government to keep inflationary tendencies in check has been accepted in principle for generations, though this has not always been reflected in effective practice.

When national money income falls too far we have depression and unemployment. Whether national policy should concern itself with positive measures to remedy this sort of situation has been controversial until much more recently. With the passage of the Employment Act of 1946, however, the maintenance of high employment as an objective of federal policy was written into the law of the land with the concurrence of representatives of the major political faiths.

How money income should be controlled so as to avoid at least the extremes of these two evils is the subject of a vast and sprouting literature. The excuse for still another symposium traversing this familiar territory is that economic studies of the problem generally suffer from two defects of omission: they do not give adequate consideration to the impact on other policy objectives of measures directed at the control of aggregate demand; and they largely overlook the limitations and conditions imposed on economic policy in any actual moment of history by the political, institutional, and social framework within which it must operate and by the developing trends and tendencies of the time. It is the purpose of this study to subject some of the measures commonly accepted by economists as appropriate to the control of employment and prices to systematic examination with respect to these two considerations.

The degree of agreement among economists as to what economic theory tells us about the probable effects of various measures on total spending is much greater than the heat of current controversy would suggest. The disagreements as to what are the best measures to use are real and profound. But an examination of the argument will frequently reveal that these disagreements do not spring primarily from differences of economic analysis. Rather they spring either from unrecognized differences of emphasis as to the importance of other objectives affected by purportedly "economic" measures or from differences in judgments as to how economic measures will work out "in practice" in the light of actual current political and social conditions.

There is a fairly widespread intuitive recognition that measures designed to affect the level of spending are likely to affect at the same time our progress toward other goals—economic, political, and social —at least as important as the goal of income stabilization. It has come to be common knowledge that the level of incomes may be influenced by such devices as taxation, public spending, price regulation, wage policy, attitudes toward competition, credit control, public exhortation, and the like. But each of these devices was originally invented for quite a different purpose, and its use to promote income control may under some circumstances frustrate our attempts to achieve such ends, for instance, as an equitable distribution of real income, the widespread diffusion of political power, the development of satisfying patterns of individual achievement, or the establishment of secure and peaceful international relations. The recognition of these conflicts of objectives, while it affects the views of economists and others on public policy matters, is seldom very explicit or systematic. One of the deplorable consequences of the development of separate social sciences—economics, political science, sociology, law, etc.—is that it is so difficult for the policy adviser or decision maker to judge any proposal in terms of the *total* values sought by a democratic society. The proposal is usually explicitly judged by reference to the norms of only one discipline—economic welfare, sound political administration, equitable legislation, or what have you—but the judgment is colored by powerful amateur hunches as to "incidental" effects.

This failure to examine explicitly and systematically the total implications of a contemplated act leads to fruitless disputes between people who have broadly similar patterns of objectives and a common technical apparatus of analysis within their own special field. Two economists might agree, for example, on the following if faced with these separate propositions out of context: 1) other things being equal, a certain increase in tax rates can be so designed as to reduce total spending by approximately the same amount as a certain reduction of public highway expenditure; 2) in these troubled times adequate facilities for national defense are essential; 3) the concentration of too much control over resources in the hands of the federal executive threatens the dispersion of power essential to effective democracy. Yet faced with the problem of what to do about inflation they may argue bitterly and emotionally, one in favor of a tax increase and the other in support of a reduced public roads program. The first may have formed the habit of associating public expenditure with an undesirable concentration of control while the second happens to link it in his mind with the necessity of an adequate highway network for military pre-paredness. But their argument will in all probability take the mislead-ing form of a technical dispute between economists as to what is, on purely economic grounds, the more appropriate device.

This does not imply that if the noneconomic aspects of the alterna-tives were systematically explored the two men would necessarily come to complete agreement on policy. Explicit differences as to the relative importance of conflicting goals or the relative strengths of the immeas-urable forces at work might very well persist on which the debate would continue to flourish. But even if this were the result much would be gained by illuminating the true sources of the conflict. Until econo-mists can learn to talk and think freely and in an orderly fashion about the total implications of the measures they advocate their policy rec-ommendations are bound to be half-baked and conflicting. But they must have the help of political scientists, lawyers, social psychologists, and others to assist them in drawing out the noneconomic implications of what are conventionally regarded as "economic" problems. It is one purpose of this study to focus attention on some of the conflicts of ob-jective which are implicit in the discussion of measures designed to in-sure full employment without inflation.

The other theme, related but different, around which the studies in this volume are woven is that the effectiveness of employment-creating or inflation-preventing measures cannot be established by abstract economic analysis alone, but is conditioned in a crucial manner by the way in which our American economic, political, and social institutions are presently in fact operating, by the character of public responses to policy measures and to the situations they create, and by the policies we currently feel impelled to pursue in superficially quite unrelated areas. Economic analysis must, like any science, examine the interac-tions of the forces it studies in simplified models lifted out of any de-veloping historical context and stripped of what from the analysts' point of view is extraneous detail. But when we apply analysis to policy formation we are dealing no longer with "an economy" unanchored in time and space but rather with the United States in the year 1952, a complex actual society at a particular stage of its evolution with its web of interacting institutions in process of moving in certain directions. To influence that development, which is the aim of policy, we need an understanding of the total context and not just of the economic model.

This second theme thus stated certainly has none of the glamour of novelty. It is a common observation among economists, for instance, that a really sensible and flexible tax policy is impossible under a political system involving the separation of powers, in which tax changes must be made by a large deliberative body subject to strong special-interest pressures. Again, everyone concerned with the design of the President's Economic Report is aware of the importance of knowing precisely how it and other government pronouncements and measures affect the expectations and attitudes of big businessmen, small businessmen, labor, farmers, consumers, etc. And we have all been dramatically impressed on several occasions during the last ten or fifteen years with the way in which the necessity of paying increasing attention to national security can radically change the whole character of the problem of controlling the national money income.

But considerations of this sort, which ought to occupy a central position in discussions of economic policy, usually hover about the periphery of the analysis or are relegated to footnotes because the author feels that they are outside his special field of competence. It is only natural that we should pay most attention to those phases of a subject which we can talk about most easily and confidently. The parts of the problem we choose to work on are determined not so much by their relative importance as by the tools we happen to have in our kit. This is perhaps especially true of economists, who have designed more elaborate and superficially more precise tools than most other social scientists and who consequently find it particularly tempting to play exclusively with their own toys whatever their relevance. It is another purpose of this study to force economists to bring noneconomic considerations out of parentheses and into the central core of their thinking, and to encourage noneconomists to focus their skills and their understanding of other aspects of American life on what are conventionally regarded as economic problems—specifically in this instance the problem of maintaining full employment without inflation.

2. Income stabilization means many things to many people. A word of explanation is called for as to what we conceive our title, *Income Stabilization for a Developing Democracy*, to mean. Half of the problem is how to avoid major depressions with the heavy involuntary unemployment and loss of production that accompany them. This great policy issue so impressed itself on the minds of some of those who passed through the grim thirties that they still have only depression night-

with commodities suited to his own particular tastes. Controversy over ends almost never arises, of course, at this level of abstraction because the symbols used are quite universally accepted as the ones to which appeal must be made to justify any operating model of Utopia. But this study has been undertaken in the conviction that they have a content specific enough to be of use in the selection of policies most likely to be consistent with democratic values. Whether this conviction is well founded the reader must judge from the pages which follow.

3. In the early stages of this enterprise it became apparent that the pursuit of the two objectives of the study we have described would involve us in two dangers, both of which it was necessary to avoid if the study was to be fruitful. The first was that the process of establishing a common ground of fundamental social goals with which income stabilization should be consistent would mushroom into one or more volumes on ultimate social philosophy which would exhaust the time and patience of the participants and leave no room for the discussion of the subject of the study. To establish the full consistency of a set of policy recommendations with one's major objectives clearly requires the construction of a rather detailed Utopia. It was agreed that our intent was not to write a treatise on social philosophy but to make some sensible comments on the problem of how to stabilize incomes in the America in which we currently find ourselves. Accordingly we decided to take what was on our statute books, the Empoyment Act of 1946, as a point of departure and consider only such policies and measures as seemed reasonably possible within the context of our present social and political structure. In this sense the symposium is intended to be practical, and the chapters on objectives, political and social framework, and the like are intended to be suggestive rather than exhaustive. Their purpose is to raise some issues particularly relevant to income stabilization policy and to indicate the nature of the goals we take to be generally acceptable rather than to explore basic ethical foundations in a complete or novel way.

On the other hand, to be completely practical is to make no recommendations at all, or at best only trivial ones. There are always excellent reasons for believing that virtually every proposed measure will fail of its objective or cannot be made politically acceptable or is administratively unworkable or that we cannot possibly know enough about its probable total effect to pass a sound judgment on its desirability. The indications were all too disturbingly clear in our early discussions that the attempt to introduce "noneconomic" considerations into the analysis of economic policy might well degenerate into a competition to see who could adduce the most compelling reasons for believing that a proposal which made sense on economic grounds was "practically" impossible, unworkable, or unwise. It is no doubt similar experience with the depressing effects of this sort of game which has led some writers to adopt the view that anything is as "practical" as anything else, and that the only sensible course is therefore to put forward what are frequently referred to as "bold" proposals without reference to practical objections or noneconomic considerations.

It is an error, however, to identify with timidity an attempt to see a problem in its developmental context or to regard as bold a refusal to consider more than one aspect of it. That most policy problems are complex is a function of the problems and not of our approach to them. It may be sound strategy for the proponent of a measure to oversimplify as a technique of persuasion, but it is inexcusable for the analyst to let himself be fooled by his own magic. Thus though the first awareness of the manifold aspects of a policy problem is likely to be depressing, such enlarged vision is essential to sound judgment. Furthermore, one's depression in the face of complexity is no excuse for inertia. The complexity attaches not only to the course of action under discussion, as public debate frequently implies, but to all alternatives including that of doing nothing. The selection of the most desirable alternative, which may be very bold in the sense of departing from past practice, is facilitated rather than impeded by an examination of the difficulties and resistances which may be involved in *all* the alternatives.

Hence our decision to treat the problem of income stabilization in a practical setting and to consider the noneconomic implications of measures to achieve it is not to be interpreted as reflecting either determinism or opposition to proposals which are radical in the fundamental sense. The full complexity of some of the problems discussed has not been generally recognized, and in some cases the essays which follow do not get much beyond attempting to portray this complexity. Clear and vigorous policy proposals in such cases must await further analysis. It would serve no useful purpose in a study of this kind to suppress genuine uncertainty for the sake of a Program. Nevertheless, we have sought to avoid wherever possible the lame excuse of the lazy or timid academic that "it all depends . . ."

In one respect it is hoped that the extension of the frame of reference attempted in these studies will be useful even where policy proposals do not emerge. We have turned up a surprising number of areas in which further advance in understanding seems to await the collection of evidence which we do not yet have but which we now have the techniques to gather. The authors of the separate studies have attempted to highlight the kinds of research which are most pressingly needed. A few of them have been generally recognized for some time, but in many cases the importance or the feasibility of needed research emerges from the application to our problem of the techniques of social sciences other than economics.

4. The idea of getting various social scientists to comment on a common problem is, of course, not a new one. There have been many attempts to achieve a cooperative approach to social questions, but the results are usually singularly disappointing. Very little purpose is served by bringing together in a single volume a series of essays such as would normally be published by their authors in their respective trade journals. It is not enough to have an economist write on economic aspects, a sociologist on sociological aspects, a political scientist on political aspects, etc. The economist must in the process become something of a sociologist, political scientist, psychologist, etc., and the practitioners of the other black arts must master some of the mumbo jumbo of economics if they are to arrive at anything more than a series of incommensurable and unrelated propositions.

The problem of devising a mechanics to achieve this blend, a kind of intellectual Waring mixer, is a difficult one to which we do not pretend to have found the whole solution. Our tentative procedure in the preparation of these essays was the holding of a joint seminar. The permanent members of the seminar were for the most part on the faculty of Yale University, drawn from various departments and research institutes, some of them contributors of written material but many of them not. Each contributor met with this seminar on several occasions during the preparation of his essay and in addition discussed special phases of his problem informally with interested individuals. Usually for one of the sessions on each topic a number of particularly qualified special guests were invited to comment on a draft manuscript. The purpose of this was to badger, threaten, and wheedle each contributor into writing an essay not solely from the point of view of his own specialty but reflecting at least an awareness of a much wider range of problems.

As the reader will discover, success in this effort varies from chapter to chapter. Some of our experts proved able to cross disciplinary boundaries with surprising agility. Some were quite willing to *talk* about problems outside their field but had powerful inhibitions against committing their insights to writing. Still others felt there were too many unsolved problems right in their own bailiwick to make an expedition into someone else's worth while. All concerned found the experience educational, though the uneven result does not fully reflect the benefits derived by the participants.

5. The plan of the study is as follows: Part I is devoted to preparing

the ground. Chapter 1 suggests a classification of values relevant to our policy problem; Chapter 2 places the problem of the economic role of government in America in its political-historical setting; and Chapter 3 describes, primarily for the benefit of the noneconomist, the essentials of the language economists use when talking about income stabilization.

Part II is devoted to a discussion of the chief instruments of policy usually regarded by economists as appropriate to the control of inflation and depression. Chapters 4 through 9 consider economic forecasting, fiscal policy, tax policy, monetary policy, public spending policy, and various other ways of influencing investment outlay. The primary emphasis in these chapters is necessarily upon the economic aspects of these instruments, but every effort is made to introduce noneconomic considerations wherever they are relevant.

Part III is concerned with policies which, while not directed primarily at income stabilization, nevertheless have an important effect on our progress toward that goal and are in turn influenced by the measures discussed in Part II. The policy areas considered here are the control of competition, policies toward labor, and the broad question of what rate of economic development we wish to achieve. This is an illustrative rather than an exhaustive list. Major policy areas omitted which are closely related to income stabilization are our national security policy, our international economic policy, and our agricultural policy.

Finally, in Part IV, some noneconomists take up more systematically than was possible in earlier parts some of the implications of income stabilization upon which other disciplines can throw light. The relation of income stabilization policies to the political process is examined in Chapter 13. The contribution which can be made by the developing science of communication and attitude research is considered in Chapter 14, and some of the administrative problems of coordinating all the governmental activities impinging upon income stabilization are taken up in Chapter 15.

The last chapter represents an attempt to distill the essential reactions of a group of key representatives of the public to the problem and to its treatment by the other authors.

PART ONE:
THE FRAMEWORK

CHAPTER I. *Objectives for Economic Policy in a Democracy*

BY MAX F. MILLIKAN

I. The Values Underlying Policy

1. *Two basic principles*

Almost everybody feels strongly about the subject of this volume. Readers will approach it with a wide range of attitudes, most of them having considerable emotional content. These will range all the way from exasperation at the notion that income stabilization is any of the government's business to surprise that there should be any dobut that it is the government's most important responsibility. The contemplation of particular measures will arouse even more violent controversy.

One of the convictions which led to this undertaking was that the smoke of the battle conceals much more fundamental agreement than is generally supposed. Certainly few would quarrel with the proposition that continued and repeated periods of mass unemployment such as we had in the 1930's would destroy the basis for whatever stable society we may hope for. Similarly, inflation of the violence experienced, for example, in Germany after World War I is incompatible with anybody's idea of Utopia. The evil consequences of both of these states of affairs have been described so persuasively that we cannot find the explanation for controversy about policy in disagreement about these evils.

Another explanation is popular. As pointed out in the Introduction, measures to stabilize incomes impinge on other goals which we regard as important. Possibly disagreement about income stabilization springs from radically different social objectives. Perhaps America is basically divided as to what kind of society it wants. Beneath the superficial general allegiance to such symbols as democracy, freedom, and liberty may lie ideas of where we should be going which are in such basic conflict as to be incapable of compromise. In this case the emotion poured into disputes about such detailed matters as Federal Reserve open market policy should be taken as symptomatic of a very fundamental clash of ideologies. If this is so it is a waste of time to argue policy issues at the level of particular measures. The only road to consensus in this case would be to expose and thrash out explicitly the conflicts of social philosophy or settle them by the brute force of majority rule.

There is a third possibility. We may all agree on the evils of deep depression and rapid inflation. Most of us may be able to agree on a set of social goals (if we can forget for the moment our individual preferences as to just how they should be labeled). But we may not have had much practice in thinking through the implications for *all* our goals of a measure directed to an apparently limited objective. One man happens to be impressed by a sinister implication, another by a favorable one. Patient and unexcited probing may reveal to each that both implications are correct, that the problem is not choosing between good and evil but weighing the net effect of a mixture. If this explanation of many policy disputes is correct, the road to agreement lies in deciding what our common goals are and dispassionately examining the impact of proposed policy measures upon all of them. The chapters in this volume are intended to be helpful in this process as applied to the problems of national income stabilization.

This requires patience. The pressure to do *something* about a problem as pressing and vital as unemployment or inflation is intense. A classification of social goals may well seem an academic and uninviting preface to a study of how to avoid what is universally accepted as one of the most menacing dangers of our time. But if we do not base our examination on a firm platform of first principles we shall probably fritter away our energies in irritated dispute about matters which cannot be settled without quietly going back together to a common starting point.

The task of this chapter, then, is to attempt a statement of goals commonly accepted in America in as noncontroversial a manner as possible. It is a characteristic of our age that no authoritative vocabulary is available for this purpose. It is impossible to discuss values without using words which have become increasingly ambiguous and for some people loaded with a high emotional charge. No two people would describe the goals outlined below in the same way. It should be kept in mind that what is important for the purposes of this volume is not whether you agree with the form in which values are here described but whether, by and large, you would accept the substance of the general ideas put forth.

Fortunately we do not have to spin out a complete ethic. We are concerned with the kinds of values that are likely to be of most significance for public policy, and for present purposes we propose to see how much we can do with a limited list designed to arouse a minimum of controversy.

Our first postulate immediately narrows the field. It is that *public policy should be so designed as to help every individual to formulate his own set of goals and to satisfy his particular values to the greatest possible degree so long as nobody else is hindered from doing likewise.* This can be put other ways. It amounts to saying that society should encourage each responsible adult to be the arbiter of his own welfare. As we shall see, this principle gives us guidance in only a limited number of situations. Where the self-professed interests of two or more people are in conflict other norms must be introduced. But if one or more people can, from their own point of view, make themselves better off without making anyone else feel worse off they should be encouraged to do so. This last formulation is one commonly used in defining economic welfare but it can be applied to values like power and respect as well as income. We may call this postulate, for short, the principle of free value choice.

The virtue of this principle is that it permits us to put aside for the time being the problem of judging personal values that do not affect interpersonal relations. If we believe in giving people what they want (instead of making them take what someone says is good for them) we can evaluate many policies by whether they do this without reference to ultimate ethics. A policy which interferes with free value choice has, on this basis, a mark against it whatever the values chosen. True, in this as in most ethical matters we are not completely consistent. Men and women who are democrats in public life are frequently autocrats within the family, imposing value judgments by authority rather than inducing them by persuasion. Again, we pass laws restraining people from suicide even though in many cases no one but the victim would suffer. But in most such cases of interference with private value choice the basis for the interference is that others are likely to be affected. The solitary alcoholic cannot be trusted to remain solitary.

It is important to remove a common misunderstanding about this principle of free value choice. It does not imply, as is sometimes suggested, either that people in fact know what is good for them or that anyone who accepts the principle is thereby prevented from criticizing other people's values. Nor does it imply that public policy should accept currently popular values as ultimate and refrain from positive attempts to change them. What it does assert is that such efforts, private or public, to alter other people's value systems must proceed by persuasion and not by compulsion. The principle dictates that policy should be devoted to giving people what they want. But it may at the same time be energetically attempting to change what they want by pointing out unrealized alternatives, by publicizing the consequences of misconception, by stimulating conscious reexamination of values, and in many other ways.

The principle of free value choice is thus concerned not with ultimate ends but with means, in the same sense in which democracy is an objective directing not what all of our social decisions shall be but the way in which they shall be arrived at. The test of a man's belief in the principle is not whether he agrees that the values of others are good for them but whether, believing others to be misguided, he is willing to submit his views to the test of voluntary acceptance. It is an essential condition of democracy that the individual's freedom to choose, in such a conflict, must take precedence over what anybody else thinks is good for him so long as his choice hurts nobody else.

Democracy is sometimes identified with a system of majority rule, but it is important to recognize that majority rule may violate the principle of free value choice in important ways; 51% of the people can give the other 49% not what they want (with respect to all sorts of values) but what the 51% think they ought to want. Where minority desires can be satisfied without loss to the majority the principle dictates that this should be done. But majority rule will not insure it, and with a smug or indifferent majority is almost certain to thwart it. Even if the majority believes in free value choice, the voting mechanism implied by majority rule is in many cases too crude and blunt an instrument by itself to bring about a close adjustment of resources to the infinite variety of individual values. We shall consider later some of the more strictly economic implications of these points.

A common initial reaction to this first postulate is that it is all very well as far as it goes, but that in most situations other people are affected, often adversely, by a man's pursuit of his own goals, so that this principle is of negligible practical importance. Actually it is a much more powerful and efficient principle than at first appears. To give an example from economics it permits us to conclude at once that any system of uniform rationing which provides equal amounts of each commodity to each consumer is unsatisfactory where there are any differences of tastes. This can be shown by the fact that under such a system consumers will, if an opportunity is provided, make many swaps which will alter the commodity distribution to everyone's mutual satisfaction, Jack Spratt giving up his ration of fat for his wife's of lean, etc. In esthetics one man's desire to paint or write music in a certain way seldom interferes with anyone else's wish to do it differently (though an attempt to force others to look at or listen to the product may have to be restrained in the social interest!). Hence we can conclude that restrictions on the nature of artistic output such as are common in some countries are a violation of our postulate. It is clear that the gratification of individual desires for affection, respect, and enlightenment is often possible without a redistribution of values which leaves somebody worse off. Examples will multiply themselves as we proceed.

This is not to say that there are not a great many cases where what have been called distributive problems arise. They are obvious in the economic sphere wherever the distribution of wealth or income is in question. Power frequently appears to be obtainable only by depriving others of it, or of some other value such as wealth or respect. The enlightenment or physical well-being of some may be possible only at the economic expense of others, and so forth. In cases in which the distribution of values among people is in question there is another postulate which we usually associate with democracy: that *commonly sought values should be shared or dispersed equitably throughout the community and not highly concentrated in a single group or class*. The democratic notion of the dignity of the individual human being carries with it the idea that there should be available to all an opportunity to participate in the pursuit of the various kinds of satisfactions people seek, that physical well-being, creature comforts, control over the institutions of society, the respect and affection of fellows, the development of skills and capacities, the growth of knowledge and understanding should not be monopolized or closely held but widely distributed throughout the community.

This postulate is more difficult to define in precise operational terms than the first. To say that values should be shared, for example, is not to say that in some sense they should be shared *equally*. What criteria are we to adopt to determine whether they are shared sufficiently widely to be compatible with democracy? Is it the actual attainment of these values or the opportunity to pursue them that we require to be shared? If the latter, how are we to define opportunity? If this goal is really to have meaning we must find ways of measuring how far any actual situation deviates from the ideal, or at least which of two situations is closer to it. How can such measurements be taken? Economists have devised indexes of varying degrees of suitability to measure the extent to which income is shared, but what of power or respect? These are questions with which the various social sciences are wrestling at the moment. To pursue them further here would take us too far from our theme. We must be content with the vague and connotative statement of our postulate given above and hope that it conveys enough content so that most readers can say, "I agree, with reservations." We may term it for convenience the principle of shared values.

2. *A classification of values*

In developing a set of objectives particularly relevant to economic policy to give content to the foregoing two principles, it will be useful to have a classification of some of the major sorts of values commonly sought by individuals. For convenience we propose to adopt a classification employed by Harold Lasswell. We may quote from his *Power and Personality.*[1]

> Participation in the making of decisions (power) is a value; access to goods and services (wealth) [*or income*] is a value. . . . *Well-being,* in the sense of bodily and psychic integrity is a value. *En-lightenment* is the finding and spreading of knowledge. There is *skill,* the acquiring and using of dexterities. *Respect* covers what is often called social class position. *Affection* includes friendship and also sexual intimacy. *Rectitude* is the value of morality. This is a representative, not an exhaustive, list of values. It is not a ranking of values in order of importance in American or any other culture. We assume that the relative position of values varies from group to group, from person to person, and from time to time in the history of any culture or personality.

A word or two is in order to clarify aspects of this classification which will be of particular importance for our later discussion of economic policy. Economists, in order to make their discipline manageable, have set up the construct of the economic man, an individual pursuing the values of wealth or income, if not to the exclusion of other values at least independently of them. In its policy recommendations, therefore, what economists call "welfare economics" has as a rule taken the maximization of this income value or its equitable distribution as the prime criterion for policy selection, on the ground (usually implicit) that other values were not the concern of the economist and could be dealt with by other than "economic" policy. But even the briefest consideration of the above list of values makes plain that what is thought of as economic policy affects the extent and distribution of these other values in endless ways, and that the effectiveness of economic policy is in turn conditioned by what individuals do in pursuit of these other goals.

Though this point has not yet adequately influenced the structure of formal theory, it has become so widely recognized that a few examples selected at random should suffice both to clarify the value list and to illustrate its internal interrelations.

These interactions of values have become a matter of great practical

1. (New York, Norton, 1948), pp. 16–17.

concern, for instance, in problems of labor relations. Here economists can properly be charged with having led businessmen astray for some years. Economic theory conventionally abstracted from all but pecuniary incentives in its concept of the worker. He was pictured as balancing in his mind the attractions of *income* against the unpleasantness of working for it. The researches of such people as Elton Mayo, T. N. Whitehead, and E. Wight Bakke have documented what common sense should have told us from the start, namely, that employee motivation is affected by many other values such as respect, enlightenment, and the use of skills. Men would seek some employment in pursuit of these other values even if their incomes did not depend on it. The realization of this fact has revolutionized the art of personnel management.

With reference to *power*, it is important to note that this refers to participation in the making of any important decision and not merely those decisions carried out through the institution of government. Every institution, public or private, is in one aspect a power complex. The sharing of power in labor unions, fraternal organizations, business firms, etc., is as important a subject of study as the distribution of what is conventionally referred to as political power. Employees are pursuing the value of power when they seek some voice in decisions affecting the work situation, just as businessmen pursue power in attempting to extend the range of their economic control. Astute economists have often been troubled by the observation, inconsistent with the basic assumptions of most economic theory, that businessmen frequently seek power at the expense of income, expanding their enterprises, for example, when this is probably not profitable. The relations between distribution of power and governmental economic activity are at the heart of many disputes about income stabilization measures.

The forms of *respect* and its distribution have been much less thoroughly studied than those of power or income, though its importance in superficially economic problems has become increasingly apparent in recent years. Loss of respect has been shown to be one of the evils of unemployment probably as important in many cases as loss of income, and policies to relieve unemployment must, as is now recognized, be such as to relieve the loss of respect that accompanies it as well. It is for this reason among others that soup lines and make-work projects are no longer regarded even as suitable palliatives for unemployment.

In many situations unemployment could be reduced if people could be persuaded to move from areas of job shortages to those of labor shortages. Their reluctance to move is frequently based upon an unwillingness to forego the hard-won respect, standing in the community, and acceptance in their particular group which they have painfully achieved.

Enlightenment is obviously related to economic policy in a great many ways. If we accept this value we shall be chary of methods of directing the economy which involve, in effect, producing desired reactions (on consumption, investment, or other economic variables) by fooling people as to the true state of affairs. On the contrary, it has recently been urged that some of the causes of instability could be removed or mitigated by the wider spread of understanding of the current economic scene. The President's annual Economic Report called for in the Employment Act represents a significant milestone in the history of economic policy, since for the first time in the United States it is accepted as a responsibility of the executive branch to keep the Congress and the people informed as to the general economic condition of the country. How this new policy tool should be used is one of the questions which has occupied us throughout this study and to which Harold Lasswell pays particular attention in Chapter 14.

The availability of opportunities for satisfying the *skill* value is, as we shall see, peculiarly wrapped up with income stabilization policy. If the desire to make full use of inherent and acquired capacities and talents is to be widely satisfied, there must obviously be ample employment opportunities. There must also be an effective mechanism for either creating the kind of jobs wanted at the times and in the places where people with special skills are looking for them or for bringing about changes in the kinds of skills acquired. Neglect of this value has been responsible for the disappointing results of many schemes for increasing labor mobility and reducing unemployment through labor exchanges and the like. Unwillingness to accept a job which does not make use of the applicant's special training is sometimes regarded as unreasonable inflexibility, but it is a reflection of a widely sought value. Furthermore, attention to the satisfaction of this value is a prerequisite to the success of an income stabilization policy. For income stabilization requires a balanced relation between money flows and physical output or productivity, and productivity depends in an obvious way on both the development of appropriate skills and the utilization of those available.

The intimate connection between productivity and *well-being*, physical and psychic, is by now a commonplace of industrial management. Vitamins have been correlated with absenteeism and emotional tensions with industrial accident rates. From another point of view, the objective of equitable income distribution frequently derives from the basic value of shared well-being: "Every citizen is entitled to a minimum standard of food, shelter and medical care." Since a major part of the incomes of many people is used to attain well-being, there will be many cases where an attempt to draw a line between income and well-being will look like hairsplitting. But the same may be said of the relations between well-being and other value goals. The goal of national security, which in the proximate sense is a power goal, derives in part from the desire of the individual to protect his home, his person, and his way of life from attack. Deprivations of respect and affection can easily lead to mental illness. On the other hand, well-being is often pursued as a means to another end. Health promotes income, strength is sometimes required for power, and a good figure may secure the respect of beauty contest judges. That these value categories overlap or that they are sometimes means and sometimes ends does not upset their usefulness as a check list of things for policy makers or policy advisers to keep in mind.

Affection should not be confused with respect. An employer treats an employee with respect when he accords the employee status as one entitled to basic human dignity, when he avoids racial, religious, or other discrimination, when he acknowledges that the employee has rights and standing as a person. The relationship becomes one of affection only when there is personal warmth, which may be present with or without respect. Southern slaves very often were accorded great affection, but by modern standards they were deprived of respect. The employee of the modern corporation may find himself the recipient of a considerable degree of respect without adequate opportunity in the work situation for relations of affection with either employers or fellow workers. A reminder that affection is a widely sought value which may conceivably be influenced not only by death but also by taxes may lead the policy maker to useful if unfamiliar insights.

Two instances may be cited of the importance of considerations of *rectitude* in economic policy. Much of the discussion of measures appropriate to income stabilization is concerned with the appropriate size and method of management of the public debt. Now for many people debt is a matter not so much of economics as of morals. Whatever its consequences in specific circumstances, debt for such people is a Bad Thing, for oneself or for the government of the country with which a good citizen of a democracy identifies himself. Any amount of logical argument may be powerless to affect this ethical judgment which, as long as it is strongly held, must be accepted as part of the value pattern of the electorate. Policy makers believing the creation of government debt under some circumstances to be a desirable device to assist in income stabilization, for instance, may attempt to reconcile government debt with rectitude in the public mind in a number of ways. They may try through education to alter the public's value scale; they may emphasize that public debt is really not debt at all in the same sense as private debt and thus reduce the affective ethical tone of the term; they may abandon debt creation as an inflationary device and substitute direct money creation which has different (though probably not much more favorable) ethical connotations. But the ends of democracy cannot be served if these rectitude values are not given full weight. This is true not only because it will be difficult to secure acceptance at the polls of policies regarded as immoral, but also because, even if such policies are successfully promoted, it is undesirable to secure an increase in incomes at the expense of widespread feelings of guilt if the latter can be avoided.

Another example of the intrusion of rectitude values into an "economic" problem arises in connection with proposals to manipulate the rate of saving in the community in order to stabilize incomes. We shall be devoting a good deal of attention to such proposals in later chapters. Here it is the extent and intensity of a moral approbation of thrift which must be investigated and allowed for in the design of policy if it is to be truly democratic. If thrift is widely regarded (and this needs further objective study) not merely as a sensible way for a rational man to spread his income over his lifetime and protect himself against contingencies but as a Good Thing in itself, a mark of the moral man, almost of the religious man, in short as one of the ultimate virtues, then real tensions and unhappiness may be created, for instance, by a government campaign to persuade people to buy more. The conflict of values thus produced does not promote the total objectives of democracy.

It must be remembered that in listing these eight boxes into which some kinds of values can be sorted—income, power, respect, enlightenment, skill, well-being, affection, and rectitude—we are describing not a pattern of actual values with detailed content but merely a formal classification to assist us in breaking into manageable groups the values that people in fact pursue. To do otherwise would be to violate our first postulate, the principle of free choice of values. Within each of these categories people choose the most widely different value patterns. For some the essence of real income is a car with white sidewall tires, for others a first edition of William Blake, and for still others a chance to lie on the sand in the sun. Many people are normally little concerned with political power but insist on having a determining voice in deciding who shall be admitted to the club in which they spend a good part of their time. Enlightenment may be sought in Plato, *Organic Gardening Magazine,* or the Kinsey Report. Individually we each have views of varying intensity as to which of these values are more admirable or important, and we are free to try to persuade others that we are right. But for the purposes of this study we are concerned only to note that these categories of objects of desire exist and tentatively to affirm as generally acceptable our two principles: that people should be helped to pursue them in their own fashion whenever the deprivation of others is not involved and that the opportunity to pursue them should be shared wherever a problem of distribution arises.

Note that we are not even making the value judgment that everyone *should* pursue values in each of these categories, that respect, skills, well-being, and the others are in some form inherently good things. Rather we are making the working hypothesis that as a matter of observable fact the great bulk of the population *does* pursue goals which can be thus arranged. There may be some individuals whose aversion to decision-making is so great that they would be quite willing to be deprived of all power and have every detail of their lives determined by others without recourse. There may be others for whom no form of respect is of consequence or for whom no principles of rectitude have any force. But so long as these kinds of values are sought quite widely our two principles (free value choice and shared values) require that democratic policy should take full account of them in all their interactions.

Many readers would prefer a different classification of values from that we have given. Values are many-dimensioned. Whatever simple machine we use to slice this complex web into pieces will cut across strands which have peculiar importance for some people. For example, there is no explicit mention in the list just given of the goal of security against the future so prominent in current discussion. This is not still another value to be added to those already described but rather a particular aspect of all of them. We want our power, our income, our respect, our well-being, etc., all to be secure against the risk of future deprivation.

Again many will miss values more explicitly oriented to the group rather than to the individual. Is there not something in the idea of national security, for instance, beyond the protection of the individual members of the community? Should we not add the values of group solidarity, of participation in a common enterprise, of the preservation of a culture and a social organism which is much more than the mere sum of its parts? Is not the sense of belonging to a larger entity something we have overlooked in our list? Again the answer is no. Most of what is important in these so-called group values is implicit in the categories we have described. The values of power, respect, enlightenment, psychic well-being, affection are all values deriving from interpersonal relations, whose satisfaction depends primarily on the structure of the group in which the individual finds himself.

We have the choice of starting with individual values and deriving the group structure necessary to their satisfaction or classifying group goals and then showing how they relate to individual fulfillment. I confess to a preference for the former procedure. If we start with group values there is always a danger that they will come to take on a somewhat mystical independence of the people composing the group. I take it to be an axiom of Western liberalism that groups are important primarily because of the way in which they shape and mold the lives of individuals. True, we must not let our individualistic ethic blind us to the fact that each person is what he is largely because of his place in the social organism of which he is a part. But to say that individuals are inseparable from the groups to which they belong and derive their primary satisfactions from group relationships is not to say that it is the group and not the individual which matters.

But the particular classification of values which we have chosen is not fundamental to our purposes. There are many perspectives from which we can view the values we would all broadly accept. We have no room here to elaborate on alternative formal schemes, but the labels are incidental. Our purpose is to illustrate the theme that policy must be built on a broader and more fundamental base than can be given us by any one discipline such as economics.

3. *Economic policy and economic functions*

Economic policy may be thought of as policy which employs measures primarily designed to affect the size, composition, and distribution of wealth and income. Most such measures have effects, sometimes of great importance, on other values, and similarly measures which by this definition are not a part of economic policy often influence income in significant ways. It is not possible to separate policies into watertight compartments according to which values they actually affect since most policies affect most values. Nevertheless, it is possible to make a workable, practical classification according to the value at which the *primary* expected effect of the measure is *directed*. Economic policy looked at in this way is nearly but not quite what the term implies in common discussion. For instance, insofar as antitrust measures are proposed primarily because monopolies are regarded as interfering with the equitable distribution of power they are power policies and not economic policies. Again, a Fair Employment Practices Act dealing with racial and other discrimination in employment is a part of what we might term respect policy, although it controls what are usually thought of as economic contracts and may have very far-reaching economic effects. On the other hand, a program of public information is a part of economic rather than educational policy if its main purpose is to persuade people to behave in such a way as to minimize fluctuations in the national income. It is not necessary for our purpose that the boundaries of the area of economic policy be theoretically sharp so long as they permit us to exclude some questions from its domain.

We can best describe the way we think an economic system ought to behave if we first look at the functions every economic system in fact performs. The complex of things we call an economic system must decide, one way or another:

1) How much employment there will be.
2) What resources will be used for.
3) How much the economy will save.
4) What techniques of production will be used.
5) How the product will be distributed.

Every economic system, be it capitalist, socialist, fascist, primitive, feudal, or whatever, makes all these decisions, explicitly or implicitly. Let us see what they involve in a little more detail.

How much employment? The system determines *how much* work will be done by the people making up the society, or how the total available man-hours are to be divided between income-producing effort and other activities such as leisure, recreation, sleep, etc. Since with given techniques the volume of employment determines the level of output (or total income) of the community, we can describe this same function another way as that of determining how much total output the system is to create.

What will resources be used for? It determines *what kinds* of output are to be created. Most labor and most physical resources can be used in the production of any one of a number of goods or services. The economic system provides, consciously or otherwise, a mechanism for selecting which goods or services each resource is to help produce. Since labor is a resource, this includes the function of deciding at what jobs each of the people in the community is to be employed. Economists call this the function of resource allocation.

How much will the economy save? One set of decisions about resource use raises special problems which justify our including these decisions in a separate function. They are the decisions as to how much and which of the available resources are to be used to produce immediately consumable goods and how much to expand and improve productive plant and equipment and build up stocks which will make possible greater future consumption. This is usually called the function of determining the community's rate of real saving.

What techniques will be used? Once it has been decided what each resource shall help produce, the system must also provide a way of deciding *how* it is to be done, what techniques are to be used to transform inputs into outputs. This is different from the function of resource allocation. Allocation involves deciding, for example, how much steel shall be used in automobiles, how much in houses, etc. Determining techniques means deciding whether parts shall be stamped or cast, whether assembly shall bring the parts to the unit or the unit past the parts on a conveyor, whether operation shall be in one, two, or three shifts, and the like. It includes in addition to physical techniques the techniques of personnel management, the determination of conditions of work, the design of incentives, etc.

How will the product be distributed? Finally an economic system provides a mechanism for determining how the total output of consumable goods and services is distributed among the people of the community. This may usefully be separated into two parts.

The first, the function of general income distribution, is to decide what share of the total output of goods and services in general each member of the community is to have without reference to what specific goods are included in that share. This is what is commonly thought of as the distribution of income, and commonly measured by indicating what proportions of the population receive money incomes (or their equivalent) between certain limits (as, for example, 23% receive between $2,000 and $3,000 per year, etc.). The system must decide this distribution of purchasing power not only as between income classes but also as between geographical areas, between functional groups (workers, farmers, executives, etc.), between ethnic groups, and so on. These are all aspects of general income distribution.

With general income distribution determined, however, there is still the problem of what the detailed commodity composition of each person's income is to be, of how each particular good is to be allocated to particular consumers. This we may call the function of commodity allocation. General income distribution has to do with how big each person's package is; commodity allocation has to do with what is in it. Two people may be made equally well off (i.e., given equal incomes) by giving one a bag of oranges and then giving the other a quantity of apples which is (by some standard) worth as much. Or the oranges and apples may both be divided equally between the two, or some other division which gives roughly equal total values may be settled upon. It is the function of commodity allocation to decide questions like this. These two aspects of the distribution of the product of an economy are in practice inextricably mixed up with each other, but in formulating objectives it is useful to separate them in our minds.[2]

It is not intended to imply that these functions are in any sense independent of one another or clearly separable in any complex real situation. A change in techniques will commonly involve a change in resource allocation, probably a change in employment, probably a change in the rate of saving and investment, and very likely some alteration of the distribution of income and the allocation of commodities. Similarly a change in the performance of any of the other functions will have repercussions on all the interrelated variables of the system.

It is also worth emphasizing again that whereas every society in fact performs all of these functions in some way or other, their performance is by no means always an object of conscious policy, governmental or otherwise. The result may be random, it may be logical but "unplanned" as the commodity allocation of a competitive economy was believed to be by the classical economists, or it may be centrally designed as most of these functions are in the Soviet Union. Whatever the machinery by which these functions are performed, however, most people have expressed or implicit views about what the result should be. We have classified the functions in the above fashion because we believe this classification points to useful distinctions among the various different and sometimes conflicting goals of economic policy.

As we proceed with the discussion of these goals we shall try to relate them to the two fundamental postulates assumed above and to show their relation to the kinds of values already described. Our purpose, however, is not to engage in a vigorous and detailed defense either of the substance of the goals proposed or of the particular labels and distinctions adopted. The intent is not to persuade anybody but rather to focus on our problem propositions which most people already accept. Hence if there is wide disagreement with the *substance* we should not argue but rather revise the offending parts. Whether the *form* is appropriate can be tested only by the use to which it is later put.

2. Footnote for economists: I am quite aware that if one scrutinizes it closely the concept of generalized income distribution independent of the commodity composition of income either has no precise meaning or no great significance for small income variations in a community where tastes differ. It will be impossible in such a community, for example, to get agreement on the equality in the welfare sense of two real incomes of differing commodity composition. The Italian will pick the one with olive oil and the Englishman the one with Brussels sprouts (cf. Paul Samuelson, *Foundations of Economic Analysis* [Cambridge, Harvard University Press, 1947], p. 225). Nevertheless in the real world the cases where *inequalities* are unambiguous for a wide range of bundles of commodities are sufficiently numerous to make this distinction useful for policy.

II. Six Objectives of Economic Policy

1. *Minimum unemployment*

The first objective we wish to distinguish is concerned with the way in which the function of determining the volume of employment is performed. It may be briefly stated as follows: It is desirable that *the amount of involuntary unemployment should at all times be as small as it can be made consistent with the attainment of other primary objectives.* We may call this the objective of minimum unemployment.

This objective is by no means identical with that of full employment as the term is used by some writers. In certain contexts the purpose of mentioning "full employment" is to make the reader feel warm all over rather than to denote any objective state of affairs. Since this is not conducive to clarity of analysis it is reason enough to avoid the phrase if possible. However, in more careful writing there are at least three elements sometimes included in the notion of full employment which it is desirable to distinguish in the design of policy. This goal sometimes implies 1) that everybody who wants a job should have it; 2) that everybody should have a job that provides what by some standard is an "adequate" income; and 3) that the job situation should in each case be one that would satisfy, as far as possible, the individual's aspirations for power, respect, enlightenment, well-being, exercise of skills, and other nonincome values. For reasons which will appear presently it is convenient to separate these various elements and refer to the first only as the objective of minimum unemployment.

To illuminate these distinctions further we may think of a spectrum of possibilities. At one extreme is a man working at a job which yields a satisfactory income, a job which makes full use of his capacities, which he enjoys, and which fulfills his notions of a satisfactory working life. Such a man is clearly employed. At the other extreme is a man out of work though willing to do any job he is capable of doing wherever he can get it and at minimum rates. Such a man is clearly unemployed involuntarily. In between lies a whole range of people, some of them working at jobs which do not satisfy them, others not working because the obtainable jobs they could get do not quite meet their conception of what a job ought to be or what they should be paid for it. Presumably everybody would like to see all job seekers clustered at the extreme end of the spectrum which we have labeled "employed" and which might more appropriately be called "fully employed."

But for a number of reasons it will serve clarity to break the continuum of possibilities into pieces covered by the three separate objectives of *enough* jobs, the right *kinds* of jobs, and jobs which *pay* properly. One such reason is that at least rough figures are available on how many people are seriously looking for jobs, that is, on the magnitude of involuntary unemployment in a gross statistical sense, whereas little or nothing has been done on the extent of malemployment or on the volume and nature of additional employment applications that would be forthcoming if job opportunities were widely redesigned to appeal to aspirations now frustrated. If new *kinds* of jobs were offered, based on research into the kinds of work people like to do, the labor force might attract many people who are not now listed as unemployed, as occurred during the war. Ways of measuring these potential additions to the labor force have not, however, been worked out.

Another reason for these distinctions, perhaps more important, is that most of the instruments of policy which economists have regarded as appropriate for an attack on the employment problem have been suggested by the existence of unemployment as the statistics now define it and are directed at the elimination of this particular evil. Most such measures probably have a limited or ambiguous effect on the "adequacy" of employment in the broader sense suggested above. If we speak too loosely of "full employment policy" we may be led falsely to expect a set of measures rather narrowly directed at a particular disease to cure many of the other evils the economy is currently heir to. There is no reason to suppose that a little dose of compensatory spending or a bit of fiddling with the credit structure will transform a humdrum sweatshop into an exciting adventure in living, but this is the impression one gets from some writing on the subject. Distinguishing what we shall call ideal employment from minimum unemployment emphasizes that a positive attack on the broader problem will require the development of quite a different kit of tools than those in the conventional full employment expert's bag and should focus attention on the necessity for developing some of these new tools.

As to whether jobs pay enough, this question, as we shall see later, is obscured rather than illuminated by looking at it as part of the unemployment problem. It is the broad problem of the standard of living and of the productive capacity of the economy. The standard of living cannot be determined by fiat, but is affected by how the functions of resource allocation, income distribution, the design of techniques, etc., are performed. It may be most usefully considered after we have set forth some objectives relating to these other functions.

The distinctions suggested above are not always easy to make. A precise definition of involuntary unemployment is not easy to give in the abstract, though in practice it is not too difficult to measure. Clearly for the purposes of our objective of minimum unemployment everyone actually working full time is to be regarded as employed however much they may be champing the bit. Clearly, likewise, no one should be regarded as unemployed who is not seeking some kind of work somewhere, although if "ideal" employment were realized opportunities might be opened up which would attract many such people. The difficult cases are those of people who are seeking work but have more or less stringent reservations as to the kind of work they would accept or who are working but would like to work longer or harder if they could find more work to do.

For a man's unemployment to be regarded as involuntary must he be willing to pull up his roots and move to another region? Must he be willing to change his trade and abandon skills in which he has invested time and perhaps money? Must he be willing to take a job which changes his status in the community and reduces the respect accruing to him? These are questions which are faced daily by those who must administer unemployment insurance systems. The theorist cannot provide the administrator or statistician with many general rules beyond the question-begging suggestion that a man's unemployment should be regarded as involuntary if he is "reasonably" flexible as to the type, location, and circumstances of jobs he would accept. In practice most people who regard their own unemployment as involuntary are "reasonable" about their standards, so that within broad limits we can leave it to the statistician to determine what detailed definitions will make the statistics of unemployment least ambiguous, most consistent, and most obtainable.

Situations may develop in which we have set our standards of "suitable" employment too high. They may then become a real obstacle to fitting the pool of available unemployed into urgent vacancies even over a considerable period. In such cases the economist should suggest a downward revision in the standards. An example of this not infrequently met in practice is the case of a region which for sound economic reasons is suffering a decline in activity requiring an outward shift of population. But as a general matter it will serve clarity to regard the problem of fitting the particular man more effectively to the particular job as a separate problem distinct from that of minimizing unemployment. If we recognize this other problem we can as a rule accept the definitions of the fact-gathering agencies as to what unemployment in their sense is without danger of overlooking serious maladjustments between people and jobs.

Similar considerations apply to qualifications as to the wage scale a man must accept. In economics generally an article is not regarded as part of the available supply unless it is being offered for sale at approximately the current price. Similarly we may regard involuntary unemployment as existing whenever, in the language of the Employment Act, there are people "able, willing, and seeking to work" at approximately the going rate of wages for the kinds of work they are capable of doing. In some few situations it may seem desirable to define "suitable" standards at a pay scale slightly below what has been customary, but in general it will be less confusing if we do not identify our objectives with respect to the average and minimum standard of living with the goal of minimizing involuntary unemployment.

The relation of this objective to our fundamental postulates and our value system is too obvious to need lengthy elaboration. The direct effects of unemployment on the values of the persons unemployed are pervasive, extending as a rule to incomes (loss of remuneration), power (reduced participation in decisions affecting the work situation), respect (degradation to a lower social class), enlightenment (reduced comprehension of one's place and function in society), skill (deterioration through lack of practice), well-being (inability to afford adequate food and medical care), affection (loss of companionship of co-workers), and rectitude (sense of guilt and personal responsibility for failure). Some of these losses can be made good in whole or in part by measures taken by society other than the provision of employment, but they cannot all be so dealt with.

If a man can be put back to work, and if the value of what he then produces is at least as great as the payment he receives, then the desirability of employing him follows unambiguously from our first postulate, the free choice of values. For under these circumstances things can be arranged so that no one else suffers any deprivation through his reemployment. The fact that he is seeking work at the going wage is evidence that he regards himself as better off employed, and this desire can be satisfied without making anyone else worse off. In most situations these conditions will be satisfied. There are, of course, cases in which the social productivity of the involuntarily unemployed would, if they were put to work, be below the value of the going wage. The wage could not then be paid out of the man's product, and somebody else would have to be deprived of the balance. However, even in these cases the man usually produces *something* useful and hence the deprivation of others required is less than if the unemployed were taken care of by mere transfers of funds from others. It is, of course, desirable that employment opportunities be provided which will be so productive that they will not raise these difficult distributive questions.

Indeed, it is worth pointing out here that there are circumstances in which the values created for others by the employment of a man are so great that they outweigh his own *dis*inclination to take a job at the ruling wage. In such cases the principle of shared values may provide some justification for involuntary *employment*, for forcing a man into an occupation against his preferences. The outstanding example of this in American society is compulsory military service. An all-out mobilization for common defense may require some drafting of workers as well as soldiers in the social interest. These cases are dangerous, however. If the values created for others by a man's employment justify them in offering him enough to make the job attractive—that is to make his employment voluntary instead of involuntary—this will normally be the better course. If the added social values created by his employment are not sufficient for this, there is real question as to whether the employment can be defended on democratic grounds.

2. Ideal employment

Our second objective is concerned with the relation between employment opportunities and people's nonincome values. It may be described by saying that *each person who seeks it should have a job which, to the greatest extent possible, supplies him with the degree and forms of respect, power, well-being, enlightenment, skill acquisition and use, affection, and rectitude which he seeks.* We may call this the objective of ideal employment.

The nature of this goal should be clear in a general way from the discussion of the preceding section. It is another dimension of the broad goal of "full" employment which must be added to the objective of minimum involuntary unemployment. We seek a better adjustment of the worker to his job for two reasons. The first is that such an adjustment will probably result in a higher output from the worker which will increase the income available to him and to the rest of society. The second is that it is one of our primary criteria of welfare that the kind of noneconomic satisfactions people get from the work process itself should be maximized.

The first of these functions, the adjustment of the worker to his job so as to increase *output,* has been recognized as the business of economic policy for some time, though it had to be forced to the attention of economists by psychologists, personnel management experts, and others. It would not be necessary to introduce the goal of ideal employment to cover this function. It is included in any proper conception of good resource allocation and maximum efficiency of resource use. In this context labor is a factor of production like any other, and its use in ways which will produce the biggest national income is merely "good business." If a happy worker is a productive worker then soft music in the factory, a company health program, and an educational campaign to explain the worker's role are justified by productivity considerations.

As soon as we broaden the scope of our objectives from the maximization of income to the satisfaction of a wider list of value goals, the adjustment of the worker to his job becomes not merely a means of facilitating high output but also an important end in itself, growing directly out of the principle of free value choice. The amount and distribution of power, respect, enlightenment, etc., are as much a concern of democratic policy as the amount and distribution of income.

What has to be reexamined here is the extent to which these things are a concern of *economic* policy, which we have defined earlier as policy which employs measures primarily designed to affect income. The most mechanical of the classical economists were always careful to insist that their economic models were intended to explain only one *aspect* of human behavior. The economic man was never thought of as anything but a piece of a man. But income stabilization policy cannot take as its goal the curing of all the ills of humanity. It would surely make our task much easier if we could limit the scope of our inquiry, as is usually done in economic studies, by relegating these nonincome goals to the province of other kinds of policy than economic.

Unfortunately our progress toward the goal of ideal employment is so intimately dependent on virtually every decision we make regarding what on the narrowest definition is purely economic policy that we cannot separate the two. There has been a tendency among economists to distinguish not merely between economic and other *aspects* of people's behavior but between people's economic and noneconomic *activities.* The utility of this distinction rests in part on the possibility of indentifying these activities in practice. If people's behavior as buyers in the market place and sellers at their place of employment can be described as solely economic, their reactions in bed or on the golf course can be regarded as largely irrelevant to economic problems. It is becoming increasingly apparent, however, that the more or less intangible satisfactions of employment affect so intimately and are in turn so directly influenced by purely economic institutions and behavior that they must be regarded as part of the fabric of economic relationships. As we have already discovered, we cannot even define unemployment without some reference to these matters. And when we adopt a labor policy or a tax policy or a government spending policy because of its expected effect on the level of incomes we may be sure that it will have effects, sometimes powerful, on the distribution of other values in the employment situation which we must take into account.

The objective of ideal employment adds another dimension to economic policy. If people are not employed in the jobs at which they would be most *productive* there is only one sort of remedy—to alter their jobs. But if the difficulty is that their aspirations are not satisfied by their existing employment there is an alternative course of action—to attempt to change their aspirations. This idea is at first startling to some who find in it a suggestion of totalitarian manipulation of mass public opinion for ulterior purposes, but it need carry no such sinister connotations.

As we emphasized in laying down our first principle of free value choice, the role of public policy should not be conceived in a purely negative way as the protection of the individual's right to choose, but should accept the positive obligation of providing him with an improved understanding of alternatives on the basis of which to make his choice more intelligently. Insofar as employment aspirations are inconsistent with what is feasible, it is surely a democratic objective to inform and educate the public to the facts so that they may form a more realistic conception of the economic role they should play. If ten million women are desperately unhappy because they are stenographers, telephone operators, and cooks instead of movie stars, a little accurate information on how many jobs there are for movie stars and precisely what they involve may contribute a good deal to ideal employment without shifting the employment of a soul. If an industry is shifting from one region to another a little public advice about the probable course of the shift and the character of available jobs elsewhere may reduce frustration and increase mobility among employees otherwise aspiring to stay put at all costs. These are but relatively trivial examples of the kinds of considerations introduced into policy formation by a recognition of this objective.

3. *Consumer-guided allocation*

Our third objective relates to the way in which the economy performs the functions of allocating resources to the production of different goods and services and then allocating the goods and services when produced to different consumers. We may state it as follows: *Resources and commodities should be so allocated that no change in their allocation is possible which would make somebody better off by his own standards without making somebody else worse off.* We may call this the objective of consumer-guided allocation.[3]

It is immediately apparent from this rather involved way of stating this objective that it is merely the direct application of our principle of

3. It is better known to economists as the principle of consumer sovereignty.

free value choice to the values classified as income values. It is perhaps less clear what it means in practical terms. The resources employed by an economy at any moment are being used in a certain pattern to produce a certain collection of outputs which are being handed out to the members of the community in certain ways. This objective states that if the pattern could be shifted around in any fashion so that after the shift someone said, "I like what I am getting better," and *everyone* else (not just a majority) said, "I like it at least as well as what I got before," the shift would be a good thing. Stated in these general terms the principle sounds perhaps both too obvious and too trivial to be worth putting down. Would not any change which would increase anyone's real income and reduce no one else's be put into effect immediately? Yet economists have increasingly come to realize that many of the most serious evils of actual economic systems can be described as violations of this principle.

Let us look at some examples of situations in which the objective is not satisfied. Assume that in a free market economy two companies agree to divide equally a certain market for, say, steel. One company is much less efficient, wasting facilities, raw materials, office space, and so on. If resources were shifted from the inefficient to the efficient company the same resources could produce more steel and make some people better off. There would be more than enough extra output to compensate the owners of the inefficient firm for any losses resulting from the shift. The market-sharing agreement prevents our reaching our objective.

Again assume a monopoly selling, say, warm woolen shirts is able to separate its customers and charge $6.00 per shirt to a group of outdoor workers needing such shirts badly and only $3.00 a shirt to a group of office workers who can be induced to buy them only by the low price. If the two groups of purchasers could get together the outdoor workers would probably like some more shirts at $4.50 and the office workers would prefer the cash to some of the shirts they have bought. A trade at this price would make everybody better off. Economists can prove that price discrimination almost always involves a violation of the principle of free value choice. The more important industrial cases are a great deal more complex than this, but the principle is the same.

Assume the commissar of food in a centralized economy decides to determine by "democratic" procedures what kind of bread to make and distribute. A ballot is handed around inquiring whether people would rather have white bread or whole wheat; 80% vote for white, so the commissar has a mandate from the people to produce white bread. He decides it would be too costly and complex to produce both kinds. The ballot might refer to several other kinds of bread as well, but it would be too confusing to list all the kinds found in an "unplanned" market. In this example consumer guidance is not being made effective since resources could be reallocated to everybody's satisfaction. A more obvious violation of our principle would, of course, occur if the commissar of public health ruled that, whatever the public wanted, only whole wheat bread would be produced because of its higher vitamin content.

A government wishing to eliminate unemployment decides, on the basis of a report that the people are ill-clothed, to put the unemployed to work repairing old clothes for distribution among the less fortunate. Suppose that if they had distributed money instead of clothes the recipients would have spent it at amusement parks, and the unemployed labor would have been absorbed in the construction and operation of merry-go-rounds. The old clothes program, a step closer to our objective than leaving the labor unemployed, would still not achieve a consumer-guided allocation of resources.

These are merely random examples of the great number of ways in which an objective which may sound obvious in the abstract can fail of achievement in practice because of ignorance of the consequences of a change, ignorance of the precise character of individual tastes, the inertia of bureaucrats, the imperfections of a market, an unwillingness to accept the principle of free value choice, a lack of official imagination in conceiving alternative solutions to a problem, or for a multitude of other reasons.

A reader who is persuaded that the principle of consumer-guided allocation is not trivial may nevertheless have serious doubts as to its validity and implications. We have dealt with some of these in our general discussion of the principle of free value choice above, but some further elaboration of these comments as they apply to consumer-guided allocation may be helpful.

First let us refer again to the question of whether we can regard the objective of a consumer-guided allocation as meaningful in a society in which a substantial volume of resources is devoted to manipulating the wishes and desires of consumers. In the picture of the economic system commonly drawn in the texts of twenty-five years ago the tastes of consumers were generally regarded as an independent datum, a fundamental index of the basic wants and needs of the members of the community whose satisfaction might be taken as the primary object of economic activity. There was only one way of satisfying these wants, which was to produce the goods and services wanted in the largest possible quantities. The modern science of social psychology and its applied counterpart in advertising practice have made it clear that the apparent discrepancy between wants and satisfactions may be reduced in another way—by manipulating the basic wants themselves. As long as consumer demand could be taken as a measure of fundamental requirements of the human spirit reflecting the goals of independent rational individuals the satisfaction of that demand could be regarded as a dignified and worthy objective. It is a little more difficult to look upon the labored creation of a public clamor for Thinsies or Tabu, and its satisfaction, as fulfilling the essential purposes and destiny of Western civilization.

Nevertheless if we regard the objective of consumer-guided allocation as only one of our objectives, and as suggested earlier look upon it as an objective relating to means and not ultimate ends, it retains validity and can gain acceptance in a world of advertising and propaganda. Thus interpreted it does not imply that the existing pattern of consumer tastes is necessarily admirable, or that the allocation of resources dictated by that pattern is the best allocation in some fundamental sense.

All it implies is that if some other allocation is to be achieved it should be achieved through a change in consumer tastes rather than through more directly dictatorial or authoritarian methods. This leaves full scope for attempts to shape the wishes of consumers to goals regarded as more noble or more satisfying (or more profitable to sellers) through education, persuasion, propaganda, or "public opinion management." It is wholly consistent with the view that it is an important function of public policy to guide the education of consumer tastes to more rewarding patterns. But it implies that we regard it as of the utmost importance that if we wish to change the allocation of resources we must do it by persuading the body of consumers that they wish such a change; indeed, we regard it as so important that if we cannot persuade them, we are willing to abandon the proposed reallocation altogether. As stated earlier, we believe this objective to be fundamental to the conception of democracy.

An apparent lapse in the application of the principle occurs when someone's purchases are made for him by some other person or institution. Examples are the housewife's food purchases for the family or the consumer cooperative's purchases for its members. Such cases must be examined closely to determine whether the lapse is real or formal. If the purchasing agent is really an agent, highly sensitive to the varying values of the people for whom the buying is done, the arrangement may be merely a convenient mechanism. But if mother buys all turnips when father prefers parsnips and they are just as cheap, there is a real if trivial violation of the principle of free value choice. More serious violations sometimes occur when a cooperative is controlled by persons with positive value judgments which differ from those of some of the membership.

It is sometimes urged that people do not know what they want until they have tried it, and that it may be justified sometimes to force unwanted goods upon consumers in the belief that once they become acquainted with them they will prefer them. This should be recognized as a violation of the principle of free value choice. A strict adherent to that principle would insist that here likewise the proper route is persuasion, and that if people cannot be persuaded to be experimental they should be left alone. There may be rare and extreme occasions when experiment is very costly and when the evidence is overwhelming that the expected taste will develop, but the burden of proof in such cases must rest heavily on the advocate of force.

Nonetheless it should be emphasized that the objective of consumer-guided allocation not only permits but itself requires changes in tastes and in the flow of commodities available to satisfy them. For allocation and distribution are not optimum as long as the possibility exists of changing either of them in such a way as to leave somebody in a position which, after the change, will be regarded as "preferred" without leaving anyone else worse off. This requires constant experimentation with new kinds of outputs which might be preferred if consumers knew about them. This meets the objection frequently raised against the whole pattern of values implicit in classical economics: that it was a static pattern making no provision for the objective of progress, of improvement in the kinds of goods and services produced, and the techniques of their production.

Professor Schumpeter has argued convincingly that it is in the dynamics of economic change, the process of development and innovation, that we find both the distinguishing characteristic and the primary defense of the capitalist mechanism for which much of classical economics was an apologia. If our objective were to stop with the satisfaction of existing known wants there would be no room for this ideal. But an economic system which leaves unexploited possibilities of creating and satisfying currently nonexistent wants is failing to achieve the objectives of consumer-guided resource use as we have defined it. The system must, of course, have some mechanism for sorting out those potential new wants that will be preferred from those which, by this standard, would not justify the allocation of the necessary resources. If the want does not develop or cannot be nurtured to the necessary degree the innovation must be abandoned. But without the dynamics of innovation optimum allocation will not be achieved.

It is as important to recognize the limitations of this objective as a criterion for policy formation as to understand its wide applicability. It cannot help us to settle problems involving redistributions of values among people. Where one alternative is better for one group and another for another group we cannot choose between them by an appeal to consumer-guided allocation. There are, in other words, a great many ways of allocating resources and outputs, each ideal from the standpoint of this objective but each corresponding to a different distribution of rewards and deprivations among individuals. To choose between such allocations we require additional objectives which will permit us to make comparisons between the values of different people, to say when indulging Paul is worth the implied deprivation to Peter. The principle of shared values, as we shall see, gives us help in some situations of this kind, though by no means in all.

It is difficult to know where to put the emphasis in discussing this limitation of the objective of consumer-guided allocation. The average layman almost certainly underestimates how far we can go in policy matters without raising distributive problems. It is a primitive reaction of common sense that in order to give something to a person you must take it from somebody else. It was one of the great virtues of classical economics that it emphasized that a trade did not, as the medieval writers thought, have to be at someone's expense but could benefit all parties to it. Noneconomists still need to be impressed with the number of ways in which, with a little imagination, things can be shifted around to everyone's benefit and no one's harm.

Even economists have given too little attention to ways in which a change which appears to involve a deprivation can be turned into one of universal benefit by compensating the parties deprived out of the more than ample gains of the immediate beneficiaries. If, as economists have been unanimous in insisting for a hundred and fifty years, the abolition of tariffs benefits the community more than it harms the owners of protected industries, why does it not make sense for the community fully to compensate those damaged by tariff reduction and thus remove their opposition by turning a distributive problem into one of universal gain? As a practical problem this might raise insuperable administrative difficulties, but the possibilities need to be looked into with care. There are a great many other fields where this principle of buying off the opposition out of the profits of those benefited would make the criterion of consumer guidance applicable.

On the other hand, many economists have no doubt exaggerated the extent to which distributive problems could be isolated from those of allocation. The rock on which what is now called welfare economics is founded is the notion that voluntary exchange must benefit all parties to it or it would not take place. Starting from this foundation a large and growing literature has been devoted to examining what kinds of markets, what kinds of industrial organization, what kinds of pricing, etc., would maximize this mutual benefit, that is, would provide ideal consumer-guided allocation for any assumed income distribution. Problems of distribution could be left to one side for separate treatment because, by definition, voluntary exchange could not involve deprivation for any of the parties willingly taking part in it.

One weakness in this view, as the British economist A. C. Pigou pointed out, was that many transactions affect the values of persons other than those voluntarily taking part in them. This has been aptly termed the "neighborhood effect" of a transaction. The most familiar example he adduced (appropriate to the British nineteenth-century tradition in which he was reared) was the smoke from railway engines, which greatly increases the laundry bills of those living along the right of way. An example perhaps more congenial to the internal combustion age is the damage to property resulting from the purchase of large quantities of alcoholic beverages. These are instances of deprivations of *income* to third parties which, following Pigou, economists have come to recognize. When we extend our value system to the range of other values outlined at the beginning of this essay the number of cases where a voluntary transaction may do some third party harm is vastly increased. In the field of residential and industrial construction the well-being of third parties both physical and psychic is intimately concerned. The more obvious neighborhood effects are sometimes recognized in building codes and zoning regulations, but many community planners would hold that the impact of the physical character of a town or factory on the psychic well-being of the inhabitants is much too subtle and pervasive to be controlled by these devices. Monopolistic agreements frequently deprive third parties of power, labor contracts affect the skill opportunities of those not party to them, sales based on race discrimination deprive broad groups of respect, etc. The reader can multiply examples for himself.

We shall consider later some other policy implications of these neighborhood effects, which can of course be positive, benefiting third parties, as well as negative. What is important here is that many problems which look as though they could be solved by appealing to the objective of consumer guidance alone turn out upon closer examination to involve distributive aspects. In an economy mobilized for war or near war the number of transactions which have a neighborhood effect is obviously greatly increased. National defense is inherently a neighborhood problem and not an individual one. The number of situations in which individual preference can be allowed to operate through the market is inevitably reduced. This does not mean, however, that the objective of consumer guidance is irrelevant to these problems but merely that other objectives play a greater role than in peacetime. It is important, especially if mobilization is prolonged, that we employ control devices that permit the maximum degree of consumer guidance consistent with our defense goal.

The relation of this objective to income stabilization policy should be obvious. The immediate purpose of any measure adopted to increase incomes and employment is to put resources to work. There is a tendency in some analyses of the unemployment problem to suggest that this is all that matters, that the objective of minimum unemployment is the only one of importance. But it makes a great deal of difference what they are put to work at. The objective of consumer-guided allocation is one of the criteria for attacking this problem. Similarly measures to avoid inflation—monetary policies, tax policies, and the like—have repercussions on resource allocation which must be tested against this norm. Examples will emerge in subsequent discussion.

4. *An optimum rate of saving*

Our fourth objective relates to the function of determining the community's rate of real saving. As pointed out earlier this is a special instance of the function of resource allocation which concerns the decision as to whether resources are to be used to produce immediately consumable goods or to produce goods for future consumption (capital goods and inventories). Some writers would see no necessity to separate this particular form of resource allocation out from the rest, contending that consumer tastes should guide this decision as they should all other allocation decisions. But as we shall see there is real question as to the meaning of a consumer-guided rate of saving and considerable dispute as to the validity of such a principle. In stating our objective we will therefore dodge this issue, merely assuming that *there is some rate of saving or accumulation which is best for the community* without specifying how it is to be determined. We may call this objective the optimum rate of real community saving or, for short, simply the optimum rate of saving.

One reason for separating out this objective for special treatment is that many of the policy instruments economists have proposed as useful in the stabilization of income are instruments which operate directly on either the savings desires of the community or on the decisions to produce capital equipment of private industry and government. There are, however, some more fundamental reasons. These can best be explained by reviewing the way the classical economists thought savings decisions were related to other allocation decisions in the economy.

The classical economists believed that under certain conditions a free competitive market mechanism would direct the allocation of resources (with greater or lesser efficiency) in a way in general consistent with consumer-guided allocation. Individuals balanced their desires for goods against the prices of those goods, which in turn were a measure of the social cost of producing them. An increase in the desire for one good would lead to greater demand for it, and a shift of resources into its production until the cost of applying still more resources to producing it began to exceed the value consumers put on additional quantities.

In an exactly analogous fashion consumers were thought of as guiding the choice between production for present use and for future use. Each individual was pictured as basing his decision as to how much of his income he would save on a subjective comparison of the satisfactions to be derived from consuming now with those to be secured from having more to consume at some specific future time. The rate or price at which these two kinds of satisfactions could be traded was determined by the rate of interest, which offered a premium for the postponement of consumption. All the individual savings decisions taken together were believed to dictate the allocation of real resources between current production and capital accumulation (or what economists call investment). The connecting link between individual saving and community investment was the rate of interest which controlled the amount of real capital goods produced. When this mechanism was working properly, the interest rate was the price which insured that resources would be allocated between present and future production in just the way consumers wanted them to be. When consumers wanted to postpone more consumption, their added savings would drive down the rate of interest, drawing more resources into capital goods activity and vice versa. The volume of capital accumulation was determined by the consensus of consumer preferences between current and future consumption in the light of the comparative costs of these two ways of using resources.

There are many flaws in this picture as a description of the actual savings-investment process in a modern economy. The most prominent in current discussion is the failure of the mechanism always to induce precisely the amount of capital accumulation which the public's desire to save at full employment income levels would require. It is now recognized that an increase in the public's desire to save (which is the same as a decrease in their desire to consume *now*) may lead not to more production of capital goods but to less total production and employment. This problem will be discussed further in Chapter 3.

For our present purpose we are not concerned, however, with this particular defect in the model. Let us suppose that policy is successful in achieving the objective of minimum involuntary unemployment, and that we have high production incomes. The question we must then raise is whether the total amount of money that the public decides to save out of its money income really does give a clear indication of how consumers want resources allocated between present and future consumption. If it does, then a thoroughgoing acceptance of the principle of free value choice would compel us to accept this volume of money saving as a measure of the optimum rate of real saving (assuming we had achieved a proper distribution of income in the first place). It would then be a policy objective to see to it that the actual rate of production of capital goods (i.e., of real investment) was at the level indicated by the public's saving desires. Attempts to manipulate artificially what economists call the public's propensity to save, or to achieve a different rate of real saving from that which it would suggest could then be said unambiguously to be in conflict with the principle of free value choice, and an important principle of stabilization policy would be established.

Unfortunately there are at least two compelling reasons for believing that the community's propensity to save out of money income does not reflect its choice between current and future production. The first is that in an uncertain world many individual savings decisions result much more largely from vaguely precautionary considerations than from preference as to the timing of consumption. The individual saves not because he wants to substitute known future consumption for known present consumption but rather because he wishes to accumulate a reserve against possible but unformulated contingencies. But in many cases no real saving by the community is needed to provide the individual with this sort of protection. His desire to avoid risk can be met by insurance schemes which reduce his propensity to save without affecting the optimum allocation of resources between current and future production.

In the operation of an insurance scheme some people save by paying premiums while others, the recipients of benefits, dis-save by consuming more than their current income. When such a scheme is available the excess of saving over dis-saving may be sharply reduced below what it would be if each individual had to build up his own reserve from which to meet contingencies. In other words, the pooling of risks makes it possible to provide a given degree of protection against contingencies with less sacrifice of consumption than if each person had to build up his own reserves. This risk-protection motive for individual saving thus has no bearing on the optimum rate of saving for the community.

This is quite a different point from the contention that the propensity to save does not reflect time preference because saving is controlled by habit, custom, and public opinion. This is true to some degree of all expenditure patterns. As pointed out above, to accept consumer guidance does not imply that current consumer tastes are rational or ideal, but that an ideal allocation of resources should be sought through the persuasion of consumers. The essential difference in the case of saving decisions is that there are valid rational reasons why individuals should wish to save amounts different from those dictated by pure time preference. Therefore even in the ideal case in which consumers have been educated intelligently to pursue what are in fact their best interests, the individual propensity to save is not a good index of the desires of the community with respect to the optimum real rate of saving for the group.

The second thing which sets savings decisions apart from other allocation decisions is the fact that in a modern community a substantial part of the total money saving is performed by business institutions. Ideally one might hold that the decision of a corporation not to pay out all of its earnings merely reflects indirectly the common decision of the stockholders to save. In practice, of course, the motives for corporate saving are in many cases so far removed from the time preferences of the owners that they may be regarded as virtually independent of them. For this reason we are in need both of special criteria for the ideal rate of group saving and of mechanisms other than the present price system for establishing it.

These difficulties in determining the rate of capital goods production (real community saving) wanted by consumers have led some economists tacitly or explicitly to the view that there is no such thing as an optimum rate of saving, that it fundamentally does not matter what the real rate of capital accumulation is, and that therefore any manipulation of the rate of investment which will favorably affect our progress toward some other goal, such as minimum unemployment, is a good thing. This, of course, does not follow. The fact that the classical indicator of the optimum rate of saving cannot be relied on does not mean that there is no such optimum rate.

This becomes clear if we consider extreme cases. We would all presumably agree that we want continued growth in our total capacity to produce, and that some net investment in capital goods is necessary for such growth. A rate of saving as low as zero would be universally agreed to be less than the desirable rate. On the other hand, a rate which absorbed as much as 30 or 40% of our resources would imply a reduction in standards of living which almost everyone would agree is not worth it. The problem is how to narrow the limits of this range by criteria which will be sensitive enough to be helpful in deciding between alternatives less dramatically far apart.

The failure of the classical indicator, far from leading us to abandon the whole concept of an optimum rate of saving, should spur us to redouble our efforts to find some general way of defining it and, failing this, should make us examine with particular care individual proposals to manipulate the rate of saving to achieve another end such as income stabilization to make certain that such proposals are not in obvious conflict with whatever limited ideas concerning a good rate of saving we may have in a particular situation. Paul Samuelson considers this problem further in Chapter 12.

5. *Maximum technical efficiency*

Our fifth objective has to do with the function of selecting techniques of production. *Techniques should be such that the maximum possible output of any commodity is obtained from given inputs of resources, or alternatively that a given output is obtained with minimum quantities of inputs.* This we may call the objective of maximum technical efficiency. It concerns not what commodities are produced nor what resources are used but rather what methods of production in the broadest sense are employed.

This objective is a direct corollary of the principle of free value choice. If total output can be increased without changing input, one or more persons can clearly be made better off without hurting anybody. Similarly if everybody can enjoy the same flow of goods and services with less effort or sacrifice on someone's part, somebody gains and nobody loses. The only important qualification we must make to the familiar statement of this objective is that input and output must be interpreted in terms not merely of income but of the whole range of values pursued. If increased physical output is obtained with the same physical exertion but with deprivations of respect to the worker, input in the sense relevant to this objective is not unchanged. The sharing of power between management and employees may in some instances reduce physical output but it may be justified in spite of the reduced physical efficiency of the operation. Fortunately in most instances the satisfaction of nonincome values increases purely economic efficiency rather than the reverse, but each case must be examined with the entire value scale in mind.

Jurisdictionally minded economists have regarded the problem of increasing technical efficiency as lying outside their province. Economics texts often begin with the statement that the economist assumes given tastes, given available resources, and a given "state of the arts." Productive techniques are taken to be part of the data of the economist's problem rather than one of the variables it is his business to explain. This probably goes back to an identification of "techniques" with mechanical inventions, thought up by clever, if slightly eccentric, individual inventors like Eli Whitney and Thomas Edison for reasons which psychologists can possibly explain but economists must regard as outside their ken. The available knowledge of mechanics at any time, on this interpretation, can be regarded as a "given" resource like iron ore or petroleum deposits.

This preoccupation of economists with problems which start from what they call "given production functions" has led many of them to underemphasize what may be one of the principal obstacles to the achievement of higher levels of output. For the problem of productive efficiency is, of course, much broader than mechanical invention. In the first place invention in the modern world of great industrial laboratories is no longer a matter of bright ideas coming more or less accidentally to isolated men in garrets or workshops. The rate at which new discoveries are made depends in a fairly predictable way on the resources devoted to research and discovery. Thus the progress of invention itself is directly influenced by economic policies which encourage or inhibit business research expenditures. We are greatly in need of more information on how these research outlays are affected by such factors as taxes, subsidies, the interest of the military, the degree of competition, etc.

In the second place, as Professor Schumpeter has so rightly emphasized, pure invention is only the first, and a rather minor, step in the process of technological change. Once the invention is available it must be applied, businessmen must have the foresight to see its virtues and the courage to risk its adoption, production methods must be readjusted to take fullest advantage of the new technique, old equipment to which firms have committed funds must be scrapped, men must be retrained and the opposition of groups with a vested interest in the old process overcome. These and many other steps are necessary before a change in technical knowledge is reflected in industrial practice, before, in Professor Schumpeter's terminology, an invention becomes an innovation.

That these things do not happen as a matter of course is apparent to anyone familiar with American business practice. Why, in spite of competitive pressure, the availability of capital funds, and similar favorable factors, do methods of production generally admitted to be antiquated and inefficient persist in some of our major industries? This is a question which any agency responsible for economic policy must ponder. It seems reasonable to suppose that the climate of business sentiment, shaped and influenced by economic policy and especially by income stabilization policy, has an important effect on innovation in this broad sense.

Finally it has come to be realized in recent years that productive efficiency is determined by much more than physical engineering. It is as important to use *people* correctly as to devise new machines and new methods of plant organization. This art of human engineering has developed rapidly of late but its application in the business world is still in its infancy. We have already discussed (section 2 above, p. 82) as a fundamental goal which would be accepted by most Americans the objective of ideal employment, of providing for each individual employment opportunities which potentially indulge his entire range of values as far as possible. What we are here concerned with is the somewhat different problem of getting the greatest quantity and quality of output from our human input. It is one of the happy discoveries of recent research that by and large these two objectives are complementary rather than conflicting. Giving people what they want turns out to be one of the best ways of increasing their productivity.

This is well illustrated by the broadening of the structure of incentives offered by progressive management to include not only income (the wage) but power (participation in decisions affecting the work situation and the development of the enterprise), respect (recognition of the human and social status of the employee), well-being (protection of employee health and safety), enlightenment (information about the purposes and prospects of the firm, its economic position, the kind of social contribution it is making, and the relation of the employee's job to the rest of the business), skill (adjustment of the worker to jobs for which he is fitted with provision for learning new desired skills up to the capacity of the individual), and so forth. By offering a worker not merely an income but some or all of these other values as well a firm can greatly increase his economic efficiency. The effect of income stabilization policies upon this structure of incentives and thus upon worker productivity is therefore something to which policy officials should give serious consideration. It is not enough, for instance, to counter depression and inflation by manipulating aggregate purchasing power if the employment provided thereby is uncongenial in any of the ways suggested above to those seeking jobs. It is not enough, first because the objective of ideal employment is itself overlooked and second because productivity is restricted so that more employment does not produce much more output.

Another dimension of the problem of human engineering to which less attention has been paid is concerned with what makes for high productivity in the managerial staff. What determines the focus of attention of business managers? Is the failure of inventions to become innovations a consequence of the fact that executives are not spending their time on the right problems, that they are not directing their attention to the places where it is most needed? The design of policy can have a great influence on this aspect of efficiency. It is not merely that controls should be so devised as to impose a minimum of red tape and lost motion on businessmen. More important, perhaps, is the desirability of not focusing the attention and imaginative energies of managers too heavily on relations with controlling agencies. The history of many subsidized industries is an object lesson in how the process of innovation can be retarded when the minds of executives are diverted from production problems to relations with government. This is, of course, a problem which extends beyond economic policy to the legal and social environment of business.

A more subtle problem is how the efficiency of management is affected by the extent to which the manager's own work situation satisfies his value pattern. Ideal employment may well be as important to managerial productivity as to employee efficiency. For example, businessmen as a class undoubtedly felt deprived of respect by the New Deal. The intense antagonism to the Roosevelt program which developed among businessmen was due not so much to the effect of New Deal measures on business profits as to the suggestion in much New Deal literature that to be a businessman was to be a selfish money grubber. It would be interesting to know to what extent the energy expended in hating "that man in the White House" reduced managerial efficiency during the thirties. These examples may serve to suggest ways in which income stabilization policy may be framed to take account of the objective of maximum technical efficiency.

6. *Optimum income distribution*

Our sixth objective concerns the way in which the function of determining general income distribution is performed. Unfortunately there appears to be no simple way which would be widely accepted of describing what we mean by the "best" distribution of income (and wealth). This does not mean, however, that there is no such thing, or that notions of what is a proper income distribution do not have a profound and pervasive effect on all kinds of policy decisions. We shall find it convenient to refer to this goal, however it may be defined, as the objective of optimum income distribution.

Although we have not yet found a generally acceptable way to describe quantitatively exactly what we mean by optimum income distribution, we could get broad agreement on a good many things the objective involves. Difficulties in formulating criteria of equity in the abstract will not prevent a surprising consensus of opinion as to which of two particular income or wealth distributions is the better. Policy makers are required daily to make decisions concerning the sharing of the social product which they are frequently able to defend to the approximate satisfaction of a large majority. Somehow we arrive at a scale of income tax rates, apportion government aid to individuals, establish income criteria for housing programs, etc. This suggests that there is more common ground here than we can easily summarize in a formula.

The difficulties of delimiting this common ground in general terms are formidable, and we cannot undertake here to do more than suggest a few of the bench marks preliminary to a more complete survey. The objective is clearly an application to the limited sphere of income values of the general principle of shared values laid down at the beginning of this essay, and is subject to all the ambiguities and confusions attaching to that idea. Furthermore, the distribution of income must be viewed not only as a *consequence* of economic organization to be judged by ultimate standards of equity but also as an important *determinant* of our progress toward other goals. In any practical case we must consider not only whether a given distribution is good in itself but also whether it fosters production or reduces social unrest or discourages dictatorship or is an instrument to some other end.

This suggests one limit to the notion of an optimum income distribution we can probably all accept. As a practical matter it is doubtful whether many thoughtful persons would regard absolute equality of incomes as optimum. There is the familiar difficulty that people's needs differ for reasons beyond their control—people in the North need more hot water bottles than people in the tropics. But even if we interpret equality in the Marxist fashion as equality in relation to individual need there is a further problem which arises from the twofold nature of personal income as both a source of value to the individual and a prerequisite to his productive activity as part of the community's resources.

For example, a strict application of the principle of equality would mean that the President of the United States would live in an average small house where his advisers and official visitors could not be efficiently received, that he would put up his own screens in the spring and polish his own car, and (if he was that kind of a man) he would do a good many errands downtown for his wife. Regarding him as a consuming man we might defend the proposition that he deserves no special treatment just because he happens to be President. But regarding him as a vital instrument of government, as a valuable national resource, it is clear that if we have chosen him well it would be an unconscionable waste to allocate his energies to sweeping his garage. This is but an extreme example of the consequences for income distribution of an efficient division of labor. As Adam Smith insisted, specialization is capable of increasing output enormously. To produce a high national standard of living the inputs of individuals into the productive process must vary greatly in character. But inputs and outputs are inextricably intertwined in the welfare position of the individual. Traveling salesmen see the world, professors have long summer "vacations," and labor leaders frequently escape the monotonous routine of the workers they represent. Wherever men specialize there will be some inevitable differences in their incomes, broadly conceived, which are a necessary concomitant of the efficient use of their special capacities and skills.

There is further the question of incentives. The incentive effects of income discrepancies are today used in two ways. Firstly, income differentials still play some role in shifting resources, particularly labor, into more urgent and away from less urgent uses. Expanding industries bid workers away from contracting industries by offering them better pay and conditions of work. It may be, as some writers contend, that income differentials are a poor tool for this purpose, but we have not yet devised an effective substitute.

Secondly, any scheme which guarantees equal incomes must of necessity eliminate the use of income as a stimulus to productivity. To a lesser degree any scheme which reduces differential rewards for productivity weakens the stimulus. How important this factor is, is a matter of fact which requires much further study. There is an abundance of violent opinion and a paucity of reliable evidence. We have come a long way in recognizing the importance of nonincome incentives. On the other hand, our experience with Europe immediately after World War II appeared to show that in that society at least the bait of consumers' goods was necessary to call forth high production.

We can now draw one boundary of the goal of equalization of incomes which would probably secure widespread acceptance. If it can be shown that starting from a particular income distribution a further equalization would reduce output so much that those at the bottom of the income scale would clearly be worse off after a redistribution intended to be in their favor, then the redistribution is undesirable. In other words, optimum income distribution requires any degree or type of inequality which can be shown unambiguously to benefit the poor as well as the rich. This follows directly from the principle of free value choice, since in this case inequality makes everybody better off. Whether this condition is actually of any help to the policy maker in practical situations depends on whether we can develop reliable and objective evidence as to the impact of distribution on productivity. It is certainly worth devoting resources to research in this field if we can thereby establish acceptable policy criteria where today there are none.

Leaping across the terrain we can see the outlines of another boundary on the other side. Income inequalities, pushed to extremes, undoubtedly interfere with productivity as much as excessive equalities. The mirror image of our first boundary would be the principle that a redistribution in favor of the rich which, through its impact on productivity, leaves the rich worse off would clearly be undesirable. The masters of a slave state benefit from a policy of keeping their slaves fed, healthy, and warm. But this boundary is probably entirely off the map of the country we live in. The Nizam of Hyderabad (an area of extreme inequality) would undoubtedly feel worse off if he were to make over half his income and wealth to the people of his erstwhile realm.

By adopting a slightly more controversial position we can bring the upper boundary of inequality closer to home. We may tentatively suggest that wide acceptance could be found for the view that a reduction in inequality is desirable whenever it raises the *average* real income, i.e., whenever it increases total production. And we can bring still another important class of cases within reach of our criterion if we are willing to say that any reduction in inequality is desirable which leaves the level of average real income unchanged.

We could not gain support for this last proposition from those who believe that the presence of a wealthy class in a society is essential to the development of certain kinds of desirable nonincome cultural values. Only the rich, so runs the argument, can encourage the arts, literature, science, and illustrate a concept of gracious living. Whatever the merits of this view in a society with a low standard of living like that of the Medicis, it probably has few adherents in an economy like ours in which the average man has both time and money to devote individually or through his social institutions to culture.

There is still a strip of territory between our two boundaries where we have established as yet no general criteria for choosing whether distribution A or distribution B is the better. We have no way of telling from the conditions so far developed whether a change which benefits the poor but lowers the average standard is a good thing or not. How wide this strip of territory is can be determined only by empirical studies yet to be made. It is the suspicion of the present writer that it is narrower than is often supposed. We could narrow the range a good deal further by defining the concept of the distribution of income more precisely. So far we have characterized it by only three measures, the top income, the bottom, and the average. Much depends on the details of the distribution through the middle ranges, on the distribution by function and geographical area as well as by size group, on the opportunities offered individuals to move from one income group to another, on the stability and risk attaching to incomes of different sizes, etc. By looking further into these and other characteristics we could undoubtedly draw a tighter and tighter net around the idea of optimum income distribution, so that while we might not be able to capture the animal we could confine him in a small enough pen to get a pretty clear idea of what he looks like. This is not a task appropriate to this volume. We have pursued the investigation this far merely to indicate that we do not have to relegate the concept of optimum income distribution to the relativist limbo of each man's private whim. It is wholly possible that by patient effort coupled with empirical research we can develop some generally acceptable standards which will offer policy guidance.

Two further comments are in order as to the meaning of the objective of optimum income distribution. An attempt is sometimes made to bypass the difficulties raised above by interpreting the principle of shared values in terms of equal *opportunity* to acquire such values as income. This is a plausible goal, which can usefully be employed to attack certain kinds of simple discrimination, such as racial or religious qualifications for employment or advancement. Applied to a broader range of problems, however, the concept of equality of opportunity turns out to add other ambiguities to those we have already discussed. How are we to determine by what standards opportunities are equal?

In our American society people's opportunities depend on their geographical location, on the degree and nature of their basic abilities, on their personal contacts, on luck and chance, and on many other factors which cannot by their nature be equalized. If we equalize opportunity in the conventional sense of removing such barriers to it as social caste, inadequate education, inherited poverty and the like, it is not at all clear that what we would regard as an equitable distribution of income will automatically follow. Again the problem of selecting in practice those policies which will promote equality of opportunity is a good deal simpler than that of formulating useful broad generalizations about it. The complexities of the theory of equal opportunity are suggested here merely to indicate that our objective would not really be rendered any more precise by substituting "equal opportunity" for "optimum income distribution."

The second comment is that income must not be interpreted narrowly as money income as measured by the internal revenue authorities. It is obvious, of course, that income furnished in kind (such as farm produce consumed on farms) must be valued and added. Apart from this routine statistical qualification, however, it is important to remember that the distribution of assets (wealth) is as relevant to our objective as the distribution of money (and imputed) income. Income distribution and asset distribution tend to be correlated, but there are important instances where they diverge. Since assets represent potential consumption (as well as a source of other values such as power and sometimes respect), their equitable distribution is as important as that of the currently accruing income stream.

This objective is related to income stabilization in a number of ways. In the first place, many of the evils resulting from a failure to stabilize incomes are reducible to inequities in income distribution. Unemployment, as we have seen, is undesirable for many reasons, but not the least of these is that in the absence of relief measures one group in the population, the unemployed, receive an intolerably reduced share of a reduced national output. In an inflation maldistribution becomes the central villain of the piece. Indeed if it were not for maldistribution (and the threat of ensuing depression) all but the more violent inflations would be relatively harmless. Everyone is familiar with the plight of such persons as widows and college professors forced to live on a fixed money income in a period of rapidly rising prices.

Secondly, a great many of the measures available to policy officials for dealing with depressions and inflations have important repercussions on income distribution. Almost any tax measure and almost any major governmental expenditure impinges on income distribution in more or less important ways. The effects of monetary policy are less obvious but they can be significant. One whole class of measures proposed for stabilization involves direct manipulation of the distribution of incomes in order to affect the volume of consumer spending. Included in this group are proposals to increase wages relative to profits on the theory that a larger percentage of the wage dollar is spent than of the profit dollar, and counterproposals to increase profits relative to other functional shares on the ground that higher profits mean a larger volume of investment spending. The merits of this type of controversy will be considered at various points later in this symposium. What is relevant here is that these arguments are so often conducted without specific reference to the objective of optimum income distribution itself. The fact that optimum income distribution is difficult to define in the abstract does not relieve policy officials of the obligation to consider whether the effects of a proposed measure on income distribution are desirable in themselves.

The prevalence of proposals to stabilize output and prices by redistributing incomes suggests a danger to which we are exposed by the difficulty of defining objectively an ideal income distribution. A measure whose purpose is income redistribution will almost always be controversial. On the other hand, everybody is in favor of avoiding depression and inflation. If, therefore, you want to redistribute incomes you had better do it in the name of income stabilization or some similarly innocuous objective. Much of the difficulty economists have in reaching agreement as to the effects of income distribution on the level of employment arises from the fact that the disputants are not really primarily interested in the explicit object of their dispute, but are battling over unexpressed assumptions as to ideal distribution. Policy formulation is likely to be clearer, more consistent, and less self-frustrating if these unexpressed conflicts are made explicit. Better to confess that we have a goal that cannot be objectively tested than to pretend that we are concerned only with quite different matters.

A rough test is available as to when this particular divergence between real and stated aims is present. Since depressions are associated with too little spending and inflations with too much, most income stabilization measures are reversible. If a redistribution of incomes in one direction should be a good antidepression measure, a redistribution in the other direction should be a good anti-inflation measure. If a man who argues for wage increases in a depression will agree that wage reductions are a good anti-inflation device you may criticize his logic but you can be fairly sure of his honesty. The almost universal failure of redistribution proposals to pass this reversibility test suggests that in the literature on income stabilization policy concealed objectives play a large role.

III. THREE INSTITUTIONAL COROLLARIES

1. *Primary use of the private market*

The set of objectives for economic policy that we have outlined so far —minimum unemployment, ideal employment, consumer-guided allocation, an optimum rate of saving, maximum technical efficiency, and optimum income distribution—have been developed without reference to the institutional or political structure of society. These are objectives that might be pursued in a capitalist, socialist, communist, corporative, or managerial state. None of them is *by definition* incompatible with virtually complete laissez faire or with virtually complete state ownership and operation of the economy. Nonetheless, most people have strong views as to the kind of society in which these objectives are likely to be most nearly attained. The conviction that certain institutional arrangements must be preserved for various reasons is one of the most powerful considerations in all kinds of policy formation. It is necessary, therefore, to extend our list of objectives to include certain commonly accepted notions as to what the organization of our society should look like.

It is necessary to preface this supplementary list with two observations. The first is that it is not easy to draw a line in practice between what we wish actively to promote as an ideal of social organization and what we are willing to accept as an inevitable trend. We are all to some extent determinists, at least in the short run. What it is feasible to accomplish depends on the developing situation in which we find ourselves. It is easy to affect its development a little, difficult to affect it a good deal, wholly frustrating and "impractical" to ignore altogether the powerful forces already at work at a given time in any society. The assumptions which the operating policy maker adopts about the institutional framework within which he must operate will always, therefore, be a compromise between what is desirable and what is inevitable. The supplementary "objectives" listed below reflect this compromise. They all exhibit the Marxist confusion between what one would like and what one predicts. This confusion is perhaps logically deplorable but it is an unavoidable aspect of the statesman's art. We should try to be as clear about it as possible, but we cannot do without it.

The second observation is that this essay is not the place to construct and defend a complete social and political philosophy. The corollary objectives listed below (like those already developed) are intended only to identify and classify in a useful manner a set of conditions believed to be widely accepted by thinking people in America. The selection and classification, furthermore, have been made solely on the basis of the light they may throw on the problems of income stabilization policy. The comments made concerning the objectives are intended only to explain what is meant and why it is relevant and not to defend or justify.

The first institutional condition which we assume is generally regarded as desirable in America is that *the bulk of the decisions as to the allocation of resources and the production and distribution of individual commodities should be made by a market mechanism participated in by private individuals buying and selling for private account.* We may refer to this as the objective of *primary use of the private market mechanism.*

There are three critical words in this statement of the objective. The first is "primary." It has always been recognized, as Francis Coker demonstrates in Chapter 2, that there are some allocation decisions, such as how many policemen there should be, that cannot from their nature be made by a price system. The area of the economy in which governmental allocation is recognized to be appropriate has been growing. We shall discuss the criteria for delimiting it presently. This objective is intended to suggest that that area is still not dominant and should be kept rather vigilantly within bounds.

The second key word is "market." This is intended to imply the use of an effective price system as the major instrument of allocation. If properly interpreted, the phrase "free price system" could be substituted for "market mechanism." In this event, however, "free" should not be taken to imply the absence of any controls over buyer and seller whatever. The price system must be free in the sense that prices are permitted to perform a genuine allocating function which is not impeded by such devices as price control and rationing. It may, however, require considerable government control and supervision of a market to insure that prices are free in the sense intended.

The third significant word is "private." There are proposals for the extensive use of "free price systems" by socialist states. Such proposals omit one of the key elements of this objective, the idea that the market mechanism should operate in a framework of primarily private ownership and that the operations of production and exchange should be undertaken primarily for private account. The reasons why this is deemed to be desirable will occupy us in a moment. Here we are concerned only to make clear that the objective we are discussing includes both the "market" element and the element of private ownership. The objective might be loosely identified with the maintenance of "capitalism" or "free private enterprise," but these phrases have acquired too many ambiguous overtones to suit our purposes.

Capitalism has come to be widely defended on political grounds as a bulwark against authoritarian systems of various kinds, but it is important to remember, as Francis Coker emphasizes later, that this defense is a comparatively recent development. The political philosophers of the nineteenth century believed in the private market mechanism as a device to achieve principally economic rather than social or political results. It is useful to consider in what respects the classical economic defense of capitalism has been weakened by twentieth-century developments in the world of both theory and experience.

It was believed by the classical economists that virtually all of the objectives of economic policy we have outlined would be more nearly attained under a private market mechanism with a minimum of government interference than under any other alternative. It was implied that a private competitive system would automatically produce minimum unemployment, a consumer-guided allocation, an ideal rate of saving, maximum technical efficiency, and the most equitable general distribution of income. There are isolated pockets of faith where a last ditch defense is still being put up for this view, but American expert and public opinion has for the most part abandoned several of these ramparts.

The Employment Act of 1946 elevates to the level of official government policy what the majority of economists have believed for some years, namely, that special action by the government is required to prevent the system from developing, cyclically and perhaps chronically, intolerably high levels of unemployment. Reasons for believing that the capitalist machinery for determining the rate of saving is inadequate are given above (section II–4, p. 41). We have accepted in our income tax laws and possibly in other legislation such as minimum wage laws the conclusion that the distribution of income resulting from a free market determination of the prices of human services is not the most equitable. Finally, few would contend that the free market mechanism achieves a close approach to the objective of ideal employment as we have defined it. If we are to stay within the realm of generally acceptable propositions we cannot defend the private market mechanism primarily on the basis of its superior performance of any of these functions.

There remain the two objectives of consumer-guided allocation of resources and maximum technical efficiency. If there is to be any *generally acceptable economic* basis for the defense of the mechanism it must be sought in its alleged capacity to bring us nearer to these two goals than any presently known alternative.

The position here advanced is that in fact a majority of Americans would agree that a primarily free and private production and market system (in a suitably controlled environment) does the jobs of allocation and technical advance well enough to justify its preservation. It follows from this proposition that anything which directly interferes with the system's performance *of those functions* is in conflict with an accepted objective.

It should be unnecessary to reiterate the now familiar point that the maintenance of capitalism does not imply a policy of laissez faire in the old-fashioned sense of an absolute minimum of government intervention. As implied above there is among capitalist apologists pretty general acceptance of intervention to maintain employment, redistribute income, improve the character of employment opportunities, and even affect the rate of saving. Beyond this, however, and within the sphere of what are still regarded as the prime economic functions of the market mechanism, three more types of intervention are consistent with its preservation.

The first of these is called for when private transactions have a strong "neighborhood effect" (see section II–3, above, p. 40), that is, when such transactions affect the values of persons not voluntarily parties to the transaction. Sometimes these neighborhood effects are so strong and so pervasive that there is a case for abandoning the market mechanism in favor of direct governmental allocation, but in other instances market procedures can be used if they are so regulated that injury to third parties is prevented, or injured persons compensated. Zoning laws and smoke ordinances are examples of regulation in the interests of the "neighborhood."

Secondly, intervention is called for to promote competition in private markets. It has become pretty commonly accepted that in many fields the free market will not satisfy the objective of consumer-guided allocation without positive state controls designed to establish and maintain competitive conditions and to prevent monopolistic restrictions of various sorts.

Finally, our conception of the areas in which the private price system, however regulated, cannot be expected to allocate resources effectively and in which therefore direct allocation by government authority is called for has enormously broadened. These points will be expanded in subsections 2 and 3 below, pp. 60–68.

The acceptability of this private market objective depends in an important way upon the dynamic interpretation we have given to the objectives of consumer-guided allocation and maximum technical efficiency. We have already referred to the fact that many people feel that the peculiar virtue of the private market mechanism lies in its capacity not only to adapt resource use to rapidly changing techniques and patterns of taste, but also actually to stimulate technical advance and the maturing of wants much more effectively than other institutional devices. It is here that the importance of the incentives associated with private property is alleged to be particularly great. Since the development of new and more rewarding wants is an integral part of the objective of consumer guidance and the invention and design of new and better methods is essential to the maximization of technical efficiency, the dynamic advantages of the private market mechanism are implied in the assertion that it is the best presently known instrument for achieving those two objectives.

When we broaden our perspective from income values to the full value scale outlined earlier in this essay (section 2, p. 18) it is at once clear that there are other defenses of the private market mechanism than those we have described. Since we are concerned only to identify goals and not to defend them we can give only one or two suggestions as to the trend of the broader argument.

The principle of free value choice implies that individuals should be left with the maximum liberty to pursue their own ends. But economic activities and "noneconomic" activities are inextricably interconnected. The private market mechanism (suitably controlled) is widely believed to leave the individual more degrees of freedom in his economic activities than other systems with which we are familiar. This implies more degrees of freedom with respect to values other than income values: freedom to change employment, to choose between working for others or working independently, to choose between secure and risky patterns of life, to decide between occupations which maximize respect and those which maximize power or income, freedom to use one's resources to acquire skills, or to invest heavily in physical well-being, or to multiply opportunities for relations of affection, etc. Many would defend the market mechanism as an organizing principle for the economy on the ground that it is more likely than other systems to render the principle of free value choice effective over the whole scale of values and not merely in the domain of income.

Again it would be argued by many that there is at least a greater possibility of wide *sharing* of certain nonincome values under a private market mechanism than in other systems. If, for instance, ultimate responsibility for all economic decisions rests with a single agency, the state, this organizational principle implies an extreme concentration of proximate power. Even if the state is organized along genuinely democratic lines so that "popular will" effectively directs the broad outlines of policy, managerial efficiency will require that a great many decisions be controlled from a very narrow base. This makes an effective sharing of power administratively very difficult even if officials are genuinely concerned to promote it. To be sure, great concentrations of power may also occur within the private sector, but there is at least a possibility of dispersing them through public policy whereas concentration of some degree of responsibility is inherent in government-operated enterprise.

Thus we may argue that the principle of shared values has a better chance under a predominantly private market mechanism than under alternative systems.

The particular importance of this objective for income stabilization policy is that income stabilization is probably a good deal easier in systems which abandon the private market mechanism. In a centrally controlled economy unemployment can very simply be avoided by merely providing that the state will forthwith employ any unemployed person. Similarly the control of inflation is simple if enforcement is adequate since any rise in prices can be forbidden by decree. The second of these measures is invariably inconsistent with the use of a private market mechanism and the first is very likely to be, since it may well lead to a rapid expansion of the governmentally directed portion of the economy. It is very likely, therefore, that some of the measures proposed for stabilizing incomes will conflict with this objective. How to minimize such conflicts is one of the most important problems confronting the would-be stabilizer.

2. *Promotion of competition*

Many of the economic advantages alleged for the private market mechanism depend on the degree to which the private enterprise system is free of elements of monopoly. There are, further, some nonincome values which are promoted by a high degree of the right kinds of competition. In this context competition means not a dog-eat-dog struggle to do in the other fellow, but a state of affairs in which there are enough independent buyers and sellers in any market to limit the control of any one of them over price and output and to keep them all toeing the mark of efficiency. We may list as an additional institutional goal the objective of the *promotion of competition* in this sense.

It is as hard to be precise about this objective as about some of the others. It would be generally agreed by economists that the private market will produce the desired results as to allocation and technical efficiency only if there are present in a substantial number of markets adequate competitive elements. The difficulties are of two sorts. First there would be controversy as to the precise areas of the economy in which competitive forces can be encouraged with any hope of success. It has always been recognized that there are some industries in which the most technically efficient producing unit is so large that one or at most a few firms of this size can satisfy the entire demand. The public utilities are generally regarded as falling in this category, but there is no substantial agreement as to the boundaries of this class. Some economists feel that a good part of modern heavy industry is technically unsuited to competitive organization, while others contend with equal vigor that even some of the fields which we now class as public utilities could be made effectively competitive. Eugene Rostow considers some of these problems in Chapter 10.

In large sectors of another market, the labor market, effective competition has long been absent. Some of the consequences of this state of affairs are explored by C. E. Lindblom in Chapter 11. For the purpose of this catalogue of generally acceptable value judgments all we can say, therefore, is that in those areas of the economy where it can be agreed that effective competition is not technically impossible it should be promoted.

The second sort of difficulty arises from an attempt to define what, for practical purposes, is meant by competition. Here we have at one extreme a group who feel that only if the theoretical ideal of perfect competition (which is quite rigorously definable) is completely achieved will resource allocation be optimum, but that any means of approximating that condition will improve matters. On the other hand there is a group which asserts that the theoretical ideal is practically never attainable and that some kinds of imperfections of competition are much more vicious than others. This group generally works with some such concept as J. M. Clark's "workable competition." Fortunately there are a good many forms of noncompetitive behavior which both groups would recognize as producing results not in harmony with our objectives. We must interpret the promotion of competition, then, to mean the elimination of these types of monopolistic practices from those industries where there is some hope that at least "workable competition" is practicable.

There would probably be considerable support for the proposition that competition should be promoted even beyond the point where it is economically more efficient for reasons associated with nonincome values. The concern for small business, for the "little man," in American policy derives from something more than a faith in the economic virtues of competition. There are a good many elements in this concern, some of them not wholly rational, but it is not difficult to see how some of them are introduced by a broadening of the value scale beyond income. We suggested above that one of the defenses of a private market mechanism was the probability that under such a system power would be more widely shared than under alternative arrangements. Clearly the development of very large-scale private organizations reduces this probability and should therefore be resisted.

It could also be persuasively argued that the range of opportunities for free value choice in the selection of an occupation and a way of life is likely to be greater in a society with many comparatively small units than in one dominated by a few very large organizations. In such a society it is perhaps easier for an elliptical peg to fashion himself an elliptical hole and thus avoid being forced into one of the standard square or round ones. Similar considerations apply to the free selection and wide sharing of other values such as respect. In any case, whatever the rationale of this objective, which it is not our purpose to defend in detail here, it is clearly more than merely an economic corollary of a preference for a market system.

3. *Optimum level of government expenditure*

The last objective we wish to discuss relates to the question of what proportion of the community's resources is to be allocated to end uses by the mechanism of direct public spending rather than by the private market. We may refer to it as the objective of *an optimum level of real government expenditures.*

In strict logic it is superfluous to state this objective separately since it is implied in the objectives we have already set forth. The objective of primary use of the private market mechanism implies that government direction of resource use should not be indefinitely expanded. On the other hand one of our more fundamental objectives, such as consumer-guided allocation, will in some cases turn out to be most effectively promoted by governmental rather than private allocation. In each instance a careful review of the impact of government allocation on each of our basic objectives is needed to guide the policy maker.

This objective is separately listed here solely because it is central to the proper design of employment policy. Government spending of various sorts is one of the most commonly proposed instruments for the control of the volume of employment. Its effects on our other objectives are very frequently lost sight of because of its obvious relation to the employment problem. To say that one of our objectives is an optimum level of real government expenditures is a way of emphasizing that there are many important reasons apart from employment policy for selecting any given level, and that these other reasons should be seriously considered. It is convenient to have this shorthand term to refer to the total impact of all of our other objectives upon the particular institutional device of public resource use.

As with the objectives of optimum income distribution and optimum rate of saving there is no brief and simple way of stating in the abstract how the optimum level of real government expenditures is to be determined. But again more agreement is possible in particular cases than this theoretical impasse would suggest. A few hints as to some of the relevant considerations are all we have space for here.

We must first distinguish between government *enterprises* which make full use of the market mechanism in the distribution of their product and government output which is furnished to the community free or for nominal fees. In the former category ownership is public rather than private but the market mechanism can still be employed to determine what and how much is produced. If government enterprises follow appropriate rules for determining their prices and outputs, consumers determine through the market the volume of resources to be allocated by such enterprises just as though they were privately owned. The principal defense for such government ownership, commonly in the public utilities field, is that in such areas the objective of the promotion of competition cannot be attained for technical reasons and therefore the *private* market mechanism will not produce desirable results and must be supplanted by a *public* market mechanism. This is not an issue which vitally affects employment policy. By government expenditure we shall therefore normally mean expenditure incurred in producing goods or services to be distributed otherwise than through a market.

Many expenditures of this type can be justified by reference to the objective of consumer-guided allocation. Doubt as to whether the private market allocates resources properly arises wherever the neighborhood effect of a transaction (discussed in section II-3 above, p. 34) is important. That mechanism can be expected to produce desirable results only in cases in which a buyer can satisfy a value by purchase from a seller without affecting in an important way the value position of third parties. We have already mentioned that where the neighborhood effect is strong the private market may either have to be regulated or replaced.

In some cases it is not technically possible to separate the commodity or service into units which can be supplied separately to individuals (or to firms serving individuals). There is no way of deciding who gets how much of the services of a battleship or a mosquito control program, nor is there any way in which an individual can choose separately to forego these services when they are being provided to others. In such cases allocation of resources to the service by government through the voting process rather than by the price system is clearly in order. Since at least a minimum of services of this type is probably preferred by nearly everybody to the things the same resources might provide through the market mechanism, *some* real governmental expenditure is called for by the objective of consumer-guided allocation.[4] We will come back to how much presently.

In other cases the supply of separable units of a service to individuals or firms might be conceptually possible but is deemed to be practically too difficult or costly. This is the case with streets and highways, where it is ideally possible to determine who uses them but where, except in special cases, the charging of a price for the service would not be practical. The vagueness of criteria of practicality suggests that these cases should be examined with particular care.

Finally there are cases where there is no technical or practical obstacle to the purchase of a good or service by an individual or firm from a seller, but where the effects of the transaction on third parties are pronounced. If this neighborhood effect is negative, that is, if the third parties are injured by a transaction—as in the construction of unsightly or dangerous buildings, or the exhaustion of a resource by wasteful exploitation—there is a strong case for controlling or regulating the market but no a priori case for replacing it. On the other hand, if the neighborhood effect is positive, that is, if the total value to the community is greater than that to the parties directly involved, it may be desirable that the good or service be provided even though the private market would not provide it. Public expenditure may be the only effective method, as is probably the case, for instance, with education. There is clearly no technical obstacle to the private purchase of educational services by individuals, as is evidenced by the fact that a thriving private market for such services exists. On the other hand, if no public education were available a much smaller proportion of our resources would be devoted to this service. The defense of public education rests on the contention that the indirect benefits to the community of the additional services provided justify foregoing the things which the resources used could otherwise produce. There is a further defense on grounds of income distribution which is dealt with below.

If the optimum level of real governmental expenditures were to be determined solely on the basis of the objective of consumer-guided allocation, then, two steps would be necessary. First we would have to decide what activities had a strong neighborhood effect. This would tell us in what areas government expenditure might be appropriate. It would then be necessary to decide how far these activities should be carried. With respect to the first of these steps, there has undoubtedly been a trend in recent decades toward the recognition of an increasingly broad

4. This may seem to the noneconomist to stretch the concept of what he thinks of as the consumer. Here, as in economics generally, a consumer is anyone whose values are satisfied (i.e., who derives "utility") from a given use of resources.

list of activities which affect the interests of the community at large. This trend will probably continue. It is the natural result of more penetrating and thorough analyses of all the indirect effects of a social event. Indeed some socialists would rest their case for primarily public ownership on the contention that neighborhood effects are so pervasive in all economic transactions and so impossible to deal with by regulation that we should abandon the private market objective altogether. As indicated above, it is a premise of this study that this view would not be widely accepted in America today. Nevertheless the growing recognition of the existence of more and more kinds of neighborhoods effects suggests that much more thought could profitably be devoted to devices for taking account of such effects within the private market mechanism.

Once the appropriate *areas* for government resource use have been agreed upon the ticklish problem remains of how far the government should carry activities within those areas. Here at the moment we have no alternative but to depend on the voting process. This is unsatisfactory for a number of reasons already touched upon and developed further by Victor Jones in Chapter 13. The direct ballot is a much less sensitive device than the "dollar vote" for adjusting resource use to a wide variety of values and especially to minority values. Furthermore, it is impractical to employ the direct ballot in making the bulk of the decisions as to the volume and direction of government spending. At best many such decisions can be made only through a representative body which is at least one step removed from the complex pattern of values of the constituents. In many cases voter preference must make itself felt through successive layers of legislative and administrative machinery which may screen out all but the simplest and most powerful values. The "first-handedness" of choice on a market is one of its major virtues.

If we are serious about the objective of consumer-guided allocation, however, there are steps that can be taken to estimate more closely what level of real government expenditures is optimum from the point of view of that objective. The alternatives involved in public as opposed to private use of resources can be presented to voters in ways which will render their choice more conscious, explicit, and informed. Much more sensitive methods can be designed of determining the pattern of consumer values in areas where the price system is not appropriate. Market research has made great strides in estimating these patterns for private producers in advance of a real live market test. There is no reason why such methods cannot be refined and applied to resource allocation by public bodies. The technical problems involved in determining the intensity of an individual's preference for ten dollars' worth of public parks as compared with ten dollars more to spend in the department store or ten dollars more put into public education are knotty and we shall never solve them completely. But given the objective of consumer-guided allocation there should be no insuperable conceptual difficulty in defining what we mean by an ideal level and pattern of real government expenditures. Dahl and Lindblom spell out one set of possible criteria for this purpose in Chapter 8.

Our difficulty is likely to be one not so much of defining this ideal as of keeping it before us in policy deliberations. In periods of involuntary unemployment the notion that government resource use is *alternative* to anything else tends to be suppressed. It is true that in the emergency of a depression there is no time for extensive sampling surveys and delicate computations of the relative marginal utilities for different groups of a myriad of different ways in which resources could be employed. The urgent thing is to employ them. Nevertheless, if we have developed at our leisure some concept of what proportion of our resources should be governmentally allocated *at full employment,* we have a quick guide in depression as to where to put the emphasis in recovery policy.

Similarly, in an inflationary period we need criteria which will give us guidance as to where to apply the brakes. Arguments as to the relative merits of economy in the public budget and restriction of private spending by tax and other measures cannot be resolved except by appeal to some notion of a proper division between public and private resource allocation.

There is another of our objectives, optimum income distribution, which is frequently regarded explicitly or implicitly as a justification for government expenditure. Public education, public housing, public medical care, and the like are frequently advocated on the ground that this is the only way such services can be provided to people who otherwise could not afford them. It is important though difficult to examine this argument with some care. It is important because it sometimes conceals a fundamental rejection of the principle of consumer-guided allocation, and such conflicts should be brought to light. It is difficult because income distribution objectives are so often hidden behind a façade of less controversial goals.

The argument frequently takes off from an attack on the idea of the dollar vote expressed in the market. This is not a fair vote, it is said, because some people have so many more votes than others. Low cost houses will never be built privately because those who need them do not have the money to express their need effectively on the market. *Therefore*—and this is the step that bears watching—they should be built by the government. Now if the case is really nothing more than a plea for a more equal income distribution, the conclusion does not follow. It is always possible to redistribute incomes not by building low-cost houses but by simply redistributing incomes. This can be done by redesigning the tax system or by direct subsidy payments to bottom income groups if necessary. One can test whether supplementing low incomes is really a major argument in favor of, for example, public housing by inquiring whether the proponent would be equally willing to see an amount of money equivalent to the subsidy turned over to prospective tenants, without strings, in lieu of the opportunity to rent an apartment. If the answer is yes, then the objective of primary use of the private market suggests that such a cash transfer would be a better method of effecting redistribution than a government building program.

If the answer is no, there are a number of possibilities. One is the contention that there are important neighborhood effects of housing, so that it cannot be left to purely private transactions. In this case we are back to the argument of the last section, and it is the neighborhood effects and not the redistribution effects which justify public construction. Another possible reply is that people cannot be trusted to buy the kind of houses they ought to live in even if they have the money. This is a clear rejection of the objective of consumer-guided allocation, and it is the desire to impose some other norm of allocation which justifies the public building program and not income distribution. Or the answer may be that housing is one of those fields in which for technical reasons competition cannot be effective, in which case again the distribution argument is irrelevant.

There is one line of reasoning which gives it relevance, though it is a dangerous one. This is that while redistribution of cash income would be as good as or better than the more indirect method of subsidy to housing, it would not be politically acceptable. If this means that the electorate can be brought to understand and visualize the maldistribution of income only when it is dramatized in terms of health or housing, there is some plausibility to the argument, though educational devices are available less drastic than major government expenditure programs. On the other hand what you may really be saying is that you are sure in advance that the voting majority disagrees with your ideas of an optimum income distribution, and you have concluded that it must be secured by pretending it is something else. We need not debate whether this is consistent with democratic principles.

We conclude that the objective of optimum income distribution is a shaky foundation on which to build a justification for government resource use, though it undoubtedly supplies much of the emotional drive behind the pressure for many kinds of public spending.

We cannot leave this discussion of the optimum scale of public economic activity without observing that however it is delimited there is every prospect that it will grow larger with the passage of time. As our conception of values broadens and along with it our understanding of their interrelations we are going to discover more and more kinds of neighborhood effects. A man's income may be unaffected by a deal between two other people while his power or respect position may be sharply influenced. Thus the sorts of activities in which there is a case for public direction of resources will probably multiply in number. At the same time the extent of those already regarded as inevitably in the public domain will expand. The most obvious case in point is the resources devoted to national security and especially to the development of atomic energy. If, as we think most Americans believe, the private market mechanism has distinct virtues, these probable developments underline heavily the importance of continued scrutiny of the criteria for public resource allocation and the vigorous application of those criteria to proposals to achieve full employment by public expenditure.

IV. ALTERNATIVE POINTS OF VIEW

1. *Other ways of describing the goals*

There are many other objectives which are relevant in some degree to the design of income stabilization policy, some of which are brought out in succeeding pages of this symposium. But this list is believed to comprehend most of the goals which would be widely regarded as the aims of *economic* policy, and more especially of income stabilization policy. Certain of these goals are commonly expressed in terms somewhat different from those we have used. It may therefore be well to indicate briefly how other common formulations of our objectives relate to the classification here suggested.

Let us look first at the two goals which are usually regarded as the primary concern of income stabilization policy itself, namely, avoiding depression and avoiding inflation. Clearly the first of these is merely another name for our objective of minimum involuntary unemployment, though the way we have put it is somewhat broader, covering not only the general unemployment associated with depressions but also the "frictional" unemployment which may be consistent with something like "good times." Our desire to avoid inflations is more interesting and complex. As we shall see, depression and inflation may be considered analytically as symmetrically opposite phenomena, the one resulting from too little spending, the other from too much. The evils which they bring in their train, however, are not similarly symmetrical. An inflation is not a time when there is too much output or too much employment in any simple sense. In fact, in extreme "galloping" inflations both output and employment may, as in depression, be reduced well below their optimum levels. In milder inflations, however, unemployment is at a minimum and output is at something close to the full employment level.

What then disturbs us about an inflation? Part of the resentment it stirs up is irrational. Everyone complains about rising prices even when they are accompanied by incomes rising even faster. We wrongly assume that our incomes would go up anyway and that the price rise therefore entails a net loss of purchasing power. Even if the real evils of inflation were eliminated most of us would coninue to be angry at it. There are, however, real evils of several sorts. In the first place, inflation tends to distort income distribution from the patterns found in periods of stable prices. This distortion is usually of a kind which everyone would agree increases inequities. The distribution of income in an inflation is uncertain and haphazard and hence most unlikely to be optimum, and groups with fixed or inflexible money incomes always suffer a decline in real earnings.

Secondly, all but the mildest inflationary movements increase the uncertainties of the business planning process and consequently interfere with efficient production. With costs, prices, and availabilities changing rapidly it is difficult for the businessman to estimate, and even more to achieve, that combination of inputs which will promote maximum technical efficiency. Thirdly, inflationary periods spawn political pressures which make it difficult to maintain competitive conditions in private markets. There is likely to be powerful support for proposals to halt the inflation by the brute force method of direct price control, an explicit repudiation of the objective of primary use of private markets. More subtly, strong pressures develop for the intervention of government in price formation in various less direct ways—by persuasion, publicity, and the like. There are also incentives not present in more stable periods for collusive action among private groups of buyers and sellers. Finally, one of the most persuasive arguments against inflation is that it contains the seed of subsequent depression and unemployment. This is not the place to reproduce the argument, but there is good reason to believe that inflations produce distortions in the price structure and in the pattern of resource use which ultimately make the avoidance of depression much more difficult.

It is stated to be an objective of the Employment Act of 1946 to promote "maximum employment, production, and purchasing power," and these phrases recur often in the economic reports of the President and his Council of Economic Advisers. They obviously cannot be taken literally. We do not want to squeeze out of the population the maximum number of man-hours of work that they could physically perform, nor to make anybody work who does not want to at going rates. Clearly "maximum employment" must be taken to mean either minimum involuntary unemployment or some combination of that objective with that of ideal employment. Similarly, "maximum production" as a goal must be interpreted as being subject to the proviso that the "right" balance exist between work and leisure. In this sense, maximum production means minimum involuntary unemployment combined with maximum technical efficiency. Maximum purchasing power carries, perhaps, the added implication that we want not only "high level" employment and output but also an appropriate distribution of that output, an idea that is covered in our objective of optimum income distribution.

Another common formulation of our economic objectives is in terms of a high standard of living. This may mean one of two things. It may mean that the average real income per person should be as high as possible, in which case it is simply the idea of maximum production in another form (maximum production divided by the population or the number of families). Or it may imply that the average standard should be high, not in the purely statistical sense of the word average, but in a broader sense suggesting that the bulk of the people should enjoy that standard or that there should be some minimum standard below which nobody should fall. This again adds a distributive element taken care of by our objective of optimum income distribution. Once we have determined the volume of employment (or man-hours of labor), the allocation of resources (including labor) to different uses, and the technical conditions of production we have determined the total volume of output and thus for a given population the average standard of living. If, further, we then specify an optimum distribution of the available output among the people, we thereby determine how much the smallest income in the community will be or, in other words, the minimum standard of living.

There is some danger in starting with the concept of a particular average or minimum standard of living as a basic objective in itself. Since such standards are already completely implied in our other objectives it is likely that independently adopted standards will be inconsistent with those objectives. For example, a higher average standard than that implied by full employment and maximum technical efficiency could only be secured by forcing people to work more than they wanted to. Similarly an excessively high minimum standard may be achievable only by an income distribution more equal than the optimum, one for example which reduces total output sharply. Standards lower than those implied by our other objectives do no harm, perhaps, but are superfluous and understate the possibilities.

2. *Social planning versus classical liberalism*

The most serious obstacle to the understanding and acceptance of the classification of objectives here given arises out of the clash of two very fundamentally different ways of looking at what we mean by the goals of an economy. One reaction to our statement of what we have called objectives will be that they are not true objectives at all, but mere rules of the game, forms without content, procedure without substance. A group of persons whom we may call the social planners, deeply concerned with certain specific ills of our society—inadequate housing, poor nutrition, faulty education, and the like—will miss any reference to these problems. They will want to know where there is room in this colorless cobweb of analysis for a positive program such as Beveridge's crusade against the giant social evils of Want, Disease, Squalor, and Ignorance. A list of economic objectives, they will feel, should specify the kinds of uses to which resources should be put; it should sketch in at least the outlines of what an economy devoted to promoting the good life should look like; there should be a catalogue of such concrete aims as better health, better housing, more balanced diets, a wider spread of education, the creation of a better and more stimulating physical environment for living, the provision of adequate facilities for recreation and cultural development, etc. The principles of free value choice and of shared values and the corollaries that follow from them are all very well but they give us no clear guide as to the directions in which we should move, no list of the concrete things we should do with the abundant resources at our command. We should develop a set of social priorities to guide us in planning for balanced economic growth toward a carefully thought out ideal economy. This group will insist, to use a metaphor made famous by the late Professor Clapham, that the categories elaborated in the preceding pages are merely empty boxes incapable of containing the great dream of a better world which should be the ultimate inspiration of all policy.

There are two elements in this objection which must be distinguished. In part the complaint is valid and has considerable force. We will consider this valid element presently. But first it is necessary to dispose of another element which is the consequence of a failure on the part of many social planners to understand the concept of consumer-guided allocation. This misunderstanding is peculiarly irritating to another group whom we may call the classical liberals. They contend that the objections of the social planners are without foundation. For, they insist, there is implicit in the objective of consumer-guided allocation, taken together with the objective of equitable income distribution, a very detailed and concrete substantive list of basic wants to be satisfied. This priority system is much too complex to be summarized in a simple blueprint since it comprises the whole pattern of wants of every person in the community in full detail as it would be if incomes were equitably distributed. To set forth our objectives in terms of individual commodities and services would involve listing thousands of items of varying grades and degrees of importance to each of millions of people. There are dangers in summarizing and simplifying such a list too far, since objectives of great importance to some people are almost certain to be left out. Nevertheless, it is clear that this complex pattern of tastes gives great prominence to the broad goals regarded by the social planners as basic. Certainly better health, better housing, better food, better education, more recreational facilities are things that the consuming public wants with sufficient intensity to give expression to their wants in money demands. The classical liberals will point out that the battle against want, disease, squalor, and ignorance is not a campaign launched for the first time by Beveridge. It is essentially the fight for which most economic systems are organized. The classical liberals would not only admit but insist that the effectiveness of the free enterprise system must be judged largely on the basis of its success or failure in waging Beveridge's battle. Social planners may differ with the detailed values of the consuming public. They may feel that people would be happier if they lived in round houses instead of square ones or ate wheat germ instead of ice cream, but they cannot contend that the objective of consumer-guided allocation overlooks the goal of more adequate housing or better food.

The classical liberals can point to another weakness in the formulations of objectives frequently put forward by social planners. The concrete lists of desirable uses of resources which the latter would like to see adopted give us, paradoxically, very little help in framing policy measures affecting resource allocation. The essential economic problems are problems of *choice*. To say that we want a world in which people will be healthier, better housed, better fed, better educated, more cultured, etc., gives us no clue as to what to do with a particular set of scarce and limited resources. Should an increment of resources be applied to more housing *or* more food *or* more education, or to all three in various proportions, and if so in what proportions? Should we spend 10% of our resources on the elimination of disease and five on squalor, or five on disease and ten on squalor, or all fifteen on ignorance?

A list of concrete goals will not answer these questions for us, and yet they are the questions which are most crucial in actual policy formation. A set of objectives, to be relevant to the design of policy, must throw some light on the relative merits of using marginal quantities of resources in different alternative ways. The concept of consumer-guided allocation, the classical liberals remind us, implies not only a detailed list of desiderata but a set of scales of relative importance as well. Taken together with a properly designed market mechanism it gives in most cases very clear guidance as to which of two quantitative alternatives is preferable in a concrete situation.

This point is one which is of particular importance for employment policy. We are in great danger of falling into the habit of thinking in periods of unemployment that any constructive use of resources is better than none. This is, of course, true, but it does not follow that some particular employment, which everyone admits is desirable, is the best use to which resources can be put. There is real danger in such a period of allocating resources to projects which, in the competitive atmosphere of full employment, could never be justified, simply because no adequate examination of alternatives has ever been made. There is a tendency in some recent works on employment policy to describe all the useful things that could be done with unemployed resources as though it were necessary to persuade the reader that *some* use could be found for them. Surely the problem is how to design ways of submitting the literally countless alternative possibilities to the test of democratic choice.

But the social planners must be permitted their rebuttal. There is a valid element in their position which justifies much of their contemptuous irritation with the classical liberal. The "sovereign" consumer to whom the liberal defers so unquestioningly is not the rational and informed choosing machine of the early models, but is increasingly revealed by social and psychological study as a quivering mass of responses conditioned by accidents of experience, physical state, cultural environment, and psychic type and stabilized only by the inertia of habit and ignorance. We cannot accept his frequently foolish pattern of values as final. As suggested at several earlier points in this essay the principle of free value choice and its economic corollary, the objective of consumer-guided allocation, relate to the means by which improvements in our value systems are to be brought about and not to the ends which such systems will ultimately imply. In this sense the social planners are quite right that to insure free value choice is clearly not enough. The responsibility of the expert—economist, political scientist, psychologist, philosopher, or what have you—does not stop with the classical liberal task of insuring that people get as nearly as possible what they want. A major part of his function must be to assist them to achieve more rational and satisfying value patterns by exploring the implications of alternatives, by suggesting hitherto unsuspected possibilities, by revealing inconsistencies, and improving understanding. An important part of this process is the construction of Utopias. It is important, especially in a democracy, that people be stirred to think searchingly about the kind of society in which they want to live. The blueprints of the social planners are an indispensable element in this process, and it is essential that economists and other experts participate in the construction of such blueprints so that they may be drawn up in the light of the best scientific knowledge available.

This is important for two reasons. As the world becomes more and more complex it is increasingly difficult for the individual to decide what his own personal values are and how to achieve them. There is a strong temptation under these circumstances for him to relax into the comforting inertia of purely imitative behavior. He needs imaginative presentations of unfamiliar alternatives and searching analyses of the full consequences for him of habitual or conventional courses of action. Furthermore, as pointed out earlier, there is every prospect that the proportion of our decisions made socially through the voting process will increase as compared with those made individually through the market mechanism. This is true partly because of the growing recognition of the social consequences of individual behavior (neighborhood effects) and partly because of the increasing importance in our society of large-scale organizations which inevitably pursue their ends through political rather than strictly economic means. Voters are going to be increasingly faced, then, with the necessity of making decisions on social rather than private grounds. This kind of system can operate successfully only if the individual citizen develops values relating to the pattern of society as a whole and not merely to his own activities. These values should be based on the most expert advice he can get.

The apparent conflict between classical liberals and social planners is thus largely a false conflict. Their positions can be complementary rather than alternative. We may want the allocation of resources to reflect current tastes accurately and still insist that those tastes are unintelligent and ignoble and must be reshaped. We believe in free value choice because if we are true democrats we deny that anyone can be *sure* that he knows best what is good for somebody else. We also affirm that given time, expert help, and freedom the citizenry will ultimately reshape their value patterns in what will turn out to be sensible ways. We can therefore afford to accept the current verdict of public taste expressed either through the market or through the voting mechanism as seems most effectively to express it in each particular case. The social scientist must assist the policy maker in designing techniques to give maximum effect to these popular values. But he must go beyond this and play a leading and crucial role in the continuing process of revising and interpreting and freshening values.

Why, then, have we not laid more emphasis in our list of objectives on this latter process? Because our list is intended to be a minimum list on which very broad agreement can be secured. Insofar as particular kinds of resource use are already widely accepted as desirable, they are implied in the principle of free value choice underlying our list. Insofar as they have not yet become the object of public clamor they are not appropriate for discussion here. What is agreed is not what in some sense are our ultimate goals but rather how we should approach them. If we can resolve, or at least call attention to, certain conflicts between income stabilization policy and what is implied in the democratic process we will have done enough for one volume.

CHAPTER II. *Income Stabilization and the*
American Political Tradition

BY FRANCIS W. COKER

The Problem: PREVAILING ASSUMPTIONS OF GOVERNMENTAL INTERVEN-
TION AND THE PERSISTENT OPPOSITION TO GOVERNMENTAL INTERVEN-
TION

The participants in this symposium consider some relatively new
forms of governmental action, designed to prevent the disruptive fluctuations of income caused by an instability in the level of prices and in
the volume of employment and investment. In general the writers attempt to avoid direct governmental intervention, in the form of orders
to particular individuals in their decisions about jobs, prices, or investments. The role they prevailingly assign to government is that not of
"regulation" but of "condition-creating" through measures aimed at
achieving certain general levels of employment, prices, and investment.
Thus they consider tax changes (Chapter 6) designed chiefly not to
meet current revenue needs, but to influence the kinds and amounts of
private spending or investment; government borrowing (Chapter 5) not
to cover budgetary deficits but to increase the amount of money in
circulation; credit controls (Chatper 7) to affect the amount of credit
available for private investment; governmental expenditures (Chapter
8) timed primarily not to supply immediate community needs but to
counteract general deflationary or inflationary tendencies; loans on
farm crops (Chapter 9) not only to protect farmers from the inevitably
intense competition in agricultural marketing but also to help keep up
the general purchasing power of the community; measures of "social
security" (Chapter 8)—old-age pensions, unemployment payments—
not simply to relieve distress among wageworkers or to secure a generally more equitable distribution of wealth but also to help stabilize
the whole economy; government-imposed wage and price ceilings
(Chapter 11) to prevent the governmental supports of collective bargaining from disrupting the general program of stabilization.

In these various proposals the writers reflect a prevailing consensus
that unaided private enterprise cannot protect the community from re-

curring periods of depression and inflation and that instability of income is more than a temporary or "emergency" problem. The newer controls, most of them already in operation in some degree, are superimposed upon a wide variety of other, generally more direct, governmental interventions: such as the familiar health and safety controls, restraints on monopolies, regulation of public utility rates and services, the time-honored price controls of the protective tariffs, and the more recent interventions to fix minimum wages, police the security markets, and provide governmental loans and subsidies for needy business concerns.

Despite the insistent demands from various sections of the population for these governmental aids and regulations, there are widely held convictions that in the present volume and variety of our regulatory policies we are making manifest what should have been clear before: namely, that we are destroying our traditional economic and political system. Those who express this fear over the threatened disappearance of our system of free competitive enterprise are not in full agreement in identifying the beginnings of our destructive policy. Our excesses appear variously to have started with the Interstate Commerce Act of 1887, or the Antitrust Act of 1890, or the extended railway and anti-trust regulations of the Theodore Roosevelt, Taft, and Wilson administrations, or the expanding state and national labor legislation of the first quarter of the twentieth century, or, more definitely, with the sweeping controls initiated by the New Deal of the 1930's, when our leaders in power adopted explicity the doctrine that there are human rights superior to property rights. In these warnings there is the belief that our regulatory policy in its present scope is destroying the very rights we are attempting to protect. Gradualism in the process, it is said, only serves to make us unaware of the progressive dissolution of our traditional system.[1]

The question of how much governmental intervention is permissible or desirable is one that has always been with us. There is a tendency in current literature on the subject to dramatize our present position as at some sort of unrepeatable crossroads. This mood is not entirely new. At almost any moment of our history some of us have believed that we were at a unique point of time, when a decision to follow one path rather than another would commit us irrevocably to one or another extreme alternative. The appearance of a choice between extremes, however, has usually been much sharper in our economic and political theory than in the designs of our practical policy. The purpose of this

1. For extreme expressions of these fears see John T. Flynn, *As We Go Marching* (1844) and *The Road Ahead* (1949); Henry Hazlitt, *Economics in One Lesson* (1946).

chapter is to examine our traditional system: considering, first, some main historical trends in our economic policy and in the varieties of our traditional beliefs about private enterprise and governmental regulation; and, second, some characteristic features of our economic structure and governmental policy today and of our present-day economic theories, all appraised in relation to our traditional policies and beliefs.

I. OUR TRADITIONAL SYSTEM

1. *The colonial economy* [2]

Few of the seventeenth-century settlers of America were inspired by any intention of experimenting with novel ideas about either government or property. Economic concerns, it is true, moved many of the migrants. Thus in England, during the preceding generation, inflation, war, and changes in fiscal policy had seriously upset certain industries. And although at the time of the first settlements England was apparently emerging from this depression, many competent persons were still finding it difficult to maintain their accustomed standards of living or believed they were not sharing sufficiently in the recovery. Unemployment was still widespread; towns and parishes were overwhelmed by the task of taking care of beggars and vagabonds, and the belief was growing that England was overpopulated. America offered prospects of a better livelihood not only for ordinary laborers and craftsmen but also for farmers, professional men, and others who were willing to endure the hazards of migration.

The first immigrants settled generally in groups rather than as individuals; and in many respects the settlements were operated as community enterprises for a considerable time. Thus in Massachusetts Bay the original title to lands was vested in a joint-stock company. The company later trannferred titles to the towns. When the towns made allotments to individuals they not only restricted the owners' rights of alienation but also retained considerable areas for common use. Thus each "freeholder" had his own plot for home, garden, animal sheds, etc., while the community retained, under strict public inspection and regulation, the "common" lands that were to be used by all the families for tillage, pasturage, and lumbering.

2. On economic policies and ideas in colonial America see Joseph Dorfman, *Economic Mind in American Civilization* (1946), *1*, chs. 1–10; William B. Weeden, *Economic and Social History of New England* (1890); E. A. J. Johnson, *American Economic Thought in the Seventeenth Century* (1932); Max Savelle, *Seeds of Liberty* (1948), chs. 4–5; David Fellman, "Property in Colonial Political Theory," *Temple University Law Quarterly, 16* (1942), 388–406.

There was no idea in colonial times that the private farmer, artisan, or merchant was free to carry on his business as he pleased or that the laborer was free to demand what working conditions he considered fit. New Englanders in particular placed a high value on the private citizen's obligations both to his neighbor and to the public. Thus an artisan or merchant might be required by town authorities to help a neighboring farmer (behind in his harvesting) gather his crop, and to accept as pay the regular farm wage; and an ordinary citizen might be fined for failing to attend town meeting. Occasions for the regulation of the private economy appeared at the very beginning of our colonial life. A scarcity of workers resulted in high wages; this in turn led to high prices for the necessaries of life, or made insecure reasonable profits for the employers, or, it was believed, lured wage earners into idle or extravagant ways of living. Accordingly public authorities set maximum wages for various kinds of work; and there were some attempts to protect consumers' interests by limiting prices and profits. Some of these early regulations were soon abandoned as ineffectual: a worker ordered to accept a lower wage in one industry could find employment in another place, or he might set up for himself in farming, industry, or trade; and "supply and demand" thwarted most of the attempts to limit prices and profits. Other regulations, however, continued throughout the colonial era. Both town and central authorities intervened frequently to fix maximum interest rates, prescribe standard weights and qualities for goods brought into the market, and to limit the charges and services of millers, innkeepers, and public carriers.

Most of the colonies were particularly concerned to make themselves self-sufficient—each colony striving to keep itself economically independent of the other colonies as well as of the home country and foreign states. In furtherance of these mercantilist policies, prevailing in the later seventeenth and early eighteenth centuries, the colonial legislatures forbade the export of various raw materials (skins, wool, flax, etc.) needed by the local spinners and clothiers, and they assisted the manufacturers of various other commodities (iron, cloth, rope, leather, linen, glassware, etc.) by grants of tax exemptions, monopoly privileges, and governmental loans and subsidies. They attempted also to adjust their taxing and monetary policies to various social and political purposes. Thus to obtain greater fluidity in buying and selling and greater safety in investment, several of the colonies issued paper money (made receivable for public dues) by means of which they hoped both to correct the fluctuating values of coin and bullion and to create an ample supply of currency for the essential foreign trade.

Although the colonial leaders were prevailingly in agreement on the necessity of governmental intervention, there were often sharp differences of opinion on the proper occasions for intervention and the forms it should take. Disputes over actual policies were frequent. As the colonies expanded and prospered, the economic interests involved became too numerous and complicated to allow of even the appearance of integrated harmony such as the mercantilist ideas of the time presupposed. Tenants were often opposed to landlords, yeomen farmers to plantation owners, shopkeepers and small farmers to bankers and merchants, employers to wageworkers. The groups opposed to one another over such questions were usually concerned with immediate and concrete issues rather than with conceptions of the ideally best or rationally necessary form of economic organization and policy. Their differences ranged over a wide area, covering questions of monetary policy, rules of tenure and inheritance, forms of taxation, and the justice or expediency of governmental limitations on wages, prices, and interest rates.

There were some theoretical discussions of general questions concerning forms of ownership and the uses of wealth. In these discussions (chiefly by theologians) it was taken for granted that one of the primary reasons for the existence of government was the protection and regulation of private ownership. Puritan doctrine, it is true, associated the pursuit of worldly gains with man's baser traits. Yet, according to this doctrine, man was born with these traits and there was no way to get rid of them. Man's pursuit of wealth, moreover, might serve moral and social as well as material and selfish ends. Indeed, one of the aims of the Puritans in migrating to the New World had been to find a way to live on a higher moral plane than had seemed possible in the home country. It was hoped that a more favorable economic environment would make it easier for the people to carry their consciences into their economic affairs, private and public.

Thus although the Puritans wholeheartedly endorsed the competitive pursuit of individual wealth, they had a high sense of the community's obligation to prevent antisocial or immoral uses of property. This attitude was implicit in the multiplicity of actual regulations and explicit in the utterances of religious and political leaders. They knew no law, theory, or tradition that would deny to their governing authorities the right to regulate private property in the public interest.

The eighteenth-century arguments between the colonies and the mother country, arising out of England's colonial policy, were developed chiefly in terms of imperial constitutional law rather than in terms of a body of economic doctrine to be applied in America. In the intensification of the controversy, however, in the decade immediately preceding independence, the idiom of the American argument changed from "rights of Englishmen" to "rights of man." In the early days of independence, also, when old domestic differences between agrarian and mercantile interests broke out anew, with the lines between them more sharply drawn, the writers were driven to relate their rivalries to more general ideas concerning the scope and methods of governmental action in relation to property.

2. Our national tradition [3]

a. A COMPLEX HERITAGE; MERCANTILIST BEGINNINGS

Thus our Revolutionary and Constitutional forefathers were blest, or burdened, with a complex heritage of economic and political ideas, derived both from the experiences and beliefs of their colonial forebears and from the economic and political doctrines of seventeenth- and eighteenth-century English and French writers. They believed, on the one hand, that man was born with natural rights and that political society was a compact which no rational man would enter voluntarily except on the assurance that he would not have to surrender any of those rights. On the other hand, they also accepted the idea of "commonwealth"—the belief that the welfare of the political community was superior to the special interests of any individual or group within the community.

Our writers of the Revolutionary period, framers of the Constitution, and leaders of our first political parties were agreed that the right to property was one of man's natural rights and that the preservation of that right was one of the chief ends for which governments were established. All associated high moral and practical values with private property and attacked policies, national or state, that threatened the rights and interests of owners. But they were concerned with different sorts of property and had different ideas as to what sorts of owners should guide public policy and as to what the main economic objectives of national policy should be. For Hamilton and his followers the goal was a nation made prosperous and self-sufficient by a governmental promotion of large-scale ownership; while for Jefferson and his followers the goal was a nation kept internally free and secure by the preservation of individual ownership. Hamilton's aim was a prosperous, wealthy nation; Jefferson's, a nation of property owners. Most of our subsequent political controversies have been concerned, in considerable measure, with competing claims to property; newer against older owners, indus-

3. On economic policies and ideas in the national period see Joseph Dorfman *Economic Mind in American Civilization, 1,* chs. 12–18 and 2.

trial against landed owners, large against small owners, owners of means of production against owners of consumers' goods.

Mercantilist aims were predominant in the early policy of the national government. The national leaders were concerned to get under way the measures that would advance our national prosperity by strengthening our capitalist industry. Hamilton, John Adams, and others set forth a general social theory in support of the mercantilist policy. Their ideas concerning the nature of man were essentially the same as those of the English classical economists, formulating a scientific theory to fit the rising capitalist economy, although the practical applications were not always the same. Even if all men, according to the general theory, are primarily alike in acting in response to impulses of self-interest, they are unlike in their abilities either to serve their own interests or to pass wise judgments on the public measures designed to promote the common interests. Accordingly the men of greater wealth should direct public policy because they understand best how to serve the public interests upon which depend ultimately the promotion of private interests—of the poor as well as of the rich. Inequalities of wealth are inevitable and cannot be changed by government. But government can supply effective "incitement and patronage" in advancing the national prosperity.

In the application of such ideas, the framers of the Constitution were at pains to put into the document the provisions that would make the national government strong in its commercial and fiscal powers. The first Congress under the Constitution made effective use of these powers. It created a central bank (the government owning one-fifth of the stock) empowered not only to act as governmental agent in issuing legal-tender bank-note currency but also to carry on the general business of a commercial bank. Congress, in designing its import taxes, was influenced in part by the desire to protect our domestic manufacturers and traders from foreign competition. Hamilton set forth, in his famous "Report on Manufactures," his views as to the great advantages to be derived from a policy of governmental regulation and aid. The protective tariffs, he declared, would encourage new enterprises, attract migrants from Europe, and create new demands for the surplus products of the soil. And these and other governmental supports for domestic manufactures would, by facilitating a more extensive use of machinery, bring into productive work many potential workers—notably women and children—who are generally unable to perform the heavy manual tasks of farming.

Thus governmental intervention, at the national level, was our original policy in support of capitalist industry.

b. THE TRADITIONAL OPPOSITION TO REGULATION

In the later advocacy of a public policy favorable to private industrial enterprise, the main emphasis has been on arguments against governmental intervention; and in this we have prevailingly followed the eighteenth-century European theories. Political democracy and private industrial enterprise had come into the modern European world together; and their original ideologies had much in common. A rising business class and a new working class were alike in demanding both economic freedom and political freedom. Old restrictions—guild regulations, government-created monopolies, remnants of slavery and serfdom—had survived into the eighteenth century, along with restraints on voting rights and on freedom of religion, the press, and association. Industrial owners and industrial workers had a common interest in destroying the privileges that had been created by governmental interference. A broad doctrine of natural human rights supplied a consistent theoretical foundation for claims of inalienable property rights as well as of inalienable political rights. Spokesmen for each group could believe that if everyone were given an equal chance, in the economic as well as in the political world, each individual would reach that place in society for which he was best fitted by his ability and effort.

In America as in Europe the case for nonintervention has been periodically set forth in terms of a positive "science" of economics. It has been held that scientifically discoverable "laws" determine the behavior of men in producing and exchanging goods and services. These laws, it has been maintained, show that all men desire to possess and to excel in the possession of material goods and that the normal individual knows best how to pursue those ends for himself. Each man finds also that he can serve his economic ends only by producing goods or services that other men want enough to be willing to pay for them, so that each in serving his own interest serves also the general interest.

In opposing particular interferences, however, both academic and lay economists mixed practical and ethical ideas with their "scientific" theories. Public relief for the poor was bad, they maintained, since it tended both to increase population beyond the available means of subsistence and to reduce the total available fund of wages by reducing the capital upon which the size of that fund depended. And either public or private aid for the poor was likely to be bad because it tended to ruin the character of its recipients by encouraging the ignorance, sloth, and vice that created the need for relief. Laws to improve working conditions in factories hampered capital investment, and they were not needed: the natural law of supply and demand would compel employers to improve conditions, since, in the general prosperity furthered by free enterprise, the demand for workers would increase faster than the supply. Laws limiting interest rates were uneconomic, since they limited capital investment; and such laws were unfair, since they put no limits on other sorts of profit.

Not all of these writers were able to hold themselves to a policy strictly consistent with their hard theory. They were not in full agreement on the question of interference through the protective tariffs. All recognized that the tariffs were, in effect, governmental subsidies and price regulations. Some of the writers defended that form of regulation and aid as an exceptional necessity in our expanding industrial economy. Others maintained that to make so substantial an exception to the general principle vitiated the whole practical and moral case for noninterference. Some of the extremer critics of the tariffs called the protectionists "communists" (i.e., "socialists") since they were "price fixers." [4]

Many of our most prominent nineteenth-century theologians and moralists offered emphatic Scriptural testimony in support of the practical and academic case against governmental interference with the competitive pursuit of private wealth. The desire and the ability to get rich, they proclaimed, were reliable tests of man's moral character and social usefulness. "Historically," said President Mark Hopkins of Williams College, "the general wellbeing and progress of society has been in proportion to the freedom of every man to gain property in all legitimate ways." "Acquisitiveness," said Professor Daniel S. Gregory, was placed in us by God and for "a good and noble purpose"; each of us elevates himself morally and enlarges his contributions to society by a proper and diligent exercise of that trait. Governments exist to defend property rights, maintained President Noah Porter of Yale. To deprive a man of his property rights is "theft," declared President James McCosh

4. Ideas in opposition to governmental regulation, in the early and middle nineteenth century, were set forth by various sorts of writers. *Professional economists:* Thomas Cooper (1759–1839); George Tucker (1775–1861); Henry C. Carey (1793–1879); Thomas R. Dew (1802–46). *Christian ministers* (college teachers of religion and philosophy who regarded orthodox economic principles as essential parts of their social ethics): John McVickar (1787–1868); Samuel P. Newman (1787–1868); Francis Wayland (1790–1865); John Bascom (1827–1911). *Lawyers, businessmen, journalists, and others:* Samuel Young (1779–1850), lawyer, capitalist, politician; Stephen Colwell (1800–71), lawyer, iron manufacturer, railroad director; Jacob N. Cardozo (1786–1873), Southern journalist; Louisa S. McCord (1810–79), South Carolina essayist and poet; Simon Newcomb (1835–1909), astronomer and mathematician.

Dew, McVickar, Cardozo, McCord, and Newcomb consistently opposed the protective tariffs; Young persistently urged high tariffs; Cooper switched from support to opposition, Carey from opposition to support.

of Princeton. "In the long run," said Bishop William Lawrence of Massachusetts, "it is only to the man of morality that wealth comes. . . .
Godliness is in league with riches. . . . The race is to the strong. . . .
Material prosperity is helping to make the national character sweeter,
more joyous, more unselfish, more Christlike." [5]

It is true that we have never been able to adhere strictly to a general
policy of noninterference. In the constant shifts in practical policy between interference and noninterference, however, the theoretical case
for noninterference has continued to be set forth in terms either of abstract dogmas or of empirical generalizations held to fit all conditions.
The items in the general theory are familiar: Property owners should
be free, within certain admitted limits (assumed to be axiomatic), to
accumulate as much property as they can by what means they choose
(outside the traditional restraints of crime, tort, and breach of contract) because private property is a natural right of man. Noninterference is the only way of maintaining natural and satisfactory relations
between supply and demand. Noninterference also is the only way of
securing the socially beneficial effects of a natural selection and reproduction of the fittest individuals in a competitive struggle for survival.
And experience, illuminated by common sense, shows us the harmful
moral and practical consequences of governmental attempts to minimize the effects of an unequal distribution of wealth. [6]

In many ways a general policy of noninterference appeared to work
well during the first three quarters of the nineteenth century. Under
actual conditions it appeared to be socially desirable to rely generally
on the sorts of adjustments the doctrine of noninterference assumed to
be automatic. And much of the nineteenth-century dream of a close
connection between political democracy and free competitive enterprise seemed to come true in America above all other countries. More
and more individuals were gaining freedom to vote and freedom to

5. Mark Hopkins, *Law of Love and Law as Love* (1868), pp. 182–183; Daniel
S. Gregory, *Christian Ethics* (1875), p. 224; Noah Porter, *Elements of Moral Science* (1885), pp. 362, 385; James McCosh, *Our Moral Nature* (1892), p. 40; William Lawrence, "The Relation of Wealth to Morals," *World's Work, 1* (1900–01),
286–292. Cf. Ralph H. Gabriel, *Course of American Democratic Thought* (1940),
ch. 13.

6. For typical statements see: among economists—David A. Wells, *Recent Economic Changes and Their Effect on the Production and Distribution of Wealth*
(1889), Thomas N. Carver, *Essays in Social Justice* (1915); by sociologists—William Graham Sumner, essays in the eighties and nineties, Albert G. Keller, *Man's
Rough Road* (1932); more generally—Truxton Beale, ed., *Man versus the State*
(1916), a reprint of essays by Herbert Spencer, with comments by various public
figures (Elihu Root, Henry Cabot Lodge, E. H. Gary, and others).

pursue their own ways in religious and intellectual expression at the same time that they were gaining greater material comforts in their unregulated competition. There appeared to be many practical reasons for believing that under a policy of no governmental interference most members of the community would be most likely to apply energy and ingenuity in mastering the forces of nature and in devising and perfecting the arts of industry, and most likely to develop habits of prudence in preparing for the uncertainties of employment and the infirmities of old age.

C. THE CONTINUING DEMAND FOR REGULATION

In both our practice and our theory we have had, throughout our national history, a tradition of governmental intervention as well as of nonintervention. Prior to the national mercantilist legislation of the first Congress, the colonies and then the states had taken on the role of promoting the development of industry and commerce within their respective areas. Colonial legislatures had provided for free alienage of property and simpler forms of conveyance as means of promoting individual enterprise. The early state governments continued this policy of removing obstacles to a wide diffusion of ownership by abolishing quit rents, entails, and primogeniture. Then, in the early nineteenth century, the states, still in the interest of strengthening the private economy, found themselves in the business of chartering corporations and of granting highly remunerative property rights to these newer units of private enterprise. Thus to corporations generally was granted the limited liability for stockholders; and to various corporations other special rights were granted, such as the right to take ownership of private land, the right to issue bank-note currency, and exclusive franchises to carry on certain types of business. Then again, in order to offset these privileges and to protect the interests of both individual enterprisers and the general community, the states imposed various restraints on the corporations they had created, by limiting their life terms, restricting the amounts of their capitalization and indebtedness, and defining more specifically the scope of their powers.[7]

Meanwhile the national government was continuing the policy, initiated by Hamilton, of intervening in the private economy in order to

7. For accounts of policies of governmental intervention at the state level, in the period between the Revolution and the Civil War, see the following intensive studies of two typical states: Oscar and Mary F. Handlin, *Commonwealth: A Study of the Role of the State in the American Economy: Massachusetts 1774–1861* (1947); Louis Hartz, *Economic Policy and Democratic Thought: Pennsylvania, 1776–1860* (1948).

promote the national prosperity. There continued to be able spokesmen for the policy. Calhoun (in his early career), Clay, John Quincy Adams, and other national leaders in the early nineteenth century supported the drive toward national economic strength and "self-sufficiency" by their advocacy of protective tariffs, a national bank, national public works ("internal improvements"), various aids to the private builders and operators of turnpikes and canals, and a planned national policy for conserving and disposing of the public lands.

This explicit acceptance of governmental intervention was by no means confined to spokesmen for the Federalists, Whigs, and other mercantilist-minded political groups. Even Jefferson, firm believer in private enterprise and "limited" government, had approved public enterprise where private enterprise failed to meet essential community needs, and had advocated regulation of private enterprise where unregulated private enterprise created extreme inequality. Thus when it appeared that private banks were not providing the credit needed by small owners, he proposed the creation of a Virginia state bank, empowered to "befriend the agricultural man" with short-term loans on farm crops. He also suggested various monetary and banking reforms designed to thwart the "usurious and demoralizing purposes" of "private banks," "private speculators," and "self-created money-lenders." He was so impressed with the inadequacies of the states in this field that he, a strong advocate of "states' rights," suggested that the states might have to cede to Congress their power over banks; the national government, he thought, might be more successful in making moneylending a "useful enterprise"—more successful, that is, in keeping the amount of money in circulation "proportioned to our produce." He was one of the first to advocate governmental action to improve the means of internal transport by dredging rivers and constructing canals and roads; and here again, having first urged this task upon the Virginia legislature, he later, as President, recommended a constitutional amendment vesting this function also in Congress. He suggested various measures of direct and indirect governmental intervention (chiefly at the state level) to reduce extreme economic inequality. Thus he proposed as a means of "silently lessening the inequality of property," that "the higher portions of property" be taxed "in geometrical proportion as they rise." Where the inequality is "enormous," Jefferson declared, "legislatures cannot invent too many devices for subdividing property." And finally a government, he said, must accept its responsibility for keeping up employment. This meant chiefly, in Jefferson's time and place, finding land for the landless. "Whenever," he said, "there is, in any country, uncultivated lands and unemployed poor, it is clear that the laws of property have been so far extended as to violate natural right. The earth is given as a common stock for man to labour and live on. If for the encouragement of industry we allow it to be appropriated, we must take care that other employment be provided to those excluded from the appropriation." [8]

Mid-nineteenth-century economists, philosophers, theologians, journalists, and literary publicists set forth scientific, moral, spiritual, and esthetic arguments to explain the social maladjustments in our domestic economy and to demonstrate the need for collective action to remedy them. Man, said Henry Carey, is not exclusively, or even primarily, a competitive being. All men, he declared, have a natural desire to cooperate as well as to compete with their fellows; and they are aware that even their self-serving powers are increased by voluntary cooperation as well as by the regulatory measures of government. The laws and customs that sustain our system of free enterprise, said James Fenimore Cooper, are the product of the cooperative activities of men in society; they cannot be rationally explained by any theory that men may do as they please with their property. The useful competitions of private enterprise, said Horace Greeley, cannot rest on any theory that the free market sorts out accurately the competent from the incompetent. [9] Emerson and Thoreau, Theodore Parker and William Ellery Channing, expressed their doubts as to the net moral, spiritual, and esthetic values of the aggressive economic traits implied in the hypotheses of economic orthodoxy. They found something essentially shoddy and ignoble in that creed; and they insisted that the Scriptural exhortations to diligence and thrift were not meant to place selfish materialism above normal impulses toward charity and justice. [10] Various writers pointed out that

8. Jefferson's various proposals for governmental intervention, on both state and national levels, appear in letters and public statements covering over three decades (1784–1817); for the items indicated above see his *Writings*, Paul Leicester Ford, ed. (New York, Putnam, 1899), *3*, 423–424; *4*, 17; *6*, 98; *7*, 336; *8*, 343–344; *9*, 392–394, 415–416; *10*, 69, 91. For his statements condemning overregulatory government see *ibid.*, *3*, 223–224; *4*, 479; *8*, 123, 142, 182, 284–285, 343; *10*, 36, 45.

9. Carey's views favoring governmental intervention (in contrast with his earlier position) appear in his *Harmony of Interests* (1851) and *Principles of Social Science* (1858–59). James Fenimore Cooper's ideas on the social foundations of private property appear in his *American Democrat* (1838), section "On Property," pp. 127–133, and in ch. 27 of *The Monikins* (1835), an allegorical satire on America and England. Greeley's advocacy of governmental intervention, in behalf of farmers and wage earners, appear in several of his essays and lectures, published in his *Hints towards Reform* (1850).

10. See Emerson, "Essay on Politics" (1842), in *Complete Works* (Centenary ed., 1903–04), *3*, 177–221; "The Fugitive Slave Law," *ibid.*, *11*, 179–244; *Journals*, E. W. Emerson and W. E. Forbes, eds. (1909–11), *3*, 371, 379–380; *4*, 95, 242;

no government can protect liberties of any sort without also limiting them.

Throughout the nineteenth century both the national and state governments were continually changing their policies to fit technological and cultural changes. The development of large-scale industry, the industrialization and urbanization of the population, the shift in status of the typical breadwinner from that of owner to that of employee or tenant—these changes were constantly creating new obstacles to free competition and revealing other inadequacies in the policy of nonintervention. Governmental guarantees of legally free bargaining rights did not always appear to be guarantees of an equal chance to achieve wealth proportionate to one's abilities. Free competition often failed to secure the survival of the fittest and the elimination of the most incompetent; many individuals, neither lazy nor inefficient, appeared to be the victims of conditions that had little or nothing to do with deficiencies in individual ability or effort. The development of large-scale ownership and management in the private economy was, moreover, changing substantially the actual character of our property rights and thereby destroying the empirical bases for some of the traditional arguments against governmental intervention.

d. CHANGING FORMS OF OWNERSHIP

For our forefathers of the seventeenth and eighteenth centuries property rights meant generally rights of an individual over the land, tools, or materials with which he worked in earning a livelihood. Most of the original settlers of America owned small properties of that sort in the old country, and they came to this country with the hope of obtaining greater security of ownership here. Individual ownership of productive property continued to be a dominant feature of our economic system until well into the nineteenth century. When we adopted our Constitution, some 90% of the free inhabitants of America owned the properties upon which they worked. A hundred years ago about 80% of the citizens engaged in economic enterprise were small farmers, traders, mechanics, and craftsmen, each working with his own land, tools, and materials. Even as late as the 1860's and 70's—by which time there had been a considerable extension in the use of machines—the typical shoe-

---

5, 285–286. Thoreau, "A Week on the Concord and the Merrimac Rivers" (1852), chapter on "Sunday," and *Walden* (1854); Parker, "The Slave Power" (1850), in *Writings* (1907–11), *11*, ch. 9, and "The Nebraska Question" (1854), in *Additional Speeches* (1855), *1*, 295–380; Channing, pamphlet on "Slavery" (1835), in *Works* (1895), pp. 688–743.

making shop, flour mill, slaughtering or packing house, and textile, furniture, or wagon factory was a local enterprise, owned and managed by an individual or by a group small enough for owners and managers to be the same people.

The belief that ownership of the property upon which one works for a living is an essential factor of political liberty, and that a democracy must foster that sort of ownership, has been a familiar doctrine in our traditional political theory. Thus it was argued by Samuel Adams and other "radical" leaders in the Revolutionary period that the doctrine that protection of property is the primary end of government presupposes a wide distribution of property. Representatives of small owners opposed ratification of the Constitution because they feared that the enlarged economic powers of the national government would prevent the states from granting to farmers and other small owners some relief from the debts that threatened their ownership. It was a cardinal doctrine of the Jeffersonians that the essential economic basis for a political democracy was a society of property owners. Some of the Federalists, notably John Adams and Daniel Webster, concurred at times, agreeing that in a republic it was a part of political wisdom to maintain such a distribution of property as would, in Webster's words, "interest the great majority of society in the support of the government." [11]

Yet, despite these venerable traditions favorable to a wide diffusion in the ownership of productive property, the actual development, both in our private business practice and in our governmental policy, has been prevailingly in the opposite direction. The steady advance of familiar technological, economic, and social changes has made it increasingly difficult for the individual enterpriser to survive in most fields of productive and commercial activity. And the national government has continued to play its significant part in bringing about this concentration of ownership and power, both by its unwillingness or its inability to break up unnecessary monopoly and by the positive aids it supplies to monopoly through its tariffs and its fair trade laws.

Thus the vast majority of Americans have lost their property rights, in the traditional sense of an individual's rights over the materials and instruments with which he labors in earning a livelihood. Most of us play our parts in the private economy, not as owners or managers, but as tenants or employees, with relatively little opportunity to have our

11. For early statements of the idea that a wide distribution of individual ownership is an essential foundation of political democracy see John Adams, *Works* (1850–56), 9, 376; Jefferson, *Writings*, 3, 268–269; Webster, *Works* (1851), 1, 34–40.

interest effectively represented in the private decisions affecting the conditions under which we work.[12]

II. Our System Today

1. *Forms of ownership and the distribution of economic power*

Our economy, although still mainly a private economy, is no longer a society chiefly of individual enterprisers. The corporation has supplanted the individual as the typical owner in our present-day economy. Corporations own all our railways, nearly all of our public utilities, most of our manufacturing and mining enterprises; and corporate ownership has been spreading rapidly into the retail-mercantile, building-construction, and real estate fields. Moreover, the tendency is toward a narrow centralization of ownership and management. Big firms have been getting bigger. A hundred large corporations own over a half of our total manufacturing plants. In each of forty-odd industries, three or four companies now account for from 75 to 90% of total output. Five companies control over 90% of our rubber tire business; three companies do over 80% of our cigarette business; and a very few companies account for the bulk of our output in steel, copper, automobiles, and a number of chemicals and other products.

There are, it is true, substantial compensations for the loss of older rights of individual ownership. Although large-scale enterprise has reduced the ordinary individual from independent owner to dependent wage earner or tenant, it has at the same time provided him with a higher income, more and better goods upon which to spend his income, and safer and more varied opportunities for profitably investing his savings. In many cases, however, the enlargement of business units has gone far beyond what is needed for the most beneficial utilization of modern technological processes. A considerable part of our present-day concentration of corporate management has nothing to do with efficiency or economy in production and distribution because the concentrations bring about no combinations of physical properties and no coordination of operative activities. Many of our advances in productive efficiency and economy have been due to technological improvements largely unrelated to the size of the business units; many mergers have combined, under a single management, separate enterprises that were already adequately equipped and managed.

12. On the progressive disappearance of individual ownership of property, see F. W. Coker, "Property Rights as Obstacles to Progress," *Annals of American Academy of Political and Social Science*, 185 (1936), 133–144; John Fischer, "The Lost Liberals," *Harper's Magazine*, 194 (1947), 385–395.

These changes from small-scale to large-scale ownership have profoundly altered the character of our property rights. The ruling personnel of our larger corporations today are often able to exercise their powers arbitrarily, whether in dealing with one another or with other groups—employees, stockholders, suppliers, customers—as well as with the community at large and with the government. Although an estimated seven or more million individuals own shares in our corporate enterprises, the ordinary stockholders have no thought of influencing the direction of the larger enterprises; their several holdings, as compared with the total number of shares in any large company, are too small for that.

Labor also often wields a narrowly concentrated power in important sections of our economy. With the strong weapons of the strike-supported closed or union shop, organized labor is often able to protect union members from the competitions of a free labor market. Policy-making in the largest unions operates mainly on a national or industrial rather than on a local or individual level. The power of central management of a big union tends to reduce the economic freedom of rank-and-file workers as well as of ordinary consumers. A laborer may have difficulty in joining a union—there are financial and and other restrictive conditions to be met; and after he joins he may gain no appreciable part in decisions fixing the conditions under which he works and still less in decisions affecting the specifications and the disposition of the commodities he helps produce. Moreover, the main object of union managers is to raise wage rates. Insofar as they succeed in obtaining wage increases not justified by increased production, their policy tends (as C. E. Lindblom points out in Chapter 11, below) toward inflation and thereby toward both reduced employment and reduced production.[13]

These private rule-making groups, in corporate business and organized labor (and in other places, as in farming and the professions), play substantial parts in deciding how jobs, goods, and services are distributed and in influencing generally our economic habits, preferences, and ways of thought.[14] And government also, as we have seen, plays its part. Directly or indirectly—through wage and hour regulations, social security payments, collective bargaining supports, farm price guarantees, housing aids, credit controls, protective tariffs, etc.—it takes part in managing our economy and distributing its product. The decisions of these various private and public rule-making groups, competing or cooperating with one another, have changed some of the traditional

13. See also Charles E. Lindblom, *Unions and Capitalism* (1949), chs. 4, 5, 10, 12.

14. See Beardsley Ruml, *Tomorrow's Business* (1944), ch. 2.

processes of our private, price-profit, economy. Most of us have lost some of our former opportunities for self-direction and self-expression in our economic activities.

Yet we still have a highly competitive economy. There are still some ten million individually owned and operated enterprises. The total number of business establishments has been increasing, during the last half century, at a rate greater than the rate of our increase in population. United States Steel, which fifty years ago produced two-thirds of all the steel made in America, now produces only a third of that total. And even our largest corporations compete with one another. The Aluminum Company of America, producing half our total of primary and fabricated aluminum, competes with two American and several foreign companies producing the same thing, as well as with other American companies producing scrap aluminum, and with still other companies that produce various substitutes (zinc, steel, copper, wood) for aluminum. The Dupont Company, producing cellophane, competes with paper-making companies; and the same company, producing nylon, competes with producers of silk and cotton cloth. Gas refrigerators are in competition with electric refrigerators. Theaters, the movies, the radio, and television compete with one another. Any corporation, however big it may be, has to be alert to take advantage of new inventions, new consumers' desires. There remains also enough of an "open" market for individual consumers to make their own decisions as to what they want to buy and what they are willing to pay; these scores of millions of consumers play their part in determining the quantities, qualities, and prices of what our business concerns, big or little, produce and, thereby, in determining the successes or failures of these concerns. Thus our economy remains relatively free, operating prevailingly according to traditional assumptions of an economy of private enterprise. We still count on the "free market" to play the chief part in equating supply and demand and in bringing about generally efficient and equitable uses of our resources. A relatively large number of our citizens choose their occupations according to their own preferences and abilities, bargain freely with one another in buying and selling goods and services, and make their own decisions in spending, saving, or investing their incomes.[15]

15. See report of testimony of Benjamin F. Fairless (president, U.S. Steel) before a House subcommittee investigating the steel industry, reported in the *New York Herald Tribune*, April 27, 1950, p. 9; Roy A. Hunt (president, Aluminum Company of America), "Big Business and Competition," *United States News and World Report*, November 11, 1949, pp. 36–39; Sumner H. Slichter, *American Economy* (1948), ch. 1; Oswald Knauth, *Managerial Enterprise* (1948).

2. *The present-day opposition to regulation*

In defense of this private, competitive economy against governmental interference many of the arguments are still founded on our traditional beliefs in natural rights of ownership and in natural economic laws that determine natural relations between supply and demand in a society in which each individual is free, within the limits of his abilities, to choose the productive tasks he likes and the goods and services he wants. Only this "free," "open," market, it is said, can perform the essential function of economic calculation—letting producers know what consumers want and are willing to pay, letting cousumers know what producers are able and willing to produce and at what prices, and letting society know whether its whole economy is operating at a loss. There is in this argument no assumption that there has ever been a completely free market. The contention is rather that the general trend in Western civilization, at least since the end of the Middle Ages, has been toward the removal of limitations on the market and that this increasingly free market has been the chief factor in bringing about our steadily increasing prosperity.[16]

The tendency in this sort of argument is to rest the case against regulation solely on rationalist and empirical foundations. We act irrationally, impractically, it is said, when we call upon the state to do more, in relation to economic affairs, than protect private property and the open market against violence and fraud. By attempting more we cannot obtain either a larger total production or any redistribution that helps the people we may want to help. Regulations designed to shorten hours of labor, increase wages, reduce prices, change the purchasing power of money, or stabilize income and employment tend to bring about effects opposite to those intended. At the utmost, any planning for "social security" should not go beyond the assurance of a "reasonable" level of subsistence. Beyond that the citizen should be left to look out for himself. It is admitted, in this argument, that our humane impulses, even our sense of justice, may be offended by the sight of competent and industrious citizens suffering sharp reduction of incomes through no faults of their own. But, it is maintained, an assurance of a given income to any individual or group can be achieved only at the cost of destroying the individual initiative, self-reliance, and freedom of choice, upon which the productive efficiency of our economy depends.[17]

16. See Ludwig Von Mises, *Human Action: A Treatise on Economics* (1949), chs. 11–15, 26–27, 35.

17. Extreme views of this sort appear in the works of Flynn, Hazlitt, and Von Mises (*op. cit.*, above, nn. 1, 16). See also David McCord Wright, *Democracy and*

Some who make this rationalist, empiricist argument against governmental regulation are explicit in renouncing all "noble" considerations —specifically, all arguments founded on ideas about American tradition and Christian morality. The traditionalist, it is said, whether arguing for or against regulation, simply selects the ancestors who agree with him; and he often selects, as time-honored, only policies of very recent origin. Moral arguments also, it is said, are often fictitious. We abolished slavery not when theologians and moralists told us that slavery was wrong—other theologians and moralists continued, to the very end, to tell us that slavery was right. We abolished the morally bad institution when we discovered that it was economically bad—that is, when slave labor could not successfully compete with free labor. We stopped flogging school children when that practice ceased to be "an incentive to production," and more recently we have been abolishing child labor because child labor has been becoming inefficient and unnecessary.[18]

Yet an opposite tendency—toward an emphasis on higher considerations—appears extensively in the present-day argument against regulation. With many writers the defense of free enterprise against governmental regulation takes in some way the form of a general argument for moral, spiritual, and political freedom. Restrictions on economic freedom, it is said, lead to restrictions on these other, more basic freedoms. Thus, it is specifically contended, any extensive program of governmental control over the private economy leads to the destruction of political self-government. For the controls must be devised and executed not by officials chosen by the electorate but by appointed officials, far removed from the people. A representative legislature may define generally the scope and objectives of the plans and regulations and prescribe the formal methods for executing them. But actual application of these controls require specialized techniques of expert investigation and administration, so that a legislative body has to grant to administrative agencies a wide discretion in formulating rules and issuing orders to secure compliance with the rules. Thus, it is said, Congress, in the days of the New Deal, made such sweeping grants of powers of rule-making and adjudication that many of the administrative agencies became, in effect, independent legislative, judicial, and executive agencies, all in one. These agencies often adopted their rules without adequate hearings for the parties particularly affected, and often made

---

Progress (1948); Herbert Hoover, *American Individualism* (1922) and *Challenge to Liberty* (1934); William A. Orton, *Economic Role of the State* (1950), pp. 27–46, 66–122.

18. This is a main theme in Von Mises, *Human Action;* see especially pp. 188–192, 612–616, 719–725, 879–881.

specific orders, sustained by severe sanctions, through procedures lacking the ordinary safeguards of a fair trial.

Thus, it is argued, a planning government inevitably becomes a bureaucracy—a government by appointed bureau heads responsible only to administrative superiors. And this concentrates vast powers in the hands of the President. His wide appointive and removal power over bureau heads gives him power to dictate their most significant decisions. The wide area of social life covered by the newer regulations vastly increases the President's power to determine the voters' decisions as well; for he can influence the content and timing (e.g., before or after an election) of governmental reports in such way as to determine what the voters hear about the facts and issues bearing on the decisions they are to make at the polls.[19]

Fear of vigorous executive power is one of our oldest and most persistent traditions. Thus our first state constitutions entrusted the most essential governing powers to the legislatures, regarded as immediate representatives of the people. The governors were assigned short terms of office and little powers, with no legislative veto and only a limited appointing power. One of the strongest arguments made by those who opposed ratification of the federal Constitution was that the document gave far too much independent power to the President. The powers conferred on him, it was said, made him the "full-grown progeny" of British kings, colonial governors, and ancient Asiatic despots. Strong executive power was "inconsistent with the genius of republican government"; all the tyrannies of the past had been "executive tyrannies." [20] In our subsequent history, our most active Presidents (whom most of our historians have called our greatest Presidents) have been assailed by their contemporary detractors as tyrants and despots or (more recently) as fascist or communist rulers.

This present-day political argument for free enterprise is usually stated more generally. It is said that all other freedoms—political, intellectual, moral, esthetic—are dependent upon economic freedom. Economic competition cultivates the very traits upon which the successful operation of political democracy depends—individual initiative, self-reliance, self-discipline. Governmental planning stifles the creative urge, blocks progress, limits the free choices upon which all

19. See John H. Crider, *The Bureaucrat* (1944); Lawrence Sullivan, *Bureaucracy Runs Amuck* (1944). For balanced criticisms see Charles S. Hyneman, *Bureaucracy in a Democracy* (1950); Merle J. Pusey, *Big Government: Can We Control It?* (1949); J. M. Juran, *Bureaucracy: A Challenge to Better Management* (1944).

20. See Charles E. Merriam, *History of American Political Theories* (1903), pp. 80–82, 113–114, 153–154, 177–181.

effective political freedom and truly moral action depends. A denial of property rights is always the prelude to a denial of other rights. A managed economy requires a censored press. Benevolent government inevitably becomes paternalistic government; the service state becomes the servile state.[21]

Thus much of the older argument in behalf of the essential profit motive in a free economy gets crowded out of the contemporary debate. "We defend economic freedom," former President Hoover has recently declared, "not because of profit and greed," but because "we know that without economic freedom the freedoms of mind and spirit will perish." [22]

3. The universal demand for regulation

Yet in however comprehensive a form the argument against governmental regulation may be stated today, the theoretical differences between advocates and opponents of regulation become somewhat blurred in their practical application. Long before the New Deal of the 1930's there had been effective demands for various forms of governmental protection from the hazards that were apparently inherent in the latter-day economy and that appeared to be beyond the power of private effort to control. Maladjustments in the changing economy were continually appearing, owing in part to the unequal rates of change; the capacity to produce goods increased at times at a faster rate than the capacity to consume them; increased employment intermittently lagged behind increased production. The New Deal was, to a considerable degree, only a revival and intensification of a course of legislation that dated back at least to the administrations of Presidents Theodore Roosevelt, Taft, and Wilson. This policy, it is true, had been interrupted by World War I and by some brief postwar efforts to return to what was called the "normal" order of private enterprise. In the Congress of 1933–35, however, leaders of the Republican party, while denouncing New Deal principles, supported most of the New Deal measures: the party's floor leader in the Senate voted for all but two of the major measures enacted by that Congress; and the Republican senator selected to give the keynote speech in the party's nominating convention in 1936 had voted for all but one of those measures.

21. See F. A. Hayek, *Road to Serfdom* (Chicago, University of Chicago Press, 1944); John T. Flynn, *As We Go Marching* and *The Road Ahead;* Herbert Hoover, *Addresses . . . 1941–45* (New York, Van Nostrand, 1946), pp. 222–225, 240–241, 259; Von Mises, *Human Action,* pp. 279–285; Walter Lippmann, *The Good Society* (1937).
22. *Addresses . . . 1941–45,* p. 259.

This bipartisan advocacy, or acceptance, of extensive governmental restraints and aids has continued down to the present day. The Republican platform in 1948, while promising to reestablish "liberty," "voluntary cooperation," and a "minimum of dependence on law," also promised new laws to protect farm prices, extend rural electrification, widen the scope of social security, and develop further the nation's water resources for purposes of improved navigation, flood control, and electric power. After the Republican defeat in the 1948 election, various leaders of the party warned their followers that the party had not gone far enough or had not been explicit or persuasive enough in reformulating its program. The party needs "a tremendous lot of rebuilding," declared former Governor Harold E. Stassen of Minnesota. It "must shed some of its aloofness," said Governor James H. Duff of Pennsylvania. "It must have been some very clumsy Republican," said Governor Thomas E. Dewey of New York, "who tried to pin the label 'welfare state' on Mr. Truman's government . . . Anybody who thinks that an attack on the fundamental idea of security and welfare is appealing to people generally is living in the Middle Ages." [23]

The three Republican governors just quoted may be regarded as spokesmen chiefly for a progressive minority of the party. But conservative leaders also have come round to reminding Republicans of the humane and progressive traditions of their party. The party had taken the lead in abolishing slavery, providing pensions for veterans of the Civil War, protecting businessmen from cutthroat foreign competition, helping farmers to obtain homesteads, and, in these and other ways, indirectly serving the interests of wageworkers. More recently Senator Taft, addressing his "fellow taxpayers" (in May, 1950), reminded them of the extended legislation for agricultural reclamation and rural electrification that had been enacted under Republican auspices in the Eightieth Congress and of the housing and hospital aids and the increased minimum wages put through the Eighty-first Congress with Republican sponsorship or support. He promised that the next Republican-controlled Congress, while avoiding "the deadening regulations of government bureaus attempting to fix prices and quotas in free industries," would "not hesitate to use the power of government to prevent the abuses and excesses of a laissez-faire economic system." A Republican Congress, he continued, would protect "proper" minimum-wage levels, and it would support farm prices at levels that would keep the farmers' purchasing power "in reasonable relation to other groups in the population"; it would also intervene more generally to prevent

23. Address before Woodrow Wilson School of Public and International Affairs, printed in *United States News and World Report*, February 24, 1950.

any destruction of the general purchasing power that "could bring about another depression"; and it would "offer financial assistance to promote better education, better health, better housing, and better economic security." [24]

Thus today advocates of a planned economy or welfare state avow their intentions to make free enterprise secure, as a means of promoting the general welfare; and they propose various governmental measures designed to restore free enterprise in areas where unregulated or un-aided private business has destroyed it. Also today advocates of a free competitive economy affirm the general welfare as their criterion for appraising the results of free enterprise; and they specify the various governmental regulations and aids they accept or demand as means designed both to protect free enterprise and to promote the general welfare.

Thus, as indicated at the beginning of this chapter, as well as in Max Millikan's preceding essay, there appears to be general agreement, explicit or implied, on such propositions as the following concerning our present-day economy: increasing production, making possible a generally high standard of living, does not by itself insure full employment, or economic stability, or the most just and efficient distribution of wealth; large-scale industry tends toward excessive competition and also toward excessive concentrations of power; technological changes, which make possible the increased production and reduced costs, tend also toward other changes that create new inequalities of income not closely related to inequalities of need, ability, or effort. [25]

Many of the differences over practical governmental policy relate in part to the total scope of regulation but also to the justice or expediency of specific regulations; here it is often a question of whose income and whose security is to be stabilized or enlarged; or it is a question of how far we must accept such responsibilities as a normal rather than as an exceptional, or "emergency," governmental obligation. A constant question is how to combine governmental regulation and free enterprise or how to prevent continual deadlocks between the two principles. Obviously unrestricted private enterprise has never been possible; and governmental planning of the bulk of our economic activities is not

24. Radio broadcast from Washington, D.C., May 16, 1950, printed in the *New York Herald Tribune*, May 17, 1950.

25. For principles and proposals by individuals and groups generally identified as spokesmen for a moderated or "liberal" capitalism see Eric Johnston, *America Unlimited* (1944); Beardsley Ruml, *Tomorrow's Business*; John K. Jessup, *America and the Future* (1943); Edwin G. Nourse, *Price Making in a Democracy* (1944), chs. 1, 2, 5, and Appendix B; Sumner H. Slichter, *American Economy*. Cf. Herbert Hoover, *Addresses . . . 1941–45*, pp. 229–260.

likely soon to be tolerated and might indeed make more difficult the maintenance of some of our political and civil freedoms.

4. *Safeguarding individual rights*

We need, on the one hand, to find ways of having our private rule-making groups accept the responsibilities and opportunities created by their social power. These groups have, of course, their private responsibilities to discharge. A corporation executive must operate his business profitably to himself and to the stockholders. But he has social responsibilities also. He must see that his business is operated in such a way as to provide the wageworkers with good working conditions, with some security of income and employment, and some opportunity for a development of their individual interests. These ends may be achieved in some measure by voluntary efforts. Managers of large enterprises may come to regard management as a business affected with a public interest, or as a profession holding itself to self-imposed standards of professional ethics. The various enterprises, moreover, may find ways to make the stockholder's right of representation in management a right that can be effectively exercised. They may give their employees a definite status in the enterprises, and they may bring their customers and the public into some effective participation in the making of relevant decisions.[26]

The labor unions also have their social responsibilities now, created by their economic power and by the community's acceptance of the unions, not merely as special groups furthering their various private interests, but also as essential units in the organization of a working community. There are some signs that the unions are becoming aware of their social standing in the community. There are possibilities also of voluntary cooperation between labor and management, not only in settling their private disputes and in providing for security of employment and income in their several enterprises, but also in serving wider economic interests by increasing production, reducing costs, and conserving resources.[27]

Irresponsible use of private economic power sooner or later leads to governmental compulsions of some sort. Various interested groups call upon the government to force the corporations that make public offer-

26. See Harwood F. Merrill, ed., *Responsibilities of Business Leadership* (1948).
27. See Lloyd K. Garrison, "Organized Labor in a Free Society," in Thurman Arnold and others, *Future of Democratic Capitalism* (1950), pp. 63–90; Louis Stark, "New Pattern Evolving in the Labor Picture," *New York Times*, April 30, 1950, sec. 4, p. 10; Charles E. Lindblom, *Unions and Capitalism*, chs. 15, 18. Cf. Chapter 11 below.

ings of their securities to conduct their affairs in the interests of the rank-and-file shareholders. The government may require corporations to set up schemes for workers to share both in the profits and in the management of the enterprises in which they work. It is believed that we can check the concentration of corporate ownership and management by making big corporations smaller and by restoring individual ownership in various fields. To the former end we can more rigidly enforce the antitrust laws; and we can adopt new measures such as a law taking away the power of one corporation to buy the physical assets of another corporation, or a law designed to restore the patent system to its original constitutional objective of encouraging, rather than discouraging, competition. To help restore individual enterprisers we can make it easier for small firms to get loans, sell stock, and get government contracts; and we can help tenant farmers to become farm owners by reducing interest rates on their mortgages and establishing easier conditions of amortization.

The growing monopoly powers of large labor unions have also led to proposals for government controls. We can compel the unions to remove some of the arbitrary restrictions on union membership and some of their featherbedding and other wasteful practices; compel them to open their financial accounts to public audit; abolish their exemptions from the antitrust laws and apply these laws against unions in the essential industries; and we can provide for a freer use of the injunction to stop strikes that seriously affect the national health and safety.

There remains the issue as to whether a regulatory government will or can adopt and administer its regulatory policies through democratic methods—that is, through free elections, free speech, and the safeguards against summary, inquisitorial, administrative procedures. There may be a critical danger of too great reaction from a traditional system of "freedom of contract"—a reaction that might indeed destroy some other freedoms upon which our institutions rest. Any increase of governmental power is to some extent a surrender of individual freedom and may be a step backwards toward a social condition in which a man's economic activities are determined by his status rather than by his ability, character, or effort.

There does not appear to be much evidence that extensive economic restraints and aids by a government lead, as a matter of course, to suppression of free speech and assembly or to abridgment of rights of fair trials by the courts. The new totalitarian regimes set up during a decade and a half following World War I did not follow governments that had been overactive in relieving the stresses and strains in their private economies. They followed regimes that had been conspicuously negligent in that field. If the experiences of those countries (Russia, Italy, Germany) are determining, the conclusion would have to be that dictatorships succeed weak rather than strong governments. They show also, it is true, that extensive controls over economic life can be combined with autocratic political methods. But they do not show that such a combination must or usually does exist. Political autocracies often leave established economic structures essentially unchanged, as today in Spain; and Russia was an autocratic state for several centuries before it became a socialist state. Still other experiences, here and abroad, show that substantial changes in the private economic structure can be fostered by governments that leave political and civil rights undisturbed. Thus, for example, Australia appears definitely committed, in profession and practice, both to a planned economy and to a political system that maintains fair trials, free elections, free association, and free speech; and experiences in the Scandinavian countries and in England indicate that a society may maintain democratic methods in adopting and operating extensive programs of governmental aid and regulation.

There is not full agreement as to what are the proper liberal and democratic procedures to be followed by the agencies set up to apply the extensive governmental regulations and aids embodied in recent legislation. In the controversy over this question, one side emphasizes the dangers, of both oppression and inefficiency, in the recent "spawnings of administrative definitions and rulings," often made without hearings and changed without notice. There are, accordingly, proposals that both the routines of fact finding and the deliberations on rules, regulations, and special orders required by the newer agencies should follow the formal, slow, and costly procedures of ordinary legislative and judicial bodies. The other side wants to maintain simpler and less technical processes, in order to provide what the late Charles E. Hughes described (when he was governor of New York) as a "prompt, continuous, expert and inexpensive method for dealing with a class of questions of fact that are peculiarly suited to examination and determination by an administrative agency specially assigned to that task." "To follow the rigid requirements proposed by the critics," he continued, "would force administrative agencies having a wide variety of functions into a single mold so rigid as to bring about a widespread crippling of the administrative process."

Moderates on the two sides are inclined to agree that a considerable range of discretion has to be left to administrative agencies in formulating rules and devising procedures for their enforcement, and yet that some formal checks need to be put on arbitrary action. The two sides usually agree that we can require the boards to announce the rules under which they intend to operate, hold hearing before issuing rules and regulations that affect the rights of individuals, set up appeal boards to hear complaints, and permit the aggrieved parties to petition the courts to set aside the decisions on the grounds that they were issued without formal notice or hearing, or that they were not supported by substantial evidence, or were "clearly erroneous." [28]

We have not always objected to strong presidents or regarded vigorous executive action at other governmental levels as incompatible with democratic government. At the very beginning Alexander Hamilton offered the warning that irresponsible political action is ordinarily the product of a diffusion rather than of a concentration of authority. Power placed in a group, he said, is "more liable to abuse" and "more dangerous when abused" than power placed in one man, who can be "more narrowly watched and more readily suspected." Authority clearly placed tends to "beget a livelier sense of duty." [29] In the states a popular movement against legislative supremacy got under way early in the nineteenth century. As voting rights were broadened through removal of high property qualifications there was a shift from indirect to direct election of the state governor and other changes enlarging his power by lengthening his term and giving him a veto on legislation and an increased appointing power. He rapidly came to be regarded as "man of the people," their "watchful sentinel . . . elected by their suffrages and identified with their interests," as a delegate in the New York Constitutional Convention of 1821 expressed it. In national politics this popular demand for strong executive leadership found expression in the election of Andrew Jackson to the presidency. Jackson regarded himself as representative of the people against the legislative aristocracy; and the people appeared willing to trust him with great powers in order to insure the victory.[30] The later presidents we have generally called "great" (e.g., Lincoln, Cleveland, Theodore Roosevelt, Wilson) achieved that accolade chiefly by virtue of a dynamic leadership in the formulation and vigorous execution of programs of reform demanded by a popular opinion. During the last half century popular reform movements at the lower territorial levels have generally been associated with changes, in law and practice, greatly strengthening the powers of local chief executives. The direct primary and direct legislation came in along

28. Cf. F. W. Coker, "Freedom in America," *Ohio State University Law Journal,* 7 (1941), 258–382, at 373–375.

29. *Federalist,* No. 70.

30. Charles E. Merriam, *History of American Political Theories,* pp. 109–111, 114–115, 178–179, 182–184.

with the advent of strong mayors and strong governors, in general move-ments aimed at weakening the powers of special group interests inside or outside the government.

Recent experiences in our national policy supply us with reasons to believe that political and civil rights can be kept generally as secure in a society whose government helps direct its economic development as in a society that leaves the controls predominantly in private hands. While we have been modifying some of our economic liberties, we have at the same time been making more secure some of our other liberties. This is shown in recent decisions of the United States Supreme Court in cases initiated or participated in by executive agencies. These deci-sions have helped to establish freer voters' participation in nominations and elections, freer communication of ideas, and fairer court trials through a fairer selection of juries, a more effective right to assistance of counsel, and a stronger protection against compulsory self-incrimina-tion. While our government, during a decade and a half, has been apply-ing new forms of economic intervention we have retained substantially unimpaired our rights to talk, organize, campaign, and vote in efforts to prevent, repeal, or extend the aids and regulations.[31]

III. Preserving Traditional Values

We have maintained, from colonial times to the present, a mixed eco-nomic system, with changing mixtures of private and public enterprise and changing forms and degrees of governmental interference and non-interference.[32] "Conservatives" who have condemned new governmen-tal interventions, on the ground that they violate tradition, have gen-erally come round later to approving the interventions on grounds both of their proved benefits and of the worthy traditions they have come to represent. Sooner or later we call on government to protect our pri-vate economy from its self-destroying errors and to help it in other ways when it appears not to be able to take full care of itself.

Our earlier leaders could not have foreseen the particular economic and political changes that vast technological and industrial changes

31. See Albert T. Lauterbach, *Economic Security and Individual Freedom: Can We Have Both?* (1948); Joseph Rosenfarb, *Freedom and the Administrative State* (1948); Charles F. Griffin, *Enterprise in a Free Society* (1949); Seymour Harris, *Economic Planning and Freedom* (1950); A. Campbell Garnett, *Freedom and Plan-ning in Australia* (1950); Thomas K. Finletter, *Can Representative Government Do the Job?* (1945); Paul H. Appleby, *Big Democracy* (1945).

32. For explicit recognition of our present-day mixed economy see John Cham-berlain, *The American Stakes* (1940); Stuart Chase, *For This We Fought* (1946); Oswald Knauth, *Managerial Enterprise;* Arthur M. Schlesinger, Jr., *The Vital Center* (1946).

would bring about. But they had faith that we could somehow, with good ends in view, accommodate our policies to the changes. To appraise, in terms of our firmer traditional beliefs, the present role of government, we should probably go back of the economic determinism and social biologism of the last three quarters of a century and return to older American conceptions of society and government and thereby understand again that the state, although an agency of organized social coercion, has never been the only agency of social coercion and never solely an agency of coercion.

Typical examples of traditional American ideas on the occasions for governmental intervention appear in the following statements by two of our earliest national statesmen:

Said Benjamin Franklin (arguing, in 1789, against a proposal to amend the Pennsylvania state constitution in such way as to establish an upper legislative chamber to represent "the Property," as distinguished from "the Population of the State"):

> the accumulation . . . of property . . . and its security to individuals [is] an effect of the protection afforded to it by the joint strength of the society in the execution of its laws. Private property therefore is a creature of society, and is subject to the calls of that society whenever its necessities shall require it, even to the last farthing; its contributions therefore to the public agencies are not to be considered as conferring a benefit on the public, entitling the contributors to the distinctions of honor and power, but as the return of an obligation previously received, or the payment of a just debt.[33]

Said Alexander Hamilton (advocating, in 1791, the imposition of duties on imports in order to promote American manufactures and setting forth generally the need for governmental aid in maintaining a diversified, balanced, secure, and progressive economy):

> Experience teaches that men are often so much governed by what they are accustomed to see and practice that the simplest and most obvious improvements, in the most ordinary occupations, are adopted with hesitation, reluctance, and by slow gradations. The spontaneous transition to new pursuits, in a community long habituated to different ones, may be expected to be attended with proportionately greater difficulty. When former occupations ceased to yield a profit adequate to the subsistence of their follow-

33. From "Queries and Remarks Respecting Alterations in the Constitution of Pennsylvania" (1789), in *Writings of Benjamin Franklin*, Albert Henry Smyth, ed. (New York, Macmillan, 1905–07), *10*, 54–60, at 59–60.

ers, or when there was an absolute deficiency of employment in them, owing to the superabundance of hands, changes would ensue; but these changes would be likely to be more tardy than might consist with the interest either of individuals or of the society. In many cases they would not happen, while a bare support could be insured by an adherence to ancient courses, though a resort to a more profitable employment be practicable. To produce the desirable changes as early as may be expedient may therefore require the incitement and patronage of government.[34]

Some recent forms of governmental intervention are new, but the basic criteria and derivations are old. To explain and justify the interventions in general terms we do not have to import or invent ideas about man, society, or the economic requirements of a political democracy. We can safely hold on to a traditional belief that man in his economic activities is moved by considerations of individual or family self-interest and that this "profit motive" has great social utility, while also holding on to the belief, stressed by Max Millikan above, that in both economic and noneconomic activities man is moved also by other incentives—by a desire for power, prestige, self-expression, social approval, as well as by some concern for the welfare of others or for the general welfare.[35] We do not have to try to sort out accurately the various activities that are to be powered by these various incentives to individually satisfying and socially useful efforts. We can still accept generally the statement by one of the earliest Americans (Rev. John Cotton, in 1651) that every "lively holy Christian has a combination of virtues, strangely mixed." And a judgment expressed in a present-day business periodical that "Service" is "the path to profit" does not seem very different from a conclusion stated by another first American (Rev. John White, in 1630) that "nothing sorts better with Piety than Competency." [36]

We appear today to be prevailingly in agreement on our main social objectives: national security and prosperity; and for each citizen a minimum level of material welfare with some assurance of security of income and employment and of a reasonable chance for a constructive

34. From "Report on Maufactures to the House of Representatives" (December 5, 1791), in *Works of Alexander Hamilton*, H. C. Lodge, ed. (New York, Putnam, 1904), 4, 70–198, at 104–105.

35. Cf. Herbert Hoover, *Addresses . . . 1941–45*, pp. 240, 245, 259–260.

36. John Cotton, *Gods Way and Course* (1651), p. 119; Henry R. Luce, "The Reformation of the World's Economies," *Fortune*, 41 (February, 1950), 59–68, at 60; John White, *Planter's Plea* (1630), in *American Colonial Tracts* (1838 collection), 2, No. 3, at p. 60.

and respected role in the national economy. We regard these ends as valuable in themselves and also as means essential for an effective exercise of democratic political rights. We also prevailingly believe that to achieve the volume of production and employment required for realizing our goals we must depend chiefly upon the decisions of private individuals who compete with one another in improving the methods of private enterprise and in initiating new enterprises and new methods. We want to keep up the supply of private enterprisers, even though this may require the aid of government. We recognize, it is true, that our present-day large-scale industry, although greatly increasing total production, often creates obstacles to an efficient distribution of its vast product; but we also believe that relief from this disadvantage can be best obtained not by abolishing private enterprise but by fixing some of the general conditions under which it is to operate.

Thus historical processes, beyond our power or desire to stop or deflect, have apparently answered the question as to whether government shall intervene in our private economy. Reasons for this were stated, thirty-five years ago, by a distinguished conservative, Elihu Root, in his presidential address before the American Bar Association:

> We have only just begun to realize the transformation in industrial and social conditions produced by the wonderful inventions and discoveries of the past century. The vast increase of wealth resulting from the increased production is still in the first stages of the inevitable processes of distribution. The power of organization for the application of capital and labor in the broadest sense to production and commerce has materially changed the practical effect of the system of free contract to the protection of which our law has been largely addressed. The interdependence of modern life, extending not merely to the massed city community but to the farm and mine and isolated factory, which depend for their markets and their supplies upon far distant regions and upon complicated processes of transportation and exchange, has deprived the individual largely of his power of self-protection, and has opened new avenues through which, by means unknown to the ancient law, fatal injuries may be inflicted upon his rights, his property, his health, his liberty of action, his life itself. We have not worked out the *formulae* through which old principles are to be applied to these new conditions—the new forms perhaps through which the law shall continue to render its accustomed service to society . . .
>
> The individualism which was the formula of reform in the early nineteenth century was democracy's reaction against the law and

custom that made the status to which men were born the controlling factor in their lives. It was an assertion of each freeman's right
to order his own life according to his own pleasure and power,
unrestrained by those class limitations which had long determined
individual status. The instrument through which democracy was
to exercise its newly asserted power was freedom of individual contract, and the method by which the world's work was to be carried
on in lieu of class subjection and class domination was to be the
give and take of industrial demand and supply. Now, however, the
power of organization has massed both capital and labor in such
vast operations that in many directions, affecting great bodies of
people, the right of contract can no longer be at once individual
and free. In the great massed industries the free give and take of
industrial demand and supply does not apply to the individual.
Nor does the right of free contract protect the individual under
those conditions of complicated interdependence which make so
large a part of the community dependent for their food, their clothing, their health and means of continuing life itself, upon the service of a multitude of people with whom they have no direct relations whatever, contract or otherwise. Accordingly, democracy
turns again to government to furnish by law the protection which
the individual can no longer secure through his freedom of contract,
and to compel the vast multitude on whose cooperation all of us
are dependent to do their necessary part in the life of the community.[37]

Nothing in this chapter implies that there are, in our tradition, no
limits to the proper scope of governmental intervention; or settles any
question as to the proper forms of regulation at any given time. A government may take on more burdens that it can carry; and the means it
adopts for bringing greater freedom and security to the ordinary individual may make him less secure and free.

The general aim of the participants in this symposium is to restore
or strengthen the market mechanism, not to destroy it; to help keep up
a generally desirable level of employment, prices, and investment, rather
than to substitute governmental orders for private bargains in decisions
on particular jobs, prices, and investments. The government should,
for example, arrange its tax program in ways that favor risky new ventures or that mitigate extreme differences of wealth; it should direct

37. "Public Service by the Bar," in Elihu Root, *Addresses on Government and
Citizenship* (Cambridge, Harvard University Press, 1916), pp. 512–542, at 533,
539.

some of its expenditures toward securing more nearly equal opportunities in health, education, and housing; it should time its expenditures on essential public works in such ways as to fill the gaps in employment due to excessive market fluctuations; and it should take steps toward restraining unnecessary concentrations of corporate ownership and toward democratizing the control of technological monoplies.[38]

The participants assume that government's essential role is that of fixing general rules determining the conditions under which our natural and technological resources are to be used.[39] This role, they believe, should be not that of compelling or persuading particular persons to do particular things but that of assisting in the maintenance of conditions "within which unidentified persons may act of their own free will." [40] These seem to be the aims implicit in the quotations above from Franklin, Hamilton, Jefferson, Elihu Root, and various present-day political leaders.

38. See John M. Clark, *Alternatives to Serfdom* (1947) and *Guideposts in Time of Change* (1949); Sumner H. Slichter, *What's Ahead for American Business?* (1951); *Fortune Editors,* in collaboration with Russell W. Davenport, *U.S.A.: The Permanent Revolution* (1951); Peter F. Drucker, *The New Society* (1950). Cf. the titles listed above in n. 25.

39. See F. A. Hayek, *Road to Serfdom,* ch. 6: "Planning and the Rule of Law."

40. Margaret Mead, *And Keep Your Powder Dry* (New York, Morrow, 1942), ch. 11: "Are Democracy and Social Science Compatible, Each with Each," p. 187.

CHAPTER III. *A Primer of*
National Income Analysis

BY MAX F. MILLIKAN

I. INTRODUCTION

1. *Do economists agree?*

One of the premises of this study is that economists have got far enough with the purely technical economic problem of what causes periods of depression and prosperity so that some of the noneconomic aspects of the problem of employment policy can fruitfully be investigated. Any layman taking a cursory look at the technical literature of the field would be smitten with doubt as to whether this was so. Controversy continues to rage at what appears to be the very heart of the subject, and terminology appears, superficially at least, almost as personal to each author as ever. Yet we believe it to be true that over the last fifteen years a way of looking at the problem has been developing in the profession which identifies the forces at work (though it does not establish their relative importance) and which would be accepted by an overwhelming majority of economists as providing a useful framework of analysis.

This does not mean that on outstanding policy issues a quorum of economists can usually be found, a majority of whom will support or reject a particular proposal. It does not even mean that there is any agreement as to what causes booms and depressions. There are still many theories. But a scientific explanation or "theory" is made up of two elements. There is the armchair element consisting of a way of getting hold of the issues, a set of concepts in terms of which the data can be classified and the forces which may potentially be at work related to each other; and there is the laboratory element consisting of a set of facts or quantities which establish the relative importance in the real world of each of these forces. The facts needed to establish the relative importance of the interest rate, the tax structure, the distribution of incomes, and many other factors are still missing or incomplete. Until they are convincingly established there will continue to be differences as to appropriate policy among men of common objective which will appear as wide as ever. But the groundwork at least has been laid for a generally acceptable conceptual apparatus with which the facts when known can be analyzed to give demonstrable conclusions. It is the purpose of this essay to describe the main outlines of that apparatus.

2. Is this analysis "Keynesian"?

It is perhaps wise to issue a caveat at the start. In the development of economic ideas the approach to employment problems about to be described is probably associated with the name of Lord Keynes more frequently than with that of any other writer. In fact its roots go well back of Keynes, and under cultivation by recent writers it has grown into a plant rather different from the thorny shrub first depicted in Keynes's *General Theory*. There is another reason, however, for not referring to it as "the Keynesian analysis." In his writings Keynes was not careful to separate the exposition of conceptual tools from either his intuitive hunches about matters of fact or his positive prejudices as to appropriate policy. Many people have therefore come to identify the Keynesian approach with either a pessimistic view of the vitality of private investment or certain specific policy proposals such as deficit spending.

Neither of these has anything to do with what we may call the income-expenditure approach to employment problems. The tools of analysis which he helped to mold are entirely neutral and have no implications as to policy until applied to factual material imported from outside the ivory tower in which they were fashioned. They are susceptible of use by Republicans and Democrats alike, and can be applied equally well to problems of depression and inflation. Because he was their principal architect we may hope that some day they can be referred to as Keynesian without the improper overtones which such a reference unfortunately currently carries. Meanwhile we had better call them something else. Economists have come to call this approach, rather loosely, "national income analysis" or simply "income analysis" for short.

3. The intellectual heritage of modern income analysis

Modern income analysis can best be approached by taking a look at its intellectual heritage. It has three principal lines of ancestors. Probably the earliest type of economic instability recognized and treated by theorists was price inflation. The great historical price inflations were usually associated with radical changes in the money supply, resulting either from discoveries of the precious metals or from attempts by desperate or crafty rulers to pad their resources by making one coin into two or by simply printing increasing quantities of promissory notes. Thus the study of the price level and inflation came to be regarded as the province of the expert on money and banking, a subject set quite apart from the study of why goods and services are produced.

A second tributary stream had its origins in the increasing concern during the nineteenth and early twentieth centuries with recurring periods of unemployment and low output. It was suggested that these recurring depressions reflected some underlying rhythm or cycle in economic activity, and a separate subject of study, business cycle analysis, grew up to proliferate theories of boom and bust, each described in its own private language. A tenuous bridge existed between the money experts and the business cycle experts, but until recently many of the latter made scant use of it.

Finally toward the end of the nineteenth century increasing attention began to be paid to the more prosaic problem of how you go about measuring what we call the national income, which in turn forced a more careful analysis of just how you define it. For the most part the early investigators in this area regarded their problem as descriptive and statistical rather than explanatory and theoretical. They were merely trying to measure, not to explain.

The insulation of these three types of problems from each other twenty years ago may be appreciated by examining any representative college economics text of the period. You will find a section on money and banking which will include an explanation of how the price level is determined and what causes inflation. If the book is not too old there will be another entirely separate chapter on unemployment and the business cycle which will probably not mention either inflation or national income. Unless it is quite a recent text there will be no extended discussion of the concept and measurement of national income itself.

Yet it is the analysis of the measurement and components of national income and the relations between money income and physical output and employment which has served to bring these three strands of thought into something much more nearly approaching an explanation of why the real and money incomes of the country behave as they do, be it depression, inflation, or nervous teetering on a tightrope of "normalcy." We shall therefore begin our primer with a description of some of the key ideas involved in the measurement of income and output. We can then see how income analysis can be used to illuminate as well as to describe fluctuations in economic activity. Initially we shall restrict ourselves to situations in which money is assumed to behave "normally" and prices are stable. Finally we can take a look at how all this relates to the price level and the money system, an area in which unhappily our three streams do not yet flow quietly together to commonly accepted conclusions but where there is hope of more consensus in time.

II. The Measurement of Income and Product

1. *What do we want to measure?*

What do we mean when we say there are fluctuations in "economic activity"? What do we want to stabilize when we say we want to stabilize incomes? And how are we to measure the extent of the evil of instability and the degree of our success in combating it? A number of possibilities spring to mind. The most obvious index of what we are trying to stabilize is employment, the number of people at work at paying jobs throughout the country, or perhaps the relation employment bears to the "labor force," that is, the total number of people who want to be at work. But employment is not the sole index of economic welfare nor even a very satisfactory one. We would all like to have jobs, satisfying ones if possible, but they do not in themselves guarantee a high standard of living. Digging holes and filling them up does not make anyone better off. Individually we each tend to think of our economic welfare in terms of our money income. But a period of inflation brings home to us dramatically that money income is likewise frequently a poor measure.

What we are really trying to get at is what is in some sense the real value of all the productive want-satisfying activity going on in the economy during a given period. However it is measured we know that a depression is a time when the total output of goods and services declines sharply, and this is what matters most. In the short run this total output will fluctuate in the same direction and in roughly similar magnitude with the volume of employment. We can legitimately speak of the two rising and falling together. But in the longer run we should be getting, through increased productivity and efficiency, more and more output from the same number of man-hours of work. We need an index of this output to see whether we are achieving this dynamic goal.

2. *Money spending as a measure of physical output*

The measurement of physical output is a difficult business. If we were to itemize all the automobiles, baby carriages, packs of bubble gum, pairs of pants pressed, hours of duty of policemen, miles of highway, etc., turned out in a year we would have an impossibly long list. Also it would not add up to any meaningful total we could compare with other years. All these productive activities must be evaluated in terms of some common standard. Furthermore, from a practical point of view, this standard must be one in terms of which records are already available if our job is not to require half of us to become census enumerators. We must utilize the accounts already kept in the economy. This means we must use the money standard furnished for us for the most part by the market mechanism. To almost every productive activity there corresponds a money transaction. Work is paid for by wages, goods are sold for prices, the services of capital equipment are measured, however inadequately, by the depreciation accounts of businesses. In the accounts of the units that make up the economy we can find a record in money terms of almost every productive activity that takes place during a year. In those few cases where there is no money transaction to measure production, as when a farmer raises chickens and eats the eggs himself or a householder lives in and "uses" his house without entering a rent charge on his own or someone else's books, there are comparable money transactions in the market which permit us to "impute" a money value to home-consumed food and the rent of owner-owned homes.

The problem of evaluating national output, then, begins with the problem of finding (actual or imputed) a money transaction corresponding to every productive activity going on in the economy. If we then add up all these transactions, we have a measure of national income or output. There are three things we have to be careful about in this process.

The first is that many money transactions occur which do not reflect any productive activity at all. The sale of a share of stock by one person to another represents a transfer of ownership but corresponds to no added output in the system. A loan may facilitate production but the granting of the loan does not itself measure any productive activity. The same is true of gifts, second-hand purchases, and so forth. So in adding up money transactions to get a measure of national income we must be careful to leave out those which measure merely a reshuffling of existing wealth and not the creation of new values.

Secondly there is the related difficulty of how to avoid counting the same productive activity two or more times. Suppose an automobile is produced during the year and sells for $2,000. In the production of that automobile there will be many money transactions totaling a great deal more than its final value. The final value includes the value of some iron ore bought once by a steel company, bought again from the steel company by a manufacturer of frames, sold to an automobile company, sold again to a dealer, and finally sold to a consumer. The iron ore embodied in the car, like most of the car's other components, will thus be paid for three or four times over before reaching the final user.

During the process of production and distribution most items of output exchange against money a good many times before they are consumed. In adding up money transactions to arrive at a measure of output, therefore, we must not only omit transactions which do not really represent output, but we must also be careful to omit transactions covering output we have already counted somewhere else in the system. This creates difficulties for national income accounting. It has, however, one compensating virtue of considerable importance. Since we have a good deal of choice as to which transactions we will use to represent each item of output, we can measure the same thing in a number of different ways. Thus national income can be derived from a number of different sources and the results compared with each other as a check on the accuracy of the data. This point, as we shall see, also has great importance for the explanation of fluctuations.

Our third difficulty in using money transactions to measure real income arises from the familiar fact that the value of money itself—the average bundle of all kinds of things you can buy for a dollar—fluctuates from year to year. When all prices have gone up on the average 10%, we do not wish to be fooled by a 10% rise in money national income into thinking that the country is better off. In particular, in considering the severity of economic fluctuations, we are likely to get a greatly exaggerated notion of the violence of ups and downs from looking at the way money national income behaves, since prices usually fall with declining economic activity and rise in prosperous times. The changes in the real value of output are consequently a good deal less extreme than our money measure would lead us to believe. We will come back to this problem a little later (see section 5 below); but for the time being let us imagine that prices behave themselves and that money today is worth about as much as money yesterday or money tomorrow.

3. *The income method of measuring output*

As goods and services flow through the production pipeline the flow is metered by money transactions at frequent points between original input and final output. Which meters shall we read to be sure of avoiding double counting? There are two obvious alternative sets of meters to use—those at the input end of the pipe and those at the output end. If we make adjustments for changes in the amount in the pipeline—for goods in process—these two readings should give us the same result. Most modern national income accounting systems use both kinds of measures, each acting as a check on the accuracy of the other. When we add up all the transactions representing final output (including any increase in what is in the pipeline) we get what is commonly called national product. When we use the meters at the input end of the pipe we get what is called, for reasons which will be apparent in a moment, national income. "Product" and "income," if they are measured and defined properly, should come out the same since they are both measures of the same thing—total national productive activity during the period.

This identity of product and income is so important for the analysis of why productive activity fluctuates that it is worth explaining somewhat further. If we consider concretely just what transactions we add together to get the two totals the reason for their equivalence will be clearer. Looking first at the input end of the pipe, the work done by all the people in the community is obviously the biggest element of input. A good deal of that work is paid for, and its value roughly measured, by wages and salaries; so all wage and salary transactions ought to be included in our input measure. Farmers, professional people, small businessmen, and others who work for themselves are not paid wages, but the amounts they earn over and above their costs are a measure of their contribution to the productive process. Part of what they earn is the equivalent of a wage for the work they do and part is compensation for the risk they take and the capital they use in putting their savings into their enterprises. So the net earnings or profits of these unincorporated enterprises should be included as a measure of another element in production.

In the business corporation the contributions of capital and labor are more sharply separated out. The contributions of labor are measured by wages and salaries; those of capital are paid for in profits and interest. These inputs of capital resources into corporate business may be measured, then, by adding to the other elements of input interest paid, dividends paid, and corporate profits retained in the business, called undivided profits.

The output of any given year is produced with the help of many items of capital equipment. The productive services of this equipment are inputs without which the inputs of labor and entrepreneurial energy would be able to produce little. How shall we measure these equipment-service units of input? In the accounting of the business firm the services of durable plant and equipment are measured by adding in to the cost of goods sold an item for depreciation. For the nation, then, we can add to our other income components an item representing total depreciation of durable producers' goods or, as it is called in the official statistics, a capital consumption allowance.

Finally, a special problem arises in the case of people who own houses, land, and other resources which they do not use directly in their businesses. The services of these items of property are one of the inputs into the productive pipeline. If this property is rented, the excess of the rent over the costs of maintenance and upkeep of the property, which is called net rent, measures the contribution of these resources to production. If the property is not rented, as in the case of owner-occupied houses, there is still a service which should be measured. In the United States this is done by employing the fiction that every houseowner is a dual personality. As a houseowner he is an investor who is thought of as renting his own property to himself as a consumer of housing services. The net rent he would receive if he rented his house to someone else is estimated and added in to the total value of inputs into the pipeline.

In summary, then, the value of input can be roughly measured by adding up, in the language of our national accounts, all compensation of employees, all proprietors' and rental income (including unincorporated business and professional income, farm income, and the rental income of persons), corporate profits (both distributed as dividends and retained "undivided" in the business), net interest, and capital consumption allowances. We can now see why this measure of productive activity is called the "gross national income." For although we started out to measure all inputs into the productive mechanism, what we come out with is (with one adjustment to be considered presently) the sum of all the current money incomes of all the people and all the businesses in the community. This is not so surprising as it seems at first when we stop to think that almost all incomes are a result of the process of production in the broadest sense of the word and that almost all production gives rise to money incomes.

4. *The income and output of government*

Two slight modifications of this picture of national income are called for when we bring government into the picture. In the first place, we have covered the incomes of individuals and of business firms, but we have said nothing so far about the income of this other major economic entity in our society. The income of government is derived for the most part from taxes. Should we not add in these tax receipts to get a complete picture of total national income? Our first impulse is to say no, if what we are trying to measure is inputs into the productive mechanism. For tax transactions do not correspond to any physical input into our pipeline of production. They are a mere transfer of buying power from individuals and businesses to government. Government may use the money to build, let us say, a dam, which is certainly a productive enterprise. But the inputs involved in the building of the dam are already counted in the wages of the workers on the dam, the profits of the construction companies doing the work, etc. The tax payments themselves do not correspond to any inputs though they may make inputs possible.

So if we count as part of the incomes of individuals and businesses all the money they receive which they subsequently pay over to the government in taxes, we should not also count the income of government, since this would be counting the taxes twice. For some purposes, however, it is convenient to be able to speak of the income of government, i.e., total tax receipts, as a component of national income. We can do this logically without double counting if we are careful first to subtract these tax payments from the incomes of the individuals and businesses that pay the taxes, counting only their incomes after tax, or their "disposable" incomes as part of national income.

The other modification arises from the fact that the government pays some people money which they think of as income but which does not correspond to any input of effort into the pipeline. Unemployment benefits, veterans' bonuses, and old-age assistance payments are some of the most important of these payments that represent mere transfers of buying power from the government to individuals and do not measure any real productive effort. These payments, which are called "transfer" payments, should not be included in our measure of national production.

We have arrived, then, at one way to measure the value of the gross output of the nation during a period: add together the disposable income (income after taxes) of all individuals in the nation including the owners of unincorporated businesses, subtract transfer payments from this, add the net incomes of corporations retained in the business, add capital consumption allowances, and add the tax income of government.[1] In other words, if we conceive of the community as being made up of consumers, businesses, and governmental units we can arrive at a measure of national production by adding the incomes of these three components, or by consolidating the income side of their accounts into a statement of the national income.

5. *The product method*

Suppose we now take a look at the other method, that of reading the meters at the output end of the production pipe. The last transaction in

1. Economists will note that what is here described is the gross national income at market prices and not what the U.S. Department of Commerce calls national income, which is net national income at factor prices. I believe the former to be not only easier to describe and relate to national product but also more significant and useful.

the flow of most goods and services from initial input to final consumption occurs when the final consumer buys the good or service at retail. This is the last meter in the pipeline. In many cases it is still some distance from actual consumption. An automobile yields services for some years after it has been bought by its consumer-owner. Ideally that part of output which consists of automobile services should perhaps be measured by car miles driven rather than automobiles sold. But here, as in many other parts of our national accounting system, we must use the best information we can get at practicable cost, and for consumers' goods this means using retail sales.

As mentioned before, the United States official statistics make one exception to this rule of measuring consumer goods output at the point of sale to the final consumer. In the case of houses, which last frequently over the course of several business cycles, the distortion involved would be too great. Also in the case of a substantial fraction of the housing market, the consumer buys not the house but the services themselves through rental payments. This is done in a wide enough range of cases to permit reasonably good estimates to be made of what owner occupants would have to charge themselves if they were to collect rents from themselves at current rates.

One component of final output, then, is measured by the total spending of consumers on goods and services, including a guess as to what they would spend for rent if they had to rent their homes but excluding what they actually do spend in buying houses. As buyers of houses consumers are thought of as businessmen, and these expenditures are treated along with business spending, which we shall look at in a moment.

There is one type of final output which is never bought by consumers in a market, namely, the goods and services provided without prices by the government. The services of policemen and firemen, the production of roads and parks and dams, the maintenance of defense forces, and all the other things that government does for the people must be included as part of the productive activity of the economy. Since these things are not bought directly by the people we have no direct measure of what they would pay individually for them if they had to. Collectively, however, the community has decided that these government activities are worth the amounts of money spent on them. The best available measure of their value, then, is their cost to the government, though in particular instances individuals will complain that this is a very bad measure. We add, then, to consumer spending the spending of government for goods and services. It should be noted that this is not quite the same thing as total government expenditure, for it excludes the government transfer payments we mentioned earlier—unemployment benefits, bonuses, etc.

—which are a sort of subsidy to consumers rather than a payment for current productive activity.

Consumer spending and government spending for goods and services measure the flow of final output at the consumer's end of the pipe. If this flow were always equal to what was being put in at the input end we would have nothing further to add to our measure of output. But in fact in a growing economy such as ours the flow of inputs is normally substantially larger than the flow coming out to consumers. This is because the amount in the pipe itself is being constantly increased. This is what economists refer to as the growth of capital. It may take several forms.

In the first place, there may be an increase in the quantity of goods in process—raw materials, partly finished goods being worked on, and finished goods not yet sold to consumers. Any increase in these inventories held by business firms reflects productive activity which is not measured by the value of goods passing to consumers. On the other hand, in some periods a part of what is being consumed does not represent current product at all but merely a drawing down of stocks built up in some earlier period. So we must adjust our measure of output by adding any increase or subtracting any decrease in the inventories held by business.

In the second place, a good deal of productive activity goes into expanding the plant and increasing the equipment used to produce output. In a sense such plant and equipment are goods in process just as much as are inventories. The inputs required to build a plant emerge as output for consumers only over a period of years as the plant is used up and worn out in service, but they do so emerge ultimately or they would never be undertaken in the first place. Increases in this supply of what is called fixed rather than working capital must be added to our measure of output. Included in this investment of business in additional productive instruments is the value of new houses built each year.

These two elements of product—the change in inventories and business capital investment—correspond to what we may call net business spending. It would clearly be wrong to add all business spending to the spending of government and consumers in arriving at a measure of national output, since most business spending is made for elements that go into the things consumers and government finally buy. That part of business spending which represents the costs of goods sold in the current period is for elements of output we have already measured in adding up retail sales. Any business spending which represents productive activity and is not included in current retail sales, however, must be added in. Spending which increases inventories and spending on additions to plant and equipment (including residential housing) are the two important varieties.

Finally there is one last discrepancy between input and the ouput bought by domestic consumers, government, and business which arises from our trade with other countries. Part of what is produced in any country trading with the rest of the world is not consumed at home at all but sold to foreigners. On the other hand part of what is consumed is derived not from current production but from imports. If what is bought from abroad for domestic sale is exactly equal to what is exported for foreign consumption no adjustment in our measure is required to take account of this complication. For in this case sales to domestic consumers will overstate production by the amount of imports and understate it by the amount of exports, and since they are equal the net result will be correct. If, however, we export more than we import —investing the difference in loans to foreigners—we must add this net foreign investment to our other measures to get total product. On the other hand, if we consume more than we produce at home, importing the difference, we must subtract this net *dis*investment from our measure of national product.

This adjustment can be put in terms of another kind of spending, the spending of foreigners. If foreigners spend for our goods and services more than they receive for sales to us this net spending of foreigners must be added to the other kinds of spending which measure product. If they receive more than they spend, these net receipts of foreigners must be subtracted from total spending.

In summary, then, we can arrive at a measure of final output by adding up various kinds of spending just as we measured input by adding up different sorts of income or receipts. Considering again the three components into which we divide the economy, national product is measured by adding the spending of consumers, the spending of government on goods and services, and the spending of business on additions to capital, both inventories and plant and equipment. In this case, however, we must add a fourth component, namely, the *net* spending (excess of spending over receipts) of the rest of the world in our country.

The two ways of measuring national productive activity which we have described—by national income and by national expenditure—are illustrated in Chart I for the two years *1949* and *1950*. This chart is taken directly from the report of the Council of Economic Advisers to the President. It is prepared quarterly for the President, other executive departments, and the Congress and is available to the general public both in the semiannual reports of the council and in the monthly pub-

Chart I. The Nation's Economic Budget

1950 (BILLIONS OF DOLLARS)

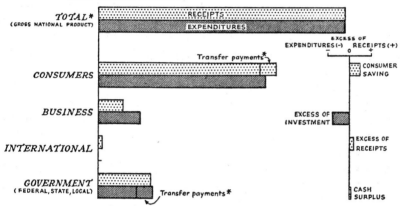

1949 (BILLIONS OF DOLLARS)

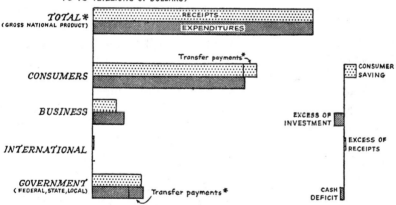

* Transfer payments are included in receipts or expenditures of the
separate accounts but not in the total gross national product.

0   50
SCALE IN BILLIONS OF DOLLARS

lication, *Economic Indicators,* obtainable from the Government Printing Office. It is worth studying carefully since successive issues of it not only describe what is happening to national product but indicate, as we shall see, the key factors responsible for the fluctuations we know as inflations and depressions. Ignore for the moment the little stubs at the right of the chart. The length of the light-shaded bars represents the magnitude of the receipts or current income of the various sectors into which we have divided the economy. Thus the disposable income of consumers (or income left after payment of taxes) was $204.3 billion in 1950, including transfer payments (the small box at the end of the bar, of $19.0 billion. The retained income of business (after tax and dividend payments), including capital consumption allowances, was $29.7 billion and the cash tax income of all government (federal, state, and local) was $60.8 billion. Adding these up, subtracting the transfer payments, and making various minor technical adjustments amounting to $6.8 billion, we get a gross national product of $282.6 billion, represented by the top light-shaded bar.

Using the other method, represented by the dark-shaded bars, we see that the expenditures of consumers on goods and services amounted to $193.6 billion, the expenditures of government came to $61.5 billion, including $19.0 billion of transfer payments (again shown as a box at the end of the bar), the spending of business for investment in inventories and capital goods was $48.9 billion. Foreigners spent on our goods $2.3 billion less than they received for what they sold to us. Adding consumer expenditures, government expenditures less transfer payments, and gross private investment and substracting our net expenditure on foreign goods we get our $282.6, representing gross national product again.

6. The identity of income and product

The reader who has stuck with us this far has been very patient in wending his way through a labyrinth of analysis which must have seemed woefully unrelated to the problem of finding jobs for men out of work or keeping prices from galloping upward in a spiral. His patience is about to be rewarded by a glimpse at how we use these tools to diagnose our ills and suggest remedies; but first one vital point must be driven firmly home. To understand the analysis to follow it is necessary to be quite clear as to why the two bars representing total income and total expenditure must always and inevitably be of exactly equal length.

This can be explained in several ways. In the first place, since they are designed as alternative measures of the same thing, namely, total national productive activity, they ought to come out equal if we have defined them correctly. The flow into the pipe must equal what comes out the other end plus whatever accumulates inside. Looking at it another way, we have measured in one case what people have received for national product and in the other case what they have paid for it. These are obviously two sides of the same set of transactions. What the seller gets for an article cannot be different from what the buyer pays if there are no other parties to the deal. If we had no relations with foreign countries, and if our data covers, as it should, all domestic buyers and sellers (including the government which takes a slice in taxes), receipts and expenditures must add up to the same total. Since we do have foreign trade, we must allow for the discrepancy this may introduce by bringing in the rest of the world as another party in our market. With this adjustment the identity of spending and receipts is preserved.

For those with a flair for bookkeeping the thing can be explained still another way. In the income accounts of a business everything that is recorded on one side as received from current sales must be allocated on the other side of the account to some item of cost or to profit. If we consolidate the accounts of all the units in the economy into one master account we can show on one side the sales or output of the economy as a whole and on the other side the costs and profits, broken down by who gets them. Unless there is a mistake in our arithmetic the two totals cannot come out differently.

In fact, of course, our sources are sometimes incomplete and our methods inaccurate. Statisticians are human, appearances to the contrary notwithstanding, and our two methods of computing national product will therefore produce slightly different results in practice. If you ask all the sellers of a commodity how much they received and all the buyers how much they paid, you will almost certainly come out with different totals. But though you get different estimates, it is still the same quantity you are estimating in both cases. If your information were all perfectly accurate and your addition correct you would come out with the same result. National product is a single magnitude whether viewed as income or expenditure.

We may digress as to the bearing of this point on a common popular fallacy. It is sometimes alleged that the economy is not creating sufficient income to buy its current output. If we mean by income the income of consumers, businesses, and government taken together this statement can never be true. Total current income is always exactly equal to the value of total current output at current prices and is therefore always just sufficient to buy current output. What may be true is that the income may be going to people or firms or governmental units that will not in fact spend it the next time round. But this is very different from saying that there is not enough income available to buy what is being produced. For every increase in output creates an exactly equal increase in income somewhere in the system.

What is true of the totals is not, of course, true of their component parts, as a glance at Chart I shows. One man may buy much more than he sells. But if he does, it is inescapably the case that somewhere someone must sell more than he buys since total sales must equal total purchases. Thus income is always sufficient so that total output *can* be bought, though it *may not* be if income receivers elect not to spend it. This gives us a hint of the central idea of modern income analysis—to examine the precise relation between the incomes of various persons, firms, and governmental units and the amounts they subsequently spend.

III. The Crucial Kinds of Spending

1. *The escape from a vicious circle*

We are now at the threshold of our main problem: Why does national product fluctuate? We could investigate the problem in two ways corresponding to our two equal measures of national product, namely, national income and national expenditure. The whole is merely the sum of its parts, so to explain fluctuations in total income or expenditure the first step is to explain fluctuations in the income or expenditure of each of the component parts of the economy—consumers, businesses, and government. Starting with the income approach we at once come up against a difficulty. The income of a consumer or a business firm depends very largely on factors beyond his control—usually on somebody else's spending. In most transactions we think of income as the passive or determined factor and spending as the active or determining one. So it is difficult to get very far by looking at why an individual's income varies. If we pursue this we are likely to come up with the answer that it is because national spending (or income) is varying. The total varies because the parts vary because the total varies. We do not make much progress galloping around this circle.

If we turn to spending we appear at first glance to be better off. The spending of individuals and businesses, and even of governments, appears to be much more directly under their control. One can decide to spend or not to spend within rather broad limits, especially these days when credit is available in so many ingenious forms. What, then, are some of the factors which affect these decisions to spend?

The first one which springs to mind bids fair to pull us mercilessly back into our vicious circle. For there is no doubt that the single, most compelling, factor determining how much consumers, businesses, and governments spend is their incomes. Patterns of consumer spending are closely related to income levels; the investment program of a business concern is shaped largely by the level of its earnings; in the realm of government the spending of local and state units depends on their tax receipts; and at the national level Congress has been reluctant to sanction much of a divergence between federal outlay and receipts.

The great bulk, then, of the spending of consumers, businesses, and governments is determined by the incomes of those various bodies. But it cannot *all* be so determined, or there could be no fluctuations in national product of the kind we are striving to avoid. For since incomes are determined by other people's spending, if everybody's spending were determined entirely by his income our circle would be closed in fact as well as in logic. The erratic ups and downs of employment, production, and output which cause us so much trouble could not occur.[2] This observation suggests the fruitful idea which lies at the root of modern income analysis: the factors responsible for economic fluctuations must be those which change *the relations between the incomes and the subsequent expenditures* of the units which make up the economy. To put it another way, we can think of changes in spending as being of two sorts: those that are a result of changes in incomes and those that occur for some reason other than because income has changed. The former we may call *induced* changes in spending and the latter *autonomous* changes. The vast bulk of the changes which occur in spending are the induced ones, but the ones which are crucial for an understanding of the sources of fluctuations are the autonomous ones. If we can isolate the areas where these autonomous changes in money payments occur, and find out something about what causes them, we shall be well on the way both to an understanding of economic instability and to a set of prescriptions for policy to mitigate it.

Look back at the right-hand side of Chart I. The lengths of the little bars or stubs shown there represent the excess of receipts over expenditures (to the right of the vertical line) or the excess of expendi-

2. Footnote for economists and mathematicians: By assuming appropriate lags between changes in income and the changes in spending to which they give rise, the closed circular flow of income and spending can be made to pulsate up and down in a regular fashion instead of remaining constant. The discovery of this mathematical possibility has stimulated the construction of numerous ingenious models, but their inventors usually admit that on grounds both of mathematics and common sense something else is needed to build a satisfactory theoretical image of the turbulent real world.

tures over receipts (to the left of the line) for each of the groups in the economy: United States consumers, United States business firms, foreigners having dealings with this country, and United States governmental units. There is no bar of this kind at the top showing the difference in the totals, since as we have seen total receipts and total expenditures must always be exactly equal (apart from mistakes in measurement). These little bars at the right labeled "consumer saving," "excess of investment" (business), "excess of investment or receipts" (international), and "cash surplus" or "cash deficit" (government) are worth very careful study, for to understand their properties is to take the first step toward understanding the causes of fluctuations.

2. *The income-spending relation for consumers*

Let us look at each of them in turn to see a little more concretely what they mean. You will note that consumer receipts or "disposable income" (including transfer payments) are greater than consumer expenditures, and that the difference ($14.4 billion in 1949), which we call saving, is therefore represented by a bar to the right of the vertical line. This reflects the fact that consumers as a whole normally spend less than their incomes on goods and services, putting the balance into life insurance, securities of various kinds, investment in homes, savings accounts, checking accounts, or in an old fruit jar on the top shelf. This is not true for everybody, nor even for the nation as a whole at all times. During any year a surprising proportion of the families of the country are spending more than they are taking in or "dis-saving." They do this by borrowing, buying on installment, using up past savings, and the like. And when national income is very low, as it was in the great depression of the thirties, enough people dissave to offset the savers and bring personal saving for the nation as a whole down to zero or even below.

Nevertheless, in spite of the amazing variety in the relation between income and expenditure for different people—and we are just beginning through studies sponsored by the Federal Reserve Board to discover how great that variety is—there is apparently considerable stability in that relation for United States consumers taken all together. The proportion of consumer income saved falls toward zero as disposable income falls in a slump and rises as disposable income recovers again, but for any particular disposable income repeated several times the amount of total consumer spending does not appear to vary by more than a few per cent. In other words, the vast bulk of consumer spending is what we have called induced, that is, it depends quite closely on the level of income. It does vary some, however. There are autonomous elements in it. People as a whole sometimes decide to spend more or to cut down their total spending even though their incomes have not changed. This is the same thing as saying that consumer saving sometimes changes without any change in income, since saving is just the difference between spending and income. We know very little about the extent to which such changes occur. If they are of significant magnitude they are clearly one of the crucial factors determining economic fluctuations, since, as we shall see presently, a small change in the community's wishes as to how much it wants to spend (or save) out of its current income can produce greatly magnified effects upon total economic activity.

It may be well to issue a warning at this point about that little word "saving," which means all things to all people. We sometimes think of our savings (with an *s* on the end) as referring to the money we have in the bank, or all our liquid assets including marketable securities, or all our assets of all kinds including life insurance policies, homes, and the like. This is not the sense in which economists use the word saving. This year's saving is defined as the difference between this year's income and this year's spending on consumption goods and services. It makes no difference what is done with the money. It is "saved," by definition, whether it is soundly invested in government bonds, recklessly put into a worthless enterprise, loaned to an improvident nephew who will never pay it back, left sitting idle in a bank, or sent to the cleaners by mistake in a rumpled suit and never heard of again. This warning is necessary because eminent economists have wasted reams of paper in learned journals arguing issues that would have been settled at once if they had agreed on a definition of saving.

One of the things, then, that we want to watch carefully in order to diagnose what is going on in the economy is that little bar labeled consumer saving. If it grows or shrinks when disposable income is not changing much this is a signal that consumer behavior may be upsetting stability.

3. *The income-spending relation for business*

Passing on to the next little bar labeled "excess of investment" (business) we observe that this extends to the left indicating that expenditures are greater than income. Recall that in this case the income of business excludes all those parts of its gross income which are passed on to others as costs or paid out to owners as dividends. What remains is sometimes called business saving. The expenditures, on the other hand, exclude current expenses associated with sales and include principally spending to build up inventories and to purchase capital goods, plant, and equipment. In the American economy in prosperous times business as a whole is increasing and improving its facilities, expanding its capacity, and adding to its inventories of goods in process as output grows. These are characteristics of a progressive economy. The money for this expansion comes partly from retained income, the business savings of our chart. But in considerable measure it comes from banks, individual investors, insurance companies, and other sources of capital.

This excess of business investment in producer's goods over business saving is much more volatile and unpredictable than consumer saving. To some degree these investment expenditures are induced like consumer expenditures. When business income is high prospects look good and management is encouraged to lay and execute large plans. When business income is low or declining many firms turn to a policy of conserving existing assets and retrenching capital investment, even when they could obtain the funds for expansion. But income is only one of many factors affecting business capital expenditures, and many of these expenditures are autonomous in our sense of being independent of the level of income. Many economists find the chief source of economic instability in these autonomus fluctuations of private domestic investment.

It should be noted that there is another possible source of autonomous variations in spending within the business sector of the economy. Businesses can alter the relation between their retained income and their investment expenditures by changing their saving as well as by changing their investment expenditures. A business will never reduce its gross income if it can help it, but it may well reduce or increase, in response to changes in circumstances, that part of its gross income which it retains. There are two major factors which determine what a business does with that part of its income that it is not compelled to pay out at once to cover current costs. The first of these is how much the business feels it should set aside out of current income to provide for the ultimate replacement of its durable assets. This capital consumption allowance, as explained above, is what the business puts down in its accounts as depreciation and obsolescence costs. This element in retained business income tends to be fairly stable and is not subject to sudden autonomous variation. Accounting practices with respect to depreciation change only very slowly and are quite unlikely to give rise to sharp variations in depreciation allowances.

The other factor affecting business saving is the decision as to what part of net income to pay out to owners and what part to retain as what is known as undivided profits. The part of profits paid out to owners becomes part of the incomes of the individual owners or stock-holders and is not therefore included in business-retained income. The payment of dividends is thus a kind of business spending, though a rather different kind from the buying of equipment. Thus the little bar at the right labeled excess of investment (business) may grow longer either because of business decisions to increase spending on inventories, plant, and equipment, or because of decisions to reduce retained income by paying out more of the profits to owners. Note that in the latter case we have something that could be described as an autonomous change in *income*. In either case changes in the length of the little bar will have far-reaching consequences for the rest of the economy.

Usually autonomous changes in business spending, whether they relate to the purchase of capital goods or to dividends, will show up as changes in the excess of investment represented by the little bar. It is possible, however, that a business may decide simultaneously to reduce its dividend payments and increase its capital expenditures by the same amount. This will increase business saving and business investment equally, with no change in the difference between them. This kind of change likewise has consequences for output and employment, as we shall see. We must therefore keep an eye on the bars at the left, as well as on the little one at the right reflecting their difference, in order to catch simultaneous autonomous changes in both business saving and spending which offset each other.

4. The income-spending relation for foreigners

Turning to the excess of foreign spending on goods and services in this country over the receipts of foreigners from what they sell to us, it is clear that we cannot generalize as to whether this will normally be positive or negative. It was very close to zero in both 1948 and 1949. This may seem surprising in view of the fact that a great many more goods were shipped abroad in both these years than were brought into the United States. The explanation is, of course, that a large proportion of our exports was paid for not by foreigners but by the United States government under the Marshall Plan. The money spent on these goods appears in the government's accounts rather than in the accounts which show foreign spending. In the year 1950, as in earlier years, the amount we actually shipped to foreigners was greater than they shipped to us. United States aid was, however, a good deal more than the difference so that foreigners sold to us for cash goods worth about $2.3 billion more than they had to pay us for.

In the years immediately preceding the inauguration of the Marshall Plan, the excess of foreign spending in the United States, over United States spending abroad, reached very substantial proportions. In 1947, for example, foreigners spent nearly $9 billion more on our exports than we paid them for our imports. The Marshall Plan has now been replaced by the Mutual Security Assistance program. It is quite probable that if these assistance programs should cease the discrepancies between foreign spending and receipts would again become an important element in the total pattern of spending.

5. *The income-spending relation for government*

Looking at the government sector of the economy it will, of course, surprise nobody to discover that all our government bodies put together sometimes have a deficit and sometimes a surplus. There was a substantial federal cash surplus in 1948, a small deficit in 1949, a small surplus in 1950, and a large surplus in the first half of 1951. State and local bodies spent slightly more than their receipts throughout this period. As in the case of the business account, the balance of receipts and expenditures—the little bar at the right of the chart—can be changed either by autonomous decisions to change the expenditures or by decisions to change the income or receipts through changes in tax policy. We can eliminate a deficit or build up a surplus either by spending less or by taxing more or by some combination of the two. We can reduce a surplus or create a deficit either by increasing spending or by reducing taxes or by doing a little of both. Ten years ago it was widely believed that the direct influence of the government budget on the flow of spending depended solely on the size of the deficit or surplus (measured by the little bar at the right) and not on how it was brought about. It is now recognized that the level of government spending and the level of taxes is important as well as the difference between the two. As in the case of the business accounts, simultaneous autonomous changes in both taxes and expenditure which leave the deficit or surplus unaffected will influence the national income. So here again we must keep our eyes on the behavior of the bars at the left as well as on the piece at the right which measures their difference.

6. *Summary: the six determinants of national spending*

This brings us to a very important proposition, namely, that fluctuations in national money income must come about through autonomous changes in one or more of the following factors: 1) the amounts consumers want to spend out of any given income (or the amounts they want to *save* out of that income, which comes to the same thing); 2) the spending of business firms of all kinds on plant, capital equipment, and inventories; 3) the proportion of their income (after taxes) that businesses decide to retain and not pay out in dividends; 4) the *net* spending (or net receipts) of foreigners on American goods and services; 5) the spending of government bodies, both their spending on goods and services and the transfer payments they make to individuals and businesses in subsidies, social security payments, bonuses, etc.; and 6) the tax receipts of government bodies. This exhausts the possible channels through which changes in income can come about. Anything which influences the level of income in the community must do so through one or more of these factors. An increase in incomes must be the result of an autonomous increase in consumption, business investment, the net spending of foreigners, or the spending of government, or of a decrease in business saving, or in taxes. And one or more of these things must change not as a consequence of a prior change in income but autonomously as a result of changes in tastes, in expectations, in institutional environment, or in some other factor.

This proposition is, of course, a tautology. It is, if you like, little more than the self-evident statement that the cause of a change in spending (or incomes) must be a change in spending. Of what use is it to us, then, in understanding depressions and inflations? The answer is that while this does not provide us with a *theory* of business fluctuations, it does give us an orderly way of classifying the various channels through which the fundamental causal factors must operate. This has several advantages. It permits us, in looking for the true causes, to take up one thing at a time, and to be sure when we are through that we have examined all the relevant pieces of the puzzle. Perhaps more important, it provides us with a check list of possible consequences of any proposed measure or event. A change in the tax structure, for example, may operate through a number of rather different channels. It will probably change aggregate tax payments, which is itself one of our determinants of spending. But it may well also affect the total amount of consumption spending done out of the community's disposable income. It is very likely to affect the decisions of businessmen as to what to spend on capital equipment, and it may alter their dividend (business saving) policies. It may impinge on our foreign trade balance. We cannot make any sensible estimate of the effect of such a measure on the economy until we have examined its impact not just through one channel but through all channels.

Again it is generally held by economists that the availability of credit is one of the important factors affecting the level of business activity. Monetary policy, after being regarded during the 1920's as the major weapon of business cycle control, is now somewhat out of fashion, but as Professor Hart argues convincingly in Chapter 7, it still has a major role to play. The mistake of many economists who exaggerated its effectiveness lay in their failure to follow its impact through the chain of spending decisions outlined above. They came to believe that there was a direct relation between interest rates and economic activity, whereas the influence of monetary factors operates only through their impact on spending. If for some reason the spending decisions of consumers, business, and government are insensitive to credit policy, as they appeared to be during the great depression of the thirties, then credit policy will be impotent.

An examination of the various kinds of spending decisions which may be influenced by credit policies may, however, suggest measures which would not be thought of otherwise. Interest rates may, as many economists now believe, have relatively little effect on investment decisions, but the availability of capital funds to certain kinds of enterprises may strongly influence the extent to which they feel it necessary to build up reserves for investment out of their own saving (undistributed profits) rather than relying on outside financing. And recent experience seems to suggest that the ease with which consumer credit is available may influence the relation between consumer income and expenditure.

The classification we have given of the six channels through which the level of economic activity may be influenced has another utility. It permits us to examine in a relatively orderly way the alternative policy measures that are available to us to influence the course of business boom and depression. The list suggests the possibility that there are measures whose primary influence will be on each of the determinants. There are ways we can influence consumption patterns, there are measures primarily directed at investment, there are special devices to encourage or discourage corporate saving, there are many policies which impinge on the foreign balance, and of course the two instruments of variation in taxes and in government expenditure are available. Succeeding chapters will be concerned with all these types of measures, and with reconciling their use for income stabilization purposes with the other objectives which must condition their design and execution.

Modern income analysis, properly used, however, should serve to highlight the fact that though a measure may be focused on one of the types of decisions mentioned, it is very likely to influence several of the other types as well. Thus though the classification of spending types we have developed serves to suggest new kinds of measures of control, it should also be used to check all the possible channels through which such measures may take effect and thus expose "indirect" as well as "direct" effects.

Before we proceed to the detailed examination of particular policy areas which is the task of succeeding chapters, there are two further pieces of the analytic puzzle to be put into place. The first, which will occupy us in the following section, has to do with how far a change in spending goes when set off by a change in autonomous spending somewhere in the system. The second, which we shall get to in sections V and VI, is concerned with how spending is related to money, prices, and employment.

IV. The Repercussions of a Change in Spending

1. *The mechanics of induced changes in consumption*

You will recall that in describing the almost vicious circle of spending and income we observed that most changes in spending are induced by prior changes in income, but that some spending changes are autonomous or independent of income changes. It follows from the importance of induced changes that when an autonomous change does take place somewhere in the system it is going to give rise to a further series of induced changes. When a business firm steps up its rate of outlay on capital goods the new spending it does at once becomes income for the people on the receiving end. But these people in turn will spend at least some of this new income and thus create income for others, who will be induced to increase their spending, thus creating still more income, and so on. Thus if consumers or business firms or governments change their rate of spending this acts like the movement of the first in a long string of dominoes, setting off changes in the total flow of spending and income much greater than the initial impulse. In order to appraise the final result of such an autonomous change we must understand more fully 1) just what the mechanism of change is, 2) how far this snowballing of spending changes is likely to go, and 3) what may accelerate or slow down the repercussions.

The mechanism of change can be examined by following through on our chart of the nation's economic budget the repercussions of an assumed change in spending. So as not to have to talk about too many things at once, let us think of a situation in which there is a good deal of unemployment and in which prices do not change much in response to spending changes. Let us also assume for the moment that the international and government sectors of the economy are not much affected, focusing our attention on the interactions between the business and consumer sectors.

Now suppose that the Pennsylvania Railroad decides that its competitive position would be improved and its costs lowered if it laid additional track along a stretch of the main line. Accordingly it lays out a program for the purchase of rails from the United States Steel Corporation calling for the expenditure of $50,000 more per month for a considerable period. U.S. Steel makes the rails to order, hiring more men and expanding production for the purpose. Now the first effect of this new rate of spending will be that the incomes of various people will be increased by a total of $50,000 per month. This will include the men U.S. Steel hires, the added men required by the firms producing the necessary coal and other materials, the stockholders of U.S. Steel who get additional profits, etc. In terms of our graph, we would expect that the top bars representing total national expenditure and total national receipts would both grow longer by $50,000 a month or $600,000 a year. The bar showing business expenditure would also grow longer by the same amount. Assuming no change in the business retained receipts bar—that is, assuming U.S. Steel pays out to stockholders all the extra profits it makes on this particular deal—the excess-of-investment bar will push out to the left by $50,000 a month.

Now this poses a problem. Total receipts are always equal to total expenditures for the economy as a whole. Therefore any excess of expenditures in one sector (represented by a stub to the left of the vertical line on our chart) must be balanced by an exactly equal excess of receipts in other sectors. Since we have assumed that the international and government sectors are not affected the only thing which can balance our $50,000 of new investment is $50,000 consumer saving. Saving must in fact have increased this amount at the same time that investment increased. This, of course, is what has happened. The employees, managers, and stockholders who have cooperated in producing the new higher output of rails have incomes $50,000 higher than before, and we have said nothing about any increase in their spending. So the difference between their incomes and their spending, which we call their saving, has increased by $50,000. But this is clearly a strange kind of saving. No one has *decided* to save that much more. The recipients of the new incomes find themselves momentarily saving, unintentionally or involuntarily as it were, merely because they have not yet got around to increasing their spending.

This state of affairs clearly will not last long. Almost at once the new recipients of income will start spending it, or at least most of it, bringing their saving down again to the desired relation to their incomes. Let us suppose that on the average they will want to save some $5,000 out of this new income each month and will spend the other $45,000 monthly. We might suppose that this would reduce total consumer saving back to within $5,000 of its original size. But how can this be? The Pennsylvania Railroad is still buying $50,000 worth of rails from U.S. Steel each month, keeping the rate of investment $50,000 higher than formerly. As long as investment remains at this level our rule that total receipts must equal total expenditures tells us that actual consumer saving *cannot* fall. If the steelworkers in Pittsburgh, the stockholders, and others are now doing only $5,000 of the additional saving monthly, who is doing the rest?

The answer is to be found, of course, by pursuing further the spending of the steelworkers and others whom we have left dangling. This money is received by grocers, automobile dealers, movie theater proprietors, and all the other people to whom the steelworkers pay their new incomes. These payments create still more income which, until the spending of these new groups is increased accordingly, becomes saving. Most of it is still unintentional saving, of course. Out of the $45,000 received in this way by those who sell to the steelworkers, they may wish to save perhaps 10% or $4,500 and to spend the remaining $40,500. This spending of $40,500 then becomes income for still other groups, who in turn will pass it on to yet other groups, after withdrawing a portion of it to add to their savings, and so on ad infinitum.

Thus an investment of $50,000 a month inevitably creates actual saving of the same amount. Initially this saving is unintentional, and those who receive the money will reduce this temporary and involuntary saving by spending the major portion of it. But the community's attempts to reduce saving are bound to be thwarted as long as the investment continues, since every act of spending designed to reduce the saving of the spender will increase the saving of the recipient by an exactly equal amount. The less people want to save the more they spend, and the more they spend the more they receive, and the more they receive the more they save.

2. *How far do the repercussions go?*

The answer to this question in the real world is complex, but we can get an idea of the answer by seeing what happens in the simple situation we have assumed. Consider what happens 1) if investment goes up $50,000 a month and stays there, 2) if on the average people want to save 10% of any added income they get, and 3) if the government and international sectors of the economy are not affected. There are two ways to see how far the process goes. The first is to follow each successive increase in income, add them all up, and see what the total is. Each time money spent by one group becomes income for another group it leads to further spending, amounting to 90% of receipts. Thus when we have settled down to the new level of income and spending created by this investment we will have each month additional spending of $45,000 plus $40,500 plus $36,450 plus $32,805, etc., each figure being 90% of the last. The items in this series become smaller and smaller the further we carry it until ultimately they get to be so small that they can be neglected. The reader who remembers his high school algebra will recognize this kind of a set of numbers as what is called an infinite geometric series. He will remember, perhaps, that it has a sum but will probably not remember that that sum is given by the formula $a \times \dfrac{1}{1-r}$ where a is the first term and r is the fraction by which it is successively multiplied. In our case a is $50,000 and r is .9, giving us a sum of $50,000 $\times$ 10 or $500,000. In other words, income will ultimately increase in our hypothetical example by ten times the original autonomous change in spending.

The other way to look at the problem, which is perhaps intuitively clearer, is as follows: The process of expansion goes on because people do not want to save the whole of the increase in their incomes which results from the investment expenditure of the Pennsylvania Railroad. They do, however, want to save a part of it. The amounts the community wants to save increase as income increases. As long as new actual saving, which in our simple case is always equal to new actual investment, is in excess of what people want to save as a regular thing, spending and incomes will grow. But as incomes grow they will ultimately get so large that people will want to save $50,000 more than they did before. At this point actual saving and intended saving will be brought into balance and no further expansion of spending will occur. Our question may be restated, then, to read, "How much must incomes increase in order to increase the amount of saving people want to do by $50,-000?" If, as we have assumed, people want to save 10% of any increase in their incomes, it is clear that incomes must increase by $500,000 in order to induce people to save an extra $50,000. As long as incomes are below this level there will be people in the community who have not yet expanded their spending by as much as they propose to do out of their new higher incomes. But when we have reached this point the community will not wish to expand its spending any further.

In this very simplified case it is clear that the ultimate impact of the increased capital purchases of the Pennsylvania Railroad depends on what proportion of new extra income people want to spend and what part they want to save. If they want to save half of any increase, it will take a rise in income of only $100,000 to bring further expansions of spending to a halt. If they want to save a third, income must rise by $150,000 to persuade them to save $50,000 voluntarily. If they want to save a fourth, an income rise of $200,000 is required and will occur as a result of the community's attempts to spend all but 25% of any increase in their incomes.

This crucial fraction is what economists call the "marginal propensity to save," and its mirror image, the fraction people want to *spend* out of increases in their incomes, is called the "marginal propensity to consume." It is important to note that what matters for our present analysis is not what people save *on the average* out of their entire income but rather what fraction of *changes* they will save. A person may well be saving only 10% of his total income, but he may at the same time be resolved to save 20% of any *increases* in his income. Or he may be saving nothing out of his present income, but a reduction in his income might lead him to use up assets to maintain consumption, consuming *more* than his income or *dis*-saving. It is what he does in response to *changes* in income which determines the final consequences of an autonomous *change* in spending.

It is perhaps unnecessary to point out that the process works the same way for an autonomous reduction in spending as for an increase. When the Pennsylavania Railroad is through with its program of rail purchase its monthly rate of capital expenditure will drop by $50,000. If no other investment increases to offset this, consumer incomes and spending will drop by a good deal more than $50,000 as the repercussions of this autonomous decline are felt through the system. People will cut their spending by somewhat less than the decline in their incomes, reducing their saving to make up the difference. The larger the share of the income cut which comes out of spending and the smaller the share which comes out of saving the further will total incomes shrink. Incomes must fall far enough to persuade people to cut their saving by as much as investment has fallen. If the fraction of the income cut which they take out of saving is one fourth, income will fall by four times the cut in investment (or $200,000 in our illustration) before it stabilizes again. It must fall this far to induce people to save $50,000 less.

At one time it was thought that private investment spending was peculiarly effective in producing these induced effects upon total income. It should be clear from what we have said above, however, that any autonomous change in spending will have a similar result. If consumers as a group decided to spend $50,000 more out of the same income as before, the repercussions through the system would follow in like fashion. This $50,000 spent by one group of people would become income for another group, who would in turn increase their spending by some part of $50,000, creating still more income for another group, etc. This attempt by consumers to decrease their saving by increasing consumption cannot actually decrease the amount saved as long as the amount being invested by business is unchanged. What happens is that the attempt to decrease saving by increasing consumption increases incomes. This process goes on until incomes are increased enough so that people want to save out of the new higher incomes as much as they were saving before. How much incomes will increase before this point is reached depends, as before, on what part of an increase in income people want to save and what part they want to spend.

Similarly, an autonomous increase in spending by government or by foreigners will lead to the same sort of results. An autonomous change in any of the little stubs at the right of our chart will produce offsetting changes in other stubs which will lead people to spend more or less than before. Thus incomes will change further until the relation between receipts and spending in each sector of the economy is what the members of that sector want it to be. At that point a new equilibrium is reached in our circular flow of income and spending, which will not be changed until another autonomous change in spending decisions occurs.

3. Induced changes in investment

We can now indicate some of the complications that arise in the real world to modify this simplified picture of the results of an autonomous change. First, what difference will it make if we permit investment to vary after the initial autonomous change? Several things may happen to private investment.

In the first place, during the process of change there will be repercussions on inventories held by retailers, wholesalers, and manufacturers. Go back to our original example, but suppose the new orders of the Pennsylvania Railroad were met by U.S. Steel not out of new production but out of inventories of rails on hand. In this case the $50,000 purchase by the railroad in the first month would not lead to any new incomes at all but merely to a reduction in inventories held by U.S. Steel. You will recall that these changes in inventories are part of business capital investment. So the first effect of this purchase would be an increase of $50,000 in the investment of the railroad and a decrease of an exactly equal amount in the investment of the steel company, leaving investment and incomes for the economy as a whole unchanged. If the railroad's order is a big and continuing order, this offsetting inventory decline is not likely to persist. Before long the steel company will increase production to meet the new higher demand. But there may be a lag, longer or shorter depending on the steel company's estimate of the situation, before the new investment leads to new incomes.

Again, when the steel company finally does hire new workers to step up production and these new workers begin to spend their new incomes there may be another lag before this spending becomes income once again, for the retailers of Pittsburgh may not anticipate this increase in their business. The first impact of the spending of the workers upon the retailers may be an increase in retail sales which draws down the stocks retailers keep on hand. This can be described as a kind of unintended reduction in investment. If the higher level of sales had been foreseen the retailers would have increased their orders from wholesalers and manufacturers in advance, and these in turn would have expanded production to meet the higher level of sales. In other words, given time to adjust to the new situation, the retailers would not have planned lower inventories and in fact would probably have planned higher ones. But one of the reasons for carrying inventories is precisely to be able to meet these unforeseen changes in demand. Thus the investment of the railroad may be partly offset in this second phase by reduced investment by retailers. This cushioning and delaying effect of inventory change may well be present throughout the process of change in income. It affects the manner and rate of income changes, but it should not affect the final result, since these inventory changes are transitory and will normally be followed by changes in production and incomes in due course.

This emphasizes, however, the necessity for caution in interpreting changes in the little stubs at the right of our chart. As we have seen, a change in the consumer-saving stub may reflect an autonomous change in consumers' desires as to how they want to divide their incomes between saving and consumption. It may, however, reflect no change in consumer attitudes at all but merely the fact that changes in spending have not yet been adjusted to changes in incomes. In other words, we must distinguish between the level of saving people will continue to do as a steady thing out of given incomes and the amounts of saving they do in transition periods because they have not yet had time to bring their actual spending patterns into line with their new income level.

Similarly, changes in the excess of investment may reflect changes in fundamental business decisions as to the amount of capital expenditure they want to undertake, or it may reflect the somewhat "involuntary" and transitory changes in inventory investment which occur more or less automatically during a boom or slump in sales that has been imperfectly foreseen. Unfortunately the national income data themselves do not announce what the nature of the change is, and the analyst must use great caution in interpreting it.

There is another quite different respect in which changes in investment may complicate our analysis. We have taken account so far only of the changes in consumption decisions to which changes in income give rise. But it is probable that investment decisions are likewise influenced by changes in incomes, particularly in business incomes. U.S. Steel will have to replace rolling mills more frequently the higher the level of output, retailers may be induced to enlarge their stores or improve their equipment sooner if their business is better, consumers' goods producers will be stimulated by higher profits and sales to increase their capacity, the resulting orders for machine tools may encourage machine tool firms to install more toolmaking machinery, and the increase in railroad freight traffic may lead the Pennsylvania Railroad to buy more rolling stock and even to plan still further expansions of track capacity. Thus increased incomes lead to higher levels of planned investment.

We must not, of course, let this kind of general reasoning run away with us. It is tempting to suggest that a small expenditure undertaken in the bottom of a depression can snowball in this fashion into a major recovery movement, possibly carrying the economy back to full employment and beyond into dangerous inflation. But it is more realistic to expect the response to be in proportion to the stimulus. A rise in income will probably stimulate some increase in investment spending under most circumstances, but in all but the most abnormal periods the additional investment will be but a small fraction of the increase in income which set it off. If business expectations are sufficiently gloomy, and if there is a good deal of unused capacity available to meet new demands, there may be no induced investment at all. Indeed, certain methods of increasing income—some kinds of government expenditure programs, for example—may actually reduce private investment, offsetting the effects of the autonomous increase in spending.

In any actual situation we must examine the probable extent to which a change in income will have these induced effects on investment. The more investment responds to income changes the larger the repercussions of any autonomous change will be. The smaller this "marginal propensity to invest" in response to changes in incomes the smaller will be the secondary effects which follow on the initial change.

4. *Induced changes in the other four factors*

We have looked at the repercussions of an autonomous change on two of our six basic factors, namely, the relation between consumption and income and the level of business spending on capital goods. We must now take a look at the response of the other four factors to changes in income, namely, business saving, the international balance, government receipts, and government expenditures.

The effect of business saving is not hard to see. If the United States Steel Corporation does not pay out to final income receivers the entire $50,000 received monthly for new rails from the Pennsylvania Railroad, but keeps some part of it in undistributed profits or in unexpended depreciation reserves, this retained fraction will not become consumer income and consequently consumption expenditure will not go up so rapidly or so far. If $5,000 is retained by U.S. Steel, the new consumer income created the first time around by the new investment will be $45,000 instead of $50,000, and the first induced burst of consumer spending will be only $40,500 instead of $45,000. Furthermore, some part of the incomes created by the subsequent spending of these new incomes will be retained by such business firms as the retailers, wholesalers, and manufacturers who benefit from the induced spending. In other words, at each stage of the circular flow of income some part of the new flow will be diverted into business saving, so that only part of the spending of one group of consumers becomes income for another group. To the extent that this occurs, the final expansion in spending and incomes will be less than it would be if there were no business saving.

We can see this another way by looking once more at our chart. The increase of investment of $50,000 a month lengthens the stub labeled "excess of investment" by this amount. But any increase in business saving that occurs shortens this stub again. It is the *excess* of investment that creates the new income for consumers out of which is done the added saving necessary to offset the investment. If as expansion proceeds a total increase in business saving of $10,000 occurs, the *excess* of investment is reduced to $40,000, and thus the increase in consumer saving required to balance it is similarly reduced. The expansion in incomes, which continues until people want to save what they are actually saving, will thus be less.

The effect of taxation is exactly parallel. In our tax system, in which income taxes play such an important part, a substantial fraction of any increase in either business or individual income must be paid over to the government in taxes. Since it is probably income after taxes, or disposable income, which primarily governs consumer expenditure, the more is taken away in taxes each time around the less will be the expansion of consumer spending. Taxes no doubt have a similarly dampening effect on investment. A $10,000 increase in business net income before taxes may be only a $5,000 increase after taxes, and its effect in stimulating investment expenditure may be correspondingly reduced. So the effect of taxes which vary with incomes is to reduce the induced repercussions of autonomous changes in spending.

Consult the chart again. If government spending is constant, any increase in tax revenues lengthens the bar labeled "cash surplus" or shortens the one labeled "cash deficit." To the extent that an increase in business investment is offset by the resulting increases in tax revenues the change required in consumer saving to make up the difference is reduced. Since it takes a smaller increase in incomes to make a smaller volume of saving voluntary, equilibrium will be reached at a lower level of spending the higher the level of taxes.

In the international sector, the excess of foreign investment is likely to be reduced by an expansion of incomes. For increased incomes at home will lead to increased consumption of imports as well as of domestic goods. There is no reason, under most circumstances, to expect any corresponding increase in exports. In other words, we will probably buy more from foreigners as our incomes rise, but there is in general no reason why foreigners should buy more from us.[3] To the extent that, as incomes expand, part of those incomes are paid over to foreigners, the repercussions of the spending will be reduced. Spending which becomes income for Americans will once again be spent, at least in part. Spending which becomes income for foreigners may not be spent or may be spent in other countries where it does not further increase incomes here. On our chart an autonomous increase in excess of business investment is likely to be partly offset by a decrease in excess of foreign investment (to the left of the line) or by an increase in excess of receipts of foreigners (to the right of the line). To the extent that this occurs consumer-saving and consumer-disposable income will change less than they otherwise would.

Certain kinds of government spending respond quite automatically to changes in income. When a rise in national income brings a drop in unemployment it also brings a drop in unemployment compensation. It also is generally associated with declines in relief payments, work relief

---

3. This conclusion is altered, of course, in a situation in which the exchanges are controlled in such a manner that foreign purchases from us are directly dependent on our supplying the necessary dollars through purchase from them. In this case an increase in our imports leads directly to an offsetting increase in exports. This is not, however, even in the looking-glass world of today, the usual state of affairs.

projects, and even in some cases public works projects. Thus for the federal government, at least, expenditures tend to vary in the opposite direction from national income. As private spending rises certain kinds of government spending tend to contract, offsetting in part the effect on incomes of the changes in the private sector. The reactions of government spending to a change in incomes tend, like those of taxes, to slow down and diminish the induced further changes. In graphical terms, as incomes increase government receipts increase and government expenditures decline, both factors tending to reduce the length of the stub labeled "government deficit" or increase that labeled "government surplus." The change in this stub offsets in part any autonomous increase in business investment, reducing the expansion of consumer saving that is required to balance the system.

5. *Summary: what the net repercusssions depend on*

The induced changes set off by an autonomous change in one of our six basic factors are thus seen to depend on the way in which, and the rate at which, each of these six factors responds to a change in the level of national income. As we have seen an increase in income is almost certain to call forth an increase in consumption and is quite likely to stimulate an increase in investment. These two changes create still more income, which creates more spending of these types, which creates more income, etc. The larger the reactions of a change in consumption and a change in investment to a change in income, the further the process of expansion will go. On the other hand, an increase in income is likely to increase business saving, to decrease the excess of foreign investment, to increase tax payments, and to decrease government spending, and all four of these factors tend to reduce the size of the repercussions following an autonomous increase.

Similarly, an autonomous reduction in spending will reduce incomes, calling forth a secondary reduction in consumption and probably in investment, which starts off the endless series of downward movements in income. On the other hand, each reduction in income will probably cause some reduction in business saving, some increase in foreign investment, some reduction in tax payments, and some increase in government spending, and these four results will all cushion the decline in incomes and prevent its going as far as it otherwise would. The net result in both cases depends on the sensitivity of each of these six factors to income changes.

A good deal of empirical work has been done in estimating this degree of sensitivity. Quite good estimates are available as to the sensitivity of a given tax structure and of certain kinds of government expenditures to changes in income. We know less about the magnitude of the reactions of consumer spending and foreign investment to income changes, but estimates of these quantities are not lacking. In the case of business capital expenditures, business saving, and many kinds of government expenditure, factors other than income change are so important that it is almost impossible to separate out the influence of income change by itself. We are fairly safe in concluding, however, that the combined effect of all six of these factors is such that an autonomous change in spending will, under most conditions, produce a net change in aggregate income several times as large as the initiating impulse.

This analysis has, of course, policy implications. It suggests that there are three ways of increasing the stability of the flow of incomes. One is to attempt to reduce the frequency and magnitude of what we have called autonomous changes in our six basic variables. A second is to design autonomous changes in the variables over which policy has control which will offset the changes in the uncontrolled factors. A third is to reduce the sensitivity of the economy to such autonomous changes as do occur. It is clear from what has gone before that this last result would be achieved if we could reduce the sensitivity of consumption and investment to income change, or if we could increase the sensitivity of the damping factors of business saving, foreign investment, taxes, and government spending. It may be difficult or undesirable on other grounds to attempt to design measures to do each of these various things. Subsequent chapters will be concerned with exploring such questions in detail. The purpose of this analysis is merely to lay bare what the alternatives are.

6. *The repercussions of different kinds of autonomous changes*

Certain differences in the repercussions of different kinds of autonomous change deserve mention because they have been rather widely misunderstood. We can classify autonomous changes into three basic groups: 1) autonomous changes in spending, 2) autonomous changes in incomes, and 3) simultaneous autonomous changes in both spending and incomes.

The changes we have used in our examples so far are changes of the first sort. Consumer spending, business investment spending, the spending of foreigners in the United States, and the spending of government may all change autonomously. Autonomous changes in income or receipts occur in only two of our sectors of the economy. Consumers cannot, in general, decide to change their incomes by their own act nor can foreigners decide unilaterally to increase their receipts from what they sell to us. The government can, however, change its receipts autonomously by altering tax rates, and businesses can change their *retained* income by paying out more or less to stockholders.

The immediate effect of such autonomous changes in incomes is to change other incomes in the system in the opposite direction. Thus if the government decides to increase its income by increasing taxes, the immediate consequence is that the disposable incomes of business and consumers are reduced correspondingly. If business decides to increase its retained income the incomes of stockholders are correspondingly curtailed.

Finally, in the two sectors where autonomous changes in incomes are possible, it is not at all unlikely that certain decisions will involve equal and offsetting autonomous changes in spending and receipts. Governments may increase taxes in order to increase spending, or may reduce spending in order to be able to cut taxes. Business firms may reduce distribution of profits to stockholders in order to increase purchases of capital goods, or may reduce a capital investment program in order to pay out more in dividends. The three kinds of autonomous change we have distinguished will have different repercussions.

Autonomous spending decisions change national product in two ways. In the first place, the new spending itself buys new product which must be added to the national total. In the second place, as we have seen, the spending creates money income which stimulates further buying of product. When the government builds a dam, the dam is an addition to national product. In addition, those who are employed to build the dam receive more money than before and hence spend more for further product.

Autonomous changes in incomes, on the other hand, are mere transfers of income from one group to another and do not in and of themselves create any new product. Their influence on spending is entirely through the second of the two channels described above, namely, through their influence on the spending of others. A decrease in taxes of $50,000 a month does not itself constitute an increase in product. It leaves consumers and businesses with $50,000 more, and thus stimulates them to buy more, but the total effect is less than that of a business capital investment or a government expenditure on goods and services of the same amount. The induced changes are similar but the autonomous change itself does not represent new production.

Finally, when there are autonomous offsetting changes in spending and incomes, the induced effects disappear and the only change in product is that represented by the autonomous change in spending itself. Thus if government expenditure is increased and taxes are increased by the same amount, consumers and business firms are left with the same disposable income as before. The government spending has added to private incomes as much as the taxes have taken away. Private spending may, of course, be influenced by the change, but if so it is not a change in total disposable income which is responsible. The induced effects of the two sides of the decision balance out and only the direct effect of the initial spending change remains. If a dam is built and paid for with new taxes, employment is increased by the number of men necessary to build the dam and manufacture its components, but the expansion stops here. The extra incomes of the workers thus employed are just enough to make up for the reduced incomes of taxpayers. Similarly, an expansion of private investment financed out of new business saving increases output but only by the amount of the increase in investment. The extra incomes of those employed to produce the new capital goods are balanced by the reduced incomes of those stockholders deprived of dividends. There may be some induced effects of the change resulting from the fact that the spending habits of the two groups affected may be different, but again the induced changes are not a consequence of changes in aggregate disposable income.

This last category of change is important because it was thought a few years ago by those who used income analysis carelessly that only changes in the stubs at the right of our chart could produce changes in incomes. An increased balanced government budget would not change the deficit and thus would not change national product, so the argument ran. Similarly it was thought that equal increases in business investment and business saving would leave the level of activity in the economy unaffected. We can see now that this view was mistaken. These counterbalancing changes in spending and incomes will change the level of activity, though it is true that they will change it less than autonomous changes in income alone and still less than autonomous changes in spending alone.

V. The Interaction between Spending and Prices

1. *The problem*

Everything we have said up to this point has been concerned with the question of what determines the level of money spending and money incomes. But what we are really after is an explanation of what causes changes in the flow of real goods and services being produced. We have assumed up to this point that prices, the link between money incomes and real incomes, remained fairly stable so that money income fluctuations reflected real income fluctuations. But we must now face up to the fact that this assumption is highly unrealistic in many periods. Indeed, it rules out one-half of our problem, our concern with inflation, which we have defined as a rapid rise in the general price level.

Everything we have said about the determinants of the level of spending remains true if we permit prices to vary, except that two additional questions call for an answer. Firstly, we want to know under what circumstances a given change in spending and incomes will have its effect principally on the price level leaving real output relatively unaffected, and under what conditions it will reflect, on the contrary, mainly a change in real output with little or no price change. Secondly, we need to know how a change in prices, if it does occur, will influence the total level of spending. A change in the over-all price level will usually be induced by a change in total spending. If it is, we need to know whether or not the price level change will lead to further changes in spending, setting off further price changes and so on in a continuing spiral. Then, too, there are ways in which prices can change independently of spending changes, or autonomously, to use a term whose meaning should by now be familiar. In such cases we need to know whether further spending changes will be induced by such autonomous price changes or not.

2. How changes in spending affect prices

The answer to the first of these questions—what will a change in spending do to prices?—is not easy, and economists are by no means agreed as to the best way to seek an answer. No simple generalization which will cover all cases is available. The best we can do is to spell out what will happen in certain simple situations as a guide to what to look for in more complex ones.

Probably the clearest case is that in which there is an increase in spending at a time when labor and other productive instruments are close to full employment. If there are no resources available with which to increase production, an increase in spending can call forth no increase in real output and must be accompanied by price increases. Of course, resources are never fully employed in the sense that no additional production whatever is physically possible. People can always work a little harder or a little longer or a little more efficiently if they have sufficient incentive to do so, as our experience during the war proved dramatically. Nevertheless, when involuntary unemployment has been reduced to a low figure we are safe in predicting that large increases in spending will have their principal effect on the price level rather than on output. At such times it is clear that if rapid price level increases are a bad thing, policy should be directed at preventing or offsetting big increases in total demand for goods and services. Antiinflation policy at such times is antispending policy.

There are three other possibilities to examine: declines in spending in a full employment situation, and increases and declines in a situation of underemployment. What happens in these three situations depends on the way in which costs behave in response to changes in the output of the economy. The bulk of all costs are ultimately labor costs. Interest costs and rent costs are commonly fixed by long-term contract and therefore respond very slowly to changes in conditions, and are in any case a small fraction of total costs. Profits are a long-run cost for the economy in the sense that profits must be earned in a private enterprise system if entrepreneurial effort is to be forthcoming. In a competitive situation, however, profits in the short run are a residual and not a determinant of price behavior. In the sectors of the economy which are monopolistic and where prices are set "administratively" by the decisions of sellers, the views of businessmen as to desirable profit margins no doubt influence price behavior somewhat, but there is good evidence that even in these sectors *changes* in prices are influenced more by how costs behave than by sellers' notions of what constitutes a proper margin.[4] So we are left with labor costs, which are well over two-thirds of total costs for the economy, as the most significant cost element in price behavior.

What will happen to labor costs throughout the economy when spending declines in a full employment situation? This varies, of course, with different kinds of labor. In the case of the self-employed, such as farmers, small retailers, professional people, and the like, the ratio of effort to income is highly flexible. The wages of such people are not easily distinguishable from profits. They are a residual, and in many cases no probable decline in the earnings of such people will lead to any great diminution of their output. Thus with a decline in demand the prices of agricultural products tend to fall sharply, whether the decline is from a high employment plateau or is a further dip in an already depressed economy. At the opposite end of the scale are certain of the industries in which labor is highly organized, bargaining is industry-wide, and union policy resists any decline in wages irrespective of the volume of unemployment. In such situations costs are quite rigid against downward pressure and prices are unlikely to respond much to reductions in spending. In between lies a series of intermediate

4. Some economists do not accept this proposition. I am relying partly on evidence to be found in Alfred C. Neal, *Industrial Concentration and Price Inflexibility* (Washington, D.C., American Council on Public Affairs, 1942).

situations in which the effect of a decline in spending on prices depends
on the volume of unemployment, the relative strengths and attitudes of
parties to wage negotiations, the degree and kind of organization of the
labor market, and the impact of public wage policy.

Some writers believe that the attitude of business toward price change
is crucial. These economists conclude that it is possible to influence
markedly the way in which prices respond to a change in spending by
attempting to persuade businessmen to adopt the desired "price policy." Others feel that, given the business executive's objectives and his
responsibilities to his stockholders, the range of discretion in price making left him by his costs on the one side and market conditions on the
other is usually relatively small. We do not yet possess conclusive evidence on this question to determine the truth from the facts. It is the
present writer's hunch that there is less room for the adoption of widely
different price policies by business firms than is often assumed, but
this cannot be demonstrated with finality. If I am wrong, business attitudes toward correct pricing must be added as an important factor in
determining the result.

Although clear-cut theoretical propositions are not available in this
matter, the following broad generalizations probably represent as close
to a consensus as there is on what determines price level behavior in the
American economy of 1952:

1) When there is a great deal of unemployment both of labor and
of other resources, increases in spending will increase output a good
deal more than they will increase prices in the manufacturing sector of
the economy.

2) As unemployment declines, as bottlenecks appear, and as the
bargaining power of labor increases, the expansion of spending will
impinge more and more on prices and less and less on output. In certain
sectors of the economy marked inflationary tendencies may show themselves while there is still substantial unemployment.

3) There is a notable asymmetry in the behavior of prices between
increases and decreases in spending. Decreases are much less likely to
reduce prices than increases to raise them. This is true to some extent
under all conditions but more especially when unemployment is low.

4) Not only are price decreases less likely to be induced by declines
in spending than increases by expansions, but when they are induced
they occur much more slowly and are more easily reversed by a reversal
of spending.

5) The development of industry-wide bargaining, coupled with the
practice adopted by both management and labor of basing wage and
price policy on a few key wage and price determinations, has greatly

increased the probability that the price level will move, chiefly upward, not in response to changes in spending but autonomously in response to labor-management bargains. This point is further developed by Mr. Lindblom in Chapter 11.

3. *How changes in the price level affect spending*

To appraise the effect of changes in spending on prices is only half our problem. For changes in prices are almost certain in their turn to influence spending decisions. Here is an area where we must pick our way, with great care and resolve, around numerous siren fallacies. It will be easier to focus on a correct solution to this problem if we first expose the more subtle and alluring of these intellectual seducers for the hags they really are.

The first and worst is the idea that the lower the price level the more people will buy. In its simpler forms this amounts to denying that the price level will affect the volume of money spending at all. For if money spending is constant and the price level falls, the same spending will inevitably buy more goods and services. This is a peculiarly seductive error because, when applied to an individual commodity taken by itself, it becomes a respectable truth. To analyze what happens to the sales of one commodity when its price changes we can legitimately assume that the incomes of buyers of that good will be unaffected by the change. If your income is unchanged and something costs less, you will usually be strongly tempted to buy more of it.

The error in applying this reasoning to the output of the whole economy lies in forgetting that for the system as a whole income and spending are the same thing. If you assume that money income will not be affected by a general change in the price level, then of course money spending, which is just another way of looking at income, cannot be affected either. But prices directly affect money incomes. The price an article brings on the market is essentially the sum of the incomes earned in producing it. If prices fall and output does not change, the income earned in producing that output will fall too. If all prices fall, including the price of labor, then wages, profits, rents, etc., all fall by the same amount. And for the economy as a whole these things all play double roles. Wages are a cost and at the same time they are a source of purchasing power. A wage reduction cuts costs, but it also cuts incomes, unless employment and output expand sharply. Will they in fact do so? We are back in the vicious part of our circle. If output expands, money income may be maintained permitting purchase of the new output. But if output does *not* expand, money incomes will shrink and the price reduction will not call forth increased buying.

A fallacy which beckons invitingly at this point involves assuming what we are trying to find out. If we assume for purposes of argument that money incomes remain constant, then a fall in prices means an increase in output, employment increases by as much as prices have fallen; and spending is unchanged. In other words, if money income is constant, money income is constant. On the other hand we could see what happens if output or employment is unaffected. In this case incomes go down by as much as prices, spending drops proportionately, and real income is unchanged. In other words, if output is constant, output is constant. Neither of these propositions helps much in telling us what is likely in fact to happen. How can we investigate this problem without finding ourselves chasing our tail each time we think we are getting somewhere?

This circle is in fact the same one we got into at the beginning of our analysis of spending when we noted that spending depends on income and income depends on spending. The escape is the same one we found then, namely, to concentrate our attention on what happens to the *autonomous* elements in spending. Is a price change likely to affect the *relation between* consumer incomes and consumer spending? Is it likely to change the excess of business spending over business saving? Will it alter the foreign balance? How will it modify government receipts and expenditure? Whatever the immediate effects of a change in prices, these factors will determine its ultimate effect.

How will they behave? There is no single answer. We are forced to take refuge in "it all depends . . ." We can get some notion of what it depends on. Forgetting about the impact of price change on the foreign and government sectors for the moment, let us look at investment and consumption in turn. If all prices fall by a somewhat similar amount, the simplest assumption is that people will discount the change in the value of money and try to do the same real things they wanted to do before. Businesses will continue to carry out the same investment projects, but they will cost less, and the money value of investment will accordingly be less by the amount of the price fall. Firms will want to save about the same proportion of the same real profits, which again means a decline in business saving in money terms. From the consumer's point of view, if his money income were to fall at the old price level he would probably feel unable to save as big a fraction of it as before; but if prices fall too, so that his standard of living is maintained, he might be expected to maintain about the same relative saving in real terms, which means less saving in money terms. If all these things are cut in money terms by as much as prices fall, the level of real income and output will be unaffected, and our price change will change spending by an equal proportion. Note in passing that should the state of affairs be as here described, proposals to expand output and employment by forcing or inducing all-round price declines throughout the economy would fail of their objective. Spending and incomes would fall by as much as the price level and nothing would be accomplished.

Variations from this simple conclusion are possible and even likely in both directions. Consider the impact of a price fall on the expectations of spenders, be they investors or consumers. If the price fall is taken as evidence that further declines will follow, autonomous spending may dry up markedly. There may be a general postponement of purchases in the hope of getting better bargains later. On the other hand, if the price declines are expected to be followed shortly by increases, they may stimulate a swelling of autonomous spending by those who wish to take full advantage of temporary bargains.

Another factor at work is the effect of the price level on the value of the public's holdings of cash and other liquid assets. A 20% drop in prices means a similar increase in the value of a given bank balance. People and firms who thus feel richer because their cash balances are worth more may be stimulated to spend more than they otherwise would have on consumption or investment and thus to expand spending as a whole.

Again, much spending and much saving is fixed for one reason or another in money terms. Individuals do a good deal of their saving in the form of life insurance or premiums on past installment purchases, both involving fixed money payments periodically. These cannot easily be reduced if the price level falls. Business firms calculate what they must set aside for depreciation on the basis not of what their assets are worth today in money terms but on the basis of what they cost in some earlier period. This tends to keep business saving abnormally high in periods of falling prices and thus to depress spending. On the other hand, contracts let in a high price period may continue over into a period in which prices have fallen, helping to maintain a high level of spending.

For a country which depends importantly on foreign trade still other considerations enter in. A cut in the domestic price level does not cut foreigners' incomes as much as it cuts those of the domestic populace. Hence there is good reason to expect, in the short run at least, that the excess of sales to foreigners over purchases from them (net foreign investment) will rise, and with it the level of spending. What will happen to the government deficit or surplus depends on the precise design of the tax structure and on the nature of the government's spending obligations. There is no reason to expect one result to be any more likely than another.

All these possibilities, and many more which we omit for brevity's sake, are described not purposely to confuse the reader but to emphasize the conclusion that there is no a priori probability that a change in all prices together will alter output and employment either one way or the other. It may do either depending on the circumstances of the case. In this writer's view, the uncertainty of the effects of a price level change on spending and output makes proposals to control either inflation or depression by direct action on prices unwise unless more positive methods are, for one reason or another, not available.

4. *How changes in relative prices affect spending*

There are few economists today who believe it desirable to attempt to influence spending by measures to change the general price level, but there are a good many who are convinced that the relations between different sets of prices are of the greatest importance in determining the level of spending. The most common form of this argument is that a "balance" between wages and prices is essential to insure the ideal level of expenditure, but the argument is also applied to the relations between agricultural and industrial prices, investment goods and consumption goods prices, and many other categories.

There is no space here to consider all these relative price problems, but the analysis of one, the wage-price problem, may serve as a sample of how one would go about it. Again, it is necessary to begin by stripping the cloak of plausibility from one or two common fallacies. Two opposing arguments are common. The first is that an increase in wages relative to prices means an increase in real incomes for the community, since wage earners can buy more. If real incomes go up, consumption spending will go up and all the induced expansions we described in section IV will follow. The most important thing to be clear about in examining this argument is that an increase in wages relative to prices does not constitute in and of itself an increase in the community's real income but rather a redistribution of it. If wages are increased relative to prices, this means that while wage earners' incomes are increased, those of profit, rent, and interest receivers are reduced. This redistribution may change the amount of consumption the community wishes to do out of a given income, but it does not automatically change total incomes. In other words, insofar as an increase in wages changes the relation between income and consumption for the community as a whole, it may change total spending.

The opposite fallacy focuses on wages in their role as costs of production. The argument here is that with a given market an increase in wages relative to prices reduces the prospects of profit to be anticipated from new capital expenditures. Investment spending will therefore drop, bringing with it a decline of incomes and subsequently of spending in the manner described in section IV. The key to the weak link in this chain is the phrase, often omitted from statements of the case, "with a given market." For if wage increases do redistribute income in such a way as to stimulate consumption, the market will not be "given" but may be expected to expand. In this case what happens to investment depends on the relative impact on investment of increased sales on the one hand and decreased margins on the other.

There is no one answer to this double problem, but the direction in which an answer is to be sought is clear. Once again we examine the sources of autonomous change in spending and try to see what the effect of the relative price change on each is likely to be. Neglecting the foreign and government sectors for simplicity, we need to consider the impact of a wage increase (with product prices unchanged) on the relation between consumption and income, on the level of business saving, and on the level of business investment. On the whole it is probably safe to assume that in most cases a shift from property income to wage income is a shift from richer to poorer people. This is not nearly so obvious as it appears at first glance. Property income is the main source of support not only for widows, orphans, and old people living with difficulty on the proceeds of life insurance and annuities but also for a great army of small shopkeepers and other little businessmen who cannot by any stretch of the imagination be classed as in the upper income brackets. The high salaries of movie stars and corporation presidents, on the other hand, are a part of wage income. Nevertheless, let us see where we get on the assumption that an increase in wages relative to prices distributes incomes on the whole more equally. Because the rich obviously save a much higher proportion of their incomes than the poor, one is tempted to conclude at once that such a redistribution will have a powerful effect in increasing the amount spent on consumption out of a given total of income.

But caution is required here. Suppose that when old moneybag's profits go down by $1,000 a month he salts away $200 less in his idle bank account and pares down some of his luxury expenses by $800 a month, perhaps by laying up his yacht. And suppose that when his hundred employees find their incomes increased by ten dollars a month apiece each increases his purchases of food for his family by eight dollars and puts the other two dollars into making up back payments on the three-piece living room suite they were about to lose to the finance company. In this case there will be no change in aggregate consumption or in aggregate saving as a result of the redistribution. The proportion of the *change* in income devoted to saving is the same for both groups. What matters, as was pointed out in section 3, is not the *average* amount or the proportion saved in the two income groups but the way saving changes with changes in income. Such evidence as we have seems to show that this "marginal propensity to consume" varies much less between income levels than the *proportion* of income consumed. How much it varies is still a matter of dispute, so that no reliable statement can be made as to how much effect redistribution of the kind described here will have on the income-consumption relation.

The direction of the effect on corporate saving is fairly clear. An increase in wages relative to prices will almost certainly reduce profits, and a reduction of profits will almost certainly reduce undivided profits. The impact of this factor by itself on spending is unambiguously to increase it, though we need much more evidence to determine the magnitude of the effect.

Investment spending, on the other hand, is very likely to be reduced. This will depend on the previous level of profits. If they have been very high before the change, the depressing effect on investment will probably be smaller than if profits have been low to begin with. This effect operates through a number of channels. In the first place, for firms which are too small, too venturesome, or too jealous of outside interference to seek adequate funds for investment from the banks or the capital market, undivided profits may be the prime source of money with which to carry out plant and equipment expenditures. Any reduction in business saving forced by a decline in profits in such firms will restrict investment by nearly as much. Secondly, a reduced profit margin may well make a risky investment seem less attractive, even if it is partly offset by larger sales. In the third place, a wage change of this kind may be depressing not so much because of its specific effect on current earnings as because it is a troubling indication of the sort of trend which gives businessmen bad dreams.

The net effect of all these influences cannot be established by logical argument alone. It requires much more careful measurement of relative magnitudes than economists have succeeded in making up to now. Further, the magnitudes are not constant but themselves depend on changing circumstances. If you believe, as some economists do, that a level of investment as high as that we have been experiencing for the last few years cannot be maintained anyway, whatever the relation between wages and prices, you may conclude that a mild redistribution in favor of wages will not depress investment much more than it would be depressed anyway by other forces, and that the expansion of consumption which would result from this redistribution is the only way of filling the gap in spending which the decline in investment will inevitably create. On the other hand, if you feel, as some other economists do, that redistribution will not affect the consumption-income relation much and that investment is powerfully affected by profit margins, you may conclude that some widening of the gap between wages and prices is called for to stimulate the volume of spending needed for full employment. Or again, your estimate of the situation may be that spending is likely to be excessive for some time to come, pushing us continually toward secular inflation. In this case you may welcome higher wages and lower profits *because* you think they will reduce investment a lot and not increase consumption much, or you may oppose them because you fear they will increase consumption greatly and not dampen sufficiently an excessive zeal for investment.

Finally you may perhaps conclude, as this writer does, that it is rather silly to base any policy proposals on evidence as fragmentary and conflicting as that we now possess about the effects of relative price movements on spending, and that we had better eschew attempts to influence relative prices *for stabilization purposes* until we know a little more about what their consequences are. If this is your conclusion, all it can be hoped that you will carry away from the discussion of this section is a little clearer idea of what the factual questions are to which we need better answers on which to base a positive analysis.

VI. The Interaction between Spending and the Money Supply

1. *How monetary factors affect spending*

Many readers will be puzzled by the fact that we have said nothing to this point about the banks and the quantity of money. Twenty years ago an analysis of fluctuations in economic activity quite commonly started with an examination of the money supply, and banking and monetary policy was frequently held to be crucial in determining the course of prices and employment. To understand why the emphasis has shifted, and why there is some danger of the pendulum swinging too far in the opposite direction of underrating the importance of monetary forces, it will be well to take a look first at just how monetary factors *can* influence incomes, and second to reappraise what the significance of that influence is likely to be.

Our procedure will be the one which should by now be familiar of examining the impact of monetary factors on the various kinds of autonomous spending decisions that we have distinguished as determining, among them, the level of incomes. Let us look first at investment. We noted in section III that business spending on plant, equipment, and inventories is normally in excess of business-retained income. The problem which at once suggests itself is, where does the money come from? One obvious source of funds, especially for the financing of short-term needs, is bank loans. The ease or difficulty of obtaining loans from banks may then have an important effect on business investment decisions. If no alternative source of funds is available, and if banks refuse to grant a loan, a firm may be prevented from undertaking an investment project which it would otherwise carry out.

Economists often speak as though the method used by banks to expand or contract their outstanding loans was to lower or raise the rates of interest they charge to borrowers. A contraction in loans is described as being accomplished through a rise in the rate of interest which chokes off loan applications and an expansion through a fall in interest rates which encourages new borrowing. Actually most banking institutions do not consciously use the rate of interest they charge as a device to control the volume of commerical loans. Rather they vary their requirements as to security and collateral and as to the eligibility of loans with varying degrees of risk. We shall speak, therefore, of changes in the availability of capital rather than in the rate of interest, although the terms are used interchangeably by many economists. Of course, a restriction in the availability of capital from banks will usually raise many of the interest rates ruling on negotiable loan instruments since people will sell such instruments to obtain funds when they cannot get them from banking sources. These sales will depress the prices of such things as government and corporate bonds, thus raising the effective interest rate.

There are, however, many other sources of funds for investment besides banks and currently retained earnings. One possibility is to borrow directly from the public by issuing stocks or bonds, or arranging financing privately with individuals, or investing institutions like insurance companies. The availability of capital from these sources can clearly be influenced in important ways by banking and monetary policy. If potential lenders are highly liquid it will be easier to induce them to lend than if a shortage of money has led them to employ all their liquid reserves in enterprises of their own. A tightening of credit by the banking system or a decrease of liquidity forced by a contraction in the supply of liquid assets available will make it harder to obtain funds from nonbank as well as from bank sources.

Another possible source of funds for a firm planning investment outlays is its own liquid and semiliquid assets. It may have little or no undivided profits of the current period to draw on, but all businesses have part of their assets in more or less liquid form. They may decide that they can get along with a smaller cash balance than they have been carrying and use the difference to buy equipment. Or they may own government or other securities that they can sell to raise the money. Or they may reduce their accounts receivable by tightening up on their terms and conditions to purchasers who have been buying from them on credit. These things will also be influenced by the availability of capital in the market. For if securities bearing high rates of interest have been available the firm probably does not have much idle cash, most of its liquid assets being in the form of marketable securities. If interest rates are high, however, and especially if they are expected to fall again in the future (raising the prices of securities held), selling those securities now to obtain money involves the risk of a substantial capital loss as compared to holding them. Finally, if bank credit is hard to obtain, customers will find it hard to reduce their accounts payable to the firm, and good business relations may make it very unwise to try to contract credit supplied to buyers.

Thus there is no doubt but that if credit is contracted *enough* and the community's liquidity reduced enough, the difficulty of obtaining funds for investment can be the factor on which the investment-spending decision turns. On the other hand, in a period in which credit is quite easily obtainable and people and firms are quite liquid the availability of credit may never be a consideration at all in the investment-spending decision. In the decision-making process attention comes to be focused on what promise to be the serious obstacles to the success of a venture. If the availability of capital is not a serious obstacle, it tends to drop out of the focus of attention altogether. In this case moderate changes in credit terms and liquidity may have no effect in inhibiting or encouraging investment.

The availability of credit may, of course, influence business saving quite markedly. If it is hard to come by the funds required for investment in any other way, an obvious alternative is to withhold them from the stockholders. Again, there are many other motives for business-saving decisions, and this one is likely to be prominent only when money is scarce. This may, of course, be true for some firms when it is not true for the economy generally. The smaller and riskier businesses must depend on internal financing to a much greater extent than the larger and more stable concerns. Anything which makes funds more easily available to such enterprises may be expected not only to expand their investment but also, in some cases, to contract their saving. We still know very little about the magnitude of these effects in practice under various conditions. A few empirical studies of the importance of "the rate of interest" for business investment and saving have been done, but they are inconclusive.

The influence of credit conditions on the relation between consumer income and expenditure is probably much greater in this day of installment selling and widespread charge accounts than it was in an earlier period when cash purchases made up a larger proportion of total sales. Just how important it is is another of those elusive quantitative questions on which a great deal depends and to which we do not yet have the answer. The recent direct regulation of consumer credit by the Federal Reserve Board appears to have affected consumption, but it is very difficult to isolate the size of the effect of this variable in a period when so many other things were changing so rapidly.

There is another way in which monetary factors may influence the income-consumption relationship. When individuals own large amounts of liquid assets such as cash balances, marketable or redeemable government securities, savings accounts, and the like they may feel less pressure to set aside funds from current income as a precaution against contingencies. A high degree of liquidity may thus encourage a level of consumption higher, relative to income, than would prevail if people had not acquired a large supply of government bonds and had not been able to build up substantial cash balances. Again we do not know the magnitude of this effect, but recent experience suggests that it may be significant. In the postwar period consumption has been a good deal higher relative to income than the prewar experience would lead one to expect. Individuals have also been abnormally liquid in recent years as a consequence of their being forced to accumulate liquid assets during the war by the shortage of consumable goods. Other factors, however, may be responsible for part of this apparent correlation.

We will pass over the impact of monetary factors on foreign spending, which is treated by Mr. Hart in Chapter 7, and refer briefly to the government sector. There was a time when the relation between government spending and tax revenues might be influenced by monetary conditions. The government must borrow if it spends more than it takes in for any considerable period of time, and the terms on which it could borrow were at one time an important consideration in deciding whether a spending program was a good idea. This is still true of some of the smaller governmental units in cities and towns, but federal government borrowing, instead of being limited by credit conditions, is now a principle determinant of those conditions.

The government can borrow from individuals, from the banks, or from the Federal Reserve banks. Under current conditions the banking system almost automatically absorbs whatever government securities private lenders do not wish to absorb. And in the process the banking system at the same time automatically creates new money. The situation is essentially the same as though the Treasury were to print up new money to cover any deficit in the government budget and to retire old money out of any surplus. In this sector of the economy, therefore, the relation between income and spending is clearly a cause and not an effect of changes in credit conditions. The spending decision is the initiating force. It may be modified somewhat out of consideration for its probable effects on the credit structure, but it is never limited or conditioned by the difficulty of obtaining the necessary funds.

2. *The significance of monetary factors*

Having examined the channels through which monetary factors can affect spending decisions we are now in a position to appraise the significance of those factors and to explain why they have dropped out of fashion as star performers in the drama. It should be clear from what has gone before that money factors will be the yes-or-no factors in spending decisions of all kinds chiefly when money is scarce. This condition has not obtained in the United States since 1933. In this period the banks have almost continuously had excess reserves which put them in a position to respond readily to additional demands for funds. This does not mean that everybody who wanted a loan could get it. Difficulty of borrowing has no doubt inhibited many a business gambler from taking a long shot. But in these cases the deterrent is more properly described as a high risk of loss than as a shortage of money. In a sense, any investment that does not take place can be described as inhibited by the fact that somebody would not put up the necessary cash. But this is not the same thing as saying that there is a general shortage of funds for investment or consumption.

The older monetary theorists, and even Keynes himself, were accustomed to speaking of the banking system as "determining" the quantity of money. Monetary policy consisted, then, principally in manipulating the quantity of money—meaning currency and bank deposits—in some desired fashion. If money was scarce this manipulation of the money supply might be expected to have a critical effect on many kinds of spending decisions and thus ultimately on the level of incomes, of output, and of prices. This chain was often regarded as so tight that one could omit the intermediate links in exposition and speak for brevity of the relation between the supply of money and the price level, or the level of output. The depression of the thirties and the events of the forties emphasized two things. First, they brought home to everyone how dangerous it is not to examine each link in the chain and particularly the link connecting the availablity of money with spending decisions. For these events made clear that the reaction of spending to changes in monetary conditions is not automatic and that under certain conditions there may be no such reaction.

Second, they illustrated the fact that under modern conditions the causal chain often runs in the opposite direction from spending decisions to the quantity of money. The spending decision is fundamental and often comes first, and the banking system reacts by making available whatever funds are required. It is clear that this is the case with the spending decisions of government. But as Mr. Hart explains it is also largely true of the spending decisions of business and consumers at the present time. When the banks have ample excess reserves and when the Treasury and the Federal Reserve System stand ready to provide any additional reserves required to prevent interest rates from rising, the quantity of money is determined not by the banking system but by the demand of borrowers. Thus under present circumstances most changes in the money supply are induced by changes in spending and do not take place as a result of autonomous decisions of the monetary authorities or changes in the supply of the precious metals.

It would be a mistake to conclude from this, however, as some economists have done, that monetary policy is powerless or that monetary factors do not now and never will again have any influence on the spending-producing process. In the first place the almost perfect elasticity of credit to demands for it which obtains today is itself a consequence of conscious policy. The banks can provide credit almost without limit because the Federal Reserve banks stand ready in their turn to provide reserves to the banks at will. This could be changed. There are many obstacles to the pursuit of a tight money policy by the Treasury and the Federal Reserve System, and such a policy might not be desirable on a number of grounds. New legislation might be necessary to make it effective, but it could and may be done, and if done with enough vigor could undoubtedly restrain spending decisions effectively.

Furthermore, monetary policy, broadly defined, is any policy which influences the public's liquidity position. This includes not only the control of bank credit through the conventional devices but also the control of the public's supply of liquid assets other than cash, especially government securities. The management of the public debt, which is a joint responsibility of the Treasury and the Federal Reserve System, can operate in such a way as to increase or decrease the liquidity of the public markedly and may well in this fashion influence various kinds of spending decisions. Precisely how this operates is spelled out in more detail in Chapter 7. All I am concerned to do here is to suggest that the management of the money system and of the public debt still has an important role to play in stabilization policy.

The most important lesson we should learn from recent experience with monetary theory and practice is that it is dangerous to reason about economic processes without carrying our analysis back to the decisions of the individuals who, in the last analysis, determine those processes. Money is still important, but it is important to the extent and in the ways in which it influences the autonomous spending decisions of individuals, businesses, foreigners, and governments, and through no other channel. There is no automatic connection between money and prices, for instance, except as money affects spending and spending affects prices. And each of these links, as we have seen, is composed of a number of smaller links, all of which are essential and all of which vary in their action with varying circumstances. There are no simple keys to universal truth in monetary theory or in any other branch of economics.

VII. Conclusion: How to Analyze Policies

Our introduction has brought us as far as a primer should try to go and perhaps a good deal farther. It remains only to consider what light this set of tools throws on the scope of the policy alternatives before us.

A tempting way to approach the problem of how we might influence spending so as to stabilize it is to examine each of our six basic factors in turn to see how we might affect it by public action. We could look first at what techniques are conceivable through which we might influence the relation between incomes and consumption, so as to increase consumption out of depression incomes and reduce it when inflation menaces. We could then examine devices for stimulating or checking private investment and for discouraging or encouraging business saving. We could look at the uses which could be made of schemes to change the relation between imports and exports, increasing net foreign investment when spending needed a prod and decreasing it when incomes were getting out of hand. Finally we could glance at the manipulation of the federal budget, where we would be led to the popular view that any kind of a deficit will be stimulating in a slump and any sort of surplus will help keep the lid on an inflation.

This is a procedure that is in fact frequently followed. Its great weakness is that it encourages us to look only at one aspect of a policy and to ignore many of its repercussions. It is hard to find a measure whose impact will be on one of our six factors alone. A scheme to expand consumption out of income may well depress investment by as much or more. A device to increase investment may increase business saving still more and leave spending about the same. A foreign investment plan may merely involve a diversion of spending from domestic to foreign areas. And, of course, it is apparent when you stop to think of it that virtually any change in government spending or revenue is almost certain to have repercussions on all six of our factors. If we think of a policy as a policy to affect investment, we are in grave danger of neglecting or underestimating its effects on consumption. If we think of it as focused on the foreign balance, we may overlook its impact on the revenue structure of government.

Accordingly, it seems wiser to consider a range of areas of possible policy action and examine each systematically for its total impact insofar as this can be apprehended. The chapters which follow attempt to do this.

We start, in Chapter 4, with an over-all look by Everett Hagen at how much we can tell in advance about what conditions policy is likely to be faced with in the future. In Chapter 5 Gerhard Colm examines the over-all problem of the use of the government budget as a weapon of stabilization policy. In Chapter 6 Carl Shoup goes more deeply into what we know and, more important, what we do not yet know about how taxes influence the other crucial variables described in this chapter. Albert Hart explores, in Chapter 7, how these variables are and might be influenced by monetary policy. The complex and involved effects of public expenditure both on the factors controlling incomes and on other values of importance to Americans are spelled out by Robert Dahl and C. E. Lindblom in Chapter 8. Finally, Ralph Brown examines a variety of other ways of influencing the most volatile of the variables described in this chapter, namely, the level of private investment. The framework of concepts set forth in the three chapters which end here may be helpful as we plunge into the more controversial issues which lie at the heart of the stabilization problem.

PART TWO:

THE INSTRUMENTS OF POLICY

CHAPTER IV. *The Role of Economic Forecasting in Income Stabilization*

BY EVERETT E. HAGEN

I. Economic Forecasting: A Possible Guide to Action

A rising tide of public sentiment has thrust upon the federal government responsibility for controlling the level of economic activity. By the Employment Act of 1946 the federal government formally accepted this responsibility. That acceptance, however, was not a solution to the problem of income stabilization but only a mandate for its consideration. The problem of how to stabilize is yet to be solved.

Chapters which follow discuss the effect of various types of public policy upon income, output, employment, and prices. This chapter is devoted to the more modest purpose of discussing the seemingly much simpler question, the use of one tool, economic forecasting, in deciding the timing of action to stabilize income, output, employment, and prices.

The course of economic events between V-J Day and Korea furnishes a vivid example of the dilemma faced by government administrators and legislators who must attempt to stabilize. The years 1946–48 were years of inflation, broken by a temporary lapse in inflationary pressure early in 1948. Unemployment was typically at or below two million, an abnormally low level in an economy as large and as dynamic as ours. But at no time during this period were economists sure that the inflation was not about to end abruptly. In the last half of 1948 aggregate demand did begin to decline. From autumn 1948 to mid-1949 wholesale prices fell by 9%;[1] prices paid by consumers, by not quite 4%.[2] Unemployment rose to four million. Majority opinion among students of economic conditions was that output and income would fall further, but that majority was divided concerning the depth of the downturn and the speed of recovery from it. A respectable minority among professional economists (see, for example, Sumner Slichter's occasional articles in the *New York Times Magazine*) held that the fundamental underlying factors were so favorable that while major increase in unemployment

1. August, 1948, to July, 1949.
2. September 15, 1948, to July 15, 1949.

was possible it was not probable. Only a salutory shakedown in prices was in prospect. That minority turned out to be correct—except that even the price structure proved more sturdy than they had anticipated. Prices fell little further and by January, 1950, were turning up again. Unemployment fluctuated moderately, hit a seasonal peak of 4,700,000 in February, 1950, then declined. The rally thus antedated Korea by half a year. Defense did not provide the turning point; this was a peacetime recovery from a very minor recession.

This situation illustrates what Professor Hart has called the "cryptic character" of full employment.[3] The continuance of full or high employment, like the continuance of inflation, is *always* uncertain. Full employment at any time is sustained in part by various types of economic activity which are only temporary—by a housing boom which will presently satisfy the demand for housing units, and come to an end, or a boom in factory construction to meet new levels of demand which, when it has created sufficient capacity, will taper off, or a burst of road and school building which will reach the limit of needs or finances or both, or some other type of activity which must come to an end (or, more probably, by a combination of several of these temporary props). As one of these declines in volume another must replace it or a recession will occur. But while it seems inevitable that sooner or later no sufficient replacement will be forthcoming for some important type of economic activity which is declining, no one can foretell even approximately when such a decline will occur, or when it occurs whether some rising activity or activities will have vigor enough to take the place of the withering one. A forecast that the end is approaching is as dangerous as a forecast that it is not.

These remarks concerning full employment apply with even more force to inflation as we have known it in the United States. Nothing is surer about inflation than that it will come to an end—and that nobody knows when.

Under such circumstances, even though forecasting is hazardous or worse, the course which the Congress ought to follow in carrying out its mandate to stabilize *seems* clear enough. Prompt action should be taken *after the fact*. When unemployment has increased, or when inflation is under way, the Congress should take stock of the situation and legislate measures to counteract the unemployment or the inflationary pressure.

This seemingly simple prescription, however, is too simple. Adopting remedial measures after the event has hazards. The chief of these is that

3. Albert G. Hart, "Timing and Administering Fiscal Policy: How to Give Relevant Counsel," *American Economic Review*, 38 (May, 1948), 430–442. See especially pp. 431–433.

planning and enacting legislation, putting it into effect, and then waiting while it bites into the economic situation may cover such a time period that a measure which was adequate while it was being planned is insufficient or futile by the time it takes effect; or a measure which was appropriate when planned may be positively wrong by the time it takes effect.

The time involved in planning and enacting legislation is especially long in the case of tax and spending policies, which in most circumstances are the most direct and powerful tools by which to influence employment and output. (The impact of monetary policies is far less certain, both in timing and in magnitude.)

After the President has prepared his budget, Congress independently duplicates—or, because of the coordinate position of the two houses, triplicates—much of the process of investigation and analysis followed by him in preparing it. Because Congress guards jealously its "power of the purse," this independent consideration of budgetary matters is followed even when the President and the two houses of Congress are controlled by the same political party. When opposing parties control, the degree of duplicate consideration is intensified.

This time-consuming result of our Constitutional separation of powers requires that the budgetary process begin, in the executive branch, almost a year before the beginning and almost two years before the ending of the fiscal year to which it applies. It is worth noting that the Reorganization Act and the Full Employment Act, by focusing attention on integrated or over-all Congressional consideration of the federal budget and its economic effects, *in addition* to the traditional bill-by-bill consideration, may tend to prolong this budgetary process.

These statements apply with especial force to expenditure changes. The length of time required for the preparation of tax legislation is somewhat less; but here too, because of the American legislative structure and because of the conflicts of interest which exist concerning tax legislation, the process is time-consuming, except for emergency action taken without review of the entire tax structure. But emergency action cannot be expected regularly. The prolonged delay in tax legislation which occurred in 1951 is a much more typical event than the speed of tax action in late 1950.

On humanitarian and ethical grounds the total time period involved is too long for involuntary unemployment to be endured. In addition, a cumulative downswing may have set in which makes the problem much worse than it need have been if speedier action had been taken. If a goal is set of preventing unemployment in excess of (say) six million, then preparing specific measures after a downswing has clearly begun will be inadequate, for the downswing may carry unemployment far beyond six million before the countermeasures take hold.

And if delay is unfortunate in the case of unemployment, it is equally evil in the case of continuing inflation. For during the period of planning and enactment of legislation to check inflation, a cumulative spiral may develop. Never is it more true than when fighting inflation that lost time is never found again.

In some situations action taken after a time-consuming process of planning and enactment will have an even more extreme defect. Not all economic swings are indications of a continuing trend; some reverse themselves. As a result, a measure developed by Congress after a certain situation was faced may come into effect at a time when conditions have changed, so that its effect is perverse. Congress reduced taxes immediately after the war, in anticipation of a recession. But the recession did not occur, and the tax reductions in fact came into force during a period of inflationary pressure and increased that pressure. On the other hand, in 1948 Congress passed a tax-reduction bill over the President's protest that it would be inflationary. But a recession occurred, and the increase in demand resulting from the tax reduction was salutary in 1949.

The only way in which the time involved in legislative and administrative processes can be shortened, if the planning begins after the event to be countered has occurred, is by hasty improvisation. Alternatives to waiting until after the event must be considered. One such alternative is to have permanently on the law books measures which will counter economic fluctuations whenever they occur.

Such built-in devices to counter fluctuations in employment and income are of two kinds, which may be called *active* and *passive*. By passive measures is meant measures which are actually in force at all times, but which have a different effect in prosperity or inflationary boom from that in depression, because they affect the individual consumer or business firm differently at different times, depending on the degree of his prosperity.

Unemployment compensation is an example. An employed worker does not benefit; if unemployed a worker draws compensation which offsets a part of the decline in his income and keeps his spending from falling as low as it otherwise would. Agricultural price support measures are another example. If the demand for the farm products covered by the price-support program declines, and the price drops, government loans or purchases set a floor under the fall and check the fall in farm income. If demand and farm prices (and farm income) rise, government support is withdrawn.

Progressive income taxes on individuals are among the most powerful of these passive built-in stabilizers. The more progressive the tax structure, the greater the stabilizing effect. In time of inflation measures such as price supports and unemployment compensation exert no positive anti-inflationary effect. At best they have merely the negative virtue of ceasing to contribute to demand, as employment becomes full and farm prices rise above support level. But as inflation proceeds a progressive income tax does more. It takes a bigger bite of money income as it rises, thus checking demand and cutting into the inflationary spiral. Indeed, a progressive income tax alone, if well enforced, would stop any inflation at some point—provided that the government refrained from spending its swelling receipts. On the downswing, as income falls, income tax liability falls faster, so that the income after taxes of an individual falls by less than does his income before taxes. Or, put in another way, his buying power falls by less than his income. Thus demand is partially sustained and the fall in output and employment partially checked—provided only that the government does not curtail its expenditures as its revenues fall.

It is because such measures are in effect that recent swings in economic activity in the United States have not been more extreme than they have. Without the progressive individual tax, inflation in 1946–48, and indeed in 1950–51 also, would have been more severe than it has been. And these devices could be improved, to make them more effective.

It is an important characteristic of these passive devices that they can only *temper*, but never *prevent* or fully counteract, a fluctuation in economic conditions. So long as an unemployed person suffers a partial reduction in his income, his expenditures will decline and the curtailment in his buying will cause unemployment to spread. The government cannot consider fully sustaining his income, for that would cripple the incentive to work. No responsible person, I think, has seriously proposed automatic income-sustaining measures which would fully maintain a person's income when the market for his services has shrunk and he is not making his normal contribution to production.[4] Nor has anyone seriously proposed that a tax law should take *all* of an inflationary increase in income, for to do this would also cripple incentives.

If automatic devices are to assure a reasonable degree of income stabilization, what is required is *active* devices which provide that *new*

4. Farm price support sufficient to prevent any fall whatever in farm prices would completely prevent market prices from exercising their function of turning producers from the production of commodities in lesser to those in greater demand. And only this degree of support extended to all commodities and services would prevent any fall in income and employment.

measures shall automatically go into effect when income or employment falls and shall be terminated or reversed when income rises. For example, a tax law might provide that tax *rates* should be reduced, not at any specified date, but automatically (on announcement by the appropriate official) when unemployment rose. Such a measure, by positively increasing private spending power, instead of merely lessening its rate of decline, might check the rise in unemployment completely. Similarly an automatic rise in tax rates, when prices rose by a certain percentage, could if sufficient in amount positively reduce total demand and completely check the price rise. The President might be authorized by Congress to set in motion certain preplanned public works projects, if unemployment exceeds a certain number. Or the Federal Reserve authorities might be granted additional authority to control credit expansion, effective in cases of a specified rise in prices.

Other devices could be cited.[5] It is the opinion of the present writer that such active, automatic measures are necessary to an adequate income stabilization policy. But it should be recognized that they would require the forfeiture by Congress of prerogatives which both on selfish political grounds and for deep-seated reasons of governmental theory Congress would not under present circumstances give up. Congress would have to give up, in some degree, the power of the purse. Congress would have to delegate either to the operation of blind economic forces, or to administrative discretion, the initiation of new expenditure programs or of changes in tax rates. These are radical and far-reaching steps, which Congress would and perhaps should be loath to take. Even in the field of monetary control, where discretion has traditionally been granted to administrators, the 1949 Congress refused to continue such minor grants of discretion as the power of the Board of Governors of the Federal Reserve System to control the terms of consumer credit, or the power to impose reserve requirements slightly above the previous statutory limits. Only under the pressure of events in 1950 was the former power restored.

Hence it is doubtful that the alternative of active, automatic devices is feasible. It is therefore worth while to devote a chapter to sober consideration of the final alternative, the forecasting of economic conditions in order that measures may be adopted by Congress in anticipation of economic changes and thrown into effect in time to counter an undesired change.[6] If this were feasible, it would at the same time preserve Congressional prerogatives and make possible effective action.

5. For a brief discussion of some devices, see my paper, "The Problem of Timing Fiscal Policy," *American Economic Review*, 38 (May, 1948), 417–429.

6. For purposes of employment policy, attention must be focused on the problem of forecasting employment and unemployment *on the average in the United States*

II. The Present Status of Forecasting

A forecast, if known with confidence to be accurate within a fairly narrow range of error, would be the sound basis for a firm set of policy proposals designed to meet the known prospective course of events. (Insofar as the forecast caused changes in public policies, which alter the course of events, the events forecast would not in fact occur.)

1. *Criteria for a usable forecasting method*

a. IT MUST POSSESS GREAT ACCURACY

The forecasting method must have an unusually high degree of accuracy if forecasts are to be used as bases for decisions to inaugurate changes in stabilization measures. In most social sciences a high probability that a forecast a year in advance was correct within 5% would be high accuracy indeed. For some business purposes, such as production scheduling, and for some public purposes, such as anticipating the demand for Tennessee Valley Authority power or the number of cases to be presented to a court of law, a forecast which had say a 2-to-1 chance of being within 5% or even 10% of the correct value would be useful. *But this moderate margin of error is too great to permit the forecasts to be used as a basis for the formulation of public policies designed to influence the level of output, income, and employment.*

That unusually great accuracy is needed for this purpose is readily seen from a simple example. Suppose that the forecast which seems most probable is employment of 57 million and unemployment of 4 million, but that it is agreed that there is a considerable probability that the employment forecast may be in error by 5%, or about 3 million. There is a significant chance that the correct forecast of unemployment may be either 1 million or 7 million. Unemployment will not literally fall to 1 million; for without a system of rigid price controls a high demand for goods will not push unemployment down this low. Instead, such a forecast would imply that fairly intense inflationary pressure will exist and prices will rise. On the other hand, unemployment of 7 million indicates that fairly serious deflationary influences and fairly serious

---

as a whole. It is true that employment and unemployment do not change uniformly throughout the country. Fairly small changes in the national unemployment total may hide larger fluctuations in certain industries or in certain areas. Unemployment may exist in a given region or a given industry which improvement in general business conditions will not remedy. But in spite of these important variations concealed within the national totals, the predominant unemployment problem in the United States, when there is one, is almost certain typically to be nation-wide unemployment, and in this chapter only variations in the national total will be discussed.

unemployment will exist. The policy implications of the two alternative forecasts are diametrically opposed. In such a circumstance the
forecast obviously furnishes no basis for a single line of public policy.
It does, of course, furnish the useful conclusion that public policy must
be prepared to meet either serious inflationary or serious deflationary
tendencies, or any condition lying between them.

If the forecast indicates unemployment of 9 million, the consequences
of error are of course much less serious, for the general nature of public
policy is clearly indicated, regardless of where within the probable
margin of error the correct forecast lies. In such a circumstance, however, prospective conditions are probably sufficiently clear to common
sense analysis so that the more elaborate forecast is unnecessary as a
basis for policy judgments.

b. ITS ACCURACY MUST BE DEMONSTRABLE

Not only must the forecasting method be highly accurate: it must
meet a more exacting test. Its accuracy must be demonstrable at the
time the forecast is made.

In the past most forecasting of economic events has been a product
of "informed judgment." Men of experience have reflected and then have
expressed their opinions concerning future developments. Each person
may have stated explicitly the reasons for his judgments; but the reasoning was subject to dispute. Valuable though such judgments often
are, this sort of forecasting will not do as the basis for public policy.
Men of experience disagree. The most informed of judgments will err
seriously concerning economic prospects, as anyone is well aware who
has observed the forecasts before or since the war by government officials, or by professional economists, or by leading business executives.
If forecasting is to be based merely on that intangible, informed judgment, then each legislator and each administrator will exercise his own
judgment. It will often be difficult to arrive at a consensus; and where a
clear majority opinion is reached, the majority will not be certain
enough of its own prediction to make major changes in public measures in anticipation of future events. For if the future is clouded, it is
less embarrassing to have left matters unchanged than to have acted
rashly and been proved wrong. Further, this diffidence will be justified;
the majority will frequently be wrong.

Forecasting will therefore not be acceptable as a basis for governmental action if the forecast is merely a consensus of informed opinion
or the judgment of any economic authority, no matter how revered.
It will be necessary to develop an accurate *objective* method of forecasting—objective in the sense that it is based on verifiable data and is ca-

pable of being stated so precisely that any trained worker, starting with a given set of facts and using the method, will arrive at the same forecast of the level of employment at, say, 12 months hence and the same estimate of the margin of error in the forecast. With such a method, the accuracy of the forecasts can be checked, and if accuracy is proven by experience the forecasts can be used with confidence. Only if such an objective method of proven accuracy can be developed can legislators and administrators be expected to accept the responsibility of using it as a basis for adopting economic measures in anticipation of events which have not yet occurred.

2. *The passing of the barometric method*

Up to the recent past the most popular method among professional forecasters was a "barometric" one. A search was made for an economic series, or a group of them, which in the past had moved up or down in advance of movements in business conditions. If one was found the question was asked whether there was any logical reason why changes in this item should precede changes in business conditions. If the answer was yes, to the satisfaction of the forecaster, such a series was accepted as an indicator of changes in business conditions.

One of the most interesting of such barometers was the price of steel scrap. The logic is as follows: good times are almost invariably accompanied by business expansion and a high level of industrial construction and of equipment purchases. These types of activity use steel, and when they are planned orders for steel will increase. Increased orders for steel will increase the demand for steel scrap and send up its price even in advance of the increase in steel output. Thefore, a rise in the price of steel scrap may be taken as a harbinger of a rise in the level of economic activity. Conversely, a decline in scrap prices heralds a decline in business activity. By and large this logic is reasonable; but unfortunately a sufficient number of other circumstances also affect the price of steel scrap, so that on a number of crucial occasions its use as an indicator led to grievous error.

Another barometer was stock prices in general or the prices of selected groups of stocks. The logic here was that the smartest observers of business conditions operate on the stock market; when prices of most stocks (or a significant group of stocks, such as industrials) rise or fall, it is as a result of an informed and "smart" consensus which is probably correct.

That the stock market, like other barometers, is an unreliable one is an oft-told tale which need not be restated here. With the repeated failure (mixed with some successes) of the barometric method, in recent years there has occurred a renewal of hope that the basic causes of economic fluctuations are coming to be well enough understood so that forecasts can be based directly upon analysis of the causes at work rather than upon the discovery of some barometer.

3. *The influences which determine the level of output and employ-ment*

a. A DETAILED ANALYSIS OF CAUSAL RELATIONSHIPS

It will be useful at this point to review the analysis of national spend-ing and income given in the preceding chapter in order to explain its relation to the problem of forecasting. As Mr. Millikan has explained, analysis of the causal factors in business fluctuations may begin with consideration of the four great markets for the goods and services pro-duced in the economic system, namely, sales to consumers, to business enterprises for capital purposes, to foreign buyers, and to government.

Of all of the goods and services produced in the United States (or any other country), the bulk are purchased by consumers. In addition to purchases of services and goods of various degrees of durability for use currently or in the near future, consumers spend a good deal on pur-chases of new houses. These housing expenditures are grouped, for purposes of convenience, with business investment.

Business enterprises, in addition to producing or purchasing goods for resale to consumers, also spend for various types of physical plant and durable equipment and at times to increase their inventories and to build houses for rental. This is a second main source of demand for the output of the economic system.

Foreign buyers create a third source of demand, their net demand being measured by the excess (or deficiency) of their purchases from the United States over their sales to the United States.

Finally, the various units of government—federal, state, and local—not only produce many services with the labor of their own employees but also purchase goods and services from private business enterprises.

The expenditure figures from Chart I, Chapter 3, representing the total output in the United States in 1950, are reproduced in the table below. Gross private domestic investment is further broken down into four categories.

Consider again the influences which seem to be the major ones deter-mining how high the level of each of these types of expenditures will be. Tracing even the major influences for forecasting purposes is a fairly complex process; but when it has been completed some important gen-eral conclusions may be drawn.

GROSS NATIONAL PRODUCT IN THE UNITED STATES, 1950

billions of dollars

Personal consumption expenditures (consumer purchases of goods and services)		193.6
Gross private domestic investment		48.9
Nonfarm residential construction	12.6	
Other construction	9.6	
Producers' durable equipment	22.4	
Net change in business inventories	4.3	
Net foreign investment (net exports of goods and services; the excess of sales to abroad over purchases from abroad)		−2.3
Government purchases of goods and services		42.5
Total		282.7

The largest single category is consumer purchases. The expenditures of all consumers in the United States combined during any given time period depend primarily, as we have seen, upon the income remaining to consumers after paying taxes (consumer "disposable income") during that same period.

These expenditures will of course vary somewhat even when disposable income does not, but the relationship between expenditures and disposable income is not nearly as erratic as one might suppose before examining the data. On the contrary it is rather dependable. It is true that the living habits of the people, their attitudes toward saving and spending change gradually from generation to generation and even from decade to decade, as new products and new possibilities of comfort, health, and pleasure develop. But at any one time those habits are not erratic, and the amount which all consumers in the country will spend at a given level of disposable income, or the amount by which consumer spending will increase or decrease if disposable income goes up or down, can be forecast without too great error, provided that circumstances other than the level of income do not change so as to interfere with the forecast.

This, however, is an important proviso. For many other influences which do change must be taken into account in forecasting consumer expenditures, and some of these influences are difficult to evaluate.

For example, during a depression the level of consumer expenditures depends not only on the level of income but on the standard of living to which consumers become accustomed during a preceding prosperity period. People spend more out of a given income if they have previously received a higher one and grown accustomed to a higher living standard than if they had not done so. Economists feel, however, that they

have learned enough about this trait of human behavior so that in forecasting consumption they can allow for it without too great error—
though unless and until another depression occurs it will not be possible to test whether this confidence is justified.

Aggregate consumer expenditures in the nation are also influenced
somewhat by the degree of inequality in the distribution of the income
among the families and individuals of the country. This fact, however,
does not cause as great difficulty in forecasting as was once feared, for
several reasons. In the first place, the degree of inequality in the distribution of income does not vary tremendously from year to year.
There is a material change between prosperity and depression, but this
can be allowed for. Secondly, a change in the degree of inequality in
income distribution does not affect aggregate expenditures out of a
given aggregate amount of income, in the country as a whole, as much
as was once thought. Finally, the surveys of the spending and saving of
families and individuals at various levels of income have furnished a
basis for judging the effects on spending of any given amount of change
in income inequality.

When we come to making allowance for influences not directly related to income, influences responsible for the "autonomous" changes in
consumer spending described in Chapter 3, the problem becomes more
difficult. Consumer expenditures at any given level of income depend
upon the amount of cash or assets readily convertible into cash (called
liquid assets), such as government savings bonds; they also depend
upon the accumulated shortages or stocks of consumer durable goods—
automobiles, household electrical appliances large and small, and the
like. The ownership of cash and other liquid assets influences spending
not only because these assets may be converted into cash and spent but
also because even if these savings are not spent their possession makes
their owner freer in his spending out of current income. This is known,
but too little is known about the precise degree to which ownership of
liquid assets affects spending to permit very accurate allowance for it.

It is obvious that if shortages of consumer durables exist, spending
for them will increase and that as consumers stock up, their purchases of
durables will decline; but too little is known to permit accurate estimate either of when purchasing of such items will taper off or—more
important—of the degree to which, as it tapers off, it will reduce total
consumer spending on the one hand, or on the other merely cause a
shift of spending to other types of goods and services.

The influence of accumulations of liquid assets and the influence of
shortages of consumer durables are apt to be great at the end of a major

war. They are among the many circumstances causing extreme difficulty in forecasting at such a time.

The third type of influence affecting consumer expenditures—in addition to those relating to income and to assets holdings—is expectations concerning future income, future prices, and the availability of goods. It is clear that such expectations are very important at some times. Consumer expenditures fell more sharply than did consumer disposable income, between the fourth quarter of 1948 and the first of 1949, and it has been said that this occurred not only because consumers had satisfied the bulk of their deferred demands for durable goods but also because, anticipating a continuation of the decline in prices which had begun, they were holding off for lower prices. During the third quarter of 1950, following Communist aggression in Korea and the initiation of a major rearmament program in the United States, purchases by United States consumers rose far more than did income, presumably because of fear of goods shortages or of price rises or both. To predict such "buying sprees" in anticipation of higher prices and shortages or consumer "strikes" in anticipation of lower prices is extremely difficult. Anticipations are subjective psychological phenomena, and economists and statisticians have as yet developed no precise method of measuring their intensity or their effect upon consumer behavior. Forecasts of the effects of such anticipations upon consumer spending are therefore very crude indeed.

Of course, this list of influences is not complete. Consumer expenditures also depend upon a variety of other influences, such as the relative prices of various types of goods and services, including rents; upon the weather, style changes, etc.; but the influence of these various factors upon *total* consumer spending seems to be either fairly small or very temporary. The dominant influences, typically, are those mentioned in preceding paragraphs.[7]

These paragraphs have discussed the influence upon consumer expenditures of consumer disposable income, consumer asset holdings, and consumer expectations. Of these three types of factors the most important at most times is the level of disposable income. Changes in disposable income are more often the causal factor in large changes in the level of consumer expenditures than are the other two factors.

But what determines the level of disposable income? It depends in

7. Consumer expenditures also depend upon governmental regulations, such as the tightening up or relaxing of permissible terms of consumer credit and housing loans, by action of the Board of Governors of the Federal Reserve System. Such regulations may cause difficulties varying from minor to extreme for the forecaster.

part on the amount of special government payments, such as GI aids, social security payments, farm price supports, and upon the level of taxes. It depends also upon corporate dividend payments. By far the most important determinant is the volume of production in the country. Consumer income goes up and down as production and employment go up and down.

This is the apparently vicious circle examined in the last chapter. Consumer expenditures are the largest single determinant of the level of output and employment; but the level of output and employment is the most important determinant of the level of consumer income and therefore of consumer expenditures. As we have seen, however, the vicious circle is not real. Consumer expenditures and the level of output do not simply raise each other by pulling on each other's bootstraps. Other autonomous influences are at work helping to determine the level of output.

Consider next the four categories of "gross private domestic investment"—residential construction, other construction (commercial, industrial, and miscellaneous), purchases of producers' durable equipment, and increases in inventories.

Some new houses are built by consumers for their own occupancy, but the great majority of houses and apartments are built by commercial builders for rent or sale. Much the same influences affect both classes of construction, for it is of course the prospect of sale or rental to consumers which determines the volume of housing construction by commercial builders. The dominating factor which causes the volume of housing construction by commercial builders to rise or fall is of course change in the anticipated profitability of housing ventures. Possession of capital or ability to obtain it is a limiting factor, but since capital becomes available to the housebuilding industry when profit prospects are attractive (unless competing uses of capital are too lush) and ceases to be available when they are not, expected profitability is the touchstone in this respect also.

Expected profitability in turn depends upon the scarcity or excess supply of existing housing units on the one hand, and construction and financing costs on the other. If housing units (i.e., houses plus apartments) are in excess supply, rentals and sale prices will be low, and the amount of construction will be small; if housing units are scarce, rental rates, sale prices, and hence the amount of construction activity will all be high.

The relative scarcity or availability of housing units—the "vacancy ratio"—will be determined by the relationship between the number of families seeking housing units and the number of housing units in exstence. This relationship is liable under certain conditions to fairly sudden changes of which the forecaster must beware. For while the number of housing units in existence is a given quantity, which needs no forecasting, the number of families is not a biologically determined figure which can be depended on to increase steadily from year to year as the population grows. Instead, economic adversity will cause marriages to be postponed and will cause families to "double up" (forming one family for housing purposes), so that over a period of several years the number of families increases little or even declines, though the population is rising. Then with improvement in economic conditions families may undouble and the marriage rate jump, so that an increase of several million in the number of families seeking separate housing units—an increase which normally would cover six or seven years—may occur in half that time.

An increase of, say, a million in the number of families seeking housing units will cause only a moderate increase in housing construction if there are several million housing units standing idle, but if the number of families has increased enough so that the housing situation is fairly tight (if the ratio of vacant units to the total number has fallen below 5%), a further increase of a million families will cause housing scarcities in many places throughout the country and initiate a housing boom. Thus it is not merely the absolute increase in the number of families seeking housing but the precise relationship of this to the number of housing units in existence which is important. Once a sufficient number of housing units have been built so that the housing situation is loose again, the housing boom will taper off, though other forces cause high prosperity to continue and the number of families remains large and even continues to grow gradually. The 1920's illustrate these tendencies of housing construction activity. In the early twenties a housing deficit appeared, and housing construction activity soared. Then, because the deficit in housing needs had been more than made good, housing construction declined rapidly after the record years of 1925 and 1926, even though the number of families continued to grow gradually and their income remained high. Following 1929, as the number of families seeking housing units shrank, construction activity fell to only a small fraction of the 1925–26 level.

The scarcity or excess supply of housing, and the consequent prospects for rental rates and sales prices, constitute only one blade of the scissors which determine the volume of housing construction. How high a housing boom will swell, and how low the amount of construction will fall, in depression, also depends on construction and financing costs.[8]

8. And for apartment buildings, operating costs.

Financing costs depend upon the rate of interest. For many house-builders this depends directly upon the terms of housing loans or loan insurance furnished by the federal government; for others it depends upon the money market in general, which in turn is controlled by the monetary authorities. Thus the forecaster need not forecast interest rates; he can only assume that they will remain constant unless the forecast itself indicates general economic conditions of inflation or unemployment such that the monetary authorities should take action affecting the money market in order either to check inflation or to stimulate employment.

Housing construction costs depend upon wages in the construction industry and on the prices of building materials. Building materials prices are fairly rigid or "sticky"; that is, they do not vary from prosperity to depression to prosperity as much as do prices of, say, agricultural products. But they do vary and their variation is fairly closely related to the tightness of the economy as a whole. Thus a forecaster who had a basis for forecasting economic conditions in general would also be able to forecast with some degree of confidence at least the general trend of building materials prices. Much the same situation is true of wages in the construction industry. Construction workers in large cities are almost completely unionized and strongly resist reductions in wage rates; but various bonuses vary considerably from prosperity to depression, and the pressure for increases in wage rates will be effective in a boom but not in depression. Thus the variation in this element of construction costs is fairly closely associated with the degree of tightness or looseness of economic conditions.

This analysis suggests that aside from the number of houses in existence, which is given by past history, the amount of housing construction depends largely upon general economic conditions, but in a fairly complex way—a high level of demand for housing leading only to a temporary boom. While the nature of the influences affecting the volume of housing construction suggests that it would be easy for forecasts to err, there is nothing in the nature of these influences to suggest that accurate forecasting is intrinsically impossible.

Other types of private domestic investment will be considered in somewhat more summary fashion.

Expenditures by business firms for new productive plant and equipment seem to depend to a large extent, though not entirely, upon the prospect for profit from the investment [9] and upon either the posses-

9. This comment should not be taken as acceptance of the conventional assumption of classical economic theory that economic man is moved solely by the profit motive. Modern psychology has demonstrated clearly that the motivations of human behavior are far more complex than this.

sion of liquid assets sufficient to finance the investment or ready access to the capital market. A business enterprise will often undertake a new project, or a project of expansion or modernization, if it has the ready cash, even though in the same circumstances the banking community would not consider the venture safe enough to lend the money.

Economists do not know enough about business behavior to generalize with certainty concerning the bases on which businessmen judge profit prospects. It seems probable that in part they do so simply by an empirical rule-of-thumb consideration of the level of recent profits and the trend in them, but that in greater part they judge the future level of sales in some way (most commonly on the basis of recent trends in sales and any unusual elements in recent sales, such as deferred demand) and compare it with productive capacity. The desirability of added construction and equipment purchases, if this analysis indicates tightness or shortage of capacity, is then considered in the light of construction costs (and financing costs, especially if the money must be borrowed).

These considerations indicate why there are sometimes temporary spurts of commercial and industrial construction and of equipment purchases, just as there are of housing construction. If somehow our growing economy has entered a period of sustained prosperity, there may be a steady pressure of expanding sales on productive capacity, and plant expansion may continue fairly steadily for, say, a decade or more. But on the other hand if the economy has swung up from depression to press hard and fairly suddenly upon productive capacity, there may be a sudden great need for added capacity. This may lead to a temporary rate of plant construction and expansion well in excess of the rate which the economy needs year after year. Such a boom in business construction will end fairly abruptly (construction not ceasing but falling to a more moderate level) when the urgent needs have been met.

Such a burst occurred after World War II. Shortages of productive capacity appeared throughout the economy, and expenditures for plant and equipment soared. The burst of plant expansion was not concentrated into an even shorter period than it was, mainly because, while some firms rushed to expand at once, others, thinking the unprecedented level of demand only temporary and hoping that soaring construction costs would turn down, held off. As the boom in demand proved fairly durable, many of these others executed their expansion plans after one or two years of delay, thus prolonging the construction boom.

This brief description, of course, ignores many minor factors affecting business investment. Even assuming that it is a fairly accurate summary of the major factors, it indicates the complexity of the conditions which a forecaster must judge.

Business prospects at any time will of course vary widely from industry to industry. A forecast which considers the factors mentioned in the preceding paragraph only in the aggregate, for the economic system as a whole, will presumably suffer from a greater margin of error than one which is able to analyze each major industry group separately —agriculture, mining, public utilities, and so on.

Construction on farms and purchases of equipment by farmers, for example, depend to a much larger degree than other business investment upon the current income and the liquid assets of the person making the investment.

Other nonresidential construction and other purchases of durable goods—by hospitals, private schools, and a variety of other nonprofit institutions—seem to depend largely upon the general level of income and business activity in the country as a whole, which affects the income and financial condition of such institutions.

The volume of purchases for addition to inventories is at times an important temporary factor in a boom. At times, too, reduction in inventories is an important factor in a recession. Waiving inventory speculation for the moment, decisions to expand or contract inventories depend upon *changes* in the level of sales. If sales rise, inventories must be increased or the higher rate of turnover will create repeated shortages. There results not only an increase in orders to match the increased rate of sales but a temporary additional increase in orders to increase inventories. When inventories have been built up, orders will be reduced even though the high level of sales continues. Similarly, if sales decline, orders will temporarily decline even further and will then be increased, when inventories have been reduced to the desired level. Inventory cycles may thus exaggerate more basic movements in the level of economic activity.

The sectors of economic activity discussed so far have been analyzed almost wholly in terms of economic causation operating within our economic system. This, however, is not true of the remaining sectors, the excess or deficiency of exports over imports and government employment and purchases. The relationship between imports and exports depends not only upon the level of economic activity in this country but also upon world economic activity and in times like the present upon American governmental policy. The relationship cannot be forecast, therefore, without a judgment concerning both world economic conditions and the noneconomic factors affecting future governmental policy decisions.

Some historians assert that governmental policies (and therefore taxes and government expenditures) are determined largely or wholly by economic influences—by the economic interests of the dominant class or classes, for example; but though this theory obviously contains a large element of truth, it is equally obviously impossible to state any relationship which will enable one to forecast government expenditure or taxes directly from economic conditions.

b. THE EFFECT OF LABOR UNION ACTIVITY

One final factor which affects business decisions to invest, and to a lesser extent consumer expenditures perhaps, deserves separate mention—the influence of labor union activity. Other supply factors—productive capacity and the labor supply—have been given their place in the analysis; but what of the influence of labor organizations? What effect, for instance, did the successive rounds of union demands for wage increases have upon business activity after the war?

Part of the answer is that union activity affects the general level of wages and prices, and the relationships between various prices, much more than it affects the level of output and employment. Most wage increases are apt to be passed along in price increases, or may prevent a reduction in prices which would otherwise have seemed advantageous. Suppose that widespread union pressure for higher wages results in a price level, say, 8% higher than it would otherwise have been. Insofar as through wage increases consumer income in the aggregate has risen with prices, the physical volume of consumer purchases will be little changed. And if banks have plenty of excess lending capacity, so that it is fairly easy to borrow the added funds needed to cover higher costs of construction and equipment, the level of business construction and equipment purchases may not be greatly affected.

Any individual businessman faced with an aggressive union is apt to get a partial and somewhat distorted impression of this process. The pressure of the union's demands upon his costs, and particularly the anticipation of future pressure, deters him from making expenditures for capital purposes, he is sure. However, an increase in money incomes throughout the economic system increases his market and enables him to charge a higher price, so that this offsets in whole or part (or may in certain cases more than offset) the direct effect of union activity upon his calculations. The businessman often does not reflect that this increase is a result of the same wave of union activity which increases his costs.

However, collective bargaining certainly does in a number of cases increase wages *at the expense of profits*, rather than at the expense of prices. For the country as a whole, wages are somewhat higher and profits somewhat lower because of union activity than they would otherwise be. This effect, plus the psychological effect of the anticipation of perpetual future pressure, certainly has some net depressing influences on business expenditures for capital purposes, even though this is less than a businessman is apt to think.

Further, price rises themselves are apt to lessen the aggregate amount of goods and services purchased, even though income also increases. It was noted above that the possession of cash or other liquid assets stimulates business expenditures which would not be made if bank loans had been necessary. Insofar as a price rise reduces the purchasing power of liquid asset holdings, it will tend to reduce somewhat the physical volume of construction and equipment expenditures undertaken by business enteprises. Similarly, the reduction in the purchasing power of consumer liquid asset holdings reduces the physical volume of consumer purchases, though such evidence as is available suggests that this effect is not great.[10]

On the other hand, insofar as union activity causes a shift from profits to wages, corporate undistributed profits may be decreased and total consumer income increased somewhat; and a reduction in the inequality of the distribution of consumer income is apt to occur (even though wage earners with fairly high wage incomes are apt to get the largest increases). Both the increase in consumer income and the change in the distribution of income will increase consumer expenditures. However, as has been noted above, a moderate shift in the distribution of consumer income does not seem to have any marked effect upon total consumer expenditures, so that this effect will not be great.

The net effect of union activity upon the level of business activity is thus difficult to measure. For forecasting purposes, what is important is the effect of any intensification or diminution of union activity.[11] One rough way of measuring this would be to assume that union activity increases with an increase in the percentage of all wage earners who are union members, and to include in one's forecasting system the assumption that as this percentage increases, business expenditures for plan-

10. In the postwar period of "overfull" employment and inflationary pressure this depressing effect of an increase in the price level upon expenditures mean that there was somewhat less inflationary pressure remaining, after wage increase had raised the price level, than there would have been at the lower price level. Indeed, the inflationary pressure at the lower price level would have tended to raise prices even if wage increases had not led the way; so that much, though probably not all, of the price increase which was popularly associated with wage increase would have taken place even if unions had not existed.

11. Since a forecast will be concerned with forces causing *change* in total expenditures "next year," compared with "this year."

and equipment will be adversely affected. This is a very rough and uncertain rule, in view of the other factors which affect union activity and of the difficulty of distinguishing between any possible effect of union activity upon business decisions and of various other factors. However, union activity should be kept in mind as one possible causal factor but one difficult to measure.

C. FOUR GENERALIZATIONS CONCERNING THE CAUSAL FACTORS

Out of this brief item-by-item analysis of the major causal factors affecting the level of economic activity, four generalizations of importance to forecasting may be drawn.

One is that the analysis of the influences determining the level of various types of output does not indicate threads of causation leading to one single central focus. There is no one key indicator or barometer which will furnish guidance concerning the whole economy. There is no royal road to forecasting.

In the second place, the analysis suggests that forecasting of most if not all sectors of economic activity may be possible on the basis of *objective* relationships. For example, the level of housing construction depends largely upon prospects for profits from the sale or rental of housing, which is a subjective evaluation of the future. But if that evaluation in turn depends primarily on the relationship between the number of families and the number of existing housing units, knowledge of the number of housing units plus an accurate forecast of the number of families may make it possible to pass directly to an accurate forecast of the level of housing construction. Similar *objective* relationships have been suggested above for other sectors of economic activity. If it is possible to estimate from past experience *how great a change* in each sector of economic activity (e.g., housing construction) is caused by a given change in some objective causal factor (e.g., number of families, relative to number of housing units), then it should be possible to develop a purely objective method of forecasting.

The third general statement is that, to an impressive degree, all sectors of economic activity other than governmental activity and foreign trade depend either upon conditions inherited from the past (productive capacity, the existing number of housing units, etc.) or upon the general level of economic activity and changes in it. But since the general level of economic activity is simply the sum of economic activity in all of these sectors combined, this statement means that to an impressive degree all sectors of economic activity *depend upon each other*. This mutual interdependence of the various sectors of economic activity is the most striking single fact developed by modern students of "econometrics" or economic measurements. The level of output and employment almost anywhere in the economic system depends in major degree upon the level of activity elsewhere in the system, because all parts of the system are interconnected by income flows, mutual demand for productive resources, and price relationships. It is of little use to try to forecast output and employment by examining six or eight or any other number of economic sectors separately, forecasting the level of each in turn, and then adding the results. *No sector, it seems, can be forecast until the other sectors have been forecast first.* What this indicates is that it is necessary to make quantitative forecasts of activity in all sectors of the economy *simultaneously, taking account of the interrelationships between them.* This is the keystone of modern forecasting.

Finally, it is clear that governmental activity and foreign trade have mainsprings which lie outside the field of United States economic activity, so that in these sectors at least purely objective methods of forecasting are impossible. The would-be forecaster must not only enter some degree of judgment about world conditions; he must also go outside the realm of economics entirely into analysis of the considerations which govern public affairs.

4. *The econometric method of forecasting*

a. MUTUAL INTERDEPENDENCE AND THE NEED FOR PRECISE STATISTICAL RELATIONSHIPS

The fact of mutual interdependence between various sectors of economic activity does not imply a lifting-oneself-by-one's-bootstraps effect, so that any level of economic activity will sustain itself. Instead, as Chapter 3 has indicated, there is some one level of economic activity, and only one, which will tend to be brought about by the interrelationships within the economic system. This can be made still clearer by a grossly simplified example. Suppose that after surveying economic conditions a forecaster had decided tentatively in June, 1949, that the average level of output in the United States during the coming twelve months would be as follows:

	billions of dollars
Consumer purchases	177
Residential construction	7
Other private construction	9
Business purchases of equipment	20
Increase in inventories	0
Net exports (excess of sales to abroad over purchases from abroad)	2
Government purchases (including payrolls)	41
Total gross national product	256

The tentative forecast of gross national product is $256 billion. However, the forecaster might have noted, after the necessary calculations, that this level of output would yield consumers an aggregate income, after paying taxes (and after including any special government payments to consumers) of $188 billion; and that out of that level of income, judging by recent experience, consumers would spend not the $177 billion initially estimated but $2 billion more. The estimate of consumer purchases would therefore have had to be revised upward. But this increase in consumer purchases would increase total output, which would increase consumer income, causing a further increase in the estimate of consumer purchases. After a succession of adjustments the forecast of consumer expenditures might therefore be increased to $181 billion; of gross national product to $260 billion; and of consumer income after taxes to $190.5 billion.

But the forecaster might have decided that at this higher level of purchases inventories would not be adequate. He might then have increased the estimate of change in inventories from zero to $.7 billion and the estimate of gross national product accordingly. But this increase in output would increase consumer income, consumer expenditures, and total output somewhat further.

With demand estimated at this higher level the forecaster might have felt that a moderate upward movement in prices which he had not anticipated would appear. He would then have to decide how this would affect expenditures. Further, at this higher level of income, is the estimate of residential construction too low? What about business construction and equipment purchases? If the estimates of these are revised, the total changes and a whole round of secondary adjustments must again be made. So the process would go, with each change in any one item setting off a series of necessary changes throughout the entire area of the forecast.

The important point is that the process of repeated adjustments could finally result in a forecast, every sector of which was consistent with every other sector—in which, for example, total output, consumer income, consumer expenditures, prices, inventory changes, net exports, and business expenditures for construction and equipment would all be "in line with each other." It is reasonable to believe that there is some one level of each and under any given circumstances, only one level, which the interrelationships between the various sectors will in fact bring about.[12]

12. The thinking of some readers concerning the influences which determine the level of output and employment is probably couched in terms of the relationship between saving and investment. These readers may wonder why the relationship

However, though there is some one level, the forecaster has no reason to be sure that he has correctly forecast it. His final forecast was the product of a series of tinkerings, and as the process is sketched above the judgments involved are sufficiently imprecise so that the forecast might be considerably different from what it would be if some other student of economic affairs had done the tinkering—and both might be considerably different from the course of events which the future will in fact bring about.

At least two difficulties cause this considerable margin of error.

1) In making the various adjustments it is necessary not only to have analyzed the causal relationships correctly but also in addition to estimate *by how much* a change in each causal factor will influence spending. This necessity has been referred to above. If disposable consumer income decreases by $10 billion, by how much will this tend to decrease consumer spending? If liquid asset holdings of consumers increase over a period of time by $50 billion, by how much will this tend to increase consumer spending? If total sales of business enterprises decline by $10 billion, how much will profits fall? If profits fall by a given amount, by how much will this reduce expenditures for new plant and equipment? If interest rates fall by $\frac{1}{4}\%$, as a result of some anticipated change in monetary conditions, by how much will this affect expenditures for new plant and equipment, if at all? And so on. Informed analysts may differ considerably concerning the precise numerical relationships involved.

2) Even if some precise estimate of every relevant relationship were arrived at, the piecemeal adjustment of each item throws the estimates of other items out of line, and it is extremely difficult to get the forecasts of all of the items entirely consistent with each other so that there is a basis for confidence that a reasonable over-all estimate has been arrived at. So many relationships are involved that the human mind has difficulty in coping with all of them at one time.

Mathematical and statistical techniques can give aid in solving these problems.

---

of saving to investment has been largely ignored in the discussion to this point. The answer is that the level of output which the interrelationships between the various factors at work will bring about is a level at which saving equals investment, in the ordinary sense of those words. Analysis like that above is an alternative to "savings-investment" analysis. But to analyze the effect of the various factors upon aggregate expenditures is simpler than, and in fact theoretically preferable to, analyzing their effect upon saving and investment.

b. DETERMINING THE STATISTICAL RELATIONSHIPS

The only way in which objective estimates of the quantitative relationships can be arrived at is by analysis of past data.[13] In the past, what change in profits was associated with a given change in the volume of sales? What change in plant and equipment expenditures was associated with given changes in profits, in the relationship between sales and productive capacity, in interest rates, etc.?

Obviously, the first step is to obtain data for each factor involved for as many years as possible. Some factors must be ignored for lack of data. For example, no known data will furnish a reliable clue to the quantitative effect of consumer anticipations concerning price or income changes on consumer expenditures. As another example, data do not exist for liquid asset holdings of business firms in separate industries, or (except for a few recent years) for business firms as a whole, separately from the liquid asset holdings of consumers; so that it is impossible to make a reliable analysis of the effect of possession of liquid assets on investment.

Even when as many as possible of the desired data have been gathered or estimated, analysis of the relationships is difficult simply because many changes occurred at once. If business expenditures for new plant and equipment increased from $13.5 billion in one past year to $15.4 billion in the next; and at the same time total sales in the economic system were up by $6 billion; profits were up $1.6 billion; capacity was up by $5 billion as a result of last year's plant and equipment expenditures; construction costs fell by 3%; and interest rates fell by ⅛%—if these various things occurred, how much of the change in business expenditures for plant and equipment is attributable to each? Suppose that each of the five causal factors—sales, capacity, profits, construction costs, and interest rates—is expected to change in a future year, by varying amounts. How much weight should be given to each in forecasting the plant and equipment expenditures which will result?

The analysis of such relationships is one branch of econometrics. The analysis should be made, of course, not only for one year but for all years for which there are data. Conclusions based merely on one year may be badly in error because of some unusual development in that year or perhaps because some of the data for that year are somewhat in error.

The analysis should be made, for all years, for each of the sectors of output. What influences are the causes, and in what amounts, of the observed changes in consumer expenditures? residential construction?

13. Unless surveys such as those of consumer intentions to buy, or of the investment plans of business enterprises, are regarded as objective estimates.

business expenditures in various industries for plant equipment? changes in inventories? [14] What change in disposable consumer income will result from a given change in gross national product? in special government payments? What influences are the causes, and in what amounts, of the observed changes in interest rates? corporate profits? residential rental rates? changes in the price level? And so on. Until recently it was thought that changes in any one item could be explained by relating the data for that item, over a period of years, to the data for items believed to exert an influence on it, by the statistical technique of "multiple correlation." For example, the change in consumer expenditure caused by given amounts of change in disposable personal income, in liquid assets held by consumers, and by the previous level of expenditures, to which consumers had grown accustomed, could be analyzed in this way. Statisticians now know, however, that because of interrelationships between all of the items in the economic system treating one dependent item and the causal influences which affect it, separately from the remaining dependent items and the causal factors affecting them, will give inaccurate estimates of the relationships. *The relationships between every dependent variable and its group of causal factors must be estimated simultaneously.* The very complex statistical procedure by which this can be done is known as the "method of maximum likelihood." [15]

When the analysis has been completed, a statement will be obtained (in the form of a mathematical equation) for each sector of economic activity—consumer expenditures, housing construction, etc. The statement will indicate by how much activity in the given sector will rise (or fall) with a given change in each causal factor. To cite a simple hypothetical example, the analysis may indicate that the volume of inventories held by all business firms in the United States, combined, will be increased (or decreased) by $1 billion for each $7 billion of increase (or decrease) in the volume of goods sold; that they will be increased by a given small amount for every .1% fall in short-term interest rates; and that there are changes in inventory holdings (presumably due to swings in business expectations concerning the future) which are not accounted for by changes in sales or in the interest rate and which it does not seem possible to account for objectively.

It should be observed that the change in inventories depends upon

14. Net exports and government purchases of goods and services cannot be analyzed in this way, since they depend on many factors other than economic changes in this country. See page 186 above.

15. It has been shown by statisticians that the method of maximum likelihood also has a bias of its own. No known method will give entirely accurate estimates of the true relationships.

the change in the level of sales, while the change in the level of sales depends in part upon the change in inventory holdings (for additions to inventories require purchases of the goods held, i.e., *sales* by some other firm). Hence, neither the level of sales nor the change in inventories can be forecast before the other. The two must be forecast simultaneously.

One important limitation of this statistical analysis should be noted. No known statistical technique will insure that the forecaster has analyzed the true causal factors affecting each sector. The results may indeed give some suggestions concerning this. If there are large or apparently systematic changes in the activity being analyzed (e.g., additions to inventories) which are not explained by the causal factors which were used in the analysis, this may suggest to the forecaster that he should seek other causes; and if changes in some presumed causal factors seem to cause only slight changes in the activity being analyzed, this may raise the question whether there is a true causal relationship. But these indications are by no means infallible; in the main the forecaster must depend upon logic rather than statistics for the selection of the proper causal factors.

Two sectors of the economy cannot be analyzed by this statistical procedure. These are net exports (or imports), that is, the excess (or deficiency) of sales to abroad over purchases from abroad, and governmental expenditures. Neither can be estimately merely on the basis of economic relationships within the United States; each depends in part on noneconomic factors or on circumstances outside the United States. (However, past data for both of these factors have entered *as causal factors* into the explanation of changes in the level of other sectors.)

The volume of net exports depends in part upon world conditions, including both the level of economic activity abroad and the international policies of our own and other governments (such as the European Recovery Program). It also depends in part upon the level of output and income in the United States (which affects one-half of the picture, our imports). Therefore, the volume of net exports cannot be forecast in advance of the general forecast of gross national product in the United States; the two must be forecast simultaneously. For simplicity, however, an approximate estimate of the probable level of gross national product can first be made and a forecast of net exports based on this. This forecast can then be used in the final forecast of gross national product.

A basis for forecasting tax revenues can be arrived at by including the relationship between tax revenues and the level of economic activity in the method of maximum likelihood. However, if this is done, allowance must be made for changes in tax laws, which have affected the relationship. Further, a political forecast must be made of any change in tax laws which may be in effect during the period to which the forecast applies. Certain types of government expenditures also vary automatically with changes in economic conditions. Examples are unemployment compensation and farm price supports. The effect of economic conditions upon these expenditures can also be analyzed by the method of maximum likelihood; but as in the case of taxes allowance must be made for changes in laws concerning these expenditures which have altered the relationship, and a forecast must be made of further changes in these laws which will affect future expenditures.

Other government expenditures, which are determined from year to year by presidential recommendations and Congressional action, must be forecast on the basis of a judgment of that action.

C. MAKING THE FORECAST

When the procedures just described have been completed, the necessary ingredients for a forecast are at hand. Assume for convenience that the forecast is for a one-year period in the immediate future. The ingredients are:

1) Knowledge of varying degrees of precision of the stocks of consumer and capital goods (automobiles, other consumer durables, number of housing units in existence, stocks of inventories, productive capacity in various industries) on hand as the year begins; and of the cash and liquid assets in existence. These stocks of goods, of productive facilities, and of liquid assets are among the factors which will determine the level of economic activity during the coming year.

2) A forecast of net exports and of governmental tax revenues and expenditures.

3) Specific estimates in mathematical form of the network of quantitative cause and effect relationships between all of the major factors affecting the level of economic activity.

With 1) and 2) determined, there is only one level of gross national product and its components and of the incomes derived from it which the set of relationships referred to in 3) can result in. This level can be determined by a fairly simple mathematical process.

The method thus meets the first test suggested earlier in this chapter for a forecasting method. Any forecaster using a given set of relationships is bound to arrive at the same forecast. But the method is still subjective in the sense that the set of causal relationships assumed depends upon economic analysis concerning the appropriateness of which economists may and probably will disagree. The proof of the method must be in its results. It must meet the second test, namely, accuracy. What can be known about the accuracy of a forecast derived by such a method?

d. SOURCES OF ERROR

It is evident that there will be some margin of error, for the forecasting method described cannot take all causal factors into account.

1) Some factors must be omitted because even though the forecaster knows or believes that they have an influence, he cannot derive any quantitative measure of them or of their effect. This is conspicuously true of certain types of expectation concerning the future. Swings in business sentiment concerning the future of prices certainly cause bursts of accumulation or decumulation of inventories—commonly referred to as speculative. Yet it is extremely difficult to state objective changes in economic conditions, which can be forecast, causing these speculative inventory movements. There probably are similar elements of anticipation concerning the future which influence the level of consumer expenditures or of business plant and equipment expenditures, which slip through the meshes of the forecaster's objective analysis and cause changes in the level of output and employment which he has not forecast.

There may be other known omissions. In the complexity of life, minor forces must be ignored to obtain a clearer statement of the important ones. Some factors thought to be minor must be excluded to keep the statistical analysis within manageable bounds.

2) But there may also be sins of omission or commission of which the forecaster is not aware. The basic analysis of cause and effect relationships may be faulty. The modern study of economics is only two centuries old; the concept of a general equilibrium of mutually interacting forces which determines economic conditions at any given time, little more than two generations; the intensive study of *quantitative* economic relationships, only a single generation; and the specific development of a system of econometric relationships designed to explain the level of output and employment (and of the statistical techniques known as the method of maximum likelihood), hardly a decade. Under these circumstances it will not be strange if the system of cause-and-effect relationships embodied in recent econometric models is found to be at fault. The sins may be both of commission and omission. Some lines of causation may be incorrectly stated, simply because of the inadequacy of analysis to date in this field; and some important causal factors may have been excluded because of deficiency in the analysis.

The omission of influences, which turn out in fact to be important, results not merely in making the analysis incomplete; it may render inaccurate the statistical analysis of the factors which are considered. If one important causal factor is in fact omitted, the result may be to associate with one or more of the others a larger share of the causation than is actually the case, thus leading to an erroneous forecast of the effect when that causal item varies.

3) There may be errors in the past data from which the quantitative relationships between components were estimated. Many of our economic data for past years are estimates rather than precise measurements. In witness of this, note the magnitude of many of the revisions in data made by the Department of Commerce in its 1947 supplement to the survey on National Income. Insofar as the data used are in error, the relationships estimated from them may be inaccurate and the forecasts based upon them in error.

4) It is possible that the economic system may have changed, so that causal relationships which held true in the past will no longer do so. The forecasting method sketched here is based on the assumption that human reactions to economic circumstances will, in general, be the same in the future as in the past—or that if those reactions were gradually changing, that gradual change will continue.

Surely in general these assumptions are correct. Folkways are deeply rooted; human behavior changes only gradually. But there may be exceptions. Perhaps the war gave many persons glimpses of new standards of living, so that a higher percentage of each added dollar of income will be spent. Perhaps the enactment of broader social security legislation, such as health insurance, or the adoption of a public housing program will further change spending habits. Perhaps the gradual increase in the wage earner's share of the production dollar was associated with a growth in the strength of labor unions' bargaining position, which has now been checked. In any of these cases a forecast based on the assumption that the future can be judged by the past will prove in error.

The method of forecasting discussed here can be adapted to changed relationships. Wherever it is felt that a changed relationship has entered into economic behavior, the new relationship can be introduced into the forecasting process. But by virtue of the fact that the new relationship *is* new, its estimation is hazardous. The greater the number of relationships derived from past experience which must be altered because it is felt that human behavior has changed, the greater the risk of error.

5) Finally, the forecasts of government expenditures and of net sales to foreign buyers—the two forecasts made not as a part of the general analysis but separately, as special cases—may be in error. If so, the error will be reflected in the over-all forecast.

e. THE MARGIN OF ERROR

The existence of some error in forecasts will not invalidate their use as a basis for action by Congress or the executive branch. The basic question is how great the margin of error is apt to be. The remarkable degree of precision necessary in such forecasts, if they are to be used as a basis for social action, has been noted.

The proof of the pudding is in the eating, and it may be assumed that the reliability of forecasts by the method described—which I shall refer to hereafter as the econometric method—can be determined only by making forecasts year by year for a considerable period of time and seeing how they turn out. Fortunately, this is not necessary. For, unlike informed judgment, which is typically correct, by its own appraisal, in explaining retrospectively events which have already occurred, the econometric method can be checked against the past. Using the system of relationships which have been derived, and using actual data for net exports and government revenues and expenditures for a given past year, a "hindcast" of gross national product employment, the price level, etc., can be made for that year. When similar hindcasts have been made for a series of past years—presumably for all years whose data were used in estimating the relationships—the estimates of gross national product (or of any component in which there is especial interest) can be compared with the actual past data and the error in each estimate noted. From this series of results a statistical estimate can be made of the probability that *any* such hindcast taken at random will be within any given margin of the correct figure. Since for several reasons forecasts may have a greater error than these hindcasts, this procedure will furnish a minimum estimate of the probable error of a forecast.

The Cowles Commission, an institute for research into the theory and practice of economic forecasting, has made such tests of sets of relationships developed at the commission.[16] The Cowles Commission has been the center of research into the methods described above. With the best forecasting apparatus developed at the commission so far, the chance is at least one in three that a hindcast of gross national product for a twelve-month period would be in error by 5% or 6% or more. This is therefore a minimum estimate of the margin of error in a forecast of the average level of output for an immediate future twelve-month period; the error by the end of the twelve-month period may be greater.

The margin of error in forecasting employment may be greater than that concerning output. For if the change in labor productivity from

16. See Lawrence Klein, "The Use of Econometric Models as a Guide to Economic Policy," *Econometrica*, 16 (April, 1947).

one year to the next is incorrectly forecast, there will be error in estimating the amount of labor which will be needed to produce the forecast volume of output. This error may either counteract or reinforce any error due to an incorrect forecast of output.

The minimum probable margin of error in present forecasting methods is much greater than the permissible margin. The brief conclusion to this long discussion, therefore, is: in its present stage of development economic forecasting is much too inaccurate to be used as the basis for changes in stabilization measures.[17]

This fact should not lead to undue pessimism. The work of the Cowles Commission and that of other researchers in this field is experimental; no one can say that great improvements in methods and in results may not be achieved within a relatively short time. But for the time being, at least, no objective method of forecasting (and no other method) is sufficiently accurate to be used confidently as a basis for public action.

At this point some reader may object that this conclusion could have been reached much earlier. The much-publicized forecasts of depression during the reconversion period—to one of which the writer was a party —were so greatly in error as to leave no question concerning the possibility of accurate economic forecasting.

In answer to this objection, it should be noted first that the reconversion period was a very special situation, not typical of that faced in peacetime forecasting, and second that the reconversion forecasts were made by very crude methods. Techniques have developed considerably even during the relatively short period between then and now. The experience of the reconversion period is of little relevance in testing the accuracy of the forecasting method described in this section.

III. Steps toward More Accurate Forecasting

If greater accuracy is to be achieved, what is the path toward this goal? This section suggests possible steps forward.

1. More work needed

The basic prescription for lessening the margin of forecasting error is simple: *continued work on the problem.* Compared to the course of development which has led to major advances in other fields of study, the amount of informed human effort which has so far been devoted specifically to this problem is trifling. Attempts to improve the understanding

17. This statement should not be taken to imply that the forecasting now being done by various private economic consultants is necessarily too inaccurate to be useful for various other purposes.

of the influences which determine economic decisions of various sorts are now going forward in a number of universities and other research centers; it cannot be doubted that they will bear some fruit.

This research must take the form not merely of the application of thought by an informed expert sitting at a desk—a form of research whose value should not be underestimated—but also of statistical research and work "in the field." On the one hand, there is needed the accumulation and refinement of data, the improvement of statistical techniques, and the statistical testing of tentative hypotheses; and on the other, surveys by competent analysts of the procedures by which business decisions are actually made and the motives which influence them, and of the influences which motivate consumer behavior. If, for example, business executives typically act not so much to maximize profits as to maintain or improve the relative position of their firm in the industry (and whether this is true remains to be determined), this fact has relevance to an explanation of the forces which determine the rate of business construction and equipment purchases. If spending by the typical consumer is importantly influenced not only by the amount of his disposable income, and the other influences mentioned earlier in this chapter, but also by the level of his income *relative to other incomes in the community* in which he lives, this fact affects the behavior of consumers when the level of income changes. These and other plausible hypotheses concerning economic behavior which have been advanced recently must be explored.

Research must take the form of cross-fertilization between theory and empirical study. If some new explanation of the motives affecting business decisions seems plausible, how can it be tested statistically? If the statistical testing furnishes partial verification, but suggests certain peculiarities in the data for some years, what new hypotheses are suggested or what questions arise which may be resolved by further field work? The combination of inductive and deductive reasoning is as essential in this field of analysis as in any other science.

a. THE NEED FOR NEW TYPES OF EQUIPMENT

Some of the statistical analysis which might prove to be fruitful waits at present upon physical equipment not yet available. Theoretical analysis has suggested empirical investigations of increasing complexity. The empirical work is greatly hampered by the burdensome statistical manipulations which are required. For example, the method of maximum likelihood is computationally so burdensome as to make its application to the study of various complex sets of relationships almost completely impracticable, if the only equipment available is ordinary electric calculators or business machines using punch-card techniques. And the electronic computing devices developed recently, and widely used for intricate problems of mathematical computation in other fields, are in their present form not well suited to maximum likelihood analysis. The development of electronic machines adapted to this use, which is entirely practicable, would immediately eliminate this computational restriction upon the advancement of econometric analysis. Research to perfect the necessary modifications in electronic computers is now under way.

b. AN EXAMPLE OF STATISTICAL EXPLORATION WHICH MAY BE FRUITFUL

The experimental forecasting so far done has been based entirely or almost entirely upon relationships between annual data. The use of quarterly and even monthly data may make possible improvement in forecasting, since annual averages may conceal various ups and downs in the data which would reveal significant relationships. In addition to involving more burdensome computations, the use of quarterly or monthly data involves collection of sufficiently complete sets of such data, analysis of them to reject series which are simply estimated from annual data and so furnish no added information, and finally working out the mathematical procedures necessary to allow for the effect of purely seasonal variations in the data and to make it possible to apply the maximum likelihood method to a mixture of annual and quarterly or monthly data.

In general, forecasting based mainly on quarterly data will be most accurate in estimating conditions for only one quarter in the future. The chance of error would be compounded as added quarters were added to the forecast. However, improvement in forecasting for longer periods— say for a year—may be possible by use of a method which in a sense is a compromise between the use of annual and of quarterly or monthly data. At the time when any forecast based on annual data is made, something more is known than merely the average level for the year just ended (and for previous years) of income, output, employment, etc. In addition, conditions *at the end of the year just ended*—i.e., at the moment the forecast is being made—are known (even though as was noted above many of the data for the year's end are incomplete and subject to error). The relationships at the end of the year between consumer income and consumer expenditures, between business inventories and sales, between prices, profits, sales, and business investment, and so on—between all of the components of economic activity—indicate something more about prospects for the coming year than does merely the average of conditions during the year.

At present, forecasts based merely on "informed judgment" take account of those end-of-the-year conditions, but it has not been possible to do so (except as they affect the annual average) in the more systematic methods of forecasting. If a procedure can be derived for superimposing the end-of-the-year relationships methodically upon the system of analysis based upon annual data, so that they enter systematically into the forecast, the results may be improved. Whether or not this is possible is beyond the mathematical competence of the writer; it is certainly a topic which should be studied.

c. "QUANTIFYING THE NONQUANTIFIABLE"

A principle fondly asserted repeatedly by one of the early students of educational psychology is that "whatever exists, exists in some amount, which is subject to measurement." In a certain limited sense this is true, and one of the possible paths of improvement in economic forecasting is to devise ways of measuring certain phenomena and their causes which at present seem nonquantifiable.

The most conspicuous class of such nonquantifiable factors is anticipations (both of businessmen and of consumers) concerning the future. Are there swings in such anticipations, not based upon objective factors in any way which is now understood and therefore not allowed for in the econometric forecasting apparatus, which play an important part in changes in output and employment?

The fact that such nonquantifiable influences may exist should not necessarily lead one to the conclusion that their importance is great. In the past references to such influences has often been a mask for ignorance, just as savages attributed storms to the anger of the gods out of ignorance of the true causes. If one does not know why a certain change has occurred, it is often convenient to attribute it to "speculation," or to "bearish business sentiment due to foreign political developments." This is the kind of game which financial page writers play in analyzing the previous day's stock market activity, and of course the explanations may at times have substance; but they need not be accepted without critical examination by social scientists. It may well be that, as understanding of economic relationships grows and as mathematical analysis of them becomes more refined, the area of variation which it seems appropriate to attribute to such influences will steadily shrink. For example, there have been numerous periods of accumulation and later unloading of business inventories in the United States during the 1920's and 1930's. Ten years ago it was fashionable to attribute them in the main to speculation; now, on the basis of improved data and analysis, it seems more reasonable to attribute most of them simply to lags in the adjustment of inventories to changes in the level of sales.

Yet, whatever degree of debunking of "psychological" factors, waves of pessimism and optimism, and the like, may be appropriate, it remains true that an unsolved problem exists here.

Concerning consumer anticipations, survey techniques [18] which attempt to measure attitudes rather than merely record opinions are now in use. But to date they have made so little progress in the quantitative measurement of attitudes that it can only be said that they may hold promise of improving understanding in this field.

d. THE USE OF SURVEYS OF PROJECTED BUSINESS PLANT AND EQUIPMENT EXPENDITURES

Possibly the best way of dealing with business attitudes and intentions is to short-circuit the entire problem by the use of surveys which obtain information concerning business plans for near-future expenditures for plant and equipment, without attempting to identify the causes which affect those plans.

These are expenditures for which in the main (though not in all cases) fairly definite plans are made by business enterprises in advance—by large enterprises, some considerable time in advance. This being so, it is the most obvious common sense to suggest that the process of economic forecasting should include direct surveys of business enterprises in which they are asked their plans concerning expenditures for plant and equipment.

There is a considerable margin of error in forecasts of such expenditures by the econometric method—that is, in forecasts based upon study of the statistical relationships which have prevailed in the past between business profits, sales volume, plant capacity, etc., and if forecasts of the level of these expenditures could be made on the basis of surveys of business plans, this one stroke would do much to improve the accuracy of economic forecasting.

Several such surveys, dealing with a one-year or shorter time period, are now made. Following the lead of the Department of Commerce and the Securities and Exchange Commission, both *Fortune* and *Business Week* are now conducting such surveys. More recently, the McGraw-Hill Corporation has surveyed corporate expansion plans for the next five years. The survey conducted jointly once a quarter by the Depart-

18. Such as those used by the Public Opinion Research Center at the University of Michigan.

ment of Commerce and the Securities and Exchange Commission is perhaps the most promising for forecasting purposes. Each quarter, this survey inquires concerning expenditure plans for one quarter in advance, and during the first quarter of each calendar year the survey inquires concerning plans for the entire year.

Useful though this survey is, it has certain defects which could readily be corrected if more funds were available. The sample is probably not sufficiently representative of business enterprises which do not report to the SEC; and it is not now possible to reconcile the past data for capital expenditures by business enterprises as published in this survey with data for what appear to be the same expenditures, but in fact relate to a somewhat different total, which are presented in the tables of gross national product published in the *Survey of Current Business* of the Department of Commerce.

Since its initiation at the end of the war, the usefulness of this survey has been greatly increased by the inclusion since 1948 [19] of questions concerning *the level of sales which was anticipated in making the plans concerning plant and equipment expenditures*. With this information, adjustment can be made of the probable expenditures for plant and equipment if the final forecast indicates that the level of sales will be higher or lower than businessmen anticipated when they made their present plans.

Even with this information, using such a survey effectively is a very difficult matter. It should not be assumed that reported plans for plant and equipment expenditures can be either taken at face value or used after merely a *simple* adjustment for change in the level of sales from that anticipated. There will be a discrepancy between present plans to spend and future expenditures which will actually be made, even if sales develop precisely as expected. Some plant and equipment expenditures, which were not visualized at the beginning of the year, will be made during the year as needs become clearer; some which were not planned for lack of funds will become possible because funds are more freely available than was anticipated; new firms not included in the survey will make such expenditures; and some firms included in the survey will be unable for a variety of reasons to make expenditures they had anticipated.

The SEC-USDC surveys to date show that large firms have estimated fairly accurately their plant and equipment expenditures for the ensuing quarter (and even for the ensuing year), while smaller firms have tended to underestimate theirs. This may be because smaller firms plan less far in advance, or because large firms are sophisticated enough to

19. Since 1947 for corporations registered with the SEC.

add an allowance for "expenditures not yet planned," while smaller firms are not, or for some other reason. The change in a firm's plans, as sales expectations change, probably depends upon this firm's liquidity, on what is happening to this firm's sales relative to those of the entire industry, and on other factors. Accurate forecasts of plant and equipment expenditures probably cannot be made, on the basis of surveys, until enough experience has been gained to adjust the survey results on the basis of these and other factors.

Yet, in spite of these necessary adjustments, it is easy to exaggerate the degree of error which will necessarily be involved in the forecasts. And it must be remembered that even if the margin of error is at first fairly great, that margin may be reduced as experience increases. If the funds can be obtained and the necessary ingenuity and technical competence applied to the task, and if the cooperation of the business community can be obtained through creating an understanding of the importance of the project, development of an improved survey of business intentions to make expenditures for plant and equipment probably would afford a greater advance within a short period of time in the accuracy of economic forecasts than any other step which could be taken in the near future.

e. THE NEED FOR BETTER DATA

A more pedestrian method of making possible a certain degree of improvement in forecasting would be to improve economic data. Improvement both in the speed with which data become available and in their accuracy would be helpful. Greater timeliness of data would be useful to all forecasters but of greatest advantage for very short-run forecasting. For many types of economic data reasonably reliable estimates (few data are complete, most are estimates) are not available except after a lapse of some months, so that data for a three- or six-month period just ended, which are basic to a forecast of the near future, are themselves based on incomplete information. Reduction in this time lag for many economic series is possible without exorbitant increase in cost, though any speed-up in collection or processing of data is apt to involve some increase in expense.

Further, even after enough time has elapsed for the process of data collection to be complete, some types of data are less accurate than would be desirable. Though the United States undoubtedly has the best economic statistics of any major country, even United States data are subject to inaccuracies which may appreciably weaken the forecasts based upon the data.

Since almost all important economic data originate in the federal government, these observations apply especially to federal statistics. The improvements suggested here cannot be obtained by exhortation nor, in general, by improvement in administration. Data collection is an expensive operation, and by and large an essential step is that Congress shall be persuaded to appropriate more generously for these unspectacular statistical activities.

For the purpose of improving the data currently collected and advancing the time of their availability, more funds are needed for the Bureau of the Census and the Office of Business Economics in the Department of Commerce, for the Bureau of Labor Statistics, and for units in other federal agencies which exercise parallel data-gathering and estimating functions. More money must be appropriated both for basic censuses and for the current operations of statistical agencies. Frequent complete censuses of industry and trade, and frequent sample censuses of consumer income and expenditures, are needed to furnish the bench marks to which intervening current estimates can be tied. In recent years Congress has refused to finance industry and trade censuses even of the scope and frequency of prewar ones. This is a penny-wise and dollar-foolish policy.

2. *Are there ultimate limitations on the accuracy of forecasting?*

The general philosophic question remains to be asked whether, when all possible improvements in analysis and techniques have been made, the nature of human economic life sets ultimate limits to the possible accuracy of forecasting. To a believer in a mechanistic universe the answer is, "Absolute accuracy is conceptually possible." If cause begets effect, and if every effect is totally determined by antecedent causes, then our ability precisely to forecast the future is limited only by our understanding of the past and the present.

But some developments in the physical sciences place this rigid mechanistic theory in question. Heisenberg's principle of the indeterminacy of certain aspects of the behavior of physical matter is no longer useful in the physical sciences (if it ever was); but the theory which suggests that light consists neither of impulses of matter nor of ethereal waves, but of "wavicles," particles whose movement in space is in the nature of a "probability distribution"—this same theory may by extension suggest that even with omniscience a forecast of human action cannot be unqualified but instead can only be a statement of the degree of *probability* that human behavior (either of one individual or of a large number) will be within specified distances of a certain value. If the "probabilistic" rather than mechanical nature of scientific truth be granted, the ultimate limitations of forecasting need further philosophic analysis. But even if such conceptual limitations exist economic forecasting has not begun to approach them.

3. The "feedback" effect

One last difficulty which economic forecasting may encounter perhaps deserves discussion—the feedback effect.

In the early days of radio reception, when countless high school boys were constructing their own receiving sets, an improved hookup known (if my uncertain memory is correct) as a regenerative hookup came into vogue. The electrical impulse coming from an amplifying tube was fed back into the tube so that the impulse was reamplified. One result of this feedback, however, was that if the set was tuned ever so slightly above or below the frequency of the broadcasting station being received, instead of precisely on it, electrical impulses raced crazily through the circuit so as to produce a squeal or howl in the earphones, and in addition broadcast impulses which interfered with reception for blocks around.

Some persons fear similar effects from the feedback of economic forecasts into the economic system. Even if forecasting is otherwise entirely accurate, what will happen when consumers and business executives react to the forecast?

It should be noted that this effect will be of no concern when the millennium is reached—when the accuracy of forecasts is accepted by everyone, including legislators and administrators, and when corrective measures are at hand. For a forecast of an increase in unemployment of five million will then not be an unqualified forecast but a statement that unemployment will increase unless the government takes corrective action. And if corrective action is expected, and is expected to be effective, the forecast will not interfere with the public's expectation that prosperity will continue.

It is the effects of forecasting at a time when the announcement of a forecast does not bring the accompanying expectation that government can and will take effective stabilizing action which deserve consideration.

First, it should be noted that a forecast of prosperity cannot of itself sustain the prosperity. That is, if underlying economic conditions, correctly analyzed, indicate a recession, announcement that prosperity will continue will not preserve the prosperity even though the announcement is believed. A nation cannot normally "talk itself into prosperity." On the contrary, when depressions have occurred, it has typically been true that even though everyone had anticipated the continuance of prosperity there would not have been enough expenditures, in the aggregate, to sustain the prosperity.[20] Thus the feedback effect is not in itself a cure for economic ills.

Nor is a correct forecast of depression apt to cause the depression to be deeper than if the forecast had not been made. If an unheralded recession occurs, and after a time the fall reaches a bottom and conditions level off at a depressed level, this implies that at that level aggregate output and aggregate demand are in balance. If instead of being unheralded the recession were announced in advance, such an announcement is apt to do little more than cause the adjustments to the lower level of output to be made more promptly than would otherwise be the case.[21] The announcement, if the reaction to it was panicky, might of course cause the drop in activity to overshoot the mark and to bobble up and down before settling at the depression level. Such unnecessary fluctuation would in general be undesirable; the circumstances under which it would be apt to develop are too complex to be discussed here.

Whether or not an *incorrect* forecast of a depression could of itself cause one is a more difficult question. It is an economic axiom that a decline in output and income will ordinarily result in a smaller decline in expenditures. Therefore, if the underlying economic circumstances are such as to sustain prosperity, and if a $30 billion cut in output and income occurs because of an incorrect forecast that a recession is in prospect, aggregate demand will fall by less than $30 billion. As a result, at the lower level of output producers will find that demand is high enough to make an increase in output advantageous and the economy will spiral back up to full employment.

However, this is not necessarily always the case. For some of the expenditures which are sustaining prosperity may be due to plant expansion which is occurring because productive capacity is too small to serve the prosperity market. But if a bearish forecast causes a reduction in demand, this may cause cancellation of the plans for plant expansion and this, combined with the fall in consumer spending, may be sufficient to keep aggregate income and expenditures in the economic system at the depression level until such time as some fortuitous circumstance or some measure of public policy caused employment and output to rise again and thus caused the revival of the plans for expansion.

20. Admittedly, it would be difficult to summon historical evidence to prove conclusively such an "iffy" statement, but I think almost all economists would agree that it is true.

21. Whether such an acceleration of the onset of a depression would make its total duration longer than otherwise, or whether recovery as well as the recession would be advanced correspondingly, is a question too complex to be discussed here.

Though these undesirable feedback effects are possible, the possibility should not be given too much weight; the effect would occur only if the forecast was rather generally believed and in that case a strong demand for counteracting public action would immediately arise. This fact, however, indicates an opposite danger. An incorrect but generally believed forecast of depression, if it caused expansionary public action, could cause inflation; and an incorrect but generally believed forecast of inflation, if it caused the government to take deflationary (i.e., counterinflationary) measures, could cause a depression.

The moral, of course, is that forecasting cannot be the basis for changes in stabilization measures, unless and until it attains an assured high degree of accuracy. If forecasting gains a *moderate* degree of accuracy, it may become the basis for a strong request by the President to the Congress for "stand-by powers," by which to throw measures into operation if the contingency which seems probable should arise. This seems a likely middle ground before forecasting gains an even firmer status, if it ever does so.

IV. The Uses of "Conditional Forecasting"

So long as economic forecasting remains a highly imperfect instrument (and it may always remain so), no public body charged with the responsibility for forecasting can appropriately do more than make conditional statements about the future. Such statements might, for example, note potential demand in certain sectors of the economy and comment that under certain conditions this demand might come onto the market and cause inflation. Or under other circumstances the forces which are sustaining high employment might be noted, and the probability noted that if certain of these forces decline serious unemployment will appear, unless public policies are formulated to meet the situation.

At certain junctures such a forecast might be a warning light, focusing the attention of the nation on critical problems. In the present stage of economic knowledge, however, the forecast would typically be so hedged about with qualifications that it would amount to little more than an analysis of the factors which affect economic activity and would partake only slightly of the nature of a prediction.

Perhaps, therefore, the main beneficial effect of well-informed conditional forecasts is to give legislators, administrators, business executives, and the public generally a better understanding of the operation of the economic system and therefore of the way in which economic circumstances may be controlled or influenced by public or private policies. An examination of leading business publications indicates how greatly that understanding has improved in the past fifteen years, but indicates too how stubbornly certain ancient beliefs and prejudices die, especially those relating to fiscal policy.

The annual and midyear Economic Reports of the President to the Congress (together with the appended report by the Council of Economic Advisers to the President) can play and I believe are playing an important part in this process of education of noneconomists. In my judgment these reports (which present conditional forecasts) have been of progressively increasing educational value. Early reports did not distinguish clearly and consistently between adjustments needed to stabilize prices, output, and employment, and those which might have destabilizing effects under the circumstances existing but were regarded as desirable because of other social welfare aims. To some degree an impression was created of ex parte advocacy of certain measures. Recent annual reports, however, are not subject to this criticism. The reports are the more useful because the more or less technical report of the council to the President is now separated from a twenty-page nontechnical report of the President to the Congress.

If these reports receive the attention they deserve, their continued presentation will steadily improve the economic understanding of community leaders throughout the country.

CHAPTER V. *Fiscal Policy and*
the Federal Budget

BY GERHARD COLM

I. FISCAL POLICY: THE EVOLUTION OF AN IDEA

The great depression dramatized the dilemma in which Western capitalism found itself in recent decades. The free enterprise system had unleashed tremendous productive forces which carried the technical revolution from one field of production to another and from one region of the world to another. The standard of living in the industrial regions of the world showed great gains. It brought into sight an age of plenty.

On the other hand, there was a growing threat of instability. The expectation that the economic system of free enterprise and free markets would bring about steady and full utilization of all resources gave way to a growing fear that instability and periodic depressions are the price that must be paid for freedom and progress.

The earlier hopes that the government could steer an otherwise free economy solely through the device of a deliberate central bank policy were shaken by the experiences during the boom of the twenties and the depression of the thirties. Many people began to wonder whether liberal institutions and rapid and sustained economic progress were compatible with each other, or whether sacrifices with respect to one were necessary in order to gain the other.

In this situation what has come to be known as fiscal policy was proposed as a means to overcome depressions. It was greeted with enthusiasm as it promised to combine steady economic and social progress with the maintenance of basic economic liberties. It appeared as the true middle-of-the-road policy that avoided the fatal mistakes of a do-nothing policy without choosing the equally fatal policy of economic regimentation.

This is not the place to describe how this idea of fiscal policy grew out of modern theory and recent experience,[1] but a brief explanation

1. There is extensive literature on this topic, particularly with respect to the relationship between Keynes's theory of employment and Hansen's theory of fiscal policy. See, for instance, *The New Economics: Keynes' Influence on Theory and*

may be in order. In its simplest form fiscal policy is conceived as a means to counteract the economic instability that is caused at times by active purchasing power exceeding the supply of goods at existing prices or at other times by the sum total of demand falling short of potential supply. If inflationary tendencies prevail, the government increases taxes or curtails expenditures, thus reducing purchasing power. In periods of deflation and underemployment the government decreases taxes and increases expenditures, thereby adding to active purchasing power and effective demand. If the government succeeds in influencing the total stream of purchasing power and active demand, production will be forthcoming in the right amount and composition, and no other government regulation is needed to stabilize the economy and promote economic growth.

Fiscal policy seemed to be the ideal tool which could repair the basic defect in a laissez-faire economy without any specific interference with the free decisions by management of what and how to produce, by labor where to work, and by consumers what to do with their money. No new government powers would be needed except an adaptation of conventional government activities, namely, collecting revenue, spending money, and managing the debt.

Like all great ideas, the concept of fiscal policy was characterized by its simplicity. Little of that simplicity is left in present-day discussions about the actual role that fiscal policy may play in an endeavor toward stabilization of income and employment.[2] A survey of our experience with fiscal policy during the depression, the war period, and the postwar and rearmament period may help to focus on some of the problems that have been encountered in the attempt to adopt fiscal policies as a stabilization device.

1. *The great depression*

Government expenditure and revenue policy during the great depression can only to a limited extent be regarded as a test of the effective-

---

Public Policy, Seymour E. Harris, ed. (New York, Knopf, 1947), and *Income, Employment, and Public Policy,* essays in honor of Alvin H. Hansen by Lloyd A. Metzler, and others (New York, Norton, 1948). Arthur Smithies has treated the subject of this chapter in "Federal Budgeting and Fiscal Policy," in *A Survey of Contemporary Economics,* Howard S. Ellis, ed. (Philadelphia, Blakiston, 1948).

2. The recent report on *National and International Measures for Full Employment,* submitted by a group of experts appointed by the Secretary-General of the United Nations (December, 1949), presents a very clear though still oversimplified exposition of these problems. (See also the discussion of this report in the proceedings of the Eleventh Session of the Social and Economic Council of the United Nations in Geneva, July, 1950.)

ness of fiscal policy. The contraction in incomes, investment, and employment certainly called for support of purchasing power in order to bring the downward spiral to a halt. Actually, tax rates were not reduced but rather increased. Particularly, state and local taxes were increased, contributions to social insurance were initiated, and some other federal taxes were raised.

Expenditures by the federal government, on the other hand, were increased rapidly. A large part of the emergency outlays, however, were designed to enable farmers, homeowners, and businessmen to meet their debt obligations and to avoid bankruptcy and foreclosure. Most of these outlays simply substituted a federal debt for a private debt without a substantial addition to current purchasing power. Furthermore, the effect of the increase in purchasing power generated through federal expenditures was largely offset by the curtailment in state-local expenditures so that the total additional government "net contribution" to purchasing power was only of limited size.

Additional government expenditures for public works create, primarily, additional income of workers and contractors on and off site; these workers and contractors spend some of their additional income and, as a secondary effect of government expenditures, incomes are created in the hands of grocers, bakers, millers, and so on. (See Chapter 3.) During the period of recovery, the national income increased between two and three times as much as the government net contribution. This seemed to corroborate Keynes's theory of a "multiplier"—if one ascribes much of the recovery in national income to the effect of government expenditures, which is not an unreasonable assumption for this period.[3]

The concept of pump priming, which was used during those years, implied, however, more than this multiplier. The pump-priming theory held that the increase in consumer purchasing power and demand would induce a genuine revival of business investment. To the extent that investment began to rise, it was hoped that the recovery movement would continue under its own momentum and that the government net contribution could be safely reduced or discontinued. Investment, however, rose only very moderately, not enough to carry the recovery movement forward under its own steam. Thus the pump-priming or the "acceleration" effect of government spending did not materialize to a sufficient extent. The recovery movement did not become self-sustaining. As a

3. For an attempt to classify government expenditures according to their effect on national income and capital, and for an attempt to measure the effect of such expenditures, see Gerhard Colm and Fritz Lehmann, "Public Spending and Recovery in the United States," *Social Research, 3* (May, 1936).

matter of fact, a reduction in the government's net contribution to purchasing power in 1937 coincided with the beginning of a serious recession.

In response to the 1937–38 recession, the first systematic plan of fiscal policy for purposes of stabilization was devised by the administration, but only partly adopted by Congress. There was still considerable unemployment when the defense effort began to supersede the recovery effort.[4]

This incomplete success of the government's fiscal policy in inducing a self-supporting recovery movement has been attributed, first of all, to the fact that the size of the net contribution was not large enough. While emphasis was on additional expenditures, taxes were increased. A combination of tax reduction and increased expenditures would probably have exerted a greater effect on purchasing power and business investment.

Reflecting upon the consequences a different policy might have had during the depression, one should not forget to take the mores of the time into consideration. The majority of the people demanded bold leadership and appreciated the pursuit of new types of policies. It is difficult to say, however, whether a still bolder policy would have frightened people and created a negative economic effect. Nevertheless, irrespective of what could have been done during the thirties, it is important to recognize now that the size of the *net* contribution of the government to purchasing power probably was not adequate to offset the strong deflationary tendency.

Perhaps even more important the policy of the depression period was not exclusively or mainly a recovery policy. Under the circumstances of the period it had to be a reform policy also. As such it antagonized large sectors of business and created a climate that was unfavorable to the resumption of business investment.

Finally, the business community did not expect the recovery policy to last very long. Before each election it expected a change in administration and basic policy and waited for a political change before embarking on economic expansion.[5]

4. The 1937–38 recession and revival offers excellent material for a study of fiscal policy. Extremely interesting is Marriner Eccles' dramatic story of these events in his memoirs, *Beckoning Frontiers* (New York, Knopf, 1951). A valuable analysis of the possible causal relationship between these events is given by Kenneth D. Roose in "The Role of Net Contribution to Income in the Recession and Revival of 1937–38," *Journal of Finance, 6,* No. 1 (March, 1951).

5. A comparison of the attitude of business during the recovery of the thirties with that during the recovery of late 1949 and early 1950 demonstrates dramatically

Thus it can be concluded from the experience of the thirties that an effective fiscal policy:

a) Must bring about changes in taxes and expenditures of sufficient size to restore purchasing power to the level at which business investments are forthcoming.

b) Must be coordinated with other nonfiscal policies in order to avoid self-defeating inconsistencies in policy.

c) Must be coordinated with state and local policy to prevent local policy from counteracting national policy.

d) Must be regarded as a policy that has such general popular support among various groups of the population that it can be expected to be continued in one form or another, irrespective of the party in power, as long as it is needed.

These are some of the lessons which can be learned from the experience of the depression of the thirties. In addition, the failure of the government-spending and deficit policy of the depression to lead to self-sustained prosperity gave rise to a discussion of the impact of a government stabilization policy on the federal debt. Under the pump-priming concept, the deficits incurred during the period of slackening private activities should be offset by surpluses during the subsequent periods of self-sustained prosperity. The budget could be balanced, if not each year, then over the cycle, that is, over a period of several years. In this case no permanent increase in the national debt would follow from the use of fiscal policy as a stabilization device.

The experience of the depression did not confirm this notion. Nevertheless, the failure of goverment deficits to initiate a period of renewed self-sustained prosperity suggested to Alvin Hansen [6] and others that fiscal policy had to serve not merely as a temporary anticyclical device but possibly had a more permanent active role to play in promoting economic conditions of steady growth.

In line with Keynes's theory, it was argued that the economy is in balance if total demand equals, and grows in proportion to, total potential supply using all available resources. People either directly purchase goods and services for their personal consumption or save. Net saving by individuals or corporate business offsets outlays for producers' goods

the influence of the "confidence" factor. The importance of this factor has been brought out in the *Fourth Annual Report to the President* by the Council of Economic Advisers, December, 1949.

6. Alvin Hansen, *Fiscal Policy and Business Cycles* (New York, Norton, 1941).

such as plant and equipment, tools, residential houses,[7] commercial buildings, and other investments. The economy is in balance on a high level of activity if the amounts persons and corporations wish to put aside as savings are equal to the amounts persons and corporations wish to use for investment. In that case the sum of direct consumer and indirect business demand is equal to the potential output, and the economy proceeds on a full employment level. Hansen maintains that there is at least the possibility that in a "mature" economy the amount people and business managers wish to save from full employment incomes and profits may be larger than the amounts they wish to invest—year in, year out—through additions to their plant and equipment, inventories, houses, or foreign investments. As long as that is the case we have the threat of a downdrift in economic activity.

Such a tendency of potential oversaving or underinvestment could be counteracted, for example, by tax legislation that curtails saving more than spending, or by public investment that supplements private investment. In order to be most effective some part of this public investment should be financed by government borrowing, so that the government would put into active use some of the nation's saving that is forthcoming at a high and rising level in income and profit.

This concept leaves at least the possibility that a compensatory fiscal policy may lead to a permanent increase in the absolute size of the national debt. According to Evsey Domar [8] and others this does not mean a necessarily increasing debt *burden*. The burden of the debt is determined by the interest rate charged and its relationship to taxable incomes. If private and public investment result in a steady expansion of productivity and income, the tax base grows more than the interest the government has to pay on the debt (particularly if a part of the new issues are placed with the central banking system at nominal interest rates). A moderate permanent net addition to the debt over the cycle, such as might be needed to balance the nation's saving and investment on a level of high and expanding activity, would not necessarily be a cause for alarm.

This debate was in full swing when the relatively limited spending programs for recovery gave way to the large-scale programs for defense

7. Construction of residential houses, as explained in Chapter 3, is regarded as investment and the use of the houses as a consumer service. It has been found statistically convenient to treat all residential housing as if it were built for rental purposes even though in the case of owner-occupied houses the landlord and the tenant are identical persons.

8. Evsey Domar, "The 'Burden of the Debt' and National Income," *American Economic Review*, 34 (December, 1944), 798–827.

and war spending. The issues were not solved but postponed for the time being; and the much-discussed depression debt was dwarfed by the huge increase in debt that resulted from the war.

2. World War II

While a concept of fiscal policy only gradually emerged from the experience of the depression, the financing of World War II was considered from the beginning in the light of its possible contribution to economic mobilization and stabilization.

At the beginning of the defense program the President recommended only moderate tax increases in order to permit an expansion of economic activities and absorption of unemployment. At the same time less essential public works and work relief were drastically reduced in order to channel employment into essential lines of industry.[9] With the stepping-up of the defense and war program, the President recommended a drastic tax program with sharper tax increases than Congress was ready to adopt.[10] The recommended tax increases, and particularly those that were enacted, could absorb only a part of the inflationary gap that had resulted from the creation of incomes far in excess of available goods left for civilian use.

Economic stabilization during the war had to rely largely on nonfiscal methods of control, particularly price and wage controls, allocations, and rationing. Tax increases, however, reduced the inflationary gap so that the task to be performed by nonfiscal stabilization devices became manageable.

Two main lessons were learned from the wartime experience with fiscal policy:

a) Some further increase in taxes, and particularly the use of compulsory saving, would have made the wartime stabilization more effective and would have reduced some of the postwar difficulties. Nevertheless, fiscal measures sufficient to accomplish stabilization with lesser use of nonfiscal controls would have had to be so drastic that the tax rates would probably have interfered with incentives to work.[11] It is

9. See the *Budget Message of the President,* January 3, 1941.

10. See the *Budget Messages of the President,* January, 1942, and the following years.

11. At very high tax levels the same tax measure may, on the one hand, absorb purchasing power and thereby have a deflationary effect and, on the other hand, impair incentives to produce or induce cost (e.g., wage) increases and thereby have a price-raising effect. Only a case-by-case analysis can determine the point at which the price-raising effect of a tax measure begins to outweigh the deflationary effect. It is not likely that this point of diminishing anti-inflationary effect of taxes was reached under the tax rates that were adopted in the United States during the

possible that a much more drastic tax policy would have been feasible only if a system of national service had been adopted so that there was less need to rely on income incentives.

Furthermore, fiscal policy alone would have been a very blunt instrument for curtailing the demand for scarce goods. In the light of the limited possibilities of shifting resources from one use to another, shortages in various products or services were very uneven. A carefully devised tax program could have curtailed various types of consumption in different degrees. Nevertheless, as serious wartime scarcities made it necessary to husband available resources and to channel them into the most urgent use, wartime fiscal policies had to be supplemented by nonfiscal measures of control such as allocations, rationing, price and wage controls.

b) The wartime experiences made it abundantly clear that it is important to consider changes not only in the net government contribution but also in the type of expenditures or taxes that are to be changed, and that direct as well as indirect effects of fiscal measures must be considered.

It was recognized, for instance, that taxes imposed on the masses of consumers would be most effective in limiting demand. Such tax increases, however, may make the pressure for wage increases irresistible, and these wage increases may nullify the fiscal effect of the tax increase. A compulsory saving program might have been more desirable in this respect than very drastic income or excise taxes imposed on people in the lower brackets. Curtailment of profits, on the other hand, did not have a very great direct effect on active demand but it had a restraining influence on wage demands. Even the moderate wage controls of the war period would hardly have been politically feasible without a drastic limitation of profits through taxation and renegotiation of war contracts.

Thus economic stabilization during the war required not only an increase in taxes and limitation of the budget deficit but a careful consideration of the direct and indirect effects of the specific tax devices that were used.

3. *The postwar period*

Most fiscal analysts who speculated about postwar problems during the war expected that, after a transitory period of postwar inflation, lack of purchasing power and deflation would again be our major problems.[12]

war. These problems are considered further by Carl Shoup in the chapter which follows.

12. I do not intend to discuss here the various errors in forecasting that were made. A few economists in this country and some foreign observers expected a de-

It has been suggested that the government's willingness to remove controls rapidly after the war and to discontinue the excess profits tax must be partly attributed to the erroneous expectation of a postwar depression.

The business advocates of decontrol and tax reduction, on the other hand, based their case not on an expected depression but argued that these measures would increase the incentives for more production and would combat inflation by increasing supplies. They grossly exaggerated the degree by which tax reduction and decontrol would stimulate production.

I believe that the decision to remove controls quickly was influenced more by the belief that it would be good politics to get rid of unpopular measures as rapidly as possible rather than pursue an antidepression or an anti-inflation policy.

Nevertheless, it is very likely that different fiscal policies would have been recommended if the growing international tension and the intensity and duration of postwar inflation had been correctly foreseen. The fact remains that erroneous forecasts were very detrimental to the cause of fiscal policy in the long run.

The administration began its systematic drive for new anti-inflation measures in 1947, after a tense world situation made it clear that the postwar reduction in defense expenditures could not be continued and that substantial programs for foreign economic and military aid would have to be adopted. What was actually accomplished was a delay in the adoption of further tax cuts until 1948.

For a short time very large surpluses of federal cash receipts over payments were achieved. The cash surplus in the calendar year 1947 amounted to almost $6 billion. During the first half of the calendar year 1948 it was running at an annual rate of $12.5 billion, but later in 1948 the surplus declined under the impact of the tax reduction granted through the Revenue Act of 1948 and the rising trend of federal expenditures. Under the impact of the recession in 1949 the surplus was transformed into deficits, which lasted until the outbreak of hostilities

---

pression to begin immediately after the end of major military operations. Most economists, however, expected a period of postwar inflation that would follow brief and temporary "frictional" unemployment immediately after demobilization and cancelation of war contracts. Postwar inflation has lasted longer than most economists expected. But it should be remembered that all statements about the probable postwar development were predicated on the assumption of a true peacetime budget and not on budgets that reflected high and increasing international tensions. See Michael Sapir, "Review of Economic Forecasts for the Transition Period," in *Studies in Income and Wealth* (New York, National Bureau of Economic Research, 1949), *11*.

in Korea stimulated economic activity and again created growing budget surpluses in the second half of the year 1950 and the first half of 1951.

The large cash surplus of the years 1947 and 1948 probably was one of the factors that helped to limit the inflationary pressure. More surprising is the fact that a surplus reaching at times an annual rate of more than $12 billion did not cause an actual contraction of the whole economy. If economists had been asked in previous years what the economic effect of even a temporary $12 billion budget surplus would be, most of them, I am sure, would have answered that it would throw the economy into a downward spiral. In explaining the relatively mild effect of this very large surplus, three facts ought to be considered:

a) The effectiveness of a budget surplus as an anti-inflationary device depends not only on the types of revenues that are being collected but also on the type of monetary and credit policy that is associated with the budget surplus. Actually, the credit policy of these years mitigated and partially offset the anti-inflationary effect of the budget surplus.[13] The anti-inflationary effect of fiscal and credit policies is also reduced when business is able to use liquid assets and retained profits for financing its expansion and working capital needs.

b) To the extent that the budget surplus resulted from the inflationary increase in incomes and profits, it mitigated the inflationary impact but could not reverse it.[14]

c) A budget surplus may be effective in absorbing excess purchasing power, but it is less effective in counteracting inflationary pressure that works through the wage-price spiral. The inflationary movement of the postwar years cannot be explained solely by the fact that large spending created excess purchasing power; the size of the inflationary price rise must be explained to some extent by the fact that an initial price rise induced wage demands and that the wage increases in turn were translated into further price increases, and so on. This process, it is true, could work only as long as money and credit resources were sufficient to support the rising price level. Nevertheless, fiscal policy is not an effective device for counteracting a wage-price spiral. The "inflationary bias" which may be characteristic of a high employment economy of the future is likely to operate largely from the cost and price rather than from the demand side. This possibility certainly limits the effectiveness of fiscal

13. I do not deal with the relationship between fiscal policy and monetary policy in detail in this essay, since it is the subject of Chapter 7. Recognition of the fact that credit policy in part offset the anti-inflationary effect of the budgetary surplus does not mean that another credit policy would have been feasible or desirable.

14. For further discussion of this point, see section III-5, below.

policy as a stabilization device and requires the use of other supplementary policies." [15]

d) The simplified concept of fiscal policy assumed that budgetary changes are the most powerful causal factors in economic development. Budgetary changes, however, are not only causes but also results of developments in the private economy. In the post-Korean period powerful inflationary pressure originated in the private sector of the economy,[16] resulting in budget surpluses. This effect was reinforced by the increase in taxes adopted promptly after the Korean outbreak. It appears likely that the budget surplus in 1950–51 has mitigated the inflationary pressure, but it was not powerful enough to prevent it. Nevertheless, the increase in taxes was probably one of the factors that aided in halting the inflationary price rise early in 1951.

Postwar experience also demonstrated that changes in the budgetary situation alone are not always a sufficient means for avoiding a recession. The government cash surplus declined from $12 to $3 billion (annual rate) from the first to the second half of the calendar year 1948.[17] This drastic change in the budgetary situation did not prevent the development of conditions which led to the recession in 1949. The change in the budgetary position was due in part to the reduction in income tax rates which largely affected taxpayers in the high income brackets and did not have a substantial impact either on mass consumption or business investment. To the extent that the decline in the cash surplus was due to an increase in government expenditures, it certainly added to the support of the economy and the mildness of the subsequent recession.

The recession of the first half of the year 1949 was characterized by a sharp decline in manufacturing production and a drastic change from inventory accumulation to inventory liquidation. Incomes and sales, however, dropped much less. The President, in his Midyear Economic Report of July, 1949, recognized the changes in the economic outlook that had taken place since his previous report of January, 1949. Recessionary forces had been developing, but it appeared likely that the sharp curtailment in orders and inventories without a corresponding decline in sales would lead to an early recovery without large-scale government

15. See Hearings on the January, 1950, *Economic Report of the President* before the Joint Committee on the Economic Report, January 17–20, 1950, p. 72.

16. It should be remembered, however, that the increase in consumer and business demand following the outbreak in Korea and the Chinese intervention took place in anticipation of rising defense expenditures and resulting shortages.

17. *Midyear Economic Report of the President*, July, 1949, p. 45.

interference. The President's fiscal recommendations were adapted to this analysis. He withdrew his earlier request for large tax increases and recommended a limited reduction in especially harmful excise taxes. Thus he accepted a budget deficit as an undesirable but unavoidable fact, pointing out that any attempt to balance the budget either by increasing taxes or slashing expenditure programs would aggravate the recessionary forces and might result in still larger deficits.

The President emphasized, on the other hand, that as long as economic activities were still high and market adjustments still had a chance of raising the level of activity, additional large-scale increases in government programs and large-scale tax reductions would be premature. However, government cash payments rose further, partly because of the "automatic" increase in transfer payments to farmers and the unemployed. At the same time the tax yield declined and cushioned the drop in disposable profits and incomes. The cash deficit in government (federal, state, and local) operations of $2.5 billion in 1949 and $3.4 billion in the first half of 1950 (annual rate) was probably not the sole or main factor, but it was at least a contributing factor in halting the decline and supporting the recovery movement. While the recovery movement did not restore a full employment level of national income up to the beginning of 1950, it can be assumed that the shift in the budget helped to mitigate the impact of the recession.

The role that fiscal and budgetary policies played in counteracting inflation and recession in the postwar period still remains to be analyzed in detail. What evidence we have permits, however, some tentative conclusions.

During the thirties it was thought by some economists that the government net contribution, which is essentially the cash deficit or cash surplus, was one of the main causal factors in the economy influencing the generation or contraction of purchasing power, but the experience of recent years has demonstrated that a surplus or deficit per se is not a factor sufficient to explain movements in aggregate incomes or in employment. An analysis of the nature of the changes in government transactions and in the private sectors of the economy is necessary before any conclusion can be drawn as to the causal relationship between changes in the government surplus or deficit and changes in the economy as a whole.

Government not only adds or deducts purchasing power in general but in specific ways affects personal incomes and expenditures, business profits and investments, and international transactions. Government activities may promote or impair dynamic processes developing in the private economy. Government policies, therefore, should be viewed in the light of all the factors which in their interplay make for a steadily growing economic life.

With respect to the dynamic influence of government programs the "program effect" and the "spending effect" should be distinguished. The program effect of a road program, for instance, refers to the effects of the new roads on costs of transportation of farm products or on the tourist trade and the automobile industry. The spending effect of the same program refers to the wages and profits created in the hands of construction workers and the construction industry and the secondary effects resulting from the spending of these wages and profits. Only the spending effect is usually referred to in fiscal policy considerations.

Moreover, changes may originate in consumer demand or business investments or international transactions, which in turn affect government budgets. Traffic between the public and the private sector of the economy moves not on a one-way but on a two-way street. In other words the effects of government budgets must be analyzed in the whole of the Nation's Economic Budget. Stating this prerequisite of effective fiscal policy is easier than pursuing it. Indeed, the interrelationship between public and private economic action is an area in which extensive further research is required.

Recent experience has suggested one final important lesson with respect to the idea of fiscal policy. The original prescription was simply that fiscal policy was to offset either a clearly inflationary or deflationary situation. Conditions, however, are not always of such a character that the conventional concepts of inflation and deflation can be used adequately to describe actual economic conditions or the economic outlook.

At the beginning of 1950, for instance, unemployment rose while economic conditions appeared to be almost booming. With the available resources, a considerably higher volume of goods and services could have been produced. Yet general economic conditions were not of a nature that suggested an antideflationary fiscal policy as a desirable remedy. There are situations which call for adjustments in prices and costs, and in the rate of investment and consumption, rather than for changes in fiscal policy. Such adjustments involve more than merely the absorption of or the addition to purchasing power as it is needed to compensate for inflationary or deflationary processes that are clearly under way.

At the beginning of 1950 the economy was in the process of shifting from a postwar catching-up boom to a sustainable peacetime prosperity pattern. But again the problem of the necessary long-run adjustment was postponed by the worsening of the international situation and the attack on South Korea. Again economic policy had to be oriented toward aiding a mobilization program and combating the threat of inflation. The problems of a deficiency in purchasing power moved further into the background and were overshadowed by those of allocation of resources to the most pressing needs. The urgency of defense procurement gave emphasis to a more general shift in the problem of the postwar era as compared with the depression and recovery period of the thirties. During the thirties, attention was focused on the actual or threatening lack of demand to match the increasing power to produce. Only gradually people began to realize the tremendous amount of production that would be needed to develop and conserve natural resources, modernize the productive plant of the nation, provide decent homes, and meet the demand of consumers that is forthcoming from a more nearly equal distribution of incomes. To this was added after the war the need to make a contribution to reconstruction abroad and to economic expansion in the underdeveloped areas of the world. The problem has been shifting from the creation of outlets for production to one of mobilizing productive resources and channeling output into the most urgent usages. While both these aspects of the problem may, to some extent, exist at the same time, the shift in emphasis from one to the other has important consequences for the task of fiscal policy.

4. Conclusion: a modified concept of fiscal policy

From fifteen years' experience with fiscal policy, the following conclusions can be drawn:

a) Fiscal policy, a combination of deliberate changes in expenditure programs, revenue and tax programs, and debt management policies, is well suited to aid in counteracting general inflationary or general deflationary tendencies.

b) The fiscal policy of the federal government must take into account, and must be coordinated with, the fiscal policies of state and local governments.

c) Fiscal and nonfiscal policies must be coordinated so that they complement each other and do not act at cross purposes.

d) Inflationary and deflationary tendencies may result from economic maladjustments in the price-wage-profit or investment-consumption relationship. A policy that is suitable to combat an inflationary or a deflationary movement may not remove the maladjustments that cause these movements. It is desirable to use fiscal and other policies to iron out the maladjustments before they lead to inflationary or deflationary movements.

e) If maladjustments have not been prevented in time and lead to inflationary or deflationary movements, then fiscal policies should be used at least as a temporary stabilizing device until more basic adjustment policies have been worked out. Fiscal policies are not adequate devices for combating the inflationary bias which may occur under a full employment policy.

f) The effectiveness of fiscal policy is increased when the community understands its working and has confidence in (and therefore anticipates) its results.

g) Fiscal policy must be related to the long-range requirements of allocation of resources to improvement in the standard of living, to expansion of the productive plant of the nation, to adequate defense needs, and to aid economic development abroad. Emphasis on each of these objectives varies, depending on the foremost needs of each period in the life of the nation.

There is no doubt that the task of fiscal policy, as indicated in these conclusions, is much more complex than is suggested by the simple formula proposed in "functional finance." Recognition of this complexity does not imply, however, that fiscal policy is unimportant. While sustained and steady growth of income and employment and a rational allocation of resources cannot be achieved through fiscal policy alone, it is equally true that these objectives can best be achieved with the aid of fiscal policy in a political and economic system that tries to give widest scope to individual responsibility and initiative and to minimize direct regulatory action of the government. The contribution that fiscal policy can make toward these objectives cannot be finally appraised before the budgetary procedures are examined through which fiscal policy must be realized.

II. The Federal Budget: The Evolution of an Institution

Budget principles and budget procedures were developed historically as a means for legislative control of government operations. They were designed more to check arbitrary use of funds than to promote effective implementation of government responsibilities.

Until 1921 the federal budget was determined exclusively by Congressional action based on uncoordinated submissions of estimated departmental requirements. Budget making was regarded as a Congressional prerogative. The whole history of Congressional efforts to control expenditures has been, as Lucius Wilmerding stated, "in large measure self-defeating." [18] It took a long period of bitter experiences and mounting federal expenditures before Congress was ready to recognize that an executive budget formulation was essential for efficient gov-

18. Lucius Wilmerding, *The Spending Power* (New Haven, Yale University Press, 1943).

ernment and that legislative control is ineffective unless it is based on effective executive control.[19]

1. *Establishment of an executive budget*

The development of the executive budget of the United States government is closely related to the spectacular rise in the size of the budget in recent decades. The Budget and Accounting Act was adopted in 1921 at a time when total federal expenditures had increased from approximately three-quarters of a billion dollars before World War I to around $5 billion. The drive to wind up wartime expenditures helped to overcome final resistance to the establishment of an executive budget in the federal government. The emphasis was on economy and efficiency.

The Budget and Accounting Act was designed to establish an effective executive scrutiny of departmental budget requirements before transmittal to the legislature. In order to increase incentives for economy and efficiency the act prescribed that expenditure and tax recommendations be combined in one document. If proposed expenditures were expected to exceed revenues under existing legislation, then the President was to make a specific recommendation either for additional taxes or for borrowing to cover the deficit. If, on the other hand, revenue under existing legislation was expected to exceed proposed expenditures, the President was to make specific recommendations whether taxes should be reduced or the surplus used for debt redemption or other purposes. It is significant that the requirement of the Budget and Accounting Act to include specific proposals with respect to revenue and debt policy has been neglected more often than followed. This requirement is essential for a coordinated fiscal policy.

The Budget and Accounting Act did not clearly define the place of the Bureau of the Budget in the executive establishment. It was established as an agent of the President but placed in the Treasury Department for housekeeping purposes. This lack of clarity impeded the effectiveness of the budget process as a device for policy coordination and for the formulation of fiscal policy.

2. *The budget as a management arm of the President*

The Reorganization Act of 1939 made the budgetary process a center of presidential coordination of the far-flung activities which are the responsibility of a growing number of departments and agencies. During the New Deal years federal cash expenditures had increased from

19. Harold D. Smith, "The Budget as an Instrument of Legislative Control and Executive Management," in *The Management of Your Government* (New York, McGraw-Hill, 1945).

a level of $3–4 billion to $8–9 billion. In 1929 total federal cash expenditures were 3½% of the national income; in 1938 they had increased to 12%. It was recognized that the federal budget had become one of the most important factors influencing the national economy. Yet recovery policies were largely treated as emergency measures, formulated outside the regular budget and appropriation procedures and adopted largely by lump-sum authorizations and appropriations.

Only in the latest phase of the New Deal period was the potential significance of budget and fiscal policy recognized. This change in attitude was dramatized by the transfer of the Bureau of the Budget to the Executive Office of the President and by giving it a number of functions which were related to top coordination but only indirectly related to the budget function proper. They included coordination of legislative proposals and statistical programs and administrative management. It is significant that shortly after the transfer of the Bureau of the Budget to the Executive Office a Division of Fiscal Analysis was established within the bureau with the function of analyzing the impact of budgetary operations, expenditure programs, tax programs, and debt management on the economy as a whole. During the war the Fiscal Division became instrumental in preparing programs for economic stabilization.[20] The coordination of fiscal policies was, however, far from effective, largely because the coordinating role of the Bureau of the Budget in relation to the Treasury Department was not generally recognized.[21]

The Budget Bureau's function of preparing the executive budget was supplemented by at least some control of *budget execution*. After appropriations have been enacted, the Budget Bureau establishes quarterly allotments of the appropriations and sets up reserves out of appropriations. Budget execution is still based largely on the Antideficiency Act of 1905, which was designed to assure that an agency stay within its authorized limits in incurring obligations. This act has been amended only recently in the General Appropriations Act of 1951 (Public Law

20. See *The United States at War*, pp. 250 ff., prepared under the auspices of the Committee of Records of War Administration, by the War Records Section, Bureau of the Budget, 1946.

21. The conflict is again demonstrated by the recommendations of the Commission on the Organization of the Executive Branch, February, 1949, as contrasted with the recommendations of the commission's own task force. The same conflict existed between the report on "Financial Control and Accountability," by A. E. Buck (*Fiscal Management in the National Government*, Pt. 1, The President's Committee on Administrative Management, No. 2 [U.S. Government Printing Office, 1937]) and the final recommendations of the President's Committee on Administrative Management (the Brownlow committee) that laid the groundwork for the Reorganization Act of 1939.

759, section 1211). In spite of attempts to develop a system of executive control, appropriations have been frequently considered as a "vested right," if not a mandate, of the agency to spend the money rather than as an authorization to be used under the supervision of the Chief Executive.[22] The system of allotments and reserves could be developed into an important instrument of fiscal policy, but it has been used for that purpose only in rare instances.[23] The provision in the General Appropria-

22. Harold D. Smith, *op. cit.*, pp. 90 ff.

23. At the beginning of the defense and war program during the years 1941 and 1942 and in subsequent years, an attempt was made to use the system of budgetary reserves for curtailing public works and work relief in order to adjust actual spending to rapidly changing conditions. One assertion of executive budgetary control is expressed, for instance, in the following statement by the President which he issued when approving the Flood Control Act on August 18, 1941: "In approving this bill I wish to make it clear that during the present emergency I do not intend to . . . approve allocations of funds for any project which does not have important value in the national defense." The right of the President to withhold funds from spending has been challenged repeatedly.

The clash between the interpretation of appropriations as a Congressional mandate to spend, on the one hand, and the responsibilities of budget execution, on the other hand, was dramatized in a hearing before the Subcommittee of the Senate Committee on Appropriations. The Budget Director, testifying before this subcommittee on February 18, 1944, said: "It is only a part, as I see it, of budget administration that we put on our books and have knowledge of money appropriated to an agency which the agency, because of war conditions or some other reason, cannot spend. For example, in connection with the CCC program, at the beginning of the war, the same issue arose. . . . We showed we were setting up funds according to a curve, which curve corresponds to the falling off in enrollment in the CCC camps, because of the initiation of the war and the defense program and the requirements for manpower." To which the chairman, Senator McKellar, replied: "Well, you admit it is a practice. . . . You are operating this practice absolutely without authorization of law. You are treating the Congress of the United States with absolute—not disrespect—but contempt when you undertake to say, after the Congress has made an appropriation of money and directed the executive officers what to do with it; when you come along and overrule the Congress and put it in a place where the executive officer whose duty it is to expend this money cannot expend it. You put yourself in the place of the Congress, Mr. Smith. I want to say with all due respect that you have no legal right, moral right, or any other right, to overturn the action of the Congress that has been approved by the President of the United States. . . ."

Mr. Smith: "Mr. Chairman, I would hesitate very much to have this record show, without any response from me, that I treated the Congress with contempt or that I am violating the law."

Senator McKellar: "You are doing both."

Mr. Smith: "I am sure this committee does not want us to countenance the expenditure of funds, even though appropriated, which would be wasted."

Senator McKellar: "You have no more authority in reference to appropriations that are made by the Congress, that the President has signed, and that our ad-

tions Act of 1951, mentioned above, should help greatly to clarify the powers and duties of budget execution.

Until 1945 government corporations represented a serious gap in the executive control of government operations. Government corporations performed not only quasi-commercial functions but to a considerable extent (and in some cases without clear reason) also some administrative functions. An important step toward completion of budgetary control was the adoption of the Government Corporation Control Act of 1945, which established "business-type budgets" for corporations wholly owned by the federal government. Inclusion of these operations in a comprehensive system of budgetary control is an important step toward the development of institutions for more effective fiscal policy.

The development of the budget from $8 to more than $40 billion, and of the Budget Bureau from an agency designed to screen departmental requests to a general management arm of the President, was associated with a rapid increase in the Budget Bureau personnel from about 100 employees in 1939 to more than 700 employees in 1946. Budget Bureau personnel has declined to about 500 employees in recent years in spite of the increase in the size of the federal budget.

The broader concept of the role of the budget as a monetary expression of the President's program as a whole, and as an important factor in the national economy, was also reflected in the Budget Messages of the President. Until 1939 most budget messages had been largely financial statements. Subsequently they became state documents in which the

---

ministrative officers have been directed as to what to use them for; you have no more authority over those appropriations than you have got over the man in the moon; not a particle."

Mr. Smith: "I think I am carrying out the law."

Senator McKellar: "You go on talking; and I do not think you mean to be disrespectful, but that is very disrespectful."

Mr. Smith: "I think it is important to realize where you have under the Anti-Deficiency Act a requirement that no department can run a deficiency, it is very necessary at times when we set up reserves to keep a department from running a deficiency. . . . We have in the main only used those reserves for the purpose of seeing that a department does not run into a deficiency. . . . When the war came along and materials were not available, enrollment in various programs such as the CCC, as I pointed out, fell off quickly. I am sure the Congress did not want that agency to spend money unnecessarily. We acted on behalf of the President in setting up these reserves, because under his general powers, he is responsible for the administration of all these appropriations acts passed by the Congress."

Explaining what a reserve is, Mr. Smith's assistant, Mr. Lawton, said: "That money is money that, because of various changes that may have taken place since the appropriations were made, will not be required to carry out the programs of those agencies during the current year. . . . That money reverts to the Treasury at the end of the second fiscal year after the close of the fiscal year."

President laid before Congress and the country the broad outlines of his national program in furtherance of the country's political, social, and economic objectives. This development reached a climax in January, 1946, when President Truman combined the State of the Union and the Budget messages in one document that dealt with his political, economic, and fiscal program as a whole.

Besides the Budget Bureau, The Reorganization Act of 1939 established the National Resources Planning Board in the Executive Office of the President. While the National Resources Planning Board prepared valuable studies in the field of resource development and fiscal and economic policies, the planning was not closely related to the operations of the government. It did not make itself an indispensable cog in the government machine.

When the board was terminated by Congressional action in August, 1943, the Budget Bureau's responsibilities as a main coordinating and programing arm of the President were further increased. On the other hand, there were created various wartime coordinating agencies such as the Office of Economic Stabilization and the Office of War Mobilization and Reconversion. As a matter of fact, the Budget Bureau's methods of quiet coordination had to be supplemented by a more dramatic organization and the appointment of individuals who would command a very high popular prestige for their task. It was obvious that during the war the budget lost some of its significance as an instrument of control. Specific targets such as the number of planes, ships, etc., and military strength were more important than dollar appropriations and estimates of expenditures as an expression of the war programs. Allocations of raw materials were more effective than budgetary controls in directing resources into the most desirable channels. But these competing wartime coordinating devices were regarded as a temporary affair. Whether similar instruments of direct coordination are needed in peacetime is a question examined by Thomas Emerson in Chapter 15.

3. The peacetime budget and the policy of economic stabilization

In any case it became clear during the early postwar years that the federal budget could be reduced drastically from the wartime peak, but that for a considerable time it would remain at a level several times higher than the prewar years. Budget expenditures, which exceeded $8 billion in 1939, amounted to $40 billion in the fiscal year 1949 and approximately $45 billion in the fiscal year 1951. They amounted to $66 billion in the fiscal year 1952 and, under plans available at this time, may rise above $75 billion in 1953 and $80 billion in 1954. The importance of budgetary decisions for the government, for the country, and to some extent for the world has been increased beyond expectations.

The postwar years brought two important organizational developments, namely, the establishment of the legislative budget through the Legislative Reorganization Act of 1946 and the establishment of a procedure for appraisal and formulation of economic programs through the Employment Act of 1946.

To some extent the establishment of a Joint Committee on the Legislative Budget was intended to complete the budgetary reform that was initiated by the Budget and Accounting Act of 1921 and the Reorganization Act of 1939.[24] Following adoption of the Budget and Accounting Act, Congress replaced the large number of independent appropriations committees by one committee in each house. However, there remained a lack of coordination among the subcommittees dealing with the various parts of the budget and between the appropriations committees on the one hand and the committees dealing with revenue on the other. These four committees were combined into a joint committee that was supposed to examine the President's budget with respect to expenditures, revenues, and debt transactions as a whole and to recommend to Congress ceilings for appropriations and expenditures. The Senate and House then were to incorporate their over-all budget ceilings in a concurrent resolution which was intended to serve as a guide for the work of the appropriations and finance committees.

This procedure did not work successfully during the first few years after its adoption. There was a technical difficulty arising from the fact that the act calls for a ceiling on *expenditures* while Congress acts on *appropriations*. Expenditures in any one year result in part from obligations which have been authorized by appropriations of previous years. More important than this technical difficulty, which could well be solved by considering the budget over a number of years, was a political difficulty.

During the first two years the intent to develop a procedure for legislative coordination was intermingled with the desire of the legislature to assert its own independence.[25] Obviously a committee of more than 100 members without an adequate staff is not in a position to re-do within a few days the work done by a large Budget Bureau staff in

24. See George B. Galloway, "Reform of the Federal Budget," Library of Congress, Legislative Reference Service, Public Affairs Bulletin 80, April, 1950.

25. See Jesse V. Burkhead's somewhat exaggerated statement in "Federal Budgetary Developments: 1947–48," *Public Administration Review*, 8 (Autumn, 1948), 269: "Certainly the whole Reorganization Act is shot through with a primitive philosophy of putting the Administration in its place."

several months of intensive work. Nevertheless, an examination of the budget as a whole, considering the expenditure as well as the revenue side, should certainly have a place in the legislative procedure. It should bring home to the legislators and the people the relationship between government programs on the one hand and the methods of paying for them on the other.[26] Yet the Legislative Reorganization Act of 1946 has not yet found a workable solution. It would be most unfortunate if the attempt to improve legislative consideration of the budget and its financing should be dropped because of the failure of this particular plan.

Another development deeply affecting the relationship between fiscal policy and budget procedure was the adoption of the Employment Act of 1946. This act stated that it should be a responsibility of the government to "utilize all its plans, functions, and resources for the purpose of creating and maintaining . . . conditions under which there will be afforded useful employment opportunities, including self-employment, for those able, willing, and seeking to work, and to promote maximum employment, production, and purchasing power." The act thereby established by statute a function of government which during the years of depression, recovery, and war had been recognized as a necessity even though no permanent agency was formally charged with the coordination of economic policies needed for that purpose. Throughout the Congressional debates on the "full employment bill," the great importance of fiscal policies in a policy of economic stabilization was recognized. Several legislators thought of combining the functions to be performed under the proposed full employment bill with those performed under the Budget and Accounting Act in an agency in the Executive Office of the President which would concern itself with the national economic budget as well as with the federal budget. Another group in Congress preferred the creation of an independent commission for economic stabilization.

As a compromise the Employment Act of 1946, as finally adopted, established the Council of Economic Advisers in the Executive Office of the President. It also established the Joint Committee on the Economic Report in Congress, to provide a general guide and coordination for the specific work of the various legislative committees on legislative proposals that have an impact on employment, production, and purchasing power. It was specifically intended that the recommendations of the Joint Committee on the Economic Report should serve as background

26. The proposals of the Committee for Economic Development in *Taxes and the Budget: A Program for Prosperity in a Free Economy* (New York, November, 1948) emphasize this important aspect of budgetary policies. See also *Tax and Expenditure Policy for 1949* (May, 1949) by the same organization.

for the Joint Committee on the Legislative Budget so that economic aspects could be taken into consideration. This phase of the plan is still in process of evolution. Perhaps it could be made to work better by combining the functions of the Joint Committee on the Legislative Budget with those of the Joint Committee on the Economic Report.

By combining both functions the difficulty of proper timing and proper staffing in connection with the work of these committees might perhaps be overcome. The task of the Joint Committee on the Economic Report requires in any case that it examine over-all fiscal policy as related to economic conditions. This committee is of a more manageable size and is perhaps better staffed for doing a coordinating job; it might become more effective if it is given additional responsibilities. Through the emphasis on the economic aspects of the budget, it could easily avoid any overlapping with the work to be done by the appropriations committees and their staffs. Quite in line with the functions given to the Joint Committee under the Employment Act, it could make its own deliberations and investigations more fruitful by maintaining closer relationship with the various legislative and appropriations committees. High-caliber members can be expected to devote their time to an advisory committee only if it functions as a responsible steering committee and if they can be certain that its advice will be given most serious consideration by the various legislative committees.

The Employment Act made it a responsibility of the President to report to Congress at least once a year, with the assistance of the council, 1) on the levels of employment, production, and purchasing power needed to accomplish the purposes of the act, 2) on current and foreseeable trends in order to detect whether they are likely to meet or fail to meet the required levels, and 3) on the economic program of the government, appraising the economic effects of existing programs and recommending changes in programs which are needed to accomplish the purposes of the act.

The duty to review and recommend programs that have an impact on employment, production, and purchasing power naturally included fiscal policies. In this respect the council obviously was given the responsibility of advising the President in addition to the responsibility vested in the Budget Bureau. Since both agencies are in the Executive Office of the President, it was possible to establish close and harmonious collaboration.

There are now three documents transmitted to Congress at the beginning of each session: 1) the traditional State of the Union Message, which presents to Congress the highlights of the President's foreign and domestic program; 2) the Economic Report, which details the President's economic program, based on an analysis of economic objectives and the economic outlook; and 3) the Budget Message, which has been developed toward a more detailed statement explaining and justifying the various specific government programs on the basis of a functional classification.

Even though there are now three separate documents, they are much better interrelated than were the State of the Union and Budget messages in former years. This has been accomplished not only through close cooperation between the Budget Bureau and the Council of Economic Advisers but also through the close cooperation of these agencies with the President's White House staff.

The development of the budgetary institutions was largely determined by the need to improve the means of legislative control and administrative coordination in the face of rapidly increasing expenditures and a growing complexity of the federal establishments. These developments, first of all, were designed to improve the budgetary process while, as Arthur Smithies stated, "the requirements of good budgeting are by no means identical with the requirements for a positive fiscal policy." [27]

Nevertheless, improved budget procedures, and particularly a system of controlled budget execution, make the consideration of fiscal policy aspects of the budget more feasible. The establishment of a Council of Economic Advisers in the Executive Office of the President and of a Joint Committee on the Economic Report in Congress has created institutional channels for consideration of these aspects. However, the establishment of these agencies in itself has not removed all of the basic difficulties of orienting budget policy toward the objective of economic stabilization. In the next section some of the conflicts between the idea of fiscal policy and the institutions of budgetary procedure will be discussed.

III. Implementing Fiscal Policy through the Budgetary Process

The idea of fiscal policy, as sketched in the first section, has a short-run and long-run aspect. In the short-run it is the adaptation of government expenditure, revenue, and debt policies to the task of offsetting fluctuations in private activities. In the long-run aspect it involves the use of the same policies for the purpose of promoting self-sustained growth of the economy, thereby reducing the instability that causes cyclical fluctuations. Fiscal policy as a cyclical compensating device and, even more, as a long-run stabilizing device must be supplemented by other means of economic policy. Fiscal policy must be realized largely through budg-

27. Arthur Smithies, *op. cit.*

etary procedures and budget policy must be related to the national economic objectives.

Budgetary procedures, as sketched in the preceding section, were developed largely as a means of legislative control and administrative management with little consideration for economics and specifically for cyclical variations. Improved legislative and administrative budget controls to some extent have made the budget procedure a more suitable instrument of fiscal policy. In some respects, however, the idea of fiscal policy clashes with other objectives of government policy that enter into budget-making and with the traditional manner in which budgets are determined and executed.

In this section there will be presented a survey of actual or apparent conflicts between fiscal considerations and other considerations that enter into the content and operation of the budget. Some suggestions will be offered for possible reconciliation of conflicting objectives and institutions. It must be recognized, however, that not all conflicts can be resolved and that the need to compromise between various objectives of policy will remain one of the characteristics of day-by-day fiscal operations.

1. *Conflict of objectives: economic versus noneconomic objectives*

The size of the federal budget and major changes in it are controlled largely by what we may term noneconomic programs of the government. All programs of the government have, of course, political, social, and economic aspects. The aspect of foreign policy is predominant, for instance, in programs for national security and foreign policy. These programs, though "noneconomic" in their origin and purpose, are obviously "economic" in their impact, and the determination of their size is of course not exempt from economic consideration. In the 1950 pre-Korean budget, for instance, four major programs of the government—national defense, international commitments, veterans' programs, and interest on the public debt—required almost three-fourths of the budget total. All other activities of the federal government devoted to social welfare, health, natural resources, including atomic energy, agriculture, transportation, communications, housing, education, labor, finance, commerce and industry, and the costs of general government absorbed about $12 billion or approximately one-fourth of the budget.[28]

The international situation forced the government to step up defense and foreign aid programs while private business was engaged in a post-

28. *Budget Message of the President for the Fiscal Year 1950*, January, 1949.

war investment boom. But obviously expenditures for purposes of foreign policy could not be delayed until the postwar boom began to peter out or until defense and foreign aid or veterans' programs could be fitted nicely into a compensatory fiscal policy. Obviously fiscal policy has to be adjusted to the necessity of these national objectives rather than having these national programs determined in a way that fits into a policy of economic stabilization.

Of course, it would be wrong to say that noneconomic government programs are or should be determined without any consideration of the economic situation. The determination of these programs must take account of the political urgency of these objectives on the one hand, and of the sacrifices that result from diverting resources from other uses on the other hand. This diversion can take the form of curtailing other government programs or of diverting resources from private use. Even before the aggression in Korea, the armed services believed that substantial increases in defense expenditures were desirable in the interest of national security. It was argued, however, that under conditions of virtually full employment a drastic increase in defense expenditures would have required a substantial curtailment of government expenditures not directly related to defense, or a substantial increase in taxes, and possibly the adoption of some direct price and wage controls and allocations to prevent more serious inflation.[29] While everybody agreed that no costs—in terms of money, curtailment of desirable peacetime programs or inconveniences of control—were too high to meet an actual emergency, balancing defense requirements and other objectives of government policy were believed necessary to meet a period of possibly prolonged international tension. No judgment is passed here on the question of whether economic considerations actually resulted in a curtailment of defense expenditure proposals, which proved unfortunate in the light of subsequent events. In any case it is absurd to contend that the increase in defense expenditures was initiated in order to forestall an otherwise unavoidable depression. What economic considerations there were, were all on the other side.

Another example is the formulation of the foreign aid program (Marshall Plan) in 1947. Before a final legislative recommendation was made, the President asked the Council of Economic Advisers to examine the

29. See Edwin G. Nourse, "Economic Implications of Military Preparedness," an address before the National Military Establishment Joint Orientation Conference, November 10, 1948, reprinted in *United States News and World Report*, 25 (December 10, 1948) and "The Impact of Military Preparedness on the Civilian Economy," an address before the same body on April 5, 1949, reprinted in *United States News and World Report*, 26 (April 15, 1949).

domestic repercussions of such a program, while other groups and agencies examined the needs of foreign countries and other aspects of the program. The council submitted such a report in October, 1947, pointing out the feasibility of a sizable foreign aid program but recommending monetary and selective direct controls which would be needed for its implementation.[30]

The fact that economic considerations must enter the deliberation of such noneconomic programs places a great responsibility on the economist. One danger results from the view which regards economic considerations as predominant and subordinates essential national objectives to an ironclad rule of "sound finance." [31] It would be equally wrong if noneconomic programs were determined without consideration of their fiscal impact. The fact that noneconomic programs may require a sustained effort over a considerable period of time, and depend more than ever on popular support, makes it imperative that the fiscal, economic, and social implications of such programs be fully considered in their determination.

2. *Conflict of short-range versus long-range economic policies*

A possible conflict of objectives exists not only with respect to economic versus noneconomic objectives but also within the field of economic objectives itself. During the postwar years the federal government deferred many public works and social programs although there was no question about their long-range desirability. The longer the postwar boom lasted and the longer the policy of deferment was continued the more voices were heard which questioned that policy. It has been pointed out that it would be absurd to defer, for instance, urgently needed school buildings while building materials are being used for commercial construction of lesser social urgency. Similarly, it would be absurd to defer construction of hydroelectric power facilities if a real power shortage is a bottleneck in the expansion of needed supplies such as aluminum.

30. *The Impact of Foreign Aid upon the Domestic Economy,* a report to the President by the Council of Economic Advisers, October, 1947.

31. Against this view was directed President Roosevelt's statement in the Budget Message of January, 1942, four weeks after Pearl Harbor: "There need be no fiscal barrier to our war effort and victory." Perhaps it may be useful not to forget that Hitler's initial success in Europe was greatly aided by a "conservative" financial philosophy of the democratic countries of western Europe during the thirties. Adequate defense preparation was directly hampered in these countries by fear of budget deficits—during the depression. The Nazi's own war preparations were not taken seriously enough because the leading statesmen of the democratic countries were told by financial experts that the "unsound" methods of Nazi finance were bound to result in an early collapse.

As a matter of fact, during the period of postwar inflation public works of state and local governments and some of the most urgent federal projects were initiated in spite of the general policy of deferment. A strict fiscal policy of deferment of all public works in periods of full activity implies the belief that private activities in principle have priority over all government economic and social programs; in accord with that philosophy, government programs would be undertaken only when private activities were not using all available resources. It would be absurd to argue that the people must wait for a depression before they can obtain urgently needed services of public undertakings. Many economic and social programs of the government obviously do not belong in the category of deferrable demand. The decision as to which public undertakings should be deferred in a period of high business activity must take into consideration the social and economic urgency of the various projects. The fact that not all public works can be regarded as deferrable per se limits the variability of government expenditures.

The urgency of needed public works and the desirability of postponing them were in especially serious conflict in the postwar years. Once the public works deferred during the war have been completed and the most urgent demands have been met, the conflict between short-range and long-range economic objectives will become somewhat less troublesome.

Besides the existence of high priority public works and other local developmental programs which have been deferred, the standard of relative usefulness in itself is subject to change. It is obvious that at a time when idle resources are available programs become desirable which were regarded as deferrable in a period of full employment. This principle appears sensible not only in the interest of economic stabilization but also from the point of view of reasonable financial management. Resources are expensive in terms of social accounting as well as in terms of actual prices when they must be bid away from private use. They are inexpensive in slack periods. Many public works, such as irrigation projects, are managed on a self-supporting basis. They are supposed to be financed, at least partly, by farmers through payments of fees for water use. Fees computed on the basis of construction at peak prices may be prohibitive; if constructed at somewhat lower prices they may be tolerable. Even though market prices and costs should not be the determining factor in public activities, they partly reflect the relationship between benefits and economic costs and to that extent should be taken into consideration.

The contention that sound policy precludes a cyclical variation in expenditure programs (except for so-called "built-in flexibilities" to be discussed later) cannot be maintained on theoretical or practical grounds.[32] Even if expenditure programs were to be determined strictly by their social benefits in relation to economic costs, they would have to be varied because that relationship itself is not independent of the business situation.

In practical political terms the reconciliation between short-run and long-run objectives of economic and social policy does not appear impossible. In a dynamic society there will always be desirable new economic and social programs, or an expansion of existing programs, in the discussion stage. In prosperous times there should certainly be no absolute embargo against the adoption and expansion of economically and socially urgent government programs. Under conditions of full employment, the merits of additional programs must be such that they are clearly preferred to private programs with which they may compete for labor and material. They also require financing by additional taxes designed so as to work as an effective brake on private activity. Under depressed conditions, the tempo in the adoption of needed programs can be speeded up. Their relative costs then are lower, measured in terms of government cost accounting, tax burdens, and social accounting. It may be difficult to accomplish an expansion and contraction in government expenditures depending on the ups and downs in private activities. There is, however, such a large backlog of highly desirable improvement programs that it is feasible to plan for faster progress in periods of slackening business conditions and to hold to a somewhat slower progress as long as business activity remains high. In the postwar years we had a tremendous backlog of work to be done in housing and urban redevelopment, in transportation, educational and health facilities, and the development and conservation of national resources. Only very inadequate progress has been made on these programs during the postwar inflation. The rearmament program again forced postponement of many desirable projects. They can be developed as soon as we have passed the peak of defense preparations, serving short-run requirements by pursuing long-run needs.[33]

Only if desirable and needed programs are prepared in advance and ready for adoption will an administration be able to resist the demand for less desirable emergency programs in case of a depression. There

32. An uncompromising suggestion in this respect was made by Milton Friedman, "A Monetary and Fiscal Framework for Economic Stability," *American Economic Review*, 38 (June, 1948). The position of the Committee for Economic Development is less extreme but tends in the same direction; see *Taxes and the Budget, op. cit.*, and *Monetary and Fiscal Policy for Greater Economic Stability* (New York, December, 1948.)

33. See the *Midyear Economic Report of the President*, July, 1952, pp. 118 f.

is the danger that in case of a depression pressure for all kinds of payments will develop. It is true that for the immediate impact on demand a quick outpouring of money is more important than a careful selection of projects. For the long-run effect, however, it is very important that additions to expenditures be truly productive. If they add to productivity and thereby to the future tax base, they will be self-liquidating in the broadest sense of the term.

3. *Conflict of short-range versus long-range tax policies*

Every argument which limits the use of short-run variations in the rate of government expenditures becomes an argument for exploring the desirability of short-run variations in tax policy for purposes of economic stabilization. In this area too we run into a conflict of objectives.[34]

Some statements made by A. P. Lerner and Beardsley Ruml have suggested that it is the main purpose of a national tax policy to regulate the flow of purchasing power. Taxes should be low enough to permit the purchase of everything that can be produced and high enough to prevent inflation.[35] If that were the sole or the main purpose of taxes, then our tax system and, even more, our tax ideals should be basically revised. Then the most effective taxes would be those that have the greatest direct bearing on consumption because their reduction would free purchasing power and their increase would absorb purchasing power much more effectively than any change in progressive taxes. There would really be no ground for maintaining progressive taxes in the tax system.

Obviously, tax policy, no less than expenditure policy, must consider other long-run economic and social objectives as well as price stabilization. A wartime experience may be mentioned to illustrate a possible conflict between these objectives. When an anti-inflationary fiscal program was under discussion during the war, a modified sales tax was suggested for consideration. The tax proposal was devised so that the

34. The revenue side of the budget is not discussed in any detail because of the treatment of tax policy in Chapter 6.

35. See, for example, A. P. Lerner, *Economics of Control* (New York, Macmillan, 1944), ch. 24. Reference is made to Lerner because the position he takes in the work referred to is the most uncompromising and therefore particularly suitable for an argument about the principles. See also various statements by Beardsley Ruml, such as, ". . . our taxes should be as low as they possibly can be without putting the value of our money in danger of inflation." National Tax Association, *Proceedings of the 37th Annual Conference* (1944), p. 167. Both authors have recognized other specific purposes of taxation and the need for nonbudgetary devices for stabilization.

buyer could obtain refunds in bonds or cash on a per capita minimum of taxable purchases. Such exemption was believed necessary for reasons of equity and in order to reduce the effect of the tax on wage demands which would have nullified much of its anti-inflationary impact. Nevertheless, the proposal was turned down because of the opinion that a sales tax once admitted to the family of respectable federal taxes would probably be retained even at a time when the specific fiscal argument was no longer applicable.

In expenditure and tax policy those measures are best that reconcile the requirements of both short-run and long-run policy objectives.

4. Conflict in jurisdiction: federal versus state and local programs

One of the definite lessons to be derived from the experience of the great depression and the war and postwar period is that an effective fiscal policy cannot be limited to the operations of the federal government alone.

State and local financial policies tend to aggravate rather than to counteract cyclical fluctuations. During the depression state and local governments were forced to curtail expenditures and to raise tax rates. One scheme after another was devised to aid state and local undertakings—with only partial success and much criticism. Without the various aid programs curtailment of state and local services would have been much more drastic.

During the war ample revenues and the limitations on spending (because of physical restrictions) created budgetary surpluses and temptations to reduce tax rates. Tax reductions could be kept within limits because many governors and state legislatures responded to the appeal for voluntary state cooperation in the national anti-inflation program. After the war, when the appeal to cooperate in a national program of anti-inflationary fiscal policy was less effective, state and local bodies rapidly spent much of their wartime surpluses and contributed substantially to the inflationary pressure. The absence of federal-state-local coordinating machinery constitutes one of the most serious limitations on an effective national fiscal policy.

A possible step toward such coordination might consist in the establishment of flexible grants-in-aid. The federal government pays about $2.5 billion per year to state and local governments in the form of grants for a variety of purposes. That is about 6% of the federal budget but almost 15% of state and local receipts.

An element of flexibility could be introduced into the federal-state-local relationship if the federal government were to contribute a lower percentage of state-local outlays as grants for specific programs in booms and a higher percentage in depressions.[36] Although such flexibility provisions may not be feasible in the case of all programs, they do appear feasible in some and could at least contribute to the prevention of cyclically "perverse" fluctuations in state-local spending. Beyond that, at least in the case of some programs, such provisions might induce countercyclical timing of expenditures even at the state and local level.

Flexible grants-in-aid for state and local public works might be a useful instrument for building up a "shelf" of state and local public works projects. The trouble with a shelf of public works is that as soon as worthwhile projects are prepared in blueprints, local pressures become active urging their immediate execution, irrespective of the business situation. An incentive for a more reasonable policy could be created if the federal government would pay nothing or merely make a nominal contribution to such projects when undertaken in times of prosperity, but a larger percentage contribution when conditions are less favorable. Such flexible grants for public works may aid in developing the kind of national public works policy embracing all levels of government recommended by Dahl and Lindblom in Chapter 8.

5. Conflict in procedures: requirements of legislative control versus the need for flexibility of government expenditures

The budget procedure was developed, as pointed out above, as a means of legislative control of government operations. The legislative machinery with its committee setup and public hearings is not designed for quick action except in cases of obvious emergency. Appropriation and tax legislation must usually be initiated a considerable time before the expenditures are to be made or tax changes become effective. For stabilization purposes, on the other hand, it is necessary that fiscal policy be adaptable quickly to short-run changes in the economic situation.

From the point of view of fiscal policy, it would be most desirable if the executive branch were given the authority to change the rate of expenditures within given statutory limits in the same manner in which the Federal Reserve System, for instance, is authorized to change reserve requirements within certain limits. Such delegation of authority obviously must be reconciled with the purpose of legislative control. A workable democracy requires that both the legislature and the executive share in the responsibility for stabilization policy. Thus some reconciliation

36. See the Report of the Joint Committee on the Economic Report, March, 1949, pp. 37–38. For a detailed discussion see James A. Maxwell, *Federal Grants and the Business Cycle* (New York, National Bureau of Economic Research, 1952).

between the objectives of fiscal flexibility and of legislative control must be worked out.[37]

The so-called built-in flexibilities achieve this purpose to some extent. An example is the unemployment insurance program which provides by law that disbursements must be made to those who have a rightful claim. Since these payments are made out of trust accounts no problem of appropriation is involved as long as the fund is not exhausted. Payments rise and fall automatically with the rise and fall in unemployment. Built-in flexibility also exists, though with somewhat less automatism, where basic legislation requires periodic appropriations to implement it. If prices for farm products fall rapidly and remain low over a considerable period of time, authorizations or appropriations will be needed to permit payments under farm price support legislation. Congress is usually prompt in appropriating money that is necessary to meet clearly defined legislative commitments.

We have in our present government machinery many more built-in flexibilities than we had at the end of the twenties. Thus we have cushions today which we did not have at the beginning of the last depression.

Several students of fiscal policy who are concerned with the conflict between the requirements of legislative control and the need for flexibility see the solution of the problem in exclusive reliance on such built-in flexibility.[38] Built-in flexibility has a special appeal because it seems to accomplish the job of a compensatory fiscal policy without the need for special legislation or the delegation of authority to the executive. Advocates of this theory argue as follows: If business activity shrinks, tax yields diminish and certain spending programs are stepped up automatically. Thereby a government cash deficit is created. If the cash deficit is financed by bank borrowing, it may create an inflationary (or reflationary) force that tends to restore a high employment level. The opposite is true with respect to a budget surplus that is the automatic result of inflation. It leads to the possibility of debt redemption and credit contraction. Built-in flexibility should achieve stability if mere

37. See G. L. Bach, "Monetary-Fiscal Policy Reconsidered," *Journal of Political Economy,* 57, No. 5 (October, 1949), p. 387: "But to assume congressional renunciation of direct control over the power to tax and the power to spend, except possibly for some delegation of authority over timing of prearranged programs, appears to have little relevance to reality. Formulation of a workable monetary-fiscal policy must recognize the stubborn fact of congressional prerogatives."

38. See Milton Friedman, *op. cit.;* Committee for Economic Development, *Taxes and the Budget, op. cit.;* G. L. Bach, *op. cit.* Built-in flexibility should be distinguished from the "formula" flexibility for tax rates that will be discussed below.

changes in the potential money supply are sufficient to regulate economic activities. Those who doubt the effectiveness of changes in potential money supply will assign to built-in flexibility only a somewhat more modest role. They will contend that a mere passive response of government operations to changes in the private economy will mitigate the change but cannot possibly reverse its direction. A deficit that *results* from a drop in income acts as a cushion but cannot turn the drop into a rise.[39]

Unemployment compensation restores only a fraction of the normal earnings of a worker. It reduces the income loss due to unemployment. Farm price support gives the farmer less than prosperous markets for farm products but reduces the impact on income of farm surplus production. Built-in flexibilities in themselves, therefore, cannot be relied upon exclusively to stop a deflationary spiral and restore full employment. They mitigate a drop in incomes but must be supplemented in case of need by legislative or administrative flexibility which will permit an affirmative variation of expenditure or tax programs.

A possible way of reconciling the goal of legislative control with that of executive discretion would be to distinguish three types of expenditures in the budget. One type would include current operations of the government for which appropriations would be made on a strictly annual basis.

A second type of expenditure would be for public works and economic development. Appropriations for these purposes would be made, let us say, on a five-year basis, with executive discretion to vary the speed of program execution in line with economic requirements. In order to preserve the desirable legislative controls, it could be provided that the program be subject to annual legislative consideration for the subsequent five years, and that each year the President should report if actual obligations or expenditures in any one year fall considerably short of or considerably exceed the obligations or expenditures which were scheduled for that particular year under the five-year program.[40]

---

39. A deficit that follows from a drop in incomes and tax yield has been called a *maintenance* deficit, which is distinguished from a *stimulating* deficit. See G. Colm and F. Lehman, *op. cit.* For a critical discussion of the Committee for Economic Development proposal, see Alvin Hansen, *Monetary Theory and Fiscal Policy* (New York, McGraw-Hill, 1949), pp. 175–183. See also "Federal Expenditure and Revenue Policies," Hearings before the Joint Committee on the Economic Report, 81st Congress, 1st Session, September 23, 1949, p. 9.

40. See Harold D. Smith, *op. cit.*, pp. 96 ff. See also Gerhard Colm, "Comment on Extraordinary Budgets," *Social Research*, 5 (May, 1938), 168 ff. Of interest is the provision in the Housing Act of 1949 which authorizes a six-year program of 810,000 units of public low-cost housing, or 135,000 a year, but permits the Presi-

In a third type of expenditures, the quasi-commercial outlays of government corporations, the greatest degree of administrative discretion should be permitted. Like the Reconstruction Finance Corporation or the Tennessee Valley Authority, they should be authorized to adapt their activities promptly to changes in economic conditions. While these agencies should be free of too specific legislative direction, they should be geared into a national development and stabilization program. It has been the experience in many countries that the directors of government corporations often want to be "masters in their own houses" just as much if not more than directors in private corporations. In other words the activities of government corporations must effectively be made subject to executive control, without depriving "business-type" operations of the government of the desirable flexibility. The Government Corporation Control Act of 1945, to which reference has been made above, is a step in that direction. Proposing different rules for the appropriation procedure concerning these different types of expenditure programs is not intended to suggest breaking down the budget in three separate parts.

6. *Conflict in procedure: requirements of legislative control versus the need for flexibility in government revenues*

As Carl Shoup devotes the next chapter to the role of taxation in economic stabilization policy, only a short comment on flexibility in tax policy will be made here.[41]

Recently, proposals have been made to introduce formula flexibility into the tax system by providing for changes in tax rates when an index of production or unemployment (or any combination of indices) indicates that a substantial change in economic activities has taken place.[42]

While very good arguments in favor of formula flexibility have been advanced, there are probably more valid reasons against adoption of that plan under present circumstances. First of all, we know too little about what kind and amount of tax change would be called for when unemployment has reached a certain point. Much more fiscal policy by trial and error will be needed before we are ready to crystallize a definite scheme of flexibility in legislation.

---

dent, after receiving advice from the Council of Economic Advisers, to vary the number of starts for any of the six years to between 50,000 and 200,000. Even though this provision had no practical consequence, it may well be regarded as a significant landmark in economic legislation.

41. See also G. Colm, "Full Employment through Tax Policy?" *Social Research,* *18* (November, 1940).

42. See "Federal Expenditure and Revenue Policies," Hearings before the Joint Committee on the Economic Report, *op. cit.*, and *National and International Measures for Full Employment, op. cit.*

Second, legislation must consider a variety of objectives and, depending on the particular circumstances, different tax measures may be needed in conditions which appear statistically similar. Formula flexibility may not be flexible enough.

Third, formula flexibility assumes that short-run changes in tax rates can be entirely separated from the changes which are in the long-range interest in an improved tax system. If a situation calls for tax reductions, those will be most desirable which will aid in the immediate situation and at the same time be justified as a long-run improvement of the tax system.

Finally, legislative prerogative with respect to tax legislation is even more sacrosanct than with respect to the power of the purse.

The case may be somewhat different with respect to payroll contributions. They are not regarded as part of the general revenue and are appropriated to special social insurance funds. If the present recommendations for an extended social insurance system are adopted, payroll taxes will increase within a few years to an aggregate of about 10–12%. A variation in this percentage could have a very significant economic effect. There may be fewer objections to an administrative flexibility in social insurance contributions paid into trust accounts than in general taxes. Increases in social insurance contribution schedules by legislation in the past have been repeatedly "frozen" by legislation on short notice, and Congress has recognized that possible future deficits in the funds must be met by appropriations from general Treasury funds. It is perhaps significant that the wartime coalition government in Great Britain also identified social insurance contributions as the most suitable instrument of a flexible tax policy. Still, such variations in social security rates can at best make a moderate contribution to a stabilization policy.

If a delegation of power to vary the rates of either taxes or social insurance contributions, with or without a formula, does not appear acceptable, it is not entirely unrealistic to envisage simplified legislative procedures for enactment of specified changes within a short time. On request of the President, or on its own initiative, the Joint Committee on the Economic Report could, for instance, be authorized to recommend temporary changes in tax rates for purposes of an anticyclical policy. In this case a representative of the Joint Committee might testify before the Ways and Means and Senate Finance Committees and the hearings could be limited to a minimum. The legislation might provide that the changes would be for a specified limited period. If changes were intended to become permanent, the limiting clause would have to be eliminated by ordinary legislation, presumably after hearings which would be more detailed and extensive than those held under the simplified procedure.

I believe that neither built-in flexibility, nor formula flexibility, nor delegated flexibility can be the full answer to a cyclical tax policy. To a large extent we must depend on improvements in the normal procedures of tax legislation and on a much closer cooperation of the executive and legislative branches in economic stabilization policy.

7. *Conflict in procedure: mechanism of budget making versus the need for flexibility*

One specific difficulty with a cyclical consideration of expenditure policy follows not so much from the conflict with legislative control as from the sheer mechanical requirements of budget making. On what assumptions with respect to economic developments should the budget requests of the various agencies be prepared?

With the Call for Estimates, a policy letter formulated by the budget director is sent to the agency telling them by what assumptions they should be guided in preparing their requests for the ensuing year. These assumptions must be formulated more than two years before the end of the period for which the estimates are prepared. The attempt to base the budgetary requirements on anything like a realistic economic forecast seems to be utterly impossible. First, we do not now have, and I doubt that we ever will have, the ability to make a reasonable forecast which covers a period two years hence, for reasons discussed by Everett Hagen in Chapter 4.

Second, even if forecasts were more reliable than they are it would be difficult to base the budget preparation on them. Budget preparations, for instance, for the fiscal year ending in June, 1955, begin in the spring of 1953. Let us assume, for discussion's sake, that at that time experts expect that business conditions are likely to decline so that at least for part of the fiscal year 1955 depressed conditions should be assumed. Such a "forecast" can only mean that the experts expect a business contraction under the assumption that current government policies continue and that no effective stabilization program of the government is initiated. Under the Employment Act the President would have to make recommendations to Congress to counteract a depression as soon as such a forecast can reliably be made. Assuming the government initiates such counteraction in time, the outlook for the fiscal year 1955 would appear quite different. The downward tendency may be halted or reversed, depending on the promptness and effectiveness of the program. In any case basing the budget preparation on the assumption of a depression in the next fiscal year for purposes of the formulation of departmental requirements would really imply failure on the part of the President or the Congress to take effective measures to forestall or counteract an anticipated depression.

Therefore it appears preferable that the budget as a whole should always be prepared under the assumption of approximately full employment. This budget would show expenditures and revenues, disregarding the effects of a possible business recession. For programs which would be initiated or increased immediately if business should begin to slacken, a contingency appropriation should be requested so that a minor fluctuation does not make it necessary to ask for a deficiency appropriation. This contingency reserve should, however, be impounded, to be released only by specific presidential action. This would make it unnecessary to base the budgetary requirements on any specific forecast, but would make funds available to the President which would be needed in case of a mild depression. In case of a severe depression, however, the President would have to submit to Congress a supplementary or deficiency request for funds for additional programs along with other recommendations for economic and fiscal policies as they would be formulated under the Employment Act.

It is important for Congress and the public to recognize clearly the basis on which budgets are formulated. If a hypothetical full employment basis is used, later revisions may not be due to erroneous estimates but to a discrepancy between assumed and actual events. The budget should be thought of less as a forecast than as a working plan which is designed as the basis for later adaptation to unfolding economic conditions.

8. *Conflict in accounting*

The conduct of fiscal policy requires different accounting guides from those needed for program formulation and program control.

Program formulation requires estimates of costs for a program as a whole. For deciding whether a program is worth undertaking, and especially for comparing various alternative programs which are under construction, true cost estimates are essential and, as far as possible, appraisals of the benefits to be derived from the program. If, for instance, construction of a dam is under consideration, estimates of the costs and benefits of the whole project are more essential than an estimate of expenditures which would have to be made in the first year.

Program control requires statements which relate the legislative authorization to appropriations, obligations, and actual expenditures. These statements permit a review of the legality of a government activity, of the progress made in its execution, and of the unobligated appropriations and unliquidated obligations (which are factors to be considered in computing the need for new appropriations and for estimating future expenditures).

Financial planning requires estimates of cash expenditures and cash receipts which have an impact on cash balances of the Treasury, and the need to borrow and the possibility of redeeming outstanding indebtedness.

The data developed for program formulation and program control must be adjusted before they can be used as guides for financial planning. While appropriations and obligations for expenditures and tax liabilities are most important for program formulation and program control, financial planning must be based on cash expenditures and cash receipts. Furthermore, accounting according to administrative organizations may very often lead to double counting. Money may be appropriated to trust accounts and reported as budget expenditures or as a reduction from gross receipts.[43] On the other hand, the trust accounts reflect disbursements of these accounts to recipients. The purpose of this administrative accounting is control and supervision. Adding up these administrative accounts does not necessarily give any meaningful totals. Meaningful totals are needed, however, for financial and fiscal planning.

For financial planning, therefore, statements are needed which 1) reflect only cash transactions, 2) include disbursements of all the various government accounts, including accounts of government corporations and trust funds, and 3) eliminate transfers from one government account to another. Such estimates have been called the *consolidated cash statement*. This statement presents meaningful totals.

The consolidated cash statement is not only an instrument for financial planning but also for *fiscal policy*. Fiscal policy views the government budget as an aid in balancing the nation's economic budget. Fiscal policy considerations, therefore, require new concepts and new classifications in government and national economic accounting. Statements are needed for past, current, and future periods that portray the relationship between the government accounts and the national income and expenditure accounts. We must know what money is being spent in a way that adds to the funds available to individuals, businesses, state and local governments, or foreign countries, and what revenue is received through absorption of funds from the same groups.

Traditional budget accounting was developed as a tool for program

43. Most receipts from payroll taxes are directly appropriated to the social insurance funds and appear in the budget as a deduction from gross receipts rather than as expenditures.

control, program formulation, and financial planning. One cannot say that the budget for the United States has been clearly devised to serve any one of these purposes. It includes cash and noncash transactions, disbursements to the public, and internal transfers.

The various purposes of government accounting should be more clearly distinguished. We need cost data for program appraisal; we need data for purposes of budget control; we need data for financial planning and fiscal policy. No one set of figures can serve all these purposes. The consolidated cash budget and the nation's economic budget were designed for purposes of financial planning and for guidance of fiscal policy.

Fiscal policy requires not only the development of appropiate totals of budget transactions but also of suitable classifications. With respect to new classifications, the requirements of fiscal policy reinforce the need for a classification by character of expenditure. Such a classification distinguishes between expenditures for current operations and those expenditures which are of an investment nature and hence represent benefits which will be realized in future periods.[44] Furthermore, the fiscal analyst needs expenditures classified according to type of goods and services which are bought (object classification) and also a classification by type of recipients of the money paid out.[45]

The conflict between the conventional accounts and the accounts needed for fiscal policy can be reconciled because the same basic data can be processed in different ways so as to supply various statements each serving its own purpose.

9. The human conflict

Perhaps the hardest conflict resides in the fact that the job of conventional budget determination and of fiscal policy requires different attitudes. The people whose job it is to screen budgetary requests and

44. For an example of such a classification see the *Budget of the United State Government for the Fiscal Year 1952*, pp. 969 ff. For a corresponding discussion related to Great Britain see J. R. Hicks, *The Problem of Budgetary Reform* (Oxford Clarendon Press, 1948). Hicks deals especially with the problems of accounting for nationalized economic activities in Great Britain. They are of lesser importance in this country, but some corresponding problems exist with respect to, for instance the Post Office Department, Tennessee Valley Authority, and other agencies with quasi-commercial activities. For a full discussion of the policy use of national economic accounting in various countries, see *Income and Wealth*, Series I, Erik Lundberg, ed., International Association for Research in Income and Wealth (Cambridge England, Bowes & Bowes, 1951).

45. As a sample of classification of expenditures by type of recipient, see Table A-8 in the *Midyear Economic Report of the President*, July, 1952, p. 134 f.

determine either budgetary recommendations or Congressional appropriations must be in a frame of mind which is quite different from that of those who can be most effective in the formulation and determination of fiscal policies. The legislator who has the job of examining budgetary requests usually assumes that the agencies are asking for too much. They know by experience that a good executive who is devoted to his task wants to do the best possible job, and the best possible job requires money. He wants efficiency, too, but he usually wants efficiency not in order to reduce the amount of money needed but to do a better job with the same amount.

Thus the legislator feels called upon to counteract this natural drive toward expansion. Of course there is also the tendency that legislators want more money appropriated for purposes in which their constituents are particularly interested. But the expenditures in which a legislator has a particular interest need not be the same as those for which the executive is making his request.

The same is largely true with respect to an efficient screening of budgetary requests on the executive side. True, the Budget Bureau is an important management arm of the President and wants to see that the President's program is implemented by budgetary allowances. The late Budget Director, Harold D. Smith, often emphasized that he no longer regarded it as the main function of the budget director to act as the "watchdog of the Treasury," but that he felt the budget director is responsible for implementing the President's program in the most efficient and economical manner. Nevertheless, a comparison between agency requests and final budget recommendations shows that the Budget Bureau has continued to perform its watchdog functions effectively. Budget examiners by the very nature of their job must adopt a critical attitude toward budgetary requests and often regard the amount of dollars they are able to cut from a departmental request as a measurement of their effectiveness. There is certainly an urgent need for an effective performance of this screening job.

As long as the economy is in a state of inflationary pressures, the attitude of legislative or executive budget examiners coincides largely with the requirements of a restraining fiscal policy. In a period of threatening or actual business contraction, however, fiscal policy may require the stepping-up of government activities rather than curtailment. There is certainly the danger that in such a period the fiscal policy view and the budget view may clash. To some extent such a clash did occur at the beginning of the thirties when Budget Director Douglas showed little enthusiasm in implementing the President's recovery program.

As a matter of fact, it would be utterly erroneous to have a looser attitude toward budget requirements in a period of underemployment than in a period of high employment. We need stabilization policies but the attitude toward budgetary screening should always be strict and conscientious. In the postwar years the Budget Bureau's policy letter accompanying the Call for Estimates has emphasized the need for tight budgeting in an inflationary period. It cannot be imagined that the Budget Bureau would or should ever send out a policy letter that did not ask for tight budgeting. Programs should always be executed with a minimum amount of money. What should be changed is the size and character of the *programs* rather than the attitude toward economy in budgeting.

The President's program should be determined after consideration primarily of long-range and secondarily of short-range economic and noneconomic objectives and the total costs involved. The budgetary review should insure that these programs are formulated and executed with the greatest economy at all times. The Executive Office of the President must assist the President in both these functions, namely, the formulation of a program that takes account of economic requirements and also the most economical implementation of his program. The Executive Office needs two types of people: those who have the attitude and imagination to be able to assist the President in program formulation and those who have the attitude and conscientiousness of the budget examiner.[46]

Whatever the best administrative relationship may be between these two groups within the Executive Office, it is clear that both attitudes must be blended if a national program is to be formulated that fulfills the necessary functions of supporting an expanding economy, assure that waste is eliminated, and that the nation receives the highest possible value from each dollar spent.

IV. An Appraisal of the Scope and Limits of Fiscal Policy

We started this essay by describing the simple idea of fiscal policy as a steering mechanism that could keep the economy on an even keel merely by proper timing of changes in government expenditure, government taxes, and debt management. A review of the experience with fiscal policy during the depression, the war, and the postwar period was used to illustrate some of the complications and limitations which must be recognized in the use of fiscal policy as a device for economic

46. Thomas Blaisdell, Jr., probably had the distinction between these two attitudes in mind when, in a speech before the American Society for Public Administration in Washington, D.C., March 11, 1949, he said: "The Budget Bureau methods are those of the control of the purse strings. The methods of the Council of Economic Advisers must be those of leading strings."

stabilization. We distinguished between fiscal policy as a short-run compensating device designed to *offset* fluctuations in private business activities and fiscal and other economic policies as long-run adjusting devices designed to reduce the *causes* of economic instability.

We also emphasized that a national program pursues a variety of objectives. The objectives of fiscal policy clash to some extent with other objectives and must be reconciled. Fiscal policy must be executed largely through the budgetary process, which again requires reconciliation of various purposes.

Yet it would be wrong to conclude from these complexities that fiscal policy as a stabilization device is only of minor usefulness. The purpose of this final section is to summarize the potential usefulness of fiscal policy and to reemphasize the arrangements in our legislative and administrative procedures which may become necessary in order to make full use of this instrument.

It is true that fiscal policy in its original and simplest conception is designed to combat inflation or deflation. This means that compensatory fiscal policy is more suitable to combat the results than the causes of economic maladjustments. It would be preferable, at least under peacetime conditions, if these maladjustments themselves could be prevented before they cause large swings of inflation or deflation. What, then, are these maladjustments and to what extent can fiscal policy contribute toward straightening them out?

It has been pointed out that an economy sustained at high levels of activity may have an inflationary bias that works through the mutual effect of prices and wages. In order to reconcile a continuing high level of employment, approximate price stability, and free collective bargaining it appears necessary to develop a long-range wage and price policy with participation of business and labor.[47] This solution requires further development in collective bargaining within the general framework of a national stabilization policy. The other alternative, namely, permitting inflation to develop and then counteracting it by an anti-inflationary fiscal policy, is obviously much less desirable.

In a similar way active purchasing power may be hampered at times by a business price policy of large profit margins and retained earnings above those justified by investment needs. In such a situation the lack of active purchasing power can, of course, be offset by a reduction in taxes or an increase in government spending. But again it would be more desirable to reinforce competitive forces and to correct the price policy that is responsible for the deflationary trend.

47. G. Colm and M. Young, *The American Economy in 1960—Economic Progress in a World of Tension,* Washington D.C., National Planning Association, December, 1952, 180 pp.

With respect to economic maladjustments that may lead to periodic depressions, most business cycle analysts emphasize the heavy swings from expansion to contraction in private business investment as one of the contributing main factors. Again there are two possible courses of action. One attitude accepts these swings as the natural way in which the economy grows by leaps and bounds and attempts to mitigate the impact of these fluctuations on the economy as a whole by a compensatory government fiscal policy. The other attitude tries to promote conditions in which there is a chance that business management may modify and "regularize" its policies of investment planning.[48]

In the long run, success in the latter endeavor is crucial for a permanently successful stabilization policy. We cannot be too sure, however, that this objective can be reached within a very short time. Business investment in the postwar period had to make up for past deficiencies and to bring productive capacity in line with a greatly increased level of income and demand. Depleted inventories also had to be replenished. Steady economic growth does require a continued high level of investment. The national security program also requires emphasis on expansion in productive capacity, although on a selective basis. Yet we must be prepared for the possibility that a period of high business investment may be followed by a period in which business investments contribute *relatively* less to total demand. While it would be desirable in such a situation to adopt a policy that supports investment, and adds to consumer income and expenditures, we must also be prepared to engage in compensatory fiscal policy in case total demand should contract or fail to expand sufficiently.

In the light of existing price and income rigidities and historically determined income distributions, we cannot be sure that the forces of the market and decisions by business and labor alone will bring about needed adjustments. Therefore it is necessary for the government to support such adjustments by policy measures when necessary. These might include price and wage policies, social security policies, long-range government investment programs, and tax revisions. In other words, fiscal as well as nonfiscal measures may be necessary to support these needed adjustments in basic market relationships.

Even though in all these respects it would be most desirable to adopt

48. The latter attitude was expressed in the *Second Annual Report to the President* by the Council of Economic Advisers, December, 1947, p. 18: "If the swings from expansion to contraction of private business which we have had in the past were to continue, offsetting operations would be too big to be left to 'compensatory' Government policies. Economic stabilization can be achieved within our private enterprise system only if management accepts the responsibility for a more stable practice in planning its investment and operative programs."

policies that effectively combat maladjustments before they lead either to inflationary or deflationary developments, it is not likely that we will always be wholly successful in such efforts. We must, therefore, be prepared to use remedial fiscal policies to the extent that we fail in our preventive policies.

It has been pointed out repeatedly that very important structural changes have taken place in the American economy during the last fifteen years. We have on our statute books programs that have an automatic built-in anticyclical effect. Progressive tax laws result in anticyclical changes in tax revenue without any change in rates. Social security programs and social assistance programs result in anticyclical variation of disbursements without any new legislation. Farm price support programs act in the same direction. Federal deposit insurance, changes in margin requirements, and several other programs add to the stability of the economy.

The President's Economic Reports of July, 1949, and January, 1950, have noted the fact that personal incomes and personal consumption have maintained a high level while industrial production dropped sharply in the first half of 1949. This has been rightly attributed in part to the effects of these various cushions that have been built into our economic system. An economy with a very large government sector is probably in itself more shock-resistant than an economy with a smaller government sector.

On the other hand, it must also be recognized that a $300 or $400 billion economy is in some respects more vulnerable than a $100 or $150 billion economy. Business investment, which has been running at an extraordinary absolute and relative amount, is a very volatile element in the economy; also many items of consumer expenditures are of a deferrable character and they become more important in an economy at higher levels. Therefore, it would be foolhardy if we did not prepare fiscal policies to be ready to counteract either inflationary or deflationary trends that may develop under peacetime conditions. General acceptance of the government's determination to iron out heavy fluctuations by fiscal policy becomes in itself a stabilizing factor, particularly of business investment, and may help to bring about those adjustments which might minimize inflationary or deflationary fluctuations. The possible "announcement" effect of a determined policy of stabilization on the behavior of individuals and business certainly deserves extensive study and attention.

A program of fiscal preparedness cannot rely on built-in flexibility alone. It must provide for positive action. Built-in flexibility must be supplemented by legislative and administrative flexibility. The less we can rely on the accuracy of economic forecasts the more it becomes necessary to emphasize the need for institutional arrangements that permit prompt action.

One of the unavoidable defects of the recovery policies during the thirties was that they were regarded almost wholly as the responsibility of the executive and at best tolerated by the legislature. The effectiveness of fiscal policies depends largely on the belief that they will be consistently pursued. This belief will be strengthened if the legislature and the executive share in the responsibility for their formulation. Close cooperation between the coordinating agencies in the executive and legislative side of government, namely, the Council of Economic Advisers and the Joint Committee on the Economic Report, is essential in this respect.

The main suggestions for increasing flexibility that are made in this chapter relate to the formulation of a five-year program of developmental government investments, of flexible grants-in-aid, and of the provision for some contingency expenditures in the operating budget. It is felt that on the revenue side social security contributions may be the most suitable tax for variation in accord with business conditions.

The need for flexibility relates to expenditures as well as tax programs. In a depression the more conservative advocates of fiscal policy will usually favor tax reduction (because they may feel that taxes have been too high anyway and they prefer to have individuals or business spend additional money rather than the government), while the more progressive advocates of fiscal policy will think first of government programs which they wish to see increased (because they may feel that these programs should have been adopted long ago and they may fear that taxes, once reduced, may limit desirable government programs in the long run).

No dogmatic statement can be made that variation either of expenditures or taxes is preferable. If there are certain taxes which are particularly undesirable in a given economic situation (e.g., taxes that form costs of production or highly regressive taxes), then their repeal may have highest priority. When private construction is dropping, additional public construction may be next on the urgent list. Under a system of progressive taxes, general tax reduction probably adds less to active demand than an increase in government expenditures. If available expenditure programs are concentrated, e.g., in construction, the sharp increase in these programs beyond a point determined by available resources will drive up costs rather than volume of construction. Before that point is reached other spending programs or tax abatements, particularly in the lower brackets, become more effective. Thus a combination of expenditure and tax measures is most effective economically in the short run and may be most effective in furthering long-run objectives at the same time. The specific combination will always depend on economic conditions, administrative preparedness, and legislative and political feasibility of the various elements of the program. Corresponding considerations apply with respect to curtailment of spending programs and increases in taxes in case of inflationary developments.

Basic legislation should enable the executive, always with Congressional approval or veto power, to meet moderate fluctuations. If the situation becomes serious and emergency measures with respect to government programs or taxes should be called for, the executive should formulate and present a specific program for legislative consideration.

The Employment Act of 1946 has provided machinery on the executive side through the Council of Economic Advisers, and on the Congressional side through the Joint Committee on the Economic Report, which should facilitate the formulation of stabilization programs and the integration of fiscal and nonfiscal measures. Even more important, the Employment Act, the United Nations Charter, and other international commitments have recorded a solemn expression of determination by the government to do everything in its power toward economic stabilization. The implementation of this policy objective requires adjustments in our institutional arrangements and attitudes.

Some suggestions for needed institutional adjustments have been made in this essay. Some readers may believe that our proposals are too drastic. They should remember that an attempt to achieve economic stabilization is a new responsibility of the government that cannot be met without equipping it with the necessary tools. Other readers will find that our suggestions have been too cautious. They should remember that there is no point in proposing tools unless we are convinced that there is the professional and administrative ability to handle them and the political determination to use them. Determination and ability to use new policies depends, at least partly, on the seriousness of the situation that must be mastered. No attempt has been made in this essay to forecast the strength of inflationary or deflationary conditions which may develop. We have emphasized the direction in which we ought to search for solutions rather than how far it will be necessary to go in that direction. The answer to that question, I believe, must be left to the future and will be determined largely by the democratic process of trial and error.

CHAPTER VI. *Taxation and Fiscal Policy*

BY CARL S. SHOUP

I. Effects of Taxation on Consumption, Saving, and Investment

1. *Assumptions concerning cash balance, debt, and expenditures*

This chapter is concerned with the effects of taxation on consumer spending, investment spending, saving, and the volume of work, all in relation to the problems posed by unemployment and inflation. It does not analyze the effects of a government deficit or surplus. In the assignment of topics for the seminar, it was agreed that the general problem of fiscal policy would be divided into these two parts; Mr. Colm has covered the second part in Chapter 5.

It is therefore necessary to specify just what the present analysis takes for granted. To study the effects of a tax is to make a comparison, explicit or implicit, between two situations, in one of which the tax is present, in the other, absent. But if a tax is removed, at least one other magnitude in the economy must change also: the government's cash balance, its expenditure, its debt, or its other tax revenue. Any public finance change always has at least two sides to it.

The solution adopted here (except for a brief excursion in section III below) is to assume that all these other public finance magnitudes remain unchanged, in the two situations that are being compared. This assumption is useful only if the analysis is restricted to the following types of comparison:

1) A single taxpayer is examined under a given tax and under no tax; the accompanying change in the government's cash balance, debt, or expenditures is so slight, and its effects so dispersed, that its influence on the taxpayer in question may be ignored.

2) The composite situation of a large body of taxpayers is studied under one tax and then under an alternative tax raising the same revenue, so that the government's cash balance, debt, and expenditures may be assumed to be quite unchanged.

3) The composite situation of a large body of taxpayers is studied under one tax and under the same tax changed slightly in revenue (through an assumed change in rate, base, etc.); the effect of the tax at

the margin (of the tax) is studied, and, as in 1) above, the change in the government's cash balance, debt, or expenditures is so small and its effects so diffused that the consequences for the taxpayers as a group may be ignored.

2. Current amounts of tax revenue in the United States

The Department of Commerce estimates that for the calendar year 1950 the federal, state, and local governments levied taxes to a total of $69.8 billion. This total includes a small amount of nontax receipts. Since the gross national product for the year was $283 billion, and the national income, $239 billion, it is evident that the economic effects of the present tax system are of substantial importance. Personal tax payments accounted for $20.5 billion; corporate profits tax accruals, $18.6 billion; indirect business tax accruals, $23.8 billion; and contributions for social insurance, $6.96 billion.

By far the larger part of the tax revenues, some $50.5 billion in 1950, accrues to the federal government. The remaining $19.2 billion, which went, in 1950, to the state and local governments, is nonetheless large enough to have a significant effect on the national economy.[1]

3. Some definitions

a. INCENTIVE EFFECTS AND DISPOSABLE-INCOME (WORKING-CAPITAL) EFFECTS

Before considering the studies that have been made, it is useful to draw a distinction between the incentive effects of a tax measure and the disposable-income, or working-capital, effects.

The incentive effects of a tax are the impairment or strengthening of incentives to work an additional hour, or save an additional dollar for investment, or undertake an additional risk in order to invest a dollar already saved, in view of the tax consequences of such action. The effect is at the margin of the taxpayer's activity. As the marginal tax rate is increased, the individual taxpayer's disposition to work the last hour or invest the last dollar that he was planning to work or invest suffers a change, normally a diminution. Applying Hicks's terminology, we may call these the substitution effects of the tax. Pigou includes them within his somewhat broader category of announcement effects.

The disposable-income effect (on an individual, nonbusiness, taxpayer) or the working-capital effect (if the taxpayer is a business con-

1. Figures in this section are from "National Income and Product Statistics of the United States," Supplement to the *Survey of Current Business*, 31 (1951), by the Department of Commerce.

cern) results from the fact that the tax takes a certain amount of money away from the taxpayer. Because it does so he is induced to modify his action; he has less money than before. Under this type of effect the taxpayer is not regarded as having any choice between paying or not paying the tax, in contrast to the first effect, where he is viewed earlier in the game, so to speak, while he is still making up his mind whether or not to undertake the action that will make him taxable. He pays the tax; his disposable income (or working capital) is decreased; he must therefore restrict his consumption (or investment) spending, or his saving, or obtain more income, or perhaps some of all three. These are the income effects (Hicks). They include what Pigou calls the distribution effects.

The contrast between the two effects can be seen most clearly by comparing the results of a heavy poll tax, say $1,000, with those of an income tax having a zero rate up to, say, $3,000 and a 100% rate on all income above this amount. Suppose that the taxpayer is earning $4,000 before the tax. If the poll tax is imposed, his disposable income is decreased, for the moment, to $3,000; as a result he will probably decrease his consumption expenditures and decrease his saving, and also increase the amount of his work in order to earn an extra $100 or so. All of these effects are disposable-income effects; they arise because his disposable income has been changed. There is no question of deciding whether or not to do this or that in view of the tax that will thereupon attach; the tax has to be paid in any event.

In Pigou's terminology the initial decrease in the disposable income to $3,000 and the resulting contraction of consumption and saving are distribution effects; they reflect the way in which the total tax bill is distributed among people in different economic situations. The $3,000 is viewed as being spread over "different sorts of purchases . . . in the proportions in which an untaxed [$3,000] . . . man of the same temperament as himself would distribute his income." [2] The added work and added income are, however, classified by Pigou as announcement effects.

Bergson and others (see section 6-a below) similarly assume that if an individual with $4,000 of disposable income (to use the case above) pays an additional tax of $1,000, the effect on his saving and consumption may be estimated by noting how much saving and spending has been habitual with individuals whose disposable incomes have been $3,000.

If an individual with $4,000 income pays a $1,000 poll tax, we may

2. A. C. Pigou, *A Study in Public Finance* (London, Macmillan, 1949), p. 56. See also *ibid.*, pp. 64–65.

assume that the last dollar of his disposable income (which is tentatively $3,000) means more to him than did the last dollar of his $4,000 income; it has a higher value, measured against leisure and the irksomeness of labor. Before, he did not think it worth his while to work an extra hour to earn an extra dollar or, rather, he was on the margin of indifference in this matter. Now, therefore, he does think it worth while to work an extra hour or maybe more. The marginal utility of money to him has risen. Suppose that he works 100 more hours a year than before; his disposable income, after the poll tax, is $3,100, not $3,000. To determine the effect of the $1,000 tax on the saving and consumption of the $4,000 earner, it is not sufficient to ascertain how a $3,000 man distributes his income between saving and consumption. A more nearly relevant pattern is that of the individual with a disposable income of $3,100. Even then the comparison is only partly justified. The two men cannot be of "the same temperament" (including similar abilities), else they would both have been earning $4,000 before the tax. After the tax is in force the taxpayer, with a disposable income of $3,100, will be working more for it than the person with whom he is being compared, and this fact alone makes it difficult to derive the former's consumption-saving pattern from that of the latter.

But if, instead of the $1,000 poll tax, there is imposed an income tax with a rate of zero up to $3,000 and a rate of 100% beyond, the taxpayer in this illustration will decrease his work, not increase it. He will decrease his work by one-fourth, so that he will be earning just $3,000.

To move from the extremes of a poll tax and a 100% marginal-rate income tax to the customary type of progressive-rate income tax: such a tax has both incentive and disposable-income effects. Suppose the tax carries a personal exemption of $1,000, taxes the next $1,000 at 10%, the next $1,000 at 20%, and all above $3,000 at 30%. The incentive effect of the 30% rate induces the taxpayer to decrease his work; but, supposing that he does not tend to reduce his income below $3,000, there is the disposable-income effect of the 10 and 20% rates and so much of the 30% as he remains subject to; this induces him to step up his work. If he was working 4,000 hours to start with, we may imagine him deciding, on the basis of the incentive effects alone, to reduce his working time to 3,200 hours, but, upon considering the disposable-income effects (the increased marginal utility of money to him), striking a balance between the two kinds of effect and settling on 3,400 hours of work.

b. REPERCUSSIVE EFFECTS

If the study is not confined to the tax collected from one taxpayer (comparison 1 in section I-1 above), its scope might include the possible effects on any given taxpayer's income, consumption, saving, and investment that is produced by the reactions of all the other taxpayers considered in the aggregate. If, for example, a sales tax is supposed to be substituted for an income tax, the aggregate reaction of taxpayers, in the first instance at least, might be a decrease in consumption spending. The accompanying decrease in total spending would of course have some effect on the income, consumption, saving, and spending of any given taxpayer, an effect in addition to that which he experiences through the direct impact of a tax on him. These repercussive effects, as they will be called here, will be referred to occasionally in the present chapter, but most of this field is left for discussion by other authors in this book.

4. *The function of taxation in relation to investment and consumption*

A possible misconception needs to be eliminated at the start. Whatever the aims of a sound tax system may be, the avoidance of any repression of private expenditures for consumption or of private expenditures for investment is certainly not one of them. Indeed, if a tax system did nothing at all toward discouraging private spending, the economy would be in recurrent, and perhaps long-continued, states of inflation as the government, consumers, and business bid unceasingly against one another for the limited volume of resources. "Every tax discourages some kind of production," remarked the English economist Edwin Cannan, writing in 1901, "because the aim of taxation is to divert a portion of the productive force of the community from producing what individuals desire as individuals to producing something else which they desire in their corporate capacity." [3] We cannot therefore choose between alternative taxes yielding the same total revenue on the grounds that one of the taxes discourages consumption, or discourages investment, less than the other tax. Some such discouragement is necessary to compel a release of productive resources that may then be devoted to producing things for the government. Otherwise the government has to go into the market and pull these resources forcibly away from private use by the process of bidding against the private sector, using for this purpose money borrowed from the existing stock and also, no doubt, money newly created for it by the banking system or the printing press.

The question is, rather, given a certain amount of resources that the private sector must relinquish (for producing things for private use), and therefore a certain amount of discouragement of private consump-

3. "Equity and Economy in Taxation," *Economic Journal, 11* (December, 1901), 476.

tion and private investment that is necessary, how much revenue shall be raised in the process of achieving this amount of discouragement by taxation? Tax A may compel the needed release of resources while raising fewer dollars in revenue than tax B, which compels the same release of resources. The choice between the tax measures will involve the following considerations: It is desirable to select the tax that discourages total output (output for government plus output for private use) the least; the preferable tax is the one that meets certain tests in distributing sacrifice among individuals (and this may conceivably involve selecting a tax which imposes the greater total of money sacrifice—a point distinct from the minimizing of decrease of total real output); the choice must be made in the light of aims with respect to the public debt and monetary liquidity; and perhaps other major issues are involved. This point will be developed somewhat more in the next section, where the need for a new unit of comparison is discussed. In general, the division of labor in the present volume has placed these topics in the areas staked out for Mr. Colm, and Mr. Hart. A few more remarks in that field are offered in section III of the present chapter; here it is merely necessary to avoid any presumption that, because a certain tax may decrease private consumption or private investment less than some other tax, per dollar of revenue, it is thereby the better tax.

5. *Allocation of resources and full use of resources: need for a new unit of comparison*

One purpose in studying the effects of taxation on consumption, investment and saving, and income is to understand how taxation influences the level of involuntary unemployment. In policy terms taxation is studied as a means of maintaining full employment without inflation. But the study may instead be focused on the optimum utilization of resources under conditions of full employment; the first problem is assumed away, or abstracted from, and in policy terms the search is for a tax system that will facilitate effective choices by individuals among expenditures on various kinds of commodities, their choices between spending and saving, and their choices between work and leisure—one that will, in some sense or other, maximize satisfaction.

The second group of problems involves us in sacrifice doctrine, welfare analysis, and similar topics, which have been so thoroughly treated by Pigou, among others. On the whole the present essay will not proceed far in this direction, since the chief concern of the volume is the problem of unemployment in its broadest terms; but occasional reference will be needed to the effects of tax measures on sacrifice and welfare, with the added justification that Mr. Millikan has reminded us of the importance of keeping in mind the allocation of resources under full employment.

Alternative tax measures are commonly constructed with the proviso that they yield the same revenue. This is an appropriate procedure for subordinate governmental units that are narrowly limited in their ways of raising money; often, if they cannot get the means of payment for their employees, creditors, and suppliers from tax revenue, they cannot get it at all, or at least not on terms that provide a sensible alternative. It may also be an appropriate procedure for much of the sacrifice-doctrine analysis. But when the discussion centers on degrees of employment, and on inflation or deflation, equality of revenue-raising power is no longer an appropriate unit for comparison. A more relevant unit would be the extent to which the tax forces a reduction in consumer spending or in investment spending; that is, the extent to which the tax forces the private sector of the economy to release economic resources that the government may then hire. Thus, if inflation is under way, the aim is to force the private sector to release its hold on a certain volume of resources, so that the combined demands of government and the private sector for manpower and materials will not continue to drive prices up. The alternative tax measures to be considered should then have the same resource-releasing effect.

The choice among them may be made after weighing the differences in amount and distribution of sacrifice (which, as noted above, does not arise merely from being forced to give up the current use of resources), the effect on the public debt, the stock of money and the rate of interest, the relative ease of administration, and other relevant matters. On the basis of such considerations the tax measure that gives the largest revenue may be selected—but it might turn out that the preferable tax measure (among those with the same resource-releasing power) is the one that gives the smallest revenue. There is no a priori rule in this matter to be applied in advance; we cannot say that, among taxes having the same resource-releasing power, we shall always want to select the one that yields the largest revenue.

Similarly, if the background is one of deflation and unemployment, and it is desired to encourage the private use of resources for private purposes, the appropriate choice is between two or more tax measures that have the same negative resource-releasing power (normally, tax decrements, not tax increments; see section 6-b below).

In such analyses a comparison of tax measures raising the same amount of revenue is not very useful; it is like comparing all automobiles of a green color, when the aim is to select an automobile that will hold five persons.

Unfortunately, our knowledge of the resource-releasing pressure exerted by a particular tax (at a particular time and place) is very limited. As will be shown in the section immediately following, it is of course too inadequate to allow us to draw up a table showing the number of units of resource-releasing power in an increment or decrement of rate of each of the major taxes at each of several rate levels (the marginal resource-releasing power). We cannot even rank various tax changes in the order of their resource-releasing power, or group together all tax changes that have roughly the same resource-releasing power. But this lack of knowledge is no reason for carrying on the abstract discussion in terms of equal revenue-raising units. Utilization of the new, if yet unmeasurable, unit of comparison in abstract discussion would help avoid the impression that is sometimes given in current analyses (as noted above) that, of two taxes that raise the same amount of revenue, the one that causes the lesser discouragement of private use of resources for private purposes is somehow necessarily the better. Moreover, the analyst would be constantly reminded how little he does know of the resource-releasing power of any given tax measure, especially regarding its power to force business firms to release resources from the process of gross capital formation.

In practice it must be confessed that comparisons are usually made, and will continue to be made, between alternative tax measures that yield the same amount of revenue. Practice departs from abstract analysis because of the lack of quantitative data on resource-releasing power and because of a lack of understanding of the importance of the resource-releasing function. In practice, then, it is admitted that the analyst, when called on for advice, will have to deal with differences (vaguely estimated) in resource-releasing power of two or more equal-revenue tax measures.

6. *State of knowledge on topics listed above*

The state of knowledge with respect to the degree to which any particular tax increment forces a reduction in the taxpayer's consumption, saving, or investment, or a change in his income is very unsatisfactory. However, a superficial distinction, and perhaps something more than that, may be drawn between a) consumption and saving, b) investment, and c) income in this regard. Numerical calculations have been made to estimate the amount of a tax increment that is likely to come out of consumption and out of saving. A considerable body of reasoning about possibilities has been constructed with respect to both the incentive and the working-capital effects on investment, but it has not been possible to make numerical calculations as in the analyses of consumption and saving. The effect of taxation on the taxpayer's willingness to work, and thus on his income, has been studied relatively little even in terms of possibilities. The following paragraphs attempt to summarize what has been done in each of these three divisions. In the nature of the material the summary will be easiest, and probably most useful, with regard to the research on consumption and saving. The qualitative, directional conclusions reached in the other fields are not so readily summarized.

a. ESTIMATES OF EFFECT OF TAXATION ON CONSUMPTION AND SAVING

Sample surveys have produced data on how consumers at successive income levels dispose of their incomes—so much to taxes and, of the remainder, the disposable income, so much to consumption expenditure and the rest to saving. Utilizing these data, Abram Bergson, Richard B. Goode, and others have imagined additional taxes being imposed, or existing taxes being lightened, at each of several income levels. A hypothetical increase in tax would drive the income recipients at one level of disposable income down to a lower one. How much of their smaller disposable income would they spend? The same percentage as do those whose disposable income is in fact that small? If this is a tenable assumption, the effect of the additional tax is readily computed. From the family budget data, the amount of change in disposable income from one income level to the next lower one is seen to be accompanied by a certain decrease in amount of saving and a certain decrease in spending. An additional tax, of the same amount as this decrease in disposable income, would therefore come out of saving and spending by these amounts.

This technique is suited primarily for a study of changes in the personal income tax. The family budget data on which it rests show personal taxes—not sales taxes or other business taxes that affect the family's consumption and saving in real terms through an increase in prices of the things they buy. And of course the technique has nothing directly to do with corporate saving.

For an increase or decrease in the entire tax system, involving changes in all the major taxes, Nicholas Kaldor uses a technique that is somewhat different in form though much the same in substance. A marginal propensity to save is estimated for each type of income. Thus, one propensity is computed for investment income, another for wages and salaries, and another for undistributed profits. For this last category the propensity to save is naturally said to be 100%. The estimates for the other types of income are based on budget studies and time series that yield an indication of the multiplier. The proportion of the total tax revenue that comes from each type of income is estimated. The corresponding marginal propensity to save is applied to each proportion. The result is the percentage of a proportionate change in total tax revenue that would come out of saving.

Bergson's computations indicate that an income tax increment equal in total to 5% of the aggregate family income of 1935–36 would come 61% out of saving, if the new tax were laid at rates as progressive as those already in existence. If the additional tax were simply at a flat rate of 5% on all incomes, only 30% of it would come out of saving.

Goode's study is based on 1941–42 family budget data. The tax that he is testing is that part of the corporate income tax that may be assumed to reduce the individuals' disposable income through its effect in curtailing dividends. His computations indicate close to half of this part of the corporation income tax came out of the individuals' spending, the other half, therefore, out of their saving.

Kaldor, using British data, and studying the effects of a uniform percentage increase in all taxes, direct and indirect, concluded that 27% of such a tax increase would have come out of saving, 73% out of consumption.

These computations give some general idea of how large a proportion of a tax increment may come out of saving (or spending), but the conclusions probably have too large a margin of error to be very useful in choosing among alternative fiscal policies in practice. There are at least two reasons for this:

a) There is insufficient evidence on the degree of stability over time of the propensity to consume. At any given income level it is not safe to rely on 1935–36 or 1941–42 family budget data in 1952. Obviously, more frequent and detailed budget studies are needed.

b) To assume that the taxpayer will act, at the new, low disposable-income level to which he has been driven by a new tax, just as does one who has been at that level for some time is to ignore the likelihood of lag in adjusting one's spending and saving habits to a change in disposable income.

b. QUALITATIVE CONCLUSIONS

The incentive effects on consumption, saving, investment, and work, and the disposable-income or working-capital effects on the last two have been the subjects of a great deal of qualitative analysis, but no numerical estimates have been attempted. The amount of qualitative analysis in these fields has been so vast that a comprehensive summary, no matter how skeletonized, is out of the question here; but an attempt will be made to cover certain issues that seem to be of particular interest.

1) CONSUMPTION VERSUS SAVING: INCENTIVE EFFECTS. An individual may be considered as continually engaged in deciding how to allocate his net worth among three alternative uses: spending for consumption, maintaining it in liquid form (i.e., with the prospect of little or no income on the saving), and maintaining it in investments, in the market or financial sense of "investment," not in the narrower national-income sense. And if he does decide to maintain his net worth, he may do so either with a view to consuming later or with the intention of a perpetual or at least indefinite maintenance of his position.

The usual type of personal income tax affects the taxpayer's choice among these alternatives. Abstracting for the moment from the liquidity alternative, it may be shown that the income tax disturbs the relative rewards open to the individual from consuming his marginal dollar of net worth and maintaining it with a view to receiving an investment return. For purposes of this analysis, it is necessary to cast the discussion in terms of the disposition of income rather than net worth; the time period is expanded backward to include the acquisition of the income that gives rise to the marginal increment of net worth. The income tax is presumed to be of the usual kind: it does not grant exemption to the part of income that is saved and it does not exempt income obtained from investment, as distinguished from income obtained from work. The reward for saving is decreased, relative to the reward for consuming. If, before the tax was imposed, the individual was on the margin of indifference between a) devoting his last $100 of income to immediate consumption or b) devoting it to investment for one year in the expectation that he would thereby be able to spend on consumption $105 at the end of the year, then the introduction of a 10% income tax will change his option to a) devoting $90 of income to immediate consumption versus b) devoting it to investment for one year with the expectation of spending on consumption, at the end of that year, $90 plus 5% interest minus tax on the interest, or $94.05. The choice between $90 now and $94.05 then is not the same as a choice between $100 now and $105 then. In the first case the individual gains 4.5% in amount of consumption if he waits a year; in the other case, 5%.

If the individual is choosing between consuming now and saving and investing forever, the difference becomes more pronounced.

This fact, that the reward for saving is reduced relative to the reward for consuming at once, has been obscured off and on throughout the past several decades by strenuous debate over, first, whether the income tax causes "double taxation" of saving and, second, whether as a policy matter the income tax should be altered so as to exempt saved income (or, alternatively, the income from investments). The terminological difficulties inherent in the first point have led, or helped to lead, to an apparent denial, by more than one authority in taxation, of the fact just adduced. On the other hand, the policy conclusions reached by some of those who have recognized that fact are not, in the present writer's view, inevitable consequences, even on grounds merely of allocation economics or full-employment economics and hence apart from the political and social consequences of, for example, concentration of wealth.[4] It is not certain how any given taxpayer will react to a relative decrease in the reward for saving. Some taxpayers might increase their gross saving and decrease their consumption rather than the reverse.

Similarly, the income tax decreases the reward for saving and investment as compared with that for saving for liquidity; the rewards of liquidity are not realized in terms of income, for the most part, and hence are not subject to the income tax. The liquidity that is induced by a hope of being able to invest at a lower price later is more or less of an exception to this rule.

A tax on the taxpayer's entire net fortune, including his holdings of cash, would not discriminate in this way between holding money and holding income-bearing assets. In this sense a tax on capital value discriminates less against investment, even in the national-income sense, than a tax on income.[5] Still, it cannot be said that a tax on capital would have no incentive effect at all on employment-creating investment. There is always the alternative of spending more of one's net worth for consumption and thus investing less. A very low-rate tax on net worth would probably induce little if any increase in consumption, however, and such a tax is a promising one if it is desired to exert a given amount of resource-releasing pressure on the private economy with an accompanying large volume of revenue rather than a smaller volume. But this aim, as noted in section 4 above, is not to be taken for granted.

When there is a prospect, and especially when there is certainty, that the rate of an excise tax or other tax on sales or production is going to change in the near future, consumers will react accordingly. A prospective increase in the rate will stimulate buying, partly at least at the expense of later buying. Conversely, a prospective decrease will induce a decrease in buying for the time being. So well recognized is this tendency that governments usually take measures to block it. In the United States, when the tax is collected at the manufacturing level, the govern-

4. Pigou's treatment, *op. cit.*, ch. 10, "Income Tax and Savings," is notably free from both kinds of clouding of the issue.

5. See M. Kalecki, "Three Ways to Full Employment," in *The Economics of Full Employment* (Oxford, Blackwell, 1945), pp. 44–45.

ment's weapon is a tax on floor stocks of wholesalers and retailers. This kind of tax has a considerable history with respect to liquor. If the tax rate is to decrease a floor stocks refund is indicated, but there has been little if any experience with such a measure.

This device does not, however, block the tendency of the ultimate consumer to anticipate the tax. For that aim the British practice is the only effective one: the change in rate is kept a secret until the day it is to go into effect. This method is unavailable under the political and parliamentary organization of the United States.

The tendency of consumers, or retailers or wholesalers, to anticipate a change in tax rates may be included among the incentive effects of taxation: the government announces that if you act in a certain way, you pay less tax.

2) INVESTMENT: INCENTIVE EFFECTS. In this section investment is used in its national-income sense: the purchase or, when speaking of the economy as a whole, the creation of capital goods. Gross investment, not net, is the main object of study, since it is gross investment that is more closely correlated with employment, but some possible differences between the incentive effects on gross and net investment will be noted.

One incentive effect of the income tax has already been discussed in the preceding section: the decrease in relative reward for investment as against saving in liquid form or consumption. A second effect is to make risky investments less attractive relative to less risky investments. Risk is here defined as the degree of dispersion of possible outcomes. Suppose two alternative investments; in one, the chances are equal that, if $100,000 is risked, $100,000 additional will be gained or $80,000 lost. In the other, the chances are equal that, if the same amount is risked, $5,000 additional will be gained or nothing lost. If a 50% income tax is imposed, and the taxpayer has no other source of income, the comparison becomes one of (A) chances equal that $50,000 will be gained and $80,000 lost; (B) chances equal that $2,500 will be gained and nothing lost. Venture B is now more attractive, relative to A, than it was before, in the sense that a large number of B ventures would yield a 1.25% return, against a minus 15% return on a large number of A ventures, whereas formerly it was 2.5% against (plus) 10%. If the taxpayer was on the margin of indifference before, he will presumably—though we cannot say for sure—be inclined toward the B venture now. No doubt investors cannot compare ventures on any such precise basis, and the example must be taken as illustrating a tendency of thought rather than the exact thought itself. Very little is known about what inducements are necessary for risk-taking or how potential investors compare different ventures. The history of stock prices on the market shows how a continual shifting of preferences at the margin is going on and to what extremes of willingness and unwillingness investors are prone at different moments of time.

Insofar as the investor has other sources of income against which he can offset the loss if it does occur, in somewhat the same range of tax rates, the income tax transforms a risky investment into a relatively riskless one instead of discriminating against it and a riskless investment. The dispersion of possible outcomes is reduced. The supply of risky ventures is decreased and that of low-risk ventures increased. The net result might be some change in total investment. But the supply and demand conditions for high-risk and low-risk investments, viewed as rival uses of funds, has not been explored sufficiently to allow of any further conclusions here.

Very high income tax rates on profits may produce just the reverse of the incentive effects usually attributed to that tax. The wartime excess-profits tax is an illustration. Management can purchase certain nonmonetary benefits with its money outlays, usually in the form of relief from various strains, including the bother of trying to estimate just how much money gain a given outlay will net. Under a marginal tax rate of 80%, there is a strengthening of the inclination to make these deductible money outlays in order to obtain nonmoney, nontaxable benefits. There is even, if we are to believe some businessmen, the non-monetary satisfaction of seeing that the money does not go to the government.

If the management expects the tax rates to go down in later years, it may of course be justified, on a purely monetary calculation, in making outlays now that will increase the gross receipts later, provided the outlays are conventionally of a "current" type—expensed, not capitalized —hence deductible now in computing the amount subject to the high tax rate. This is quite a different type of incentive effect from the non-monetary case just noted; it is to be grouped with the investment in inventory that occurs when a rise in an excise tax is anticipated.

A distinction was drawn above between gross and net investment. The difference between the two is replacement investment. A guess may be hazarded that the management usually has a more inelastic demand for replacement than for new investment, whether it is price elasticity or risk elasticity or some other consideration that is in question. To see the business firm actually shrink a bit in size is to experience much more psychic loss than to see it fail to grow a bit in size. Of course if it grows in size in other measures, as in sales, it may shrink in terms of investment, as in fact occurred in more than one giant concern during the latter 1930's, without evoking the resistance just postulated. But a shrinkage on all counts injures the management's prestige or at least its sense of self-satisfaction. Hence the profits tax rate may go fairly high before the management gives the order to whittle the concern down to a smaller size so that the stockholders may have a part of their capital investment returned to them in liquid form to be held that way, or invested in less risky enterprises, or spent for consumption. Admittedly, these remarks are pretty much conjecture, based only on general observation of what the business community says and does.

3) INVESTMENT: WORKING-CAPITAL EFFECTS. A tax on a business firm usually leaves it with less cash or other liquid assets than it would have had if there had been no tax. The only exception to this statement occurs when the tax is completely shifted without any decrease in unit sales, surely a rare case. If the firm is to continue with the investment that it would have undertaken but for this cash drain, it must borrow or sell an additional equity interest, except in the instances where a large enough cash reserve is habitually carried to meet just such problems. The fact that the management was willing to invest the concern's own cash is no guarantee that it can persuade outside investors that this is a wise use of money. Investment may thus be blocked through a cash drain caused by the tax.

The taxes of chief interest in this connection are the personal and the corporate income taxes. It is not known which of the two is likely to have the largest aggregate effect. The partnerships and proprietorships pay no income tax as such, in the federal system, but the inclusion of their entire current earnings in the incomes of their owners subject to tax must in many cases make unavailable for investment by these firms substantial sums of money that otherwise would have been so spent. There is indeed a kind of counterworking of forces that tends to limit the seriousness of this problem. The higher the marginal tax rate applicable to the total taxable income from all sources of the owner(s), the greater the cash drain; but the fact that a high rate is applicable indicates that the owner is relatively well-to-do and, unless the business earnings are his sole income, is thereby perhaps better able to advance money to the concern in spite of the tax than is the owner of small income. Nevertheless, there seems to be a real danger that the working-capital effects of the income tax system are much more serious for the unincorporated concern than for the corporation; and the tendency to encourage large-size firms at the expense of smaller ones may be greater than is generally realized. Here is an area in which a great deal of research is needed.

The pressure on the unincorporated concern may be especially strong in periods of rising prices, if the first-in first-out method of inventory accounting is followed. Almost all of exceptionally large profits may need to be retained in the business if the concern is not to shrink in physical size; the inventory must be replaced on the new high cost level. The universal practice of computing deductible depreciation on the basis of historical cost poses somewhat similar problems.

4) LABOR: DISPOSABLE-INCOME AND INCENTIVE EFFECTS. The fact that money is taken from the taxpayer raises the marginal utility of money to him. The marginal disutility of work remains unchanged; hence he tends to accept more work and less leisure. If, contrary to the stipulations in Sec. I(1) above, the analysis were broadened to include the effects of substantial changes in tax revenue and an accompanying change in services rendered by the government, the net result might be less work, not more. The free consumer goods coming to the individual from government would lessen this need for an additional dollar of income, diminishing the marginal utility of money to him. And if the government services were services to business instead of being consumer goods, the resulting fall in the market price of privately produced goods would lead to the same result (if the business owners, or other factor owners, kept the benefit of the government services by refusing to lower prices, the marginal utility of money to them would decline as their money incomes increased). But these considerations may be neglected, within the framework chosen for the present analysis; for these purposes, then, an increase in tax will be said to tend to increase work, and a decrease, to decrease work, so far as the disposable-income (distributive) effects are concerned.

It is quite otherwise, of course, with regard to the incentive effects, the effects at the margin. The tendency here is to induce a reduction in the amount of work. The fact that the worker must share with the government the proceeds of his last hours of work will raise the marginal value of leisure relative to that of the proceeds of work.

While there is general agreement on the directions of these tendencies, there is as yet no substantial agreement on whether they are important, quantitatively, in the aggregate. At one extreme is the view expressed by Pigou:

> With the great majority of people, once their occupation is decided upon, the quantity of work which they do is only to a very limited extent within their own control. Their hours are fixed by rule; the intensity of their efforts in many cases by custom and tradition; their age or retirement by pension arrangements. . . . Moreover, in the higher walks of industry wealthy men in control of large concerns are often much more interested in the success of their concerns as an index of capacity and a means to power than in variations in

the amount of their net private incomes, which are in any event ample.[6]

At the other extreme are those business representatives who seem to intimate that there is a danger that the top posts in American industry will go begging because the heavy income tax rates cut so deeply into the executive's compensation.

The present writer's impression is that, at income tax rates in effect in 1949, the incentive effect in deterring work was of somewhat more importance with respect to the wage-earning group than for those in the high-salary positions, chiefly because so many of the former are paid on a piece-rate basis or have an occasional opportunity to work overtime for extra pay. The reduction of work at the executive level is more of a long-term phenomenon and occurs chiefly only through a) less active striving for the top positions, so that on the way up the concern gets less work out of the rival aspirants to the few prizes; b) earlier retirement, which, however, may or may not result in "less work" in the sense of work of a given grade of efficiency. (It is not uncommon to hear the complaint that the top executives stay on too long for the good of the firm.)

It is not only the income tax, of course, that weakens the worker's incentive to go overtime or speed up under a piece rate. A substantial general sales tax should have somewhat the same result; it cuts the real purchasing power of the worker's marginal earnings and thus makes a little more leisure a little more attractive.

A fixed poll tax has only disposable-income effects; an income tax with an exemption almost equal to the worker's present earnings from labor has only an incentive effect. All of the important revenue-raising taxes exercise both pressures, since they take money away and at the same time make it harder to get. It would require a great deal more knowledge than we now have, or seem likely to get in the near future, to ascertain, for example, whether five points off the present individual federal income tax would, on balance, increase or decrease the supply of labor.[7]

II. Countercycle Changes in Taxation

If a tax reduces its revenue demands on taxpayers as business and employment fall off, and increases its revenue take on the upswing, it has a countercycle action in the broadest sense. But defined in this gen-

6. *Op. cit.*, pp. 69, 70.
7. See Carl Shoup, "Problems in War Finance," in Lester V. Chandler and Donald H. Wallace, eds., *Economic Mobilization and Stabilization* (New York, Holt, 1951), pp. 191–201.

eral way countercycle action is found in almost every tax. As the tax base diminishes in the aggregate, owing to the decline in economic activity, the tax revenue of course falls off. Something more than this simple trait of moving in the same direction as business activity is meant when a tax is said to be cycle-sensitive, or to possess "built-in flexibility."

At least three chief measures of cycle-sensitivity have been employed, explicitly or implicitly, since this subject began to be discussed intensively about twenty years ago.[8] The percentage fluctuations in the revenue of one tax may be compared with those of other taxes.[9] The fluctuations in the yield of a tax may be compared with the fluctuations of some index of general business conditions.[10] Or, the fluctuation in the revenue of the tax may be compared with the fluctuation of the base of this tax: changes in personal income tax revenue during the cycle could be compared, for instance, with changes in taxable personal income.[11]

There are five major ways in which the cycle-sensitivity, however defined, may be increased for a given tax:

1) By adjusting the structure of rates and exemptions without changing the total yield in the initial period. The adjustment that gives a greater degree of cycle-sensitivity is not necessarily one toward a greater degree of progressivity.

2) By defining the tax base so that it includes elements that appear largely in good times and not in depressions (for example, capital gains, under the income tax).

3) By requiring tax payments to keep pace with tax accruals instead of lagging behind several months or even a year or more. This refinement is applicable chiefly to the income tax.

4) By speeding up the payment of tax refunds, at least so far as the re-

8. The earliest reference in the extensive bibliography on this subject compiled by Jean Marchal (see n. 10, below) is Fritz Neumark's monograph of 1930, *Konjunktur und Steuern* (Bonn, K. Schroeder), except for a reference to an article by Vilfredo Pareto in 1913.

9. As in *Facing the Tax Problem* (New York, Twentieth Century Fund, 1937), pp. 322–329, where William Vickrey devised a technique that compared the ratio of maximum yield to minimum yield, both with and without allowance for trend.

10. See Jean Marchal, *Rendements fiscaux et conjoncture* (Paris, 1942), Annexe III, describing the coefficient of correlation between revenue-yield fluctuations and business-index fluctuations.

11. See Richard A. Musgrave and Merton H. Miller, "Built-In Flexibility," *American Economic Review*, 38 (March, 1948), 123, where the concept of "income elasticity of the tax yield" is defined as the ratio of the percentage change in personal income tax yield to a given percentage change in personal income and is expressed as the ratio of the marginal tax rate in the initial period to the average tax rate in that period.

funds are due to the tax system's not being on a completely pay-as-you-go basis, or to a carry-back of either a) losses, b) deficits in normal profits (excess profits tax), or c) unused personal exemptions. This measure, too, is significant chiefly for the income and profits taxes.

5) By changing the tax rates, the exemptions, or the definition of the tax base as business conditions change.[12]

1. *Rate structure, exemptions, and tax base*

a. PERSONAL INCOME TAX

Without specific assumptions as to the distribution of taxable income, in the initial period and in the second period, and the rate schedule that is assumed to be in force initially, it cannot be said, in general, whether the tax will be made more or less cycle-sensitive (in any one of the three senses noted above) if the rate structure is made more progressive. The same uncertainty applies to an increase in the personal exemptions. But in general, and under conditions that have existed in the United States, it seems likely that the progressive rate scale and the personal exemptions have each served to increase the cycle-sensitivity of the tax, compared with what it would be under a flat rate, or no exemptions, and producing the same revenue in a given year.

An earned income credit probably reduces cycle-sensitivity. In other words, a differential tax on investment income probably reduces cycle-sensitivity, since it seems likely that the total of dividends and interest will fluctuate by a smaller percentage in future cycle swings than earned income. Profits from unincorporated business, including rentals, partake of both earned and investment income characteristics.

Taking account of capital gains and losses instead of ignoring them, in computing taxable income, increases the revenue response to cycle changes, provided the gains are included in full and are taxed as other income and provided also that the capital losses are allowed as deductions from other income. If, on the contrary, capital losses are deductible only from capital gains, and may be carried forward several years for this purpose—as is virtually the case with the federal tax and exactly the case with the New York State personal income tax—the result may be little if any more instability in revenues over the cycle than if gains and losses were ignored.

The profits and losses of unincorporated firms are included in full in the returns of the owners for the year in which they occur. This feature is an important reason for the degree of sensitivity that the personal in-

12. For still other factors affecting the cycle-sensitivity of taxes, see Marchal, *op. cit., passim.*

come tax now possesses. The sensitivity is increased appreciably if, as in the present federal law, the business loss may be carried back to offset the profits of an earlier year, when the loss is so large that it exceeds the taxpayer's income from other sources for the current year. Only the excess of the loss is carried back, of course. This device gives rise to refunds of tax paid in previous years, refunds which are paid to the individual income taxpayer in a year when his net income is negative; a negative tax is thus imposed in depression. If, on the contrary, the loss is allowed only to be carried forward, to be offset against the profits of subsequent years, the result is to stabilize rather than unstabilize revenues. No refund occurs; the carry-forward merely results in the taxpayer's paying a smaller tax in prosperity than he would under no carry-over, or under a carry-back.

An individual may receive so little income in a year of depression that his personal exemption and credit for dependents is more than enough to cover his net income. If he is married, with three children, for example, his exemption and credits will total $3,000 under the present federal law. If his net income is only $2,500 there is $500 of his exemption that he does not need; it has gone to waste. If this excess could be carried back and applied against taxable income of previous years, to produce a refund of some of the tax paid in those years, the sensitivity of the personal income tax to cycle swings would be greatly enhanced. Whether such a carry-back of unused personal exemptions is justifiable, taking all tax considerations together, involves issues of equity not discussed in this chapter.

Except for the carry-over provisions the individual's income for the particular year in question is the tax unit; no account is taken of what his income was in past years or may be in future years. Of two persons, with the same total income over a period of years, the one whose income fluctuates the most will pay the most total tax over the years, because the rate scale is progressive (personal exemptions have been treated in the preceding paragraph). If it is desired to take the same total tax from both, a system of averaging personal income over a span of years is required. The question arises whether the adoption of averaging would alter the cycle-sensitivity of the tax and in which direction. Cumulative averaging will, in general, increase cycle-sensitivity, but under certain types of rate progression and certain kinds of wide fluctuation in income cycle-sensitivity will be lessened.[13]

13. See William Vickrey, "The Effect of Averaging on the Cycle-Sensitivity of the Yield of the Income Tax," *Journal of Political Economy*, 53 (September, 1945), 276; and Richard E. Slitor, "The Flexibility of Income-Tax Yield under Averaging," *Journal of Political Economy*, 54 (June, 1946), 266–267.

b. CORPORATION INCOME TAX

The degree of progression in corporation income tax rate schedules is usually very limited, and often there is no progression at all. Large exemptions at the bottom of the rate scale are also uncommon, if only because they are an invitation to artificial split-ups of a corporation into several smaller ones. But progression and exemptions, as already noted, do not necessarily tend to make the yield of the tax fluctuate more. Moreover, the base of the tax is inherently unstable and could be made more so by restricting it to undistributed profits. There might even be a carryback of negative undistributed profits in a period of depression.

Inventory and depreciation accounting are important factors in determining the degree of cyclical stability of a tax on business profits, including of course the profits of unincorporated concerns, subject to the personal income tax. The recent trend toward "lifo" (last in, first-out) inventory accounting tends to reduce the cyclical swings in stated profits. Cycle-sensitivity would also be reduced by a change from depreciation on a historical cost basis to depreciation on a current replacement basis, but this alteration in the measurement of profits is not likely to be accepted—in contrast to lifo inventory accounting, which has spread rapidly in the past decade.

c. EXCISE TAXES

The major federal excises are those on distilled spirits and cigarettes. The former is inherently sensitive to cycle swings, the latter relatively insensitive. The spirits tax could be made still more sensitive if the present specific rate were changed to an ad valorem rate. A similar alteration in the cigarette tax would have less effect, but the change might not be negligible. And if the ad valorem rate itself were graduated, sensitivity might be still further increased. Under the present system the rate is equivalent to a regressive ad valorem tax; the cheaper liquors and cigarettes pay a tax that is a larger per cent of their price than the more expensive brands.

d. GENERAL SALES TAX OR GENERAL SPENDINGS TAX

A federal general sales tax would probably fall somewhere in between the income tax and the present cigarette excise in its cycle-sensitivity. If the sales tax were equipped with personal exemptions to consumers, a device that might not be practicable except in the form of per capita tax "refunds" to consumers, the sensitivity would be increased. A general spendings tax, collected from the consumer on the basis of a return made out by him, could have progressive rates and personal exemptions.

But it would be less sensitive than the income tax, for it would be an income tax with savings exempted; and savings fluctuate by a larger percentage than does consumption, in most cycle changes.

e. PAYROLL TAXES

The payroll taxes imposed under the old-age benefit and unemployment compensation programs carry no personal exemptions and are levied at a flat rate. Like a general sales tax, they probably fall somewhere in between the income tax and the excises.

f. DEATH AND GIFT TAXES

The death and gift taxes vary with the cycle insofar as the price level changes substantially, especially the level of security prices and real estate. But collection commonly occurs some time after the event that gives rise to the tax, at least under the federal estate tax, so the significance of this restricted cycle-sensitivity is still further reduced. Moreover, the death and gift taxes, in their present form, play a minor role in the fiscal system.

g. CUSTOMS DUTIES

The customs duties, too, are now a minor part of the revenue-raising system. The fact that some of them are imposed on a specific rather than an ad valorem basis tends to dampen their cycle-sensitivity. An exception would occur if the specific duties rose so much in ad valorem terms, as prices declined, that they shut out imports to a degree that caused a substantial decline in revenue. In any event, this is not the kind of revenue decline that is sought as a countercycle fiscal policy, except for the short-run effect of stimulating home industries, and even this view requires an assumption that it is permissible to fight a depression by exporting unemployment.

h. PROPERTY TAX

The localities, and to some extent the states, depend on the property tax, which has become largely a tax on real estate. Assessors generally do not follow the cyclical swings of the market closely in valuing the properties, even where a genuine reassessment is made every year. In terms of tax liability, then, the property tax is one of the least sensitive in the entire system. In terms of tax collections the story is different. Delinquencies were so widespread and so long continued in the 1930's that the property tax did not cut into purchasing power during the depression to the extent that might at first be thought. Moreover, when good times arrived, a large part of the delinquent taxes was paid up, resulting in collections exceeding 100% of the current year's levy, in some recent years. Delinquency, however, is not an admissible way to create cycle-sensitivity. As a substitute a federal agency might be set up to loan money to property taxpayers with the property as security, to pay state and local property taxes, but there are obvious limitations to this device. Altogether, the property tax hardly ranks as one of the more promising automatic countercycle taxes.

2. *Requiring tax payments to keep pace with tax accruals*

During World War II the federal personal income tax was put on a current basis; all taxpayers, except farmers, are now required to pay the tax as it accrues during the year. They do so either through having the tax withheld from their wages or by paying quarterly installments, during the year, of the estimated tax that will accrue for the whole year. If the system were still on the prewar one-year lag basis, an initial recession year would find the taxpayers trying to scrape together the money to pay a large tax computed on the previous year's income, with a consequent strengthening of the deflationary forces. There would be no such effect if each taxpayer were provident enough to lay aside the tax money as the tax accrued, but such foresight would be too much to count on. With tax rates as high and exemptions as low as they now are, the former system of collection might easily have resulted, in a recession, in the degree of delinquency noted above under the property tax, except, no doubt, without any substantial recovery of past-due taxes in the succeeding boom.

So long as business continues down the deflationary pressures are weakened by requiring the tax on year A to be paid in year A rather than in the succeeding year B. But on the upswing the contrary result obtains. Suppose a series of years with income and tax as follows: A, $4,000, $400; B, $3,000, $300; C, $4,000, $400; D, $5,000, $500. Under current-payment and one-year lag sets of rules, the taxpayer pays as follows:

Year	Current Payment	One-year Lag
A (recession)	$400	(not specified)
B (trough)	300	$400
C (first recovery)	400	300
D (second recovery)	500	400
E (third recovery)	(not specified)	500

Once the trough is passed, recovery is stimulated by a one-year lag system compared with a current-payment system. It is only when the economy passes into an inflationary boom period and while it is in the downswing phase of the cycle that pay-as-you-go is a countercycle weapon, compared with a one-year lag. However, the other advantages of the pay-as-you-go system, or at least of the payroll-deduction part of it, are so substantial that the considerations just adduced are not likely to lead to a suspension of the system at the bottom of the next recession unless it develops into a deep depression. But in that event—suppose another 1931 or 1932 arrived, for instance—there would be substantial pressure to abandon the pay-as-you-go system, especially since a move back to the old method of payment would automatically result in a year of no tax payments.

The corporation income tax is not on a pay-as-you-go basis. However, it appears to be a well-established practice on the part of many corporations, at least with regard to the larger part of the total tax collected, to keep a current-assets position that is consistent with the accruing tax liabilities.

States and local units might reasonably require somewhat more prompt payment of the accrued property tax than is commonly called for under present laws. The other major taxes in the federal-state-local system, except the estate and gift taxes, are already on a current-collections basis, or close to it, or are too small or too irregular in their cyclical behavior to justify much trouble in changing from the existing system.

3. *Speeding up the payment of tax refunds* [14]

The tax refunds in question here are of two kinds: those that arise from the carry-back provisions and those that are caused by overwithholding or overestimating the estimated tax for the current year. The former applies to both the corporate and individual income tax; the latter, to the individual income tax only.

Suppose that a corporation has made profits in years A and B. As year C opens the corporation foresees an operating loss for the year. It anticipates a loss carry-back. It may estimate the tax benefit to come from the carry-back and apply it against the installments yet to be paid on the tax on year B income. Still, it may have a refund coming to it; the carry-back tax benefit may be so large that it exceeds the quarterly installments otherwise to be paid in year C. The refund of the excess cannot be made until year D, under present law. An "expedited adjustment" may then be applied for, and the refund must be paid within ninety days, if there are no material omissions or errors in the application. Perhaps some way could be found to grant this tentative refund sometime during year C, thus countering the deflationary pressure at once and helping the concern maintain its solvency.

If the business concern is a proprietorship or a partnership, it pays

14. Since these paragraphs were written, the carry-back under the federal income tax law has been restricted to one year.

no income tax as such, but its owners are paying currently on an estimated basis. If year C promises to be a deficit year, they pay no estimated
(current) tax during year C (abstracting from their other sources of
income). But this does not take care of the refund that may arise from
a carry-back of the year C loss. The owners have to wait until year D
before applying for a refund of taxes paid on the incomes of years A
and B. Here, too, it might be possible to grant tentative refunds to the
business owners during year C.

Somewhat similar problems are posed by overwithholding and over-
estimation of estimated personal income tax. Suppose that year C is a
prosperous one for the first six months, but a sharp recession develops
at the middle of the year. Employees are discharged or put on short time
or reduced pay. In many cases it will transpire, by the end of the year,
that the employee has had more deducted from his wages in the first half
of the year than he owes for the full year. This is almost sure to be the
case with those who become unemployed. Under the present law they
cannot apply for a refund of the tax overwithheld until January 1 of year
D. It might be possible to provide for prompt tentative refunds as year
C progresses; the refunds might be made through the same offices that
send out unemployment compensation checks if adequate federal-state
coordination on this point could be developed.

Many business owners, professional men, and others who filed estimated tax declarations in March of year C, paying quarterly installments in March and June, would become sure that, owing to the recession, their tax liabilities for the year would turn out to be less than the
amount they had already paid in the first two installments. But they too
cannot apply for a refund until January 1 of year D. Tentative refunds
made during year C would aid in maintaining the solvency of many
business concerns and would also ease the deflationary pressure on these
taxpayers viewed as consumers.

4. *Changing the tax rates, exemptions, or definition of base as business conditions change*

The anti-inflationary, antideflationary tendencies arising from the
cycle-sensitivity of any particular tax can be complemented by raising
rates, lowering exemptions, and broadening the definition of the tax
base in times of inflationary pressure, and by the reverse measures in
times of unemployment.

a. CHANGING THE DEFINITION OF THE TAX BASE

Changing the definition of the tax base back and forth from one phase
of business conditions to another has not been seriously considered, indeed, scarcely even mentioned. An extreme example of such a measure

would be the inclusion of capital gains and losses in the income tax base during inflationary periods and the exclusion of them in depressed periods. This procedure would doubtless be considered too inequitable to be tolerated. Yet somewhat the same result is reached by the common practice of allowing capital losses to be deducted only against capital gains of the same year; capital losses tend to occur in years when capital gains are scarce. Finally, the same kind of equity issue is present, although in less acute form, in all proposals for countercycle tax changes, whether affecting the definition of the base, the exemptions, or the rates.

In any event, it appears that the conflict of aims involved in changing the tax base with changes in business will not be a major one; for most taxes there is only a narrow variation in the definition of the base that is permissible without encountering injustice or administrative difficulties. Moreover, in some instances a countercycle change in definition of tax base would carry within it conflicting tendencies even for fiscal policy alone. Undistributed profits are usually larger in prosperity than in depression, from which it might be concluded that, considering only the countercycle issue, it would be well to include undistributed corporate profits in the corporate income tax base in prosperity but remove them in depression. But the taxation of undistributed profits tends to turn them into dividends, with a net result that may be more inflationary than anti-inflationary.

b. CHANGING THE EXEMPTIONS

Some taxes carry exemptions, or could be made to do so, which could be varied with business conditions.

The chief example is the federal income tax; a per capita exemption from income of $600 is allowed for each person, including dependents. Most of the issues here are also encountered in changing the income tax rates and will be covered in the rate-change section below. The chief difference is that an increase in exemptions, in contrast to a decrease in rates, removes some taxpayers from the tax rolls; and, of course, a decrease in exemptions during a boom period would add taxpayers. The number of taxpayers involved is likely to be large, even for small percentage changes in exemptions, under modern income taxes, which reach down into the densely populated levels of income.

The distribution of the tax relief or tax pressure, through a change in the exemption, also differs from the distributions that can be obtained under changes in rates. In general, for a given revenue change an alteration of the exemption is likely to have a stronger effect on the taxpayers near or below the existing lower limit of taxable incomes and on the well-to-do taxpayers, while a change in rates of the kind that would probably be utilized as a countercycle instrument would have a stronger effect on the middle or lower-middle group of taxable incomes.

The federal corporation income tax does not now carry a specific exemption, but could be made to do so if proper safeguards were devised against splitting up one corporation to obtain a multiple-exemption benefit. An increase in such an exemption during a depression would doubtless be of material assistance in maintaining the solvency and hence the employment-supplying power of a number of small corporations, but there are several facts that seriously limit the net effectiveness of such a change. The increase would not influence the actions, not even the dividend actions, of large corporations or of many small ones that enter the depressed period in a highly liquid condition. Unless a similar fluctuating exemption were granted to unincorporated concerns, competitive relationships might be disturbed; it is doubtful that any proposed change in the exemptions under the personal income tax would be large enough to eliminate this factor.

The federal estate and gift taxes carry specific exemptions, but, for reasons advanced in the section above on cycle-sensitivity, it is quite unlikely that countercycle variations in these exemptions would be significant for fiscal policy.

The excise taxes and the customs duties do not, with minor exceptions, allow of specific exemptions, to say nothing of variation in such exemptions.

The payroll taxes for old-age benefits and unemployment compensation do not contain specific exemptions. They might do so and the exemptions might be varied with business conditions, but such a plan would raise important problems of fairness in distribution of the tax burden. The two taxes do, however, contain open-end exemptions on the top; that part of the wage earner's earnings for the year that exceeds $3,000 (unemployment tax) or $3,600 (old-age tax) is exempt. Conceivably, these limits could be raised or lowered as countercycle instruments. There are equity issues arising here, too.

The old-age tax applies to earnings in establishments employing one or more workers; the unemployment compensation tax draws the exemption line higher up, depending on the state (the federal credit is set in terms of employers of eight or more). Countercycle fiscal policy would be served by varying even this exemption, but the equity disadvantages are so evident that the possibility is useful chiefly as illustrating the fact that fiscal policy aims must in some cases be overridden by other considerations.

If the property tax were a true tax on net worth, it would offer an in-

teresting field for countercycle changes in exemptions. As it is, the kinds
of specific exemption granted under the property tax are hardly suitable
for any such use. The chief example is the exemption granted in some
states for small or moderate-sized owner-occupied residences (the so-
called "homestead exemption").

C. CHANGING THE TAX RATES

More powerful and more flexible than changes in the definition of
the tax base or the exemptions are changes in the tax rates. However,
at least two major economic limitations to rate changes may be noted
here; the equity and noneconomic aspects are deferred to section IV.

The first limitation applies to the income tax. The tax rate has an upper
limit beyond which it cannot go in practice: 100% of the current income.
This limitation is not absolute; a rate of more than 100% can usually be
met by people with high incomes, since they normally possess liquid
capital assets to draw upon. But most of the income taxpayers would
find it impossible to pay such a rate or indeed any rate approaching
100%, and many more could do so only by forced sale of illiquid assets.
No doubt the same kind of varied and uncertain upward limit exists for
all the major taxes, but it seems more evident in the income tax.

The second limitation refers to taxes on sales, whether an excise tax
on a particular product or a general sales tax. The rate of such a tax
would be raised, under countercycle fiscal policy, when too much buying
was going on or was threatened. But the prospect that such a rise in
rate would occur would itself stimulate buying, as consumers and business buyers sought to get in ahead of the tax. Similarly, the prospect of a
reduction in rate would slow up buying. These reactions would tend to
negate the fiscal policy aims near the peak of the boom and during the
recession. As recovery progressed these same reactions would be beneficial, if it is assumed that rates would undergo some increase before the
recovery was completed; the prospect of the rate increase would stimulate purchasing and thus speed up the recovery. But even here there
are undesirable economic features insofar as the result would be an uneven series of bursts of spending, leading to confusion among businessmen on inventory policy.

This shortcoming of the excise tax or sales tax has been mentioned by
fiscal policy analysts, but in the present writer's opinion there has been
a tendency to underestimate its importance. The tradition of secrecy in
the British budget and, in the United States, the extensive use of the
floor stocks tax (and the contemplation of floor stock refunds if excise tax
rates are to be reduced) are evidence of the respect that public finance
students and administrators have for the consumer's alertness.

Tax rates may conceivably be lowered to zero; and one of the implications of much fiscal policy discussion is a complete suspension of all taxes as soon as unemployment becomes serious. It is somewhat surprising that this implication has not been brought more into the open for analysis. If, abstracting from all considerations except the goal of full employment, it is good to lower tax rates in order to induce a recovery (assuming that some degree of depression has already developed), why would it not be better to lower all taxes to zero so that recovery might come faster? The hesitation to advocate such a move, a hesitation that may be inferred from the lack of discussion of it, may reflect merely a belief that until the public's comprehension of fiscal policy develops further they would become highly confused when the measure was put into effect. It may reflect a disbelief in the willingness of Congress to restore the tax system promptly once recovery had been attained. But there are some purely economic considerations, too, although they are not of a kind that are given a prominent place in most of the Keynesian macro-economic model-building type of analysis that has proved so useful in developing fiscal policy discussion. Here the present essay is in danger of trespassing on fields allotted to others in this volume, and in any event the present writer has not developed his thoughts far enough to be very helpful; but it seems likely that the segmented nature of the economy, the lack of complete mobility of the factors of production, and the lack of close substitutes for many of the things consumers want would lead to a strong upward move in prices in some parts of the economy while the rest was still in some degree stagnant, despite the temporary removal of all taxes. The financing of any such tax holiday would of course have to be done by the federal government through that modern equivalent of the printing press, the central and commercial banking system.

But the logic of the problem will not even let us stop with this taxpayer's paradise. There is a taxpayer's heaven beyond. Tax rates can be lowered below zero. Negative taxation is another name for bounties or subsidies. If we may exercise the privilege of scholars and explore the fantastic in order to draw implications from it for the practical, we may inquire what would happen if all tax rates were lowered to, say, minus 10% or a specific equivalent. The producer of distilled spirits would get, say, $1 for every proof gallon he turned out, instead of paying $9 or $10; the wage earner would receive from the government $1 for every $10 he earned (and receive it, doubtless, through negative withholding). This thought is explored briefly in Chapters 8 and 9; its only claims to be considered a tax measure are: 1) it is a transfer expenditure, not a real expenditure, and 2) the amount and distribution of the outlay are some kind of a function of the amount the government collects when tax rates are positive.

Further consideration of the zero or negative tax level is given in section III below.

d. TIMING OF THE TAX CHANGES; ADMINISTRATIVE DISCRETION

1) FREQUENCY OF RATE CHANGE. Taxes differ somewhat in the frequency with which their rates and exemptions could be changed. If we disregard possible confusion and misunderstanding on the part of the taxpayer that might easily result from frequent changes in the rate of a tax—even if the changes were all in the same direction—there still remain some problems.

There seem to be two chief issues on this level of analysis. One of them concerns exemptions and rate graduation, and refinement of base; the other, the floor stocks question.

If the tax is simply one on sales or production, at a flat rate, the length of the time period for which the tax is imposed at a given rate is not particularly important. But for the income tax, in contrast, it is all-important. Suppose that fiscal policy considerations dictated one schedule of progressive rates for the first half year and a lower one for the second. Is the taxpayer's liability for the entire year to be found by computing two independent tax returns, one for each of the half years? If so, the need for carry-over of losses and the pressure for averaging individual incomes would be increased, especially in seasonal activities. It would seem preferable to compute the liability directly on the year's income as a whole, applying to it an average of the two half-year rate schedules, or some third rate schedule close to but not quite as low as the second half year's schedule. Or the half-year rate schedules could be regarded as both purely tentative, the government being free to establish, at the end of the year, whatever schedule for the year as a whole the then current economic conditions seemed to indicate; refunds or additional payments might then be in order on a large scale. These difficulties are not by themselves controlling, but they are substantial.

One possible misunderstanding may need to be considered here. It might be thought that the chief consideration, in ascertaining how frequent the changes in rate might be, is the frequency with which the tax is normally paid. The personal income tax illustrates the point. That part of the tax that is collected by withholding contrasts with the part that is paid only every quarter as estimated tax and still more sharply with that part paid by farmers, who need pay nothing on the current year's income until January 15 of the year following. If on April 1, for instance, it was decided that tax relief must be given as promptly as possible through a rate reduction, the decision could take effect as to withheld taxes within a month (under a tax administration that had been organized especially to handle countercycle changes quickly); as to estimated nonfarm taxes, within two and half months; as to farmers, not for eight and a half months. These statements are of course only approximate; some farmers, for example, who had been guiding their current spending activities by the thought of the tax payment to come next January would relax their thrift upon the announcement of the tax change (unless they feared a reverse change before the year was up!).

But considerations such as these tell against not the frequency with which a tax rate may be changed but the usefulness of changing it at all. If the time lag between decision and effect is substantial, damage may occur either from a series of frequent, small changes or a single large change. A small change by itself has less effect, good or bad; a series of small changes can cumulate to much the same effect as a single large one. Or perhaps the conclusion should be that, insofar as the particular tax shows a large time lag between decision and effect, it is a poor instrument for countercycle policy and, if used at all, must be used sparingly, with an eye to frequent reversal of policy and hence in a way that precludes it from being very effective even if the guesses all turn out right.

The floor stocks question concerns the excise taxes and a hypothetical federal sales tax if imposed at a substantial rate, say 10 or 15%. Here, among the major excise taxes, there would be a nice balance to be struck between frequent small changes in rate and infrequent but substantial changes. If the changes in rate were too frequent, the repeated floor stocks taxes or floor stocks refunds would become an intolerable nuisance; if a single change were too substantial, the rush or withdrawal of the public in order to buy cheaply, under the circumstances outlined in a preceding section, might work against instead of with the countercycle policy. But the smaller the change in tax rate the less is the public reaction and the less is the need for a floor stocks tax or refund. The optimum pattern of change might be a large number of prompt, small alterations without provisions for floor stocks.

The same problem and the same considerations apply to a general sales tax, especially a general retail sales tax, except that it may be assumed that for a general sales tax a floor stocks tax or refund would be impracticable in any event.

2) AUTOMATIC CHANGE VERSUS CHANGE AT DISCRETION OF THE EXECUTIVE BRANCH OR CONGRESS. At one extreme Congress might legislate a series of potential tax changes, to go into effect automatically as certain

economic indexes reached specified levels. At the other extreme, Congress might delegate authority to the executive branch to order changes in rates and exemptions, within specified limits, at its discretion. Various combinations in between are of course conceivable.

Here we reach several borders of the field of the present essay; one touches the domain of the political scientist; another, the territory, as yet largely unsurveyed, of the economist who would have the task of selecting the proper index or indexes and specifying the degree of tax change to accompany specified changes in the index. Lack of expert competence and limitations of time and energy all prohibit the present writer from exploring these issues in any detail here. But they are mentioned to prepare the ground for section IV, which deals with some of the conflicts of aims that would arise under a countercycle policy of tax change.

III. RELATIVE ROLE OF TAX ADJUSTMENTS IN FISCAL POLICY

In section II-4-c above the following question was raised: If a recession occurs and if a lowering of tax rates is deemed desirable as one method of checking the recession and promoting recovery, why not lower the rates still further, with the aim of promoting a still quicker recovery? Within the framework of the logic that supports a recommendation for a lowering of tax rates, is there any reason why the entire tax system should not be suspended until complete recovery has occurred? Outside this framework, objections to such a suspension can readily be found: conflicts with standards of fairness in the distribution of the tax burden over the entire cycle; administrative difficulties; impairment of state and local independence, if their tax system were somehow to be included in the prescription; and so on. But within the fiscal policy framework itself, is there any logic to a tax system in operation except at full employment?

Inflation, arising from the segmented construction of the economy, was seen to be one possible barrier to operating a recovery program under the forced draft of a zero tax level. But a more fundamental issue of fiscal policy is involved; it concerns the relative roles to be played, in recession, by decrease in taxes and increase in government expenditures.

Here, too, somewhat contrasting views may be found. Which view is taken depends partly on whether the analyst believes that the problem is primarily one of secular stagnation, that is, long-lasting periods of unemployment, or whether it is one of cyclical fluctuations around or just below a level of full employment. In the former case Mosak remarks, "We shall concern ourselves primarily with such measures as greatly expanded programs of social security and provision for adequate housing, adequate hospital care and adequate education. We shall support more Tennessee Valley Authorities, slum clearance, and urban redevelopment." [15] There is no proposal here to eliminate the tax system first and then resort to increased public spending only if tax elimination is not adequate. The reason why no such proposal is made is that "the choice between different measures for achieving full employment can be made only in terms of their relative marginal social utilities," [16] and the marginal utility of tax reduction, or, rather, of the use of resources that would follow from tax reduction, is to be balanced against the marginal utility of an increase in education, hospitals, etc.

The other view, set forth by Hart, does not directly compare the marginal utility of tax reduction with that of public expenditures. Instead, an optimum distribution of the economy's resources among private and public use, assuming full employment, is set as the standard: so much to private consumption, so much to private investment, and so much to government use, the amounts being set by a comparison of the marginal utilities of each. The tax system is then put at a level that (together with monetary policy) allows full employment. "The common sense of public expenditures is to carry them to the margin at which they are of equal social value with alternative private expenditures of equal amount, irrespective of revenues; revenues and transfer payments (together with monetary policy) can then be used to keep the economy at full employment." [17] Suppose, for example, that at full employment the national income is $200 billion; and suppose further that it is somehow determined that the optimum distribution of resources is: consumption, $150 billion; private investment, $20 billion; government services, $30 billion. Let corporate profits and business taxes be disregarded, to simplify the illustration; consumers' income, before personal tax, is $200 billion. If consumers will spend $150 billion out of a disposable income of $170 billion, then $30 billion of tax shall be levied; but if, instead, consumers will spend $150 billion only if their disposable income is $190 billion, then only $10 billion of tax shall be levied, for only so can there be maintained the optimum amounts of the three types of product, already set by a calculation that has nothing directly to do with tax amounts (private saving, $40 billion, will then equal, as it always must, ex post, investment, $20 billion, plus government deficit, $20 billion). And if the consumers will spend $150 billion only if their disposable income is

15. Jacob L. Mosak, "National Budgets and National Policy: A Final Reply," *American Economic Review*, 36 (September, 1946), 639.

16. *Ibid.*, p. 638.

17. Albert Gailord Hart, "National Budgets and National Policy: A Rejoinder," *American Economic Review*, 36 (September, 1946), 633.

$210 billion, the tax system must be suspended and replaced by subsidies to consumers—transfer payments—of $10 billion, according to the logic of Hart's prescription.

Actually, these two approaches are not different, on the mechanical level of using equal marginal utilities as the test. In Hart's system, as in the one described by Mosak, taxes are what they are because another dollar decrease in tax would cause an increase in consumption or private investment and necessitate a reduction of a dollar (or fraction) in public expenditures to maintain full employment without inflation. By hypothesis, the new situation would be less satisfactory than the old. Still, there does seem to be a difference implicit in the two approaches, or perhaps it is more nearly accurate to say that the two approaches raise, without solving it, the question: Who is to determine when the marginal social utilities of the various types of product are equal? In some vague sense we may imagine the balancing process going on in the mind of the taxpayer. That process is given a somewhat more explicit recognition in a method that feels its way toward the optimum-allocation, full-employment level by comparing the marginal utilities of successive increments of tax reduction and of government expenditures on goods and services. The other method is apt to create the impression that the relative marginal utilities of private goods and public goods can be set at equality without regard to how much the tax burden is and, hence, without regard to its marginal impact. The particular items of private expenditures displaced by an increment in government expenditure will depend in part on who is being hit how hard by how much of a tax system. In terms of the illustration above: if the marginal utilities of consumption, investment, and government services are equal at 150, 20, and 30, respectively, when consumers' propensities are such that 30 of tax is called for, they are not likely to be equal if consumers' propensities are different (e.g., if 10 of tax is necessary).

A more important problem, however, is posed by the fact that there has been no plan devised to make possible a comparison of the respective marginal utilities.

Two conclusions seem justified. First, the question of the relative role of tax reduction in a depressed economy is primarily a problem not of obtaining full employment but of optimum allocation of resources. Second, the economist has not offered a solution as to how such an optimum allocation is to be determined under a system in which a part of the product is distributed by government, so that there is for this segment of output no internal comparison, within the individual, between what one gets and what one sacrifices to get it, a comparison that is an essential feature of welfare theory in economics.[18] Moreover, can there be much reason to believe that economists, working alone, will ever develop usable standards for an optimum distribution under these circumstances? Is this not the case where the political scientist, and perhaps also the sociologist, must participate in setting the standards for an optimum allocation of resources, or in devising mechanisms that will register what the standard is? And in view of the intelligence-quotient distribution, considered in the light of the demands that the modern industrial system makes on one's intelligence and adaptability, a psychologist's counsel would be welcome also.

IV. CONFLICTS BETWEEN FISCAL POLICY AIMS AND OTHER GOALS

Fiscal measures that are considered with a view to preventing large-scale unemployment may conflict with other economic aims, or with goals that lie outside the field of economics. Some of these conflicts are noted here; the list can hardly be exhaustive, in view of the slight amount of attention that has been devoted so far to unearthing the potential conflicts and evaluating them.

1. *Conflicts with standards of equity in distribution of taxes*

a. LEAST AGGREGATE SACRIFICE VERSUS INCENTIVE EFFECTS

The best-known case of a conflict with standards of fairness in distribution of the tax burden is found in the problem of how to follow the optimum distribution of sacrifice, insofar as it calls for least aggregate sacrifice, without at the same time destroying incentive. Pigou concludes that least aggregate sacrifice is found to be preferable to equal sacrifice, on the basis of the ultimate or intuitive standards that he accepts.[19] Least aggregate sacrifice calls for lopping off 100% of the top part of the highest income until it is reduced to the level of the next highest income, then lopping the second income, and the first one further until both are down to the level of the next highest income, and so on—a marginal rate of zero up to a certain level and 100% beyond that level. No one seriously proposes such a tax, but let us explore the purely economic conse-

18. For a critical review of theories of public expenditure and tax distribution that have attempted to utilize marginal equilibrium analysis to explain public finance in terms so applicable to the private sector, see Erwin von Beckerath, "Formen moderner Finanztheorie," in *Festgabe für Georg von Schanz*, Band I, 1–19. (Tübingen, Mohr, 1928). The theories criticized include those of de Antonio Viti de Marco, Knut Wicksell, Emil Sax, Erik Lindahl, and F. Y. Edgeworth.

19. A. C. Pigou, *op. cit.*, Pt. II, chs. 4, 5, and 6.

quences of it. Taxation is needed in order to check private activity, or, rather, private activity directed to producing goods for the private sector of the economy (see section I above). The fact that such a tax would check this kind of activity is not therefore a count against it. But insofar as it also checked activity by private persons on behalf of the government the conflict would reappear. Suppose, however, that the suppliers of goods and services to the government do not have incomes high enough to put them in the 100% bracket. What objections to the tax would remain? The tax would raise no revenue; but a sovereign government can resort to borrowing or to creating money, which (the argument runs) could not cause inflation as long as private demand was sufficiently dampened by the tax. This reasoning is of course all on a formal, highly abstract level but consistent within itself. What, then, is the real difficulty with such a tax? Presumably the danger is to be found in the ever-increasing liquidity in which the economy would be floating or, if the government financed itself by borrowing from a stock of money unchanged in amount, in the high interest rates. This is not the point to pursue the chain of reasoning, which soon gets complicated. The purpose here is merely to suggest that perhaps the familiar conflict between the least aggregate sacrifice goal and the goal of an economy employing its resources fully and with an optimum allocation of resources among competing ends, is a somewhat different kind of conflict than what has hitherto been suggested.

b. PENALIZING INDIVIDUALS WITH FLUCTUATING INCOMES

A countercycle tax policy calls for high tax rates and low exemptions in prosperity and low tax rates with high exemptions in periods of unemployment. Unfortunately for the canons of fairness, the tax relief goes to those who need it least, that is, those who still have some income. And the extra heavy taxation of boom times strikes most severely those who could not benefit by tax relief in depression; at least this is so insofar as the trades that suffer most from depression get rather higher than usual pay in periods of prosperity. At any rate, as between two individuals who get the same total income over the cycle, one in uniform amounts year by year, the other all in a lump in prosperity, it is evident that a countercycle tax policy will take more money from the taxpayer with the lumpy income though welfare analysis might conclude that he was, if anything, worse off than the man with the steady income, even before tax.

Under a personal income tax it might be possible to eliminate this differential by some system of averaging, involving refunds; but countercycle changes in the rates of the corporation income tax, the sales tax, the excises, and the property tax (especially on business property) could hardly be purged of the injustice in question.[20]

C. DISCRIMINATING BETWEEN THOSE WHO ARE COVERED AND THOSE OUTSIDE OF THE OLD-AGE BENEFIT SYSTEM

It is sometimes proposed that the rates of the payroll taxes levied under the federal old-age benefit program should be varied counter-cyclewise. So long as the old-age benefit plan does not have complete coverage, the uncovered part of the public are in danger of an unjust exaction levied through general taxes, like the income tax, to cover a deficit in the old-age account. There is nothing in a countercycle variation of payroll tax rates that necessarily leads to a larger deficit in the fund than would occur under a stable rate, but the chance is there and needs to be considered before payroll taxes are made part of the fluctuating-rate system.

Many of the state payroll taxes for unemployment compensation contain merit rating provisions that reduce the tax rate when a firm has a continued record of high employment. These provisions, however useful they may be on other grounds, tend to enhance the cycle swings instead of dampening them.

2. *Conflict with optimum distribution of political power*

Action under a countercycle tax policy could be taken more swiftly if Congress delegated to the executive substantial power to alter tax rates or even completely suspend certain taxes. Whether such a program would give better results than one formulated at the cost of some delay but with the benefit of deliberation by many persons—congressmen, businessmen, economists, and others called for hearings—is not to be taken for granted; but, if it is decided that promptness of action is of the essence, what conflicts arise with political goals in delegating taxing powers to the executive?

This is a question to which answers must be suggested chiefly by those authors of the present volume who are particularly qualified to discuss the political-science aspects of taxation. The history of democratic in-

20. The problem here is analogous to, though not quite the same as, that of "discrimination according to age," which occurs when an event that does not recur regularly, like war (we still suppose), calls for higher taxes. "The extraordinary, temporary income-tax rates become a special tax on those who happen at that particular time to be at the peak of their earning power but also [if the income tax is being compared with a sales tax] at the peak of their saving." Carl Shoup, "Taxes Available to Avert Inflation," in Shoup, Milton Friedman, and Ruth P. Mack, *Taxing to Prevent Inflation* (New York, Columbia University Press, 1943), p. 95.

stitutions shows how concerned the representatives of the public have had to be in the past over the amount of financial power that could safely be entrusted to the executive branch. Any system that delegates much power over tax rates will have to be reasonably proof against the occasional careless or dishonest executive, and particularly proof against anyone who would deliberately seek to use the new device as a means of fastening himself securely in a seat of power. At this point it seems that the economist and the political scientist must sit down together for some long and arduous sessions. What indexes are available by which the delegation of power over tax rates could limit discretionary action by the executive branch? What combination of rules based on such indexes would give the optimum mixture of freedom to view each falling-off in business or inflationary pressure in the light of the circumstances peculiar to the particular case, without giving the executive too much opportunity to turn the mechanism to an illegitimate use? What person, or group of persons within the executive branch, would have the effective power to make the decision? Should it be the body that has the most intimate knowledge of the tax system, the Treasury Department, or should it be some group that is continually analyzing the state of the economy as a whole, like the Council of Economic Advisers? If it is to be a body of the latter type, is it safe to continue to have it located within the Executive Office of the President, where it does not feel free to criticize publicly any past action of the President or other branches of the executive? It might be better to have the discretionary power rest initially in some economic council appointed jointly by the President and Congress and owing intellectual allegiance to neither but rather to the public as a whole. The final decision would presumably have to be made by the President, though it is possible to conceive of the council itself being granted by Congress the final discretionary power over tax rates —if someone can devise safeguards to prevent such a council from becoming disquietingly powerful.

The specific issue of constitutionality needs to be discussed. If delegation of the power to fix tax rates is deemed advisable, must the Constitution be amended before such delegation may be made?

3. *Conflicts with aspects of social psychology*

No attempt should be made to institute a system of fluctuating tax rates until it is reasonably clear that the system would not cause so much confusion, or invoke so much irrationality, in businessmen and income recipients generally that the net result would be unfavorable. Here the economist feels somewhat at a loss, and although he is not sure just whom to turn to, he suspects that it may be those who have made social psychology or some allied field their specialty. He can only instance the irrational behavior that has accompanied fiscal policy in the past and ask what it may indicate for the future.

For example: in December, 1947, just before Christmas the Treasury and the Federal Reserve Board surprised the government bond market by announcing that the Federal Reserve banks would henceforth support the market at a somewhat lower price than theretofore; the peg was moved down an appreciable distance. This brought forth a flood of selling of marketable bonds, for reasons that can be judged rational, whether or not future events show them to have been correct. But it also produced some turning in of savings bonds, Series E, by uninformed, timid individuals who had heard that government bonds had gone down and thought they had better get out before anything more happened. Actually, of course, the savings bonds were not at all affected, since they are by contract redeemable at the option of the holder at a fixed schedule of prices, depending on the age of the bond. This reaction was very limited in size and probably not widespread geographically, but that it happened at all illustrates the need for taking the irrational into account in making any policy decision on fiscal matters.

What would be the reaction of wage earners who found their take-home pay fluctuating because of changes in the withholding tax decreed by executive order or by frequent changes of law by Congress? Especially, what would be the reaction when the changes were upward, without there being any change even hinted in the rate of government spending? Would it be a very difficult task to educate them to the idea that the government should give them tax relief when times are hard and increase their tax burdens in good times, quite apart from how much the government is spending?

Would such a tax program affect businessmen's decisions unfavorably, owing to the element of uncertainty it might be said to inject into their planning—or would it be a systematic kind of uncertainty which would not really trouble them?

Would general public resistance to tax increases be so deeply rooted that in practice a program of up-and-down tax rates would be nothing but a program of tax decreases? If so, the resulting inflation might produce a worse depression than what would result from a fiscal policy that kept tax rates stable at a fairly high level.

The present writer's rather uninformed attitude is one of restrained optimism on such matters, but the economist could do with a great deal of advice from his colleagues in related fields.

4. *Conflicts with the federal system of government*

If the kind of tax policy discussed in this chapter is to be effective, must the present federal system be modified substantially and would the modifications be of a kind that would impair some of the values we now receive from decentralization, including a degree of local responsibility and interest in self-government?

The states and localities are blocked at almost every turn if they try to adopt a countercycle tax policy. Fundamentally, this is because they are small units in a large economy, with a free flow of persons and goods from one unit to another.

1. They cannot rely heavily upon the most cycle-sensitive tax of importance, the personal income tax, because of the relative ease with which the taxpayer may move elsewhere to live or work and because some of the investment income of the taxpayer may arise in other areas, making it difficult to check outright evasion and occasionally involving constitutional inhibitions on the power to tax. The fact that the federal government imposes a heavy income tax is also a factor, but probably a minor one, since it allows the deduction of state and local income taxes paid in computing income subject to the federal tax—a device which markedly reduces the net added burden of a state or local income tax (it provides what amounts to a hidden form of federal aid to those states and local units). Despite the difficulties involved, however, the local income tax promises to continue spreading in the near future—an indication of the financial problems especially facing the cities. Not with a view toward promoting a countercycle program but simply to finance needed local services, several of the larger local units will probably make their system more cycle-sensitive in the near future.

It is a commentary on the complex constitutional inhibitions and intra-community conflicts of interests that several of the major industrial states, which could do a better job with the income tax than the local units, are not now imposing a general personal income tax and show no indication of doing so—for instance, Illinois, Pennsylvania, Indiana, and Ohio. Meanwhile, Columbus, Toledo, Philadelphia, and some seventy small local units in Pennsylvania are imposing personal income taxes of a sort. And it is just in the agricultural South, where an income tax is bound to be the least effective, that it is the most widespread; every state in the South except Florida, Tennessee, and Texas imposes a personal income tax.

2. Even if the states and localities could make use of the personal income tax, it would not be to the interest of any one of them, acting alone, to adopt such a tax on the grounds of its automatic countercycle

effect. When incomes decline the taxpayer is automatically relieved of some tax; but the use he makes of the funds thus spared may not benefit the state or locality concerned. He may spend the money in a way that relieves unemployment, not in his own state or local unit, but elsewhere. Narrowly considered, Nebraska's interest does not lie in releasing funds that will be spent on automobiles manufactured in Michigan. If all states and localities could act together, the common interest would of course be served; but such concerted action, however desirable, raises the question of how far the governmental system should depart from the rather decentralized structure that now characterizes it. Similar considerations are relevant in any plans for changing state and local tax rates on a countercycle basis. However, an important qualification must be made. Some of the larger industrial states, like New York, Pennsylvania, and Illinois, would probably suffer so little "leakage" in tax relief that, even from their own points of view, it might be to their interest to follow a countercycle tax policy, within fairly narrow limits. The recently enacted tax-reserve funds in California and New York State are a small step, but at least a step, in this direction.

3. To the extent that the state and local tax system has shown countercycle characteristics, the result has not been welcomed, even by some of those most concerned with fiscal policy.[21] The power of the localities to borrow is too limited (and, as Hansen and Perloff have pointed out, the burden of debt interest is so often a real one, the interest going to creditors outside the community), that a decline in tax yields is usually accompanied by a drastic slashing of expenditures, and the net countercycle effect may be a minus quantity. Moreover, where the decline in tax revenue reflects widespread delinquency, as it did under the property tax in the 1930's the countercycle effect is purchased at too high a price in terms of community morale and morals.

In the event of another substantial recession the borrowing problem of the localities is likely to be still more troublesome than it was in the 1930's. By the time the next recession threatens, the localities will be relying more largely than before on cycle-sensitive taxes. How will Philadelphia or New York City continue their services when the income tax or sales tax revenues decline sharply?

This chapter can attempt no solution of these problems. The country will be fortunate if any progress at all is made on this aspect of the full-

21. Thus Alvin H. Hansen and Harvey S. Perloff, *State and Local Finance in the National Economy* (New York, Norton, 1944), p. 51, speak of "the devastating effects of business depression on state and local finances," with respect to the decline in tax collections of all state and local units from 1930 to 1933 and the rise in tax delinquency.

employment issue by the time the present wave of prosperity starts to recede, so entangled are the fiscal policy aspects of state and local finances with important (in some cases perhaps overriding) issues of local autonomy. But the facts adduced here on taxation alone may suggest that we need a prompt start on an official survey of federal-state-local relationships that could promise to conclude with action, not merely another report, and that we need it not so much because the federal-state-local tax system is complex, or "overlapping," or detrimental to interstate business, or too heavy, in some sense, in the aggregate (although all these questions need continual reexamination), but rather because the states and localities are rapidly getting themselves into a cycle-sensitive condition without achieving a corresponding power to use surplus funds or new borrowing. So, if another powerful depression strikes, there may occur a panic-inspired slashing of expenditures and raising of tax rates that will surpass those of the 1930's and push the economy further downhill. One thing seems certain: if the federal government does not now take the lead in designing the necessary measures to forestall these reactions, nothing will be done. The state and local units are not able to work together to initiate such measures, if only because the kind of measures that will be most effective must be in large part embodied in federal laws.

CHAPTER VII. *Monetary Policy for Income Stabilization*

BY ALBERT GAILORD HART

I. MEANING OF MONETARY POLICY *

Monetary policy, as is indicated by placing this discussion between one of taxation and one of public expenditures, is a sector of the "monetary and fiscal" area. Specifically, monetary policy is policy which influences the public's stock of money and money substitutes, or the public's demand for such assets, or both—that is, policy which influences the public's *liquidity position.*

In terms of instrumentalities, monetary policy is policy toward:

1) Bank credit.
2) Loan policy of government agencies.
3) Treasury cash surplus or deficit.
4) Public debt management.
5) Interest.
6) Business expectations.
7) Monetary standards.
8) Various sundries, chiefly possible taxes on liquid assets.

As the list (particularly items 3, 4, and 5) implies, monetary policy is concerned with instrumentalities which are also the business of fiscal policy. But monetary and fiscal policy are concerned with different aspects. Fiscal policy is concerned with the sources and destinations of government receipts and revenues, measured as flows—billions of dollars per annum. Monetary policy is less concerned with the composition of the budget and looks at the cash surplus or deficit in terms of its cumulative effect on the public's liquid assets. Fiscal policy is concerned with interest disbursements as an outflow from the Treasury, monetary policy with interest rates as an incentive factor in business. Monetary policy is interested in various taxes—but not in terms of their potential

* This paper was drafted early in 1949. Rather than rewrite it, I am attaching a series of footnotes, marked by asterisks to distinguish them from the notes of the original paper, to comment on the interesting changes that have taken place between early 1949 and mid-1951. A.G.H.

yearly revenue yield so much as their effect on the public's urge to hold various types of assets.[1]

In drawing the line between monetary and fiscal policy for this discussion, I am not trying to eliminate this overlap. It is more urgent, in such a book as this, to make sure that important relationships are taken into account than to minimize duplication; so I am taking a broad view of the jurisdiction of monetary policy.

II. How Powerful Is Monetary Policy?

Twenty-five years ago monetary policy was in fashion. It was widely believed, and still more widely hoped, that gentle nudges by the Federal Reserve System could avert both inflation and serious depression. In the late 1930's fashions in policy discussion were very different and there was little confidence or even interest in monetary policy.

I write this chapter in the belief that the reaction was much overdone and that monetary policy makes a great deal of difference in the working of the economy. On the other hand, I believe that the intensity (though not ordinarily the direction) of the effects of monetary measures is highly unpredictable. In consequence my main emphasis in this chapter is on keeping monetary policy from compounding economic instability rather than on an active monetary policy designed to forestall or correct maladjustments in the economy from month to month.

1. *Grounds for undervaluing the power of money*

Why was there such a sharp "deemphasis" of money after the 1920's? Partly, undoubtedly, because economists and the public were struggling to understand the new problems of fiscal policy, of international economic policy, and then of war; so that discussion naturally focused on the new and left the old in the shadow. Partly it was an undiscriminating reaction to the fact that after the strong claims put forward for monetary policy as a stabilizing force, the "new era" prosperity broke down so completely. Among economists, however, the most important reason for the change of emphasis is doubtless a change in theoretical position, produced by the infiltration of Keynesian ideas.

Before discussing the theoretical issue I want to stress that the experience of the interwar period did not justify deciding that monetary policy is powerless. True, monetary policy did not prevent prosperity from breaking down after 1928; nor did monetary policy succeed in "re-

1. I have presented a full-dress discussion of economic stabilization policy, focused on money but also dealing extensively with fiscal policy, in A. G. Hart, *Money, Debt and Economic Activity* (New York, Prentice-Hall, 1948), Pt. V, pp. 415–519.

flating" prices and restoring prosperity in the 1930's. But the lessons of this experience must not be misconstrued. They do not show that monetary policy is powerless but rather that mistakes in monetary policy can be disastrous.

It should never be forgotten that the great depression of the 1930's was marked by the greatest monetary deflation in a century—that of 1931–33. There is room for debate on the wisdom of monetary policy during the 1920's and even in 1930. But the policy of tight money adopted in 1931 was simply suicidal. The chronic panic which ruled from the autumn of 1931 to the spring of 1933, with hoarding of paper money and of gold and with thousands of bank failures, was the product of avoidable errors in monetary policy.

There was a monetary policy of reflation in 1933–36; and it did fail to give us full recovery. But this is far from being conclusive evidence that monetary policy is powerless. In the first place, the previous deflation had landed us in a situation which monetary-fiscal policy should never be asked to cope with. Activity was at such a low ebb that modern equipment was standing idle and financial incentives could do little to restore investment in producers' durable goods. House rents were so low relative to construction costs that construction was very hard to stimulate. Economic breakdown had gone so far as to disrupt many business organizations; and overcautious policies were natural for those who had barely escaped being wiped out. In the second place, monetary policy in 1933 centered on devaluation of the dollar—a process which had much less domestic monetary influence than its doctrinaire advocates expected and which blocked efforts to get international cooperation for world recovery. In the third place, many of the economic policies adopted in the early stages of the upswing were directly restrictive of output (crop restriction, soft coal controls, and many National Recovery Administration codes). In the fourth place, many measures were taken which increased the public's demand for liquid assets, thus offsetting much of the growth in the stock of liquid assets. The higher price level created through wage-raising, farm-pricing, and NRA codes worked in this direction. So did the uncertainty created by necessary reforms of labor relations, security markets, and taxation.

In short, the downswing of the early 1930's testified to the effectiveness of a mistaken monetary policy. The incompleteness of the upswing testified to the limited effectiveness of a rather garbled monetary policy under very difficult conditions.

2. *Theoretical skepticism of the role of money*

Perhaps more important than interwar experience in the recent skepticism about the role of money is a theoretical oversimplification linked with the Keynesian notion of "liquidity preference." In the Keynesian analytical "model," a very simple causal chain is set up: National product and employment are determined, given a "prospensity to consume function," by "investment." Investment is determined, given a "marginal efficiency of capital function," by the rate of interest. The rate of interest is determined, given a "liquidity preference function," by the stock of money; *or* the rate of interest may be set by a policy decision if the authorities are willing and able to endow the public with the stock of money it will elect to hold (under its liquidity preference function) at the rate set.

According to this theoretical simplification, the stock of money (or by extension the stock of liquid assets) can affect economic activity only via the rate of interest. This view gives the stock of money a rather trifling role. In the first place, policy may act directly on interest, making the stock of money merely a by-product. In the second place, interest policy itself has come to be deemphasized, on the basis of various rather flimsy field studies of business decisions which seem to show that interest plays a minor role and of the limited volume of investment developed under low-interest policies during the 1930's. The policy upshot is a contention that wise monetary policy consists simply in keeping interest rates low and steady.

This preoccupation with interest is reinforced by the fact that so much of the monetary policy discussion is in the context of day-to-day Treasury debt management, Federal Reserve operation, and commercial banking. The Treasury has adopted low and stable interest rates as its symbols of success in debt management. Opposition to the low and steady interest line springs chiefly from commercial bankers. Their obvious financial stake in higher interest rates may lead skeptics to underrate the merits of their case. In any event, they are inclined to accept the notion that interest is the kingpin of monetary policy, so that the discussion they generate does not help much to correct the lack of attention to supply and demand of liquid assets.

On closer inspection the notion that interest is the only significant link between the public's liquidity position and its expenditures for investment and consumption does not stand up. This view of interest implies a "perfectly competitive" capital market, on which every firm and every household can borrow or lend as much as it chooses at a market rate of interest. The capital market is not like that and cannot be. Actually, borrowing power is limited by "capital rationing" rules, which limit the ratio of borrowings to equity capital to a maximum (different for different types of business but pretty definite for each type) which it is difficult or dangerous to exceed. Creditors insist also on the maintenance of respectable liquidity ratios. Ability to invest depends on possession of a margin of liquid assets, or on ability to get new funds either by equity financing (plowing in earnings or floating stock), or by a mixture of equity financing and borrowing. Ability to get new outside funds, in turn, depends on potential security buyers or lenders having a margin of liquid assets. Besides these effects of liquidity on investment, we also have to allow for direct effects on expenditure and saving by consuming households. A household with inadequate liquid resources (excess demand for liquid assets) plans to build up its position by holding down current outlays and setting aside part of income. A household with more than adequate liquid resources can relax the safeguards on its liquidity; it can budget closer to income and be less insistent on providing for unexpected outlays by cutting other outlays below the budget.

With given consumer needs and a given field of investment opportunities—and with the given interest rates—the propensities to consume and to invest will therefore be strengthened by any event which creates an excess supply of liquid assets. Experimental evidence for this proposition is offered by the high ratios of consumption to disposable income—and of investment to activity—in 1946–48, despite scarcities of goods and services which made it unusually hard to spend. By the same argument any event which creates an excess demand for liquid assets will weaken propensities to invest and consume. These theoretical findings indicate that monetary policy can take hold on events through other channels than interest changes.

3. *Uncertainty of monetary influences*

Both history and economic logic say that monetary policy can have a powerful impact. But we lack a basis for gauging that impact closely. Traditionally, economists have relied on the stability of the "velocity of circulation of money"—that is, a ratio of "transactions" to money stock. But this stability is too rough to give more than the order of magnitude of the effects of monetary changes. On the record, we can expect the dollar value of annual gross national product to be between $1\frac{1}{4}$ and $2\frac{1}{4}$ times the public's total holdings of currency and bank deposits (checking plus saving)—most of the time probably between $1\frac{1}{2}$ and 2. But this basis of estimation is so crude that it admits of either a rise or a fall of several tens of billions between 1938 and 1949.

Historically, the prewar and interwar periods show a very clear-cut agreement in direction of movement (with exceptions only for swings very small in duration or amplitude) between production and the public's liquid holdings. But there was a great deal of variation in the relative magnitude of these movements. Under different conditions, even the direction of the relation may possibly diverge. The postwar leveling off of liquid assets in 1948 did not prevent a rise of both activity and prices relative to 1947; and many analysts (of whom I am one) hold that if we had had a slight decrease instead of a substantial expansion of liquid assets during 1946–47 we would still have enjoyed output expansion—though with a smaller rise of prices.[2] This belief is based on the existence in 1946–47 of a huge stock of liquid assets left over from the war and on widespread indications that there was a strong excess supply of such assets.

A classification of reasons for doubt as to the magnitude of effects to be expected from specified monetary measures includes the following:

1) Many possible measures affect both the stock of liquid assets and the demand for liquid assets *in the same direction*, so that their effect on *net demand* for liquid assets may be ambiguous.

2) Many monetary influences are likely to take hold with a lag rather than instantaneously. People do not complete their adjustments to new monetary situations in a few hours or days; but how many weeks or months it takes is uncertain. This fact is a handicap not merely in forecasting effects of future measures but in gauging effects of past measures.

3) We are now over twenty years away from our last experience of anything like a stable peacetime prosperity, so that our basis for forecasting "normal" behavior is unusually weak, for lack of comparable experience.*

4) The strength of the "disturbances" of the demand for liquid assets which monetary policy may have to offset is unpredictable and

---

* If we take 1949–50 as approximating a stable peacetime prosperity, deflated per capita holdings of currency plus deposits (using the wholesale price index as deflator) work out at about 700 1926 dollars. The percentage rate of increase since 1926 (when the figure was $425) is slightly less than from 1906 (when it was $265) to 1926 and considerably less than from 1923 to 1929. This suggests resumption of long-standing trends. On the other hand, if we exclude time deposits, the growth from 1926 to 1949–50 appears much faster than from 1906 to 1926 or from 1923 to 1929.

2. Currency plus demand deposits rose 11%, the foregoing plus time deposits 12½%, all the foregoing plus government bonds in the hands of the nonbank public 5%, from the end of 1945 to the end of 1947. The official cost-of-living index rose 27%.

hard to gauge even for the present and recent past. This is because the "precautionary" and "speculative" motives for holding liquid assets are linked with people's expectations of the future—about which we do not yet know very much except that expectations are volatile.

This uncertainty, as will appear below, points to caution in laying out monetary policy.

III. LIMITING THE INSTABILITY OF BANK CREDIT

The "inherent instability of bank credit" has been blamed as the primary cause of business fluctuations by some investigators. Most students of fluctuations would not go so far but would agree that the instability of credit has sharpened both upswings and downswings of business and has contributed to the breakdown of prosperities. For a number of reasons (notably the institution of Federal Deposit Insurance, higher reserve requirements, the increased importance of government debt among bank assets, and the greater prevalence of medium-term amortized loans) the instability of bank credit is less than in the 1920's. But as will appear from the analysis below the problem is far from solved.

1. *Bank credit as a destabilizer*

The case against bank credit as a destabilizing force in the economy is very simple. Suppose there is a downturn in business activity. (We need not ask why; the question is what happens next.) Such a downturn creates incentives for banks to contract credit. Customers who a few months ago could pass the tests of credit-worthiness cannot now pass the same tests: falling prices of commodities, securities and real estate that might secure loans reduce people's borrowing power. Profit incomes out of which borrowings might be paid off shrink first and fastest of all types of income. The classes of firms most dependent on bank borrowing are particularly likely to develop "unsound" ratios of inventory to sales and to find collections worse on their credit sales. Thus under a mechanical application of unchanging credit rules for separating the sheep from the goats, many who were formerly sheep will be turned by a downswing of business into goats.

Besides, a downswing leads bankers to reexamine their credit standards and tighten them up. Therefore in a downswing now loans are refused, old loans are called, established lines of credit are curtailed, and doubtful bonds are sold off. Bank customers are forced into "distress sales" of assets held as security for loans, while normal sales are interfered with because the buyers cannot borrow, as planned, to make their purchases. Experience under tightening credit leads the stronger firms to build up cash so as to insure against having to borrow later. Thus the "business-like" operation of banks during a downswing tends to reduce the stock of liquid assets and to increase the demand for such assets: it tends to generate an excess demand for liquid assets, which is a force curtailing the public's expenditures and thus reinforcing the downswing.

If the banks push their loan contraction extremely hard, credit may freeze: inability of one group to borrow blocks the sales of those now in debt, so that bankers' efforts to collect loans may make collection impossible. Almost complete paralysis of the economy may ensue, as happened in 1933. (It should be said, however, that at present our banking structure rests so little on business debt that it is not as deflatable as it used to be, and bank deflation could not reach the catastrophic lengths of the 1930's.)

In the other direction, bank loan expansion reinforces an upswing of business. With unchanging credit standards any expansion of dollar sales builds up the collateral value of business assets and the debt-supporting power of business profits. Besides, relaxation of fear on an upswing is apt to extend to bankers and ease their credit standards. When a country is in extreme depression, of course, this expansive force of banking has its advantages. But it is peculiarly apt to help expansion of physical volume turn into inflation. If prices are still rising when physical volume reaches capacity, the rise of prices in itself increases the dollar value of the collateral business can put behind loans and increases the nominal value of the profits in sight for loan repayment. The small-business sector which most depends on bank financing is apt to be drained of cash by extension of credit to its customers, by expansion of facilities, by withdrawals of profits, and by the need to replace inventories at higher prices (after selling previous stocks at prices based on lower acquisition costs). Thus the increased credit-worthiness generated by the price rise is matched by an increased "need" for credit. If banking follows its natural bent, it will reinforce the boom by adding to the public's stock of cash assets and by increasing lines of credit. In case the boom takes hold strongly on sectors such as the stock market or the real estate market (where much of the claim to bank credit embodied in the value of the public's nonliquid assets is normally not exercised), the resulting inflationary tendency may be very strong.

2. *The tempering effect of reserve requirements*

What keeps the instability of bank credit from breaking down the economic system is a stabilizing influence which works through bank reserves. Shortage of reserves can stop credit expansion. Piling up of excess reserves can create incentives for bankers to stop and reverse credit contraction.

Consider first the limit on credit expansion. Commercial banks have to meet legal requirements for reserves against deposits—at present roughly a fifth of deposits [3] for the "member banks of the Federal Reserve System" which make up the overwhelming bulk of the commercial banking system. These reserves have to be held in "reserve funds—meaning a checking account with a Federal Reserve bank. There are serious penalties for any member bank which lets reserves fall below requirements for more than a few days at a time.

Any bank which expands loans or buys bonds loses reserve funds by doing so. The check drawn to pay for the new asset is ordinarily deposited in some other bank,[4] and when it is collected its amount is subtracted from the lending bank's reserve balance at the Federal Reserve. To expand credit, therefore, a bank must either hold *excess reserves* over and above requirements or must get more reserves by borrowing at its Federal Reserve bank.[5]

If banks insisted on operating exclusively with *owned reserves*—that is, if they refused to borrow reserves—the reserve limit to credit expansion would be rigid. To the extent that they are willing to operate with borrowed reserves, and that the Federal Reserve will allow bank borrowings to expand, the limit becomes elastic. Historically, the degree

3. At this writing (early 1949) requirements on checking deposits are 26% for downtown banks in New York and Chicago ("central reserve city banks"), 22% for downtown banks in other financial centers ("reserve city banks"), 16% for other ("country") member banks. Weighting by the amount of checking deposits held, these requirements average about 21%. On savings ("time") deposits, the requirement is 7½%; the average for checking and savings balances combined works out at about 17½%. [Requirements have changed fairly often but not very widely since 1949.]

4. If the borrower takes the proceeds of the loan as a credit to his balance at the lending bank, his use of the proceeds will soon result in a flow of checks to customers of other banks, and the outcome is substantially the same as if the borrower was not a depositor.

5. Banks which borrow ("rediscount") are not necessarily those which are expanding credit at the moment. The impulse to borrow arises from a shortage of reserves, implying that cash withdrawals over the counter and through check clearings are running ahead of the inflow of cash over the counter and through deposit of checks on other banks. A bank may get into this condition not only by expanding its earning assets but through shift of the public's balances from one bank to another, increase of paper currency outstanding outside banks, gold exports, etc. Insofar as such forces generate rediscounts by banks which are not expanding credit, there may be a growth of reserve funds which will permit a growth of reserves (and hence of lending power) without rediscounting for fortunately placed banks which enjoy a growth of deposits.

to which banks are willing to use borrowed reserves has generally risen in a boom; and the Federal Reserve has checked the growth of borrowed reserves not by setting a fixed maximum but by intensification of deterrents to rediscount.

In the other direction, since reserve requirements are a minimum and not a maximum, there is no possibility of a rigid limit to credit contraction. True, from the founding of the Federal Reserve System to 1932, member banks were ordinarily "loaned up" so that excess reserves were trifling; but during this period they were operating with large and fluctuating amounts of borrowed reserves. In the 1930's—and also in pre-Federal Reserve banking—banks held substantial excess reserves much of the time. Since World War II excess reserves have again been small relative to required reserves. But the reason has not been that banks were fully loaned up but rather that holding Treasury bills and Treasury certificates (with a sure market at the Federal Reserve) offered a bank all the advantages of excess reserves plus interest at about 1% per annum.[6] Thus banks have held only a modest working balance of excess reserves and have put what was left over into those securities.

In a process of bank deflation three forces are generating loan contraction. In the first place, bankers are trying to avoid holding assets on which prospective interest yield fails to offset the likelihood of default by the debtors. In the second place, some loans bankers would be glad to make (or to renew) are not available because strong business firms need less funds in a depression. In the third place, some visibly sound loans are being called or refused because bankers want to pay off borrowings at the Federal Reserve and to build up a margin of excess reserves against contingencies. As credit shrinks, the decline of deposits relative to reserves generates excess reserves,[7] and this produces a counterforce. This counterforce can do nothing directly to induce loans which offer no expectation of net return after reasonable loss allowances. The counterforce is also ineffective to make strong business firms need loans. But insofar as the driving force of deflation is bankers' sense of inadequate reserves, the accretion of excess reserves is a direct remedy. If it goes far enough the excess will begin to burn the pockets of the bankers; rather than see potential lending power fail

6. During the 1930's interest yields on these assets were bid down to a small fraction of 1%; and even at these token rates banks could not find enough such assets to absorb their excess reserves.

7. This argument assumes that the credit deflation does not lead into a panic which eventuates in hoarding of paper currency and in transfer of funds abroad. In such a situation (which we had in 1931–33) deflation worsens the bank reserve situation instead of improving it.

to yield any income, they will try to tempt sound borrowers by more attractive credit terms and will use ingenuity in the search for new types of loans to offer. Furthermore, they will be willing to bid higher for bonds—both for issues outstanding and for new issues contemplated. If credit contraction is once arrested and reversed, the first two loan-contraction forces can also be turned off: apparently "unsound" loan propositions now become "sound"; and recognizably sound concerns which saw no need of credit on the downswing will reappear as borrowers.

3. *Federal Reserve influence on the reserve position*

The Federal Reserve has several ways to affect bankers' incentives to expand or contract credit—notably open-market policy, reserve-requirement policy, and Federal Reserve lending to member banks.

The key Federal Reserve power is that of "open-market operations." By buying government securities on the open market, the Federal Reserve can increase banks' owned reserves dollar for dollar. The checks drawn to pay for these securities are deposited in member bank reserve accounts [8] and serve either to enlarge those accounts or to pay off rediscounts. In the first case, the total of owned plus borrowed reserves rises; in the second, owned reserves replace borrowed reserves. Since banks are reluctant to depend heavily on borrowed reserves, either outcome places banks in a better position to expand private credit by making loans or by buying bonds from nonbankers. In the other direction, the Federal Reserve can decrease owned reserves (forcing the banks to choose between a shrinkage of total reserves and an increase in borrowings) by selling securities on the open market.

The reserve position can be changed also through the Federal Reserve power to modify required minimum-reserve percentages—a power which was somewhat extended by legislation of August, 1948.[9] An increase of reserve-requirement percentages which increases the aggregate of reserves required by $1 billion will force member banks to reduce their excess reserves by $1 billion, or borrow $1 billion, or borrow part of the $1 billion and let excess reserves decline by the remainder.

8. If a bank is the seller of the securities bought, it gets a check in direct exchange. If the seller is not a bank but (say) an insurance company, the bank where the check is deposited acquires a fresh deposit liability with its noncash assets unchanged. But in either case the collection of the check adds to one bank's reserve balance without depleting that of any other.

9. The possibilities for modifying reserve requirements may be expressed in tabular form as at bottom of following page:

In the other direction, a lowering of reserve-requirement percentages turns part of what was required reserves into excess reserves (part of which may then be used to retire rediscounts).

Besides Federal Reserve influences on the commercial-bank reserve position, there are Treasury influences. To begin with, the Treasury as well as the Federal Reserve is a buyer and seller of securities.[10] In fact, security dealings on Treasury account are on a vaster scale than those on Federal Reserve account. The Treasury buys nearly $1 billion weekly of maturing Treasury bills; every few weeks it has to confront maturities of Treasury certificates and Treasury notes (sometimes in lumps of several billions); and once or twice a year it must either buy in Treasury bonds which become "callable" or resolve to postpone buying them in till their final maturity two or there years later. On the selling side, the overwhelming bulk of these maturities have to be covered by exchange with new securities or by selling new securities for cash. The accounts for the fiscal year ending June 30, 1948, showed total public debt receipts of $121 billion and total public debt expenditures (gross purchases for redemption) of $127 billion! Even allowing for paper transactions within the government, Treasury open-market operations are very large relative to those of the Federal Reserve; as will appear shortly, the best way to analyze open-market operations is as a joint responsibility of the two agencies.

Another Treasury influence results from current-account transactions—revenue receipts and current cash outlays. Taxes are received chiefly from the nonbank public (only incidentally from bankers), and salaries, veterans' benefits, supply purchases, etc., go to the nonbank public. But a cash surplus (such as the Treasury has had in recent years) permits the Treasury either to have an excess of security redemptions over security sales or to pile up a bank balance in the Federal Reserve banks or, at its option, in commercial banks. The accumulation of a

	1935 level (present minimum)	1935–47 maximum	present maximum	February, 1949 actual level
	per cent	per cent	per cent	per cent
Time deposits	3	5	7½	7½
Checking (net demand) deposits:				
Country banks	7	14	18	16
Reserve city banks	10	20	24	22
Central reserve city banks	13	26	30	26
Weighted average, with Dec., 1948 composition of deposits	8.1	16.2	19.5	17.6

10. The Federal Reserve banks, since they act as "fiscal agents" for the Treasury, actually execute both classes of dealings.

balance at commercial banks makes little difference to their reserve position; [11] but as soon as the Treasury's "calls" for transfer of funds to disbursement accounts held at the Federal Reserve come to exceed the inflow into its commercial-bank balances, member banks are forced to hand over reserve funds to meet the Treasury's net transfer to its Federal Reserve accounts. Thus the apportionment of Treasury balances between Federal Reserve and commercial banks, as well as the growth or shrinkage of balances through current-account and debt transactions, affects the reserve position. [12] A smaller influence emanating from the Treasury is its supply of small change, silver coin, and silver certificates (largely one-dollar bills) for hand-to-hand circulation; expansion of these items leads to Treasury deposits at the Federal Reserve, which are transformed into reserve funds when they are used to buy securities or meet current outlays.

To complete the picture of influences on the reserve situation, mention should be made of three factors not directly controlled by policy— the monetary gold stock, bank till money, and paper money circulation outside banks. When there is a net inflow of paper money over bank counters (as happens, for example, after the Christmas shopping rush), bank till money grows; and commercial banks are able to build up their reserve balances by depositing unneeded paper money at Federal Reserve banks. Most of the increases [13] can be added to excess reserves or used to retire rediscounts. Gold inflow works in like manner. Newly produced or imported gold is sold to the Treasury, and Treasury checks

11. Treasury balances at commercial banks, which receive the inflow from withholding tax collections, etc., are subject lately to the same reserve requirements as the nonbank public's checking accounts; so that it does not matter to the bank in terms of reserve requirements whether the taxpayer or the tax collector owns the funds so long as they are held in the bank.

12. During the war, the Treasury's commercial-bank balances often exceeded total reserves of the banks. The anti-inflationary power that could have been exerted by transferring part of these balances into disbursement accounts at Federal Reserve banks was largely frittered away, however, during 1946. Treasury balances at commercial banks stood at $24.6 billion at the beginning of the year and $3.1 billion at the end. The drop of $21.5 billion corresponded to a net reduction of $22.1 billion in the amount of federal securities outside official and Federal Reserve hands. (Several minor reconcilement items are neglected here.) Of this shift, $16.3 billion represented canceling out deposits against securities in commerical-bank ownership, and $5.9 billion (net) the handing over of deposit balances to private ownership in exchange for securities owned by nonbank investors. Treasury balances at Federal Reserve banks were allowed to drop from $1.0 to $0.4 billion—a fact which reflects on the seriousness with which the authorities took the monetary side of inflation control in that crucial year!

13. Not quite all, since the net paper money inflow ordinarily involves an equal net growth of customer balances subject to reserve requirements.

drawn in payment flow into member bank reserve accounts.[14] Outflow of paper currency over bank counters and gold exports, of course, have reverse effects.

4. *Nullification of reserve controls through price supports on government securities*

The account just given implies that open-market operations are undertaken at the initiative of the Federal Reserve authorities, with the objective of changing the commercial-bank reserve position as policy may require. Monetary control through the reserve position becomes impossible if the Federal Reserve surrenders the initiative to commercial banks and lets them bring about such open-market transactions as will adjust the reserve position to their convenience. The "commitment" of the Federal Reserve and Treasury to support prices of government securities has given this initiative to commercial banks since the end of the war, thus nullifying reserve controls.*

Even in the absence of any price-supporting market operations the Treasury would be bound to pay off its securities as they mature.[15] When securities mature, of course, the Treasury normally replaces them

---

* The dropping of this commitment in early 1951, together with evidence of Treasury willingness to accept somewhat higher interest rates on both short- and long-term securities, went far to restore the initiative to the Federal Reserve.

14. *Exception:* sometimes the proceeds of gold imports go into the accounts of foreign banks with the Federal Reserve, and monetary effects in this country are deferred till these balances are reduced.

15. At the beginning of 1949, for instance, the Treasury's debt (exclusive of securities in the hands of the Federal Reserve and other federal securities, included the following (billions of dollars):

	Total	At commercial banks in Treasury survey	In other hands
Due before March 31, 1949:			
Bills	6.7	2.8	3.9
Certificates	7.4	3.4	3.9
	14.1	6.2	7.8
Due or callable in the rest of 1949:			
Certificates	13.0	5.6	7.4
Notes	3.3	1.2	2.1
Bonds callable in 1949	6.0	4.4	1.6
	22.3	11.2	11.1
Total due or callable in 1949:	36.4	17.4	18.9
Due or callable in 1950:	13.1	8.5	4.6

The $17.4 billion banks could add to reserves in 1949 by failing to replace any maturing securities compares with aggregate reserve requirements at the same date of $19.1 billion.

with new securities—either by exchange or by selling new securities for cash to pay off the old. But no particular banker or other holder is obliged to replace his maturing securities with new ones. By relying on the "runoff" of government securities held, a banker with inadequate cash reserves can restore his position within a few weeks or months. In doing so he shifts his problem of finding cash to the Treasury, which must shift it to others by finding new holders for its replacement securities.

If the Treasury and Federal Reserve are in agreement on keeping interest rates low, this means that the public (including the bankers) absorb whatever part of the refunding securities it cares to, at the maintained rate, and any residue is absorbed by the Federal Reserve.[16] If the Treasury and Federal Reserve agree to avoid increasing Federal Reserve holdings, they can do so—but only at the expense of offering high enough interest rates on new issues to make it worth while for bankers to forego private loan opportunities to buy bills and certificates. Since Treasury redemptions are much the same thing as Federal Reserve open-market purchases, and Treasury sales of refunding securities much the same thing as Federal Reserve open-market sales, we can look at open-market operations as a *joint* responsibility of the two official agencies [17] and consider the flow of securities between official hands and the market. If official policy aims to determine the banks' reserve position by security dealings, it has to subordinate interest policy to getting a net outflow of securities onto the market when bank reserves are to be tightened and getting a net inflow from the market when bank reserves are to be eased. If interest-rate policy is to be put in the forefront, the two official agencies must let banks take the initiative in adjusting their reserve position, so long as they have more in short-term government securities than they feel prudence requires as a "secondary reserve." [18]

16. As a matter of window dressing, the Federal Reserve can keep interest rates on new treasury bills and certificates at the desired level, without actually appearing as purchaser at the moment of issue, by buying bills and certificates which were issued a few weeks previously. These purchases create a vacuum into which new issues can be sucked. A spread of a few hundredths of 1% per annum in interest yields between brand-new and slightly older bills is shown by market experience to be enough to find buyers for new bills, so long as Federal Reserve willingness to buy presently is clear.

17. Security dealings of the Treasury on account of government "trust funds," and loan operations of government credit agencies, should also be taken into account as open-market operations—insofar as they are not simply intragovernmental dealings.

18. A long bank tradition calls for holding some assets which can reinforce cash reserves quickly by "runoff," as a "secondary reserve," but holdings of short-term government securities have expanded so far that they must be interpreted (like the

Federal Reserve commitments to "support" prices of longer-term Treasury bonds create other ways in which bank reserves can be replenished. During the active support operations of 1948, the Federal Reserve seems to have aimed to support long-term Treasury bonds at prices slightly above those corresponding to a 2½% yield but not below par.[19] A bank which ran short of reserves could sell price-supported bonds and thus push the Federal Reserve into providing fresh reserve funds by taking up these bonds. Credit expansion also generated bank reserves through the interaction of life-insurance and savings-bank lending and the bond support. An insurance company which wished to expand its mortgage loans could dump government bonds on the Federal Reserve supports, thus causing creation of fresh reserve funds and facilitating expansion of commercial bank loans.[20] While the bond-support operations were in progress, the Federal Reserve authorities took a good deal of satisfaction in the fact that short-term securities flowed out onto the market almost as fast as bonds flowed in from the market, so that there was no sharp growth of bank excess reserves. But this does not prove that the combined effect of operations in long-term and short-term securities was to keep banks short of reserves in a way that limited credit expansion. Purchase of long-term securities under the bond-support program gave the bank a constant inflow of excess reserves. Each bank was able to hold enough to facilitate any expansion of credit to private debtors that caught its fancy and put the excess of the excess (so to speak) into short and medium-term securities yielding 1% or so.

---

excess cash reserves of the late 1930's) as assets held in default of the availability of any profitable alternatives. Late in 1948 banks held about $2.4 billion of till money (coin and paper), and about $20 billion of reserve balances with Federal Reserve banks (of which about $1 billion was excess over legal requirements). Their government security holdings included over $6 billion due within 3 months, a further $9 billion due in 4 to 12 months, and a further $10 billion due or payable in 13 to 24 months.

19. Support buying by the Reserve banks in the most active period centered in 2½%-coupon "bank-restricted" bonds, which were held a fraction of a point above par. There was also a good deal of buying of 2%-coupon "bank eligible" bonds of rather short maturity, at prices around 101. A 2½% yield basis for the 2%'s of September, 1950–52, for instance, would have been at a price rather below 99, as compared with the support price of 101¹³⁄₃₂. Two issues of 2¼%-coupon bank restricted bonds were supported at 100¹⁄₃₂—that is, at a 2¼% yield basis. None were allowed to drop below par.

20. In the 12 months from October, 1947, to October, 1948 (covering the active support period), Federal Reserve bond holdings grew by $11.3 billion. Of this $3.7 billion is accounted for by reduction of bank-restricted holdings of life insurance companies and mutual savings banks.

The underlying ease of the bank position was shown clearly in September, 1948, when the Federal Reserve authorities increased reserve requirements by $2 billion. Commercial banks entered the month with excess reserves of $900 million and ended it (after absorbing the reserve-requirement increase) with nearly $800 million. The trick was done by shifting to Federal Reserve and other government ownership somewhat over $2 billion of bank-held Treasury securities.[21]

5. Restoration of control by releasing interest rates?

We have worked ourselves into a position where government securities held by banks are substantially similar to excess reserves—except that insofar as banks abstain from converting them into cash reserves they collect interest. The amount of excess reserves banks feel they need (including secondary reserves) is in most cases well below the sum of excess cash reserves plus government securities. Thus the limit on the amount of private credit banks extend is simply the prospect of profit on loans and bond purchases. This creates just the sort of situation where business fluctuations can reinforce themselves by inducing parallel fluctuations of bank credit.

Looking at bank holdings as equivalent to excess reserves, two remedies suggest themselves. The first is to make these securities less like reserves by making their prospective return competitive with that from ordinary earning assets.* The second is to convert them into required reserves—which will be considered in section III-6.

As I mentioned above, if the Treasury and Federal Reserve insist on maintaining specified interest rates on the different classes of government securities, they have to let the market decide how much will be outstanding. The initiative in open-market operations thus passes out of the hands of the Federal Reserve and into the hands of commercial banks. If the authorities wish to decide the amount outstanding, and thus recover the initiative, they have to offer an interest rate at which the market will willingly accept the desired quantity. If pro-

---

* Policy has gone a long way in this direction since 1949; and most of the statements in the previous paragraph should now be made in the past tense.

21. Commercial banks covered in the Treasury survey reduced their holdings of Treasury securities during the month by $2.1 billion (net). These banks held $2.4 billion of the bond and note issues maturing that month and put $1.9 billion into the new notes issued in exchange, taking $0.5 billion (net) in cash. They took another $0.6 billion (net) in cash from their holdings of Treasury bills. They sold off (net) $0.5 billion of their Treasury certificates and $0.2 billion of their notes previously held. The remaining $0.4 billion was raised by sales of Treasury bonds. See *Treasury Bulletin*, November, 1948, p. 32, and December, 1948, p. 32.

spective earnings are high enough to be competitive with business loans and industrial bonds, banks cannot afford to pass up the chance to hold these assets; and the Federal Reserve can thus control the bank reserve position by selling such securities. To be competitive with business loans and industrial bonds as earning assets, government securities need not yield equal interest rates. In view of the absolute certainty that interest and principal will be paid on schedule, and of the ease and simplicity in administration, government securities would be markedly preferable to other assets at equal interest rates.

The drawbacks of raising interest rates to restore monetary control are serious, however. The effect on the federal budget would be substantial. Not counting the holdings of the Federal Reserve and other government agencies, the interest-bearing debt totals about $190 billion, so that a 1% rise in the average rate paid would cost nearly $2 billion. About $30 billion out of the $190 billion is short-term debt at rates of $1\frac{1}{4}\%$ or less; another $25 billion is debt at rates of $1\frac{3}{8}\%$ to 2%, maturing within five years. Refinancing at 2% all the debt which matures within the next five years would add $0.3 billion to the interest charges; at 3%, $0.9 billion. At rates higher than 3%, the budgetary cost might pile up still more rapidly, as it would be profitable for the holders to redeem part of the outstanding savings bonds to buy higher-yielding securities. The Treasury opposition to higher rates rests largely on this question of expense.*

Another objection to raising interest rates is that it implies lower bond prices. Our largest single outstanding issue of bonds—the $2\frac{1}{2}$'s of December, 1967–72, with roughly $8 billion in the hands of the nonbank public—has ranged in price in the last three years from $106\frac{1}{2}$ to $100\frac{1}{4}$, with a yield range only from 2.13% to 2.47%. On a 3% yield basis, these bonds would be priced at about 91; on a 4% yield basis, in the low 80's.† Most of our outstanding bonds mature earlier and consequently have a narrower potential price range. But remembering the outcry when 4% Liberty bonds fell to a price of about 82 (a yield basis of about 5.7%) in 1920, the authorities feel the public needs to be shielded against a recurrence. To my mind, the need for such shielding is overrated. The vulnerable small bondholder has bought savings

---

* This argument should be qualified by the fact that well toward half of added interest income is apt to be recaptured by income taxes.

† The exchange offer of early 1951 led to a sharp reduction in the public's holdings of these bonds. The largest issue now outstanding (the $2\frac{1}{4}$'s of June, 1959–62, with roughly $3 billion outside banks) has shown a range of fluctuation from $104\frac{5}{8}$ (a yield of 1.9%) to $96\frac{13}{16}$ (a yield of 2.6%).

bonds, redeemable rather than marketable, and does not need to worry about the market. Larger bondholders do not suffer if they hold bonds to maturity—and need incentives to do so.[22] Bondholders as a whole have probably lost heavily through the obstacle which low-interest policy set up to inflation control in 1946–48; as between protection of the nominal value of their bonds on the current market and protection of the purchasing power of their interest and principal, the latter is more important.

The most serious objection to using higher interest rates to restore control of bank credit, to my mind, is psychological. If once rates rise substantially, it may be next to impossible ever to get them down again, because the nonbank public may be led to expect high rates to continue.[23] In this case, any rise of bond prices (corresponding to a fall in "yields") will make much of the investing public "bearish" on bond prices and thus will tend to generate an excess demand for cash assets. A serious obstacle to the financing of new construction may also result. My sense is that this consideration rules out the surrender of the *symbols* of low interest rates. The Treasury should avoid floating any bonds with coupon rates higher than the $2\frac{1}{2}\%$, which applied to most of the wartime bank-restricted issues, or allowing any really dramatic discount on the market. I infer that a "support" of government bond prices is probably justified on this ground—but a few points below par rather than above par.[24]

6. *Restoration of control by security reserves?*

Turning in the other direction, if bank-held governments are so nearly the same thing as cash reserves, why not recognize that new situation by *requiring* banks to hold a supplementary reserve in such securities? This proposal, first brought into prominence by Professor Lawrence

22. A special problem is the position of commercial banks holding bonds whose market value sags below par. Insofar as they hold bonds to maturity, all the protection they need is application of the modern standard of bank-asset valuation by ultimate investment value rather than current value; paper losses can be disregarded. If an outflow of deposits from a particular bank forces it to sell bonds, the paper loss must be realized. But it would be easy to design special safeguards for banks in this position.

23. The barriers to interest changes are thus asymmetrical: the barrier to an increase is political, that to a decrease psychological.

24. This position was taken in the Committee for Economic Development staff report, Melvin G. de Chazeau, Albert G. Hart, Gardiner C. Means, and others, *Jobs and Markets* (New York, McGraw-Hill, 1946), pp. 92, 96–99, 123. It still seems to me sound policy.*

Seltzer,[25] has also been supported officially by the Board of Governors of the Federal Reserve System.[26]

Plainly such a requirement would solve the Treasury's refinancing problem so far as its securities were included in the reserve. As reserve securities matured, the banks holding them would need an equal amount of new reserve securities to replace them, so that a refunding issue would find its market automatically. By the same token, the Treasury need not pay high interest rates on such securities in times of tight credit. Instead, the government would have to face the question of what rate of return banks were entitled to as a reward for their services to the public.[27]

To restore monetary control, the security-reserve requirement must be so designed as to leave no substantial margin of reserve-eligible securities in excess of requirements—either in bank hands or outside bank ownership. Since nonbank holders own a substantial share of every class of government securities, the workmanlike way to do this would be to extend reserve eligibility only to bank-held securities registered at the outset as part of the reserve, plus later issues of securities tagged as reserve eligible when issued. As a practical matter, banks should be given the option of transforming their reserve securities into a special

---

* This is one point at which my policy position has shifted with changing conditions. Experience since 1949 has brought out the likelihood that there will be at least intermittent inflationary pressure for many years ahead, because of unsettled world conditions. I find myself in hearty approval of moves to get coupon rates above 2½% on securities (like the 2¾% nonmarketable bonds of 1975–80, issued in 1951 in exchange for marketable 2½'s of 1967–72) whose buyers accept a substantial sacrifice of liquidity. The importance of anti-inflationary monetary tools is enhanced by recent developments; the likelihood of "stagnation" in which a tradition of low interest would be helpful is reduced.

25. See L. H. Seltzer, "The Problem of Our Excessive Banking Reserves," *Journal of the American Statistical Association*, 35 (March, 1940), 24–36. Suggestions of John K. Langum, chiefly in connection with discussion of the Committee for Economic Development, have also helped form the ideas presented here.

26. Board of Governors of the Federal Reserve System, *Annual Report*, 1945, pp. 7–8; Marriner S. Eccles, "The Current Inflation Problem—Causes and Controls," *Federal Reserve Bulletin*, 33 (December, 1947), 1461–1463. Mr. Eccles proposed a requirement not to exceed 25% on demand and 10% on time deposits, which I should regard as inadequate.

27. Banks provide the public—for the most part free—with check-handling facilities and other valuable services. Unless it is public policy for banks to finance these services through service charges on customers, they must finance them through earnings on their assets. This policy issue regarding bank earnings is already implicit in the "management" of interest rates through public debt policy. The pretense that bank earnings are set entirely by an impersonal market rather than largely by public policy is wearing thin; if a security-reserve requirement were instituted, this pretense would have to be abandoned.

interest-bearing balance at the Federal Reserve, and superior convenience would probably lead most banks to embrace this option.

How stringent the resulting control of the volume of bank credit would be depends on whether the security-reserve requirement is strictly separate from the cash-reserve requirement, or whether it allows substitution of excess cash reserves for security reserves. On the former basis, if the central authorities refuse to expand the stock of reserve securities, they can completely block credit expansion.[28] On the latter basis banks may acquire extra lending power from such sources as a reflux of paper currency from circulation unless the combined cash-and-security reserve requirement is pushed clear up to 100%. At first glance it may seem as if this were impossible without depriving small business of access to bank loans and thus seriously damaging the economy. But various analysts, including Allan Sproul (president of the Federal Reserve Bank of New York) [29] have pointed out that a security reserve may be applied on the "ceiling reserve" principle—that is, requirements may be applied to total deposits (*less an exemption.*) Applying this principle would permit pushing combined cash plus security reserves clear to 100% on additions or subtractions from the base amount of deposits,[30] if the exemption is large enough to cover the initial amount of nonreserve assets.

28. Roughly, the system would amount to rationing the privilege of holding deposits and using reserve securities as ration tickets. To take an extreme example, the security-reserve requirement might be set at only 1%, and a stock of reserve securities created at the outset by offering to issue each bank free just enough to constitute 1% of its deposits subject to reserve. No expansion of deposits subject to reserve could happen thereafter (without subjecting banks to penalties for reserve deficiency) unless the central authorities consented to sell additional reserve securities. If the deposits subject to reserve were defined as total deposits less cash assets, this system would set a rigid maximum to the total of bank-earning assets.

As the illustration implies, on this system of completely separate cash reserves and security reserves, a low reserve percentage in securities would be as effective in setting a maximum as a high percentage, so long as no new reserve securities came into existence.

29. Statement before the Joint Committee on the Economic Report, May 12, 1948. It should be pointed out that Mr. Sproul in the same statement opposes "an increase to 100 per cent or anywhere near it"; but he is concerned with reducing the "leverage factor in our present system of proportionate reserves" as a matter of long-run policy, "as a means of reducing the dangerous expansibility and, at times, destructive contractability of a money supply based on low reserve ratios."

30. The discussion which follows covers the substance of the policy possibilities popularized by the late Irving Fisher in his book *100% Money* (New York, Adelphi, 1935), on the basis of pioneering work by the late Henry C. Simons. Fisher proposed to require banks to hold 100% cash reserves and to provide banks with cash by purchasing their government securities; to let banks keep their government securities and count them toward the reserve is not substantively different.

If all bank-held government securities are included in the reserve, this 100% ceiling reserve would call for basing the exemption from reserve requirements on the amount of net private credit (loans plus nonfederal bonds held, minus capital funds) held by each bank at the starting point.[31] Perhaps this arrangement could be made into a two-way stabilizer for bank credit, by providing for a permanent reduction of the bank's exemption whenever its net private credit outstanding fell below the base figure. If such a clause could be made effective [32] it would place any bank which had reason to curtail loans to some of its customers under very strong pressure to place the corresponding credit with other borrowers or to sell part of its exemption to another bank which had reason to expand.[33] Failing such a clause, we would have to rely for a check to bank deflation on excess reserves burning the pockets of the banker—an effect which would be much more reliable if a billion-dollar contraction of loans increased excess reserves by a billion dollars than now when it increases them only by a fraction of a billion.

A ceiling reserve arrangement with exemption would safeguard the legitimate interest of small busines in access to bank funds. True, credit might well be tighter for small business when there was an upswing of business volume. But it would be easier in a slump, which would reduce hazards for small business. After all, the small business interest is in *reliable* access to bank credit—not in having easy credit on the upswing at the cost of being cut off from credit whenever business suffers a setback.

Another alternative would be to include in the reserve only short-term government securities and to base the exemption on net private credit plus long-term government bonds held at the outset. Again it would be possible to insure against credit contraction as well as undesired expansion by providing that any bank's exemption would be reduced permanently by a reduction of the assets on which the exemp-

---

31. On every bank's statement, deposits are necessarily equal to the sum of cash assets, plus government securities, plus net private credit, plus the excess of miscellaneous assets (banking house, accrued income, etc.) over miscellaneous liabilities. To avoid creating hardship cases it would be expedient to set the exemption 1% or 2% higher than net private credit, to cover the excess of miscellaneous assets over miscellaneous liabilities.

32. The question is whether such a rule could be so framed as to block off fictitious loans made only to keep a bank's exemption alive. (Banks might even pay borrowers who would hold the whole loan proceeds on deposit, if the rule were as stated in the text.) Very probably the safeguards needed to block this loophole would offset the advantages of the exemption-reduction device.

33. Unless exemptions are transferable, in our unit-banking system, an exemption system will create artificial incentives for bank mergers and an artificial regional allocation of loan funds.

tion was based. This would also safeguard the economy as well as the previous arrangement against any cyclical deflation of the volume of the deposits. But it would permit a cyclical fluctuation in the *composition* of assets; in a business recession banks could curtail loans outstanding without loss of future lending privileges, on condition that they bought more government bonds on the market as they liquidated loans. This difference might make a business recession a period for shaking down those concerns which depend especially on bank financing; so that the former arrangement with the exemption based on private net credit strikes me as superior.

What if a substantial security reserve requirement proves politically acceptable, but a 100% requirement (cash plus reserve-eligible securities) on deposits above an exemption is rejected? Is such a halfway arrangement adequate to restore reserve control and limit the instability of credit? The answer is yes—but with qualifications. In the first place, the reserve position will still be out of control if the requirement leaves outstanding any substantial margin above requirements in reserve-eligible securities, or in nonreserve government securities which the authorities feel bound to support on a low-interest basis. In the second place, the lower the cash-plus-security reserve ratio on an additional dollar of deposits, the less effective is an exemption based on base-period private net credit in insuring against later credit deflation, for two reasons: a) The lower is this ratio, the smaller must be the exemption in order to make the aggregate requirement absorb the excessive volume of secondary-reserve securities now in bank hands. If the exemption can be only a small percentage of base-period net credit, it becomes less important to the bank; reduction of the exemption will not close the door to reexpansion of credit after a contraction. b) While with a 100% reserve requirement any bank which loses deposits has an equal amount of reserves released and can thus avoid liquidating nonreserve assets, a fractional-reserve system forces a bank losing deposits to liquidate some nonreserve assets (or to borrow) unless it has excess reserves to start with.

Despite the qualifications just noted, any rise in reserve requirements reduces the instability of bank credit. This instability hinges largely on the possibility, which exists for the banking system as a whole, of basing several dollars of additional loans and deposits on one dollar of initial excess reserves.[34] The expansion coefficient for credit on excess reserves, roughly speaking, is the arithmetical reciprocal of the reserve-requirement percentage; to make a more precise estimate, this reciprocal must

34. For analysis of the multiple expansion possibilities of excess reserves, see A. G. Hart, *op. cit.*, pp. 63–76, especially 73–74.

be corrected downward to allow for the probability that as bank deposits expand, part of the increase will "overflow" into paper money circulation outside banks or into foreign currency systems. Prior to 1936, when 10% was a common reserve figure, but rather above the average reserve, economists took 10-to-1 as a rough estimate of the credit expansion coefficient. Under 1947 requirements, about double those in 1935, a Federal Reserve estimate [35] put the coefficient at 6-to-1; my own estimate is lower, about 3 or 3½-to-1. If we had a 50% average requirement for cash plus security reserves on deposits in excess of an exemption, the coefficient could not exceed 2-to-1. A drop from 6-to-1 (or even 3½-to-1) to less than 2-to-1 would mean a marked reduction in credit instability.

7. Restoration of control by "qualitative control"?

Before summing up on the problem of curing credit instability, I must comment briefly on the widely favored policy of controlling credit instability chiefly by regulations about installment credit, stock exchange credit, and if possible mortgage credit, inventory loans, and the like. If control through interest rates is taboo because of Treasury opposition, and control through security reserves is left out of account for fear that it may prove unpopular, we come back to such qualitative controls by default. But I regard them as a definite third choice.

It is true that the lines of credit to which this policy is addressed are linked with key factors of business instability. Stock market speculation, on occasion, has spread boom psychology broadcast. Durable goods purchases financed on installments have contributed to the speed of rise of upswings which became top-heavy and to the inflationary pressure in the full employment period 1946–48. Real estate credit (if we dared regulate it) [36] also has many sins to its charge. Above all, credit financing of inventory expansion looks as if it would be worth combating—but unfortunately no workable control schemes seem to be forthcoming.

35. *Federal Reserve Bulletin, 33* (December, 1947), 1461.
36. National banks used to be debarred from mortgage lending; but this prohibition was dropped long ago to put national banks on a par with more laxly controlled state banks. The great trouble with regulating mortgage loans under present conditions is the necessity of going beyond commercial banks to regulate other lenders. True, stock-exchange credit controls apply to brokers and installment credit controls to mercantile lenders, as well as to banks. But mortgage credit controls would have to cover the sacrosanct life insurance companies and mutual savings banks. In addition, they would have to face the inconsistencies between monetary policy and the mortgage-financing policies of government agencies concerned with housing and with veterans' affairs.

These controls strike me as doubtful, partly because of their special impact on particular groups of people whose behavior may contribute no more to instability than that of other people control cannot touch directly. Besides, these controls are open to evasion because many loans of the sort they aim to reach can be labeled in other ways. The basis of regulation is ordinarily either the "purpose" of the loan or the character of security posted. But purposes are not directly observable, and the borrower can often substitute other security or borrow without any specific pledge of collateral. This leakage around the edges of the controls impairs their effectiveness and enhances their unfairness. My view is that in fact these controls cannot do much to mitigate economic instability, and that their main function is to enable the monetary authorities to keep busy even though their central job of monetary stabilization is left undone! * 37

8. *Correcting destabilizers versus countercyclical operations*

I have been talking in terms of controls designed to make bank credit less of a destabilizer in the economic system—that is, preventing or limiting undesired expansion or contraction of the public's cash holdings through changes in bank credit. If controls are adequate for this purpose, could they not be used to bring about a desired expansion of credit—desired, that is, by the monetary authorities for the sake of effects on employment and price levels? The answer is yes, but with qualifications. The meaning of the answer, however, varies among the three main types of policy that might be contemplated: 1) adjustment of the long-run trend of money supply to the public's needs; 2) getting favorable monetary by-products from fiscal policy; 3) countercyclical credit policy.

1) As to long-run trends, the sort of control system suggested above would not put monetary policy in a strait jacket. If there is a long-run need for expansion of net private bank credit (a matter we need not prejudge here—I am inclined to doubt this need), it can be cared for by enlarging the banks' exemption. A workmanlike method would be to enlarge each bank's exemption from the ceiling-reserve requirement by a stated percentage each year. If there is a long-run need for more

---

* Experience under the installment-credit and real-estate credit restrictions of 1950–51 suggests that I may have underrated their potency. The spectacle (in the summer of 1951) of Congress trying to legislate auto sales-credit terms, however, confirms my instinct that over time these controls will prove a morbid type of intervention.

37. I do see a use for such controls in pushing bank loans into long-term as against short-term forms; see below, p. 337.

cash to run our expanding economy—and if expansion of bank-credit exemptions does not fill this need—more cash may be provided year by year through Federal Reserve purchases of securities (or official buying of gold, etc.), increasing deposits, actual reserves, and reserve requirements at commercial banks by identical amounts. The problems of long-term monetary policy will be examined in section IV below.

2) Suppose it is national policy to reduce economic instability through the built-in flexibility of fiscal policy—by designing taxes and governmental expenditure policies so that a slump will shift the government's cash operations toward a deficit and an upswing will shift them toward a surplus. The countercyclical effect of such a swing in the budget will be strengthened if the implied change in the public's liquid assets takes place in the most liquid class of these assets—bank deposits. The control system suggested above lends itself admirably to this purpose. All that is necessary is to finance the cash deficit by drawing on Treasury balances at Federal Reserve banks (replenishing those balances if necessary by selling new securities to the Federal Reserve) and to accumulate the proceeds of the cash surplus in Treasury balances at Federal Reserve banks (using these balances if they grow excessive to retire securities held by the Federal Reserve). This will mean matching the federal cash deficit month by month [38] with an equal growth in deposits, actual reserves, and required reserves at commercial banks. The same reasoning applies if a surplus or deficit arises from discretionary (rather than automatic) fiscal adjustments.

3) The idea of trying to get banks to expand credit in a slump and contract credit in an inflationary boom is tempting. But I am inclined to be skeptical. The effects of efforts to expand or contract credit are bound to come in with a lag, so that such a policy depends heavily on forecasting, and with bad luck or bad management its timing may be as often wrong as right. Besides, the fact that policy toward bank reserves is weaving back and forth may make banks less responsive. Experience shows, for example, that a reduction of bank reserve requirements is likely to be viewed as temporary and thus to generate a demand for excess reserves out of which to meet a later restoration of higher requirements.

I am more sanguine of the usefulness of discretionary countercyclical policy addressed to the public's *demand* for cash assets (paper currency and bank deposits) as distinct from the banks' *supply* of such assets. If an inflationary drift gives evidence of an excess supply of cash,

38. Seasonal fluctuations in the cash deficit or surplus, however, need to be taken up to avoid useless disturbance of the economy; see above, pp. 314–315.

the public's holdings can be made less liquid by floating long-term securities to redeem short-term securities. This means pushing down the price of long-term securities—i.e., pushing up their interest yields—so that it may be described as use of interest increases to combat inflation. But I should be inclined, following Henry Simons,[39] to put more stress on the fact that at lower prices the holders of such securities will be more interested in holding onto them to avoid taking capital losses now and be in a position to capture capital gains later on. In the contrary situation where business is sagging, issue of short-term securities to redeem long-term securities can increase incentives for capital formation—not only by lowering interest but by creating incentives to switch now from bonds to other assets before the capital-gains prospect again becomes unfavorable.

IV. Long-Term Monetary Policy

The discussion so far has run chiefly in terms of mitigating the destabilizing effects of monetary changes within business fluctuations. This leaves untouched a number of problems which must be faced if we are to have a coherent monetary policy in the long run, notably:

1) International monetary relations.
2) The gold standard.
3) The possibility of a commodity standard.
4) The debt problem.
5) Possibilities of making the demand for liquid assets less of an autonomous source of economic disturbance.

These will be taken up in turn.

1. *International monetary relations*

The position taken above on the desirability of eliminating the instability of bank credit has serious implications for international monetary relations. The nineteenth-century mechanism for keeping international trade in equilibrium used to rely heavily on credit inflation and deflation. A country gaining gold was supposed to permit the resulting growth of bank reserves to expand credit, raising its level of prices and incomes and thus shifting the balance of payments on trade account in a way that would check the gold inflow. A country losing gold was supposed to permit the resulting drain on bank reserves to shrink credit, lowering its level of prices and incomes and thus checking the gold outflow. It is conceivable, of course, that a monetary authority which had brought its domestic credit situation under control by such a device as

39. See H. C. Simons, *Economic Policy for a Free Society* (Chicago, University of Chicago Press, 1948), pp. 220–239.

a 100% ceiling reserve would use its power to vary the domestic stock of cash in this traditional way.[40] But the whole implication of the sort of monetary policy discussed in this paper is that policy aims to avoid imposing either unemployment or inflation on the economy. Under the existing fractional-reserve system, there is some tendency for the traditional type of international adjustment to make itself felt in the teeth of policy; for a gold outflow or inflow increases or decreases bank excess reserves by three-quarters or so of the dollar volume of the flow (about a quarter being absorbed in required reserves on the primary change in bank deposits), so that it takes an active counterpolicy of open-market operations to keep credit reasonably stable. From the standpoint of domestic economic stabilization, this is a nuisance which a 100% ceiling-reserve system would eliminate.

Failing this sort of adjustment mechanism, however, the nation's international trade relations must be kept in balance by some other mechanism: either a) varying controls of the physical volume of foreign trade or b) exchange control—affecting proceeds of current transactions as well as capital transfers—or c) changes in currency parities at the International Monetary Fund. Insofar as the United States elects not to make any of these types of adjustment, foreign countries must. In the present world of "dollar shortage," if we count on effective blocking of private capital transfers by exchange control, American exports will be determined by the sum of American imports (including gold imports) and American grants of dollar credits; so that the export balance on trade account will be determined by the sum of gold imports and dollar credits. This guarantees us against any major economic disturbances arising from the foreign trade balance except such as we ourselves choose to set up through our foreign credits. But it implies a trade-adjustment mechanism resting on trade and exchange controls exercised by foreign governments—and of types which on the whole the United States resents. If we aim both to stabilize domestic credit and to dis-

40. A gold outflow under such a system would involve a "primary" deflation of the domestic stock of liquid assets, since somebody would draw checks to buy the gold for export, and the resulting transfer of funds from the buyers to the Treasury would be a net shrinkage of "demand deposits adjusted." If this primary monetary change was too small to produce any significant effects on prices and incomes (as it almost surely would be), the policy of simulating the effects of old-fashioned bank adjustments to gold flows would call for capturing private funds by some combination of a Treasury cash surplus and security sales to the nonbank public. These funds might then be transferred from commercial banks to the Reserve banks, with a corresponding retirement of reserve securities, or might be held idle (as official balances with commercial banks) till a reversal of the trade situation called for an adjusted act in the opposite direction.

courage permanent establishment of such trade controls abroad, we are committed to find ways to contribute to trade adjustment by some combination of variable-exchange-rate policy [41] and foreign investment policy.[42]

2. *The gold standard*

Under present conditions it is hard to say whether the United States and other major countries do or do not have a gold standard. In terms of standard terminology the United States at present operates a provisional, limited gold-bullion standard; [43] some other countries, including

41. The persistent "dollar scarcity" suggests that probably we should revalue the dollar upward—that is, lower our price for gold. Refusal to do this will apparently either perpetuate the tensions which keep foreign trade in a regulative strait jacket or else force downward revaluation (increases of gold prices) in most other countries, risking a scramble for advantage which may start a new phase of international economic warfare.[*]

42. If, for example, development programs we are prepared to back through the World Bank and otherwise will take a total of $15 billion over the next decade, it will ease the world currency situation if we can increase our financing in years when dollar shortage is most intense (for example, because crops here are good at a time when crops abroad are bad) and reduce our financing in years when the dollar shortage eases. Obviously it is hard to reconcile such flexibility in timing with the basic needs the program is aimed to fill and with employment and price-level developments in the various countries involved. I do not myself know enough about the character of these investment opportunities to have a reliable judgment as to whether much can be contributed to international monetary stability in this way.[†]

43. The components of this mouth-filling term need clarification: *gold standard:* an arrangement under which the value of an assigned quantity of gold and currency unit are kept equal by means of official offers to buy and sell gold at stated prices; *provisional* because we are not fully committed to keep the existing ratio of 1 ounce to $35 (though we have done so since 1934), and because we are not fully committed as to the nature of the "limitations"; *gold-bullion standard* because our monetary authorities deal in gold bars rather than in gold coin, and no gold coin circulates; *limited* because: 1) we prohibit private ownership of monetary gold except in transit; 2) we sell gold only for stated purposes (export to designated countries through authorized channels, industrial use; 3) we also limit to some degree the sources from which we will buy gold.

Exchange control which scrutinizes the purposes for which funds are transferred abroad—much more intense elsewhere than in the United States—implicitly adds further limitations.

[*] This was written some months before the devaluations of 1949 and the inflation of 1950–51. Since these changes, I would not maintain that the dollar was seriously undervalued.

[†] This was written before the United Nations, Department of Economic Affairs report (by John Maurice Clark and others) on *National and International Measures for Full Employment* (1949) and consequently takes no account of the proposals made there.

Britain, have the same—with more emphasis on "limited"; others have dollar-exchange standards or sterling-exchange standards; [44] and some are off the gold standard map. Some people advocate moving back toward an unqualified gold standard, by such steps as firmer commitments to the permanence of the gold price, restoration of private ownership of gold—perhaps even reintroduction of gold coins. Others advocate moving away from gold by withdrawing our standing offer to buy or even ending gold purchases altogether.

Advocates of the unqualified gold standard rely heavily on a notion of "automaticity" which I find unacceptable. An "automatic gold standard" is visualized as rolling all monetary decisions into one package: if all major countries agreed to adopt one and followed its "rules," there would be no trouble maintaining balance in international trade, and all central bank and Treasury monetary decisions could be read off from the existing gold situation and the rule book. Unfortunately, the rules imply that each country must have an extremely flexible internal price structure, or be quite prepared to accept heavy unemployment rather often, or both.[45] Few countries will accept these implications today. Besides, the rules imply willingness to hold a sizable part of national assets in the unremunerative form of gold reserve; countries which feel poor (either because they are undeveloped or because of war losses) will balk. The consequence is that outside the United States there is no large body of gold-standard advocates. (In Britain it was necessary to defend the Bretton Woods agreements to a Parliament with a Conservative majority by insisting they did *not* restore the gold standard!) The alleged virtues of automaticity depend on international adherence to the gold standard and its rules, which will not be forthcoming.

An independent argument is that restoring the private ownership of gold would be reassuring to business opinion in the United States. In time of inflationary pressure, furthermore, an offer to exchange gold for bank deposits might drain off part of the pressure to exchange bank deposits for physical goods. On the other hand, any buyer of gold could actually gain only if he was allowed to profit from future increases in the price of gold—or if gold he acquired somehow disappeared from

44. An exchange standard maintains equality between the domestic and a foreign currency unit by buying and selling offers—which again may be provisional and limited. With the institution of the International Monetary Fund, the difference between dollar-exchange standards and gold-bullion standards becomes somewhat hazy.

45. The American deflation policy in late 1931, which I described above as "suicidal," was apparently adopted on the ground that it was called for by gold standard rules.

his list of visible assets and later cropped up among the assets of his heirs without paying estate taxes. To provide a vehicle for speculation on a rise in the gold price, or for speculation on ability to escape taxes, has obvious drawbacks which to my mind outweigh the psychological advantages of restoring private gold ownership.

The basic argument for curtailing or eliminating gold purchases is that it is a pity to put productive resources into mining and processing a mineral which is never to be used. Ultimately, we may suppose, this waste will be cut off. But it strikes me that the next few years are not the time to take any positive steps. The psychological argument raised above in another connection also has force in favor of preserving what is left of gold standard symbolism. The success of economic stabilization procedures will depend in good part on public confidence in their "soundness." So long as we keep the gold-certificate-reserve requirements of the Federal Reserve banks at or below the present 25% (I should prefer 10%), our links with gold will not hamper policy appreciably; and in fact we shall have no difficulty keeping gold reserves at levels tradition regards as sound. Another argument against choosing this time to cut ties with gold is that the United States market for gold is a major source of dollars for Canada and South Africa, and through them for the Marshall Plan countries.

To sum up the gold situation, it seems to me that the present *form* of our gold arrangements is satisfactory for the nearer future. But we should consider for the near future a reduction of our gold price and a reduction of our gold-reserve requirements, and for the longer future an eventual cessation of gold purchases.

3. *Commodity currency possibilities*

Proposals for a radically different monetary standard have developed in recent years under the leadership of Benjamin Graham.[46] The central notion is to have a monetary authority which will buy a composite bundle of commodities whenever the price of the composite falls below a stated level. The commodities have to be standardized articles which will stand storage, so that the list to enter the composite turns out to be a fairly small group of important agricultural and mineral raw materials. This device would result in a rough stabilization of the prices of the included commodities—and also of the incomes of their producers—though leaving room for some of the included commodities to drop in price on condition that others rise.

The income-stabilizing aspect of the plan is attractive from the stand-

46. B. Graham, *World Commodities and World Currency* (New York, McGraw-Hill, 1944).

point of economic stabilization. Widespread confidence in its price-stabilizing efficacy, furthermore, could transform commodity speculation from a potentially destabilizing to a reliably stabilizing influence. The main drawbacks of the plan, aside from its unfamiliarity, strike me as lying in the danger that it might be overrated to the neglect of other lines of policy and that political pressures on prices might break through it.

Discussion of the plan tends to be too much isolated from discussion of other monetary problems and of fiscal policy. But plainly other policies would determine the state of the commodity reserve. To accumulate enough commodities to be safe in setting up a standing offer to sell the composite at a stated price, the monetary authority must start buying either in a major business downswing or at a moment when bumper crops permit heavy accumulation without serious inflationary effects. A large enough crop bulge to create a reserve is unlikely.[47] A situation where a reserve could be piled up, then, must be a situation where fiscal policy has failed to avert serious unemployment—or else a situation where the goods going into the composite are overpriced relative to (chiefly) the wage level, so that a perceptible degree of inflation will be necessary to bring the price structure into line.[48] In short, the opportunity to install this policy can be created only by overpricing farm products or by a failure of other economic stabilization policies!

Once the plan is under way, any tendency toward secular unemployment will induce a secular piling up of the commodity reserve. Any tendency toward a chronic excess of demand over supply will tend to drain away the reserve.[49] To keep the reserve within moderate limits,

47. A quick survey of the crop-production index of the Bureau of Agricultural Economics from 1909 through 1946 shows in 35 years only 8 in which crops exceeded the average for the preceding 3 years by as much as 10%, and only one (1937, on the recovery from the great drought) where the excess was over 15%. Thus, if consumption is to be kept in line with the general trend of production as indicated by recent experience, there can rarely be opportunities to put much into stock. On the other hand, 1948–49 experience suggests present support prices for farm products may be high enough to cause stocks to pile up.

48. The political-economic strategy of the Graham Plan might be described as one of launching the plan on the strength of the tendency of farmers to have the government fix prices too high to get the whole crop consumed; and thereafter dissuading farmers from pushing their prices further (as other prices come up into line), using the argument that the Graham Plan provides safeguards against serious troughs in farm income, so that farmers need not try to push up the peaks.

49. On this and the following paragraph, see my analysis in A. G. Hart, *op. cit.*, pp. 452–456, 484–485. I have left out of account there, as I do here, certain complications that ensue in case of currency devaluation if the scheme (as Graham proposes) is made international and hitched to the International Monetary Fund.

therefore, implies that other elements of monetary-fiscal policy (with the help of the stabilizing influence of the commodity reserve on farm incomes and on commodity speculation) can keep the economy on an even keel. The stabilizing effect of the program itself is not likely to be strong enough to keep the reserve within bounds.

A more serious difficulty is the danger of breakdown in case of persistent political pressure toward increasing wages (relative to productivity) and farm prices. The plan itself contains no safeguards against such pressure except the implicit commitment that if an upward drift of the price level in general deplete the reserve, other lines of policy must come into play to restore it. This means in everyday language that monetary-fiscal policy would resist inflation by generating unemployment. The alternative would be to surrender "just this once" to the price-boosting forces and raise the price of the commodity composite. The possibility that we might some time have to do this would not be enough to justify rejecting the scheme—such a price-boosting process would be at least as inflationary under any alternative system; but the scheme could not be recommended unless there was ground for confidence that such devaluations of the commodity standard could be rare. In the present state of price-wage policy, I would not venture to give assurances that devaluation would not be frequent.

4. *The debt problem*

A strong case can be made out that the economic system would be less vulnerable to fluctuations if financed more on equity and less on debt. Contrary to widespread impressions, the focus of danger in the debt structure is short-term debt rather than long-term debt. One side of the danger is the fact that short-term creditors tend to regard short-term receivables as nearly equivalent to cash and are open to disillusionment which may suddenly raise their standards for the amount of paper money and bank deposits they need. The other side is the fact that short-term debtors (including debtors under long-term contracts whose maturity is approaching) tend to rely on renewal or refinancing to settle their obligations and are vulnerable to shocks if a tightening of credit puts them under pressure actually to reduce their debts.[50]

On the other hand, we have the awkward fact that savers who get their incomes from salaries, professional practice, interest, and dividends show great reluctance to put their savings into physical assets or equity securities—that is, they insist on becoming creditors.[51] At the

50. See A. G. Hart, *Debts and Recovery* (New York, Twentieth Century Fund, 1938), pp. 6–17, especially 14–16.

51. Even in the 1920's the proportion of investment in new facilities financed

same time, businessmen are reluctant to absorb additional outside funds (whether debt or equity) unless they can match them with comparable amounts of reinvested profits. Under favorable conditions, these peculiarities of the financing process [52] may make no trouble. Three sets of such favorable conditions have been at work since World War II. 1) An abnormally high level of business profits has enabled business to save heavily out of profits and thus to absorb debt financing without weakening its financial structure. 2) Construction of housing has been very rapid. A house is the one sort of physical asset on which the types of individual savers mentioned are willing to spend their savings directly—and borrow to boot. 3) Retirement of government securities held by business (amounting to over $2 billion a year over and above the shrinkage in securities held to offset accrued taxes) has enabled business to transform financial into physical assets without any need of net new financing. All these factors may be regarded as abnormally favorable in the last few years. There may be serious debt trouble ahead—particularly if specialization of the housing sector reduces long-run prospects for using individual savings there.

Remedies are not easy to prescribe. If we were setting up an economic Utopia, we might perhaps try to design its institutions so that nobody could save without taking responsibility for embodying his savings in an increase of physical wealth. If we are not going to prohibit unembodied saving, we can try to get it converted more efficiently into physical assets by equity-financing channels; but progress along this line has been discouragingly slow (with the one exception of the flow of life insurance funds into housing). Or conceivably we can tax unembodied saving—compare the tax-on-cash possibilities considered below. To the extent that we fail to siphon individual savings across into business we

---

by sale of new equity securities (preferred and common stocks) was fairly low. A large proportion of the dollars reported as going into purchase of new issues were a stage army—proceeds of new issues being used to buy in old issues, and thus coming around to buy new ones again. See G. A. Eddy, "Security Issues and Real Investment in 1929," *Review of Economic Statistics,* 19 (May, 1937), 79–91. His finding is that out of $8 billion of security issues classified as "for new capital" by the *Commercial and Financial Chronicle* about three-quarters was to buy in existing securities rather than to buy new physical assets. The proportion used to buy in existing securities was considerably higher for stocks than for bonds and notes; almost half of the new bonds and notes apparently were for real investment, as compared with one-sixth of the stocks.

52. I am drawing here not only on my own work reported in *Debts and Recovery* but on G. Colm and F. Lehmann, *Economic Consequences of Recent American Tax Policy* (New York, New School for Social Research, 1938), especially pp. 43–56, and on Homer Jones' forthcoming CED research study *Facilitating the Flow of Savings into Private Investment* (in press).

create a synthetic need for a government deficit; for if individual savers insist on increasing their creditorship, somebody has to increase his debtorship—if not business, then the government.

One specifically monetary problem in the field of debt policy is whether to encourage or discourage the further growth of debts of businesses and individuals to banks. If such a growth is the only way to get investment opportunities used (or to get them used without a dangerous concentration of power in "big business"), it must be accepted; but substitutes for debt financing are worth cultivating.[53] Insofar as we must have a growth of debt, long-term forms (business term loans; bond issues in preference to loans, amortized rather than lump-sum mortgages) are less likely to lead to economic instability. Increasing the proportion of debt in stable forms is one useful task for the "qualitative" instruments of bank-credit control.[54]

5. *Policy toward demand for liquid assets*

Economists used to feel that the demand for stocks of paper money and bank deposits rested entirely on the "transactions motive." Recent theoretical thinking and recent monetary history point toward the importance of the "precautionary" (or "margin-of-safety") motive and the "speculative" motive. These additional motives make the demand for such cash assets a destabilizing force in the economy—capable of increasing relative to actual stocks and creating a deflationary scramble for liquidity, or of decreasing and making a prosperity situation inflationary.*

If the transactions motive did in fact dominate the demand for cash assets, this demand would become a stabilizing force. For if the stock of cash assets were prevented from shrinking in a business downswing, by such methods as a 100% security-and-cash reserve with an exemption, the reduced business volume would produce an excess supply of cash, which would try to transform itself into income-yielding assets. Similarly, an inflation would produce an excess demand for cash, which would help limit the inflation.

Now there are methods for stripping the public's cash requirements down to a transactions basis. One is inflation. If prices are visibly on the upgrade it is much better to hold physical assets or equity securities, which will share in the rise, rather than cash (or debt securities), which

---

* The post-Korea inflation of 1950, and the check to inflation in the spring of 1951, are attributable in good part to fluctuations in the demand for liquid assets.

53. The CED report of Homer Jones, referred to above, is a promising source of constructive suggestions.

54. See above, pp. 326–327.

will not. A continual creeping inflation, if we could organize it and insure its continuance, would have this effect.[55] The question remains, of course, whether inflation would keep on creeping if it was known that creeping inflation was a goal of policy. The second main method is that of taxing the ownership of checking deposits and close substitutes.[56] Without committing us to price inflation, this would change the *relative* advantages of cash and physical assets or equity securities in the same way.[57]

Either of these lines of policy would go far, incidentally, to restore potency to interest policy as a regulator of investment in physical assets.[58] A creeping inflation at the rate of 5% per annum would require interest rates, if lenders were not actually to lose purchasing power, something like 6%. Such a rate would be no more burdensome to the borrower than 1% at stable prices. But a 6% rate would be far enough above the "floor" created by the option of holding cash and earning zero interest to give plenty of room for varying interest rates. The alternative policy of a tax on cash would remove the floor at zero, and make it much simpler for policy to vary interest rates in and below the range recently experienced.

The difficulty of the creeping-inflation policy is typified by our recent experience. During 1946, 1947, and the first half of 1948, prices were advancing faster than the specified rate of 5%; but interest rates and security prices showed little tendency to register expectations of further rise. To persuade people to believe in a *steady* rise in future would be very hard.

To convince the public of the reality of a (say) ¼ of 1% tax monthly

55. This suggestion is advanced rather tentatively by W. S. Vickrey, "Limitations of Keynesian Economics," *Social Research*, 15 (December, 1948), 416.

56. The proposal comes from Arthur Dahlberg, *When Capital Goes on Strike* (New York, Harper, 1938). Cf. my discussion in *Money, Debt and Economic Activity*, pp. 443–447, 457.

57. How far the tax should be extended to cover assets other than checking deposits and paper money is a moot point. My feeling is that taxing time deposits would be desirable, because of the ease of switching deposits from one form to the other. Taxation of life insurance cash values, savings, loan "shares," etc., would have merit as a way of discouraging disembodied savings. From the same standpoint, taxes on bonds other than those of government might be considered. Taxes on government securities would not be very crucial; in the absence of such taxes, attempts to convert bank deposits into governments would pull down the interest rate government pays on refinancing issues.

58. This point is the main concern in Vickrey's article just cited in *Social Research*, December, 1948. He is inclined to argue that either policy would make monetary policy capable of stabilizing the economy without much reliance on fiscal policy. I cannot agree.

on their average bank balances, once such a tax was enacted, would be no trick at all. On the other hand, it is hard to see how such a tax could be introduced by degrees. Even its introduction at $\frac{1}{20}$ of 1% monthly would be taken as a signal of higher taxes in future and would be apt to decrease the demand for cash appreciably. I infer that this possible line of policy (rather like the Graham Plan) is something in reserve, which can be brought into use in case a serious slump develops in spite of more conservative countermeasures of monetary and fiscal policy.*

6. General monetary strategy

The general upshot of this discussion, it seems to me, is that monetary policy should not try to be too clever. Despite all allegations to the contrary, monetary policy makes a great deal of difference, and doctrinaire arguments to demonstrate its insignificance are irresponsible. Accepting its importance, we must also accept the fact that the intensity and timing of its results are hard to gauge.

The main rule we can set up for monetary policy is that it should not run counter to the general needs of fiscal policy and of economic stabilization. Monetary policy should not be exerting inflationary pressure when employment is full and prices are in motion upward, as it did in 1946–48. Neither should it be exerting deflationary pressure when unemployment is rife and prices not rising (as in the early 1930's). What it should do when prices are rising and unemployment serious (as in early 1937), or when prices are falling and unemployment low but suspected of being on the increase (as in early 1949), is not so easy a question. But it will not be a gross error to try to avoid exerting pressure either way.

To avoid being forced into policy errors like those of 1946–48, monetary policy should aim to avoid "commitments" to stabilize security prices—whether by having securities redeemable, by having much of the government debt in short-term form subject to frequent renewal, or by supporting the bond market. This implies that whenever employment is high, unless prices are falling seriously it would be sound policy to refund maturing securities held by nonbank owners into long-term

---

* The discussion above implies that there will be fairly frequent periods of economic contraction, when measures to reduce the demand for cash balances will be helpful. If on the contrary there is fairly steady inflationary pressure, it will be urgent to avoid a shrinkage in the demand for cash.

Fortunately, efforts to avoid expansion of the supply of cash through bank-loan expansion tend also to increase the demand for cash for transactions purposes: for reduced assurance of getting loans forces firms and households to have a longer transactions horizon. Open-market sales of bonds, pushing their prices to a discount, tend to uncover speculative demand for cash.

issues. It might also pay to buy out the right to redemption of savings bond holders by special offers.[59] This policy would increase interest outlays somewhat. But if the outlay on bank-held securities was held down by installing a security-reserve system, this objection would not be fatal. The essential thing is to avoid making increased interest simply a handout to security holders, but to exact from them in exchange a substantial reduction of their power to compel monetary expansion by claiming contractual rights.

The main way to avoid moving in the wrong direction is to make headway with the reduction of credit instability, along the lines suggested above. A security reserve—if possible a 100% cash-plus-security reserve, with an exemption based on initial private net credit—should be a main objective of policy. Qualitative controls can be used to increase the proportion of bank receivables which are long-term or medium-term rather than short-term debt. If a reasonably noninflationary long-term policy toward wages and farm prices can be evolved, arrangements for installing a commodity-reserve system can be planned and set up as a stand-by measure to be brought into force in case of an intractable slump.

V. Monetary Reorganization

The monetary strategy sketched above obviously calls for some reshaping of monetary legislation. It is now forty years since the last full-dress consideration of the fundamentals of monetary policy (the study of the National Monetary Commission, arising from the panic of 1907 and issuing in the Federal Reserve Act of 1913). Consideration should plainly be given to:

1) Establishment of a new temporary commission, as proposed in many quarters, to reframe monetary and fiscal policy.
2) A suggested pooling of monetary and fiscal operating responsibilities (which I am inclined to oppose).
3) Reframing the mandate of the Federal Reserve System and the allocation of monetary powers between it and the Treasury.
4) Adjusting Federal Reserve relations to commercial banks (and to nonbank credit institutions) to reduce the instability of credit.
5) Planning of stand-by arrangements for use in specified circumstances should they arise in the future.

59. It would be simple, for instance, to declare a dividend of 1% of face value on all outstanding savings bonds not redeemed in the next year—by providing for an increase of 1% of face value in all scheduled redemption values listed on the bond and applying later than one year from the announcement.

1. *The proposed monetary and fiscal policy commission*

The case for setting up a temporary official commission to play the role of the prewar National Monetary Commission is a very strong one. As between proposals (for instance, from Winthrop Aldrich of the Chase National Bank) for a Monetary Commission and proposals (for instance, from the Committee for Economic Development) for a Monetary-Fiscal Commission, the latter strikes me as strongly preferable. As will appear shortly, I am skeptical of the idea of setting up a single operating agency covering the whole monetary-fiscal field; but agencies in the two parts of the field must have a joint strategy to be effective, so that a temporary planning agency should cover both fields.

The need for such a commission is largely to set before the public the basis for a consensus on questions about which agreement can readily be reached. A great deal of information on key questions is in the newspapers every week; but information written up as "spot news" does not help much toward coordinated thinking. The Council of Economic Advisers is in a position to give the public background data on large policy issues; but it has to concern itself chiefly with the near future. A commission with a life of three to five years, well-staffed, with jurisdiction over a large but well-defined long-term problem, using the procedure of public hearings and publishing findings of fact and analysis from time to time as well as final recommendations, can do much to focus public opinion.

Not all the issues need only to be clearly analyzed to be settled. Some issues must plainly be postponed till there is a clearer basis for their settlement; in such instances the function of such a commission is to show in advance how future experience can be used to tell us what to do. There will be other issues where it is hard to see which of two or several solutions is preferable, but where some decision must be reached if debate on these issues is not to get in the way of settling others—for example, the issue of reorganizing our arrangements for bank examination. Here an authoritative commission, by proposing a reasonable solution without any pretense that it is perfect, can keep the channels of policy-making from getting clogged. As our problems shake down, some issues—including a few of those I have treated above as fairly clear on the merits—will doubtless prove hard to agree upon. Here the task of a commission will be to find workable compromises and avoid unworkable straddles.

2. Suggested pooling of monetary and fiscal authority

Proposals have been made [60] for setting up both in Congress and in the executive branch focal points for the joint consideration of monetary and fiscal problems. It is true that in Congress the separate Banking and Currency Committees, Appropriations Committees, and taxation (Finance and Ways and Means) committees consider pieces of the policy problem out of perspective. But the institution of the Joint Committee on the Economic Report, with its staff, and of the rule (so far not fully effective) calling for a Legislative Budget provide foci for economic policy as a whole and may have eliminated the need for a monetary and fiscal committee as visualized two years before this new machinery came into being.

Similarly, on the executive side we now have the Council of Economic Advisers; and there is enough flexibility in the Executive Office of the President to admit of a good deal of concentrated attention on broad economic-policy problems. The Treasury and Federal Reserve have sometimes been at cross-purposes, and the Treasury in particular has shown a distressing lack of monetary-fiscal perspective. But my impression is that this is partly a question of the subject-matter grasp of individuals in responsible posts (who would produce much the same result if differently grouped) and partly the result of an awkward allocation of responsibilities between the Treasury and Federal Reserve. Given a temporary commission to look ahead into longer policy perspectives, and the sort of reallocation I suggest below, I doubt that setting up (say) a monetary-fiscal Assistant President would be a great improvement—unless by bringing to power some first-rate man who could score a comparable improvement from a top post in the Treasury or Federal Reserve.*

3. Federal Reserve mandate and allocation of monetary powers

The mandate of our monetary authorities needs to be reformulated. When new basic monetary legislation is passed, it should assert the authority of the federal government over money—and over banking and related activities as part of the monetary system. It should instruct the Federal Reserve authorities to use their banking powers and debt-

---

* This diagnosis is confirmed, it seems to me, by the tremendous improvement of Treasury-Federal Reserve relations and firming of Federal Reserve policy in 1951. These gains seem to have sprung largely from the intelligent intervention of Senator Douglas and from the Treasury's assignment of Mr. Martin to clear up the dispute.

60. Notably by B. Ruml and H. C. Sonne, *Fiscal and Monetary Policy* (Washington, D.C., National Planning Association, 1944), pp. 30–32.

management powers, in cooperation with related agencies, toward the prevention of mass unemployment and of inflationary price increases. The rather vague instruction to "accommodate commerce and industry" could well be replaced by a more specific instruction to safeguard the access of small business to bank credit, so far as compatible with broader policies of economic stabilization.

The most promising remedy I can see for the pull and haul arising from the division of debt-management powers between Federal Reserve and Treasury is to transfer debt management to the Federal Reserve. The security-reserve arrangement (even if the reserve ratio adopted stops well short of 100%) would be a long step in this direction. For if banks preferred the convenience of holding their security reserve in the optional form of an interest-bearing deposit at the Federal Reserve, the Federal Reserve would find itself stepping in as intermediary—becoming owner of Treasury securities and setting up its own interest-bearing debt as an equivalent. A further step would be to authorize the Federal Reserve to issue its own bills, certificates, notes, and bonds and float such securities (instead of new Treasury securities) to replace on the open market such Treasury securities as mature. (New Treasury issues would thus be taken up entirely by the Federal Reserve, so that the vestiges of old rules barring Federal Reserve purchases of new issues would have to be swept away.) Finally, all Treasury checking accounts would naturally be concentrated at Federal Reserve banks; the counterpart of this would be to authorize the Federal Reserve to carry deposit balances at commercial banks, so as to avert monetary disturbances as Treasury balances vary. This arrangement would center in the Federal Reserve the open-market powers now shared with the Treasury,[61] and permit (if desirable) a separation between the interest charges entered in the federal budget and the interest rates affecting the market.

The Treasury's more narrowly monetary functions (gold dealings, provision of small change, etc.) are so nearly automatic that there is no need to include them in the transfer of monetary powers to the Federal Reserve. Our relations with the International Monetary Fund require us to maintain standing offers to buy and sell gold or equivalent

---

61. One important exception: while I would recommend complete displacement of Treasury bills, certificates, and notes by corresponding Federal Reserve securities, it does not seem to me that complete displacement of Treasury bonds by Federal Reserve bonds would be expedient. My reason is that patriotic appeals (more readily organized around the Treasury than the Federal Reserve) are a main reliance for bond sales in emergencies and for the maintenance of the rather doubtful stability of the public's United States savings bond holdings.

foreign currencies; this implies that any eventual reconsideration of our remaining gold standard arrangements must be international rather than merely national. We should stand ready to consider an upward revaluation of the dollar (reduction of our gold price) if recommended by the International Monetary Fund. Opening the door of public opinion for such a step is one major assignment for the suggested Monetary-Fiscal Commission.

4. *Federal Reserve relations to private credit institutions*

The most important question of Federal Reserve relations to private credit institutions is the adjustment of reserve requirements to reduce the instability of credit. As I have argued above, the most promising solution here is to adopt a security arrangement. The higher the required percentage of reserves the greater the contribution to economic stability up to 100% for a cash-plus-reserve securities.

Any intensification of reserve requirements of course creates competitive advantages for credit institutions exempt from the requirements. The continuance of "nonmember banks" which are free from our basic monetary controls is an anachronism; and membership in the Federal Reserve System might as well be required of all. Nonbank credit institutions (notably savings and loan associations and life insurance companies) are rapidly taking on banking functions. Their business is different enough from banking so that an identical pattern of control would not fit well. But as a safeguard against their reviving the "inherent instability of bank credit" in new forms, it would be desirable to assert the power of federal monetary authority over the banking side of their operations and to apply the security-reserve requirement to them.[62]

The continuance of qualitative controls over particular types of credit makes sense—chiefly to steer such types of credit into crisis-proof form and secondarily to damp the ardor of certain key speculative markets. On both counts, extension of such controls to real estate loans (of nonbank credit institutions as well as banks) deserves serious consideration. If inventory loans could be segregated, they would also be a good

---

62. The base for the requirement, in the case of savings and loan associations, would naturally be the excess of their redeemable shares plus surplus over their base-period mortgage loans; for life insurance companies, the excess of policy loan-cash-and-surrender values plus surplus over mortgages and nongovernment bonds. Insofar as insurance companies chose to sell pure insurance (notably term insurance), so that no reserves were set up in a form policyholders can borrow against or recover substantially in full by surrender, they would not bring themselves under monetary control.

field for special treatment; but my judgment is that there is no workable way to identify such loans for control purposes.

5. *Stand-by arrangements*

As may be seen from the discussion above, a number of promising monetary tools have been suggested but never brought at all close to operation. This applies especially to the commodity-reserve-currency suggestion (Graham Plan) and the tax-on-liquid-holdings suggestion (Dahlberg Plan). In both those cases the inventors have gone a long way toward designing workable methods of operation. But I doubt very much that they have gone far enough so that workable legislation could be drafted. And certainly they have not settled the problems of coordination of their plans with other instruments of economic policy.

One of the most important tasks of the economic profession, and of the proposed Monetary-Fiscal Commission, is to work out the best way of using these devices if and when they come to be needed—that is, as I pointed out above, in case of a serious and refractory slump. The public needs to be persuaded to take such ideas seriously. And the bankers and others who might be inconvenienced by their application need to be brought into counsel as to how to mitigate the inconvenience if they become necessary.

This exemplifies the side of the economic stabilization problem which is most important of all—getting sustained and dispassionate attention to the problem from the public. Economic stabilization cannot be just a technical operation carried on by a few experts in the background without much attention from the public. Neither can it be the program of some one economic group or coalition of groups, carried on in the teeth of opposition (or even incomprehension) from a substantial minority. It has to reflect a reasoned consensus about the national interest, applied with the good will of the great bulk of the nation. Forethought about measures that may be needed in time of trouble must be widespread to give us this consensus.

CHAPTER VIII. *Variation in Public Expenditure* [1]

BY ROBERT A. DAHL AND
CHARLES E. LINDBLOM

In 1949, before the Korean incident persuaded us to adopt partial mobilization, government expenditures accounted for more than one out of every five dollars of gross national product in the United States. They amounted roughly to 9% of gross national product in 1929, to 49% during the war, to 23½% in 1949.[2] The mere size and the variability of aggregate government expenditures both create potential disruptive forces in the economy.

Can we take advantage of the size and variability of this component part of gross national product in order to stabilize the economy? Can the planning of public expenditure become an effective tool of income and employment policy?

I. Public Expenditure and Fiscal Policy

Public expenditure as an arm of fiscal policy can change the level of income and employment in three ways, one of which is much more important than the other two.

1) With no change in the total volume of public expenditures, variations in the specific purposes of these expenditures may depress or encourage particular industries or sectors of the economy with consequent repercussions on the total volume of employment and income. For example, government investment in steel capacity may, depending on how it is done, either depress or encourage private investment in steel with repercussions for the level of spending in the whole economy. In the 1920's public investment in highway construction was a stimulus to the automobile and allied industries, and this expansion was in turn a stimulus to the general level of productive activity.

2) Increases or decreases in the total amount of public expenditure

1. The authors wish to express their appreciation to Mr. Allan Cartter for his research work and help in preparation of the manuscript for this chapter.
2. The 1949 figure is from the *Economic Report of the President to Congress,* January, 1950, p. 6. For other figures see U.S. Bureau of Foreign and Domestic Commerce (Department of Commerce), *Survey of Current Business,* July, 1947.

exactly equaled by tax increases or decreases will also influence the level of income and employment. If, for example, government expenditures on public works are increased during a depression and tax receipts are increased by the same amount, total national income may rise by the amount of increase in expenditure. Common sense, it is true, would seem to dictate that the increase in government spending is at the expense of private spending reduced by taxation. But as was explained in Chapter 3, the increased taxation may draw in part on savings and thus add to the national income when spent by government on new goods and services.

If, however, the increase in government expenditures financed out of increased taxes is merely for transfer payments, the net effect on spending may be zero, since taxes may draw upon savings only to transfer these funds into the hands of other individuals who also save them. No new goods and services are called forth by government transfer payments.

Of course, if transfer payments financed by taxes effect a redistribution of income which results in more spending and less saving in the economy, national income will be increased by the increase in public expenditures. And redistributive effects of public expenditure on goods and services may heighten the effects already described.

3) But the most important way in which variations in public expenditures may affect the level of income and employment is when these variations are not offset by equivalent changes in tax receipts. That is to say, changes in public expenditure can be a method of running a deficit or a surplus. As has been explained in Chapter 3, the expansion or contraction of credit represented by a budgetary deficit or surplus represents a net increase or decrease in the volume of spending in the economy.

Acting through a budgetary deficit, public expenditures can bring to bear on the economy a) the primary effects of the spending itself, b) the secondary effects of consumer spending when consumers begin to spend the income they have earned from working, say, on a public works project, and c) tertiary effects of new private investment induced by increased consumer expenditure. Conversely, restriction of expenditure can throw these processes into reverse to forestall inflation.

Only when public expenditures create a deficit or surplus do these secondary and tertiary effects come into play. When public expenditures are financed by increased taxes, the secondary and tertiary effects of the increased expenditure are offset by the effects of the reduced income of taxpayers.

Where changes in public expenditures are a technique of running a budgetary surplus or deficit, what is significant is not so much the expenditures themselves but the increases or decreases in total spending represented by the deficit or surplus. But increases or decreases in total spending might also come from variations in private spending induced by tax variations while government expenditures were held constant.

It follows that objections often brought against the variations of public expenditure as a stabilization technique are no more applicable to public expenditure than to variation in taxation. The issue is the deficit or surplus—not the alternative chosen to achieve it. For example, many of the objections to a large national debt are, if valid at all, valid as objections to low taxes as well as to high expenditures. For it is not the expenditures but the deficit that makes the debt.

But by the same token the claims made for deficit financing cannot be used to justify variations in public expenditure unless these variations can be shown to afford a method superior to tax variation—or a necessary supplement to tax variation.

Our grounds for emphasizing the role of public expenditures in an unbalanced budget rather than their role in a balanced budget are simply that a balanced budget approach to public expenditure requires an extremely large volume of expenditure as well as a heavy tax burden to achieve the desired expansion in income during depression. But we do not mean to rule out the possibility of a balanced budget approach to public expenditures, and what we have to say about public expenditures in this chapter is for the most part applicable to variation in public expenditure either by the balanced budget route or the unbalanced budget route.

In any case public expenditure policy is a tool of fiscal policy, and thinking about expenditure policy must therefore be anchored in thinking about fiscal policy in general, discussed by Gerhard Colm in Chapter 5. And no more can be claimed for expenditure policy than can be claimed for fiscal policy, of which it is a part. The limitations of fiscal policy are made explicit in Chapter 5. In particular, expenditure policy is incapable of dealing with instability arising from high costs rather than autonomous disturbances in spending, a possibility discussed in Chapter 11 on labor policy.

Speaking in very simple terms, at least two questions require answers before a program of varying public expenditure for stability can be decided upon. 1) Is it desirable to create a budgetary deficit or surplus as a method of stabilizing the economy? 2) Is variation of public expenditure more desirable than variation in taxation as a method of creating a deficit or surplus? It is the second of these questions with which this chapter is concerned. The strengths and weaknesses of tax variation as a stability instrument are discussed in Chapter 6; we propose here to assess the strengths and weaknesses of expenditures as a stability device by raising the question of what criteria might be developed for determining how much, when, and for what.

II. CRITERIA FOR PUBLIC EXPENDITURE: HOW MUCH, WHEN, AND FOR WHAT?

Even if public expenditures had no effect on the stability of the economy, their importance in providing goods and services should impress us with the necessity for clear thinking on how much is to be spent by government, for what purposes, and where. Table 1, which gives the last federal expenditure plan drawn up before Korea, discloses the vastness and variety of government functions for which public expenditure is necessary. The mere length of the list is a reminder that *a* decision on the level of public expenditure is never made. Instead almost countless decisions are required.

In the absence of a market mechanism by which everyone may choose those goods and services for which he is willing to pay, as is done for nongovernmental expenditures, how can a people democratically and intelligently decide on what goods and services they wish to support through governmental expenditures? And how can they intelligently determine the volume of "transfer" expenditures—payments made by government not for goods and services but directly to supplement private incomes, e.g., unemployment benefits and veterans bonuses?

1. *An extreme view*

Most of us are not entirely aware of the role which public expenditures have played in antidepression policy in the past. During the depression of the 1930's when the federal government undertook what was then considered a huge public works program, government expenditures on public works projects actually declined for some years rather than rose. Local and state governments reduced their public works construction activities by more than the federal government increased its public works activities. For a time, therefore, the impact of variations in public works expenditures was presumably the opposite of what had been intended and what was commonly supposed to be the case.[3] The very difficulty of making intelligent choices in this field has led

3. Total expenditures for new public construction by federal, state, and local government units declined from $2,776,000,000 in 1930 to $1,354,000,000 in 1933 and did not rise to the 1930 level again until 1936. See Alvin H. Hansen and Harvey S. Perloff, *State and Local Finance in the National Economy* (New York, Norton, 1944), p. 50.

TABLE I. Estimated Federal Government Expenditures for 1950, by Major Program *

millions of dollars

NATIONAL DEFENSE
Department of Defense, Military Functions:

Pay and Support of Active Duty Military Personnel	4,590
Operation and Maintenance of Equipment	3,224
Civilian Components	705
Research	630
Military Procurement	2,425
Military Public Works	299
Industrial Mobilization, Administration	487
Unexpended Reimbursements from Mutual Defense Assistance Program	−50
Civil Functions	250

Activities Support Defense

Stockpiling	580
National Advisory Committee for Aeronautics	56
RFC	−81
Other	33
Total	13,148

INTERNATIONAL AFFAIRS

Conduct of Foreign Affairs	246

International Recovery and Relief

ERP and Other Foreign Aid	4,062
Aid to Occupied Areas	831
Aid to Korea	93
RFC (Loan Repayment)	−38
Aid to Refugees	90
Other	23

Foreign Economic Development

Export Import Bank Loans	71
Inter-American Development	11

Foreign Military Assistance

Mutual Defense Assistance Program	160
Greek-Turkish Aid	195
Philippine Aid	221
Total	5,964

VETERANS SERVICES AND BENEFITS
Readjustment Benefits

Education and Training	2,718
Unemployment and Self-Employment Allowances	153
Loan Guarantees	61
Other	105
Compensations and Pensions (VA)	2,243
Insurance (VA)	518

millions of dollars

Hospitals, Other Services and Administrative Costs

Construction	225
Current Expenses	882
Total	6,905

SOCIAL WELFARE, HEALTH, AND SECURITY

Assistance to Aged and Other Special Groups

FSA Public Assistance	1,146
FSA Vocational Rehabilitation and Other	28
School Lunch	83
Retirement and Dependents Insurance	613
Promotion and Public Health	270
Crime Control and Correction	93
Other	54
Total	2,297

HOUSING AND COMMUNITY DEVELOPMENT

Aids to Private Housing

HHFA	−189
RFC	1,002
Department of Agriculture	20
Public Housing Program	
HHFA	118
RFC	−1
General Housing Aids	7
Slum Clearance and Community Development	49
Total	1,006

AGRICULTURE AND AGRICULTURAL RESOURCES

Loan and Investment Programs

Department of Agriculture

CCC	1,533
FHA	26
REA	362
Other	6
Other Agencies	3
Other Financial Aids	
Department of Agriculture	
Conservation and Use	285
Removal of Surplus Commodities	86
Sugar Act	63
International Wheat Agreement	82
Agricultural Land and Water Resources	64
Other Developments and Improvements	161
Total	2,671

NATURAL RESOURCES

Atomic Energy	673

millions of dollars

Land and Water Resources
    Corps of Engineers   486
    Bureau of Reclamation   334
    Bonneville Power Administration   42
    Other Interior Department   43
    TVA   52
    Other   7
Forest Resources   79
Mineral Resources   55
General Resources Survey   16
Fish and Wildlife Resources   28
Recreation   29
    Total   1,845

TRANSPORTATION AND COMMUNICATION
    Promotion of Merchant Marine   162
    Provision of Navigation Aids and Facilities   381
    Promotion of Aviation   188
    Provision of Highways   515
    Regulation of Transportation   15
    Other Services to Transportation   44
    Postal Service Deficit   569
    Communication   10
    Total   1,894

FINANCE, COMMERCE, AND INDUSTRY
    Business Loans and Guarantees (RFC)   153
    Promotion and Regulation of Business
        Department of Commerce   28
        Antimonopoly Programs   7
        Rent Control   22
        Other   7
    All other   7
    Total   225

EDUCATION AND GENERAL RESEARCH
    Promotion of Education
        Office of Education   34
        General Services Administration and Interior   8
    Educational Aid to Special Groups   7
    Library and Museum Services   11
    General Purpose Research
        Census and Census programs   53
        National Bureaus of Standards   12
        Other   1
    Total   125

LABOR
    Placement and Unemployment Compensation Activities
        Department of Labor   137

	millions of dollars
Railroad Retirement Board	10
Federal Security Agency	37
Mediation and Regulation of Labor Relations	12
Labor Standards, Training, and Information	23
Total	219

GENERAL GOVERNMENT

Legislative Functions	43
Judicial Functions	27
Executive Direction and Management	8
Federal Financial Management	
Bureau of Internal Revenue	230
Customs Collection, Debt Management	136
General Accounting Office	36
Government Payment toward Civilian Retirement	301
Other General Government	353
Total	1,223

INTEREST ON THE PUBLIC DEBT	5,725
RESERVE FOR CONTINGENCIES	50
Total Budget Expenditures by Major Functions	43,297

* Taken from "Budget Message of the President," *The Budget of the United States Government, Fiscal Year Ending June, 1951.* The figures as they appear here have been somewhat simplified by consolidating some items under the major sub-headings. For a complete breakdown see "Summary and Supporting Tables," *ibid.*

some economists to suggest that it is too much to hope that public expenditures can be varied intelligently to stabilize the economy. Their proposals and arguments are impressive.

One economist has suggested the following policy with respect to public expenditures: [4]

1) Expenditures on goods and services entirely on the basis of the community's desire, need, and willingness to pay for these services. Changes in the level of expenditures solely in response to changes in the relative value attached by the community to private and governmentally provided services. No change in response to fluctuations in business activity.

2) Predetermined transfer expenditures as exemplified by present systems of old-age unemployment insurance. No changes in response to business fluctuations. Payments under the system would, of course, in fact be larger in periods of unemployment.

He then proposes to put fiscal policy to work through variations in

4. Milton Friedman, "A Monetary and Fiscal Framework for Economic Stability," *American Economic Review,* 38 (June, 1948), especially p. 248.

government tax receipts and transfer payments which would automatically occur as incomes rise and fall, assuming that the government's primary tax source is the progressive income tax.

If such a program does not seem to capitalize on the possibilities of varying public works in the "right" direction, it at least avoids the major possibility that government expenditures will actually be varied in the "wrong" direction—that is, in such a way as to aggravate instability. The possibilities of perverse variations in expenditure due to errors in forecasting are avoided. Given the present state of forecasting as discussed in Chapter 4, this is no small gain.

Tax variation has, of course, one major advantage over public expenditures as a technique of running a surplus to head off an inflation. Public expenditures cannot be cut as much as taxes can be raised.

2. Specific relevant criteria

If we were to accept the argument that the best to be hoped for is a predetermined nonvariable level of public expenditure, what presumably are the criteria for determining the level and allocation of expenditures?

Now if we examine this question we soon discover that any full answer is dependent less on technical matters than on our value assumptions. This book represents an attempt to discover whether a democratic society and a stable economy can live at peace with one another. None of us is interested in achieving a stable economy at the price of democracy; nor do we wish to resign ourselves to the proposition that American democracy is so incompetent that it must forever adopt policies that will lead to needless economic instability.

This book is written because the contributers and presumably most Americans want two things—and we believe these are implied by traditional democratic values. First, we want public policy, including stabilization policy, to be democratic, in the sense that it accords with the preferences of the greater number of adult citizens, as determined by public debate, citizen activities, political parties, elections, and legislative action. We do not believe that we can have democracy without "politics"; we do not want a stable economy without democracy; therefore, we do not want a stabilized economy without politics. Secondly, however, we also want public policy to be competent or, to use a more technical word, rational. To behave competently, or rationally, is to behave efficiently, in the sense that the most competent or rational action in any given situation is the one best designed to achieve one's goals. Competent or rational action is also economical action, in the sense that one "gets the most for his money," or more technically achieves most of his goals with the least cost to his goals. As Bernard Shaw once put it, economy is getting the most out of life, and economy is the root of all virtue.

Now it follows from all this that stabilization policy might be competent or rational—in the limited sense, say, of being the correct policy to maintain maximum employment without inflation—and yet not be at all democratic. And stabilization policy might be entirely democratic, in the sense of being in accord with the preferences of the greater number of citizens, and yet not be at all rational or, in other words, designed actually to achieve stability. Pretty clearly, then, what we want is stabilization policy that is both democratic and competent. We assume most of our readers want to achieve both these goals, too. Therefore we do not think it is necessary to engage in an excursion into ethical theory in order to postulate these goals. Hereafter, we shall simply refer to the achievement of both of them together as "democratic rationality." If a reader disagrees with this aim, then he has picked up the wrong book.

Now if democratic rationality were ever to be satisfactorily approximated in the case of public expenditures, three things would be required:

1) Citizens and political leaders should know the probable consequences of proposed expenditures. Predictability is such an elementary prerequisite to competent action that no further stress on the importance of this criterion is necessary.

2) Citizens and political leaders should be able to estimate the probable satisfactions to be gained from various alternative expenditures. In the case of public expenditures, this is one of the most difficult criteria to satisfy, because decisions are often made without any clear understanding either of what alternatives might have been obtained for the same expenditure or of the probable satisfactions to be derived from the expenditure.

The principles of consumer-guided allocation set forth in the first chapter as an objective of economic policy are, as economists have argued, in many respects carefully designed to meet the criterion of rationality. But how can we achieve "consumer guidance" in the case of many proposed types of expenditures where decisions must be made through the mechanisms of political democracy rather than "consumer sovereignty" via the market? What this aspect of rationality seems to require is that where the market is a satisfactory mechanism, policies which permit consumers to express their preferences on the market are preferable to those which do not.

For a variety of reasons the market is not always a satisfactory mechanism. For example, public expenditure on education represents a kind of investment in human beings which, in the absence of slavery, is unprofitable for the private investor. Citizens may quite rationally prefer that the size and purpose of such expenditures *not* be determined by market choices. In these and similar cases, where the balance is on the side of public expenditures determined through the political process, there is great need for political mechanisms which so far as possible permit choices to be made by citizens and political leaders with a relatively clear understanding of the alternatives open and of the probable net satisfaction from each of these alternatives.

3) But to accept this last value proposition is to require some rethinking of the techniques of public expenditures in stabilizing employment in a society like ours. Perhaps among those who advocate public expenditures for stabilization purposes there has been a tendency to overlook the irrationalities that may be inherent in the attempt to decide all aspects of full employment policy at the national level. It is one thing to argue that citizens and their leaders should stabilize the economy through *government* action. It is quite another thing to argue that the *federal* government must have the exclusive role.

Most of us are capable of considerable competence about the things that are near and familiar to us, and we are correspondingly less competent as the alternative choices become more unfamiliar, more distant from our daily experiences and observations. The housewife who makes out her weekly shopping list ordinarily can appraise the alternative costs and benefits much more intelligently than the same housewife writing to her congressman urging him to support the construction of a post office in her home town, or a bigger appropriation for river and harbor work. Anyone who has ever attended a town meeting in a relatively small New England town can have little doubt that a competent decision among competing choices is much easier at that level than when these same citizens march to the polls in November and attempt to choose among two great national camps of competing political elites. If it is the introduction of garbage collection by town authorities, or the building of a new school, or the purchase of a new school bus, citizens can weigh the relative advantage of one expenditure over the other; what is more, they are compelled to compare the relative costs of each.

Unfortunately, there is little likelihood that these conditions can be duplicated at the national level. There, most decisions must be made by political leaders crudely responsive to citizens, mostly acting in organized groups, with only limited capacity for weighing alternative expenditures—and particularly for weighing costs. Because the same individuals do not both receive the benefits and pay the costs; or, because they do so at widely separated times with no comparison of one with the other, competent action is extraordinarily difficult.

Nor is it only a question of competence; it is also a question of democracy. If people do not have preferences, or if they cannot articulate their preferences, or if they cannot communicate their preferences to their leaders, or if they cannot compel leaders to follow their preferences—then, willy-nilly, decisions will be made by those leaders who *do* have preferences and *are* capable of acting on them. The criterion of *democratic* rationality would demand that public expenditure policy be based on active and widely shared preferences rather than the preferences of a group of leaders acting with the passive acquiesence of an apathetic mass. In a later section we shall argue that this aim requires a gamble on the potentialities of local democracy.

Nevertheless it is not possible to maximize democratic rationality simply by giving exclusive decision-making powers on public expenditures to local communities. For if competence in many kinds of particular expenditures is often at its best at the level of the town meeting, it is impossible to arrive there at the *aggregate* of expenditures necessary to stability for the economy as a whole. In the absence of some stabilizing mechanism for the economy as a whole, it is entirely unlikely that decisions made at the town meeting level throughout the country, taken in conjunction with thousands and thousands of other small unit decisions both public and private, will automatically achieve an aggregate expenditure of the amount necessary for economic stability. If there is any level of policy-making where the alternatives available to the nation as a whole can be reasonably understood, it must be the national level—Congress, the executive branch, the national parties, the electorate of the entire country.

Then, too, there are many specific kinds of expenditures for which the local level is an irrational, even an impossible, form of organization—national defense, highways, flood control, reclamation, and irrigation, to name only a few. Here, rational choice-making requires selection among alternatives by citizens and their representatives acting as members of a larger unit of government—state, regional, or national.

In following out the threads of the criterion of rationality, therefore, we come to these conclusions. 1) A relatively competent decision as to the aggregate *level* of government expenditures can only be made by citizens and their leaders acting through the federal government, presumably through Congress and the executive branch. 2) A relatively rational decision among alternative objects of expenditure can only be made, in a very considerable number of cases, through rather large units of government—states, regions, or the nation. 3) But for many purposes maximum rationality in choosing among alternative *objects* of stabilization expenditure can best be achieved by citizens acting in smaller-sized units of government.

This suggests an important recommendation. *Objects of stabilization expenditure ought to be selected in the smallest jurisdiction that is technically able to act and which is representative of the relevant preferences. At the same time, the aggregate amount of expenditure and the proportions to be distributed to the various units of government should be made at the national level.* It goes without saying that such a recommendation also implies a great deal of consultation between big and small units of government, advance planning, and improvement in political and administrative mechanism, particularly at the local level—reforms we shall discuss in a later section.

All this amounts to proposing that one aim of public expenditures for stabilization purposes should be to stimulate a renascence in local democracy because the goal of democratic rationality can be approximated only if expenditures are based upon a vigorous examination of preferences in small units of government where, if anywhere, informed discussion and relevant action are possible.

3. *A broader view of the role of public expenditures*

Probably most economists disagree with proposals to hold expenditures constant throughout the cycle and would consequently enlarge the list of criteria to take account of the more powerful role which they believe expenditures can play in stabilization policy.

The author of the proposal discussed earlier in this chapter is careful to point out the difficulties in his own program. He has written: "The proposal may not succeed in reducing cyclical fluctuations to tolerable proportions. The forces making for cyclical fluctuations may be so stubborn and strong that the kind of automatic adaptations contained in the proposal are insufficient to offset them to a tolerable degree." [5] If these fears should be well-founded, the case for public spending is improved, although public spending is not the only alternative.

But even deliberate reduction of tax rates in depression—reductions in revenues going beyond those automatically accomplished—may not be sufficient to offset declines in spending. Moreover, tax savings may be hoarded rather than spent, in which case public expenditures may seem to be the only recourse. And quite aside from whether tax variation is sufficient to stabilize the economy, it suffers from serious defects (discussed by Carl Shoup in Chapter 6).

Finally, because the real social "cost" of using unused resources is zero,[6] it may be rational to expand public expenditures in depression even within a formula for expenditures determined solely by "desire,

5. Friedman, *op. cit.*, p. 264.

6. Because the use of the otherwise unemployed resources does not diminish the production of other goods and services, as it would if they were employed elsewhere.

need, and *willingness to pay.*" For willingness to pay must certainly increase as cost falls toward zero. It would thus appear that expenditures should be varied as costs change. If so, public expenditures varied in such a way as to stabilize the economy have an independent justification in terms of their value relative to their costs.

What can we say as to the true costs of public expenditure? We have already said that to use unemployed resources is to incur no cost at all. But the alternative to any particular public expenditure project A is another public expenditure project B. And where it is actually possible to stimulate private investment as an alternative to public expenditure the alternative to public expenditure project A or B is private expenditure project C. Hence, while using unused resources is costless, using resources for public projects is not costless if their use by private projects is an alternative possibility, nor is the use of resources in a particular public works project costless if any alternative public or private project is possible. Conversely, of course, the cost of a private project is the alternative private or *public* project which might have been undertaken as an alternative.

Reasoning in this way in terms of cost will show that cyclical variation in public expenditure is rational. In the first place, where private investment cannot be stimulated in depression, public investment as against no investment at all is costless. It would therefore be rational to increase public expenditure in such a period. Secondly, the kinds of private expenditure which can be successfully stimulated in depression may at the margin be valued less by the community than the projects which can be financed through public expenditure. Again therefore, on a strict cost basis, public expenditures should rationally be increased during depression. Thirdly, the relative marginal values to the community of public and private expenditures may alter from depression to prosperity and from prosperity to depression. In time of depression, community needs are different from what they are in times of full employment, and the relative marginal utilities of public and private expenditure may therefore vary. (As a matter of fact, depression may be caused by diminishing private investment due to a decline in the marginal utility of private projects.) Fourthly, stimulation of private investment may not be a practical alternative in a particular situation, perhaps because of administrative difficulties, conflicts of policy, or the unwillingness of Congress to undertake the necessary legislation. In these cases, the alternative to use of resources through public expenditures in nonuse of resources, and the use of public expenditures is rational because costless.

Generally, the logic of the argument calls for undertaking in times of full employment those public expenditure projects which are judged worth their costs and scheduling projects less desired for periods in which, for any of the reasons given, their real social cost declines or their marginal social utility rises.

The force of objections to variation in public expenditure would therefore seem to lie not in any arguments that it is irrational or illogical to vary expenditure because neither value received nor costs incurred vary, for such is not the case. Rather it lies in the practical difficulties of obtaining intelligent, flexible, and democratic control over expenditures so that they may be varied when and where variation is required. Whether these practical difficulties are insuperable or not can be determined only by examination of particular kinds of expenditures and the problems connected with each. We shall specify the criteria for success and then inspect the possibilities in each area of expenditure.

4. Specific criteria for stabilization expenditure

Assuming the possibility of varying expenditures for income stabilization, what kind of specific criteria beyond those already indicated ought we to employ in arriving at decisions about the desirable magnitude, purposes, and methods of government expenditures?

Whatever criteria one might wish to propose two points seem clear.

First, in a society of diverse values, even a program of government expenditures designed to maintain, say, "minimum unemployment" should seek at the same time to maximize the other major values of the society. On the face of it, this proposition appears so likely to command immediate and widespread acceptance that to state it is merely to set forth the obvious. Yet often enough technical discussions of "full employment" seem to reflect an unconscious professional bias toward an extremely narrow set of values. All other things being equal, however, an expenditure policy that helps to secure minimum unemployment and maximizes the bundle of values we call democratic is surely preferable to one that secures minimum unemployment and has indifferent effects for democratic values. It is a part of our task, therefore, to design, so far as is possible, a general framework for policy-making that is likely to lead to the first kind of policy rather than the second.

Second, in setting forth criteria for a model policy we do not assume that in real life we shall ever wholly meet the requirements of the model. This, too, seems obvious enough. But again discussion is sometimes carried on in the light of the inarticulate major premise that a failure to meet certain postulated criteria—such as consumer-guided allocation—is enough in itself to condemn the proposed policy. We do not expect in any foreseeable time that any expenditure policy can possibly meet all of the tests we are about to set forth. All that any one can sensibly hope for is that the policies selected will meet these criteria more nearly than any alternatives available at the moment, given the state of men's knowledge, their personalities and attitudes, and their social techniques.

The additional criteria we offer are three. First, government expenditures for stabilization purposes must be highly flexible. Second, they must be coordinated. Third, they must possess "cultural feasibility."

a. FLEXIBILITY

This criterion implies at least the following:

1) Government expenditures for stabilization should be capable of precise variation in *size*. In general, it is probably much easier to design an expenditure that may be pushed upward during deflationary periods than to design one that may also be pushed downward and even terminated during inflationary periods. A government expenditure means that services are performed, values are realized, administrative organizations developed, expectations expanded, clienteles formed, interest groups created, pressures mobilized—and these cannot be easily dissolved by a change in the index of employment.

To reverse government expenditures is difficult, furthermore, if expenditures have created large upkeep expenses even when the outlays for original construction, for example, have ceased. We can, perhaps, contract the construction of public hospitals during periods of inflation, but we cannot terminate so easily the costs of maintenance and personnel.

Expenditures also ought to be susceptible to small variations as well as large. Ideally they should be capable of meeting an unwanted increase for five million unemployed, or only a half million; and, conversely, capable of being damped down to meet a moderate inflation or a tight economy bursting at the seams.

2) Flexibility requires a capacity for *speed* in varying expenditures. Ideally, *advance planning* is needed to minimize these delays. So also is an administrative and political structure for stabilization expenditure capable of speed, as well as selection of a type of expenditure that may be varied if necessary with great rapidity. Each of these points will be discussed in later sections.

3) Stabilization expenditures should be accurate in hitting the target. The targets might be a number of widely spaced industrial areas as, in the summer of 1949, certain industries or certain special sectors of the economy. Public works expenditures produce aggregate effects on over-all spending and particular effects on specific markets. It should

be possible to hit specific targets where aimed for. But public expenditures designed for their aggregate effects ought not to disrupt specific markets, as public works expenditures have often done in the past. Ideally, if structural maladjustments are to be avoided, stabilization expenditures ought to require about the same bundle of resources as private plus "normal" government expenditures had previously required.

4) The requirements specified so far impose certain demands on the decision-making process. Following Gerhard Colm's analysis in an earlier chapter, we may very roughly lump the processes for making decisions about stabilization expenditures into three types:

a) *Built-in flexibility,* when the guides to decision-making are so specific and precise that little discretion remains to the decision-makers, and the resulting decision is virtually "automatic."

b) *Executive-administrative discretion,* when some members of the executive-administrative presumably operating under relatively broad criteria are empowered to arrive at decisions without further reference to the legislature.

c) *Executive-legislative decisions,* when policy must be made by traditional law-making processes.

All other things being equal, the first has great advantages over the other two, and the second is preferable to the third. Built-in flexibility not only provides a relatively speedy method of adjustment but a relatively certain one, so that the future becomes more predictable. It has already been suggested, however, that built-in flexibility is inadequate. It is worth pointing out that it also presupposes an exceptionally high degree of advance consensus on the measures to be taken, so that the process of decision-making is virtually depoliticized.

Insofar as built-in flexibility is not enough, administrative discretion is clearly superior to executive-legislative decision-making—*provided that flexibility is the sole criterion.* But flexibility is not the only criterion for evaluating the decision-making process, and indeed in our society it is in practice one of the least important criteria.

Far more influential is the view that the process ought to be democratic, which is to say that it ought to be determined as a result of an expression of citizens' preferences. The traditional way by which preferences are registered on political issues is through executive-legislative decision-making and through the political processes presupposed by this kind of decision-making. Administrative discretion can mean either that the executive-legislative process is by-passed, or that the process has taken place before the administrative decision and has resulted in legislative guides to the administrator.

Given the values underlying the discussions in this book, it is pretty clear that we must reject the first alternative as a method of decision-making for stabilization expenditures. Ideally, then, what we need is a high degree of built-in flexibility and, where this is impossible, administrative discretion based upon criteria previously laid down by the executive-legislative and expressing such a high degree of consensus in the society that the decision becomes largely "technical" rather than "political."

b. COORDINATION

Coordination in making some kinds of decision is clearly desirable. This is in many ways one of the most difficult criteria to meet because of the extraordinarily high degree of autonomy characteristic of the American governmental structure: nearly autonomous agencies inside and outside the federal departments, semiautonomous departments, autonomous Congressional committees and semiautonomous subcommittees (particularly on appropriations), semiautonomous regional agencies, states, and communities. It is also a criterion that poses highly delicate and yet portentous questions of values, for some kinds of autonomy in the decision-making process should be inhibited, and some should not.

It is not easy to pick one's way through this jungle. If we elevate stabilization expenditures to the level of highest value, the need for coordination becomes a demand for a kind of *gleich-schaltung* that would leave little chance for any kind of democracy except at the level of the nation-state if, indeed, even there. The problem is not merely to reconcile coordination with existing democracy but to make it an instrument for an even more effective expression of citizens' preferences than is now possible.

With this as a guide, we suggest the following criteria:

1) Autonomy in the administrative branch can be a step away from, not toward, citizen control. Insofar as it is necessary to limit administrative autonomy, there need be no loss and there can be a net gain for democratic values. We propose to discuss this point in a later section.

2) Autonomy by committees within the legislature is a severe handicap to the democratic process. We shall also return to this point.

3) The real problem, then, lies with what might be called geographical units of self-government. If we may return to our earlier considerations on local government, it may be that a solution is possible here that would command the adherence of almost everyone except a contemporary Rousseau on the one side or a totalitarian on the other. It seems evident that the appropriate level of stabilization expenditures is not likely to be determined by the accidental coordination of

semiautonomous units—whether these be governmental or business. It seems equally evident, however, that once the level has been established there not only can be but, as we argued in an earlier section, ought to be a high degree of autonomy in determining the purposes for which the expenditure is to be made.

Our conclusion is therefore one that we reached earlier by another route, that in any area where democratic controls are operating, the most inclusive governmental unit should make the decisions about the aggregate of expenditures, and the unit (or units) most susceptible of registering the diversified purposes of individuals and which is technically competent to act should make the decisions about the specific purposes of the expenditures.

What does this mean? As we have already indicated, it means, first, that the final decisions as to the aggregate amount that needs to be spent for stabilization purposes within this country will have to be made through the federal government. But it also means that a great many decisions as to the particular objects of stabilization expenditure ought to be made through smaller units of government—town, city, metropolitan area, state, and region. More than this, it means that a positive and systematic effort should be made through stabilization policy to encourage decision-making at the lower levels; techniques should be developed that not only facilitate but actually stimulate the opportunities for choice among objectives of stabilization expenditure by citizens acting through the smaller units of government. In dealing with grants-in-aid in a later section, we shall suggest one such technique. Finally, it means that the communities ought to make their own ultimate decisions, not only as to purposes, but also as to the amount of local expenditures and taxes they wish to incur locally. This requires the development of a more or less neutral formula that will allocate federal expenditures for stabilization purposes among communities in such a way as to respect variations in local preferences about the range and kinds of public services they want carried on, and the amounts they are willing to tax or expend for these purposes.

But as an examination of the history of the great depression will show, it is infinitely easier to state the general principles just enunciated than to find a workable administrative and political formula for carrying them out. The Federal Emergency Relief Administration, Civil Works Administration, Public Works Administration, and Works Projects Administration all, in their various ways, represented attempts to adapt these principles to the problem of work relief. FERA was a system of grants-in-aid to states and localities; short-lived CWA and the more durable WPA were both directly operated federal agencies. Yet both leaned heavily on local sponsors.[7] For example, through August, 1937, in terms of cost about 45% of WPA projects had been sponsored by municipal governments, about 29% by county units, about 17% by state agencies, and 9% by townships.[8] WPA insisted on reviewing projects before approving them, for a variety of reasons: to keep material costs low, to insure that the projects were for public rather than private purposes, and generally to insure that federal money was "properly" spent.

On the basis of the experience of these agencies, several observations about the application of the principles enunciated above appear to be valid.

1) In the face of gigantic unemployment of the scale reached in the great depression, local control over the purposes of expenditure will tend to be displaced by federal controls. Powerful inflationary pressures evidently have much the same effect. Decentralized control over stabilization expenditures is thus best maintained in an economy of moderate fluctuations.

2) Failure of local planning and staff greatly strengthens the growth of central controls. One reason why direct government operation of the WPA type replaced the grant-in-aid system of FERA was the inability of local units to plan diversified programs, indeed to plan at all.

3) The longer the duration of mass unemployment the more that centralized control over expenditures will grow; much the same seems to be true of inflation. National agencies such as WPA rapidly develop skilled, professional staffs who routinize procedures in the effort to do a sound, professional job; they tend also to distrust the competence of local politicians and the rationality of local politics, with its graft, apathy, and machines. Hence there is strong and apparently reasonable pressure for bureaucratizing the operation; increasing bureaucratizing means increasing supervision and displacement of local amateurs by federal experts. This seems roughly to have been the line of development from FERA through WPA.

C. CULTURAL FEASIBILITY

Our third major criterion for choosing among alternative expenditure policies for stabilization purposes is "cultural feasibility"—in other words, the pragmatic question whether the policy will "work" in the American cultural milieu.

7. Cf. Edward A. Williams, *Federal Aid for Relief* (New York, Columbia University Press, 1939) and Arthur W. MacMahon, John D. Millet, and Gladys Ogden, *The Administration of Federal Work Relief* (Chicago, Public Administration Service, 1941).

8. *Ibid.*, p. 304.

1) Unless it is to be wholly Utopian, a stabilization policy proposal must be politically acceptable. The important questions are when and to whom. Our proposals ought not to run so basically counter to fundamental preferences in American society that education, clarification, public discussion, and the political process are unlikely to result in their acceptance by a political majority any time within the next generation.

2) Stabilization expenditures ought to influence the expectations of businessmen so as to induce action on their part favorable to economic stability and progress. Positively, expenditure policy ought to lead to confident expectations among businessmen that a continuous high level of incomes and spending will persist well into the future. Negatively, expenditure policy ought not to create or seem to create such violent changes in the businessman's milieu that he is "frightened," hesitant about the future, reluctant to undertake risks, and unwilling to plan ahead.

3) Likewise, stabilization expenditures ought not to be of a kind or administered in such a way that serious tensions are generated within individuals or between social groups. Thus expenditures that violate accepted mores so as to demoralize the recipient ought not to be made. This is so, even if these expenditures are rational from the point of view of stabilization and even if the recipients are thought to be irrational in feeling demoralized. Nor should expenditures be made that do in fact lead to an increase in social tensions, even if (in the minds of policy makers or college professors) this result would not take place "if only people were more intelligent." A large-scale program of direct relief accompanied by a means test may be a case in point.

4) Stabilization expenditures ought not to presuppose a kind of expert personnel and organization that is not likely to be forthcoming at the time the policy will have to be carried out. As in the defense of western Europe, what might be possible in 195— was not necessarily possible in 1949. By the same token, however, it may be desirable to envision what could be done in 195—, *if* certain not wholly improbable developments of *expertise* and organization should take place.

One final point: many proposals taken singly might meet many of these criteria. Yet taken in the aggregate they might not. In general, then, any particular proposal ought to fit in with an over-all program.

Democratic rationality, flexibility, coordination, cultural acceptability—these norms have proved to be extraordinarily demanding. In the next section we shall attempt to measure the most important kinds of stabilization expenditures against these norms. But it is perhaps worth recalling the warning at the head of this section. It would be unreasonable to suppose that *any* policy is capable of measuring up to *all* of these norms, and in the last analysis the choice to be made will require such a complicated balancing of values that a large element of subjectivity is unavoidable.

III. KINDS OF PUBLIC EXPENDITURE MEASURED AGAINST THE CRITERIA

How well do various kinds of public expenditure meet the criteria proposed?

1. *Public works*

Public works are an old favorite of the advocates of government spending. In the public mind it is possible that variation in public expenditures simply means variation in public works. But as we have already seen government expenditures cover a larger field than works projects, and many of these other kinds of expenditure are as variable as public works spending. Out of $42 billion of government expenditures for goods and services in 1949, only $5 billion was estimated for public works.[9] It is perhaps wise to begin a discussion of works projects with a caution against overemphasis on them.

How well do public works expenditures meet the criteria against which we will measure other kinds of government spending?

a. FLEXIBILITY

The fact that public works expenditures fell off after 1929 and that in our present inflationary situation they are higher than two years ago might be taken to mean that public works expenditures possess a kind of automatic perverse flexibility capable of making depressions worse and booms bigger. In an economy which has not yet fully accepted the desirability of running a deficit in depression and a surplus in inflation, low personal incomes in depression rightly call for restriction of expenditures, both private and public; and high personal incomes in inflation encourage the expansion of both. The perverse flexibility of public works expenditures is therefore a reflection of the society's unwillingness to follow an intelligent (rather than the orthodox, so-called "sound") fiscal policy and is not a necessary characteristic of public works expenditures themselves.

There are, however, serious obstacles to a flexible program of public works. Here we must distinguish between technical limits to flexibility and politico-administrative ones. In the case of public works, both have frequently been stressed, but the political problems are probably more important than the technical limitations. First, automatic or built-in flexibility is not possible, as with taxation. Either administrative or legis-

9. *Midyear Economic Report of the President*, 1949, p. 87.

lative action is required in order to set in motion or to terminate a works project; and, because needs for projects vary as time passes, it is not likely that advance authorization will be given to works projects without fresh consideration of the desirability of the project when the need for expenditure actually arises.

Secondly, because so far Congress has been unwilling on the whole to delegate administrative authority to vary the amount of public works expenditures, in actual fact legislative action is ordinarily required for this purpose. Hence, variation is slow and unpredictable. To be sure, if decisions on the level of public works expenditures could somehow be made administratively, the case for the flexibility of public works would be greatly strengthened. But such a development appears at present as rather unlikely.

Thirdly, contraction of public works expenditures in time of inflation is difficult for several reasons. Maintenance costs continue in any case. In other cases, unfinished projects constitute intolerable waste, and the community will insist on their completion. Moreover, once the community's interest in a project is aroused, it is politically difficult to terminate the project. Finally, where public expenditures prior to an inflationary situation have been running at normal, and not a high rate to counter a depression, contraction of expenditures to below normal will impose upon the community sacrifices they are possibly unwilling to make, especially in view of their high incomes. From this last point it would seem to follow that variations in public works expenditures are much better designed to curb deep depression than to head off incipient recession or curb inflation.

Finally, variability in public works expenditures has not been too successfully used to stabilize the economy because lack of coordination of policy has permitted one governmental unit to counteract the policies of another, as in the 1930's. We shall make some suggestions later as to how this may be avoided in the future; it need only be said here that this obstacle to effective variability can be overcome.

A recent statistical analysis of the flexibility of public works programs by Sherman Maisel[10] throws doubt on the usability of many kinds of public works expenditures for stabilization. Over 18 months after the passage of the Federal Housing Act of 1937, less than one-third of the number of authorized units had been approved for development by the President. Not until five years had passed were all of them approved. On the average a year elapsed between presidential approval and award of contract, and even for defense housing eight months elapsed. On the

10. Sherman Maisel, "Timing and Flexibility of a Public Works Program," *Review of Economics and Statistics, 31* (May, 1949), 151.

average, another fifteen months went by before completion of projects.

This is a historical record, and it may be objected that the time can be shortened. But the United States Housing Authority hopes only to reduce the time required for presidential approval to three months and the time between approval and awarding of contract to four months. Even this does not promise a high degree of speed, especially since the expenditure effects of public action must await actual construction and subsequent disbursement.

Chart I (see next page) indicates the time taken to expend funds on public works projects of various kinds. Based on statistical studies of previous programs, it again suggests that public works expenditures, however useful for long recessions, are too sluggish to be useful where quick action is required to head off a decline in business activity.

On the basis of his investigation of the record of public works expenditures Maisel concludes that, while advance planning may do much to shorten the time lags in public works, the more important variables are: 1) the political unit undertaking the expenditure, 2) the type of project, and 3) the size of the project. That is to say, the procedures of government, the engineering of particular projects, and the mere amount of work to be done on a project result in delays more important than those caused by lack of planning.

Parenthetically, however, advance planning as well as reform in political procedures and careful selection of type of project may well be a most fruitful method of increasing flexibility. Even if planning is not the most important variable, it is one which public policy can manipulate. Hence it becomes an important instrument for improving policy.

b. HITTING THE TARGET

A special problem of flexibility in public works, especially in antidepression policy, is the effect on particular sectors of the economy. Public works should be directed into needed sectors with such precision as to provide aid in especially depressed areas of the economy and also to avoid unintended dislocation.

One immediate limit on the precision of works expenditures is the requirement that public works expenditures must not compete with private expenditures. Such a limit often rules out directing public expenditures into the purchase of materials made surplus by declining private purchases.

This problem is seriously underestimated. It is often assumed, for example, that public construction can be counted on to bolster up the markets for the same resources left unemployed by the decline of private construction. Actually the kinds of projects which can be under-

CHART I. PERCENTAGE OF FUNDS EXPENDED IN EACH SIX-MONTH
PERIOD BY VARIOUS PROGRAMS *

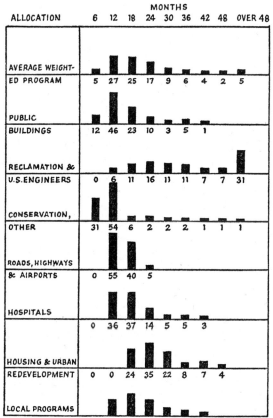

Delay between
deflation and
allocation:
Time for forecasting,
political support,
administration,
planning.

ALLOCATION	MONTHS 6	12	18	24	30	36	42	48	OVER 48
AVERAGE WEIGHT-ED PROGRAM	5	27	25	17	9	6	4	2	5
PUBLIC BUILDINGS	12	46	23	10	3	5	1		
RECLAMATION & U.S.ENGINEERS	0	6	11	16	11	11	7	7	31
CONSERVATION, OTHER	31	54	6	2	2	2	1	1	1
ROADS,HIGHWAYS & AIRPORTS	0	55	40	5					
HOSPITALS	0	36	37	14	5	5	3		
HOUSING & URBAN REDEVELOPMENT	0	0	24	35	22	8	7	4	
LOCAL PROGRAMS	0	23	32	23	10	8	4		

* Taken from Maisel, *ibid.*

taken by government call upon a significantly different mixture of resources than is used by private industry, and the dislocations of particular markets caused by public works may be very serious.

A study by Julius Margolis documents these difficulties. Chart II (see next page), taken from his study, shows the instability in consumption of certain selected materials which would have been caused by public construction over the years 1920 to 1940 sufficient to offset fluctuations in private construction.[11] This is a hypothetical chart, and it disregards the many indirect effects of deficit financing upon the markets for the commodities named. Nevertheless, it suggests forcefully the damage that may be done by public works projects.

Of course, when public expenditures are compared with tax variation as a method of running a deficit in depression, it seems clear that public expenditures can hit the target better than tax reductions. There are, however, probably more possibilities for hitting the target with taxation than are commonly supposed, such as tax refunds for business firms running at a loss and of course amortization privileges. But even so, it seems wholly out of the question to propose that tax reductions should be awarded to firms as selectively as public contracts might be offered them.

C. DEMOCRATIC RATIONALITY

One of the commonest arguments relied upon to prove the irrationality of public works is that we do not in the United States have a high priority shelf of projects to be undertaken—that a wise use of our resources precludes "wasting" them on public projects.

E. Jay Howenstine has compiled an inventory of public construction needs which attempts to encompass only those needs which must be met in various fields in order to meet standards now commonly accepted as reasonably adequate. Adding together needed projects in transportation, educational facilities, health facilities, recreational facilities, regional development, rural electrification, housing, and miscellaneous public buildings, he concludes that in terms of 1947 prices a public investment of $120 billion is required.[12]

Such estimates as these are highly subjective, as Howenstine would agree. Nevertheless, they show what a priori reasoning would suggest: that, because our wants are unlimited and our resources scarce, there

11. Julius Margolis, "Public Works and Economic Stability," *Journal of Political Economy,* 57 (August, 1949), 293–303. The chart is on p. 301.

12. E. Jay Howenstine, Jr., "An Inventory of Public Construction Needs," *American Economic Review,* 38 (June, 1948), 365.

CHART II. CONSUMPTION OF SELECTED CONSTRUCTION MATERIALS, BY TOTAL NEW CONSTRUCTION, UNDER A HYPOTHETICAL PUBLIC WORKS PROGRAM RESULTING IN A CONSTANT VOLUME OF TOTAL NEW CONSTRUCTION

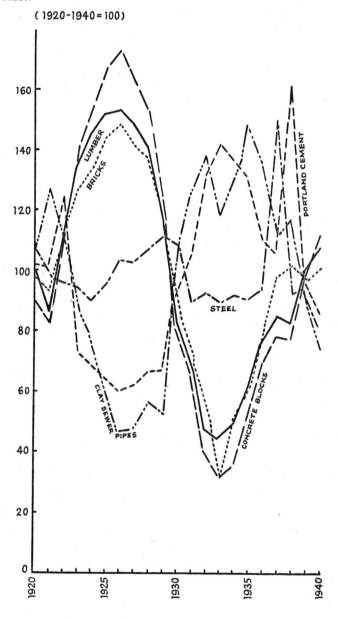

are always needs to be met in the fields of both private and public expenditures.

Yet it must be granted that there are serious obstacles to intelligent determination of the level and allocation of public works expenditures. We have already referred to the absence of the market method of casting up accounts for public expenditures. Hence governments cannot ask each citizen to indicate his preferences on public works by buying in a market at a price, a device that permits him to compare the costs he incurs with the values he receives. Furthermore, while citizens can indicate in general their preferences for public works projects through the machinery of political democracy, their choices are often less thoughtful than might be desired, because it is possible to vote for expenditures without at the same time voting to be taxed for an appropriation to support the expenditure. Many of the services of government seem to be "free" to consumers.

Moreover, great superstition surrounds discussion of expenditure on public works—public expenditure as a whole, for that matter. Strategic and economic problems are converted into moral problems by those whose prejudices for or against public works are strong. A dispassionate discussion of public works expenditures is therefore difficult for the citizen, and his decisions as a citizen do not achieve a high degree of rationality. It may be that the resulting bias has the effect of reducing the level of public works expenditure below what a more rational citizenry would tolerate, in which event the case for enlarging public works expenditures to avoid unemployment is strengthened. But we cannot know whether this or the converse is true.

There can be no doubt, however, that the lack of advance planning has resulted in expenditures which do not meet the criterion of democratic rationality. Speed of initiation and job creation potential were often more important in choice of projects in the 1930's than real need or usefulness of a project. Thus, in order to get anything done quickly, make-work projects tended to supplant public works that would have been more widely desired; and the cost of unpreparedness (in terms of poor use of resources) was many times greater than would have been the cost of planning and project selection in advance.

It has already been suggested in Chapter 1 that a rational determination of the level of public expenditures requires 1) a separation of the problems of distribution of income from those of production and 2) refinement in concepts of costs of public expenditure. On these two counts, public works expenditures have been irrational.

As to the first, public works have been proposed as a method of getting the federal government to produce goods and services (housing, as a possible example) in circumstances in which the real need is actually for redistribution of income rather than government production of goods and services. Some of these services and goods can be provided better through private markets than through public works if only income distribution is satisfactory.

In the case of housing, this argument cannot be carried very far. Additions to low income through redistribution of money income will be spent on a variety of goods and services, of which housing is only one. Consequently redistribution of money income does not guarantee a quantity and quality of housing adequate by the community's standards. Moreover, often it is politically easier to secure public policies for the production of a good rather than redistribution of income even where the latter is otherwise a more defensible policy. But with an ever-growing body of public works expenditures in our economy, it will become increasingly a source of waste and an unnecessary burden on government if income distribution problems are no better divorced from production problems than has so far been the case.

As for the second irrationality, that regarding the cost of public works projects, policy makers have vacillated between the erroneous view that the real social costs of projects in periods of unemployment are correctly represented by budgetary outlay and the equally erroneous view that all projects in time of unemployment are costless. The result has been that, on one hand, policy makers are reluctant to undertake the aggregate volume of public works that might be required in a given situation, while, on the other hand, they choose projects carelessly on the supposition that none of them is costly.

But all those irrationalities admitted, public works expenditures meet the criterion of democratic rationality better than is often supposed.

Public works expenditures may be administered so as to call upon the citizen to make choices as a member of a community in a way in which private market expenditures do not. This is no small value in a democracy, where citizens need to identify broadly with one another if they are to maintain the consensus that is a requisite of stable government. A choice so made also calls upon the citizen to consider a different range of values than he commonly considers in market choice; and, as a matter of fact, market choices are sometimes deliberately subordinated to or displaced in favor of group political choices for that very reason. Generalizing further, group political action makes possible some choices which cannot at all be made by consumer choice in a market, as in the case of many public health and sanitation services. In such cases, for all the difficulties of weighing alternatives rationally in political choice, it would seem clearly more irrational to refuse to make the public expenditure at all.

It is also true that the ideal of democratic rationality is sometimes seriously violated by market choices reflecting significant inequalities in income. This being so, political choices about public works may more closely approach the ideal of shared values and in particular the ideal of equality of power, both of which are critical values in a democracy.

Where public works expenditures are used as an antidepression technique in a situation commonly regarded as a serious crisis, the possibilities of community participation in the selection and instigation of projects, especially at the local level, and the resultant satisfying feeling that corrective action has been taken, may be therapeutically important to the community's stability and to the continuation of the consensus on which democracy rests. These intangibles are not the common values for which projects are ordinarily undertaken; but any thoughtful consideration of the importance of the values embraced in the term democratic rationality is assurance that the intangibles ought not to be neglected in appraising the rationality of public works.

We consider below some possibilities for increasing rationality in public expenditures, including public works. Market research such as is conducted by private firms to determine consumer preferences might improve the selection of projects. Decentralization of selection of projects to local and regional groups also offers a possibility of weighing more accurately in choice the wishes of those most immediately affected. If decentralization in selection were coupled with federal grants-in-aid to local and regional groups, the advantages of decentralization could be had without loss of coordinated federal control over aggregate amount and timing. The great potentialities of grants-in-aid are discussed below.

Having argued that public works expenditure often fails to meet the criterion of democratic rationality, we have nevertheless not argued that a works program cannot meet it adequately in the future. Failure to approach the criterion has been due largely to misconceptions that are gradually being destroyed by the slow but encouraging rise of economic literacy in the United States. To be sure, democratic rationality can only be approached; it can never be reached. But this is enough.

Our argument has also raised doubts as to the possibility of varying public works expenditures adequately except for deep and prolonged depressions where all else has failed and where everything must be attempted even if nothing seems promising. We have also shown that public works projects may create great instability in specific markets since they require different combinations of resources from those required by private investment activity.

It would be possible without any doubt to achieve a high degree of speed and variability in works projects expenditures if democratic rationality were not also a value. And it would be possible to direct expenditures into particular markets in such a way as to stabilize rather than unsettle them, if competitive private enterprise for the bulk of production were not equally desired. It would also be possible to direct works expenditures into those projects most desired by the community if it were not for the fact that this would unstabilize many specific markets.

Thus while it is possible to argue the virtues of public works projects with relation to many specific criteria, public works can meet some criteria only by seriously sacrificing others. Conflicts between the criteria so far discussed in the case of public works point to the conclusion that public works are a far less effective stabilizer than would be supposed from the attention given to them in recent years.

d. OTHER CRITERIA

There remain several intangible criteria against which public works should be measured. We have suggested that expenditures should not discourage desirable expectation on the part of businessmen as to institutional changes affecting them or as to the volume of spending. Public works have raised issues in businessmen's minds as to institutional changes and have not engendered any great confidence as to the aggregate volume of spending in the economy. Times change, and businessmen seem much less disturbed by public works projects than during the 1930's; but this objection to public works retains some of its force.

In part, fears as to spending and economic stability are fears of a public debt, whether created by high public expenditures or low taxes. Businessmen obviously do react differently to high expenditures and low taxes, even if these have the same effect on public debt. For example, they may fear that public works, like many other government expenditures, will restrict the role of private enterprise. We do not know enough to say whether this is a significant cause of uncertainty or not, despite the extent of speculation about it. But presumably locally initiated and rather familiar community projects, like a school or a park, are less disturbing than many vast federal projects such as the Tennessee Valley Authority.

We have also suggested that the consequences of any technique should be predictable. Obvious as this criterion is, it is also a counsel of perfection. Unfortunately, we cannot be at all confident that public works expenditures will do what they are planned to do rather than the opposite. Every dollar of public works expenditure may discourage two dollars worth of private investment. But if this seems to be an extraordinarily damaging admission, it is one which also needs to be made for every other technique of income stabilization. We can only deal in informed guesses as to probabilities. And so doing, it does not seem unreasonable to conclude that public works expenditures are as predictable in consequences as such techniques as tax reduction, transfer payments, and subsidies to private business.

In one respect they are more predictable, since public expenditures do immediately undertake the production of projects and therefore instigate the purchase of materials and labor. The alternatives just mentioned motivate spending, but they do not actually begin it.

To say that public works are predictable in consequence is not to say that desired consequences can be predicted. Again the inflexibility of public works and their impact on particular markets remain a problem.

Finally, we have suggested that any particular expenditures must be considered in the light of the whole program of government expenditure and activity. Expenditure and tax variation may be alternative methods of creating a deficit to forestall depression. But the former has the effect of doing so by enlarging the scope of government, the latter by maintaining the existing level of government activity and expenditure. This is certainly an important issue; for, at any given time, limits to the scope of democratic and efficient government are set up by the competence of government at that time. It is therefore reasonable to suggest that, given the many constant pressures upon government to take on new burdens of finance and welfare, some proposed burdens on government must be rejected. A program of variable public works may be one.

2. *Social security and veterans' aid*

Some social security expenditures can be varied with business conditions, but many cannot. Many social security expenditures can be varied, realistically speaking, in only one direction: they can be increased rather easily in times of deflation, but they cannot be decreased during periods of inflation. Expenditures of this kind include grants for maternal and child welfare, aid to the handicapped, health services, and the great variety of special measures for veterans.

Increased benefits lead to new expectations and advantageous changes in the living habits of many people. Subsequently it is difficult to threaten the security and expectations of such people by reducing welfare expenditures during inflationary periods. For the most part these groups command widespread public sympathy. What is more, as our experience with veterans and the aged shows, those who draw the benefits will probably mobilize as pressure groups; and if as pressure groups they cannot always obtain the new benefits they want, the combination of their pressures and widespread attitudes of sympathy for their position makes it highly unlikely that they can ever be deprived of what they have once gained.

So much said, it by no means follows that irreversible social security devices ought not to be used to combat deflation. If one of the aims of the dominant majority in the society is gradually increasing social security benefits and coverage (as appears to be the case in the United States), a great deal is to be said for timing the periodic extensions of social security with deflation rather than inflation. Indeed, a rational society with confidence in its long-run capacity for economic progress might well build up a shelf of social security measures to be inaugurated during periods of deflation only.

Reversibility aside, the serious disadvantage of such a proposal conceivably lies with its effects on the expectations of businessmen. This is a question on which forecasting is difficult. To the extent that an extension of social security is merely the addition of new wings to a familiar old building, businessmen may find it less threatening than some other kinds of stabilization expenditures. To the extent that it causes them to look forward gloomily to a period of ever-rising taxes and shifts in income, it may have a dampening effect.

Some very important social security expenditures, on the other hand, are not only reversible but even possess a certain amount of built-in flexibility. For example, expenditures for federal *old-age annuities* and state-financed *pensions* will be drawn on more heavily during deflation than during inflation. Thus, under the Federal Old-Age and Survivors' Insurance program, many people over 65 who had been working will, as jobs decline, withdraw from the labor market and begin receiving their annuities.[13] As the job market improves many will postpone retiring and some will even leave retirement to take jobs, thereby decreasing government expenditures under this program. However, some of the built-in flexibility may be negated by political decisions to raise the level of payments during periods of rising prices, when a demand for higher benefits will seem to be justified on grounds of individual

13. The rapid increase in total OASI benefit payments over the past twelve years as more persons have become eligible under the program somewhat conceals the degree of flexibility. Variations in the rate of increase in total payments is, however, quite noticeable. See, for example, *Survey of Current Business,* July, 1947, p. 46.

need.[14] As the proportion of our population in the over-65 group increases, this political maneuver may be increasingly feasible. The importance of old-age annuities in income stabilization is indicated by the fact that by 1964 expenditures for this purpose will reach approximately $5 billion annually.[15]

General assistance—which catches the needy who are not adequately cared for under other forms of assistance—shows a marked cyclical pattern over the past fifteen years. By 1945 total annual payments had dropped to about one-fifth the 1936–40 average, even though the average monthly payment to each recipient was up 25%. In the decade 1935–45, the greatest annual expenditures (January, 1935–December, 1935) were 17 times the lowest annual expenditures (in January–December, 1945).[16]

Because general assistance, except for scattered federal emergency grants, is a state-local responsibility, its potentialities for stabilization purposes have scarcely been exploited. Questions of differing local attitudes to one side, widespread differences in the tax resources of the various states create differences in expenditures on general assistance that are wholly irrational from the point of view of stabilization. In 1947, for example, there were almost 20 times as many recipients for each 1,000 inhabitants in Michigan as there were in Mississippi, although it is wholly improbable that there was any corresponding diversity of needs. In Tennessee the average payment was $9.61 a month; in New York, $65.45. In 30 states, state aid is less than half the local contribution, and in 15 of those states the responsibility is entirely on the shoulders of the municipal government.[17]

Here is a case where a system of federal assistance based upon certain minimum standards of local effort (such as a fixed percentage of income payments) would result not only in much more built-in flexibility but in a much greater capacity for increasing aggregate expenditures when unemployment mounts and local governments find it difficult to carry the burden.

Yet the great limitation of general assistance as a significant factor in stabilization expenditures must not be lost sight of. It is, to put it in the blunt and cruel evaluation of our society, "charity to the poor,"

14. See point 8 of the President's "Summary of Legislative Recommendations," *Midyear Economic Report of the President,* 1949, p. 14.

15. Earl Edward Muntz, *Growth and Trends in Social Security* (New York National Industrial Conference Board, 1949), p. 152.

16. *New York World-Telegram, World Almanac, 1949,* p. 314.

17. J. A. Maxwell, *Federal Grants-in-Aid and the Business Cycle* (New York National Bureau of Economic Research, Fiscal Policy Series No. 4, 1952).

and any large-scale use of it will probably seriously demoralize too many recipients (and even taxpayers) to make it worth while. It ought to remain only as a kind of catchall for the leftovers from programs that do less violence to our mores.

Unemployment compensation has perhaps the highest degree of built-in flexibility of any existing social security device, automatically expanding when employment declines and contracting on the upturn. To a limited extent, unemployment compensation also tends to hit the target, insofar as the target is the individual whose expenditures decline because he is out of a job.

Accuracy in hitting the target is, however, circumscribed in some respects. For one thing, the coverage of unemployment compensation is limited; agricultural workers, for example, are mostly excluded. For another, the target may not always be the unemployed worker—or, at any rate, not *only* the unemployed worker. Finally, because the states establish the standards, there are great differences in the average payments (from $11.10 a week in the lowest state to $22.80 in the highest) and in the maximum duration of the compensation (from 12 to 26 weeks).[18] However, it is important to bear in mind that those states which are most highly industrialized, and therefore likely to suffer the first effects of deflation, are those with the highest payments and the longest periods of compensation.

In general, it is probably correct to say that no other built-in expenditure device is as effective as unemployment compensation. Its effectiveness might be further increased by raising minimum standards. The President has suggested state minima of 26 weeks' duration and $30 weekly payments for single recipients, upgraded for dependents—this to be accomplished without federal assistance. If it should prove impossible for the states to meet a minimum of this kind, federal grants may be desirable under stipulations that will prevent a mere substitution of federal for state expenditures with no elevation in standards.

Unemployment compensation successfully meets some of the other criteria. To some extent it provides businessmen with assurance that levels of consumer expenditures will not drop violently with the growth of unemployment. The odium attached to general assistance is not today attached to unemployment compensation by most workers. For this and other reasons, it also serves to prevent a flare-up in social tensions with the growth of unemployment.

Finally unemployment compensation, like almost all the expenditures in the category of social security, directly transfers income to individuals who may then dispose of it on the market according to their own

18. See Maxwell, *ibid.*

preferences. This means not only the maintenance of consumer-guided allocation but a substantial persistence of normal patterns of expenditure and thus little of the maladjustment that may come about from government expenditures on, for example, public construction.

The central disadvantage of unemployment compensation, and indeed of traditional social security measures as a whole, is the difficulty of achieving a big enough outlay in the face of a significant decline in employment. We shall consider below a "national dividend" to remedy this deficit.

3. Miscellaneous government services

As with some forms of social security, outlays for many government services [19] can be expanded but not easily contracted; and if they can be contracted, they ought not to be. Police, fire, water, inspection, sanitation control, health services, prisons, correctional institutions, justice, traffic supervision, administrative regulation and adjudication, assessment, tax collecting, accounting and auditing, customs inspection, postal collections and deliveries—the need for these fluctuates very little with business conditions, although most reveal a secular tendency to expand. By and large, it is not too great an oversimplification to say that the outlays for these services ought to vary with changing social standards and the secular changes in the national product—but not from year to year depending on the current state of the economy.

But if these outlays ought not to be positively employed for stabilizing purposes, by the same token they ought not to be permitted to have the effect of accentuating instability—as was the case in the thirties, when state and local governments cut back their expenditures by 13% between 1929 and 1933 in a losing struggle for solvency.[20]

Yet to say so much is to imply the need for federal grants-in-aid for continuing these services during deflationary periods—and thus to enmesh us in the delicate problem of local self-government. Grants-in-aid are often said to mean "inevitably" the setting of national standards for local performance. However much national standards may contribute to a sense of tidy efficiency, if these standards are pushed into all the traditional areas of local and state self-government, they will seriously impair the capacity of local citizens to make the choices they prefer and bear at least some of the consequences.

Some people no doubt value a stable economy more than local self-government; yet others prefer the values of local self-government to the

19. We exclude at this point the whole question of variations in the public work necessary or collateral to the performance of these services.

20. Hansen and Perloff, *op. cit.*, p. 53.

deprivations imposed by federal supervision. Nor is it necessarily an adequate rejoinder to the latter group to say that, given a significant deflation, the bankruptcy of local governments will inevitably send them scurrying to Washington for assistance on almost any terms. The real question is whether this conflict of values can be avoided. In a later section we suggest that one way out of this dilemma is a system of unconditional grants for local government varied in amount according to business conditions.

One government service, however, that probably ought to be varied with significant changes in employment is education. Many young people who in prosperous times would go into the job market will in deflationary periods find education more attractive than idleness. Many if not most of these will have no unemployment compensation to draw on. And what is more, in returning to or continuing on in school they will find a familiar pattern of life that will help to reduce the anxieties and tensions generated by the frustrations of unemployment.

In a later section, we shall raise the question of educational subsidies to students as a stabilization device, but it is enough simply to note here the enormous social dangers created by youth with nothing but the bleakness and insecurities of unemployment to contemplate. Education, moreover, is probably a much more elastic kind of service than we have been inclined to think, despite the rigidity of the academic calendar. Within the huge output of normal schools and colleges there is a considerable reservoir of ex-teachers and individuals trained as teachers who, having taken up nonteaching occupations, also face prospects of joblessness during deflation.

It may well be that, as in Germany, many of these are potential cadres for political movements that capitalize on frustration and discontent; and even Machiavellian considerations would argue that it is wise to undercut such a development by providing them with meaningful and reasonably satisfying occupations.

Included in education is the training and retraining of workers, a service that can be greatly stepped up during periods of unemployment and curtailed with rising employment. Indeed, there is a whole variety of educational and cultural services that within limits can be expanded or contracted according to business conditions: adult education, government theaters, aid to artists, research, to name only a few of the more obvious ones.

To use educational expenditures for stabilization purposes pretty clearly implies federal grants-in-aid to states or localities. So far, public discussion of this problem has scarcely taken into account the possibility of varying contributions with business conditions.

4. Subsidies [21]

a. NATIONAL DIVIDEND

The proposal is frequently made that taxes should be remitted during deflationary periods, so as to help maintain the level of spending. Much less commonly discussed is the logical corollary of tax remission, namely, some form of direct transfer of income to individuals during deflationary periods, to be withdrawn as employment and production swing upward. Actually a number of government expenditures like unemployment compensation and aid to the indigent are of such a kind. But occasionally it has been proposed that something like a national "melon" should be cut when business activity declines, and everyone simply mailed a check each week by some governmental unit, presumably federal.

One such proposal is that of John H. G. Pierson; another is Kenneth Boulding's proposal for income taxation adjustable to permit negative taxation.[22]

The bizarre elements in these ideas have tended to prevent much serious discussion of their merits. From the point of view of our criteria, nevertheless, they have some significant advantages:

1) The expenditure is capable of considerable variation in size.

2) With relatively slight advance planning, the problem of speed practically disappears.

3) Provided Congressional consent can be obtained to legislation laying down the details, the policy can have a built-in flexibility easily comparable with that of unemployment compensation.

4) There is no particular problem of coordination.

5) Expenditures of this kind will insure maintenance of a consumer-guided economy.

6) The problem of choosing the specific purposes of expenditure at some governmental level is thereby avoided.

7) Except for setting the scheme up, no great problem of expertness is involved.

The proposal also has two serious disadvantages:

1) It is an open question whether the proposal would be politically acceptable. Although the idea of a dividend is widely enough accepted in American society, the paradox of receiving a national dividend only

21. Subsidies to business enterprise are dealt with in Chapter 9.

22. John H. G. Pierson, *Full Employment and Free Enterprise* (Washington, D.C., Public Affairs Press, 1947), pp. 35–73. Kenneth Boulding, *The Economics of Peace* (New York, Prentice-Hall, 1945).

during depression and never during prosperity presupposes a grasp of modern economic theory that, if one takes recent Congressional debate as a criterion, is certainly not evident now.

However, if the system were established as a family allowance for the purpose of income stabilization, payments would be made in prosperity and depression alike, although the rate level would be varied according to business conditions and presumably coordinated with variations in income tax rates. Such a system might become politically acceptable.

2) The national dividend will lack flexibility insofar as it cannot be easily adjusted to meet the special needs of depressed areas or sectors of the economy. It will help to control only aggregate expenditures in both deflation and inflation.

At a number of points, the results are not wholly predictable.

1) It may be argued that the plan would leave the structure of the economy and of government almost wholly intact. It will be replied, however, that the dividend will surely become a political football. What is to prevent the party in power (it will be asked) from handing out a national dividend just before election and thereby "bribing" the electorate? In weighing the force of this objection from the standpoint of democratic rationality we must distinguish carefully between the elements of democracy and rationality.

It would take a curious theory of democracy to demonstrate that giving the voters what they want is somehow undemocratic. The correct assumption would seem to be that a government which declares a national dividend before an election has every right to have its action weighed by the electorate. If this is the kind of action a majority of the electorate wants, it is difficult to see why the party should not be restored to power. Indeed, realistically speaking, the whole dynamics of the democratic system of control rests upon the existence of two or more great groups of organized politicians, each bidding for votes by making offers to the electorate; and it is difficult to see that there is anything more to be condemned if the offer is a national dividend than if it is a promise to raise tariffs or cut taxes. The fact is the national dividend will be neither more nor less political than the income tax.

It may be argued further, however, that the question is not so much one of democracy as of rationality. Will not the party in power use the national dividend even during periods of inflation? It is always possible that the electorate will prefer the bribe and its inflationary effects to alternatives that might seem more rational to the social scientist or businessman. Or voters may endorse a policy that seems to accord with their preferences in the short run even if they might have chosen a different policy could they have foreseen some of the long-run effects. In sum: the electorate may be irrational, and the national dividends may be a device peculiarly conducive to electorate irrationality. Yet this last argument, if it proves anything, proves too much. For what is true of the national dividend is equally true of any other expenditures for stabilization purposes. To argue that the electorate is too incompetent to vote on such issues is simply to argue that democracy is incompatible with a stable economy. This may be so. But it is by no means self-evident; and, as we argue in a later section, there are some grounds for supposing that "inflation by demagoguery" does not pay off.

But perhaps the danger is not so much mass bribery as manipulation of individuals by playing favors with the dividend. Certainly this possibility provides strong grounds for urging that the criterion for allocating the dividend among individuals should be as simple, automatic, neutral, and acceptable as possible. Thus a flat per capita payment may be the only kind that can prevent serious manipulation.

2) What would be the effect of a national dividend on workers' incentive? Are there limits to variability in aggregate size of the expenditure, imposed by the need to keep the individual checks low? Would the expectation of a national dividend induce a significant number of workers to avoid employment knowing and depending on national dividend checks to meet their living standards? Such an outcome could be avoided by making anyone ineligible for the check who had not registered with the employment service or had turned down a job calling for skills comparable to his own. This requirement, however, would considerably complicate the administrative simplicity of the plan. The primary safeguard against loss of incentives will continue to be the desire to improve one's economic position. The fact is that with free public education, the county hospital system, and relief, no one needs to work to live. But almost everyone does work.

3) What effect would the idea of a national dividend have on the expectations of businessmen? Is it so bizarre an idea that it would shake their faith in the future? Or, on the contrary, is its high degree of automaticity likely to provide them with a confidence that high levels of spending will be maintained?

4) What kinds of tensions, if any, would it generate in recipients? Would the "something-for-nothing" appearance of the dividend conflict with Protestant attitudes of "nothing without hard work"?

To raise these questions is by no means to dismiss the idea; conceivably it may meet our criteria more fully than many alternatives. In at least two forms the proposal might well eliminate most, although not all, of the objections and doubts we have raised. First, as already suggested, grants to heads of families based on the size of the family would go a long way toward meeting many objections. There still remains the difficulty, as with the income tax itself, of varying the rate level. Second, modifying the proposal to make it a tax-refund scheme probably would be more acceptable, might raise fewer fears about incentives, and would raise no problem of reversability. But since payments could then be made only to those who had previously paid income taxes, the aggregate amount would be less flexible. And the income groups most needing the grants might not receive them.

b. EDUCATION SUBSIDIES

We have already spoken of the desirability of expanding educational services during periods of serious deflation. One form of subsidy that meets many of our criteria is aid to students during deflationary periods. It is probably desirable on grounds of cultural acceptability to couple this aid with a work requirement, as was done under the National Youth Administration.

c. SUBSIDIES TO GOVERNMENT-OWNED ENTERPRISES

The question of government subsidies to government-owned enterprises has not heretofore been one of much significance in this country. In an economy where the government owned a sizable chunk of key industries, it is arguable that it might be desirable during deflationary periods to subsidize these key industries and thus indirectly to subsidize private industries and individuals consuming the products of the government-owned industries. This, it might be argued, would encourage the private producers to maintain their levels of production, consumers their level of consumption.

In this country, it is conceivable that the issue may someday arise in the case of the government-owned power industry. It is worth recalling that, if all the construction now authorized by Congress is carried through, by 1960 government dams and stand-by plants will have a capacity of over 20 million kws.—equivalent to about two-fifths of the total generating capacity existing in the United States.[23] Even now there are some more or less concealed subsidies involved in the role of government-generated electric power, although such subsidies have been aimed at the long-run development of certain "underdeveloped areas" rather than at stabilization.[24] But with a considerable power industry

23. The Commission on Organization of the Executive Branch of the Government, *Federal Business Enterprises, a Report to the Congress*, March, 1949, p. 53.
24. Thus according to a ruling of the solicitor of the Department of the Interior, revenues from the sale of water for irrigation and power on reclamation dams do

under its direct control in 1960, should the government take whatever losses are necessary during deflationary periods in order to provide cheap power, lower the costs of private industry, and thereby encourage continued high-level production and consumption? There are certain limitations to the proposal and certain possibilities.

First, if direct subsidies to government industry are desirable, why not to important sectors of private industry as suggested by Mr. Brown in Chapter 9? It is possible to argue that the administrative and political difficulties in subsidizing private industry are very much greater than in the case of government industry. But on grounds of resource allocation, government-produced products are no more worthy of subsidy than private.

More serious, however, is the fact that there are distinct limits to what can be accomplished for the expansion of business by lowering only one or two of its costs, such as electric power. Even if power were given away, it would probably not enable some industries in some circumstances to maintain output at previous levels. In this case, the logic of the proposal is not merely to give away, say, electric power, but to pay the consumer to use it. But this might better be achieved, if it were desirable at all, by a direct subsidy to the enterprise buying the power. Because the question of business subsidies is dealt with elsewhere, we do not pursue the point here.

All questions of direct subsidy to private industry to one side, what may be said of the proposal to subsidize government-owned enterprises? In the short run, certainly, it would violate the principle of consumer-guided allocation. But if the subsidy were in fact terminated with rising employment, many consumers might quite rationally prefer a temporary violation of this value to the manifold violation of other values imposed by deflation. The real question is, perhaps, whether the practice would be truly reversible. If not it would lead to a permanent drain of resources into the production of goods and services that could not pay their own way if consumers were free to express their preferences exclusively on the market. The early history of the tariff does not, perhaps, provide an encouraging precedent; but it must not be forgotten that a considerable degree of administrative discretion in rate-making is not quite comparable to the old system of directly establishing tariffs by legislation.

---

not have to cover interest on that portion of construction costs allocated to power. Public power advocates argued that to cover interest costs would require power rates too high for widespread utilization of power generated by the projects. Cf. Paul Appleby, *Policy and Administration* (University, University of Alabama Press, 1949), p. 127.

In any case, so long as government-owned industries remain of the size and importance presently contemplated, it seems unlikely that the proposal could have a very significant effect on the economy as a whole.

IV. Some Needed Reforms

It is not possible to say of each kind of expenditure considered that it will or will not serve as an effective instrument of stabilization. All show some prospects of success; all prove to be far from ideal instruments. We can, however, suggest the kinds of reforms which would immensely improve the possibilities of income stabilization through variation in public expenditures.

1. *Party responsibility*

Stabilization expenditures will never be more than a rather clumsy and inflexible tool for maintaining economic stability until responsible political parties, by concentrating more power in themselves, have deprived the pressure groups of some of their enormous and irresponsible power over public policy. Most American political scientists are convinced, after careful comparative analysis of British and American party systems, that there is an inverse correlation between the strength of parties and the strength of pressure groups.

The whole problem of reversability is mainly—although not wholly—a problem of pressure groups making public policy at the expense of the majority. It is one thing if the electorate is offered a reasonably clear choice of alternatives, and a majority deliberately chooses a party program of inflation that is then converted into public policy. But it is quite another when a majority of the electorate thinks it is choosing a stabilization program at the polls and ends up by choosing an inflationary program in the anteroom.

Two questions immediately suggest themselves. First, is there any reason to suppose that the electorate as a whole, acting at the polls, will behave more rationally about economic stability than the electorate in segments, acting in pressure groups? Second, is there, in any event, much likelihood of reforming the American party system?

It would carry us too far afield to answer these questions with the fullness they need. Victor Jones discusses them at greater length in Chapter 13. This much may be said here, however: Experience suggests that it is highly unprofitable for a political party to permit serious economic instability while it is in power. It is not too much to say that three years of serious deflation almost destroyed the Republican party and completely reversed a 46-year period of domination that had been seriously threatened for no more than four years. After 14 years of wandering in the political desert the Republican party returned to dominate the 80th Congress—and rightly or wrongly was evidently blamed for much of the hardships of postwar inflation. It was sent back to the desert. What all this suggests is the hypothesis that parties can win politically by stabilizing at high levels of employment and production, and lose if they are too responsive to pressure groups.

But if this is so, it may be asked, why do they give way to pressure groups? The answer may be that increasingly they will *not* do so. The plain fact is that, as E. E. Schattschneider has insisted, in an era where public policy strikes home to vast numbers of citizens, more and more it will be politically suicidal for a party to jeopardize its standing with the national electorate in order to pick up a few votes from a pressure group.

2. Executive discretion

Without responsible parties, then, it is futile to hope for the special kind of flexibility in public expenditure that is necessary for economic stability. But more than that, flexibility and precision demand that a considerable amount of discretion be exercised in the executive-administrative branch under guides laid down by Congress. Will—and ought—Congress to grant such discretion?

The answer seems to be that Congress will, and ought, to grant such discretion only to an executive-administrative in whom it has a certain rational confidence. For such confidence to exist there must be a powerful party cabinet comprising the President and his party leaders in Congress. Yet to the extent that Congress and the President represent different and conflicting electorates, each is certain to distrust the other, each is certain to have a violently differing interpretation of its mandate; and the party cabinet must, in the end, fall apart.

This difficulty, too, could be overcome only with a party system under which the President and Congressional majority receive a common and specific mandate at the polls, to which all party members adhere rather closely. Such a development may be a long way off; there is no agreement even that it is possible in the United States. Yet intelligent stabilization expenditure policy presupposes some such far-reaching reform of American parties; and it is probably not too wide of the mark to say that the reform of American political parties in turn presupposes some public issue as basic to party survival as stabilization expenditures conceivably may be.

3. *Congressional reform*

Coordination of expenditure policy must, in the last analysis, come from the party cabinet. For if coordination is impossible within the ranks of the top political leadership, it is not possible anywhere. To rely on administrative coordination under such circumstances is merely to put one's faith in the orderly deployment shown on the map, when the troops are already fleeing in disorder before the enemy. But this is not to say that coordination at administrative levels and within Congress is unnecessary, *if* the party cabinet is capable of making the final policy decisions as it presently operates. Congress is too decentralized for intelligent coordination of expenditure policy. What is probably required is a joint Congressional committee to act as a kind of Congressional general staff to insure that the left hand knows what the right hand is doing. The Joint Committee on the Economic Report might conceivably be developed into such a committee. Centralization has distinct limits, however; and, whatever the formal lines of committee organization may be, any detailed examination of authorizations and appropriations will require devolution to other committees and subcommittees. The most that can be hoped from a high level joint committee is that it will come to operate with the top party leadership in the making of basic expenditure policy and exercise ultimate committee supervision over aggregates and purposes.

It is scarcely necessary to underline the fact that this is a far cry from the present system of semiautonomous feudatories that owe fealty only to their small constituencies.

4. *New budgets*

If Congress and the President—or, if you will, the party leadership—are to act with some degree of rationality, several new kinds of budgets are required. Under the present budgetary system Congress and the President can make choices among *agencies* for expenditure; in many cases, however, they cannot, or can only with great difficulty, make choices among the *purposes* to which the total expenditures of government are put. Although Congress and the President do need an agency budget roughly of the present kind, they also need a budget that clearly reveals the purposes of government expenditures. For income stabilization it may also be desirable to have a budget organized according to degrees of variability of expenditures. Still another budget may be necessary in which investment, transfer, and consumer goods and services expenditures are distinguished. And the present budget has its uses too. It does make for rational choice to know whether the

Department of Agriculture, which has one set of attitudes and skills, is to make a given expenditure or, say, the Department of Labor, which has a quite different set. The point is that policy makers need many kinds of budgets. No nation is compelled to present expenditures in only one presumably God-given form. Some of the alternative ways in which budgets can be presented are considered in more detail by Gerhard Colm in Chapter 5.

On the whole, it is probably desirable to have budgets that separate stabilization expenditures from other expenditures. The stabilization budget will have to be marked by great flexibility, variation from year to year, and frequent deficits. These are not characteristics that necessarily lead to careful appraisal of alternative costs in the political setting of the American Congress. A legislative body that is as responsive to the demands of pressure groups as Congress needs a set of rather rigid attitudes favorable to budget-balancing. For it is only when Congress and the President vigorously attempt to balance the budget that they are forced to a serious consideration of the relative benefits and costs of alternative expenditures. Therefore it may be necessary to keep a sharp distinction between normal budget and stabilization budget, in the hope that attitudes will develop more appropriate to each than if the two kinds of expenditure were confused.

5. *Expert assistance in coordinating*

At the administrative level, there is unquestionable need for an expert agency to work out a coordinated picture of present and proposed expenditures and the aims and probable consequences of such expenditures. The natural locus for such work is, of course, the Budget Bureau. What is needed, however, is a much broader kind of analysis than the customary budget justifications, and it is at least arguable that the watchdog functions of the bureau develop a kind of mind-set that does not necessarily meet the requirements for this kind of task. Thomas Emerson states the case for a new agency in Chapter 15. However, the need for coordination is so great that, if it is possible to do so, there is more to be said for changing the mind-set at the Budget Bureau than to set another White House agency to compete with it.

Although it may seem fanciful in the light of current practice, one function of such an agency might well be to help formulate and clarify alternatives. Rationality presupposes some understanding of the alternatives available to us. For every proposed governmental expenditure, therefore, the agency ought to formulate a set of alternative purposes to which the same expenditure might be put. Theoretically the range of such alternatives is unlimited; but the *relevant* range probably is not.

It would very likely enhance political rationality if, in making an appropriation for a multipurpose dam, politicians and public knew what they were foregoing in, say, hospitals or bombers. It is difficult to see why this practice would displease anyone except those who feel sure they would dislike what politicians and public would do, once the latter *knew* what they were doing.

6. *Local government planning*

But the politico-administrative problems at the national level are insignificant in comparison with those at the state and local levels. Democratic rationality, we have argued, requires a high degree of advance planning and a great amount of local participation in choosing the purposes of stabilization expenditures at the local level. There can be no blinking the fact that at the moment local units of government are as incapable of both, as they were at the onset of the great depression. Although over the long period there appears to be growing interest in local planning, on the whole the state or local planning commission is a neglected Cinderella except when some serious crisis in local development turns rags into silk. But when the ball is over, this Cinderella returns home—and stays home. It is no exaggeration to say that the long-run results could be the demise of local government as an effective force in American society.

There are, at the moment, no federal provisions for advance planning,[25] despite the fact that we had made some significant beginnings in this direction. In 1941, the Public Works Reserve was established jointly by the Federal Works Agency and the National Resources Planning Board. Within one year it had organized a regional staff, established grounds for federal-state-local cooperation, built a shelf of about $10 billion in projects—and, when Congress cut NRPB to the bone, ceased to exist for want of funds. In 1944 the Federal Works Agency was authorized [26] to loan interest-free funds to states and localities for advance planning. These funds, which were to be repaid when construction was begun, financed plans for over seven thousand projects with an aggregate cost of $2.1 billion.[27] But the program expired in 1947, and so far no other has been authorized to take its place.

When it is remembered that plan costs average between 3% and

25. Public Law 105, Public Buildings Act of 1949, authorizes the Federal Works Administrator to use funds for "preparation of plans, sketches, working drawings and specifications," but only on limited projects included within a $40 million program.

26. Title V, War Mobilization and Reconversion Act of 1944.

27. Testimony by Jess Larson, administrator of the General Services Administration, before House Public Works Committee, July 19, 1949.

4% of total estimated costs, it seems abundantly clear that the failure to provide grants for advance planning through collaboration of all levels of government is not only to economize at present in order to waste resources in the future. It is also to dig the grave of local democracy as an effective instrument for citizen control over economic policy.

It may be argued, however, that *rigor mortis* has already set in at the local level, and there is not much likelihood of breathing life into the moribund remains of local democracy. Even the friend of small unit government will have to admit that disease has reduced American local politics to incompetence. Anyone who followed the Kefauver Committee hearings or took the time to read the preceding reports of several dozen journalists on the politics of American cities will agree with Robert Allen that things have changed very little since the muckraking days of Lincoln Steffens.[28] It is not unfair to say of American government today that graft, corruption, incompetence, and citizen apathy are inversely proportional to the size of the governmental unit. This is probably so because the size of the governmental unit is directly proportional to its present-day capacity for achieving the goals of the citizen. Thus we have got ourselves onto a treadmill, where many citizens will prefer a reasonably competent federal agency in Washington to make decisions about local expenditures because they do not trust their local ward heelers to do so. There was, for example, astonishingly little opposition to the replacement of the grant-in-aid principle under FERA by direct federal operation of work relief projects under WPA after 1935. Partisans of local self-rule had the ground cut out from under them by local apathy and incompetence in the face of a new problem. And then, because the federal agencies do come to make the important decisions, citizens are content to allow the ward heelers to run their cities.

Government expenditures for stabilization purposes, it is surely no exaggeration to say, will bind us to this treadmill for a long time to come—or break it. Whether they do one or the other will depend largely on whether or not policy makers are prepared to take the very real risks involved in securing the collaboration of local government units in the whole task of planning and operating a stabilized economy.

7. Grants-in-aid

But will grants-in-aid, on which we have proposed to place such a heavy reliance, only consummate the destruction that citizen apathy has begun? This question is not easy to answer with confidence.

It is a persuasive argument that the grant-in-aid is merely the first

28. R. S. Allen, ed., *Our Fair City* (New York, Vanguard Press, 1947).

step to extensive federal control over local functions. But if this is true it can be so only because citizens choose it to be so. If the grant-in-aid leads to federal control rather than local autonomy, it must be that citizens prefer federal control to local autonomy. If there were a profound and viable sociological basis for local self-government, it seems highly improbable that in a generally operative democratic society citizens would tolerate an "invasion" of the local domain. So once again we are on a treadmill, and once again grants-in-aid may chain us to the treadmill or destroy it. But the choice, surely, is not one that is "forced" on us; and in the view of the authors of this chapter it is worth the gamble to attempt to revivify the social base for local government by providing it, through grants-in-aid, funds without which it cannot function in a meaningful way for local citizens.

That the grant-in-aid will become the core of a new federalism is highly likely. It is important, therefore, to take careful note of the alternatives. Roughly, the more that grants-in-aid are transmitted directly to the states, the more probable it is that states will expand their functions and powers as compared with the localities. And the more that grants are transmitted directly to local communities, the more probable they are to expand their functions and powers as compared with the states. If this is a correct approximation of the alternatives, it seems preferable to strengthen the local community, which is potentially a much more manageable instrument of government, than any larger aggregate.

Yet in many cases neither existing local governments nor states are rational units for government expenditures. In some areas metropolitan authorities are needed; in others, regional authorities. It would take us too far afield to examine the problems of organizing such units according to the values of democratic rationality, and the most that can be set down here is the conviction that such a search would produce results that have not been attained so far.[29]

Specifically, we propose that the federal government underwrite an important share of the normal costs of both state and local governments during periods of deflation. This is, we think, the only way by which expenditures at that level can be stabilized—without a direct assumption of local government functions by the federal government. The important problem is to find a grant-in-aid technique for this purpose that will meet the tests of democratic rationality.

To produce a formula as a basis for stabilization grants to state and local governments is a problem of formidable proportions, and we can

29. Cf. the regional authority proposals in *The Case for Regional Planning*, M. S. McDougal, E. H. Rotival, et al. (New Haven, Yale University Press, 1947).

do no more here than allude to some of the difficulties and possibilities. Assuming that the total amount to be distributed to local government units is varied with business conditions, the problem becomes one of distributing lump sums to particular units of local government according to some kind of sensible criteria. For example, the amount granted to each local government unit could be a fixed percentage of the expenditures of that local government unit during a previous ten-year period. But this might operate to reward wealthy communities and penalize poor communities; reward static communities and penalize growing ones; reward cities that expanded government functions and penalize cities that did not; and lead citizens to speed up expenditures now to increase the future amounts of federal grants. Alternatively, the amount could be a straight per capita grant; yet this would fail to take into account differentials in local costs or range of government functions. Or some formula that combined several criteria might be worked out.[30]

Assuming that a satisfactory formula *could* be developed, there would still remain a very considerable area of special grants—for highways, to take one example—that probably could not be fitted into a pattern of stabilization grants suitable for most of the expenditures of local and state governments. Special situations of this kind would have to be dealt with separately. Yet to the extent that the number of these special grants increased, the significance of the block grant for stabilization of state and local expenditures would decrease.

From the viewpoint of democratic rationality, that is to say, the fundamental promise of the block grant to state and local governments lies in the freedom of choice it would permit to citizens at the local level. Such funds should be granted entirely without stipulations as to the way in which they might be used. Only in this way could stabilization of local expenditures be achieved without impairing the opportunities of choice among citizens at the community level. To do so much is, we concede, to gamble on the ultimate capacity of citizens to run their affairs with a moderate amount of good sense and integrity. But this, after all, is simply the fundamental gamble of democracy itself.

30. British experience reveals many of the problems and possibilities of alternative formulas, although none of the British grants was developed specifically for stabilization purposes. The General Exchequer Contribution (or Block Grant) under the Local Government Act of 1929 and the Exchequer Equalisation Grant under the Local Government Act of 1948 furnish particularly relevant experience. For a recent discussion, cf. D. N. Chester, *Central and Local Government: Financial and Administrative Relations* (London, Macmillan, 1951), especially chs. 8 and 9, Appendix A, pp. 375 ff., and Appendix B, pp. 397 ff.

CHAPTER IX. *Techniques for Influencing Private Investment*

BY RALPH S. BROWN, JR.

I. INTRODUCTION

By private investment we mean the spending of business firms for plant and equipment or on inventory. Business spending, as has been explained in Chapter 3, is a major source of the stream of national income, along with consumer spending and government spending. We know that a decline in private investment will lead to a decline in income, unless consumers correspondingly spend more and save less, or unless government contributions to the income stream are altered in one of the ways that have been discussed by other writers in this book. We also know that in the past business spending has been the least stable of the three main components of income; much of the discussion in this volume concerns the difficulty of adjusting to its variations. Therefore measures to keep investment stable, if we could discover them, would go far toward achieving general economic stability.

Investment takes added importance from the fact that its net volume measures the accumulation of capital goods, which enrich us by producing more goods. We count on private outlays for the bulk of this accumulation, though certain forms of government spending also increase the stock of investment goods. Therefore we seek first to avert fluctuations in business spending as a means of stabilizing income. But if stabilization is achieved at the high levels necessary both for prosperity and for continued growth, it is quite necessary that private investment be stabilized at a level that must also be described, however vaguely, as "high."

Against this well-understood background it is proposed to discuss chiefly the use of government credit and the use of business taxes and subsidies, in relation to business spending. These devices are of paramount interest because, as we shall see, they are fairly flexible in their application; some of them can be used to curb as well as to foster investment. As a special case we shall consider the control of investment in closely regulated industries, that is, public utilities.

The present chapter perhaps falls between two schools: it assumes that a high stable level of *private* investment is a desirable means to stable prosperity, and it argues for considerable *government* action to insure such a level. The initial assumption gathers in a good deal of free-enterprise ideology, largely comprehended in the proposition that the numerous decisions of individual entrepreneurs, through their success or failure, reflect the allocation of resources desired by the community as a whole. This critical area of private capitalism is often fenced about with signs reading, "No Government Allowed." To make the prohibition even slightly meaningful in our present situation it would have to read, "No Further Government Allowed." Then the argument could be made that we accept a large dose of fiscal policy to stabilize income; but once government begins purposefully to influence investment decisions, the decisions no longer reflect the consensus of the consuming community as they are supposed to do. Thus, it is argued, government influence negates the virtues of private investment and should be minimized. Furthermore, the intervention of government results in another shift of social and economic power to the already powerful state.

From the standpoint of another orthodoxy, the argument for limited government action stops short at futility. If the level of investment is the key to stability, then business spending is too important to be left to the businessman. The flow of investment must be directly controlled by the state; credit agencies, incentive taxation, and the like are excess baggage.

Neither of these polar positions is acceptable. Take first the hands-off policy. Without discussing the extent to which investment decisions "cause" business cycles, it seems clear that the cyclical prospect affects them. Looking down into a slump, entrepreneurs see no hope of profits, not from any defect in their own plans relative to those of others, but simply because prices and incomes are falling. Gazing up at a boom, many of them become oversanguine and ignore the likelihood that the public may be sated with their particular products. If, in conjunction with the other instruments of policy advanced in this symposium, the techniques proposed here can be used to neutralize the cycles, they can help to bring expectations into a stable perspective relative to the future. If at the same time they can be generalized in their application, so that at a given moment the impact of taxes or the availability of credit is approximately the same for all those contemplating alternative uses of capital, then the intrusion of government will in the end enhance rather than diminish the likelihood that the controllers of business spending will build the plants to produce the goods the community is willing to pay for. Accordingly, some government techniques bring us closer to the objective of consumer-guided allocation of resources.

But it is not enough to choke the (modified) laissez-faire position with a surfeit of cream. There are, after all, substantial sectors of the economy in which the free play of economic forces is not acceptable to the community, at least not to the majority's representatives. Credit and subsidies have been conspicuously extended to agriculture, housing, and some forms of transportation. The tariff shields a host of domestic manufactures. Cooperatives have tax advantages. The production of distilled spirits has heavy tax disadvantages. No blanket condemnation or approval of such departures from a wholly free allocation of resources is intended. They represent supposedly mature policy decisions; in general they will be critically examined for hints of methods to adopt or avoid and not for their fundamental wisdom.

As for government assumption of all major investment decisions, to denounce it out of hand as undemocratic would be to impugn many bright spirits. Nevertheless, within the political presuppositions of this symposium, one would be hard put to justify such a transfer and concentration of power. Certainly the goal of more widely shared power requires us to try to fashion techniques for influencing investment in such a way that, like most fiscal and monetary measures, their pressure will be impersonal and diffused. This leaves responsible individuals free, within the economic environment so created, to decide whether they will devote resources to producing bubble gum or hymn books.

However, a caveat is worth reiterating. If the appropriate political authority decides that bubble gum or hymn books have too great potentialities for good or evil to be left to the chance of the market, controls will be imposed. Such controls cannot be stigmatized as undemocratic any more than they can be brushed off as interfering with free enterprise. As noted above, there are important industries in which investment, sometimes for very good reasons, is anything but untrammeled. We have to fit such industries into our general framework.

After such a far-flung introduction it must be conceded that the measures to be discussed in this paper are, in a sense, residual. They supplement the massive weapons associated with fiscal policy (taxation, public spending, monetary controls). They complement policies determining the level of American investment abroad. Like every economic instrument, they stand in the shadow of defense requirements. At the same time, devices like government credit, business taxes, and subsidies are far from residual in the calculations of the managers affected by them. And, aside from their direct impact on business-spending decisions which is our immediate concern, these devices certainly influence that treacherous climate of opinion in which the investor blows now hot, now cold.

II. GOVERNMENT CREDIT

A panoramic survey of government credit institutions and policies should show their bearing on investment and serve as a basis for some recommendations. To describe all the thirty-odd federal agencies which either supply capital to other credit agencies, make direct loans, or guarantee private loans to business would only be confusing. We shall therefore concentrate on the three clusters of greatest importance, those devoted to agricultural finance, to housing, and to business. Within these fields it is useful to notice instances in which outright grants have been added to easy credit, for the line between loans and subsidies, it will appear, is a wavering one.

The emphasis on each device varies considerably between fields. In agriculture government has been lavish with subsidies, has erected an elaborate lending system, but has made little use of guarantees to private lenders. The last device has predominated in housing, with the result that contingent liabilities loom largest in the affairs of the Housing and Home Finance Agency. The Reconstruction Finance Corporation, which has administered most assistance to general business, has been chiefly a lender. Its major subsidy operations were wartime programs essentially directed to procurement of strategic materials.

1. *Agricultural credit*

In agricultural finance the premier agency is the Farm Credit Administration. Two of its units have a history antedating the great depression: the Federal Land Banks were established in 1916, the Intermediate Credit Banks in 1923. Together with the Production Credit Corporations and the Banks for Cooperatives (both 1933 creations) they serve as sources of capital for a network of local groups, mostly cooperative in organization. FCA agencies are, on the whole, competitive substitutes for such private lenders as insurance companies and commercial banks. More than a fourth ($1 billion) of farm mortgages and perhaps a fourth ($800 million) of other farm loans recently outstanding were financed through the FCA system.

Government support for this volume of lending comes from capital stock contributions which, for all FCA agencies, totaled $281 million in June, 1950. The Federal Land Banks recently retired all government-held stock and now finance their operations through the sale of bonds (*not* government-guaranteed) and through the stock subscriptions of the National Farm Loan Associations, which administer the mortgage loan program at the local level. It should be noted, however, that the Land Banks had almost cleared their government indebtedness in 1929, but had to be assisted in the depression with $125 million of new capital, in addition to contributions to surplus of $189 million made to compensate for the effects of moratoria authorized by Congress. It is these advances that have now been repaid. While the other FCA agencies mentioned have substantial earned surpluses, they are still dependent on their capital supplied by the Treasury.

The pattern of Farm Credit lending is, in general, one in which government capital is augmented, first, by private capital obtained on the security of farmers' obligations, second, by a growing borrowers' equity arising from compulsory stock purchases by borrowers through their local associations. The result of this combination of government sponsorship, regional management, and local administration has been to reduce interest rates and increase the volume of credit available to farmers. The cost to the taxpayer is about $6 million a year for interest on that part of the national debt represented by government capital advances, and annual appropriations of $3–5 billion to the Farm Credit Administration itself.[1]

With this program, it is desirable to compare the policies of the Farmers' Home Administration, successor in 1946 to the adventurous Farm Security Administration. Forbidden by Congress to engage in resettlement programs or cooperative farming, Farmers' Home is still dedicated, as was its predecessor, to bettering the lot of those near the bottom of the agricultural ladder. It is, however, confined to direct financial assistance within rather modest appropriations. It may make long-term loans to buy farms or to expand uneconomical holdings (Title I of the Farmers' Home Administration Act). Title II authorizes loans up to five years for "production and subsistence." Subsistence reflects the inheritance by Farmers' Home of emergency loan programs which have been authorized sporadically since 1918. They do not concern us here. Production loans, for periods up to five years, are for the purchase of livestock, equipment, fertilizer, and the like. The distinctive feature of both the land purchase and operating loan programs is that they are intended only for those who are considered not good credit risks. The basic act

1. These sums are mentioned simply as an approximation of the expense of this type of lending operation relative to others which will be described. The fact that the Farm Credit program has forced down interest rates, and does compete with private lenders, has led to critical and controversial search for subsidies, open or concealed. Compare Howard Friend, *The High Road to Socialized Credit* (National Tax Equality Association, 1946) with Earl L. Butz, *The Production Credit System for Farmers* (Washington, D.C., Brookings Institution, 1944), chs. 6 and 7.

provides (7 U.S. Code §1002, §1018(c)) that applicants must establish their inability to get funds at 5% either privately or from other government agencies.

Since the farm purchase loans are granted only when the land is bought at conservative assessments fixed by a statutory formula, inflated land values have made it of minor magnitude since the war. This program includes, however, probably the only instance in agricultural finance of the insured, or guaranteed, mortgage. For a 1% annual fee, the Administration guarantees full payment both of principal and accrued interest on a forty-year mortgage covering 90% of sale price. Half the fee goes into an "insurance" fund; the other half is for service of the loan, which is fully undertaken by the Administration, from appraisal to foreclosure. The initial trial of the scheme offered the lender 2½%. There were few takers, though the loan involved no risk and no expenses; so in 1948 the rate was raised by Congress to 3%, and a kind of secondary market, the lack of which had disturbed lenders, was created by a repurchase undertaking which the lender could invoke at infrequent intervals. The merits of guarantee plans will be discussed below in connection with their extensive use by the Federal Housing Administration. The present instance is worth mentioning as a dubious model. All the decision and supervision, as well as the risk, was left to the government agency, while the private lender is a disembodied source of pure capital, a function the government can discharge with at least equal facility and for less than 3%.

Both the Farm Credit Administration and the Farmers' Home Administration have liquidating functions with respect to various emergency programs of the thirties. They represent mortgages refinanced, and emergency loans made, in the depths of depression with no realistic expectation of repayment. "Loan" was a euphemism, when the advance was to a victim of the Dust Bowl. Farmers' Home has a reserve for losses equal to half its outstanding loans, a fact which does not make assessment of its performance easy.

For fiscal 1951, Farmers' Home had $150 million to lend and $28.5 million to spend on administration. It is impractical even to guess what part of its operating expense is attributable to the loan programs, since it has other functions. In any case, supervision and education of poor farmers are central to its mission, so that it is not comparable to a simple credit agency.

The Farm Credit and Farmers' Home Administrations exist for the sake of broadening the channels of credit available to farmers, and their effect on the volume of private investment is incidental, though far from inconsiderable. Land mortgage financing usually has to do with a mere transfer of existing assets; but production loans to farmers finance investment just as much as do term loans to manufacturers. Congress is likely to increase the resources available to farm lending agencies in hard times, and thus to create a useful contracyclical effect. Reverse attempts to curtail the volume of lending in the recent inflation have been confined largely to land mortgage financing, where the aim was to avoid underwriting and encouraging any such disastrous rise in farm land prices as occurred after World War I.

The most valuable technique to be learned from these agencies is the decentralization of FCA components. The initiative in making loans rests with local associations, subject however to supervision and standards set by the Land Banks or the Production Credit Corporation as the case may be. In the case of the latter, the expenses of the associations are met by a spread of about 4% between the interest rate charged to the borrower and the cost of money to the association (recently 2–2¼%, the discount rate of the Federal Intermediate Credit Banks). The development of borrower participation and responsibility is furthered by the requirement of purchase of stock in the association in an amount equal to 5% of the loan. In the case of the Land Banks, as has been noted, the use of association capital similarly obtained has made it possible to retire the government advances. This possibility of self-support, though it is all-important to those who deplore the use of any government funds for credit agencies, is only one virtue of the FCA structure. Local responsibility and administration lessen the weight of central authority and its size, too. Farm Credit Administration components have a total of about 3,500 employees. Farmers' Home Administration requires 5,000 to operate a program that is of slighter magnitude but requires greater direction and decision by the agency.

Two other Department of Agriculture programs should be noticed, because in their fields they make substantial contributions to investment. The Rural Electrification Administration has made loans, mostly to cooperatives, exceeding $1 billion, all of which has gone to capital formation. It is a spectacular example of the use of cheap government funds plus aggressive administration to stimulate a field of investment that private interests, before 1935, had largely neglected. Interest and amortization payments have so far been satisfactory, and capital losses to the government need not be at all large if a tolerable degree of stability in agricultural income is maintained. The cost of this program to the taxpayer, since 1935, has been an $11 million operating deficit, together with the interest on $145 million of direct appropriations for loans. REA funds are now obtained by borrowing from the Treasury. While the creation of employment opportunities accounted in part for the initial impetus to REA's creation, its outlays so far have tended to move with the cycle rather than to offset it, since they depend on the willingness of groups of farmers to incur indebtedness.

The Agricultural Conservation Program is a direct subsidy of part of the cost of soil-building and similar projects carried out by individual farmers. These activities are a form of investment, for they represent improvements to the farmer's land, which is his "plant." Payments in the decade 1937–46 were about $4 billion. How much private spending accompanied them cannot be estimated with any accuracy; the Secretary of Agriculture thought that in 1946 the farmer's share of the cost of the subsidized projects was about one-half. It would not be unfair to say that the program has been designed as much to increase farm income as to elicit the most farm spending for the least subsidy. However, to the extent that Congress continues to contract the appropriations in good times, as it has done since the war, the effects of the ACP are contracyclical.

The other major farm subsidy programs—parity payments, crop loans, and wartime subsidies—have been clearly intended to increase farmers' income and only indirectly affect investment spending, as the recipients elect to buy tractors rather than Buicks.

These lending and spending activities of the Department of Agriculture are worth attention, first because they exemplify large-scale government intervention resting on a broad base of local participation. It may be that farming both functionally and geographically is more homogeneous than the great diversity of general business (this point is made by Douglas R. Fuller, *Government Financing of Private Enterprise* [1949], p. 47). It is certainly true that the cooperative association is better developed in, and better adapted to, agricultural finance than to the present structure of trade and manufacturing, which is, at least in theory, competitive and atomistic. But the success of the agriculture programs in locating much of the burden and responsibility of administration in quasi-private organizations indicates that a monstrous bureaucracy is not an inevitable consequence of government action; and it should inspire proposals for new forms of credit agencies, under public control but not public operation, in other fields of investment.

Another reason for rehearsing the agricultural experience is to emphasize the contribution of farming to the flow of investment funds. A very rough estimate would put this contribution at 10–20% of gross investment. (Cf. Walter W. Wilcox, "Capital in Agriculture," *Quarterly Journal of Economics*, 58 [1944], 49.) There is every reason to expect that government influence will continue to be exerted by Congress through the specialized agencies of the Department of Agriculture; but there is no reason why these agencies should not be responsive to over-all policies aimed at stabilization, as well as to the peculiar fluctuations of the agricultural cycle and the peculiar pressures of the farm vote.

2. *Housing credit*

The role of government in housing finance is even more complex than in agriculture and is in such a state of flux that we have had a major housing act every year since the war. It is proposed, therefore, to do no more than indicate the main organizations, uneasily combined in the Housing and Home Finance Agency, and the main techniques, which run the gamut from supplying capital to lenders, through a variety of guarantee and insurance arrangements, to subsidies. Little use has been made of direct lending to builders or homeowners. The Home Owners' Loan Corporation, now liquidated, assumed $3 billion in defaulted mortgages during the depression, but this was entirely an emergency refinancing program, involving no new investment.

The chief instruments of federal credit for urban housing are the Home Loan Bank Board and the Federal Housing Administration. The first is not unlike the Federal Land Banks; it supplies capital to savings and loan associations. Stock held by the government is being retired rapidly; the banks can rely on the proceeds of debentures sold to the public and on stock subscriptions by the member associations. The members constitute a system of mortgage and savings banks competitive with private mortgage banks, savings banks, and others.

The Federal Housing Administration is of more interest because it pioneered in the large-scale use of the guarantee device to encourage private lenders to extend credit. In theory, the various titles of the National Housing Act relating to FHA create an insurance program, with a reserve built up from fees paid by borrowers, usually .5%, which are also used to pay FHA's operating expenses. The reserve at the end of 1949 amounted to about $270 million, partly government-contributed, against ultimate contingent liabilities of around $10 billion, representing the total insurance outstanding.[2] The latter figure is meaningless as a guide to probable liability, and the program is regarded as self-sustaining by its officials. But the reserve would surely be inadequate in the face of any general collapse, even one less severe than that of 1932.

It is not intended, however, to argue the adequacy of the insurance system as a true mutual fund, because from the standpoint of this paper

2. A guarantee program for veterans' home purchases administered by the Veterans Administration was of greater magnitude than the FHA programs over the period 1946–50. Its declining importance is a pretext for not discussing it here.

it is not essential for a guarantee program to be self-supporting in bad times. When it is decided to decrease lenders' risk in order to stimulate loans for investment in one or all sectors of the economy, someone must assume the burden lifted from the lender. A charge on borrowers adequate to meet all contingencies is not likely to stimulate them very much. There may be cases where the borrower is willing to pay, in the form of a guarantee fee, a higher interest rate than is permitted by custom or law. In all others we must begin to take note of the stubborn fact that the demand of borrowers for investment funds, especially in slack times, has to be coddled far more sedulously than the supply. Therefore guarantee fees have properly been kept at modest levels both by the FHA and by other credit agencies we shall shortly consider, for, whether or not they are levied directly on the borrower, they are bound to affect the cost of money to him and thus his willingness to borrow.

Of course the guarantor can come out on top; indeed the success of total stabilization policies in averting depression may well have such a happy by-product. The point to be emphasized is that a guarantee program concerned primarily with solvency is not likely to get results. In the following discussion no further distinction will be made between absolute guarantees and those with the suggestion of limited liability arising from mutual insurance terminology.

The mechanics of FHA guarantees typically include an appraisal by the agency, which also sets minimum standards for new construction. A mortgage up to 80–95% of appraised value (80% was the prewar maximum; some recent provisions for low-priced homes run to 95%), with statutory limits on the amount of insurance per dwelling unit ($9,450 under Title II as amended in 1950), is eligible for insurance. The insurance fee is .5%, as previously mentioned, and the interest charge may not exceed 5%. On default and foreclosure, FHA will take over the property and give the bank marketable interest-bearing debentures.

It will be seen that the lending bank has no risk at all. And should it become concerned over the size or liquidity of its portfolio, the Federal National Mortgage Association, now a component of the HHFA, maintains with government capital a secondary market for trading in insured mortgages. One result of this relief from responsibility is that the FHA must scrutinize each application and make almost the same judgments and decisions as the lender. In contrast to the specialized, autonomous Home Loan Bank system, FHA guarantees have induced a great variety and number of lenders to provide funds for urban mortgages; but the inducements are so liberal that administration cannot be left to the lender. FHA has 4,500 employees as against less than 400 federal employees in the Home Loan Bank system. Yet the volume of Home Loan Bank member mortgages exceeds that of FHA-insured mortgages; and relatively few of the former are insured.

A variation in technique is found in guarantees of loans for modernization and repair under Title I of the National Housing Act. Here FHA undertakes to pay cash on default, taking over the notes for collection, up to 10% of the amount of eligible loans made by the lender. Since these are relatively small amortized loans, the 10% guarantee is in fact quite adequate to free the bank of risk. At the same time, elaborate processing of each loan is unnecessary. Title I guarantees have probably made possible a useful though limited flow of this sort of small-scale investment. Of the blanket guarantee technique, more will be said in connection with the RFC.

Guarantees of loans for rental building have been especially pushed since the war, with a variety of statutory modifications culminating in a form of guarantee running direct to the entrepreneur rather than to the lender. This is an "insured annual return" (Title VII of the National Housing Act, added in 1948) which may turn into a substantial subsidy. For an annual fee of .5% of investment, FHA may guarantee amortization and a yield not exceeding 2.75% on rental housing. There is provision for FHA to cut its losses by taking over the property, or for the owner under certain circumstances to unload it on FHA for 90% of cost. Not dissimilar was a 1946 authorization of "guaranteed markets" for prefabricators; it collapsed after one year in the general failure of prefabricators to make a substantial dent on the housing shortage.

Direct subsidies in the housing field have been concentrated on public housing. Recent state legislation, however, makes tax and other concessions to limited-dividend rental builders. The Veterans Emergency Housing program of 1946–47 included a scheme of premium payments for scarce materials. This was a production subsidy launched in the midst of an inflation and casts little light on the present discussion.

It is difficult to assess the bearing on stabilization techniques and principles of the elaborate program meagerly outlined above. After all, the primary purposes of federal housing legislation, it may be assumed, have been the provision of better housing at lower costs than would otherwise be available and the encouragement of home ownership. An increase in investment is a collateral consequence of these objectives, and one that occurs either in good times or bad. Thus it is hardly disputable that the liberal provisions of postwar legislation contributed to inflationary pressures. This was presumably accepted by policy makers as inevitable, in view of the housing shortage and their unwillingness or inability to curtail sternly such alternative uses of resources as racetrack construction. When the Korean war sharpened the need for diverting men and materials to military uses, credit restrictions were promptly applied. The housing credit agencies, among other measures, increased the down payment required and shortened the amortization period on insured mortgages. Title VI of the Defense Production Act gave the Federal Reserve Board the power, exercised through its Regulation X, to impose a variety of similar restrictions on credit for uninsured new construction, with the concurrence of the HHFA in the case of residences. An Executive Order (No. 10161) required the HHFA to keep its restrictions equal in severity with those of Regulation X.

These restrictions, coming soon after the pre-Korean Housing Act of 1950 had further liberalized guarantee terms, dramatized the theoretical flexibility of credit aids. But would the brakes hold? The momentum of 1950, a record building year, carried into 1951. When construction did decline, it was hard to tell to what extent stringent terms had killed demand, for in the meantime the Treasury and the Federal Reserve had lowered the peg on marketable government bonds. To this measure was attributed an immediate shortage in supply of funds, since banks and insurance companies no longer found it attractive to sell government bonds to create mortgage money, even though mortgage interest rates rose slightly.

Residence building should be especially susceptible to credit manipulation for two important reasons. First, the proportion of capital cost to total cost is probably not exceeded in any other area of the economy. Consequently, housing is one of the few kinds of investment for which minor variations in the interest rate are still considered important to buyers. With 20-year or longer amortization periods, and 90% mortgages, interest payments may add up to half of the initial cost of a dwelling. Government lending can lower the interest rate, and government abstention can send it up. Second, the need for housing is so acute that an easy supply of mortgage money readily turns need into effective demand. Because of the presumed stability of residence values, lenders can be persuaded to permit ratios of debt to owner's equity that are astonishingly high—too high, some observers think, for many owners to sustain. Be that as it may, would-be owners sprout like weeds under the gentle rain of guaranteed mortgages that require only 5 or 10% down payments.

It is consequently possible to envision stabilization through government techniques of the flow of private investment in residential construction. The attempt should certainly be made, for another 10%, more or less, of gross private investment is at stake.

But if these factors are significant, one wonders why guarantees and free capital have had to be so lavishly expended on housing to get any results.[3] Guarantee plans, it may be postulated, should leave part of the risk to the lender, so that he will be spurred to exercise his classical function of choosing the borrowers most likely to succeed. A guarantee against any loss, for which the borrower pays, certainly does violence to this principle. And if the lender has no function other than to provide riskless capital and keep books, why 4½ or 5% interest? In general this paper indicates a preference for directing credit aids through regulated private institutions. But the housing experience suggests that if the lenders are monopolistically organized, they may simply absorb the aids and do little to make more attractive terms to investors. One way to scotch this snake is to have a main lending channel responsive to government policy and free of traditional alliances. The current animosity of other banks toward savings and loan associations (the Home Loan Banks' outlets) is suggestive of a possible healthy falling-out.

Even if the mortgage money market is tautly functioning, there remain other well-known obstacles to an effective relation between credit policies and investment in housing. Speculative land values, urban blight, disproportionate tax burdens all help to make housing a sick industry. Its sickness, like agriculture's, explains the degree of government intervention already reached. But it makes the lessons of intervention almost useless for generalization, unless one thinks the whole economy is ailing. If we accept all credit aids as differing from subsidies only in degree, what Charles Abrams says about subsidies to private housing is, to say the least, disquieting:

> Further government subsidy to private housing . . . would inevitably enhance the government's stake in real estate without bringing security to the owners. The housing problem of the masses would be left unsolved. Such aid cannot be justified even in theory. If small-scale home building were an infant industry, its claim to assistance might be arguable. The industry is suffering not from immaturity but from senility. In an era in which hundreds of products were brought within reach of millions through low-cost quantity production, building costs rose, more than half our families being unable to buy its product. A subsidy would be tribute to the moss-grown system of waste and inefficiency in the two-by-four operations of the average builder. Public funds dispensed to the builder would flush through into the hands of venturers, lenders,

3. For a pessimistic view that the government during the boom has "shot away" all its ammunition for keeping housebuilding at high levels, except direct subsidies, see Leo Grebler, "Stabilizing Residential Construction—A Review of the Postwar Test," *American Economic Review,* 39 (1949), 898.

and material dealers without substantial dividend to tenants or owners. It would be subsidizing waste.[4]

3. Business credit

On turning to general business investment, we must recognize that the influence of credit policies has been much diminished by the prevalence of internal financing in established enterprises. External sources of funds, however, are still important for the new or growing business and, paradoxically, for the settled public utilities, which conventionally pay out a large proportion of their regulated earnings.

As we have seen, government credit agencies can by various devices lower interest rates for different types of loans, make credit available to classes of borrowers for whom private lenders make no provision at all, or accept risks of default to an extent inconsistent with any conventional rate of interest contemplated by business borrowers or private lenders. Conversely, government agencies can, by withdrawing or damping these inducements, decrease the attraction of borrowing for investment. But we must keep reminding ourselves that any softening of credit has the same limitations as a lowering of the interest rate; it may encounter such poor expectations of profit that businessmen will not borrow at any positive rate of interest. Then subsidies (section III below) may be necessary.

Experience in the field of government credit for general business has been limited;[5] but examination of it at least takes us out of the special interests of farming and housing into measures designed foremost to raise the general level of investment in bad times. We also gain some insight into the problems of a direct lending program.

The Reconstruction Finance Corporation, established in 1932, at first concentrated its efforts on shoring up the capital structure of the railroads and the banking system. In 1934 the act was amended. Section 5d, "for the purpose of maintaining and promoting the economic stability of the country or encouraging the employment of labor," authorized the RFC to make loans to "any business enterprise where capital or credit, at prevailing rates for the character of loan applied for, is not otherwise available." A statutory requirement that all loans be "fully and adequately secured," though later modified, created a lending mill in which

---

4. *The Future of Housing* (New York, Harper, 1946), p. 359.

5. The tremendous wartime programs, notably the V and VT loan guarantees, are intentionally ignored; so are their counterparts in the post-Korean rearmament. The government is in effect financing its own purchases; and though the mechanics are in some cases adaptable to stabilization agencies, the goals are dissimilar, as are the problems encountered. See Fuller, *op. cit.*, chs. 8, 9.

a borrower was ground exceeding fine. For if he could not get bank credit at prevailing rates, he probably could not furnish security satisfactory to the RFC as directed by Jesse Jones.[6]

At the same time, another legislative authorization of direct loans was made in §13b of the Federal Reserve Act. This rather grudging enactment stated that "in exceptional circumstances" the twelve Federal Reserve banks could make industrial loans for working capital, under the guidance of advisory committees of active businessmen in each district. Again the borrower had to be unable to obtain assistance on "reasonable" terms from "usual" sources; and the loans had to be "sound."

The total amounts authorized under section 5d by the RFC were only $351 million up to June, 1939, and by the Federal Reserve banks $180 million for the same five-year period, after which recovery problems were dissipated by the war. Detailed studies indicate that some of the borrowers from both agencies could have been accommodated by commercial banks. Most of the experience, however, suggests that the two government agencies were partially filling a gap in the structure of private credit: the lack of five- to ten-year term credit for small or medium-sized businesses. Whether this gap should be closed by equity funds rather than loans, or (if by both) in what proportions, need not detain us here; neither type of financing has been adequately available. On the one hand commercial banking tradition aimed at liquidity; term loans (excepting the once-impregnable real estate mortgage) were taboo. It is true that this attitude has broken down since 1933. Competition, idle funds, and the RFC program have blurred traditional lines of separation. Commercial banks, along with other lenders, have embraced the term loan, with all its illiquidity and dependence on the success of the borrowing enterprise. But these hazards pretty much limited eligibility to large, well-off companies. At the other end of the banking spectrum, the investment banking business simply was not and is not organized to raise equity capital for small businesses. The expense is prohibitive. For stock issues of less than $1 million, the cost of flotation runs to more than 20% of the proceeds, and even up to $5 million the average cost of issues studied by the SEC approaches 20%.

The small man is thus left with limited access to the commercial finance companies and the factors; but they do not offer the long maturities and low interest of the RFC. Originally limited to 5 years, 5d loans were extended to 10, then by another amendment in 1938 time limits

6. The act, as revised in 1948, now requires only that credit be "not otherwise available on reasonable terms" and that the loan "be of such sound value or so secured as reasonably to assure . . . repayment." 15 U.S. Code §604(b).

were removed altogether. A 10-year limit was reimposed in the 1948 overhauling of the RFC Act. Federal Reserve 13b loans are limited to 5 years. Interest rates under these programs have been within a conventional banking range—$2\frac{1}{2}$ to 6%. It is noteworthy that the RFC has refrained from the flexible interest policy that varying degrees of risk would suggest; its officers felt that an unalterable flat rate (recently 4%) would diminish "the number of Congressmen and Senators we would have to contend with." [7]

In view of the variety of activities of both the RFC and the Federal Reserve banks, it is not possible to reach any clear conclusion whether the programs paid their way. The RFC, like other government lending agencies, has had the advantage of an initial grant of free capital from Congress and of access to the Treasury for 2% borrowing. With this head start, it has been able to carry on its multifarious lending activities, except for wartime subsidy programs, at a "profit." If the stimulation of credit at a time when risks are large is the function of the agency, as it certainly was of the RFC, then its operations need not be expected to be profitable. Even the 80th Congress recognized this. It trimmed the RFC of its wartime excrescences in 1948 and left it with $500 million of interest-free capital funds to lend. One reason assigned for this capital subsidy was that "at the direction of the Congress . . . the Corporation incurs considerable expense in investigating and setting up loan applications to see if it cannot interest private lending agencies in making loans which the Corporation believes private capital should make." [8]

For simplicity in exposition, the RFC–Federal Reserve programs have been described only in terms of direct loans. Both agencies, however, have participated in bank-sponsored loans too large for a commercial bank to undertake alone. Also, both have made increasing use of the guarantee device, under such labels as "deferred participations" or "commitments." The RFC guarantees obligate the agency to assume, on demand of the lending bank, a portion of the loan, usually not more than 75%. Repayments and losses are then shared pro rata by the RFC and the bank. For this protection the bank pays a fee graduated according to the extent of the guarantee (e.g., $.5\%$ for a 50% guarantee, $.75\%$ for 75%). Maximum interest rates are prescribed by the RFC—4% for the guaranteed portion, 6% for the rest.

The effect of these guarantees, like those in housing, is to enable the bank to increase the volume of loans it considers risky. But unlike the FHA insurance the bank is not entirely relieved of risk. It has its own

7. House Committee on Banking and Currency, Hearings on Government Credit, 1947, p. 60.
8. House Report No. 1836, 80th Congress, 2d Session, 1948, p. 4.

share of the loan to safeguard, and if it wants to decrease that share it must pay a higher fee.

By keeping alive the banks' interest in the credit-worthiness of its borrowers, the partial guarantee permits the RFC to rely somewhat on the lender's judgment and to dispense with some of the investigation and consideration necessary to a 100% guarantee or to a direct loan. The RFC has been at times widely criticized for the cautious and involved demands it made on loan applicants, and more recently for dispensing public funds with abandon to applicants with appropriate political backing. The need for a careful stewardship, emphasized by the irregularities disclosed in 1950–51, makes a direct loan program cumbersome.[9] Individual guarantees are somewhat more expeditious. The ultimate in administrative flexibility was briefly attained in the RFC's Blanket Participation Program of 1945–46. To speed reconversion lending the RFC undertook to accept 75% guarantees of any loan made by a bank which agreed to the terms of the program. These terms in substance required only that a loan should be made to a business enterprise for purposes similar to those of 5d direct loans and that it should not exceed $250,000, ten years maturity, or other limitations unnecessary to repeat. Because of a statutory requirement, the RFC had to review in each case the salary scale of the borrower's officers.

In a period of less than two years 11,000 loans totaling $528 million were authorized under the Blanket Participation Agreements. Banking comment, expressed in a questionnaire circulated by the Senate Banking Committee in 1948, was quite favorable, though the program was apparently opposed by spokesmen for organized bankers. In any event the BPA was intended only for the reconversion "crisis," and there would have been no excuse for its continuation through the postwar inflation.

As a device for future recessions, something like the BPA seems to have every merit. Not the least advantage is its extremely decentralized reliance on existing private agencies for administration and decision. One of the most troublesome practical problems of an agency intended to veer with the economic weathervane from great activity to total quiet is its status in periods when no credit stimulus is necessary. A direct lend-

9. It may be that honest government bankers are not reckless enough for promoting risk-taking through credit devices. Their method of selection and their sensitivity to Congressional criticism breed caution. Thus the FHA, to revert to the housing agencies, probably inhibits technological progress in the industry by its overconservative standards of eligibility for guarantees. See, e.g., *Architectural Forum,* January, 1950, p. 101. With bankers and builders both accustomed to rely on FHA financing, investment in new construction techniques is thwarted, perhaps to a greater degree than would occur if private lenders were in control. At least some of them might be venturesome; FHA's timidity is uniformly stifling to innovation.

ing program creates a large bureaucracy with the normal instincts of self-preservation, achieved only by continuing to lend when there is no need for it. But if the agency is put in mothballs the morale of its remaining custodians suffers, and it takes time to reconstruct staff and techniques. A blanket guarantee program requires a relatively small staff to start and operate, a good part of which might well be occupied after a recession in liquidating the legacies of default or in anticipating the next downturn.

4. Recommendations on credit measures

A number of over-all recommendations about the form and administration of government credit measures now emerge.

First, government should continue empirically to supply missing rungs in the ladder of credit. Well-conceived programs in aid of agriculture and housing may help to sustain the level of investment in those industries by large measures beyond the capabilities of private lenders. Or, where credit is unavailable because of some institutional defect in the banking system, government action may help to remedy it. The prewar direct loan experience of the RFC and the Federal Reserve is best viewed as a step toward the satisfactory provision of long-term credit for small business. This is an area of credit deficiency that has attracted considerable political attention, as well as varied proposals for new private institutions.[10] If a government agency jumps in first, private enterprise may then decide that the water is fine. The history of large-scale rural electrification is precisely such a case.

Second, the specialized credit agencies that we now have or later create should pay attention to over-all investment levels. Stability cannot always be the dominant consideration; welfare or security demands may require a burst of investment to be encouraged at just the time when the stabilizers would suppress it. It should be possible, however, to accommodate the tempo of all credit aids to the investment cycle with more harmony than is currently exhibited. During the great depression, when most of our credit agencies were created, their activities were uniformly and spontaneously inflationary. But during the postwar boom the RFC, for example, kept right on inflating investment, largely in the cause of helping small business.

An obvious proposal is to establish a Federal Loan Council, composed

10. In a special message to Congress May 5, 1950, President Truman proposed (unsuccessfully) an integrated program to aid small business, including government insurance of bank loans, regional investment banks under Federal Reserve supervision, broader powers for the RFC, and the abolition of the Federal Reserve industrial loan program.

of representatives of all the interested agencies. This recommendation has been made by the Committee on Economic Development, to which the Hoover Commission added a similar suggestion. If a Cabinet officer, say the Secretary of the Treasury, presided, the Loan Council could serve as a channel for executive policy guided by the Council of Economic Advisers. Whether such a council should have power to command as well as to advise is hard to foresee. For many of its member agencies stabilization would be a secondary function. On the other hand, some might have no other. How to harness such conflicting aims is a problem for the experts on public administration.

Third, the principle instrument of credit aid to general business should be a single [11] agency with a mandate generally to encourage investment when a decline is occurring and to shut up shop when times are good.

What techniques shall this agency employ? A large direct lending program, it has been pointed out, creates interests that are not easy to eliminate when the need for them lessens. The inception of such a program may also, by raising fears of government competition and prospective "socialization of credit," further distress the banking community when it is most desired to fill it with open-handed optimism. Further, if lending operations are successfully put on a discontinuous basis, the agency staff is not likely to be particularly expert in selecting borrowers (the RFC has been kept busy only because a depression was followed by a war). If cheap credit is to be extended to a number of marginal enterprises, which ones should be helped? Incorrect decisions (incorrect in that the enterprises fail) misallocate resources. Also, ill-informed lending may create spots of excess capacity which darken the expectations of existing producers and so diminish total spending when it is desired to increase it. To avoid these difficulties resort may be had to the private bankers who, whatever their other limitations, are experts in judging the prospects of borrowers.

In view of the considerations just listed, the fourth recommendation is that direct government lending should not be employed for large-scale stimulation. Direct lending powers should, however, be left with the RFC or its successor for limited use. For example, Congress (or the President if given discretion) may wish to authorize private loans in aid of some specific program without creating a specialized lending agency. Thus, the RFC heavily backed the Lustron prefabricated

11. Whether it should be the RFC or the Federal Reserve needs analysis by those familiar with the inner workings of both. The choice depends also on the technique preferred. Direct lending is alien to the Reserve Banks' tradition; a quasi-automatic guarantee would not be. No occasion is seen for continuing the present division of authority and responsibility.

house.[12] And as stated in the first recommendation above, this agency (or another) should have power to make direct loans where a gap has been found in the private credit system.

Fifth, a flexible guarantee plan, rather than direct loans, seems to be the best device for encouraging lenders. It can and should require that moderate terms be given to borrowers. However, the main problem for most entrepreneurs is likely to be not the interest rate but the difficulty of getting credit at all at a time when the economic prospect is gloomy. With a blanket guarantee the government can assume part of the lender's risk and still leave the direction of resources in private hands. Depending on the degree of encouragement needed, the maximum government participation can be varied. The fees charged can range from prohibitive to nominal, depending on the state of investment. So long as part of the risk is borne by the lender, there should be no need for agency review of the desirability of the loan.

These features of a blanket guarantee permit it to be decisively and pervasively employed. Half-hearted credit measures, it seems clear, can have very little effect on the flow of investment. Bold ones have little enough. To borrow an apt simile, increasing the supply of credit in a slump is like pushing a piece of string. Only a big sharp push will show any results, but the effort is worth the trial. If the slump is checked loans and guarantees cost little. In any case guarantees can be administered with a minimum of disturbance to the balance of political and economic power.

III. TAXES AND INVESTMENT

Professor Shoup has already pointed out (Chapter 6) that taxation is usually intended to wrest resources from private control. The fact that taxes cut into the loanable funds of savers or the investible funds of producers is in itself no indictment. Yet most proposals about taxes in relation to investment add up to a plea—or a demand—for reductions. The writer is not prepared to say that the current total tax load can or should be lightened by any major reduction of public expenditures over any extended period, though savings of the sort urged by Senator Douglas and others are doubtless desirable. As for the portion of the load that falls on investment, it does not appear that taxes as currently levied cut down investment below the level necessary to maintain employment.

12. The failure of this enterprise does not destroy the pertinence of the example. When the Lustron experiment commenced, it held great promise. By way of contrast, RFC support of the Waltham Watch Company was in response to no discernible Congressional policy. For an account of the pressures that bore on RFC in the Waltham case, see *Fortune*, April, 1949, p. 84.

This is not to say that there are no defects in the system; far from it. Nor does it deny that taxes can be used to stimulate or restrict investment. Several proposals to these ends will be reviewed. In addition, the next section of this chapter will propose a recession subsidy for private investment not unlike proposals that have been made to exempt reinvested earnings from the corporate income tax. But no attempt will be made to show that the plight of business spending warrants a permanent shift of an additional share of the tax burden to another sector of the economy.

One major concession may be willingly made. The present system probably offers too many refuges for what might be and, in interest of innovation and growth, ought to be venture capital. For instance, the continued existence of tax-exempt government bonds provides a haven for the very wealthy timid soul. In corporate finance the discrimination in favor of debt over equity, because of the treatment of interest as expense to the borrower, has been widely deplored. Within the income strata and the business organizations in which large-scale saving and investment occur, there is doubtless good ground for the complaint that the tax system stifles enterprise. As Professor Groves has observed, "There is a world of difference between $1 million in the hands of, say, Henry Kaiser and $1 million in the hands of, say, Doris Duke." Yet Miss Duke may have lighter taxes.

Taxes in relation to investment have been thoughtfully considered in books like Harold M. Groves, *Postwar Taxation and Economic Progress* (New York, McGraw-Hill, 1946). Consequently the following discussion will consist largely of brief observations on others' proposals for structural reforms in business taxes.

1. *Tax measures which stabilize business spending over the cycle*

A progressive tax structure, as Professor Shoup has reminded us in his paper, has an automatic contracyclical expansion and contraction in the flow of revenue it produces. This useful effect enhances the desirability of integrating the corporate income tax, which is proportional rather than progressive except for small companies, with the personal income tax. The great stumbling block in the way of such a reform is the necessity of reaching undistributed corporate profits. Various solutions have been proposed, and it will be assumed that a workable one can be adopted. The subject is raised here to point out that abolition of double taxation of dividends may not provide any lasting benefit to investors as a class. The slack in revenue would probably be taken up by higher personal rates; and stringent treatment of undistributed profits would invade a guarded stronghold of funds for corporate internal financing.

Both automatic flexibility and the related device of contracyclical manipulation of income tax rates are important primarily as instruments of fiscal policy. If they help to stabilize the total flow of income, the result could have only good effects on the stabilization of investment. Flexibility in tax rates would also have direct consequences for investment. Again referring to Shoup's exposition, a reduction in rates increases the supply of investible funds (working capital), at least for investors with net income. And if the taxpayer thinks of the reduction as a bonus from an expected higher tax, it may have the same psychological effect on him as a subsidy. Note, however, that it is a "subsidy" payable to all alike, whether they invest or not. On wholly rational grounds the effect of a purely contracyclical rate reduction on the anticipations of a marginal investor ought not to be substantial. For if he takes thought he will perceive that either the rate will go up again or its continuation at a low level will spell continued bad times. This and other arguments, however, may overstress the rational element in tax calculations.

An increase in rates during an inflation will in general have reverse effects. But a policy of frequently altered rates probably adds to uncertainty and may therefore depress expectations at all stages of a cycle. The case for flexible rates, as Shoup suggests, is far from clear. The uncertain impact on investment does not make it any clearer.

2. *Tax measures designed only to stimulate investment*

The most interesting proposal is for a full sharing of business losses by the Treasury, assuming continuation of a tax ascribable to business profits. At present losses may be carried forward or back two years; to get any tax advantage from a loss it must be offset by profits within the four-year period. The carry-back is a wartime legacy that was designed to tap high war profits for reconversion losses. Difficult to administer, and advantageous only to established concerns, its future is doubtful. Recent conservative proposals, such as those of the Treasury's research staff, look only to lengthening the carry-forward, say to five years.

Full sharing of losses would entitle the taxpayer to a payment for current net losses at the same rate as the tax on net income. As things stand now, imperfect offsetting of losses against profits increases risk, because the Treasury assuredly shares the winnings, but the investor may bear all the losings. E. C. Brown argues that full sharing of losses combined with 100% depreciation allowance during the year an investment was made would neutralize the effect of income taxes on the degree of risk of an investment.[13] If the analysis is accurate, the combination of loss shar-

13. *Income, Employment and Public Policy: Essays in Honor of A. H. Hansen* (1948), p. 300.

ing and accelerated depreciation would be a powerful stimulus to risky investment. Full sharing, moreover, seems entirely contracyclical in its effect on revenues. In bad times large payments to unprofitable firms would make quite a remarkable dent in government receipts. In good times taxes on full earnings would flow unimpaired.

There does not seem to be anything else stabilizing about full sharing, however. It would stimulate risk-taking in booms as well as slumps, and it does not appear that it could be withdrawn or modified periodically without becoming an administrative nightmare. An extended carry-forward meets most peoples' standards of fairness. Full sharing plus immediate depreciation seems too potent a device for permanent use unless we posit secular stagnation and an attendant need for continual inducements to investment.

Accelerated depreciation for tax purposes, used since 1917 to encourage private outlays on war facilities, is a more modest device that has received considerable attention as a general stimulus to investment. The basis for its popularity is a little mystifying. After all, the entire outlay is in any event deductible from income over some period of time. In stable circumstances the only advantage of an immediate or rapid depreciation deduction would appear to be the discounted value of a higher tax later (when no deduction was available) as compared to a lower tax now. Much recent clamor on behalf of accelerated depreciation probably derives from an expectation of instability. Since present profits and tax rates are high, the bigger deductions the better; for tomorrow's profits may turn into losses which cannot be fully offset. A more liberal carry-forward of losses would accomplish the same purpose. From another standpoint reduced taxes now, even if increased taxes later are unavoidable, mean more current working capital. This is doubtless a significant factor for an expanding enterprise, especially since the "loan" from the Treasury is interest-free. Finally, one can always hope that tomorrow's tax rates may be lower. The benefits of accelerated depreciation, then, aside from a pleasurable kind of uncertainty, seem to consist chiefly of a postponement of taxes.[14]

Preferential tax treatment of capital gains is another favorite theme for stimulating investment. The subject is too complex for adequate brief discussion, and the skeptic may wonder whether investors or speculators profit most from low capital gain taxes. In any case the tax handling of

14. Current controversy about depreciation for tax purposes raises other questions which should be separated from the stabilization issue. Chief among these problems seem to be: 1) objections to the Treasury's estimates of expected service lives; 2) the Treasury's unwillingness to let taxpayers take account of increased replacement costs.

capital gains and losses ought to be settled and stable, though it has not been so in the past. Whatever investment incentives result from one solution or another depend on the state of the law in the future when the gains from current investments are realized. Therefore the device has little or no adaptation to fluctuations.

In conclusion it may be thought that these brief comments understate the potency of tax incentives to investment. If accelerated depreciation will in fact build a blast furnace, it is pointless to insist that it is all done with mirrors. Any kind of tax saving certainly induces a warm psychological glow, which, for all we know, might not be true of alternative measures.

The chief objection to the various tax schemes discussed seems to be that, except for variable rates, they encourage investment in good times and bad.[15] If stabilization is our goal, this lack of flexibility is a decisive consideration. As a prerequisite for any kind of incentive to investment, it must be possible to withdraw or neutralize it during an inflation. As an ideal it should be possible to give the device an anti-inflationary turn.

IV. A Recession Subsidy to Private Investment

If any of the tax reforms briefly described above operated only during periods of reduced employment and income, it would be no barrier to their use that a loss of government revenue might result. The likelihood that a proposal to aid private investment would decrease revenues or increase government spending during a slump might make it a welcome complement to fiscal policy.

Likewise, the discussion of credit devices made no attempt to justify them on the ground that they are costless. Lending and guarantee schemes, though their current operations may appear to be financially successful, contain the seeds of considerable subsidies. But the most they offer to a borrower is an opportunity, at a modest rate of interest, to make an investment that he thinks will be profitable.

Favorable terms will not overcome expectations of loss. If prospective returns from investment take a downward turn, then possible government action to support business spending must look further than the diminution of risk for lenders and easy credit for borrowers. Negative expectations, if they are thought to be widespread, suggest a negative rate of interest—in blunt terms, a direct subsidy to entrepreneurs. Here we must grasp nettles. Subsidy is a thorny word, largely because it is associated with public grants to special private groups—farmers, ship-

15. Parenthetically, some of the tax proposals mentioned aim also at eliminating discrimination against new enterprise. This we accept as a desirable goal in good times or bad.

builders, railroads. It is proposed to avoid this association by a plan which, in accordance with the aims laid down in the introduction to this chapter, is nearly universal in its application to business spending for capital goods. To be sure, business spenders are still a private group. Though the plan will make the group a large one, it will not include employees or unemployed.

Because subsidies for any limited group are suspect to right-thinking people, they are usually described in other terms. Thus air-mail subsidies are said to promote the national defense, and swollen Treasury prices for silver, it has been claimed, benefit the masses of India and China (though unfortunately this has proved not to be the result at all). The most palatable way of advocating a business subsidy is to call it a tax remission, since taxes are almost as disfavored as subsidies. Recently a number of rather vague proposals have been advanced, such as permitting new investment by firms to be deducted from their taxable income. This would amount to a 40–50% subsidy to an eligible corporation, compared to other business taxpayers who did not invest. Proposals of this sort invite careful analysis of both theoretical consequences and practical difficulties. Such an analysis is clarified by treating the inducement as a direct subsidy rather than as tax relief. Of course, anyone who wishes is at liberty to use the tax relief label, and as an important point of administrative convenience an investment subsidy would in fact be operated through the Bureau of Internal Revenue.

Summarily, the proposal is this: when employment, production, investment, or some composite index decline to a point where other explicit compensatory measures are being launched, the President should have power to announce that the Treasury will pay a stated per cent of all investment outlays (with a few exceptions) for a year following.

Amplification of some aspects of this proposal follows:

1. Summary of possible effects of a subsidy on investment

The problems of administration of a private investment subsidy, it will soon appear, are more formidable than casual observation might suggest; but they would be worth tackling if the subsidy would help to prevent a depression. One cannot, however, be dogmatic about the effects. The worst consequence would be a further decline in investment, resulting from business hostility to the subsidy and uncertainty about its effects. This seems unlikely. The next possibility is that the subsidy would be substituted for private funds that would otherwise have been spent. There would then be no change in investment and the subsidy might as well be withdrawn. Third (these are points on a scale; the actual result can fall between any of them), investment out of private funds might be unchanged and the subsidy added to it. In that case the subsidy would have the same income-increasing effect as any other government spending on goods and services and might as well be continued as a complement, say, to public works. Fourth, the subsidy (it is hoped) would evoke private spending that would not otherwise be made.

Pointing to no better result than the third possibility is the argument that the cost of capital goods has a negligible effect on investment decisions, compared to the quality of expectations. Especially if there is idle capacity, a subsidy will accomplish nothing. This view gains some support from the limited studies that have been made of the elements of investment decision. In favor of the possibility that some increment of private spending will be evoked are these contentions: the grant of the subsidy, along with other measures, will improve expectations. Beliefs about profitability are not uniform in any case. There are always optimists, pessimists, and a middle group that can be influenced either way. The optimists especially include the innovators and new entrants into existing fields. The excess capacity of others does not dismay them; and a subsidy of part of the cost of capital goods would certainly make their ventures easier. Their dynamic investment in new technologies and new products is what drives existing firms to follow suit or fall behind.

2. *Eligible investment outlays*

Any business expenditure which is ordinarily capitalized and made the basis for depreciation should be eligible for the subsidy. Both individuals and corporations have to be able to justify their attribution of outlays to capital when deducting depreciation for income tax purposes. The present tax forms show only the charges to depreciation; but it would be no trouble to require those claiming a subsidy to state also the additions to capital account during the period in question. After this point complications set in. They are unavoidable in any attempt to measure investment in a given period of time or to distinguish it from other forms of spending. What follows is intended only to show the scope of the resulting problems. Discussion of possible solutions to a number of them has been discarded, in view of the hypothetical quality of the entire proposal.

a) Capital, or operating expense? Innumerable outlays require a borderline judgment. Should a new roof, for example, be considered a part of operating expense (repairs and maintenance) or a capital charge (additions to plant)? The availability of a subsidy in a given period would exert a tidal pull toward capitalization of doubtful items. This consequence can be accepted with equanimity. It is the encouragement of business spending that is wanted and, since additions to inventory do not seem feasible to include (paragraph c below), some leeway in this respect is desirable.

b) Gross or net investment? There are arguments against paying the subsidy on outlays which merely replace depreciated capital goods. First, it may be said that such expenditures are routine and require no incentive. But full maintenance in bad times is far from routine in many industries, for example, railroads. A dollar spent on replacement adds as much to income as one spent on additional equipment. The second objection is that replacements only maintain the status quo; if a capitalist economy does not expand, it collapses. Growth, however, does not depend entirely on new outlays. Improved replacements increase productivity, and, on the monetary side, any kind of investment offsets savings. Third, it might be argued that a subsidy on gross investment would result in disproportionate payments to heavy capital-using industries, such as steel, in contrast, say, to department stores. But this is in fact desirable. Industries with a high ratio of sales to capital are generally consumption and service trades which benefit promptly from any increase in disposable income flowing from a recovery program. The capital goods industries, hardest hit by a decline in investment, are the very ones on which investment subsidies should be concentrated.

The clinching objection to a subsidy based only on net capital formation is the impossibility of satisfactorily measuring the base. Depreciation charges, the accountants tell us, are a way of allocating declines in capital values. For many reasons they do not measure the amount of replacement called for in any short period. If we cannot measure replacement then we cannot say, except abstractly, what part of total capital outlays represent new investment.

There are still other serious objections, but no space in which to discuss them, to the idea that a subsidy (or a tax incentive) should be limited to new investment.

c) Increase in inventory. Without adding to plant or equipment, a firm invests when it makes expenditures on future output which exceed current income. The familiar need for "working capital" in business exemplifies this process and its affinity to capital formation. The result of such outlays in any period is accounted for by net increases in inventory, which should in principle be eligible for the subsidy. Since inventory changes are necessarily calculated in determining income for tax and other purposes, the necessary data would seem to be readily at hand.

The objection to subsidizing inventory increases arises from the relative ease of piling up inventory during a subsidized period. Since the raw materials or work in process will (it is supposed) soon be liquidated, the expectations and incentives are quite different from those relevant to plant and equipment. The subsidy necessary to encourage the latter would be an inducement to frightful bulges and dislocations in the former. Furthermore, inventory changes may reflect nothing more than price changes.

This likelihood of inventory manipulation leads to a tentative conclusion that additions to inventory (which over a long period are a minor factor in capital formation anyway) should not be subsidized.

d) Purchase of existing capital goods as investment. Suppose that A buys a used machine from B, a competitor. So far as A is concerned, he is investing whether he buys the second-hand machine from another machine user, or from a dealer, or a new machine from a manufacturer. The subsidy should not push him into a single trade channel which to him might be uneconomical.

But such traffic in existing goods, when an investment by A constitutes a disinvestment by B, might simply dissipate the subsidy in a whirlpool of trading activity having very little effect on income or output, except as idle facilities come into use. It would also suggest a rat's nest of fraudulent or near-fraudulent schemes to bilk the Treasury. Obvious examples are: wash sales—A sells a machine to B, B sells a machine to A, both claim a subsidy; fake reorganizations, with the successor corporation representing its entire capital as investment within the subsidy period, and successive transfers of the same good during the subsidy period. Each dodge that came along could probably be met with regulations and penalties, but the income tax analogies show that solutions would be intricate. The practical difficulties raised by such transactions, whether legitimately or illegitimately carried on, cannot be overemphasized.

e) Residential construction. The extension of the subsidy program to home buyers, desirable on some grounds, raises a whole new set of problems. Buyers for occupancy do not have the same motivation as entrepreneurs, and the effect on homeowners of a given subsidy rate might be wildly different than on other investors. To offer the subsidy to owners for rent and not to owners for occupancy would, however, scarcely seem admissible. The imaginative reader can conjure up other fine distinctions that would have to be made between investment and consumer purchase of durable goods.

There are doubtless other industries which do not follow conventional patterns of capital formation and for which variations might have to be made. This outline attempts only to suggest the magnitude of complications, not their detail. However, the many lines that have to be drawn can mostly be drawn in advance. By adequate rule-making it should be possible to make the administration of the subsidy reasonably automatic. The prospective investor should be able to determine his eligibility for the subsidy with as much assurance as he can forecast the income tax consequences of the transaction. Some people will say that is not very much; but are not taxes one of our chief symbols of certainty?

3. *Timing*

How to time compensatory measures is worried throughout the preceding chapters. I can only suggest here that an over-all investment subsidy need not be undertaken at the first breath of recession. General Electric's Charles E. Wilson, in a speech outlining stabilization policy at successive stages of declining production, reached a level where his first prescription was "Prayer and wholehearted practice of the Golden Rule." [16] It is at about this point that a substantial investment subsidy should be inaugurated.

It would also appear important to link the subsidy (and the flexible credit aids of section II) with over-all employment-production levels rather than with a stated volume of investment. The latter requires a judgment, explicit or not, that the stated volume is optimum. Within a stabilization program there must be room both for bursts of innovation and for secular changes. Also the primary purpose of the subsidy would be to assist in restoring the level of income; the promotion of new capital formation is a secondary goal. Investment outlays are extremely unstable, and it would be enough of a task to check the precipitous decline of a slump without trying to maintain a specific rate.

4. *Power to start and stop*

This, like other compensatory measures, might be authorized by Congress in advance, with the power to set the program in motion (or to end it) delegated to the executive branch. But since investment subsidies are recommended only after storm signals have been flying for some time, it would not be fatal to await a legislative announcement that the subsidy would be paid for an announced period. The program would then terminate automatically unless renewed.

5. *Form of payment*

The firm promise of the subsidy ought to be as effective in promoting investment as its actual payment. Therefore the lags which plague some compensatory schemes should be shortened. The typical method of set-

16. Edwin G. Nourse, *Price Making in a Democracy* (Washington, D.C., Brookings Institution, 1944), p. 523.

tlement would be in connection with income tax returns. As taxpayer, the investor could offset the subsidy against his tax and, if it exceeded his tax liability for the period, receive a cash payment.

6. Rate of subsidy

The subsidy need not and probably cannot be a very precise tool when it is intended to influence investments whose expected return is only an informed guess. The outlays which are hovering on the margin are in many cases those in which the element of guesswork bulks largest—and gathering storm clouds quickly drive them to cover. Besides, the effect on annual profit or loss of a subsidy measured in per cent of investment outlay varies with the expected lives of different capital goods.[17]

If marginal investments are as uncertain as the writer believes them to be, then the subsidy may as well start at 10% and increase in multiples thereof. It is recognized that old firms in settled industries can estimate the returns from new outlays with some accuracy and would doubtless be attracted by payments more closely scaled. Round numbers are therefore not economical. But if the time ever arrives for using this device, boldness is counseled rather than cautious experiment.

How far does boldness go? Clearly a limit on the subsidy rate is called for, if only to preserve the responsibility that comes from the fear of substantial loss of private funds if the investment proves to be misdirected. Assuming that the rate would be increased step by step if initial inducements proved unavailing, by the time it reached 30 or 40%, as an outside limit, there should be cause for alarm over the whimsical or foolish investments which such a payment might evoke. Furthermore, a failure of the capital goods side of the economy to respond to 30 or 40% injections of free funds, at a time when other potent income-increasing measures are in effect, should cause much greater alarm over the future of the enterprise system. A reexamination of fundamentals would be in order, not larger subsidies.

The cost of the subsidy would of course be quite substantial. This is equally true, it should be remembered, whether it consists of cash payments or tax remissions. If capital formation was kept up to 10% of gross national product, then a 10% subsidy would amount to 1% of gross national product, etc. Dollar figures referring to the future are not very helpful, but a range of $2–5 billion gives an idea of the expenditures

17. For example, assume a 20% subsidy on a $100 machine that must be depreciated in five years. The annual charge without the subsidy is $20, with it $16. Thus the subsidy adds $4 yearly to earnings. But with a ten-year service life, the annual saving is halved (though it continues twice as long).

probably necessary for an adequate trial.[18] It is assumed, however, that the subsidy would be undertaken only at a time when, with the budget already out of balance, quick income-creating public expenditures were desirable. The investment subsidy is proposed as a complement to unemployment compensation and to public works, but with the added hope of inducing a flow of private investment.

7. Time span of the subsidy

The time required for acquisition of a capital good varies widely. Investment in an existing machine can take place instantaneously; the building of a blast furnace or a refinery may take two years. Taking a year as the base period, to allow for the development of plans and financing, some provision would have to be made for projects commenced within the period and not completed until a date when (hopefully) the subsidy would no longer be in effect. Another troublesome question concerns undertakings already under way when the subsidy is announced. If it is administratively feasible special treatment should probably be given to such overlapping investments. The actual outlays during the period, or some other prorated share, should be subsidized.

8. Effect of a potential subsidy on investment

A proclamation of the subsidy would infallibly call forth pained outcries from those who had completed investments in an immediately preceding period. Worse, it may be feared that in an early stage of declining income the likelihood of a subsidy in the future would dry up current spending. Since the subsidy is an emergency device we hope not to have to use, this deterrent effect, though unpredictable, is a grave matter. One way to avoid it might be to make the subsidy retroactive, say, for a period of six months. Then an entrepreneur, uncertain about the future, would have less to fear from a continued decline and less incentive to delay. It may be that the improvement in expectations through the retroactive feature would justify cutting the forward period to six months, thus keeping the total period at one year, with the effective date in the middle.

A related danger, if the subsidy had a definite place on the shelf of compensatory devices, is the possibility of political pressure from prospective beneficiaries to advance its effective date, pressure which might be intensified by a strike of capital. The leaders could allege increasingly

18. If this amount was raised by additional taxes an increase in income would be questionable, though not impossible; see the analysis by J. C. Hubbard, *Creation of Income by Taxation* (1950).

gloomy anticipations until the stake had been made high enough to suit them. But it is hard to imagine such community of interest, let alone collusive action, among such diverse multitudes of corporations, individual enterprisers, farmers, and home builders. And the economy as a whole must include enough innovating firms and expanding industries to spoil the formation of a united front. One cannot, however, overlook the degree of concentration in manufacturing industries. A recent Federal Trade Commission study found 46% of the net capital assets of all manufacturers in the hands of the 113 largest. If they and their satellites are linked in the sinister networks of financial control that some investigators discern, the decisions of the controllers effectively determine the level of investment and in turn the success of any inducements to invest.

9. *Effect of a subsidy on prices of producers' goods*

The "wretched spirit of monopoly" may especially infect the sellers to subsidized entrepreneurs. These sellers, speaking generally, will have considerable unused capacity, especially if they have overexpanded in the preceding boom. They should welcome the increase in the amounts of their products demanded as a result of the subsidy, and since they can expand output with no increase in marginal costs they should not increase their prices. If, however, a capital goods industry is organized in one of the oligopoly patterns which in fact characterize many of them, and if the leaders of the industry think (as they often do) that the demand for their product is inelastic to price changes, they might in theory raise the price, pocket the subsidy, and leave output unchanged. It will be objected, and rightly, that no such callous behavior could occur in the present political atmosphere. What could occur is that the subsidy would simply relieve the industry of any necessity of reducing its prices. Since lower prices for capital goods, by and large, would have the same effect on purchasers as the subsidy, successful monopoly resistance to lower prices, if engendered by the subsidy, would seriously challenge the usefulness of the program.

The possible consequences in this respect are numerous. One guess may be hazarded, based on the widespread observation of rigid prices in the industries most concerned. Whatever the causes of price rigidity, its existence suggests that the subsidy might not obviate price reductions, *because they would occur so infrequently anyway*. If we can, for good or ill, take the prices of many investment goods as given, our worries about sellers' monopolies lessen. The antitrust club remains in the closet for use against overt sabotage of the subsidy.

10. *Alternative proposals*

With this tentative configuration of an antideflationary investment subsidy we may summarily compare a few variant subsidy proposals.

Of first interest, since it is in existence, is the Swedish scheme briefly described by Bertil Ohlin. Legislation enacted in 1938

> enables firms to set aside part of their profits into special funds, tax-free, on condition that those funds be spent in buildings and construction during a period which the government declares to be a suitable period—usually something of a depression. If the money is not spent in the course of the period when the government has said, "Now we have a time when it is desirable to invest," then the firms must pay the normal tax, plus 3% annual interest from the time when the fund was created.
>
> Why is it laid down that the money should be invested in buildings and construction? Because investment in machines may be completely written off tax free any way, any year the firm so desires. Thus, business firms do not pay taxes on the profit, which they can dispose of by writing off machinery. As to inventories, these also can be written down tax free to a very low figure.[19]

Other references to this program that I have seen are even more tantalizing in their brevity than that just quoted. A full account and appraisal would be welcome.[20] An obvious merit of the plan is that it provides a motive for refraining from investment in good times, and at the same time insures that some firms will have cash balances available when the authorities permit tax-free investment. On the other hand, only those firms with past savings appear to be in a position to benefit from the scheme. This reduces its stimulating power and seems to discriminate against new enterprises, an inequity which could, of course, be corrected by supplementary measures.

19. *The Problem of Employment Stabilization* (New York, Columbia University Press, 1949), p. 69. Cf. the plan of Morris Copeland, "Business Stabilization by Agreement," *American Economic Review,* 34 (1944), 328.

20. See J. P. Shelton and G. Ohlin, "A Swedish Tax Provision for Stabilizing Business Investment," *American Economic Review,* 42 (1952), 375–380. From this informative note it appears that the funds are not confined to use in construction, though 80% of those accumulated by the end of 1950 were so earmarked. The total accumulations at that time amounted to 0.7% of the Swedish gross national product for 1950. Investments eventually made from these funds the authors say may not be depreciated for income tax purposes, which rather reduces the incentive. On the other hand, they say the funds do *not* have to be segregated pending their use, and thus constitute a source of tax-free working capital.

One objection to the proposed subsidy is that its benefits shower on all business spenders, whether or not they need such an incentive to invest. The cost of such a program would be tremendous—a 10% subsidy at recent levels of investment would run to $3 billion for a year. If the encouragement of marginal investment is the aim, why not devise a subsidy which operates only at the margin? A conspicuously successful wartime subsidy was the OPA system of premium payments to high-cost mines. The bulk of the output was available at a price far below the marginal producers' costs. The government paid the difference between this fixed price and that necessary to bring out the wanted increments of output. It should be remembered, however, that this, or any other wartime experience which appears to offer a tempting analogy, was carried on in a full-employment environment where prices were controlled, materials were allocated, and the government, in effect, was the chief purchaser of the subsidized production. A marginal subsidy requires means for determining who is at the margin. As a by-product of a vast system of controls, this was (partly) possible in wartime. Furthermore, a marginal subsidy implies some standard of a maximum fair profit for those denied the subsidy and further implies that the less promising enterprise should be boosted to some sort of equality with the competitor who is willing to go ahead without aid. A marginal subsidy, in sum, is quite inconsistent with the postulate that the allocation of resources should be left as far as possible to private decision.

Another possibility that has received some attention is a subsidy measured by current output rather than by investment. It would stimulate industries with a low ratio of capital to output, encourage employment on existing idle facilities, and, if it took the form of a guaranteed return or a guaranteed market, allay the fear of general overproduction which was so evident in the thirties. Plans proposed by M. Ezekiel [21] and by F. D. Graham,[22] though differing in important respects, contemplate forms of production guarantees, with the government in the end obligated to take whatever the market will not. It may be doubted that the extension to all production of the principles underlying farm support prices would resolve the underlying contradictions of the Commodity Credit Corporation, which was relieved of its surplus stocks only by a war. Further objections to the Graham or Ezekiel proposals stem from the formidable administrative machinery they would require, from the rigidity they would introduce in production patterns, and from their tendency toward an inefficient cost-plus economy.

21. *Jobs for All* (1939).
22. *Planning and Paying for Full Employment* (1946), Graham and A. Lerner, eds.

A production subsidy, to avoid these difficulties, would probably approximate a flat percentage of gross receipts.[23] Theoretically, such payments lower prices and increase unit output. They of course add to the income stream. If they were granted only for a limited period, it is hard to see much effect on investment, except for inventory increases. And if the chief effect is on the price and quantity of goods available for consumption, is it not preferable to give the subsidy to consumers and let them decide directly how it shall be spent?

A consumption subsidy is of course the "national dividend" discussed in the preceding chapter. Its advantages and disadvantages do not need to be reviewed here. Its apparent interchangeability with a production subsidy shows that we have drifted away from our bearings on investment, for the effects on investment of either output, employment, or consumption subsidies would be roundabout and delayed. They are ways of increasing incomes that should be considered along with, and not in place of, an investment subsidy.

It remains to test the flexibility of the investment subsidy by considering its place in an upturn. The mechanics suggested above have been constructed with a view to ending the subsidy as quickly as possible. If downward pressures on soaring investment appear to be needed, the subsidy should ideally be convertible into a tax explicitly laid on investment. But the possibility that persons in power would in fact levy such a tax seems too remote to warrant discussion of details.

Are there more plausible deterrents to private investment in a period of inflation? A general increase in income taxes, corporate or personal, decreases to some extent the supply of savings available for investment. A direct assault on corporate retained earnings, an especially important source of investible funds, can be made by a tax on undistributed profits. We had such a tax in 1936–38, and we also have a penalty tax aimed at excessive corporate accumulations (Internal Revenue Code, section 102). The low esteem in which the 1936–38 undistributed profits tax is held by public finance experts does not encourage its wider use.

One can indeed, beg the question how to impose restrictions in a boom to offset exactly a depression subsidy. It is always *possible* to constrict the flow of private investment by a combination of general credit restrictions and taxes. If these are imperfectly or timidly invoked, then come

23. Or, as has also been proposed, payments measured by the aggregate employment of each employer. The Papen plan tried in Germany in 1932 was essentially a tax-remission subsidy measured by increases in employment. Complex in detail, it had little effect. See G. Colm, "Why the 'Papen Plan' for Economic Recovery Failed," *Social Research*, 1 (1934), 83; cf. K. E. E. Poole, *German Financial Policies 1932–1939* (1939), pp. 35–74.

direct controls by allocation of materials or by requiring official permission for investment outlays. Direct controls, of course, take us into a different kind of political economy from the one this volume hopefully envisions.

In this country we did not undertake direct regulation of investment until the need for diverting it into armaments appeared overpowering. The postwar inflation of 1945–50 drove other countries to supplement fiscal controls with licensing arrangements well before Korea. Even so, the vigor with which private investment (and along with it income) were stabilized in that half decade is unimpressive.

Perhaps the intoxication of inflation is so heady that sufficient measures will hardly ever be taken to curb investment in a boom. If this is so, then the subsidy, and indeed all the proposed measures to maintain investment in a slump, may lead to a long-run diversion of greater resources into investment than the community would otherwise choose to make. As a check on this possibility, there should certainly be continuing study of the relation of actual business spending to ideal standards of private investment outlay at full employment, with the hope of developing better guides than we now have to that elusive optimum.

Lacking such guides, we may still surmise that depressions reduce the average level of investment over a cycle below what it would be under conditions of sustained full employment. Investment, we have noted, drops during depressions in much larger proportion than any of the other components of spending in the economy. On the other hand, in a boom it is forced to compete for resources with other kinds of spending. In view of the scarcity of resources that develops during a boom, private investment may never recover all the ground lost during depression. The extreme cycle-sensitivity of investment is, indeed, an important reason for concentrating in depression periods on measures designed to stimulate it, in preference to stimulating more stable forms of spending, notably consumption.

V. REGULATORY CONTROL OF PUBLIC UTILITY INVESTMENT [24]

As a postscript, some remarks on the control of investment in public utilities may be useful. These industries already submit to a degree of regulation that makes further intervention relatively painless. If, therefore, a peacetime venture in regulated investment is ever desired, car-

---

24. Since first writing this, I have profited from the much more thorough analysis of the same proposal by D. G. Tyndall, "The Stabilization of Investment in Two Public Utility Industries," *Land Economics*, 25 (1949), 382. His paper, besides giving detailed information on the instability of investment in the electric power and telephone industries, considers the risk of creating redundant or obsolescent

riers, electric power, and communications are logical if unwilling candidates. They are also notably heavy capital-using industries. As an approximation the utilities, while contributing 10% of the national product, account for 20% of capital formation. And they are every bit as unstable in their capital spending as other heavy industries.

A venture into direct control of utility investment would breach our postulate that government influence on investment should be generalized and indirect. But the principle, as we noted when stating it, has many exceptions and can be useful without having to be universal. The public utility field itself exhibits strikingly the extent to which free investment is inhibited by policies intended to protect the public's health, pocketbook, safety, etc. Here, though there is a surprising lack of uniformity in the powers granted to state or municipal regulatory bodies and to the federal agencies (ICC, FPC, FCC, Civil Aeronautics Board), an underlying pattern of power is discernible. It is derived from the common law belief that some callings are so affected with the public interest that the state can require them to serve all at reasonable prices. Among the instruments of control usually found as developments from this rudimentary proposition, the following particularly affect investment. First, one cannot embark on a public calling without obtaining a legislative franchise or an administrative certificate of convenience and necessity. Second, many enterprises, once launched, may not be abandoned without commission approval. Third, major extensions of service require permission and, what is especially important, may be ordered to be performed if it appears that the utility is not meeting a demand within its resources. Finally, security issues frequently require approval and along with them reorganizations, mergers, or other transfers of financial control.

Now, these formidable powers were not brought into being for the sake of stabilizing investment. They are designed to insure the performance of vital services and, since efficiency demands that the services be performed by monopolies in most cases, to safeguard the public against monopolistic exploitation. Vigorously used, they would be sufficient instruments to force utility investment in bad times and check it in booms. Would it be legal or practical so to employ them?

---

facilities by attempting to anticipate demand. It surveys related problems of finance and of inclusion in the rate-base of additions made with a view to stabilized investment rather than to current demand. Of special interest are opinions which Dr. Tyndall elicited from the state regulatory commissions in New York and Wisconsin, and from the Federal Communications Commission, the Interstate Commerce Commission, and the Federal Power Commission, about the legality and desirability of regulated stabilization of utility investment. The sum of the responses was that authority and enthusiasm for such a policy were about equally lacking.

Starting at the constitutional level, it seems probable that the grant of federal power over interstate utilities found in the commerce clause is currently broad enough to justify investment controls by federal agencies. Extensions of state regulation might encounter difficulties at the hands of some state courts expounding state constitutional prohibitions against the taking of property without due process of law. It would be said that public agencies can control the decisions of utilities managers only to the extent necessary to fulfill traditional regulatory missions. To require a utility to rebuild or enlarge its plant, at a time when its "owners" thought the outlay would be unprofitable, would be confiscatory and contrary to a familiar assertion that the business decisions even of utilities are for business managers, not for commissions.

The reply to these arguments would emphasize the benefit to the utilities themselves of a stable investment policy. The electric power companies, for example, permitted dazzling long-run prospects in the thirties to be clouded by cyclical gloom and a hostile political atmosphere. The war supervened and left the power producers with expanded demand, narrow capacity margins, and the necessity of embarking on tremendous investment that could have been accomplished a decade before at half the cost. Stable expansion would obviously benefit the suppliers of capital goods to utilities—freight car manufacturers and the like—and permit them to pass on economies to their customers.

As for constitutional immunity from further regulation, the reply might run that the investment decisions of utilities are no different in character from a decision to refund bonds or any other move that comes under commission sway when the need for regulation develops.

Assuming that constitutional objections could be met, similar arguments would have to be made about the permissible scope of existing legislation. Since many statutes are couched in elastic standards, like "the public interest," new interpretations could be made to uphold investment direction. But a court would be equally justified in saying that conventional statutes do not give the regulators power to make investment stability a unique ground for decision. The mandate would have to come fresh from the legislature.

Assume all these bridges crossed, there still remain administrative difficulties. It is feasible to repress investment in a boom only if there is adequate expansion in the slump, when fading empires like the railroads would plead unavailability of credit. Here cooperation with government credit agencies could provide a solution. One of the most spectacular achievements of the RFC (and of the borrower too) was to finance the Pennsylvania Railroad's electrification program in the depths of the great depression.

Cooperation between commissions, credit agencies, and borrowers, moreover, would be a light task compared to getting the fifty-odd commissions to move in the same direction at the same time. Utility regulation is the great stronghold of the independent commission. Independence may be an asset when the commission is performing judicially, but it makes unified executive action very difficult. Legislation in each state would probably be necessary to make the commissions responsive to general stabilization policies.

We thus find that the grip of direct public control over public utilities, even at its firmest, falls short of controlling investment. New legislation to accomplish such a result is conceivable, though with it would have to come a great advance in administrative coordination.

If this seems elaborate, it still represents far fewer steps than would be required for direct control of investment in some unregulated industry. Of course, one can always contend for the clean slate, and one may even suggest that a novel program can expect only failure at the hands of, say, the Interstate Commerce Commission. These suggestions, however, do not overbalance the view that, if the experiment of direct investment controls is to be tried at all, the housebroken utilities are the likeliest candidates.

VI. CONCLUSION

All the foregoing, it should be repeated, assumes that we shall be trying to deal with both depressions and inflations. Much more attention, to be sure, has been paid to the former, because the search for remedies seems more arduous. But we have insisted that any technique for increasing investment, to be worthy of adoption, should be flexible enough to be promptly applied and promptly withdrawn. Ideally, it should be reversible—capable of positively discouraging investment in a boom.

If one was convinced that either chronic inflation or a lasting shortage of investment outlets was upon us, the task would have been easier. The dank breath of stagnation, for example, would invite discussion of certain measures that are independently appealing as aids to growth. Thus public investment in new natural resources, notably atomic energy, may create opportunities for private investment that go far beyond the modest programs discussed here. Similarly, policies of government-sponsored research, of which atomic fission is again a notable example, suggest bounteous new technologies on which innovating investment can feed. On the other hand, a conviction of perpetual inflation would permit us to throw away all the crutches described in this paper and to concentrate on finding a system for repressing runaway investment without administrative autocracy.

But we have confined this discussion to a search for workable tools, not for new horizons. We have shown how far the long road of government credit has already been traveled; it is relatively easy to open new avenues off a familiar highway. Government support for new types of lending agencies, and flexible guarantees to private lenders, are capable of adjusting the supply of credit to almost any situation. We recognized, however, that supply does not create demand when the indexes are falling. The hardest task is to persuade the investor to spend at such a time. You can pay him to spend, which is a direct subsidy, or you can reward him with tax remissions, which is an indirect subsidy. We chose to concentrate discussion on a quite hypothetical investment subsidy, the case for which may be quite unconvincing. But the exploration of its outlines and of alternatives has not been without reward. For if we isolate the investment subsidy from its tax aspects, and either a priori or on experiment find it unworkable, then there is little reason to think that less drastic measures will work any better. To be sure, we have been concerned with the quality of business expectations, a psychological mystery. The means to influence them may also be wrapped in mystery.

PART THREE:
CORRELATIVE GOALS

CHAPTER X. *Market Organization and Stabilization Policy* [1]

BY EUGENE V. ROSTOW

I. THE SETTING OF THE PROBLEM

1. *Fluctuations in income and the structure of industries and markets*

The essential ideas underlying many of the other chapters of this book constitute a thesis which has gradually spread from the classrooms of the economists to the realm of popular thought. In its most general form the thesis is that a capitalist democracy can achieve a good deal of economic stability, at high levels of employment, and a steady rate of economic progress without giving up either capitalism or democracy.

The body of ideas on which this conclusion rests can be summed up in these terms: the system of private enterprise in business and labor works extremely well in arranging for the production of the goods and services the public wants. It directs labor and resources to changing tasks in an economy which never stands still. It helps to establish prices and wages at levels which reflect market forces. But the system of private enterprise as such cannot achieve stability at high levels of employment. It is inherently and often cumulatively unstable. Bursts of investment activity in one line of development—railroads or utilities, for example— may be followed by periods of relative inactivity. If the total level of construction and investment pauses, or falls, spirals of decline may set in and spread throughout the economy. The inevitable and inherent variability of the system of private enterprise is one of its greatest assets, as a method for directing men and materials to their most productive possible employment. But it should be offset from time to time by compensating governmental action if society is to be protected against the waste and strain of excessive booms and slumps. While the market system of free enterprise tends under some circumstances to restore equi-

1. This paper contains parts of a book on the control of the economy, soon to be published by William Sloane Associates, Inc.; it is borrowed with their permission. Some passages are also taken from my article, "Monopoly Under the Sherman Act: Power or Purpose?" *Illinois Law Review, 43* (1949), 745.

librium, the achievement of economic stabilization in its general sense is not one of the functions it should be expected to perform unaided by the state. In view of the character of industrial fluctuations, the task of general stabilization can be undertaken effectively only by the national government.

This analysis of industrial fluctuations has led to the formulation of a program for using the machinery of public law in the interest of achieving a considerable degree of stability without sacrificing either freedom or progress. Part of this function can be performed only by government, through its actions in the sphere of "fiscal policy"—that is, through the ways in which taxes are collected and spent, and through banking policy, interest rate policy, and policy toward securities and commodities markets. The rest could be left in the main to free and competitive markets, policed by the antitrust laws, and to the largely unregulated negotiations of business and labor.

The problem set for this chapter is to examine the relationships among these three principal instruments of American policy—fiscal policy, the competitive market for goods and services, and the process of negotiation which produces wage rates. More particularly it is to consider whether, and on what terms, their functioning can be reconciled. Must government action in the sphere of fiscal policy, designed to prevent excessive booms and slumps, destroy private initiative in business and self-organization in labor? Do the institutions of private business and private labor make it impossible for government to smooth the fluctuations which have in the past marked the course of economic life? Or can high levels of employment be maintained under modern circumstances of political and economic organization only at the expense of perpetual deficits and of perpetually rising prices?

Most of the other essays in this symposium concern problems of fiscal policy, that is, the various ways in which the government and the banking authorities of the United States can (or could) manage the flow of national income in the interests of stability, economic development, and social democracy. Although they necessarily consider the difficulties and shortcomings of existing techniques and procedures, together they represent an affirmation of the view that fiscal policy in its broadest sense—including taxation, government spending, banking action, and special inducements to production—can be used to influence the level of national income in ways which should promote high levels of employment and, on certain conditions, prevent general inflation. The use of fiscal policy as the chief positive weapon of planning for a capitalist economy implies that, except for its tax collections, the government would leave most decisions as to the actual production of goods and the conduct of business to the authorities of private business and labor. By occasional action in the limited and rather remote sphere of fiscal policy, the national government could broadly condition the environment within which business and labor decisions are made, but not control the substance of those decisions. It could compensate for upward or downward movements originating within the economy and thus determine whether prospects for profit would be generally favorable or unfavorable to businessmen.

The notion of stabilization primarily through fiscal policy has an immense appeal to American opinion. It offers us a chance to meet the insistent social demand for protection against depression and runaway inflation without a basic change in the character of our institutions. As an instrument of planning it fits the pluralist tradition of American life. It does not require a gigantic bureaucracy, reaching into every business transaction and altering the balance of authority between the state, private business, and organized labor. No social revolution is necessary to carry it out, nor would its success require a substantial break with the continuity of our social development.

The doctrine of stabilization through fiscal policy is fully considered in Chapter 3 by Mr. Millikan. He classifies six major forms of spending, with a view to observing and identifying changes in spending which could cause changes in the level of national income. These are consumption expenditure; business investment for plant, equipment, and inventory; the retention of corporate profits; the nation's international account; government spending; and government tax collecting.

For purposes of this chapter we should concentrate attention first on private, nongovernmental spending, both for consumption and particularly for investment purposes. Variations in these forms of spending may arise for a number of reasons and because of combinations of circumstance. Variations in the volume of business spending for plant, equipment, and other capital purposes appear to be the principal nongovernmental force initiating general upward or downward movements of national income. If the dollar amount of business spending for capital purposes is less than the dollar volume of savings retained out of the income of the previous period, or more than that amount, the total flow of national income drops or expands. This can happen because the institutions for financing business, viewed collectively, have released fewer dollars (or more, as the case may be) for circulation through the capital goods industries of the economy than have previously been entrusted to them as withdrawals from circulation in the form of saving. Our banking system has the striking and on the whole useful capacity to create or to destroy money, in the form of bank deposits. And there is considerable variation in the rate at which existing funds are spent, at different stages in the trade cycle.

In the case of a downward movement initiated in this way, unemployment spreads from the capital goods sector of the economy, the total of national income in money drops, the demand for all goods is reduced, profits decline, leading to further worsening of investment prospects, then of investment outlays, income, profit, and employment. People complain of underconsumption, oversavings, or underinvestment, depending on their habits of speech. When, on the other hand, businessmen are optimistic about the future, and spend for investment purposes either their idle balances or money borrowed from and often newly created by the banking system, investment outlays outstrip the prior dollar level of savings; the level of national income in money rises; the demand for all goods increases; profits are generally earned; unemployed resources are drawn into production, and, if investment spending above the prior level of savings persists beyond the limits of full employment, all prices and costs are subjected to erratic upward pressure as shortages develop. Money income increases more rapidly than the output of goods, valued at previous prices, and the characteristic stresses of inflation emerge. Prices and profits are swollen, along with wage rates subject to effective union action or to the pressure of the acute demand for labor. Exports decline and imports rise. The country may need to export gold in order to pay for imports. In the past, at least, money became scarce and expensive on such occasions, as all business bid at once for the savings of the community and the credit resources of the banking system. People living on fixed incomes or fixed wages and salaries suffer relatively to other classes of the population. A demand develops for the direct control of prices and the direct allocation of goods, and there is complaint of undersaving, overinvestment, or overconsumption.

In either case the advocates of stabilization through fiscal policy believe the main line of governmental reaction is clear. With something between a fifth and a quarter of national income taken by all governmental units in the United States, government has an extraordinarily powerful and versatile weapon for counteracting upward or downward movements in the level of national income which start with variations in the level of business spending, or equally with variations in the share of income devoted to consumption. By offering subsidies, guarantees, or tax inducements to private investment, by varying taxes and expenditures, and by making corresponding adjustments in banking policy, the government can either add new money to the stream of income when its volume is inadequate to assure full employment, or siphon money off when the flow of money is excessive in relation to the supply of goods, and thus hope to achieve a degree of balance.

But the broad movements of the national income do not work themselves out through a mechanism of precisely conditioned reflexes. The attempt to view the flow of national income in a rather simplified mathematical way is a necessary step in analysis and helps to clarify some of the relationships among variable factors which develop through time. The growth of this analytical approach to the problem has, however, presented difficulties as well. People tend to think of one dollar of expenditure as equal for all purposes to any other. But the economy does not respond according to a mathematical formula. Industrial fluctuations are more complicated than Archimedes' law. Successful stabilization is not a trick to be carried out in the quiet offices where financial experts practice the black arts of budget, tax, and banking policy. It is an act of will in which the whole of society must share. The success or failure of fiscal policy as a weapon of stabilization will be determined not only by the skill and insight of those who manage fiscal policy but by what happens to prices and wages in the rough and tumble of ordinary business life.[2]

It is not correct, in the first place, to assume that a given amount of new money injected into the stream of income will produce a predictable volume of new income, employment, and output or that a given amount of hoarding will lead to a given reduction in the flow of income. New money added to income as armaments expenditure may lead to an altogether different over-all response of private business than new money spent as an ordinary government deficit started by a tax cut, or by a special tax remission to encourage private investment, or a huge regional power development like the Tennessee Valley Authority project, or the building of a publicly-owned steel mill, or a subsidy for private housing. Similarly, a fall in the level of income originating in a government surplus may show different symptoms than a fall beginning with a drop in private investment or a change in saving habits on the part of people at large. Furthermore, either additions to or subtractions from the flow of income will produce different net effects depending on the degree of monopoly power in markets, the way in which monopoly power is exercised, and the general state of opinion as to the future.

The approach of the monetary and trade cycle theorists, as it is represented in this book, is a first approximation to an understanding of economic fluctuations and an indispensable tool of public policy. But it is

2. See William J. Fellner, "Employment Theory and Business Cycles," in Howard S. Ellis, ed., *A Survey of Contemporary Economics* (1948), pp. 49, 75.

no more than a first approximation. For the broad aggregate flows of spending for consumption, investment, and taxes have their impact on production and therefore real welfare through markets, industries, and individual firms. Often, indeed, the general movements of the national income originate in the collective responses of firms, trade unions, and industries. Businessmen and union leaders, by their reaction to the news, start cumulative movements in the level of income at least as frequently as the central banks, legislatures, and civil servants. The organization and behavior of markets, both for labor and for goods and services, goes far toward determining the ways in which the economy responds to income changes originating either in government action, business action, or in the sphere of foreign trade. We can hope for a realistic policy of effective stabilization only by combining our examination of national income in aggregate terms with an understanding of how the firms, unions, and markets into which the economy is organized actually meet the pressure of changing levels of national income.

A program of stabilization depending on fiscal policy as its primary dynamic instrument of control can be successful only if the economy adopts wage and price policies consistent with its purposes. Experience during the last thirty years indicates that it is quite easy for price and wage policy to frustrate and offset the effects of action in the realm of fiscal policy, or greatly to increase its expense and its effect on the class structure of society.

Most economists agree that there are differences between the response of competitive and of monopoly markets to rises and falls in the level of over-all demand. These responses differ, moreover, not only in the short but in the long run. The structure of market organization has vital effects on the way in which an industry meets short-run declines in the demand for its product, on the pace at which it expands under the pressure of rising demand, and on its desire to develop and to introduce new and cheaper techniques of production. Economists are not agreed, however, as to the character of many of these reactions nor as to which general form of market organization, the more competitive or the more monopolistic, would best carry out the purposes of a program for stabilizing the economy at high levels of employment through the use of compensatory fiscal policy.

In the first section of this chapter four general cases will be distinguished: first, the situation presented when national income is falling; second, the case of rising national income, with some unemployment; third, the case of very close to full employment, or "overfull" employment, which may as a practical matter be the most important case of all for the rest of our lives; and finally the problem of attempting to maintain stability of employment at high levels without perpetual inflation. The problems of market and industrial organization presented in these four situations are comparable but by no means symmetrical. It was thought helpful, even at the risk of some repetition, to consider them separately.

Since the discussion in the balance of section I of this chapter is aridly technical in spots, it may be desirable to recapitulate its conclusions for readers who prefer to avoid economic analysis.

The argument of the next four subdivisions of this section is that effective competition has much to contribute as an auxiliary instrument of fiscal policy in programs of stabilization under the circumstances of the second and fourth cases distinguished in the preceding paragraph: the case of recovery, while some unemployment exists, and that of stabilization at high levels of employment. On the other hand, some forms of state-controlled monopoly are inevitable, if we mismanage fiscal policy in such a way as to indulge in inflation beyond the point of close-to-full employment, so that the economy is continuously under the pressure of excess purchasing power, rising prices, and costs. The same choice may well be made if certain key prices, notably wages, are advanced so rapidly by the exercise of monopoly power as to require compensating doses of inflation, and hence increases in prices generally, in order to permit employment to be maintained. The first case, that of extreme depression, is an economic disease which society should not and need not tolerate for any reason. Although a substantial drop in national income always provokes the protective reaction of monopoly, as people seek to hold their own prices against the falling tide of demand, heightened monopoly power cannot help to shorten nor to reverse a downward movement. It may make it more intense and more expensive to control by effective action in the fiscal field. On the other hand, while a competitive economy can and does react flexibly to mild downward movements of national income, flexible prices as such cannot cure a serious recession and may make it worse, if expectations of further price falls become widely held. Cumulative depressions can be cured, whether markets are organized competitively or as monopolies, only by compensatory fiscal policy or by some combination of factors which has the same reflationary effect.

The reader should be warned that several common words will be used in a special sense in the next four subdivisions. "Inflation," otherwise unqualified, will be defined merely as money newly added to the flow of income, i.e., as an increase in the money level of national income. Put more broadly, inflation can be identified as an increase in the total volume of spending for currently produced goods and services. The word will be used to identify acts of monetary or banking policy, not price movements. Thus the term inflation will imply sharp price rises and other familiar symptoms only if it takes place during periods of close-to-full employment. "Monopoly" will be used very broadly indeed, and entirely without moral or legal implications, to embrace markets in which price is effectively set by the decisions of a small number of buyers or sellers. Correspondingly, "competition" will connote market situations where sellers (or buyers) lack such power over price, even though they may have some other attributes of monopoly power. Where a more precise definition is required, it will be indicated in the text.

There are many ways of defining situations of monopoly and competition, and in actual life markets must be classified in a spectrum of closely related positions, often involving elements of both competition and monopoly. There is no clear-cut test which enables one to list most markets arbitrarily as either competitive or monopolistic. Until recently, at any rate, the wheat farmer operated in a largely competitive market setting, and the Aluminum Company of America in one which most economists would consider a position of monopoly. Between those extremes one can find markets of many types. The elements which most economists regard as significant in determining the degree and effectiveness of competition in a market are: 1) the number of sellers and their relative size; 2) the relations among sellers, whether by way of agreement or otherwise; 3) the conditions affecting the entry of new firms into the field; 4) the extent to which consumers will substitute the product of one seller for that of another.

The literature about competition and monopoly is of course one of the most controversial branches of social science, and two themes are often confused in the discussion: the presence or absence of a given degree of monopoly power; and whether or not it is being exercised in "progressive" ways. The analysis which follows will be concerned principally with the consequences for stabilization of the existence of considerable degrees of monopoly power, in the broad sense of power over price. This definition is used as a shorthand reference merely to facilitate the preliminary analysis and not in any way to exclude longer run problems of economic development, or some of the noneconomic aspects of the monopoly problem, which are considered at a later point. The identification of the presence of monopoly power in this sense is not intended to imply value judgments as to the desirability of monopoly nor conclusions for antitrust policy.

2. *Market responses to falling national income*

Let us first consider a case of falling national income. The money level of national income may start to fall for a variety of reasons. The international position of the economy may change, and the net result of all international transactions may be to reduce the number of dollars which the purchases of foreigners add to the flow of money income in the United States. Governmental units may operate at a surplus which they effectively hoard—that is, they may return less money to the stream of income payments than they withdraw as taxes. Alternatively, individuals or business corporations may spend less for investment purposes than have been set aside out of previous income as personal savings, undistributed profits, or depreciation allowances. They may postpone such expenditures in anticipation of price falls, thus holding more funds in liquid form, or they may use such funds to repay bank loans. By changing the rhythm of expenditures, and the relationship between the processes of deliberate saving and investment spending, they can reduce the dollar volume of national income, which is a function of the available volume of funds and the rate at which it is turned over as income.

As the total level of national income—that is, the total of aggregate spending or demand—drops, new stresses appear in every market. Fewer goods and services can be sold at the prices which previously prevailed. Where industries or labor unions use a substantial degree of monopoly power to keep prices and wage rates stable, or where monopoly policies are pursued by governmental authorities (as in the case of utilities and of many agricultural commodities), the impact of the drop in demand will appear in the first instance as a fall in output rather than in prices. Where industrial prices are kept unchanged, fewer goods are sold. If wages are stabilized fewer workers will be hired, where falling prices make fixed wage rates unprofitable. Where government policy assures the farmer a market for all he can produce at a fixed price, production may continue while surpluses pile up in government warehouses until the government, resisting the pressure, imposes acreage or marketing quotas or otherwise tries to reduce production.

Price stability in the face of falling demand is likely to be most tenaciously held where the prevailing price has some kind of normative value. For trade unions, where wage increases in the past have required an effort, and often a costly struggle on the part of the workers, a fall in wage rates tends to be considered a defeat. In markets dominated by a few sellers, where the price policy of each seller depends on the reactions of his fellows, the price cutter may be regarded, and may regard himself, as an unethical seller. Holding the price line in the face of considerable variations in demand, and even considerable drops in cost, has a special meaning. In part the tendency toward monopoly price stability represents an unwillingness to risk price changes which could not substantially alter the share of the market held by each seller, since he knows that his price changes would normally be followed by each of his major competitors. Price changes may, however, alter the expectations of his customers and make it more difficult to return to the previous level of prices, which sellers may view as more "normal," more "just," and more likely to correspond to the long-run level of demand. To many companies it has seemed more prudent to stay close to previous prices than to explore the actual elasticity of demand for their products at different stages of the trade cycle. They hope to make more in the long run by keeping prices higher in depressions than they would otherwise be and somewhat lower in booms. A price cut met by the others could not change the seller's share in the market but could reduce the profits of all; and the seller is deterred by the market forces making for price uniformity from considering the effect of a generalized price cut on the total quantity sold by all sellers. In studying such markets one almost invariably confronts the sincere belief that the demand for the product is inelastic, that is, that the quantity taken will not increase if prices fall nor decline if prices rise. Correspondingly, charging less than the market will bear during a boom may discourage the entry of new firms, and thus appeal to the existing firms as a prudent way to preserve the advantages of their position.

The extent to which fixed prices in particular markets (or, more exactly, prices which fall less than in proportion to the fall in income) lead to a fall of employment and output in the face of falling demand depends first on the elasticity of the public's demand for the particular product or service, in relation to its price. While the volume of most commodities and services taken by the market shows a considerable sensitivity to price, the relationship between volume sold and market price changes for each commodity and service with each change in the level of national income and with each change in the price of other commodities and services for which purchasers may alternatively spend their income. For the economy as a whole, however, such variations in response are not of central importance in answering the question before us. If the level of national income in money falls, and if certain monopoly-influenced prices are kept fixed, the net effect on employment would be about the same, even if the demand for the product sold at stable prices would at that moment remain constant. If demand remains unchanged, despite the fall in income, the same volume would be taken as before, and the income of the particular industry would not be reduced. But since income generally has fallen, less funds would be available for the purchase of other commodities. The effect of the price policy adopted would merely be to shift the pressure of falling income to other sectors of the economy.

At the same time, the industry capable of keeping its prices at a profitable level in the face of falling demand may absorb a share of the national income which in a period of decline it is unable to spend in turn. Neal's study indicates that industries where there is a marked degree of concentration do in fact retain a higher profit margin during depressions than less concentrated industries whose structure would normally permit a lesser measure of price power.[3] This fact could make possible an accumulation of undistributed profit at a time when the economy was not fully utilizing existing savings and when the individual business might have no incentive to spend its profits on new machinery or new plant. In that way the stable price policy of the monopolistic industry could contribute to further declines in the flow of national income. It would not only translate the initial fall of income into a fall in employment and output, but it could contribute to a further fall in the money flow of aggregate income by leading to further hoarding.

For competitive parts of the economy, where no seller or group of sellers has power to influence price, or in monopoly markets where a policy of price flexibility is pursued—for example, under wage contracts containing cost-of-living escalator clauses—the first impact of falling national income would be different. Prices would drop. The amount taken would depend on the elasticity of demand for the product, as affected by the general decline in income, and changes in the prices of other commodities. There are some goods so closely linked with investment activities that a fall in the level of national income may adversely affect the demand for the product at any price. In such cases even extreme price flexibility would not be capable of sustaining demand. If the initial fall in income is at all severe it would be rare, even in the case of consumers' goods, for the fall in price to stimulate an actual increase of demand during the period of falling national income, unless the public believed the drop to be transitory or at worst temporary. But it could be expected that output and employment would be more nearly maintained than in the case of markets where fixed price policies were followed.

Both in the case of fixed and of flexible price policies, however, a fall in national income would reduce profits. For industries which have substantial fixed costs, profit would fall if the same amount were sold at

3. A. C. Neal, *Industrial Concentration and Price Inflexibility* (1942), chs. 5–7. See also John D. Sumner, "Public Utility Prices and the Business Cycle," *Review of Economic Statistics*, 21 (1939), 97.

lower prices, or a lesser amount at constant prices. A fall in the amount of profit would therefore appear except in the rare cases of demand which remained constant at constant prices while national income fell; or in those equally rare cases where total costs fell in exact proportion to the drop in prices. Even where operating costs are fairly uniform for each additional unit of output, a cut in production, although matched by a proportional drop in operating costs, would reduce the total of profit for the industry, because of the presence of fixed costs.

When profits drop, even if current production is not reduced, expenditures for equipment and construction are almost inevitably affected, as is any forward buying of inventory. A decline in profits will almost certainly make the initial fall in the flow of income cumulative, unless new forces intervene to drive the total volume of aggregate demand up enough to restore profitability.

At this point in the analysis one confronts two utterly different versions of how the economy reacts. Empirical observation has established the familiar fact that in periods of falling national income prices fall more and output less in the more competitive than the more monopolistic sectors of the economy. But economists draw widely divergent inferences from these facts and use them to confirm widely divergent hypotheses about the working of the economy.[4]

4. The best statistical analysis of the problem is F. C. Mills, *Price-Quantity Interactions in Business Cycles* (1946). See also Saul Nelson and Walter G. Keim, *Price Behavior and Business Policy*, U.S. Temporary National Economic Committee, 78th Congress, 3d Session, Monograph No. 1 (1940); A. C. Neal, *op. cit.*, n. 3, above; Gardiner C. Means, *Industrial Prices and Their Relative Inflexibility*, Senate Document No. 13, 74th Congress, 1st Session (1935); National Resources Committee, *The Structure of the American Economy*, Pt. I (1939), Pt. II (1940); J. Kenneth Galbraith, "Monopoly and the Concentration of Economic Power," in Howard S. Ellis, ed., *A Survey of Contemporary Economics*, pp. 99, 109–115, and "Monopoly Power and Price Rigidities," *Quarterly Journal of Economics*, 50 (1936), 456; R. F. Harrod, "Imperfect Competition and the Trade Cycle," *Review of Economic Statistics*, 18 (1936), 84; Don D. Humphrey, "The Nature and Meaning of Rigid Prices, 1890–1933," *Journal of Political Economy*, 45 (1937), 651; Edward S. Mason, "Industrial Concentration and the Decline of Competition," in *Explorations in Economics: Essays in Honor of F. W. Taussig* (1936), p. 346, and "Price Inflexibility," *Review of Economic Statistics*, 20 (1938), 53; James Tobin, "Money Wage Rates and Employment," in Seymour E. Harris, ed., *The New Economics* (1947), p. 572; Rufus S. Tucker, "The Reasons for Price Rigidity," *American Economic Review*, 28 (1938), 41; Donald H. Wallace, "Industrial Markets and Public Policy," in Carl J. Friedrich and Edward S. Mason, eds., *Public Policy* (1940), 59, and "Monopoly Prices and Depression," in *Explorations in Economics: Essays in Honor of F. W. Taussig*, p. 346; Ralph C. Wood, "Dr. Tucker's 'Reasons' for Price Rigidity," *American Economic Review*, 28 (1938), 663. For a useful study of the relationship of profits to expenditures, see

One group of economists seems to believe that if only prices and wages were flexible enough, if only there were no elements of monopolistic rigidity in the economy, there would be no problem of unemployment. Wages and all other prices would quickly drop in response to the fall in national income. A new equilibrium would be reached at a lower money level of income, but at the same level of employment, output, and real income. While the dollar would be worth somewhat more, general economic conditions would be otherwise unchanged. In the absence of monopolistic rigidities and of long-term contracts fixing prices and costs, resilient market adjustments would reestablish a relation of costs and prices which would restore capacity levels of investment and thus full employment.[5]

It is difficult to accept this view, not only because the real world is full of monopolistic rigidities and frictions, but because the argument is not theoretically persuasive. A decline in national income means that available funds cannot buy available output at previous prices. The result must be a decline in profits or in output or both. The decline in income may have started with a fall in business spending. It will in almost every case inevitably involve such a fall in business spending, however the downward movement may have begun. If profits fall, incentives to invest either in plant, equipment, or inventory will be affected. If the scale of output falls, there can be no effective incentives to enlarge capacity; the volume of inventory required for operations will decline; and cost-reducing innovations will be even less appealing than in industries where output has been maintained. Even if one could conceive a frictionless economy, a fall in costs which exactly corresponded to the fall in

---

Ruth P. Mack, *The Flow of Funds and Consumer Purchasing Power* (1941), chs. 4–5.

5. Notably Gardiner C. Means, *op. cit.*, n. 4, above. See also A. C. Pigou, *Theory of Unemployment* (1933), *Employment and Equilibrium* (1941), "The Classical Stationary State," *Economic Journal, 53* (1943), 343, *Lapses from Full Employment* (1945), and "Economic Progress in a Stable Environment," *Economica* (*New Series*), *14* (1947), 180; Don Patinkin, "Price Flexibility and Full Employment," *American Economic Review, 38* (1948), 543. Further, and more generally, consult George W. Stocking and Myron W. Watkins, *Cartels or Competition?* (1948), ch. 7; Howard S. Ellis, "Monopoly and Unemployment," in *Prices, Wages and Employment*, Postwar Economic Studies, No. 4, Board of Governors of the Federal Reserve System (1946); Corwin D. Edwards, "The Relation of Price Policy to Fluctuations of Investments," *American Economic Review Supplement, 28* (1938), 56; Henry C. Simons, "Economic Stability and Anti-Trust Policy," *University of Chicago Law Review, 11* (1944), 338, reprinted in his *Economic Policy for a Free Society* (1948), p. 107; Paul H. Douglas, *Controlling Depressions* (1935), p. 64. A useful and critical study is reported in Rendigs Fels, "The Effects of Price and Wage Flexibility on Cyclical Contraction," *Quarterly Journal of Economics, 64* (1950), 596.

prices would not reverse, and could hardly arrest the fall in output and employment. To restore investment motives and investment spending, both profitability and close-to-capacity output must be restored. And to restore profitability, costs must fall more than prices and not merely in proportion to the fall in prices. For the previous relation of costs and prices, in the case we are considering, was one which produced less than full employment of the community's investment resources.

But there is no reason either in the workings of markets or in the facts of life to expect costs to fall more than prices. At best, if prices and costs fell miraculously together, so that nothing was changed but the value of the dollar, such a flexible adjustment might restore the previous relation of costs and prices and thus perhaps halt the cumulative decline in employment. But the absence of monopoly elements could not do more, even in the model world of pure and perfect competition. An increase of investment is, under these circumstances, essential to a restoration of employment; and it could be brought about not by restoring the old cost-price ratio, but by making it more profitable. Only by such a change could the flexible adjustments of the market lead to increases in output, which might, in their turn, restore incentives to utilize investment goods capacity for purposes of expansion.

Nor could one expect such a sequence of adjustments in the real world of the contemporary American economy. Even if the producer of a commodity has a greater degree of monopoly power than the trade union with which he deals, it could hardly help him, or the economy, in the face of falling demand, unless the relationship were general. It is hardly likely that commodity markets are sufficiently more monopolistic than labor markets to permit businessmen to translate downward movements of the national income into *increases* of profitability. Yet only such an exploitation of the situation, to secure a more favorable cost-price ratio, could lead to increases in the flow of investment expenditure, and thus gradually absorb unused resources into employment. In an economy of trade unions and large-scale industry, while prices and even wages are more flexible than is sometimes assumed, a greater drop in costs than in prices is even more unlikely than under the theoretical conditions of pure and frictionless competition.

Actually, investment decisions rest more on anticipations of future profit than on immediate relations of price and cost. It is this fact which has led some economists to the conclusion that monopolistic price stability would be a constructive force arresting the possible extent of a downward movement in national income.[6] They argue that business-

6. Alvin H. Hansen, *Fiscal Policy and Business Cycles* (1941), ch. 15; J. R. Hicks, *Value and Capital* (1939), ch. 21, and *A Contribution to the Theory of*

men anticipate considerable price movements in the more competitive parts of the economy. Therefore, when a downward movement begins, they hold off on purchases from such markets, expecting further price falls. Prices would respond rapidly to changes in the level of aggregate demand, and price movements would be exaggerated by speculation and changes in inventory policy. Thus Dean Mason doubts whether we should want a "really competitive adjustment of industrial prices to the upswings and downswings of the business cycle," since such price movements would complicate business planning and labor relations.[7] If, on the other hand, businessmen knew that price movements were to be limited by private or public price policy, that fact alone would be "stabilizing." It is hard to accept the conclusion. Surely the relevant expectation for the investment decisions of businessmen is their own expectation of profit, in terms of the expected level of aggregate demand. Investment decisions are governed not by the expected course of prices, as such, but by the expected course of prices in relation to costs and of demand as a whole in relation to capacity, given the expected cost-price ratio. Investment decisions, like many other elements in a dynamic economy, are influenced most directly by the expected future level of national income in relation to the present level. A rising national income is the most powerful engine of initiative we have; prices held stable while aggregate demand is falling could not materially stabilize the aggregate volume of investment or lead to an increase in spending sufficient to reverse the trend in income.

If the decline in profitability has come about because of a substantial fall in the flow of national income, the issue is whether a policy of maintaining prices, by private or public action, could be expected to restore profitability, in the absence of government or central banking programs to reverse the trend in the money volume of national income itself. The crucial question, therefore, is whether keeping prices pegged could lead an industry to sell enough, at a profitable price, to justify it in maintaining or expanding its capital. The most perfect control of prices—for example, in the field of utility rates—would introduce a "stable" element into business planning, in that no one would expect the price of utility service to fall further. But such expectations of stability could hardly

the *Trade Cycle* (1950), pp. 127–135; Joseph A. Schumpeter, *Capitalism, Socialism and Democracy* (1942), pp. 92 ff. Cf. Alvin H. Hansen, *Economic Policy and Full Employment* (1947), p. 133.

7. Edward S. Mason, "Competition, Price-Policy and High Level Stability," in *Economic Institute of the United States Chamber of Commerce, 19* (September 18, 1947), 29. See also Alfred C. Neal, "Pricing Aspects of Business Cycle History," *ibid.*, p. 32.

as such influence expectations as to the general level of national income, on the one hand, or of cost-price and demand-capacity relations for particular industries, on the other. While it is true that no one would have the incentive to postpone purchases of utility services in anticipation of a price cut, it is equally true that no one would have an interest in buying more utility service in a period when demand was falling merely because its price was not expected to fall further. Since other prices fall, utility service has become more expensive than before in real terms. The utility industry may remain profitable, by reason of its price policy, but at a less than capacity output. Undistributed profits, which in the theory of capitalist development should be signals for expansion, can under these circumstances merely add to the hoard of unused funds, thus further reducing the flow of income.

It seems almost a pun on the word "stability" to contend that monopolistic policies of price stability in the face of falling general demand contribute stability to business anticipations *of profit at levels of output which strain capacity* and, hence, to business expenditures for investment purposes.

It was thinking along this line, perfectly natural for individual businessmen and quite unreasonable for the economy as a whole, which stimulated great increases in monopoly and equivalent protective arrangements during the great depression of the thirties. Tariffs were raised to prevent prices from being pushed down further by the cumulative fall in income. In the United States the enforcement of the anti-trust laws was relaxed, as businessmen sought in combination to arrest the pressure of falling national income on their prices.[8] Such arrangements often stopped the fall in particular prices, at least in public. Higher tariffs may have shifted unemployment from less efficient domestic producers to more efficient foreign suppliers. But they did nothing to restore general profitability, because they did not increase, or even maintain, the aggregate flow of funds. Even when they succeeded in adding to immediate profits, those who received such profits would rarely have had any incentive either to use them for investment purposes or, more important, to seek new funds on the basis of having earned them. Yet national income as a whole could have been maintained and expanded only if the price changes led to such results. Finally, in the experiment of the National Recovery Administration, we embraced the remarkable doctrine that if prices and wages could be raised by decree, and enforced by the closer and more monopolistic organization of industries and markets, the course of recovery would

8. See, e.g., *Appalachian Coals, Inc.* v. *United States,* 288 U.S. 344 (1933); *United States* v. *Republic Steel Corp.,* 11 F. Supp. 117 (D. Ohio, 1935).

thereby be advanced.[9] We found, of course, that so long as the national income remained unchanged, the raising of prices merely reduced the amount that could be sold; and that as national income rose, the effect of the increase in aggregate demand was absorbed more by the monopolistic price rises than by commensurate increases in output and employment. Under the circumstances of prolonged depression, when businessmen see no reason to expect an increase in the level of aggregate demand, a price rise made possible by increased monopoly control could hardly lead to increases in spending and thus to an increase in national income itself. We applied the same theory to our agricultural economy, in the form of the religion of "parity price." The government undertook to change the terms of exchange between agricultural and manufactured products. It guaranteed a higher price for agricultural products by direct transfers of its revenue from those who paid taxes to the farmers, by restricting output, and by direct price fixing. So long as these subsidies were financed by a government deficit, they had some inflationary effect on the economy as a whole. As a permanent policy of redistributing income from the rest of the community to the farmers, the agricultural program could only slow up the historic shift of population from agriculture to manufacturing on which the industrial revolution, and the rate of progress in productivity depends.

Actually, monopoly industries do not seem in general to practice anything like the degree of price stability for which they are often complimented or accused. While conspicuous cases of absolute price stability over time can be found, the general pattern of monopoly pricing, revealed in a study like Neal's, is that monopoly prices move in correlation with changes in unit cost, although at a level (during depressions at any rate) somewhat more profitable than the prices prevailing in more competitive parts of the economy.[10] Of course, where the degree of monopoly control is altered—by the organization of a combination or by law—prices tend to be raised, at least while the combination or law remains effective.[11]

Thus policies of price stability, and increases in the effective exercise of monopolistic power to raise prices, cannot halt or reverse a

9. Charles F. Roos, *N.R.A. Economic Planning* (1937); Kenneth E. Boulding, "In Defense of Monopoly," *Quarterly Journal of Economics,* 59 (1945), 524; "Comments" by Ralph E. Holben, K. W. Rothschild, and Kenneth E. Boulding, *Quarterly Journal of Economics, 60* (1946), 612, 615, 619; Lionel Robbins, *Economic Planning and International Order* (1937), ch. 6; A. C. Pigou, "Stabilization in Particular Industries" (1927) in A. C. Pigou and D. H. Robertson, *Economic Essays and Addresses* (1931).

10. See n. 3, above.

11. Alfred C. Neal, *op. cit.* (n. 3, above), p. 134.

downward movement of national income any more than policies of price flexibility. The stabilization of a price or prices—the price of labor, of gold, of wheat, and of steel have all been suggested—would introduce a fixed element in calculations, but could hardly help guarantee that those calculations would come out in favor of investment spending, unless we also knew what was happening to the level of national income itself. And if some assurance could be given that income would be restored and stabilized at a rate of flow which would assure profitability, then the stabilization of individual prices would be of no interest and would probably interfere with the most economic possible use of resources by the economy as a whole.

Thus far we have been contending that while there are differences between the ways in which competitive and monopolistic markets react to drops in national income, neither type of market organization could by its own responses correct and offset declines in the level of national income in such a way as to restore full employment. Some extrinsic factor, beyond the interactions of prices, seems necessary to produce a turning point in the downward movement of national income, or to force up toward full employment an equilibrium established and carried forward at a level of considerable unemployment.

Both in the past and in this century, external events—outbursts of speculative enthusiasm for new projects, industries, or areas; discoveries of gold; effective changes in banking policy; war spending or other inflationary policies on the part of government—have been indispensable elements in the process of reestablishing full employment once income has started to decline. There are undoubtedly recurring and even cyclical patterns in the pace at which investment is made in different industries. Houses and railway bridges and new post offices seem to be built in spurts, which are followed by periods of little new construction. Machine tools and farm machinery are introduced in irregular rhythms. Industries arise and sometimes disappear. But cyclical trends of this kind seem to be superimposed on historical events, outside the pattern of market responses. The decisive pressures from the point of view of employment and output are not the hidden rhythms of cycles, but the gross external forces of accident and policy, of technology, education, and social development, which, since the end of the eighteenth century, have initiated and sustained a dramatic rate of increase in the production and productivity of the Western world and have thus permitted the Old World to be transformed.

An external factor of this kind can reverse a downward movement of national income only when it is inflationary in the sense in which that word has been used in this chapter: that is, when it is translated into an increase in the volume of money income which is not in the first instance accompanied by new output. This result can come about if existing private balances are spent rather than held; if the reserve position of the banks leads them to create new money by purchasing securities; if private or government borrowings induce the banks to create new money; or if gold is turned into the Treasury or the banks for new money, which in turn is spent. Such inflationary outbursts can lead to progress if the economy is equipped to respond to the pressure of profits with more production. There must be entrepreneurs ready and able to organize economic activity in response to new prospects for profit, and people, skills, and resources which can be put to work.

This proposition can be put in another way: the net effect of a decline in national income on employment and output in markets of different structures depends on more than the actual and expected flexibility of prices and wages in those markets. It is determined also by the response of the monetary system to the downward pressure. The ultimate factor determining the scale of the downward movement is whether the monetary system offsets the real source of the decline in income—the act of hoarding on the part of government or business which precipitated the initial fall in the demand for some products and hence in the number of men, and the amount of materials, employed in producing them.

A fall in national income, leading to a fall in the demand for some goods at previous prices, could be corrected by market forces only if the sequence of price changes in the markets of the economy leads to a reversal of the fall in income itself, although not necessarily to its full restoration. Suppose, for example, that prices fell more than in proportion to the fall in income and that people expected no further fall. The case would be approximately the same if prices fell in proportion to the fall in income, but people expected the prior level of income, and thus of prices, to be restored. Then prices might be such as to induce many people to hold goods rather than money and to borrow money (or to use balances) in order to buy or to produce goods. In either event the fall in prices could lead to a reversal of the trend, because the net result of market forces, coupled with an appropriate banking and monetary policy, would have increased the flow of income. This "positive monetary effect" of a fall in prices may work itself out either through the substitution of the factor whose price has fallen most for other factors of production or through an increase in the demand for it, according to the elasticity of that demand at the moment.[12] Flexible prices and wages

12. Oscar Lange, *Price Flexibility and Employment* (1944), pp. 7–9, and *passim;* A. C. Pigou, *Employment and Equilibrium.* See also Don Patinkin, *op. cit.,* n. 5, above; Herbert Stein, "Comment," *American Economic Review,* 39 (1949), 725;

could thus help to restore full employment only if the price falls lead to a net increase in spending and therefore to an increase in money income.

A fall in prices could lead to an increase of business spending in the remotely possible case that costs fell more than prices; or in situations where enough people were willing to bet that the initial price movement would be reversed. In the first of these two unlikely cases the increase in business income might be offset by a decline in consumers' income, unless the relatively greater fall in wage rates than prices were more than balanced by a quick increase in employment. Otherwise the fall in price, leading to an expectation of further price falls, could well reduce the demand for the commodity, and lead to further falls in employment and price. On the other hand, price rigidity attributable to monopoly policy is not stabilizing in this sense. Holding prices unchanged in the face of considerable decreases in demand would inhibit the kind of adjustments which might lead businessmen to increase purchases in the face of falling prices. Although stable prices contribute to the expectation that prices in the future may remain fixed, they do nothing to support the view that a large volume of goods could be sold at such stable prices.

The fall in aggregate income works itself out in the economy through particular price changes and particular changes in output and employment; through the impact of these primary price changes on peoples' willingness to spend their cash balances or to borrow more from the banks in order to expand purchases; and through the effect of the fall in income, prices, employment, and profit on peoples' opinion of the future course of prices and costs. Price flexibility could help to restore equilibrium only if monetary policy succeeded in achieving a flow of income sufficiently high to restore full employment. A flow of income capable of restoring employment could be lower than the level of income prevailing before the initial drop, if prices were generally lower. That kind of monetary policy could in turn help to stabilize expectations, unless peoples' view of the future becomes so fearful and uncertain as to require even more positive reassurances.

Conclusion: A regime of competition or monopoly which had flexible prices, responsive to a fall in the general level of demand, would tend to absorb the effect of a fall in national income more in price than in output. If flexible price movements and other forces created expectations of further price drops, price flexibility could accentuate the depression

Thomas C. Schelling, "The Dynamics of Price Flexibility," *American Economic Review*, *39* (1949), 911; "Comments," Lawrence R. Klein, Don Patinkin, and Thomas C. Schelling, *American Economic Review*, *40* (1950), 605–614; R. M. Bissell, "Prices, Costs and Investment," *American Economic Review, Supplement*, *31* (1941), 200.

by inducing the postponement of purchases. A system of monopoly which pursued policies of price stability would follow the opposite course, reacting to the initial fall in income more by reducing output and employment than prices, except insofar as inelastic demand for its product permitted it to absorb higher proportions of the national income than before. A system of monopolistic price rigidity could under some circumstances further accentuate the depression by permitting the accumulation of earning which might be hoarded during a depression. Neither a competitive nor a monopolistic structure of market organization as such offers much hope, without the help of positive contracyclical fiscal and monetary policy, for automatic self-corrective responses which would reduce the length of the downward movement and autonomously generate an upward movement likely to restore full employment. Finally, the fact that some prices remain fixed or stable, while others change considerably in response to changes in the level of income, might of itself complicate and inhibit structural adjustment. At a minimum, such a combination of flexibility and inflexibility would mean that the pattern of allocation of resources would be altered, with results that might deviate considerably from what people had previously regarded as rational. Under these circumstances, the rigidity of key prices would make anything like full employment unlikely until the general level of prices became profitable again in relation to the particular goods or services whose prices were kept stable. Thus full employment would hardly be expected until the level of aggregate demand was as high or higher than it had been before the downward movement began. This factor could make the process of restoring a level of national income capable of producing full employment more expensive than in a regime of more flexible prices.

3. *Price problems of a recovery*

The second case to be examined is that of an upward movement in national income initiated in a period of considerable unemployment. While the problems of recovery correspond more or less to those of recession, they are not by any means their mirror images.

For one thing, a recovery movement has an upper limit, whereas a depression does not. There are no altogether convincing theoretical reasons why a depression should ever come to an end, and in any case our experience with depressions suggests no reason why we should wait years for such self-correcting forces as there may be to take effect. But a recovery of national income cannot push the economy into producing more goods and services than is permitted by the society's stock of skill, resources, and will to work. The practicable maximum supply of skilled labor, engineers, and especially of entrepreneurs is probably reached well before factories are filled with women, children, domestic servants, and farm hands. Beyond that point, and probably before it, inflation will have lost its usefulness as a device for forcing up employment and output.

Let us then first consider the problem of recovery after a depression. The flow of money received by the public is enlarged, we may assume, either as a result of government policy in incurring deficits, which add new money to the stream of income, or as a result of a series of private spending decisions which have the same consequence. In the first instance this new money, largely received by civil servants or by those who work in the industries affected by the new private investment, will be spent primarily for additional consumption. Some is added to private and corporate balances or otherwise voluntarily saved. The industries directly affected by the new expenditure experience a bustle of activity. They may increase their output and keep prices the same, increase prices and keep output about the same, or choose some intermediate course. Whether the recovery starts in consumers' goods or capital goods industries is immaterial. Recovery in one section inevitably stimulates the other. The upturn will almost surely induce speculative purchases for inventories. As output approaches existing capacity, investment in equipment and ultimately in new factories can be expected.

Will the structure of industrial and market organization affect the response of the economy to this additional income? Will the "multiplier" be higher in a competitive than in a monopolistic economy?

All economists would agree under these circumstances that the goal of policy should be for the increase of income to result as economically as possible in an expansion of output, employment, and income until the resources of the community were close to full employment. They would tend to agree also that for the private sector of the economy, at any rate, resources should be employed in tasks which correspond to the collective judgment of consumers—or, rather, to the collective judgments which consumers would make as to the relative values of different commodities and services, if consumers could express their choices through competitive markets.

The simple textbook answer to the question is that competitive markets respond to the upward pressure of an increase in income more resiliently than monopoly markets. The individual seller in a competitive market, lacking power over the price he can charge, responds to increased demand by increasing output, and selling more at existing prices, so long as his own cost conditions make it profitable to do so. He hires unemployed workers and uses idle machines. He finances the expansion either by spending hitherto idle balances or by borrowing from the banks. Unless he is merely using funds that would otherwise have been spent, he adds in turn to the total flow of money income. Moreover, since production is carried on in a large number of relatively small or medium-sized producing units, many producers may individually miscalculate the scale of the general increase in demand. Each rushes to his banker for a loan to finance his expansion of output. He needs more inventory, more workmen, perhaps even an extra stenographer or a new truck. Thus the response of competitive industry helps to speed the general process of expansion and perhaps by the elasticity of its bootstraps to justify its own outlays for working capital. So long as unutilized capacity and unemployed labor are available, not even speculative buying for inventories can push prices up very fast. There is no motive on the part of any producer not to use capacity, or to resist technological advance. Capacity will be fully used; each producer will be under all the pressure the market can muster to reduce his costs; investment opportunities will therefore emerge rapidly. There would be no private motives for not taking them. Under these circumstances the primed pump should soon be gushing.

On the other hand, the market dominated by a single firm, or by a few firms which respond to market forces in parallel ways, presents a different picture under the circumstances of recovery. As income increases, demand for the product of the monopoly industries goes up. The price elasticity of demand for the product may continue unchanged—that is, the industry may face the same choice as before between price charged and quantity sold—or, as is more likely, the change in the level of national income, and in the price of other commodities, may alter the character of the demand for the product. For goods used in the investment sector of the economy—coal, steel, machinery, and the like—it is probable that elasticity of demand for the product is quite sensitive to changes in the level of aggregate demand, which is the most important factor influencing the investment motives of the economy as a whole and hence the demand for capital goods.

If monopoly industries seek to maximize their revenue, and take full monopoly advantage of the increase in demand, they will respond to the increase in income by raising prices, depending on what has happened, or what they think has happened, to the elasticity of the demand for their product. Their output will rise less than in the competitive sectors of the economy. Their capacity will be less fully used, and they will not be under pressure to expand capacity until the recovery movement has gained considerable momentum. Their profits will rise, but, since they are not fully utilizing present capacity, they are less likely than competitive industries to spend those profits at once for new equipment or new plants and therefore even more unlikely to add to the inflationary movement by borrowing from the banks. If monopoly industries follow such a price policy, they will tend to reduce the cumulative or spiral effect of the initial inflationary spending on national income; profits will be higher than in the more competitive sectors of the economy, but investment opportunities, incentives, and outlays proportionately less. It will take a larger and more sustained dose of pump priming to achieve full employment. And when full employment is achieved, it will be under circumstances which yield a more than competitive return to capital, and a less than competitive return to other factors of production.

In the postwar boom monopoly industries have tended to pursue policies of price restraint rather than price policies calculated to charge all the market would bear. While this tendency was not so evident during the recovery period from 1933 to 1937, when monopoly prices rose sharply—perhaps more sharply than others—it has been conspicuous since 1946.[13] This conservative tendency in monopoly industries has been intensified in recent years by their public relations policy, their labor relations and by their awareness of the possibility of antitrust prosecution. They are far more in the public eye than competitive industries. Their executives must spend a great deal of time and effort in answering the questions of Congressional committees and other bodies reflecting public concern with monopoly power. In the system of labor relations which prevails for big business, price changes and high profits often invite the prompt renegotiation of labor contracts. And there is the increasing threat that the more drastic interpretation of the antitrust laws which has prevailed in the Supreme Court during the last fifteen years will be invoked against monopoly industries which are unduly conspicuous or conspicuously profitable. Moreover, as was indicated earlier, such industries fear the creation of "excessive" capacity. They may rationally conclude that lower prices in the short-run would attract few new firms in the industry, and would thus mean higher and more protected profits for existing firms over the long run.

Where monopoly industries charge less than the market would bear, in the face of rising demand during a period of some unemployment, what are the consequences for recovery in general? The impact of increased aggregate income is felt initially more on output than on price. The goods produced by these industries become relatively cheap, as

13. See F. C. Mills, *The Structure of Postwar Prices,* Occasional Paper No. 27, National Bureau of Economic Research (1948).

prices in the more competitive parts of the economy are pushed up by the pressure of rising demand, rising costs, and purchases for inventory which speculate on the ultimate scale of the recovery movement itself. Shortages develop relatively quickly, since price is not fully used as a rationing device. The phenomenon of "grey" markets appears, in which people can profitably resell steel or automobiles at prices above those officially charged by the manufacturer. On the other hand, profits are not exceptionally high as compared with profits being earned in more competitive industries—partly because the deliberate policy of price stability leaves more of the enlarged national income to be spent for the product of those industries. There is a widespread fear that a return to more "normal" conditions would make much of present capacity redundant. And the familiar monopoly inhibitions against "excessive" expansion of capacity operate to limit even those enlargements of capacity which the relatively low profit rates would signal as economic.

4. Boom conditions at or above "full" employment

These modern paradoxes in the response of monopoly industries to inflationary forces become more pronounced as the increase in national income proceeds to the point where resources are almost fully employed, and shortages of labor, materials, and funds are generally experienced throughout the economy. The relative profitability of smaller industry becomes conspicuous, and capital is attracted to retail trade, consumers' goods, and service industries rather than to basic manufacturing capacity. We become accustomed to chronic shortages of steel and aluminum, while bowling alleys spring up at every corner, and all the stores on Main Street indulge in new and more glamorous show windows and fixtures.

That resources are not employed according to the preferences which consumers would have expressed under circumstances of competition implies a profound waste of resources, and a far-reaching failure of the market as our chief instrument for allocating capital. We are, however, used to wastes in this sense. We have always employed our resources in ways which offend the thrifty souls of economists. Deplorable as it is in a world of poverty not to get "the mostest" product at the cheapest real cost, there are economic policies which produce even more deplorable social results. The problem presented by continued inflation beyond the point of maximum effective employment is more serious than waste.

Inflation beyond the point at which high levels of employment can be sustained at reasonably stable prices exposes the economy to the unremitting pressure of excess purchasing power—that is, of purchasing power which cannot elicit more production but can and does tend to drive up prices, profits, and wages in different sectors of the economy.[14] If all wages and other payments followed suit, the result would be serious enough—a continued depreciation of the dollar internationally, an increase of imports, a drop in exports, and a loss of gold, until we reached a point at which we would decide to call a halt and once more seek internal price stability, or at least coordination with world price movements. And even that pressure for stabilization might be lacking if, as is likely in the modern world, all other countries were led to follow our inflationary lead. However, the purely domestic aspect of general inflation in this sense is the most serious argument against it. All wages and payments do not and cannot follow the trend. Many are fixed contractually. Others lack the capacity to rise. Municipalities and other government units, universities, trusts, and many forms of business do not share fully in the boom. They cannot increase their wages and salaries in proportion to the rise in prices. Internal stresses arise which may threaten the basis of society. Classes may be impoverished while others make feverish advances. The dangerous tensions of general inflation cloud every part of social and political life.

From the economic point of view, if the expectation of further price rises becomes firmly established, people become unwilling to hold cash balances, and the demand for commodities and property may be further increased, at a time when their supply may be fixed or even falling.

Under these circumstances of inflationary pressure, some economists have found monopoly policies of price restraint highly constructive. Thus, in 1947, Dean Mason remarked :

> Turning now to the second term in the subject assigned to me, i.e., price policy, I should like to consider the behavior of different prices in the price system as the economy approaches high levels of employment and output. The thesis I want to defend, at the risk of considerable oversimplification, is that wage rates and competitively determined prices are the dynamic price elements which drag along in their wake, but sluggishly and slowly, the prices of products produced in highly concentrated industrial markets. Needless to say the relative stability of industrial prices is not to any large extent to be attributed to the superior moral character or even the superior wisdom of those who determine these prices. The explanation of differences in price behavior and in price policies is to be found mainly in the differences of structure of different

14. See Wallace's "Comment," Mills, *op. cit.* (n. 13, above), p. 51.

product and service markets. As far as motives are concerned I assume that when business firms see an opportunity for profit they take it and that when labor union leaders see another dollar in the till their thoughts turn to wage rate increases. When these motives are converted into action the effect on prices and wages will depend mainly on the market structure within which this action takes place.

It should require no extended argument to demonstrate, nor statistical material to illustrate, the fact that the prices of industrial products are relatively stable. This is, of course, as true of the downswing of the cycle as it is of the upswing. Here we are concerned with the behavior of prices in the present period of more than full employment. It is not the prices of iron and steel, petroleum products, heavy chemicals, aluminum, glass or other items produced in the highly concentrated industrial sectors of the economy that have led the way in the present upswing of prices but rather grains, poultry and dairy products, textile fabrics, lumber and other items produced in what we are accustomed to call competitive markets. It is not the prices of motor cars as sold by the "big three" that have soared out of sight but rather the prices of so-called used cars sold on more competitive markets. And when the output of the concentrated industries has risen in price the cause of the rise in price is, as likely as not, to be found in substantial wage rate increases.

This phenomenon was, of course, familiar during the war period as well as after. It was the large scale enterprises of the country that gave least difficulty to price control authorities and the highly competitive industries that gave most difficulty. Whatever the nature of the monopoly problem at other times and places, at this particular juncture of incipient inflation public authorities should thank heaven for a substantial degree of concentration in the American economy.[15]

The difficulties of the argument, however strong its practical appeal, are very real. If the economy is under the pressure of a level of national income in money which exceeds the value, *at previous prices*, of all the goods which can be produced, self-restraint in price policy on the part of monopoly industries cannot help to shorten the inflation, nor even to protect society against its consequences. It can direct the inflationary pressure to other sectors of the economy, where double profits will be made in consequence, leading to even more exaggerated distortions in the pattern of new investment spending. It is hard to see what goal

15. Mason, *op. cit.* (n. 7, above), pp. 21–22.

beyond the stability of particular prices for their own sakes is served by
such a policy. Insofar as higher prices tend to encourage the demand
for higher wages, monopolistic price stability could serve a useful purpose in helping to prevent a costly and wasteful readjustment of the
economy to an entirely changed system of costs and prices. But this purpose would be realized only if fiscal and monetary authorities were
struggling at the same time to cut the flow of funds down to the level
of the value of output at previous prices. In actual experience stable
industrial prices seem to have lulled the fiscal authorities into relative
inactivity. They have argued that restrictions on credit and higher governmental surpluses were not necessary precisely because key prices
were not rising. Given the inflationary bias of American society, one may
doubt the contribution of stable industrial prices in this connection.

Moreover, in its treatment of wage increases as a dynamic factor leading to price increases, both in the competitive and especially in the
monopoly sectors of the economy, Dean Mason's widely shared position
is so elliptical as to be misleading except to his fellow economists.

It is often said that wage increases or price increases are "inflationary"
or "will lead to inflation." Higher wage rates are not in themselves inflationary; they may, however, make more inflation necessary to secure
full employment. Increases in costs do not increase prices; they merely
make it necessary for prices to be higher before people will be willing
to hire labor at the higher wages or to buy raw materials at the higher
prices.[16] What is often forgotten in popular discussions of the effect of
wage increases on prices is that wages are costs to the employer as well
as income receipts for the worker. Labor will be hired at wages which
rise faster than productivity only if employers anticipate prices which
will be profitable at higher wage levels. Wages can be won on paper
by strikes or successful negotiations, but they will be paid by industry
only if the general level of incomes permits them to be paid. Wage increases, if they increase unit costs, are "deflationary" in that they would
of themselves lead to a fall in the number of workers employed. The
usual experience near the upper turning-point of a boom emphasizes
the importance of rising wages and other costs in discouraging further
investment spending. Wage increases can be "inflationary," at a time
when a high level of investment spending is sustaining the flow of income, only if the government and the banks choose to offset them by
inflationary acts: that is, by creating more money. Unless the wage in-

16. D. H. Robertson, "A Survey of Modern Monetary Controversy" (1937),
reprinted in American Economic Association, *Readings in Business Cycle Theory*
(Philadelphia, Blakiston, 1944), pp. 311, 317: "To say that price is determined by
marginal cost is always bad theory."

creases can be financed by the activation of hoards—which is unlikely either during a boom, when hoards are low, or during a slump, when there are few liquid reserves—they can be associated with further inflation when financed by the creation of new money. More precisely, the wage increase or other cost increase will not of itself be inflationary, but it may induce the government or the banking system to take a further inflationary step. The wage increase presents society with a choice between unemployment and an inflation of all prices sufficient to make production profitable at the higher wage rate. Employment can be assured if sufficient new money is created to increase the total of income in proportion to the increase of wages. It is important in such a case to be explicit that, in the general interest of full employment, inflation has frustrated the desire of the workers for more real income.[17]

This issue is one of the most important practical and theoretical problems of effective stabilization within the institutional framework of American democracy. Wage increases beyond the limits of productivity, obtained by the exercise of the monopoly power of trade unions, may make full employment incompatible with the effective stabilization of prices and therefore create far-reaching social strains. The problem is not, of course, unique for wages. The similar utilization of other types of monopoly power could create comparable problems of underutilization of resources or maldistribution of income.

The pattern of our response to the pressures of inflation at a time of full employment is by now fairly predictable. We face a third war or at any rate a long period in which high levels of military spending will probably entail government deficits. The problem would be similar in less threatened times if full employment policy were carried so far as to generate sustained inflationary pressures. We have two general choices: we can either take enough purchasing power away from the public as taxes, or as voluntary or involuntary savings, to reduce aggregate purchasing power to about the value of all the goods we could make available *at the prices which previously prevailed*. Or we can cut civilian purchasing power down somewhat, impose direct controls over wages and prices, undertake the rationing of consumers' and producers' goods, and directly allocate credit and basic industrial commodities. We were not willing either in 1917 or during the second world war to adopt the first alternative of paying for the war out of taxes and direct savings. We preferred on both occasions to pay a large part of the cost through the "involuntary" savings of higher prices.[18] And every indication of

17. J. M. Keynes, *General Theory of Employment, Interest and Money* (1936), pp. 289–291.

18. See Chapter 3, pp. 148–158.

policy as we face the indefinite period of tension after 1951 is that we will again elect to finance a major fraction of the cost of security by further inflation.

Thus far in our economic experience the dominant parts of the population seem to think they have a vested interest in inflation. Our middle classes, unlike the prewar bourgeoisie of Europe, live more on profits and capital gains than on interest. They have never had the experience of galloping, pathological inflation. And they lack the intense faith in price stability as a social policy which had dominated middle-class thought, and even academic economics, on the Continent. Similarly, our trade union movement has until lately been more interested in wage rates than in the purchasing power of wages. While wage-freeze policies were enforced during the second world war, we have not yet come to the acceptance in trade union policy of relatively long-term wage stabilization programs of the type employed after the war with considerable success in Great Britain, Sweden, and France.

Even if by some miracle the present tensions of world politics could be resolved, long-range political indications strongly favor something close to perpetual, if less violent, inflation. The most backward politician has now learned that government deficits can do a great deal to offset depressions, and to win elections. There is no political support for the puritanical platform of occasional depressions as wholesome purgatives after the overindulgence of booms. At the turn of the century Sir William Harcourt remarked, "We are all Socialists now." In 1951 it would be more accurate for Socialists and non-Socialists alike to say that they have all become "Keynesians," at least in the sense of believing that most of the economic dislocations which produce unemployment can be cured by sufficient doses of inflation.

That the long-range prospect is definitely inflationary need not be catastrophic in itself. A well-known economist used to say that "coin-clipping" was the basic policy that men have always used to slough off the burden of their debts and get on with the world's work. Steady improvements in productivity work in the direction of lower prices. Social stability would not be threatened by a policy of price stability, even though it concealed a good deal of monetary inflation, if no more were required to assure high levels of employment. The economic question on which the future structure of society depends is how much inflation we choose to administer to ourselves. For one thing is clear: If we undertake enough inflation to generate steady price increases and consequent social tensions, and then react by adopting long-term direct controls over prices, wages, and the allocation of materials—that is, over investment decisions—we shall have profoundly altered, and almost certainly destroyed, the economic foundation of freedom in our society.

In a regime of over-full employment, where inflationary pressure forces the adoption of direct government controls over the ordinary detail of business decision, the problem of industrial and market organization has a completely different aspect than in situations of falling national income, of recovery from a depression, or in cases of attempted stabilization at high but noninflationary levels of employment. In a war economy, or an economy under sustained and severe inflationary pressure, one expects the rationing of goods and the allocation of resources to be accomplished not by the market, but by coupons and government orders. The aim of policy is to keep prices stable—so as to minimize the cost of its orders to the government, and to prevent any change in the relationship of prices and wages on which the stabilization structure is precariously built. Under these circumstances, the quality one wants in markets is not resilience and responsiveness, but discipline. We care more about whether there will be black or grey markets than whether the market extracts the last ounce of production from industry at minimal prices.

With this object in mind, the public and the government will inevitably prefer monopoly to competition, and insist on organizing the equivalent where it does not exist. Experience in two wars and in the depression adventure of NRA is altogether convincing evidence of the fact that it is far easier to control a monopoly industry in this sense than a competitive one. Fixed prices, allocations, quotas of production, divided markets, limitations on the entry of new competitors, and prices high enough to reward the least efficient will necessarily be the order of the day. There would be few incentives to reduce costs under such a regime, and few, if any, of the traditional economic justifications for private enterprise.

5. *Market policy in a regime of stable income*

There is a fourth general case to be considered, in the long run the most challenging and interesting of all—the problem of stabilization faced at the end of a recovery period, when employment is high, private investment is high, and government undertakes to see to it that the economy stays at or near its peak, without slipping into a depression or spiraling up into further inflation. This is what Professor Robertson has called the Blondinian problem, after the celebrated French tightrope walker of an earlier generation.[19]

19. D. H. Robertson, *op. cit.* (n. 16, above), p. 321.

It is not my task in this chapter to deal with the question of whether a Blondinian solution is possible at all, or whether capitalism suffers from too many diseases, organic and self-imposed, to be managed in this way by a skillful manipulation of all the controls available to a modern government.[20] Equally, it is not part of my assignment to consider whether the best course for policy under those circumstances would be to keep the total quantity of money fixed, presumably letting prices fall as productivity increased; or to keep the total of national income fixed; or to keep some index of the average price level stable, allowing the total of national income to rise in proportion to increases in productivity. Assuming that effective Blondinianism, on one or another of these bases, is a possible and desirable goal of policy, our question here is to consider whether a more competitive or a more monopolistic organization of markets would make it easier and cheaper to achieve.

If the analysis of the preceding parts of this chapter is valid, the answer depends on the level of employment the government undertakes to stabilize. If it insists on a level of national income so high as to produce perpetual labor shortages, then for social reasons we shall probably have to organize the economy into centrally directed monopolies containing all the worst features of OPA, NRA, and the system of Gary dinners. Such controlled fixing of prices would be the only acceptable alternative to continuous price increases which could destroy the class structure of society. Direct controls of this type, though in a somewhat less severe form, might also be required if prices rose so far as to remind the American public and government, as the British have had to learn, that a country's international economic position may under some circumstances actually limit its freedom to practice inflation.

If, however, we can muster up the political discipline to keep the national income steady, without committing the government to prevent every price drop or to offset every downward adjustment of output and employment, then there are distinct and important advantages in seeking to organize industry and trade in a more competitive way.

There are two classes of reasons for this conclusion: reasons of welfare and reasons of resilience.

An economy operating at close to full employment is an economy in which the classical economic virtues are really virtues. During the depression there was a case against thrift and a case for waste, if only it was financed with new money. An economy fully employed must balance its output against a rapidly surging flood of funds. It has a vital stake in producing all that can possibly be produced with existing resources, in order to minimize the risks of general inflation. Above all, by solving the

20. See Samuelson's Chapter 12.

problem of unemployment, it can concentrate on the real economic problems of increasing wealth and welfare. Saving is essential, to finance the investment opportunities which beckon to businessmen in every part of the economy. Maximum utilization of capacity is desirable, to keep goods coming forward on to the market in the greatest possible volume. And there is a premium on cost-reducing improvements in technology and in business and market organization.

The theory and experience of industrial organization suggest that there is much to be gained by enforcing more competition, if the goal of fiscal policy is effective stabilization. More competition should enlarge the real income of the community by reducing many of the wastes of nonprice competition, and by facilitating a more rational allocation of resources, and a more defensible distribution of income. Even more important, it should increase the rate at which productivity increases and the pace at which improvements in productivity are applied throughout the economy.

Productivity is not of course a simple function of competition. No one can plausibly contend that small business is invariably efficient and big business inefficient, or that monopoly power in the contemporary American economy invariably stifles technical advances.

Indeed, Professor Schumpeter has argued that monopoly power is essential to progress, and that much of the literature about economic theory ignores the obvious fact that big business has carried out the immense improvements in technique which have increased the standard of living in the United States during the last two generations. He contended that the promise of monopoly profit was necessary to induce the investments required for modern mass industry; that only monopoly industries could afford the research indispensable to economic progress; and (somewhat inconsistently) that the power of monopoly industries to control, slow up, or postpone innovations was a good thing, since it reduced the social cost of innovation in destroying the value of existing capital, a loss which almost inevitably takes place when a new technique displaces an old one.[21]

The problem of assuring society that the most rapid possible advance in efficiency is being carried out by the economic system is more complicated than Schumpeter's argument suggests.

The development, application, and adoption of new ideas by agriculture and industry is a process of many facets. The level of general education among the population, as well as the state of higher technical education in the advanced schools, are conditioning factors. The working force must be capable of accepting new methods, and the foremen and

21. Schumpeter, *op. cit.* (n. 6, above), ch. 8.

factory superintendents interested in learning and teaching them. There are crucial cultural elements in the process as well. The insecurity of American life, which is shared by all classes, is a force which strengthens the restless drive of American industry for mechanical improvement. The idea of competition is natural to a society without a fixed class structure, which makes social mobility a rule and not an exception.

These are the preliminary conditions of progress. What form or forms of economic organization can most effectively harness these social forces in order to achieve the most economic possible rate of improvement in efficiency? There are many examples of progressive management in monopoly industries and of backward technology in competitive ones. The skill, energy, and imagination of management is to a certain extent an independent element in the economic process. It may arise, and perpetuate itself as a tradition, in any firm or industry, competitive or monopolistic. Often, however, a progressive industry which appears to enjoy a good deal of monopoly power with respect to the products it makes is actually exposed to severe competition from industries making substitute commodities. Thus many Du Pont products actively compete in the market with commodities manufactured by what might conventionally be regarded as the textile industry, the paint industry, or the petroleum industry.

By and large, however, experience confirms theory in support of the conclusion that the pressure of effective competition, which gives industry strong motives for reducing costs, is the most reliable foundation for a policy of dynamic development. Society can expect a better return in steady technological advance when industry has a pressing economic interest in competitive cost reduction. The enthusiasm of the occasional monopolistic innovator is to be applauded. But continued improvements in technique are industry's most important long-term social function. It is more prudent to stimulate the quest for cost reduction by enforcing a considerable degree of competition than to gamble on the possibility that monopoly industry will happen to select management capable of organizing effective campaigns of increased efficiency.

For one must never underrate the institutional difficulties of cost reduction. It can come about through improved management as well as through changes in technique. It almost invariably calls for the dismissal and retraining of employees on a considerable scale. In a big business establishment these are strenuous undertakings, which generate formidable resistance. They should be easier to carry out if made under the goad of unmistakable competitive pressure.

One of the deep-seated objections against any proposals for carrying the policy of the antitrust laws to the point of actually making the organization of industries more competitive is that such action would turn back the clock to the horse and buggy era of industrial technique. Plans to cut the connections between big corporations, or to break up giant corporations themselves, invariably confront the charge that such action would abandon the advantages of large scale in manufacturing, and confine the economy to the methods of the individual artisan, perhaps aided by a few apprentices. It is firmly believed, often by professional economists, that the size of many American corporations is a technological necessity, required in order to gain the advantages of the modern methods in manufacturing. This belief survives tenaciously despite the availability of historical evidence indicating that the motives for the formation of many large corporations were to gain a monopoly position in markets or to permit the profitable flotation of new securities.[22] Similarly, there are suggestive, if hardly conclusive, studies to the effect that in many industries small or medium-sized firms are more profitable than very large ones and operate at lower costs, especially during periods of rising national income and high employment.[23] These studies must be treated cautiously, for many factors govern the differential profitability of firms of different size—in many instances the presence of monopoly advantage for larger firms or for smaller ones the protection of a market system of higher-than-competitive prices. As to costs, of course, the decisive question is not whether the average costs of large and small

22. See Donald H. Wallace, *op. cit.* (n. 4, above), pp. 59, 101, and *passim;* Federal Trade Commission, *Relative Efficiency of Large, Medium-Sized and Small Business,* TNEC Monograph No. 13 (1941); Rostow, "The New Sherman Act," *University of Chicago Law Review,* 14 (1947), 567, 568.

23. See Donald H. Wallace, *op. cit.* (n. 4, above), pp. 100–105; Federal Trade Commission, *Report on the Divergence between Plant and Company Concentration, 1947* (1950); Federal Trade Commission, *Rates of Return for 529 Identical Companies in 25 Selected Manufacturing Industries, 1940, 1947–49* (1950); William L. Crum, *Corporate Size and Earning Power* (1939); Ralph C. Epstein, *Industrial Profits in the United States* (1934); Corwin D. Edwards, *Maintaining Competition* (1949), pp. 113 ff.; Roy A. Foulke, *Expansion from Retained Earnings, 1940–1944* (1946); G. Warren Nutter, *The Extent of Enterprise Monopoly in the United States, 1899–1939* (1951), pp. 29 ff.; R. C. Osborn, *Effects of Corporate Size on Efficiency and Profitability* (1950); J. M. Blair, "The Relation between Size and Efficiency of Business," *Review of Economic Statistics,* 24 (1942), 125, and "Does Large-Scale Enterprise Result in Lower Costs?" *American Economic Review, Supplement,* 28 (1948), 121; R. N. Anthony, "Effect of Size on Efficiency," *Harvard Business Review,* 20 (1942), 290; J. L. McConnell, "Corporate Earnings by Size of Firm," *Survey of Current Business,* 25 (1945), 6; Clair Wilcox, *Competition and Monopoly in American Industry,* TNEC Monograph No. 21 (1940), pp. 309–314. More recent studies are summarized in M. A. Adelman, "The Measurement of Industrial Concentration," *Review of Economics and Statistics,* 33 (1951), 269, 278–285.

firms are different at a given moment but whether the industry is taking advantage of all available technological and managerial opportunities for cost reduction. Nonetheless, it is common experience in many industries that very large firms suffer a burden of heavy extra costs by reason of their size and the difficulty of coordinating their often scattered operations, and that there are few if any advantages in cost which accrue to them by virtue of owning duplicate facilities in different parts of the country. The lowest-cost firm will be of different sizes in different industries, and the most efficient size for a producing unit will change with changes in technique. In many fields, modern technical advances tend to be more available to smaller firms than in the past. Both in iron and steel manufacturing,[24] and in oil refining,[25] for example, recent developments permit efficient operations by relatively small units of production. While no generalization can apply equally to all parts of the economy, it is safe to say that we could have many more firms than we now have in many industries without giving up the cost and research advantages of large-scale methods of production. On the contrary, empirical studies in many fields support the view that very large corporations, which often have some of the advantages of a monopoly position and may be able to raise capital more cheaply than their less well-known rivals, actually operate above the practicable minimum level of operating costs.

It is sometimes also contended that only monopoly industries can afford the cost of research programs capable of yielding practical results for industrial technique. Too little is known about the history of important technical innovations to permit generalization; and perhaps no generalizations will ever be possible about a process so distinctive and individual.[26] In many instances, however, the important tech-

24. Testimony of S. D. Williams, "Study of Monopoly Power," Hearings before Subcommittee on Study of Monopoly Power of Committee on the Judiciary, House of Representatives, 81st Congress, 2d Session, Serial No. 14, Pt. 4A, Steel (1950), pp. 750 ff. See also Report of Subcommittee on Study of Monopoly Power of the Committee on the Judiciary, House of Representatives, 81st Congress, 2d Session, "The Iron and Steel Industry" (1950), pp. 69–77; "Editorial Note," *Fortune,* August, 1949, p. 16.

25. See discussion by Joe S. Bain and Rostow, *Journal of Political Economy,* 57 (1949), 55–69.

26. Note W. Rupert McLaurin's valuable work, *Invention and Innovation in the Radio Industry* (1949), "Patents and Technical Progress," *Journal of Political Economy,* 58 (1950), 142, "The Process of Technological Innovation," *American Economic Review,* 40 (1950), 90. See also "A Spark in Steel," *Fortune,* December, 1948, p. 95; Robert Schlaifer, "Big Business and Small Business: A Case Study," *Harvard Business Review,* 28, No. 4 (1950), 97, and *Development of Aircraft Engines* (1950); S. D. Heron, *Development of Aviation Fuels* (1950); Robert E.

nological advances seem to start with the independent research work of universities, government bureaus, individuals, or smaller companies. The great laboratories of larger companies then often perfect the techniques of applying the new ideas on an industrial scale. They are often delayed by the conservatism, vested interests, and habitual methods of established industrial practice. The history of the introduction of the tank during the first world war, scorned by the British Army and finally developed by the British Navy, on Churchill's personal instructions, has many parallels in the world of industry as well as of warfare. The jet engine, the air-cooled engine, the development of new methods for making steel, the technique of television—all these genuine innovations show a similar pattern of novelty forcing its way upon reluctant "big" business. In some industries, like the railway industry, advances in administration and technique seem to respond to the spectacular introduction of competition, such as developed for the railways during the depression. And all too often, as in that case, the response of the older industry is to seek protection against the newer and cheaper forms of competition by legal restrictions on their growth. Thus we find legal limitations on the entry of new firms into the trucking business and into air transport, prohibitions against the use of express highways by busses and trucks, and similar arrangements in a protectionist spirit.

Competitive industries meet the problem of research in different ways. Research in agriculture is largely, although not entirely, socialized in the United States and is conducted for the most part in state and federal agriculture stations, colleges, and research establishments. In bituminous coal mining, a competitive industry of advanced technique, private companies and privately supported research groups do a great deal of work on actual mining and combustion methods, although important pioneer work is also done by the Bureau of Mines of the Department of the Interior and by many university schools of engineering. The clothing industry, and other branches of the textile industry, seem to progress at a rate which compares favorably with that of other industries and draw for new ideas and procedures on the work of many small laboratories, inventors, and research units, both within and outside the textile industry itself.

Even in monopoly industries, however, it hardly follows that society must put up with the existing degree of monopoly power in order to enjoy the advantages of research. The size of enterprise capable of supporting adequate research facilities is far smaller than the dominant huge corporation of many of our major industries. Effective research

Wilson, "Competitive and Cooperative Research in the American Petroleum Industry," *Journal of the Institute of Petroleum*, 37 (1951), 407.

programs are supported by medium-sized firms which do not have either the size or the market power of the Standard Oil Company (New Jersey) or the United States Steel Corporation. It should not be forgotten, as the courts have lately emphasized, that competition in ideas is perhaps the most important of all forms of competition from the point of view of industrial progress.[27] The essence of advance in science is not the concentration of research facilities under a single direction, but the encouragement of independent study by persons of diverse views, most of whom tend to regard each other as highly unsound. In many industries—the petroleum industry, the steel industry, and the construction industry, for example—independent research firms have undertaken important work, often the crucial development of real innovation. The arts of management themselves, usually a decisive sphere for possible reductions of cost, have latterly been invaded with some success by the management analyst and consultant, who offers his ideas to all comers for a fee. The history of important technological innovations, insofar as it is yet available, hardly supports the view that a somewhat more competitive organization of industry would require any sacrifice in the social advantages of industrial research. On the contrary, such changes, by enlarging the scope of competition in research itself, should increase the rate at which industrial innovation proceeds.

On grounds of economic welfare, then, there is a good case for a policy of seeking effective competition in the organization of our industries and markets. We ought to be able to produce more, at lower costs, to sell the output at lower prices, and to move ahead as fast as our brains will permit toward lower-cost methods of production, if business works under the pressure of effective competition, than if considerable sectors of the economy are sheltered, as they are now, behind effective walls of monopoly power.[28]

In the setting of a program for stabilizing the economy at high levels of employment, there is equally a case for competition on grounds of resilience. It should be easier and cheaper to manage a fiscal policy of stabilization if one could count on reasonably competitive responses of price and output to movements in the level and especially in the direction of demand. Fiscal policy should be more effective as an instrument

27. *United States* v. *Aluminum Company of America, Inc.* 91 F. Supp. 333, 410 (S.D. N.Y. 1950); *Standard Oil Co.* (*Indiana*) v. *United States*, 283 U.S. 163 (1931); *United States* v. *Masonite Corp.*, 316 U.S. 265 (1942). See "Comment," *Yale Law Journal*, 56 (1946), 77.

28. See the striking testimony of E. R. Breech, executive vice-president of the Ford Motor Company, *America's Secret Weapon*, Sept. 11, 1950. For measures of the extent of monopoly, see Nutter, *op. cit.*, n. 23, above.

of planning in the economy if new firms can be organized with some chance of success, if capacity increases promptly in response to increases of demand, and if price adjustments clear the market in the face of minor shortages and surpluses.

No program for stabilizing a dynamic economy could or should keep all industry equally profitable at all times. Many forms of investment will vary in volume from year to year, even under conditions of overfull employment. Some industries should expand faster than others—housing at one point, steel at another, roadbuilding and utility construction at still a third. If the general expectations of businessmen as to the level of income are stabilized by the conviction that the government will use its power over fiscal policy to offset major movements, in the direction either of depression or of general inflation, then the flexible price movements of an effectively competitive market should prove useful in directing the constant reallocation of resources required to permit steady growth in the production of the goods and services the economy can produce most cheaply.

Stabilization can never be achieved automatically in an economy which devotes a considerable fraction of its national income to capital purposes. Investment spending is inherently variable, and there is no magic fraction of national income to be devoted to capital purposes which could be expected to be self-sustaining. The problem of the level of investment spending and of dealing with its inherent variability is not merely one of arithmetical balance between saving and investing habits, so that the level of national income remains constant. In primitive societies, and in societies without much capital equipment, the level of national income scarcely varies. Capital construction is the only way to achieve long-term improvements in the standards of living. As an economy develops and matures, its capital needs seem to become greater, not less. Depreciation and maintenance alone require prodigious amounts of capital, and in periods of rising prices conventional depreciation allowances do not maintain productive capacity. There seems to be no limit to the number of industries inventiveness can generate in a highly mechanical economy, from the production of Coca-Cola to the manufacture of deep-freeze units and even more ingenious household appliances. There is no "safe" percentage of the national product which can permanently be devoted to investment without risking "overproduction" and fluctuations. The problem of achieving stability and high levels of employment at the same time would not be notably different in an economy devoting 10% of its production to investment than in one willing to give up 20% of its production to future uses. Western societies, including that of the United States, are now suffering in general from a shortage of capital, which is far more likely to be their prevailing economic difficulty than the hypothetical capital glut against which we were frequently warned during the depression of the thirties.

Thus the ultimate problem of fiscal policy is not what level of investment to choose as automatically stable but how to achieve high levels of investment and employment without endless inflation. The inherent variability of many forms of investment will probably require offsetting action by government from time to time, whatever the level of investment chosen as appropriate. The number of times such offsetting action is required, and its cost, should be less in an economy where prices vary in response to changes of demand in a reasonably competitive way.

The economic reasons which have generally led economists and the public to support the policy of competition are basically long-term in character and have little to do with the reactions of the economy to cyclical forces. Competition should serve society better than monopoly in directing resources to the uses which consumers prefer; it subjects industry and trade to pressures leading output and prices toward equilibria which have the appeal of ethical as well as economic justification; it should give industry and commerce strong incentives for reducing costs and developing cheaper methods of manufacture and management; it should facilitate a distribution of income in accordance with productivity, and minimize both the classic offense of monopoly exploitation and the frequent wastes of monopolistic competition. Resources would be more fully used under competitive than monopolistic circumstances, and investment opportunities should therefore be greater. These are the general economic justifications for a system of private enterprise and free markets.

The ultimate elements in the American credo of competition are not, however, economic at all. The antitrust laws and the large body of statutes and decisions reflecting their philosophy are a monument to our fear of concentrated power and our yearning for a society in which economic power is at least widely scattered. In such a world, we believe, we should be protected against an oligarchy of the rich. Equally, opportunity would be freely open to talent, and men could enter the middle class at their own will and risk. The privilege of enterprise would be shared by all who wished to take it.

These social values, attributed to the invisible hand of the competitive market, can realistically be sought if fiscal policy is used to smooth inevitable fluctuations of national income, and if we follow price and wage policies which would permit full employment to be maintained at a stable or at worst a slowly rising price level.

II. Observations on Some Recent Experience

Section I of this chapter sets up a framework for analysis, but it lacks empirical evidence which might throw much light from experience on its argument. The evidence to test such an argument is not particularly easy to mobilize, since the actual course of industrial fluctuations is dominated by many factors other than the organization and behavior of markets. It may nonetheless be helpful to look back over the course of recent events to consider what the impact of market forces has been on the response of the economy to the great changes in fiscal policy through which we have recently passed.

If we start with 1929 our recent experience is divided into several distinct periods. There was an intense and cumulative deflation, from 1929 to 1932, during which national income was reduced by half, to a low point of less than $50 billion a year. There was a period of stagnation and slow recovery, from 1932 to 1935, during which the further fall in national income was arrested, and a slow rise began. Then came a period of quite rapid recovery, ending in the acute and instructive recession of 1937–38. Beginning in the spring of 1938 there was a period of recovery, which gradually merged into the war boom. In this process the level of national income in money increased roughly threefold, although the actual physical increase in output was far less. Since the war, with an interesting pause in 1948–49, the inflationary, expansionist movement has gone on rapidly and is now (November, 1950) being caught up by an inventory and private investment boom, anticipating a renewed enlargement of military expenditure, which is pushing the money level of national income toward the figure of $300 billion a year.

In the field of market structure a good many changes took place during this cycle of extraordinary events. In the early thirties labor unions were gravely weakened, as the pressure for wage reduction degenerated into a war of all against all. The early policy of the Roosevelt administration, from 1933 to 1935, was to encourage both the mobilization of labor into trade unions and of business into trade associations and equivalent combinations, with considerable monopoly power over price. Although the NRA was declared unconstitutional in 1935, in its application to business it had both a temporary effect, and for many industries a significant long-term effect, in the development of patterns of association not easily broken by the Supreme Court's decision. For labor, of course, the stimulus to union organization, especially that which developed after the Supreme Court upheld the National Labor Relations Act in 1937, has incalculably changed the structure of the American economy. With the end of NRA in 1935, the Roosevelt administration turned to the antitrust laws, and began vigorously to explore the possibility of applying them to some of the major areas of monopoly power in the field of business organization. That effort has now continued, with little interruption, for fifteen years, and has led to a variety of important decisions on the part of Congress, the courts, and the administrative agencies. The antitrust element in American public law has grown dramatically. In fact it has been deeply transformed as a factor in business policy. At the same time, and closely linked to its development, big business has pursued price policies of great moderation since the war, with the consequence that small business has almost certainly made more money on its capital than big business and has probably expanded more in the last four or five years. If this trend continues, its long-term effects on the structure of the economy will be important.

While these changes in the organization of labor and industry were taking place, we have developed an extraordinary and apparently permanent system of direct controls over many of the most important agricultural prices. The system of control is a curious combination of local and national elements, with a considerable dash of syndicalism thrown in for good measure. The basic instrument of control is advance assurance that the federal government will in effect guarantee a certain minimum price—often directly fixed by the Congress rather than by an administrative official. Controls of acreage and marketing quotas can be used where necessary to reduce production when the announced price elicits more output than can be sold at that price. So far the system has not been effective in a falling market. Its workability remains to be tested in the event that the terms of trade ever turn again against the farmer.

This is not the occasion to undertake a full history of industrial fluctuations since 1929. Nonetheless, certain observations on key points may help to define the impact of market structure, and especially of changes in market structure, on the course of recoveries and recessions during this period.

In the first place, the sudden increase in the effectiveness of monopoly controls under the Agricultural Adjustment Administration and the NRA, between 1933 and 1935, seems clearly to have slowed up the recovery in employment and output, by raising prices faster than the increase in aggregate demand. The recovery movement was based on extensive and deliberate government deficits, spent in part through a public works program. A considerable share of the increase in money income was absorbed by price increases, at a time when capacity was not fully used, and business spending for plant and equipment was therefore still low. The efforts of the AAA and of the NRA Code Authorities to raise prices directly, to restrict production, to eliminate price discriminations, sales below cost, loss leaders and the like, and to insist on price reporting all worked to restrict the possible expansion of industry in response to greater aggregate demand. In many instances, it led to direct and agreed restraints on investment in new plant or new equipment, and to actual reductions of output. Thus the cotton industry lost export markets as the dollar price of cotton was forced up, and the cotton textile industry gave ground to rayon and other synthetic fibers. Minimum prices for bituminous coal accelerated the shift to crude oil, and led the coal industry to demand comparable restrictions on oil prices. In many industries, sharp price rises were accompanied by less than proportional increases in output. The recovery movement gained accelerated momentum with the end of NRA in 1935.

The recession of 1937 offers a more complex but perhaps more significant opportunity to study the connections between market organization and the course of industrial fluctuations.

The recession of 1937 has been rather neglected in the economic literature, probably because it has been overshadowed by the events of the war and postwar periods.[29] It was, however, the first serious depression which took place in the setting of modern ideas about trade cycle policy, and most of the new economic legislation in the United States was in effect.

The recession of 1937 was extremely severe and precipitate. The drop in production and employment, especially in the capital goods sector of the economy, was more rapid than that which followed the market crash of 1929. From 1936 to 1937 national income fell about 8%, wholesale prices by 9%, manufacturing employment dropped about 13%, the index of manufacturing production about 24%, business investment for plant and equipment by more than one-third, and all private domestic investment by almost one half. Annual figures conceal the magnitude of the movement, for a considerable recovery took place during the second half of 1938, and in many parts of the economy the depression did not begin until the summer and fall of 1937.

29. See Kenneth D. Roose, "The Recession and Revival of 1937–38" (1947), doctoral dissertation on file at the Yale University Library, "The Recession of 1937–38," *Journal of Political Economy, 56* (1948), 239, and "Federal Reserve Policy and the Recession of 1937–38," *Review of Economics and Statistics, 32* (1950), 177; M. D. Brockie, "Theories of the 1937–1938 Crisis and Depression," *Economic Journal, 60* (1950), 292. The literature is fully reviewed by Roose. See also E. A. Goldenweiser, *Monetary Management* (1949), pp. 57–59; Clark Warburton, "Turning Points in Business Fluctuations," *Quarterly Journal of Economics, 64* (1950) 525, 546–548.

The recession had far-reaching international consequences, as all American trade movements do, but its origin seems entirely domestic.

Events followed this pattern. The year 1936 was one of rising production and employment. In 1935 the Supreme Court had freed the economy from the restrictive effects of the NRA. The government was operating at a substantial deficit, to which business was increasingly responsive. Total purchasing power was increased faster than output. Profits were pushed up, thus attracting more and more unemployed resources into production. Profits were still low but were above the worst depression levels and were increasing. Business investment for equipment was going up rapidly, and as capacity was approached in different industries, new plants were begun in significant volume. It was a period of considerable optimism and speculation. The elections in the fall of 1936 were President Roosevelt's greatest victory, and for a short period thereafter even his most implacable enemies were disposed to make peace. Toward the end of the year a veterans' bonus was paid out, giving an extra increase to the deficit, and dividends were forced in large volume by a special tax on undistributed profits. There were still 7 million unemployed, but people were confident that they would soon be absorbed by industry.

During 1936 the Treasury and banking authorities became concerned about the dangers of inflation. The banking system held an enormous amount of gold, in part representing the political flight of funds from Europe, in part the attractiveness of the American price of gold, fixed by legislation at $35 an ounce. And, as a result of government financial operations, the banks held reserves beyond their legal requirements. What the financial authorities feared was that if the recovery movement continued it could become an uncontrolled inflation, since the banks, by reason of their reserve position, were beyond the reach of restrictive action on the part of the central banks. Thus they decided, in a series of three steps beginning in 1936 and continuing through the spring of 1937, to increase reserve requirements, and thereby bring the commercial banks into a position where the Federal Reserve System could control further expansions of bank credit. At the same time, a considerable volume of gold was removed from the monetary base and "sterilized," on the ground that its presence in the United States was due to political rather than economic forces, and therefore that it should not be allowed to have its normal effect on prices. It was emphasized that neither the Treasury nor the Federal Reserve Board wished to tighten money rates, nor to limit the recovery movement. Their action was dominated by a fear of inflation. They were convinced that booms cause slumps, and therefore that the way to avoid slumps was to avoid booms. They were preparing for a rainy day. Their action helped the rainy day come, and sooner than they thought.

For at the beginning of 1937 the government deficit dropped rapidly, and the economy was suddenly deprived of that support, at a time when the volume of private investment was still low, and private incentives to invest conspicuously weak. In part, the change in fiscal policy was an accident. The soldiers' bonus of 1936 was finished, and on January 1, 1937, new social security taxes went into effect, removing a considerable portion of consumers' purchasing power without compensating returns to the income stream. In part, however, the decision was deliberate. The Secretary of the Treasury thought the recovery had gone far enough to survive without government support, and the government acted abruptly on that hypothesis.

The economy hesitated under the shock. Certain indexes of forward investment contracts paused in January, 1937. Profits dropped slightly. The damage could easily have been repaired. But it was made worse.

The second round of increases in reserve requirements went into effect on March 1, 1937. Although the Federal Reserve had carefully calculated that excess reserves would be large enough to meet the change, its calculations were wrong. A considerable number of banks had to sell government securities in order to meet the new requirement. The market for government bonds weakened, at a time when the normal recovery shift from bonds to stocks had introduced an element of weakness in any event. Corporate bonds, and then stocks, fell also, and the flow of new security issues was interrupted. Short and long-term interest rates rose. The Federal Reserve System stepped in to stabilize the market, but rather weakly. The spirit of the stock market, always anxious, not to say neurotic, never recovered.

Two other events during the winter and spring contributed to a basic change in atmosphere and in economic circumstances. President Roosevelt launched his assault against the Supreme Court, ending the era of conciliation and good feeling which was introduced by his election in November. The country was passionately divided. It was widely admitted that the Supreme Court had acted politically, and conservatively, in interpreting the Constitution to strike down social legislation. Nonetheless, the institution of the Supreme Court was sacred, and a political attack on it impressed many, even of President Roosevelt's followers, as repulsive and autocratic.

In April, perhaps in response to President Roosevelt's campaign, the Supreme Court surprised the country by declaring the National Labor Relations Act to be constitutional, and of wide scope in industry. That law undertook to protect labor's right to form free trade unions without interference by employers. It had been bitterly resisted. Immediately after the decision, aggressive organizing drives were intensified, especially those of the newly formed Congress of Industrial Organizations. Sit-down strikes were imported from France, and we experienced several months of severe labor conflict.

When the smoke cleared away, the basic industries of the United States, especially the automobile industry and the steel industry, had recognized trade unions as agencies for collective bargaining. A new and far more orderly era in American labor relations had begun, based on law rather than on unrestrained violence. But hourly wage rates had risen almost 25%, the inevitable counterpart under the circumstances of labor victory on the fundamental issue of union recognition.

The combination of factors was too much for the recovery movement. The government's budget was in balance or mildly inflationary. The securities markets were disorganized and business opinion depressed. The level of investment outlay was low, profits were low, and the rate of increase of national income had fallen off. The motives for private investment could not withstand a 25% increase in wage costs. The wage increases had their normal deflationary effect, and the government did not come forward with a dose of inflation sufficient to offset them. Investment outlays fell abruptly. The national income began to drop, and in the early fall the stock market collapsed, bringing home the nature of events to a bewildered public.

The increasing degree of monopoly price policy which had altered the structure of many markets during the depression can be traced in the responses of the economy to these rapid shifts in the volume and direction of spendings. Unlike the quick depression of 1921, when wholesale prices fell far more than the level of industrial production, the drop in wholesale prices was only 11% from the peak to the trough of the depression of 1937–38, while industrial production fell by one third. For better or for worse, there seems to have been less price flexibility than in depressions before 1929. The movement of agricultural prices was contained by law; wage rates were subject to the protection of effective unions; many industrial prices were controlled by cartel-like arrangements developed during the twenties and the depression.

After six months or more of waiting for conditions to improve by themselves, the government began to use its fiscal and monetary powers in the spring of 1938. Reserve requirements were reduced, gold was desterilized and public works programs were announced and begun. An effective housing subsidy was introduced, using a government guarantee of private investment, rather than direct expenditure. The economy began to respond to the stimulus of higher profits as rapidly as it had collapsed the year before.

In retrospect it is difficult to see why fiscal authorities were so worried by the specter of inflation at a time when there were 7 million men unemployed, and it is equally difficult to find an explanation for the extraordinarily abrupt change in budget policy which took place. Part of the trouble arose from faulty analysis, part from poor timing, the rest from a variety of circumstances totally unforeseen at the time when restrictive action was undertaken. On the other hand, it proved comparatively easy and cheap to reverse the downward trend after a short interval of depression. And it should be emphasized that the recovery movement of 1938 and 1939 was almost exclusively domestic, and owed little or nothing to European military expenditures, which did not affect the American economy until a good deal later.

The experience of 1937 is an important factor in postwar monetary policy. Until the end of 1950, the Federal Reserve System has been fearful of launching restrictive action which might precipitate a depression. At a time when it was, and is, fashionable to dismiss banking policy as an outmoded and rather unimportant weapon of policy, the Federal Reserve System had received a vivid lesson in the fact that although banking action may not by itself overcome a severe depression, it can do a good deal toward restricting and even reversing a recovery movement. During a depression, business will not borrow or spend money even when it is cheap. Against an expectation of falling profits and prices, no rate of interest is favorable. But Federal Reserve action, impinging both on the money supply and the securities markets, can, and in 1937 did, help to choke off a boom.

What happened in the United States in 1948–49 offers a further opportunity to investigate how much we have learned from errors of policy in 1930–35 and in 1937.

We came out of the war years with a tremendously inflated supply of liquid funds in the hands of both corporations and individuals—a money supply, at prewar rates of turnover, capable of supporting a national income of $500 billion a year, or almost twice the level so far achieved. The impact of this flood of money on the American economy followed the general pattern which prevailed in Europe, with the difference, of course, that our economy had not been disorganized by the war, so that the response in production was proportionately greater than that which resulted in Europe. Nonetheless, the supply of funds was excessive in all categories. The flow of money income was increased faster than any possible increase in the flow of goods, at a time when resources were quite fully employed. There was thus upward pressure on prices and profits and cumulative social strain.

During 1947 and 1948, with a notable political courage, President Truman fought hard to prevent tax cuts, in the interest of using the government surplus as a factor reducing the flow of available funds, or at least preventing it from rising as far as it might otherwise have done. In this policy he was successful until the spring of 1948, when the Congress passed tax reduction legislation over his veto. The effect of that change, coupled with a change in economic conditions, reversed the position of the federal budget in the economy. From the point of view of cash transactions, a federal surplus of $5.7 billion in 1947 and of $7.9 in 1948 was altered to a deficit. In 1948 a very large surplus in the first quarter was followed by moderate surpluses in the second and third and a small deficit in the final quarter of the year. In 1949, after a surplus in the first quarter—half the size of the 1948 first quarter surplus—there was a second quarter deficit of $2.5 billion, the largest deficit in any quarter since the war. There is a wide variation in this pattern from quarter to quarter, due to our erratic system of tax collections, but the remaining quarters of 1949 recorded a moderate deficit in this series, amounting to $1.3 billion for the year. For 1950 a small deficit in the first half of the year became a slight surplus in the last half.

During 1948 also the banking system undertook strenuous and on the whole successful efforts to restrict commercial credits, or at least to arrest their rate of increase. Reserve requirements were raised, and legislation was sought to enable the Federal Reserve to impose special emergency reserve requirements in addition. Consumer credit was limited and funds for the stock market reduced.

One factor, however, as Albert Hart explains in Chapter 7, has dominated the postwar banking policy of the United States. The banking authorities have been committed to a policy of pegging the interest rate on government bonds, which has meant intervention in the market, sometimes on a massive scale, to purchase securities. The volume of securities which they have thus had to purchase has been considerable, since during the recovery movement the banks naturally shifted assets from government bonds in order to be free to make commercial loans at higher interest rates and in order to meet increased reserve requirements. It is a paradox that very few people are willing to try substantially higher interest rates as a means of restricting the volume of investment spending. While interest rates are the traditional rationing device of central banking, almost all the bankers have been afraid of the consequences of allowing interest rates to rise, and the price of bonds to fall correspondingly, with all that might follow for stock prices and business anticipations. The volume of government debt is too high, the cost of government financing too serious, the stake of the banks and insurance companies in the continued par value of governments too controversial to permit uncertain men to take the risks of a freer market for funds. The result has been that the Federal Reserve Board has had to use the rather clumsy device of changing reserve requirements as a means of rationing bank credit.

Over the long run the policy of pegging government bond prices and of standing by to assure the Treasury a low, if not a minimum rate of interest, puts serious difficulties in the way of effective fiscal policy against inflation. The willingness of the central banks to buy government bonds at a fixed price, or within a zone of prices, means that within wide limits banks can always find reserves without sacrifice when they need them to make additional loans. The policy of pegging or stabilizing bond prices can thus frustrate a policy of increasing reserve requirements as a means of checking inflation.

It means that the banks and the public, not the Federal Reserve Board, make the decision to start open-market purchases. The board thus loses control over the reserve position of the banks. The member banks can replenish their reserves at will, and without cost, by selling bonds to the Reserve banks, or their reserves may be boosted without any banking initiative by public sales of bonds to the Reserve banks.

The capacity of the Federal Reserve authorities to meet this pressure will be tested during the next inflationary round of the business cycle. They have already indicated the main lines of their reaction to the problem: special reserve requirements, higher margin requirements, and other devices to hold down bank loans, together with certain rather timid steps of rebellion against the bond purchase program, and some suggestion of higher interest rates. When, in 1950, the Federal Reserve Board began to urge higher interest rates and a relaxation of its commitment to peg government bond prices, even at a higher yield, it was met with measures of violent resistance on the part of the Treasury and the President which threaten to undo the results of its extended and vigorous struggle for more independence.*

* Since this manuscript is being finally revised for publication in August, 1951, it may not be inappropriate to comment briefly on the course of events since the outbreak of war in Korea, a year ago. For six months or more after June, 1950, inflation made rapid progress despite a considerable government surplus. Tax collections outstripped estimates as income, employment, and profits rose. And the government was unable to spend money as fast as it was appropriated. In spite of this deflationary pressure from the government side, business expected an ultimate military deficit. Large-scale inventory purchases, consumer outlays for durable goods, and miscellaneous business investment expenditures were undertaken, push-

While the maneuvers of fiscal and banking policy were taking place during 1948 and 1949, other forces were at work. Our present statistical devices, being historical and ex post, give us no ready way to measure the magnitude of an inflationary gap. Nonetheless, it was quite evident in 1946 and 1947 that the level of investment spending exceeded the prior level of savings and the value of available investment goods at previous prices. In 1948, however, the relationships between factors of savings and of investment were altered. Savings rose sharply. Personal savings more than doubled, rising from $5.2 billion in 1947 to $12.2 billion, and business savings, in the form of undistributed profits and depreciation allowances, increased considerably, although less rapidly than between 1947 and 1948. While private investment spending also rose, some flattening out of the rate of increase became apparent and a moderate drop began in the fourth quarter of 1948, extending through the first half of 1949. Costs and prices rose, cutting sharply into investment plans. Several rounds of wage increases drove up wage rates about as rapidly as they increased in 1937. The net export surplus fell precipitately, by almost half, during 1948, from the 1947 levels, and the government budget surplus, which had been high in the first half of 1948, turned into a small deficit in the final quarter of the year.

Personal savings were not hoarded in liquid form. On the contrary,

---

ing up national income and prices with great rapidity. To the extent that funds were needed to finance these expenditures, they were provided by the banks, which increased loans by $10 billion, or 22%, between June, 1950, and March, 1951. This increase was made possible by an expansion of almost $5 billion in Federal Reserve bank holdings of government securities, while commercial bank holdings dropped nearly $8 billion. Thus, the long standing desire of the Reserve Board to be free of bond-pegging—the policy of obligatory purchases to preserve a fixed pattern of rates on the market—became irresistible. It was overpoweringly obvious that pegging the bond market was fuel for a disagreeably acute inflation. After a violent public quarrel with the Treasury, which was adamant in its desire to sell its securities cheaply, the Federal Reserve Board gave up its policy of purchasing government securities in order to maintain interest rates, although it was still obligated to help maintain "orderly" market conditions. Since the support program was abandoned in March, 1951, interest rates have hardened appreciably—between 10% and 15% in many instances—and the total volume of bank loans has been held almost stable. Changed Federal Reserve regulations have cut the flow of credit for private housing, and therefore the volume of housing, and helped slightly to reduce the total of consumer credit.

Thus by mid-summer, 1951, with the government still apparently running at a surplus, fiscal policy was holding the flow of national income in check. Wholesale prices fell slightly, and price wars broke out for some consumer goods, as changing views of the future altered motives for holding and buying inventory. The balance was of course most precarious, as military spending finally began to rise and a budget deficit became increasingly likely.

they were spent in unprecedented amounts for houses, cars and consumers' durable goods. Corporate profits and depreciation reserves seem equally to have been spent, although perhaps not to the same degree. Business spending for plant and equipment was high in the first six months of 1949, and fell sharply in the second six months. In that period it was some 14% below 1948 levels. On the other hand, inventories fell by more than $2 billion, in response to a more pessimistic view of the future course of prices. The decline in business spending, in corporate profits, and in the value of inventories were the most pronounced elements of the 1949 depression. Furthermore, many changes took place in the direction of capital spending. Net foreign investment dropped $7 billion in one year, while private construction rose $4 billion and trade debts fell by more than $3 billion.

What appears to have happened in 1948–49 can be summed up as follows: Toward the middle of 1948 banking restrictions on the flow of funds, coupled with steadily higher wages and raw material costs, began to weaken the conviction of business that prices would rise indefinitely. Inventory spending, the largest and most volatile component of private investment, reacted abruptly. After rising $12 billion between 1945 and 1946, $8 billion from 1946 to 1947, and $6 billion from 1947 to 1948, the total of inventories in manufacturing and trade fell $5 billion between 1948 and 1949. Actual spending for new business construction and other business purposes followed with considerably less drastic declines. These shifts in the form and direction of capital spending required many adjustments of the economy and somewhat weakened business confidence. The rise in consumer credit was halted. Falling profits in some areas appeared, the average level of corporate profits, after reaching a high in the second quarter of 1949, dropping precipitately during the last two quarters of the year. On the other hand, there were great differences between the recession of 1948–49 and that of 1937–38. In 1948 profit levels were high and the incentives favoring business spending for plant and equipment were far less vulnerable to minor variations in profit. There was, moreover, the likelihood of large public expenditures for roads, schools, soldiers' bonuses, hospitals, and other public works in the background, as well as a persistent private demand for houses and automobiles which helped to prevent pessimism from gaining much headway. The passage of public housing legislation, and the continuance of easy credit conditions for housing, helped to fortify the expectation of high levels of building. And, above all, the position of the government budget in this complex of circumstance was a positive element in the reversal of the trade movement, whereas in 1937 government budget policy was neutral or even worked in favor of depression.

The changes in spending were of great magnitude and took place at a surprising pace. Within a few months the decrease in the foreign surplus, the decline in investment spending, and the increase in personal savings apparently restored something like equilibrium in the circuit of savings and investment, and perhaps even pushed the level of investment spending below the amount of dollar savings in the previous period. The level of national income, after rising more than 12% between 1947 and 1948, fell 1.3% between 1948 and 1949, the level at the end of 1949 being 3% below the level at the beginning.

In retrospect the 1948 cut in taxes, which all the economists in the country violently opposed, turned out to have been a providential piece of prompt contracyclical action, accomplished by many congressmen who most deeply disapprove of government "planning" to control the economy and yearn wistfully for the day when—as they think—the economy equilibrated itself without conscious direction. The government deficit increased and the export surplus rose, at least until the devaluation of sterling in the fall of 1949. The banking system took a series of steps to ease credit. Business investment expenditure started to rise once more, carrying the entire economy along. The new upward forces showed themselves promptly in employment and later in profits, the definite turning point apparently being reached about October, 1949. The recovery movement continued steadily throughout the winter and spring of 1950, prices remaining stable while private housing and business expenditures for plant and equipment led in a process of expansion which before the start of the war in Korea had restored profits, increased national income 7%, and reduced unemployment from 6% to 5% of a larger working force.

Does this combination of factors prove that the American economy cannot remain fully employed without a government deficit? Or that it cannot do so, at any rate, if wage rates rise annually by more than 10%? It is always possible to assure full employment by further doses of inflation, which drive up prices and profits and restore incentives to invest. And democratic governments find that answer to the difficult questions of trade cycle policy temptingly easy and popular. But in 1948 the pressures of inflation became sinister. There were difficulties in recruiting policemen and school teachers, and university professors complained bitterly of their fate. One could readily see the implication of Lenin's celebrated remark to the effect that inflation is the quickest way to destroy a bourgeois society. Full employment at the expense of rapid increases in all prices was socially almost as threatening as mass unemployment. Clearly a full employment policy would not be satisfactory unless coupled with a wage and price policy which permitted a greater degree of price stability. British experience dramatized the cost and irritations of prolonged attempts to enforce price stability by direct controls. Our own experience illustrated the choice between unemployment and more inflation offered by the vigorous exercise of monopoly power over wages.

An equally hard question is whether even a competitive market economy could stabilize the flow of national income, and at the same time sustain a sufficient rate of investment to assure full employment close to the high level of investment spending achieved toward the end of an inflationary period. Will any fall in the level of investment spending initiate a downward movement in national income? Can a decline in investment correct itself by causing a comparable increase in consumption expenditure? Or can variations in the government's budget, and in banking policy, effectively offset the variations in investment spending which may be inevitable as inventory speculation declines, and people base their plans on an expectation of stability rather than of indefinite price increases?

It was contended elsewhere in this chapter [30] that no fixed rate of investment activity was more likely to be self-perpetuating than another, so long as it came close to people's voluntary division of their incomes between saving and consumption. On the other hand, stabilization at high levels of employment has been thought to present a special problem. During a period of recovery, while unemployed resources are being drawn into production, the rate of increase of output, and hence the demand for investment goods, may be higher than could prevail in a period when the object of policy is to stabilize money income, letting output increase merely at the rate of improvements in productivity. Will incentives to invest be as strong in an economy where people expect prices and income to be stable as in one where they expect the general level of income and prices to rise? More exactly, will income stabilization after a period of income expansion inevitably generate too few investment incentives to keep the economy's investment resources fully employed at anything like existing patterns of income distribution?

Stabilization at a point of high employment after the sharp increases of a recovery period may provoke a decline in demand for investment goods, which is greatly affected by the rate at which national income is increasing, coupled with an increase in the volume of savings, which are a function of the level of incomes. People may save more as their standard of living rises, at exactly the moment when investment demand

30. See pp. 477–478, above.

weakens. Many economists feel there are special dangers at this point of turning.[31]

Certainly any change in the rate of flow of money income will have repercussions on investment motives and presumably on investment decisions. A shift from expansion to stability might particularly affect motives for holding inventory, the biggest single element in private investment. It does not follow, however, that the economy must necessarily be too rigid and inflexible to adapt its patterns of production even to considerable changes in the magnitude of particular economic variables. The high levels of actual profit during periods of full employment justify considerable expansions of capacity even in terms of an expectation that national income will be stabilized. The problem may be altogether different, and far less significant, when stabilization is sought after a long period when resources are fully employed than in the case of attempted stabilization after a quick recovery from depression. In such a case investment has been geared not to the rapid increases in real income caused by the employment of unemployed resources, but to the lower rate of increase in output caused by investment itself. The deceleration of investment demand which would follow a shift from recovery to stabilization is only one of the inevitable fluctuations which characterize investment demand and should hardly be beyond the absorptive capacity of the economy, particularly after years of boom. This is not the occasion to examine fully this critical issue of trade-cycle theory. One might remark, however, the extraordinary vitality, productivity, and resilience of the postwar economy of the United States. Postwar experience in the United States indicates that the economy, backed by government fiscal policy, could and did absorb very great changes in different forms of economic activity without precipitating a cumulative depression. The export surplus, for example, fell from an annual rate of $8 billion a year in early 1949 to one of less than $3 billion in the first half of 1950. This shift almost entirely represents a drop in exports. The total of gross private domestic investment rose from $30.2 billion in 1947 to $43.1 billion in 1948, fell by $10 billion in 1949 (to $33 billion) and rose in 1950 above the 1948 figures. In the second quarter of 1950 (before the outbreak of war in Korea), private domestic investment was proceeding at an adjusted annual rate of $44 billion, a rise of $13 billion

31. See J. R. Hicks, *A Contribution to the Theory of the Trade Cycle* (1950); R. F. Harrod, *The Trade Cycle* (1946); Evsey D. Domar, "Capital Expansion, Rate of Growth and Employment," *Econometrica*, 14 (1946), 137, "Expansion and Employment," *American Economic Review*, 37 (1947), 34, "The Problem of Capital Accumulation," *American Economic Review*, 38 (1948), 777; Ernest H. Stern, "Comment," *American Economic Review*, 39 (1949), 1160.

(over 42%) from the low point reached during the fourth quarter of 1949. These are extraordinary variations indeed, when one recalls that the first New Deal experiment in pump priming called for an expenditure of $3.3 billion. Taking into account the difference in income and price levels between 1933 and 1950, the variations in expenditure for different purposes which the economy has been able to absorb without collapse during the last few years are of great significance. They illustrate some of the advantages inherent in the mobility and adaptability of a market economy.

At the level of experience, moreover, there is every reason to doubt the idea that investment opportunities decline in an advanced industrial society. The pace and pattern of technical advance do not follow a smooth curve of diminishing returns. And even if they did, the resources of modern central banking can readily keep interest rates at or below the level which corresponds to the physical productivity of capital investment. Indeed, the prevailing risk in Western society is that interest rates, under the influence of national treasuries, will be pushed too low —thus provoking inflationary excesses of demand for investment funds —rather than allowed to rise enough to destroy the balance between the forces of thrift and of productivity.

It should also be recalled that throughout this period businessmen uniformly expected a major depression to break out at any moment. Their thoughts of the future were gloomy reflections of their traumatic experience during the thirties. Poll after poll reported businessmen as believing that their own orders would hold up exceptionally during the next six months, although they thought that all other sectors of the economy would be depressed. While businessmen responded to profit prospects with alacrity, despite their innate fears of a big depression, their expectations, and hence their behavior, should be somewhat more stable if government ever succeeds in achieving stability for a period and if the public begins to be convinced that prolonged depressions have disappeared from American life. Surely not the least remarkable aspect of the performance of the American economy during the last decade has been the profound lack of faith of the American businessman in its viability.

It is doubtful that a program of stabilization undertaken after two periods of mobilization, and more than a decade of practically uninterrupted full employment, need precipitate an actual decline in all investment activity. It is entirely possible that rising savings could confront falling investment demand under such circumstances, despite the pressure of the tax laws on savings and of artificially low interest rates on investment demand. But there is no inherent reason why the elements which make up any particular trade cycle should be combined in such a pattern, rather than in a pattern in which one form of investment demand would rise as another declined or consumption rise as investment demand declined. In any event, if the conjuncture of circumstances did by chance—and it would be by chance—develop into a sequence of cumulatively declining income, which proved impervious to lower interest rates and banking policy, stability and a revival of adequate private investment could be restored, as in 1949, by a relatively small cash deficit, achieved by tax reductions, or by government investment expenditure, or by a combination of the two.

III. The Legal Policy of Enforcing Competition

The first two sections of this chapter have attempted to relate the problems of industrial and market structure to those of stabilization. For a variety of economic and noneconomic reasons, the public law of the United States is strongly committed to a policy of enforcing competition. Laws on the subject, reinforcing the continuous common law tradition, have been before the courts and legislatures for over sixty years and have developed in formidable complexity.[32] If under most economic circumstances this bias of the legal system in favor of competition is defensible, how adequate is the legal system for fulfilling the broad purposes of its competitive target? More particularly, what should we want to have accomplished by legal action in the interest of enforcing competition?

The concept of "planning" which animates this book depends upon three closely related tools of action: fiscal policy to stabilize the flow of income, the competitive market to direct the movement and use of resources in production, and the negotiations of labor and management to establish wage rates. As Professor Hayek has remarked:

> The functioning of competition not only requires adequate organization of certain institutions like money, markets, and channels of information—some of which can never be adequately provided by private enterprise—but it depends, above all, on the existence of an appropriate legal system, a legal system designed both to preserve competition and to make it operate as beneficially as possible. It is by no means sufficient that the law should recognize the princi-

32. For a comprehensive collection of materials see S. Chesterfield Oppenheim's, *Trade Regulation: Vol. 1, The Federal Anti-Trust Laws* (1948), *Vol. II, Unfair Trade Practices* (1950). Also, Corwin D. Edwards, *op. cit.*, n. 23, above; Vernon A. Mund, *Government and Business* (1950); Eliot Jones, *The Trust Problem in the United States* (1921); Myron C. Watkins, *Industrial Combinations and Public Policy* (1927); Milton Handler, *A Study of the Construction and Enforcement of*

ple of private property and freedom of contract; much depends on the precise definition of the right of property as applied to different things. The systematic study of the forms of legal institutions which will make the competitive system work efficiently has been sadly neglected; and strong arguments can be advanced that serious short-comings here, particularly with regard to the law of corporations and of patents, not only have made competition work much less effectively than it might have done but have even led to the destruction of competition in many spheres.[33]

The American legal system is by no means consistent even in its theoretical view of monopoly problems. In the field of labor, for broad social reasons, the law encourages the formation of trade unions in order to redress the historic inequalities of labor's bargaining position vis-à-vis employers. The law with regard to agriculture has seriously qualified the principle of competition, in the interest of assuring farmers minimum prices. In the case of public utilities, like railroads, gas and electric companies, and the communications system, we have state and national administrative bodies, with variously defined powers over the prices and earnings of companies engaged in this considerable sector of the economy. Apart from these special fields, however, the policy of the law is that the market for goods and services should be as competitive as we can make it.

The point of departure for the legal system developed for achieving this purpose is the Sherman Act, passed in 1890 by a vote of both parties, in response to a social development which had widely alarmed public opinion. The vigorous and enterprising business leaders of that era were putting together industrial empires, which in many fields came close to monopoly power. The titans of the railroad industry, particularly, seemed to threaten the country with vast combinations that would hold powers of life and death over whole regions. Tactics of coercion were freely used. Discriminatory advantages were obtained in transport costs and other facilities. Indeed, in one famous instance, competitors were ultimately forced to pay a tithe to the dominant company on every sale they made.

The Sherman Act contains two essential provisions. It declares illegal every contract, combination in the form of trust or otherwise, or conspiracy in restraint of interstate or foreign trade, and it provides that every person who shall monopolize, or attempt to monopolize, or com-

---

the *Federal Anti-Trust Laws*, TNEC Monograph No. 38 (1941); Walton H. Hamilton and Irene Till, *Anti-Trust in Action*, TNEC Monograph No. 16 (1940).

33. F. A. Hayek, *The Road to Serfdom* (Chicago, University of Chicago Press, 1944), p. 38.

bine or conspire with other persons to monopolize any part of interstate or foreign trade or commerce shall be deemed guilty of a misdemeanor. Four modes of enforcement are provided. Violations of the act are criminal offenses, and criminal enforcement has been used from time to time —usually resulting in the imposition of rather small fines. The courts naturally tend to resist criminal proceedings against respectable businessmen, and, in any case, criminal convictions cannot alter the fundamental economic structure of an industry nor materially change trade practices. Secondly, public officials can bring civil proceedings to halt activities violative of the statute. Civil suits of this character are the most important and most frequently used of all enforcement devices. The powers of the courts in equity cases are far-reaching. Flexible decrees can be developed, requiring action on the part of defendants or permitting court officers to carry out the wishes of the court. And the courts can retain jurisdiction indefinitely, investigating from time to time to see how their orders are being carried out or how changing circumstances have altered the problems presented by the complaint. In the third place, individuals injured by conduct which violates the law can sue privately, without the help or permission of a public official, and recover three times the amount of the damages they have sustained. Finally, the law provides that goods produced under conditions which violate the act can be seized, in effect as contraband. This interesting feature of the law has almost never been used and remains a curiosity on the statute books, although it may have considerable scope in dealing with restraints affecting foreign commerce.

The early years of the Sherman Act were years of experiment and also of remarkable achievement. Save for one decision involving the sugar trust in 1895,[34] a decision subsequently ignored, the government won every important case it took on appeal to the Supreme Court of the United States between 1890 and 1918.[35] In that period the antitrust law stopped the process of railroad amalgamation, which threatened to put our entire railway network under the ownership of a single group. It required the actual dissolution of gigantic holding companies which had brought together substantially the whole of the petroleum industry and the tobacco industry.[36] The example of these basic decisions served

34. *United States* v. *E. C. Knight Co.,* 156 U.S. 1 (1895).

35. Hamilton and Till, *op. cit.* (n. 32, above), pp. 130–134.

36. *Standard Oil Co. of New Jersey* v. *United States,* 221 U.S. 1 (1911); *United States* v. *American Tobacco Co.,* 221 U.S. 106 (1911). See Stocking, *The Oil Industry and the Competitive System* (1925); Reavis Cox, *Competition in the American Tobacco Industry* (1933); Richard B. Tennant, *The American Cigarette Industry* (1950); William H. Nicholls, *Price Policies in the Cigarette Industry* (1951); George E. Hale, "Trust Dissolution: 'Atomizing' Business Units of

as a powerful negative factor in business affairs. Certain lines of development were denied to ambitious men. The United States Steel Corporation, which at one time had over 80% of American steel capacity in its hands, pursued a course of prudence and restraint which had many followers. It won the suit which the government brought against it. But it was so impressed by the closeness of its escape that it has given up all attempts to gain complete control of the market. As in the oil industry and others, new companies have grown in strength, and the United States Steel Corporation now possesses only about one-third of American steel capacity.[37]

During the twenties, years in which American life was largely dominated by the attitudes and ideas of business, the doctrine of the Sherman Act was weakened somewhat in the courts. But despite several important defeats the government gained vital victories as well. And the pressure of the Sherman Act spread steadily throughout the business world, becoming an increasingly important dimension of all business decisions.

With the great depression of the thirties, business lost a good deal of its status and prestige in American thinking. More progressive, and even radical, attitudes became dominant. The Supreme Court, with new justices appointed during the Roosevelt regime, returned to an earlier and more strict application of the antitrust laws. During the last twelve years it has handed down an extraordinary number of increasingly severe and far-reaching decisions, which are having a profound impact on economic life.

The antitrust laws had meanwhile been amended and enlarged. During Wilson's first term two new antitrust statutes were passed, the Clayton Act and the Federal Trade Commission Act.

The general theory of the Clayton Act was that in the light of almost twenty-five years of experience the Congress would outlaw certain specific practices found to have an adverse effect on competition. Thus the

Monopolistic Size," *Columbia Law Review,* 40 (1940), 615; Edwards, *op. cit.,* n. 23, above; "Comment," *Yale Law Journal,* 56 (1946), 77.

37. *United States* v. *United States Steel Corp.,* 251 U.S. 417 (1920); *United States* v. *Columbia Steel Co.,* 334 U.S. 495 (1948). See Carroll R. Dougherty, Melvin G. de Chazeau, and Samuel S. Stratton, *Economics of the Iron and Steel Industry* (1937), and review by Frank A. Fetter, *Journal of Political Economy,* 45 (1937), 577, with replies, *Journal of Political Economy,* 45 (1937), 817; and *ibid.,* 46 (1938), 537, 567; Temporary National Economic Committee, Investigation of Concentration of Economic Power, 77th Congress, 1st Session (1941), Hearings, Vols. 18–27; Subcommittee on Study of Monopoly Power, House of Representatives, Committee on the Judiciary, 81st Congress, 2d Session. Study of Monopoly Power, Hearings, Pts. 4A, 4B, Serial No. 14, "Steel Acquisitions, Mergers and Expansion of 12 Major Companies, 1900 to 1950," March 10, 1950, and report, "The Iron and Steel Industry" (1950).

act prohibited price discrimination where its effect might be to lessen competition, ending some doubts as to whether this practice fell under the prohibition of the Sherman Act. It should be noted that this provision of the Clayton Act, like other of its clauses, has a different test of legality than the Sherman Act. It applies not merely when a given practice actually has restrained competition but where there is a substantial possibility that it might have such an effect. The purpose of the law is thus preventative and therapeutic. It recognizes that it is always more difficult to undo combinations than to prevent them from being born.

The discrimination clause of the Clayton Act has had a curious history. For some years it was invoked, in vain, by the old-fashioned system of retail distribution to limit the growth of department stores, chain stores, mail order houses and other competitive methods of distribution. The newer techniques of distribution had begun to revolutionize trade, and had introduced powerful factors of competition into previously monopolistic local markets. During the depression, always a force which favors protection, this section of the Clayton Act was amended in the interest of the small retailer, the grocer, and the local pharmacist, to help him against the large chain stores, which could buy and therefore sell more cheaply than he could.[38] The Supreme Court is now about to face this paradox, of a section of the antitrust laws being used to restrain competition rather than to encourage it.[39] The price-discrimination features of the Clayton Act have also been employed in a variety of industrial situations, most notably in the recent cases in which the courts have prohibited any system employed by competitors of basing their price quotations on agreed delivery points.[40] This practice, which has greatly facili-

38. See Breck P. McAllister, "Price Control by Law in the United States," *Law and Contemporary Problems*, 4 (1937), 273; John T. Haslett, "Price Discriminations and Their Justifications under the Robinson Patman Act," *Michigan Law Review*, 46 (1948), 450; Harry L. Schniderman, "The Tyranny of Labels," *Harvard Law Review*, 60 (1947), 571. See also, on a related topic, Richard H. Lovell, "Sales below Cost Prohibitions," *Yale Law Journal*, 57 (1948), 391.

39. *Standard Oil Co.* v. *Federal Trade Commission*, 340 U.S. 231 (1951). See also *United States* v. *New York Atlantic & Pacific Tea Co.*, 173 F. 2d 79 (7th Cir., 1949); "Comment," *Yale Law Journal*, 58 (1949), 969; M. A. Adelman, "The A & P Case: A Study in Applied Economic Theory," *Quarterly Journal of Economics*, 63 (1949), 238, "Effective Competition and the Antitrust Laws," *Harvard Law Review*, 61 (1948), 1289, and "Integration and Antitrust Policy," *Harvard Law Review*, 63 (1949), 27.

40. *Federal Trade Commission* v. *Cement Institute*, 333 U.S. 683 (1948). See George J. Stigler, "A Theory of Delivered Price Systems," *American Economic Review*, 39 (1949), 1143; J. M. Clark, "The Law and Economics of Basing Points," *American Economic Review*, 39 (1949), 430; Fritz Machlup, *The Basing Point System* (1949); William Fellner, *Competition among the Few* (1949), p. 298; "Comment," *Yale Law Journal*, 58 (1948), 426.

tated the predictability of prices among competitors and therefore made it easier to achieve the advantages of disciplined oligopoly, was held to be a form of price fixing and also a systematic price discrimination, in that consumers were denied in effect the natural advantage of their geographical position.

The Clayton Act also prohibits any sales or other transfers of goods, whether patented or unpatented, on condition that the purchaser refrain from dealing with a competitor of the seller, where such arrangements have the possibility of restraining any substantial part of the national commerce. This provision has been interpreted quite consistently in a most severe way. Almost every attempt to use a material advantage in one market as a lever to gain an advantage in the market for another commodity has been struck down.[41] For example, manufacturers of film projectors attempted by a patent license to prevent motion pictures made by others from being shown on their projectors.[42] The International Business Machine Company once tried in vain to prevent users of their products from buying the indispensable perforated cards from any other source.[43] Devices of this kind have been held illegal with great frequency, especially where a patent is involved. The courts are sensitive to the danger of allowing the monopoly conferred by the patent for an invention to be extended to an area not covered by the patent.

Another section of the Clayton Act attempted to limit the process of corporate growth by stock purchases. The statute was early held, however, not to apply to mergers carried out by the purchase of assets rather than of stock. This technical flaw for many years made the law almost entirely ineffective. An amendatory act to apply the provision to all mergers, whether accomplished by stock ownership or purchases of assets, has just been passed by Congress and signed by President Truman.[44] In the light of the way in which parallel sections of the Clayton

41. *International Business Machines Corp.* v. *United States,* 298 U.S. 131 (1936); *Standard Oil of California and Standard Stations, Inc.* v. *United States,* 337 U.S. 293 (1949); *International Salt Co.* v. *United States,* 332 U.S. 392 (1947). See John P. Miller, *Unfair Competition* (1941); Arthur R. Burns, *The Decline of Competition* (1936); Louis B. Schwartz, "Potential Impairment of Competition," *University of Pennsylvania Law Review,* 98 (1949), 10; Richard W. McLaren, "Related Problems of 'Requirements' Contracts and Acquisitions in Vertical Integration under the Anti-Trust Laws," *Illinois Law Review,* 45 (1950), 141.

42. *Motion Picture Patents Co.* v. *Universal Film Mfg. Co.,* 243 U.S. 502 (1917).

43. *International Business Corp.* v. *United States,* n. 41, above. See also *Carbice Corp. of America* v. *American Patents Development Corp.,* 283 U.S. 27 (1931); *Oxford Varnish Corp.* v. *Ault & Wiborg Corp.,* 83 F. 2d 764 (6th Cir., 1936); *Leeds & Catlin Co.* v. *Victor Talking Machine Co.,* 213 U.S. 265 (1909); *Mercoid Corp.* v. *Mid-Continent Investment Co.,* 320 U.S. 661 (1944).

44. P.L. 899, 81st Congress, 2d Session, H.R. 2734, December 29, 1950. See

Act are interpreted, it is safe to assume that the amended Section 7 of the Clayton Act will be an extremely important limitation on the process of corporate growth.

Apart from the substantive new provisions of the Clayton Act, there were several clauses of considerable significance. One exempted labor unions and cooperatives from the scope of the antitrust laws with respect to the special activities for which they were organized. While trade unions may be held to violate the Sherman Act, when they act (usually with employers) for the purpose of raising the price of the goods they make, they are exempted from the statute insofar as they seek only to improve their own wages and working conditions. Another fortified the triple-damage provision of the Sherman Act, thus encouraging the enforcement of the law by private litigation and adding to its deterrant force. Still another specified that if a decree under the antitrust laws was entered by consent of the parties, such a decree could not serve as the basis of subsequent private suits for triple damages, whereas an adverse decree entered after a fully contested proceeding was to be given the status of prima facie evidence in a private damage suit. Thus a powerful inducement was created to persuade businessmen to accept compromise settlements without a struggle. In fact consent decrees have been an extremely important enforcement device which has permitted the government, with its limited manpower, to deal with many more situations than would otherwise have been possible.[45]

At the same time another procedure of enforcement was established in the creation of the Federal Trade Commission, an administrative body which can make extensive studies and investigations in the field of trade policy and which can to a limited extent carry out the antitrust laws through administrative proceedings. Its decisions in particular cases are subject to review on appeal to the higher courts, but are treated with considerable deference in court and are in fact difficult to overturn. The Federal Trade Commission deals with a variety of problems apart from the antitrust laws proper. Its position has been much strengthened in

---

Report No. 1191, House of Representatives, Committee on the Judiciary, 81st Congress, 1st Session, August 4, 1949; Hearings, Subcommittee No. 3, House of Representatives, Committee on the Judiciary, 81st Congress, 1st Session, Amending Sections 7 and 11 of the Clayton Act (1949); *Arrow Hart & Hegeman Electric Co.* v. *Federal Trade Commission*, 291 U.S. 587 (1934); "Comment," *Yale Law Journal*, 57 (1948), 613.

45. M. S. Isenbergh and S. J. Rubin, "Anti-Trust Enforcement through Consent Decrees," *Harvard Law Review*, 53 (1940), 386; M. Katz, "The Consent Decree in Anti-Trust Administration," *Harvard Law Review*, 53 (1940), 415; "Comment," *Yale Law Journal*, 51 (1942), 1175.

recent years, and it has become a rival of the Department of Justice in the general enforcement of the antitrust laws.

The antitrust philosophy extends to a good many other statutes of the federal system. For example, banking legislation prohibits commercial banks from being connected with investment banks. Since 1907 railroads have been denied the right to engage in other forms of business, although they had been deeply involved in mining, oil, and other industries before that time. A degree of separation has been required also between shipping and air transport, between air transport and the manufacture of planes, and a variety of other connected types of business. Our laws governing radio express a similar viewpoint, and the distribution of government-owned property after the war proved an effective instrument for increasing the competitive character of several markets. And the public utility holding companies have been reorganized under a special statute into simplified regional systems.

Apart from the general structure of the statutes, and the various available procedures for their enforcement, what are the main elements in the code of rules which has gradually been developed under the antitrust laws?

Obviously, the organization of American industry has many elements of monopoly, and the drive for monopoly power is always strong. On the other hand, there are always new men, new ideas and techniques, and new organizations pushing to break through the neat fences which protect monopoly positions. The thrust of the antitrust laws is to tip the scales somewhat in favor of the competitive elements in American business and to orient the evolution of our economic life in a more competitive direction. What actually has been done in this realm?

In the first place, a long series of decisions on certain key business practices has meant that behavior which is commonplace in many countries hardly exists in the United States. The easy techniques of combination are denied, and those who wish to organize monopolistic combinations must depend on other and often more difficult procedures. For example, agreements among competitors to fix or to agree on prices, or to divide markets, have been consistently held to be illegal since 1897.[46] The reasoning of the court has been that it will not even consider whether the prices themselves are reasonable. The existence of the power to fix or control a price must of itself be denied, since a price

---

46. *United States* v. *Trans-Missouri Freight Ass'n,* 166 U.S. 290 (1897); *United States* v. *Joint Traffic Ass'n,* 171 U.S. 505 (1898); *United States* v. *Trenton Potteries Co.,* 273 U.S. 392 (1927); *United States* v. *Socony-Vacuum Oil Co., Inc.,* 310 U.S. 150 (1940).

which is reasonable today may be unreasonable tomorrow. Authority of this kind, the Supreme Court has recently remarked, can be exercised by the state but never by a private group.[47] This hostility to price fixing has had a far-reaching development. It applies not only to horizontal combinations among competitors, but to vertical arrangements as well. Once a manufacturer has sold his product to a wholesaler or retailer, he gives up most of his power to control the price at which it can be resold. Under the pressure of the depression, an amendatory law was passed permitting a limited exception to this principle, and a strong effort is now being made to repeal even this exception.[48] But the general principle remains. In recent decisions it has been extended to cover not only agreements to fix prices but arrangements which influence price, or narrow the market in any way, or limit the fullest development of competitive forces. Thus trade associations are forbidden to collect and circulate among their members statistics and estimates of future production and consumption, or future prices, which might well influence production plans and thus market prices.[49] And competitors cannot agree to install uniform systems of cost accounting, the effect of which might lead to uniform price quotations.

Secondly, all forms of boycotts, or refusals to deal, are severely dealt with. A recent case concerned the problem of what is called style piracy. Certain manufacturers of ladies' dresses made it a practice to copy the expensive creations of la haute couture for the stenographers' and housewives' market. Outraged by this flattery, the manufacturers of the more expensive clothes agreed not to sell to merchants who sinned in this way and circulated a list on which the style pirates figured in red ink. The Supreme Court upheld an order of the Federal Trade Commission against this plan to improve the ethics of the dress business. Whether it was legal or illegal, as a matter of civil law, to copy dress designs, it was illegal under the antitrust laws to restrict competition among manufacturers of dresses.[50]

47. See *United States* v. *Socony-Vacuum Oil Co.*, n. 46, above; *Fashion Originators Guild* v. *Federal Trade Commission*, 312 U.S. 457 (1941).

48. *United States* v. *Bausch & Lomb Optical Co.*, 321 U.S. 707 (1944); *Pepsodent Co.* v. *Krauss Co.*, 56 F. Supp. 922 (D. La., 1944); *United States* v. *Frankfort Distilleries*, 324 U.S. 293 (1945).

49. *American Column & Lumber Co.* v. *United States*, 257 U.S. 377 (1921); *Maple Flooring Mfgr's Ass'n.* v. *United States*, 268 U.S. 563 (1925); *The Sugar Institute, Inc.*, v. *United States*, 297 U.S. 553 (1936), James L. Fly, "Observations on the Anti-Trust Laws, Economic Theory and the Sugar Institute Decisions, I," *Yale Law Journal*, 45 (1936), 1339, II, *Yale Law Journal*, 46 (1936), 228; Samuel Mermin, "Sugar: A Rugged Collectivist," *Illinois Law Review*, 21 (1936), 320.

50. *Fashion Originators Guild* v. *Federal Trade Commission*, 312 U.S. 457 (1941). See also *United States* v. *Frankfort Distilleries*, 324 U.S. 293 (1945).

Thirdly, the scope of the protection given to trade-marks and trade names, and to patents, in American law has been narrowly restricted by the antitrust philosophy of the federal judges. There is a prodigious volume of litigation on these subjects, and the courts strike down these statutory monopolies on all sorts of grounds with something approaching enthusiasm. One might cite an instance, involving the word "cellophane," originally a trade-marked name for which the Du Pont Company paid a French inventor a large sum of money. The success of the product, the court said, had made the word part of the language and not an indication of the source of a product. Therefore, all protection was lost, and other manufacturers were allowed to call their goods cellophane.[51]

Fourth, there has been an extraordinary development of the effectiveness of the monopoly section of the Sherman Act, which was for many years neglected or employed only in connection with cases involving combinations in restraint of trade. These decisions have given a new start to the monopoly feature of the law and present one of the major issues of market policy in the United States today.[52] What has happened has been that in a series of perhaps ten cases, involving both small local markets and national industries, the courts have elaborated the doctrine that the existence of a certain degree of market power is an offense under the act, the normal remedy in such cases being the dissolution of the

51. *DuPont Cellophane Co.* v. *Waxed Products Co.*, 85 F. 20 75 (7th Cir., 1936). See R. Callmann, *Unfair Competition and Trade-Marks* (1945); Ralph S. Brown, Jr., "Advertising and the Public Interest," *Yale Law Journal*, 57 (1948), 1165.

52. *United States* v. *Aluminum Company of America*, 148 F. 2d 614 (2d Cir., 1945); *American Tobacco Co.* v. *United States*, 328 U.S. 781 (1946); *United States* v. *Paramount Pictures, Inc.*, 334 U.S. 131 (1948); *United States* v. *Griffith*, 334 U.S. 100 (1948); *Schine Chain Theaters* v. *United States*, 334 U.S. 110 (1948); *United States* v. *Columbia Steel Co.*, 334 U.S. 495 (1948); *United States* v. *Pullman Co.*, 50 F. Supp. 123 (E.D. Pa., 1943), 53 F. Supp. 908 (E.D. Pa., 1944), 55 F. Supp. 985 (E.D. Pa., 1944), 64 F. Supp. 108 (E.D. Pa., 1946), affirmed without opinion by equally divided court, 330 U.S. 806 (1947). See Edward H. Levi, "The Anti-Trust Laws and Monopoly," *University of Chicago Law Review, 14* (1947), 153; Rostow, "The New Sherman Act," *op. cit.* (n. 22, above), p. 567, "Monopoly under the Sherman Act: Power or Purpose?" *op. cit.* (n. 1, above), p. 745; M. A. Adelman, "Effective Competition and the Anti-Trust Laws," *op. cit.* (n. 39, above), p. 1289; Edward R. Johnston and John P. Stevens, "Monopoly or Monopolization—A Reply to Professor Rostow," *Illinois Law Review, 44* (1949), 29; John R. McDonough, Jr., and R. L. Winslow, "The Motion Picture Industry: United States v. Oligopoly," *Stanford Law Review, 1* (1949), 385; Wood, "The Supreme Court and a Changing Anti-Trust Concept," *University of Pennsylvania Law Review, 97* (1949), 309; David McC. Wright, "Towards Coherent Anti-Trust," *Virginia Law Review, 35* (1949), 665; R. Callmann, "The Essence of Anti-Trust," *Columbia Law Review, 49* (1949), 1100.

offending business unit into several parts. For example, there are eight large manufacturers of motion pictures in the United States, five of whom also owned theaters (usually the larger first-run theaters) charging higher prices than others, which can show films only after a marked delay. Together, these companies occupied a considerable share of the market. Without an express agreement the policies of these companies followed parallel lines, and they engaged in a variety of practices which the courts found illegal in themselves—devices to keep up admission prices in theaters, to lease films only in groups, and so on. Apart from these practices, however, the court said that the combination of theater ownership and film manufacture under these circumstances restricted competition among films. The companies are now being required to sell the larger share of their theaters to third persons.[53] The Aluminum Company of America, which before the war manufactured 90% of the virgin aluminum on the American market, was held to have monopolized the market for virgin aluminum. While the case was pending the government sold to other companies the aluminum plants built on government account during the war, with the result that the Aluminum Company now has only 50% of national capacity in this field. A lower court has decided, in an opinion of far-reaching importance, that although Alcoa probably does not now have a monopoly position in the American industry, as the term monopoly is defined at law, the fact that it did have one in 1940, coupled with the fact that it now has a dominant influence in the market, requires the court to retain jurisdiction, in the interest of ordering whatever steps are practicable to achieve "effective competition." After a lengthy factual review of the state of the industry, the court required a complete dissolution of the stock ownership connections between the American and the Canadian companies, and certain steps designed to weaken Alcoa's hold on improvements which might be developed by other companies using its patents under licenses.[54] This approach of the lower court, coupled with the policy followed by the government in selling the bulk of its wartime aluminum plants to independent companies, has transformed the structure of the American aluminum industry. At the other extreme, the monopoly section of the act has been used against a man who happened to be the only manufacturer in the United States of a certain type of rugs made of linen. A customer wished to buy his product in order to be able to compete with

53. *United States* v. *Paramount Pictures, Inc.*, 85 F. Supp. 881 (S.D. N.Y., 1949).

54. *United States* v. *Aluminum Co. of America*, 91 F. Supp. 333 (S.D. N.Y., 1950). See Rostow, "Problems of Size and Integration," in Commerce Clearing House, *Business under Federal Antitrust Laws* (1951), 117; "Comment," *Yale Law Journal, 60* (1951), 294.

him for a government contract. He refused to sell, so as to bid alone for the contract. He was held guilty in a criminal proceeding.[55]

What has happened in this cycle of decisions is the creation of a doctrine which threatens the existing structure of many large industries in the United States. In many fields two or three or four big companies occupy dominant market positions. Between them they produce 60% or 70% of the particular product. They follow each other's prices out of self-interest and without overt agreement. Each one knows that any move on his part would provoke a response from the others and that a price cut could not change his share of the market. Hence, prevailing policies in such markets are those of price leadership, on the one hand, and advertising and other marketing efforts, on the other. There is competition, not through price reductions, but through increases in cost. Each seller has an equal distaste for what he calls "cut-throat competition," an equal interest in the policy of "live and let live." When an industry is organized in this way, price, output, and opportunities to enter the field are akin to those which would obtain under conditions of monopoly. Sometimes, indeed, costs—notably selling costs—may be higher than in cases of pure monopoly. The necessary consequence of the market structure is that the dominant large companies, if they have a decent regard for their own interests, will act as if they had combined, even though their officers may never have talked to each other, even on the phone or the golf course. The market power of the dominant group is used collectively—pooled, in fact, for price purposes.

The open question now is whether the Supreme Court without more evidence of direct agreement, would on such a basis order the dissolution of the large firms of a basic industry. Its recent cases have emphasized market power, defined as influence over price, as the dominant factor in the offence under the antitrust laws, and have more and more consistently ignored evidence of ruthless, predatory, or coercive behavior of the type once given great prominence. Where power over price is held by a single firm, or by an open combination, the result is clear. Whether the act extends also to cases where market power is shared by a small group, whose influence is used in common to avoid price competition, is still not fully settled, although recent decisions to this effect have raised considerable concern.

What has been accomplished by these efforts to enforce the antitrust laws? Are they a façade for monopoly? Do they or can they be made to embody an adequate conception of policy on which society can rely to seek effective performance by the market of its economic functions?

55. *United States* v. *Klearflax Linen Looms, Inc.,* 63 F. Supp. 32 (D. Minn., 1945).

The antitrust laws are a serious subject. They have not been a façade for monopoly. Despite notable weaknesses in certain areas of antitrust law doctrine, particularly those affecting the process of merger, the influence of the antitrust laws on the organization of American business has been profound and important. The structure of industry has enormous historical momentum. The antitrust laws cannot work a revolution, but they can and do help to guide the development of industry and commerce in a more competitive direction.

The antitrust laws are to a considerable extent self-enforcing. As the courts clarify point after point, businessmen and their lawyers respond to a marked degree in their own decisions. Such a response would probably not occur except in the shadow of possible action by the government, or of private damage suits, which sometimes result in judgments of millions of dollars. It is too much to expect human beings to give up monopoly profits for the abstract pleasure of obeying a rather ambiguous law, subject to conflicting interpretation. There must be some real possibility of enforcement before voluntary compliance can be expected. The effect of the antitrust laws on business practice cannot be measured statistically, but it is nonetheless a reality. One might call attention in this context to the testimony of a business organization, the trade association of the American Machinery Industry, which has recently remarked:

> It has become fashionable in some quarters to disparage the influence of the anti-trust laws in the United States, or even to write them off as completely ineffectual. In our judgment this is a grievous error, as the experience of Britain without such legislation strongly attests. It is true that the interpretation and enforcement of anti-trust policy has been halting and inadequate. It is true that unfair application or administration of anti-trust laws is possible. It is true also that many fish escape the net. Yet no one familiar with the climate of American business can fail to sense the pervasive influence of anti-trust policy, which floats—to quote a phrase of the late Justice Holmes—like "a brooding omnipresence in the sky." Whatever its defects, it has helped to save American industry, by and large, from the gross and rampant restrictionism now afflicting Great Britain, certainly no mean achievement.[56]

American businessmen who have been in Europe since the war, either on private or public business, have uniformly come away with a renewed appreciation of the American antitrust laws. Their reaction is significant

---

56. William F. Yelverton and George Terborgh, *Technological Stagnation in Great Britain* (Machinery and Allied Products Institute, 1948), p. 65.

evidence of the part which the antitrust laws play in the complex cultural phenomenon of American business drive.

The purposes of the Sherman Act have not been fully realized in our economic life. Its history is one of futility and half-measures, of gallant attempts, occasional victories, frequent retreats, of false starts, and missed opportunities. Above all, it is a history marked by the absence of any planned and systematic effort to gain the basic strategic ends of the statute. Cases are brought piecemeal, in response to the pressure of complaints or the political winds.

To guide the evolution of industry and commerce in a more competitive direction is one of the vital jobs of American democracy. It cannot be done without the support of the courts. But it cannot be done by the courts alone. Our chances of materially increasing the degree of competition in the economy at large depend on the ability of the Department of Justice and the Federal Trade Commission to conceive and carry out imaginative programs of enforcement. Commodities, concentrations of power, and market practices should be selected for litigation in order of their priority, on the basis of a dynamic analysis of the way in which the economy actually works. We can expect worth-while results from our investment in the antitrust laws only if they are directed against targets of general importance to the economy as a whole.

Even if the application of the antitrust laws were planned systematically to carry out the implications of their history, would they provide a suitable economic policy for the organization of unregulated markets? How much competition do we want to prevail in industrial markets, assuming that we follow fiscal and wage policies which permit us even to contemplate the luxury of unregulated freedom in business affairs?

Clearly what the textbooks call pure or perfect competition is not a practicable goal of policy in many areas of American industry. We could come close to a great deal of competition—perhaps even perfect competition—in industries like bituminous coal, lumber, women's clothes, and many other consumers' goods and service industries. Pure monopoly situations, on the other hand, are comparatively rare in American business, especially if competing products are taken into account. But there is a wide range of business where the dominant size of one or two sellers in a market, the small number of sellers, or the effective combination of larger numbers for price purposes present important problems of public policy.

There are many strands in the pattern of the antitrust laws. Recently a good deal of the government's energy in this field has been devoted to protecting older procedures of distribution in many industries against the competitive pressure of chain stores and other mass distribution techniques. Business pricing practices, particularly with regard to discounts of all kinds, have been subjected to rigid scrutiny in the interest both of preventing the development of monopoly power and of shielding smaller business against change. There are also important groups of cases directed against specific trade practices, like boycotts or divisions of the market, and a comprehensive literature on the relationship between the antitrust law and patents, copyrights, trade-marks and trade names.

The central themes in antitrust law, however, concern the idea of market power. It is this concept which animates many of the detailed applications of antitrust law in the setting of particular problems or trade practices. The strong historical trend of the courts in interpreting the antitrust laws has been to equate violation of the law with the existence of a substantial degree of market power—whether held by one seller or a group in combination.

In viewing "market power" for purposes of the antitrust laws, the courts generally consider two factors: power over price and power to control the entry or growth of competing firms in an industry. They are, of course, closely related themes, both in law and in economics. It is hard to retain monopolistic power over price unless one has considerable assurance of protection against the entry of new rivals or the expansion of existing ones. In examining these related problems of market power, the courts have undertaken more and more direct and adequate economic examination of market forces and factors. Correspondingly, they have devoted less attention to elements of coercion or predatory action directly injurious to individuals, although such facts were formerly prominent in many kinds of antitrust litigation. At the present time facts reflecting abusive or coercive behavior are important in antitrust cases only in situations where the defendants lack the substantial degree of market power which the courts will regard as violative of the law. In such cases it is necessary to prove from their behavior that they have a "specific intent" to acquire a prohibited degree of monopoly power.[57] For the law makes it an offense not only to restrain or to monopolize trade but to attempt either feat.

While economists have generally welcomed this development in antitrust philosophy, as tending to bring legal and economic criteria of monopoly closer together, they have expressed concern as to the possibly revolutionary application of the newer doctrine to penalize progressive and effective monopoly industries.[58] Since it is clear that a considerable

57. See *United States* v. *Columbia Steel Co.,* 334 U.S. 495 (1948).
58. Edward S. Mason, "Current Status of the Monopoly Problem in the United States," *Harvard Law Review,* 62 (1949), 1265; David McC. Wright, *op. cit.*

number of markets of great economic importance are in fact dominated by a few sellers, who may often act together even without express agreement, the contemporary formulation of antitrust ideas might result in a program of enforcement which would not discriminate between dynamic and reactionary monopoly situations. Hence there have been several attempts to set out useful criteria of "workable" and of "progressive" competition or monopoly, with the view to guiding both the economic analysis and evaluation of markets and the application of the antitrust laws.[59]

The logic of the antitrust laws, as it has evolved in the opinions of the Supreme Court, rests on the famous "rule of reason"—that only unreasonable restraints of trade are illegal. In its first opinion announcing this principle, however, the court made it plain that combinations or other arrangements with power over price were "conclusively presumed" to be illegal.[60] This was, in fact, the common law view. In a related form, Coke says, it was the "ancient law before the conquest" for "Every practise or device by act, conspiracy, words or news, to inhaunce the price of victuals or other merchandize, was punishable by law." [61] In 1758 Lord Mansfield stated the common law position in these terms, the case concerning the legality of a contract among salt producers fixing their prices:

> If any agreement was made to fix the price of salt, or any other necessary of life (which salt emphatically was), by people dealing in that commodity, the court would be glad to lay hold of an opportunity . . . to shew their sense of the crime; and that at what rate soever the price was fixed, high or low, made no difference, for all such agreements were of bad consequence, and ought to be discountenanced.[62]

(n. 52, above), p. 665; M. A. Adelman, "Effective Competition and the Anti-Trust Laws," *op. cit.* (n. 39, above), p. 1289, "Integration and Anti-Trust Policy," *op. cit.* (n. 39, above), p. 27; George E. Hale, "Vertical Integration," *Columbia Law Review,* 49 (1949), 921, "Diversification: Impact of Monopoly Policy upon Multi-Product Firms," *University of Pennsylvania Law Review,* 98 (1950), 320.

59. For the clearest statement of criteria of "progressive monopoly" as distinguished from "workable competition" see Mason, n. 58, above. Definitions of workable competition are discussed in J. M. Clark, "Toward a Concept of Workable Competition," *American Economic Review,* 30 (1940), 241; George J. Stigler, "Extent and Bases of Monopoly," *American Economic Review, Supplement,* 32 (1942), 2; Corwin D. Edwards, *op. cit.* (n. 23 above), pp. 9 ff.; Jesse W. Markham, "An Alternative Approach to the Concept of Workable Competition," *American Economic Review,* 40 (1950), 349.

60. *Standard Oil Co. of New Jersey* v. *United States,* 221 U.S. 1, 65 (1911).

61. 3d. Inst., c. 89.

62. *Rex* v. *Norris,* 2 Keny. 300 (1758).

In modern cases the same attitude has been strongly restated. As was pointed out above, power over price is illegal "per se," without further inquiry into its reasonableness, since price, "the central nervous system of the economy," could not be privately controlled.[63] The courts could not keep the exercise of such power under continuous review. Prices which were set at a low figure today might be outrageous tomorrow, if private individuals kept the power to do so. The courts could not make distinctions between "good" and "bad" trusts in this sense. The existence of power over price had to be condemned. And the same reasoning has been applied where the market problem was reviewed from the point of view of excluding competitors. The existence of a power to control the opportunities of competitors is illegal under the antitrust laws, we are told, without further inquiry into the ways in which it was used at a particular time.[64]

As the law develops from case to case, it will define more clearly the degree of power over price or opportunity which the various provisions of the antitrust laws condemn. In this process, the economists' conception of "workable competition" should prove useful. For the law is aiming at a practical goal, and it will surely cut both its doctrine and its remedies to the underlying factual imperatives of each situation—geography, technology, and market structure.

Should the courts go further and undertake an evaluation of business performance as a criterion of illegality under the antitrust laws? Should the statutes be broadened to require the courts to do so? Should the enforcement agencies take considerations of this order into account in deciding which cases to bring? Several students have recently suggested that a monopolistic price structure should not be considered a sufficient criterion of illegality under the antitrust laws, nor an "effectively" or "workably" competitive market structure a sufficient goal of antitrust action. Despite the difficulties of testing and judgment involved, they would have the enforcement agencies, and perhaps even the courts, examine the adequacy and progressiveness of business performance before bringing and deciding antitrust cases.

While considerations of the progressiveness of business performance should certainly be given weight by the Federal Trade Commission and the Department of Justice in deciding which cases to bring, a broadening of the concept of illegality in the courts to require the judges to measure adequacy of business performance, as well as the existence of a prohibited degree of power over price, would present immense disad-

63. *United States* v. *Socony-Vacuum Oil Co.*, 310 U.S. 150, 226, following discussion, pp. 210–228 (1940).

64. *American Tobacco Co.* v. *United States*, 328 U.S. 781 (1946).

vantages. It would require the courts to consider not only such issues as the number, size, and relationships of sellers; their share of market capacity and of sales; conditions affecting the entry of new firms and the growth of existing firms; and the way in which prices are formed in the market but also the far more difficult problems of evaluating the performance of the industry: whether it has pursued a progressive policy in technique; whether its price policy has imaginatively explored the possibility of increasing sales by reducing prices; whether production was carried on in units and in places which permitted costs to be minimized; whether selling costs were excessive and wasteful; and whether the price policy of the industry made permanent unused capacity likely. Such an approach would make the antitrust laws all but unmanageable, for it would burden the courts with a vast load of intangible evidence, which could hardly be digested even within the present limits of big antitrust cases.

The theory of the antitrust laws has been that unregulated markets, and not the federal courts, are our main social institutions for allocating resources and guiding production. Markets are presumed to be capable of performing that function satisfactorily if they are at least effectively or workably competitive in structure: that is, if there are a sufficient number of buyers and sellers; if no one of them, nor the whole group in combination, has a decisive share of the market, taking its working structure into account; if the entry of new firms is possible; and if sellers have not combined for price purposes. The further application of the idea of "effective competition" in this sense offers ample scope for discrimination among cases of monopoly power without taking the further step of evaluating the "progressiveness" of an industry's performance. So far, the law has put its emphasis on competition as the driving force on which we depend for the progressive performance by business of its economic duties to society. Adopting criteria of actual performance would deeply alter that view. It would require the courts and administrative agencies to maintain a continuous oversight not only over the structure of markets but over the policy pursued by business. It would substitute administrative and judicial judgment for the competitive market and the decisions of businessmen in directing the course of business policy throughout the economy. The political and sociological implications of such a course would be formidable. We should have abandoned reliance on the market as our chief agency of social control in this area. Quite apart from the technical difficulties of proof involved, the safer course would seem to be to continue to move gradually toward a more competitive orientation of the economy and to rely mainly on competition as an inducement for progressive price and investment policy in business, and as a cumulative influence leading to a wider dispersal of economic power in society.

There is a further objection to adding a criterion of progressive performance to the administration of the antitrust laws. Even if the courts could effectively discriminate between "good" and "bad" monopolies, and see to it over long periods of time that the "good" trusts remained "good," such a principle would have an adverse effect on the opportunities of new firms to enter effectively monopolized fields. As the recent history of the automobile industry attests, progressively administered monopoly would foreclose opportunity even more completely than backward and inefficient monopolies, whose high prices and out-of-date techniques would often invite the entry of new firms. The entry of new firms under these circumstances would not always represent the most economic possible use of resources. But it would at least offer a counterbalance of some significance to the indefinite perpetuation of monopoly power.

The antitrust laws are not purely or even primarily economic in motivation. Their historic goal is social and political as well as economic. They aim to keep economic opportunity open for its own sake, as a means of assuring the community a large and broadly based middle class, which could recruit new members freely and steadily from all parts of the population. The process of social mobility in this sense is one of the most vital forces on which the continued development of the American culture depends. It is as important to our future, perhaps more important, than achieving a maximum of efficiency in the use of resources at any given moment.

The idea of workable competition as a test for enforcing the antitrust laws is at the beginning of its detailed development. There is no risk, so long as the Supreme Court sits, that it will be applied in a violent or destructive way. The doctrine requires a practical discrimination among situations of mild and of aggravated monopoly power. This is not an impossible task for the courts. Most legal distinctions are distinctions of degree, rather than of kind, and the new antitrust test of effective competition is no exception. Its purpose is not to eliminate all big business in the United States, nor to atomize American industry into family-sized factories. Rather it foreshadows situations in which it would be difficult over periods of time for considerable degrees of monopoly power to be perpetuated. It is most likely in application to favor the appearance of industries in which four or five relatively big firms compete with a dozen or so smaller ones, the big firms operating rather independently in a market which cannot readily be stabilized or kept under rigid discipline. By maintaining the pressure of competition on big and small business, the antitrust laws should be a force in the direction of maintaining incentives for cost reduction and for prices which reflect reductions in cost.

The steady development and exploitation of cost-reducing possibilities, both in technique and in management, are the most important economic tasks of business. The vigorous enforcement of a public policy favoring competition cannot guarantee efficient and progressive business management. In the final analysis, steady improvements in productivity are the job of management and labor together. But the law will have accomplished a good deal by maximizing incentives for seeking improvements in productivity, both on the part of business and of labor.

For the role of labor in this process should never be underestimated. Competition in business is one of the most important and effective limits on the monopoly power of trade unions. Professor Lindblom, in Chapter 11 of this book, discusses the widespread concern of many students with the wage policies pursued by trade unions. Some fear that the continued development of free trade unions threatens the future of capitalism. But trade union wage policy does often take into account the possibility that excessively high wages may lead to unemployment. That element in wage calculations becomes especially acute when the product manufactured is exposed to severe competition in its own markets.

Thus the principle of competition plays a considerable part in the strategy of stabilization. It is a necessity if fiscal policy, price policy, and wage policy are to be reconciled without state direction in a framework of reasonably full employment at stable rather than steadily rising prices.

CHAPTER XI. *Labor Policy, Full Employment, and Inflation*

BY CHARLES E. LINDBLOM

I. WHAT IS THE PROBLEM?

Fifteen years ago, the belief was widespread that stickiness of wages in the downswing of the business cycle caused business losses and thus made depressions more severe. Policy-wise, wage reduction as a cure for depression was not uncommonly advocated. Neither public officials nor economists agreed, however, in defining the problem or in proposing solutions. Many agreed with the position taken by President Hoover at the onset of the depression of the 1930's when he called upon business to maintain wage rates in order to support purchasing power.

The long debate on the responsibility of wage rigidity for aggravating cyclical disturbances seems now about to be settled in favor of those who have argued that the problem does not in fact exist—that wage rigidities are not a cause of instability and are probably a stabilizing influence in the economy. The Keynesian interest in aggregate spending in the economy was important in drawing attention to wages as income to supplement the earlier concern over wages as cost. But Keynesian and non-Keynesian alike came gradually to agree during the 1930's and 40's that wage cutting in depression is probably more disruptive than wage maintenance.

Today perhaps most economists agree that it is difficult to make a persuasive theoretical case for wage cutting as a cure for short-term cyclical fluctuations in business activity. And they agree also on the political difficulties of administering general wage reductions even if they were believed to be stabilizing.

More recently some consideration has been given to the possibilities of manipulating wage rates as a method of maintaining an already existing high level of employment and income. Since the war some trade unionists have insisted that major wage movements instigated by unions are capable of stabilizing the economy and should for this reason be encouraged by the government. Again it appears that economists largely agree that the economy can better be maintained on an even keel with fiscal and monetary policies than with comprehensive attempts to alter wage-rise relations directly either through government or union wage policy. For a number of reasons general wage movements, whether administered by coordinated union power or by government, represent an extremely crude method of controlling the total volume of spending.

Max Millikan has discussed some of these reasons in Chapter 3. Aside from certain questions of political feasibility, the primary defect of union and government wage policies alike, as compared with fiscal and monetary policy of government, is that they cannot affect spending through changes in wage incomes without also at the same time having a heavy impact upon costs of production. Thus at least their effects are uncertain, and at worst their effects will be just the opposite of those intended. Wage increases to maintain the total volume of spending in the economy, for example, may in their impact on costs of production reduce profit margins and the volume of employment. And wage cuts for the purpose of limiting spending to control a potential inflation may in some cases raise the price level. Through a consequent decrease in costs of production and the resultant stimulus to investment spending, wage cuts may encourage the very inflation which the wage adjustment was designed to avoid.

The difficulties in predicting the consequences of administered wage changes stem from the large number of variables on which the consequences depend. The state of investor's anticipations; the methods by which firms finance wage increases; the policies of the monetary authorities; the spending plans of wage earners; the relationships between agricultural prices, retail prices, and prices of manufactured goods—all will vary from one time to another and from one circumstance to another.[1] Especially important, they will vary partly as the result of the wage policy itself, yet it will be impossible to predict how.

Beyond these difficulties are several practical obstacles. In any kind of planning for stability, the government's inability to forecast with any certainty is a stumbling block. This problem is discussed in Chapter 4. It is an especially serious problem in connection with wage policy, however. What is required for government wage policy is inducements to *private autonomous* groups—namely, trade unions—to moderate or increase their wage demands in conformity with the government's desire to reach a particular wage-price relationship. Now while it should be easy to induce unions to step up their wage demands on the basis of a possibly mistaken forecast which suggests the desirability of wage in-

1. See Lloyd G. Reynolds, "Wage Bargaining, Price Changes, and Employment," *Proceedings of First Annual Meeting of Industrial Relations Research Association, Cleveland, Ohio, December 29–30, 1948,* pp. 35–50.

creases, the opposite is certainly not true. A union is not likely to abandon its demands because certain govenment economists have concluded that "perhaps" a wage reduction would help stabilize the economy.

It is difficult enough to subordinate a private group's interests to the general interest when the conflict between the two interests is more or less demonstrable to everyone concerned. How much more difficult it is when only very shaky evidence can suggest that a wage policy desired by government is more in the public interest than the union's own wage policy. Even assuming a sincere desire on the part of an autonomous private group to discipline itself in the interest of the public as a whole, effective control over its policies requires a fairly clear and accurate knowledge of what is in the public interest.

Another practical difficulty in wages policy as an instrument of stabilization is that it is sufficiently flexible only if general wage changes can be administered throughout the whole economy or very large sections of it. In the United States, however, we lack a coordinated union movement which might make such flexibility possible, for we not only have more than one major national federation but also a strong tradition of autonomy for each national and international union. For that matter, considerable autonomy is enjoyed by the locals.

A further defect in the use of wage policy as a tool for stabilization is the lack, in normal times, of government control over prices. This is only to restate in somewhat different terms a point already made. If wage-price relations are to be adjusted in order to stimulate or retard business activity, it is futile to manipulate wage rates only to set off consequent price movements which can neither be predicted nor controlled. It has already been suggested that we cannot estimate accurately the effects of wage changes on spending and business activity because wage changes affect both costs and spending. But we could increase the accuracy of our estimate if we had legal and administrative arrangements for continuing peacetime price control. This, however, requires a scope and complexity of regulation of the economy which is at odds with the basic goals of policy outlined in Chapter 1, which set the limits within which we seek to find solutions to the problem of instability. Hence this possibility must be discarded.

Finally—and this is the crux of the matter—wage policy is actually made largely by autonomous private groups who lack the motivation to subordinate their policies to the stabilization policy of the government. It is not enough that these private business and labor groups are generally restrained or somewhat moderated in their policies by the influence of government. To make wage policy a *positive* instrument for stability requires speed and accuracy of adjustment, but the kinds of influences which government can bring to bear on autonomous business and labor groups do not work fast or precisely.

It therefore appears that the best we can hope for in government policy is that it prevents union wage policy from interfering with short-run and long-run monetary and fiscal policies designed to stabilize the economy.

This in fact is the problem of government wage policy. The problem itself arises from the possibility that union power to raise wage rates will be so great as to frustrate attempts made by government through monetary or fiscal policy to maintain income stability and employment without inflation. It is of course possible that union pressure on wage rates might produce unemployment, but it seems much more probable that so far as union pressure on wage rates creates a problem it will be one of inflation.

Our common techniques for controlling inflation are suited to reducing the volume of spending on the assumption that inflation is caused by excess spending. But trade union pressure on wage rates may drive prices up from the cost side. If wage rates run too far ahead of productivity, either prices must be allowed to rise in order to maintain profit margins or unemployment results. Thus a wage-induced depression may be remediable only through inflation. And a wage-induced inflation cannot be stopped by ordinary anti-inflationary techniques without causing unemployment.

This chapter can be considered as a case study on a kind of problem typical of a "bloc" economy. It is an attempt to diagnose the problems raised by the influence of autonomous power groups over critical prices in the economy—in this case, the price of labor. The reader will put the chapter in proper perspective only if he realizes that the same general problem could be attacked through analysis, say, of agricultural prices and the power of the farm bloc in relation to income and employment stability.

II. How Powerful Is Unionism?

In the minds of some economists, this fact of union power to increase wage rates is the greatest single threat to the success of programs designed for economic stability. How serious a problem it is cannot be known until we appraise union power. It becomes necessary, therefore, to analyze the factors in union strength.

We may anticipate that an assessment of union strength may lead to any one of several important conclusions with respect to union power and to required government policy. 1) It may turn out that union power is not greater than can be controlled by the ordinary crude tech-

niques of influence and persuasion which government can bring to bear upon unionism. 2) Possibly, however, we may conclude that union pressure on wages may be such that we cannot avoid a consequent chronic but mild inflationary rise in prices year after year. (Quite aside from the wage-price problem, continually rising prices are a real possibility for other reasons, in which case pressure on wage rates may or may not aggravate the inflationary problem.) 3) We may decide that union power may be such that only government price or wage control can restrain it, in which case the required policy cannot satisfy the conditions laid down in Chapter 1 for desirable public policy. Finally, we may find that union power may not be manageable at all. In one sense or another all problems are of course "solved." But even with government wage and/or price control, in the face of union pressure on wage rates and union challenges to the successful enforcement of wage and/or price controls, it may be impossible to avoid a galloping inflation or chronic depression of such magnitude as to throw large and increasing numbers of the labor force on public employment.

As for an appraisal of union power to increase wage rates, the first fact to be recognized is that today's union movement is more powerful both in depression and prosperity than the union movement of the late 1930's, which in turn was a giant compared to the union movement of the 1920's and earlier. The union movement has grown in fifteen years from 3 million to 14 million. At the same time, union power has been to a degree coordinated either through industry-wide collective bargaining or through agreement by union leaders on a common policy to be pursued with each employer. Thus union power can instigate rough industry-wide wage movements and to a smaller extent economy-wide wage movements which, with varying success, may overcome the resistance which interfirm competition has traditionally offered to wage increases pursued independently by each local union.

But, for all its present strength, we do not really know what unionism will do with its power, nor do union leaders themselves know. It is a widespread hope and a not uncommon belief that unionism's power brings responsibility and caution to the movement. On the other hand, it may be that the union movement of the postwar years has only been flexing its muscles. It has been suggested that unionism's new power permits a new pattern of wage demands more aggressive than those yet displayed. New standards of what constitutes a "reasonable" wage demand are presumably in the making. Union groups may discover that the skies do not fall when wage demands are made which transcend the established pattern.

1. *Limits on union power*

One way to understand this new union power is to inspect the limits which might serve to restrict union wage gains which outstrip productivity. There are three major limitations. 1) Employment opportunities may be restricted as wage costs rise above competitive levels. 2) The union may not wish to pursue money wage gains which are offset by price increases leaving real wages unchanged. 3) The employer may resist the union for a number of reasons which may or may not be connected with the first two limitations listed.

It is not necessary to discuss whether, with respect to a particular wage movement taking place in such and such a circumstance and on such and such a scale, its consequences are more probably inflation or more probably unemployment. We wish only to ask the question whether either of these consequences provides any reasonable assurance that union wage gains will be kept within those broad limits necessary for income and employment stability.

It should be noted that an analysis of limits on union wage gains is quite different from a more general analysis of union wage policy. Unions pursue a wide variety of policies for a wide variety of motives. Nonwage and even nonmonetary goals occupy much of the union movement's energy. Certainly union wage policy cannot be described as a rational maximization of money income either to the union or its individual members.

For the present purposes, all these complications of union wage policy can be set aside. All we need to know is whether a reasonable possibility exists for a wage-induced inflation. This question can be settled by determining whether the external and internal limits which restrain union policy are adequate to forestall an inflation. If it emerges from our inspection of these limits that we have no reasonable assurance as to their effectiveness, government policy must take into account the possibility of a wage-induced inflation, even if it is not demonstrated that these limits are almost certain to be ineffective. Certain ineffectiveness creates a problem for policy, to be sure; but uncertain effectiveness imposes much the same problem upon government.

2. *Unemployment as a limit*

With respect to the first limitation, employment opportunities may be restricted for any of the following reasons: 1) the employer loses business to competitors in the same industry, 2) the employers in an industry lose business to other industries, 3) low-paid nonunion labor replaces union labor, 4) labor-saving machinery replaces union labor.[2]

With respect to the first of these possible limitations—restriction of employment opportunities as wage costs rise—this would present a significant obstacle to union wage gains if these gains were pursued by local unions, each acting independently of the other. For under these circumstances high wage costs forced upon one competing employer would put him at a competitive disadvantage. Even here imperfections in competition would permit some monopoly wage gains, which, though they restrict output and reduce volume of employment in the firm, do not sufficiently reduce employment to deter union policy. But to the extent that competition is rigorous, the long-run consequence of a significant competitive disadvantage is bankruptcy for the individual firm. While a union may occasionally drive a firm to bankruptcy, it will more often earlier realize the necessity of abandoning its high wage aims.

The fact is, however, that wage gains are not today commonly pursued by each local union in such a way as to create a substantial competitive hardship for the employing firm. Through formal and informal methods of policy coordination, industry-wide wage movements have become commonplace. Hence competition between firms as a restriction on union wage aims is rendered less effective, and it becomes necessary to look for a limit on unionism in loss of employment opportunities in the industry as a whole as its prices rise relative to the prices of outputs of other industries.

High wage costs forced on an industry do not wipe out the industry even in the long run, as high wage costs forced on an individual firm may wipe out the firm. The effect of extremely high wage costs on an industry as a whole is to restrict output but not to eliminate the industry. Does such a restriction necessarily or even probably inhibit union wage demands?

If, as would usually be the case, only a minority of the union's members become unemployed, it is rational for a majority to pursue wage increases at the expense of the minority. But, of course, union policy may or may not be rational in this sense.

If in these circumstances unions press hard for increases, their policy arises from no desire to exploit the minority. On the contrary, it may arise from what is sometimes considered a moral or ethical principle that it is better to have a few well-paid workers in an industry than many poorly paid workers.

2. For a more detailed and elaborate discussion of the effectiveness of these limitations than can be entered into here, see Charles E. Lindblom, *Unions and Capitalism* (New Haven, Yale University Press, 1949).

Furthermore, industry-wide wage policies may cause unemployment only in certain marginal firms whose workers constitute a small and ineffective minority within the union. Again, a union is sometimes committed to the idea that firms unable to pay "decent" wages should be driven out of business.

Actually, unemployment in the industries may not even appear as a consequence of an industry-wide wage movement. For one thing, the restriction of employment attendant upon union wage policy may simply moderate what otherwise would have been an expansion in employment. If so, the industry hires fewer new workers than would otherwise have been the case. Other potential new workers, never becoming attached to the industry, are not considered to be an industry or union problem. Union policy in railroads, for example, may be no more concerned with unemployment among new unskilled workers in the labor market who have never been employed than with unemployment among harvest hands. But railway union wage policy may actually have caused the unemployment of the one group by reducing, through high labor costs and high railroad rates, the railroad's demands for labor.

To the degree that wage movements are broader than industry-wide, that is, to the extent that key wage bargains set in motion wage movements which encompass more than one industry, consequent unemployment may more often be attributed to general economic maladjustment rather than to the wage policies of any particular union in an industry. Hence unemployment is weakened as an inhibitor on union policies.

But broad wage movements outstripping productivity will in fact probably not produce unemployment. Instead price increases are to be expected. An adequate investigation of possible limits on union wage gains therefore turns on the effectiveness of price increases as a discouragement to union wage demands, a possibility to be discussed presently.

It has been suggested that industry-wide wage policy may be more sensible and far-sighted than wage policy instigated by the local union.[3] Industry-wide wage policy generally rests on more adequate factual knowledge and on a better understanding of the consequences of wage changes than does local wage policy. Moreover, the local union can disregard many consequences of policy which the national union cannot safely disregard. But, on the other hand, what is sensible and far-sighted for union and industry is often monopoly. That is to say, a sen-

3. See, for example, R. A. Lester and E. A. Robie, *Wages under National and Regional Collective Bargaining* (Princeton, Princeton University Industrial Relations Section, 1946).

sible and far-sighted calculation of what is to be gained by alternative wage policies may lead union and management to cooperate. A joint program of wage and price increases may profit both. And management thus also forestalls the expansion of sales which might encourage entry of new competing firms.

Two further possible limits on wage policy through loss of employment opportunities are of uncertain effectiveness.

1) Competition from labor-displacing machinery may be ineffective on two counts. Most important, when wage costs rise substitution of machines for men may not reduce employment opportunities sharply enough to inhibit union policy significantly. Again, it need only be observed that, as in the case of high prices resulting from industry-wide increases, a substantial restriction of employment opportunities may not lead the majority of the union to moderate its wage policy. Nor does restriction of employment opportunities necessarily produce an absolute decline in the number of jobs available.

Secondly, and somewhat less important, union jurisiction follows innovation. Thus the union maintains control over workers on newly introduced machines. This is true of course for industrial unions, but even craft unions make relatively successful attempts to maintain jurisdiction over workers on new machines rather than simply surrender jurisdiction on the grounds that a craft or skill is no longer involved.

2) Competition from nonunion workers is fairly effectively controlled and is thus weakened as a significant limitation on union power by the union's tactics of control of the buyer. Unionism does not depend for its strength upon apprenticeship rules or other devices for restricting entry into an occupation. Instead a strike is used to impose a loss on the employer to force him, if possible, to consent to the union's terms. Hence the union often need not fear nonunion or unemployed workers except as they serve as strikebreakers. The recent tremendous growth in union membership has significantly reduced the number of nonunion workers available in any market to what is often a small fraction of the labor force required to reopen a struck plant. Yet the failure of the Packinghouse Workers in 1948 to carry off their strike successfully is evidence that the power of the unemployed and nonunion worker to break a strike is by no means wholly lost.

3. *Inflation as a limit*

Where widespread wage movements take place, and raise wage costs, price inflation is more to be expected than unemployment. It has often been suggested that unions will avoid money wage increases which fail to achieve any gain in real wages.

But price increases will not ordinarily be expected to take back from the worker all that he has gained through increasing his money wage rate. A 10% increase in wages of steelworkers will not cause a 10% increase in the price of everything the worker buys. Nor is it likely to cause even a 10% increase in the price of steel. The steelworker has in effect gained by a redistribution of income from others in the economy to himself. Even for industry-wide wage movements or for wage movements in clusters of industries, the possibility will remain open to gain at the expense of all those workers, farmers, small businessmen, or *rentiers* who bear the burden of the price inflation but do not, along with the unionists, enjoy an increase in money income.

If price increases inhibit the use of union power, it will be only because unionism develops a responsibility not only to its own membership but to the community at large. It will be because unionism accepts a broader responsibility than it has on the whole accepted up to this point. It is not at all impossible that this kind of change should come over unionism. We shall discuss the possibility in connection with the policy alternatives open to us for dealing with the problem of a wage-induced inflation. For the moment, it need only be observed that, without an assumption of a broader responsibility by unionism, price increases do not promise to be an effective limitation on union policy.

The brevity of the discussion of this possibility at this point in the chapter does not minimize the probability that the threat of inflation is itself the best guarantee against a wage-induced inflation.

4. *Employer resistance as a limit*

The last major limitation on union wage policy is employer resistance. Employer resistance is indeed a power which union power must contend with, and perhaps the burden of proof is on those who would argue that union power is sufficient to overcome it. Their fears stem from several considerations.

We have already noticed that the growth of unionism has produced a shortage of strikebreakers. It is ordinarily a foregone conclusion in a major strike today that the union will succesfully close down production, yet it was only a few years ago that an employer might reasonably expect to defeat a strike at the onset by maintaining operations in the face of it.

Furthermore, while the union has a clear-cut objective of "more, more, more, now," the employer finds in key wage settlements a suitable rule of thumb which excuses him from the necessity of formulating clear-cut wage objectives. He can with relatively small risk follow the leadership of negotiations in steel, autos, meat packing and the like, knowing that his competitors will probably do likewise. Yielding to union pressure by rule of thumb becomes increasingly easy.

This suggests another weakness. Employers simply do not wish to resist industry and national wage increases as they resisted increases for single firms alone, since they are not forced by the threatened loss of their competitive position to fight wage increases.

Finally, the change in the power relations between unions and management has put wage issues in a new light. When the weakness of unionism encouraged many employers to fight it rather than accept it, a successful method of undermining the loyalties of the union member to his organization was to resist wage increases. Today, when unionism each day brings new challenges to managerial prerogatives, management is tempted to offer wage increases in order to win the union away from its attempts to share managerial authority. Wage concessions can be recouped in price increases but power lost to the union is lost forever.

We do not draw from these considerations the conclusion that employer resistance is certain to be an ineffective limit on union pressure for higher wages. Rather we conclude only that employer resistance *may* easily turn out to be inadequate as a limit. The implication for policy is clear enough, for policy must be prepared to deal with all the major possibilities.

5. *Foreign trade as a limit*

A minor possibility of inhibiting union power is sometimes said to lie in competition from abroad. It is significant that for all Great Britain's reliance on competing effectively with foreign sources of supply, the problem of union power is considered to be a serious one for the British economy. For our economy, less dependent upon foreign trade than the British, the possibilities of inhibiting unions through threats of foreign competition seem very slight indeed.

6. *A stabilization program as a limit*

Might not the kind of income stability program being discussed in this book itself provide a check on union wage demands? The question poses two possibilities. One is that union power is somehow diminished where income and employment are stable; the other is that the motives to push for wage increases in a stable economy are weakened. Unfortunately, we do not know enough about union behavior to decide these questions.

It would seem improbable, however, that union power would be diminished by reason of a successful stabilization program. Union power may turn out to be very great in all stages of the business cycle. But if union power varies depending upon economic conditions, presumably it would be at its greatest in periods of high employment opportunity such as provided by a successful income stabilization program.

As for motives, to the extent that a successful income stabilization program ultimately diminishes the workers' feelings of insecurity of employment, the pressure for wage gains may be increased. And perhaps to the extent that wage gains are being pursued in the disguise of pension plans, employment and income security may reduce the drive to win these concessions from employers. Paul Samuelson has made reference to some of these possibilities in Chapter 12 on "Full Employment versus Progress and Other Economic Goals." We shall consider at the end of this chapter the possibilities of offering union members income and security goals through public policy as a method of diminishing pressure on wage rates.

7. *Summary*

Possible limits on union power so far discussed provide no reasonable assurance that union wage policy will not jeopardize income and employment stability. On the other hand, neither does the argument prove that union policy will do so. All we can say is that limits on union power are not demonstrably effective in maintaining wage and price levels consistent with a stability program, and government wage policy must be prepared to meet a problem of uncertain character and magnitude. In any case, what unionism can do in the future is not correctly estimated by its performance in the thirties or in the years 1945 to 1950. We may either seriously underestimate or overestimate unionism's power by excessive attention to the recent record.

One final point: We have been discussing limits which might serve to prevent wage gains from running ahead of productivity to a point which might cause inflation through high wage costs. It is perhaps worth emphasizing that the wage-price problem arises not from rising wage rates but from rising wage costs. Such an emphasis cautions us against forgetting that a rapidly rising productivity may forever forestall a wage-induced inflation. At the same time, the emphasis on labor costs points up the potential impact on the price level of employer-financed union welfare and pension schemes, vacations with pay, and other forms of remuneration which may increase wage costs without affecting the basic wage *rate*.

III. Some Unsatisfactory Solutions to the Wage Problem

Policies designed to deal with the wage problem must take account of our uncertainty both as to union power and as to the willingness of unionism to use its power. As we have said, it is possible that unions will at worst produce only a mild chronic inflation. On the other hand, it is quite within the realm of possibility that union power may produce economic catastrophe. Public policy must be designed to meet these two and other contingencies. While it would be a serious error to plan only to meet the threat of mild inflation when in fact a threat of runaway inflation appears, it would also be an error to undertake the drastic reforms which might be necessary to curb a runaway inflation if in fact unionism makes no such threat.

1. *Competitive labor markets*

One possible policy designed to meet any contingencies is the destruction of union power over wage rates, a policy which is often interpreted as the "restoration," "preservation," or "creation" of competitive labor markets and which parallels proposals for dealing with business and agricultural price policies. Almost everyone agrees that unions cannot be outlawed—nor can collective bargaining. It is therefore sometimes proposed that unionism be weakened by removing some of the protections which the law has thrown over it and by outlawing both industry-wide bargaining and industry-wide strikes.

These suggestions run into political difficulties, not only because of the political power of organized labor, but also because there is fairly widespread agreement in the United States that unionism performs many useful functions. A stabilization policy which calls upon workers and society in general to surrender the many benefits of unionism is of dubious value.

Our society is also marked by diminishing allegiance to competition. Not only do workers want to "take wages out of competition"; so also do other sellers want to shield themselves from its rigors. And as a general value the competitive system seems to be losing ground in the face of many assaults made on it. We may be in no hurry to abandon what we have of it; but, on the other hand, no political leader could expect to arouse a following for a program designed to "restore" competitive labor markets.

Congress has given thought recently, however, to imposing limitation on industry-wide bargaining and industry-wide strikes. The objection to these proposals is not that they cannot be enacted but rather that they cannot be effectively enforced. To destroy union power it is necessary to eliminate industry-wide wage movements. But industry-wide wage movements do not usually depend on formally established industry-wide bargaining; nor do these movements ordinarily depend upon industry-wide strikes.

Informal coordination among local unions under the guidance of their national organizations is enough to achieve a degree of uniformity in industry-wide wage changes. Prohibition on industry-wide collective bargaining does not attack this form of cooperative behavior, nor does it seem likely that any alternative reform could effectively prohibit consultation and cooperation among union leadership. We do not believe in arbitrary wage differentials among workers doing substantially the same kind of work. Hence it does not seem practicable to propose that we declare illegal any attempt of one union to pursue the same wage gains pursued by other locals in the same or in related industries. But even prohibition on informal consultation among union leaders would still leave wide open the possibilities of follow-the-leader patterns of wage changes accepted by unions and employers alike.

2. *Responsible unionism*

The many difficulties standing in the way of decentralizing union power and attempting to create competitive labor markets have led most students of the problem to the conclusion that public policy must pursue the opposite line of attack. It appears to them that coordination and unification of union power might make union leadership more responsible. This, they believe, offers the only hope of keeping wage rates within the limits of a stabilization policy.

Can union policies thus be made responsible to society as a whole?

In general, union leadership is already relatively responsible, intelligent, and mature—in terms of the interests of the union membership. The question therefore hinges not on the intelligence, maturity, and capacity for responsible leadership of the union officialdom. Rather it hinges on whether union policy can be made responsible to a larger group than union membership, that is, to the public as a whole.

The case for coordination and unification of power rests on what appear to be reasonable suppositions. National leadership is responsible for the entire union movement and for the consequences of this movement's behavior for the economy as a whole. It is therefore less likely to act without regard to these consequences than is decentralized local leadership. Each local leader knows that the larger social consequences of his particular policies are not great and may therefore be disregarded.

Coordination and unification may also moderate union policy by creating responsibility on the part of the national leadership for remedying inequities in income within the union movement which may arise from the ability of some unions to proceed with wage gains much faster than others. Again, with local leadership the less successful unions may protest their being left behind in the advance of wage rates, but no national leadership can be held responsible for this state of affairs.

The obstacles to developing responsibility through coordination are many.

1) We do not actually have the high degree of coordination necessary for responsibility, nor does it seem likely that it will be developed in the foreseeable future. The American Federation of Labor itself is a relatively loose federation; the Congress of Industrial Organizations, while more coordinated, is yet without unified control over its affiliates; and the AFL, CIO, Railroad Brotherhoods, and independent unions have not gone very far in the development of a unified policy which would coordinate their various wage policies.

2) For many years to come a great many wage earners will be outside any labor organization. A unified union leadership could not therefore effectively represent the whole labor force and would have no compelling motives to act responsibly toward the whole labor force.

3) For good reason trade unionism has developed as an institution to protect and pursue the particular interests of its members as a kind of minority group within the society. Its traditions and ethical values reflect its more or less intelligent and unabashed interest in a particular group. To call upon union leadership to be responsible to the whole society is to ask the union movement to achieve a rather fundamental change in purpose. Union members, like all of us, believe that they have an important stake in the general public welfare and believe that the institutions of government should protect that general public welfare. In addition they believe that they need a special organization for their special interests, and it may be unreasonable to expect them to permit their unions to be converted into one more of many agencies already designed for general social betterment rather than special protective purposes.

4) Even if all wage and salary earners were brought within the union movement and a coordinated national organization were made responsible to all wage and salary earners, it would still be rational for the new union leadership to pursue wage increases even at the risk of unemployment or inflation. In case of inflation wage earners would pay out in higher prices a substantial portion of what they had won in higher wages. But they would not always lose all they had gained. For farmers, rentiers, independent businessmen and other nonwage or salary earning groups in the population would also pay higher prices. High wages

would to some extent constitute a transfer of income from these groups to the wage and salary groups encompassed in one great union.

5) Cause and effect are lost sight of in wage changes. Wage changes do not show up immediately in the form of price increases or reduction in payrolls. In many cases wage increases will not even increase wage costs. But if they do it may be some time before the firm responds with changed production plans. The chain of events between an originating wage change and consequent changes in prices or employment in the economy is very complex. Thus it will be possible for unions to remain in ignorance of the consequences of their policies. Moreover, even with adequate information it is ordinarily impossible to prove the responsibility of wage policy for subsequent changes of prices or employment. Consequently the union is ordinarily in a position where it can ascribe unfavorable consequences to other policies and changes taking place in the economy having nothing to do with union wage policy. There will be much room for honest disagreement as to cause and effect. And it will always be possible for union leadership to rationalize.

This particular obstacle to establishing union responsibility is illustrated in the wide disagreement among economists as to the responsibility of high wage rates for the retarded recovery of the 1930's or again in the differences of opinion among economists today as to the responsibility of high wage rates for continued postwar inflation. If these contradictory interpretations of fact are possible, how can unionism be responsible even if it wishes to be?

6) A highly responsible, high-minded, and public-spirited unionism might very well be aggressively anticompetitive and hence disinclined to respect the requirements of stability in a competitive order. Unionism insists that it is morally right to "take wages out of competition." Its leaders commonly insist that the "warm human needs" of workers take precedence over the requirements of successful operation of the competitive system. Hence, while union leadership rarely explicitly asserts its willingness to follow disruptive wage policies, it is constantly defending its right to pursue such policies if and when it wishes to undertake them. And the policies thus defended are not merely hypothetical. In those instances where we can be fairly certain that union policies are monopolistic, union leadership will defend the policies in ethical and moral terms and often because they are anticompetitive, not despite this fact.

7) This suggests in turn a further obstacle. Criteria are lacking by which a responsible wage policy would be guided. In order to avoid general inflation or unemployment, wage rates must be tied at least roughly to productivity and more specifically to what might be called,

speaking broadly, "competitive" standards. But an organization which develops as its principle tactic a method of suppressing competition among sellers of labor and whose traditional slogan is "take wages out of competition" is not disposed to accept any criterion of wage adjustment which insists on subordinating union policy to the requirements of competition. And, quite the contrary, it pushes hard for the common acceptance of wage standards which relate immediately to the income needs of workers. For the union movement to accept competitive standards it must limit its hopes for improving workers' incomes to the elimination of low noncompetitive wage rates. On the record, the union movement is far more ambitious than this.

8) It has often been suggested that the "new" leadership, especially the young leadership of some of the CIO unions, can be expected to show a broader responsibility than the older leadership. Those who make this suggestion are in effect attributing irresponsibility in union policy to ignorance, immaturity, and narrowness in background and training, for they believe they see in the new leadership a better educated, better informed, generally more enlightened and intelligent leadership. The contrast drawn between the two groups has some validity. Probably union leadership is growing in its capacity to understand the economy and its problems. In part, however, the difference between the two groups is in public relations.

In any case, the new leadership, if more skilled, is as likely to pursue high wage policies as it is to pursue more moderate policies. Presumably a better trained and more intelligent leadership will be more rather than less effective in pursuing the particular special interests of the rank and file. Furthermore, the new leadership is probably more conscious of the conflict between its aims and the competitive order than is the old leadership. Hence, it is perhaps more often driven to an avowedly radical position in which, while continuing to pay lip service to private enterprise, it nevertheless looks favorably upon the possibilities of price control or other governmental powers which could be called upon to adjust the economy to the demands of unionism should union demands even produce inflation or unemployment. The new leadership is perhaps less inclined to compromise and more inclined to make wage disputes of great principle.

9) In a democratic society leadership is often held responsible by its own inhibitions; but the inhibitions which restrain union leadership may not be sufficient to deter it from inflationary wage policies. Yet such inhibitions as do restrain them are extremely important and should not be disregarded as limitations of some effectiveness.

In many cases union leaders fail to ask for as much as the employer could fairly easily be compelled to grant. The explanation of this is simply that doubts assail union leadership when it asks for "too much." In interviews union leaders will often reveal that upper limits to their wage demands are set by a vague feeling that more ambitious demands would be "unreasonable." Even when union leaders can point to no predictable employer resistance or to no other expected undesirable consequences of their demands, they nevertheless often act as though certain demands lie beyond what serious and sensible people should expect.

But it is worth noting that these inhibitions, which rest on feeling of what is customary and therefore "right," seem to reflect the leadership's idea of what it is reasonable to expect in income gains rather than what it is reasonable to impose as new costs on the employer. Hence, these inhibitions are not tied to standards which provide reasonable assurance that union wage policy will not be disruptive.

The obstacles to the development of union responsibility are of three major sorts:

1) Union hostility to the competitive system, as expressed in such slogans as "labor is not a commodity," might conceivably lead the union to pursue policies resulting in inflation where the inflation is a cost willingly incurred in the attainment of certain values, such as the mere assertion of union power in itself, income gains, security, or an extension of control over management.

2) Union wage policy may produce inflation because it has miscalculated and thereby produced unintended consequences.

3) Union policy may produce inflation because the union members gain by so doing, even if at the expense of the rest of society.

It is the second and third of these possibilities which are presumably the most serious. In view of the wishful thinking that goes into union wage policy, the second should not be at all underestimated. If there is a remedy for the second possibility, it is presumably to be found in enlightenment, which suggests that public policy aimed at providing union leadership and rank and file with necessary information might be a simple but very effective step in influencing union wage policy.

If there is a remedy for the third possibility, it is in a demonstration that in a very important sense such possibilities for gaining at public expense simply do not exist. That is to say, the solution lies in the discovery by the union movement of the possibility that, if the indirect and ultimate consequences of union policy are taken into account, gains for unionists at the expense of the general public are illusory or short-lived.

We cannot be sure that there is in the economy such real harmony of interests as these sentences would suggest. Yet it does not seem improbable that, were union policy to take into account such indirect repercussions of policy as a bad-tempered Congress, a hostile white-collar class, or the unpredictable course of inflation, it might quickly be concluded that intelligent union wage policy should always be put to the test of the public interest. But then, again, to suggest this as a possible development in the future is not to declare that such an attitude toward the public welfare has already developed within unionism or that it can be counted upon to develop in the foreseeable future.

3. *Encouraging responsibility through government action*

What possibilities exist for the development of responsible unionism may be much heightened if government can lend a guiding hand. We may therefore ask what the possibilities are for responsible policy where coordination of policy is supplemented by one or more of various possible kinds of influence which government might bring to bear.

1) One possibility is that government may exhort unions to serve the public interest. This is probably the least effective of the various policies that might be attempted. The preceding paragraphs imply that what is required is information and understanding rather than morality. Reasonableness, maturity, statesmanship, and morality are of no help to wage policy without facts as to the consequences of wage changes and a substantial comprehension of the complexity of indirect consequences of union action.

2) Government might therefore (with more attention to economics and less to morality) announce a general intention to restrain wage increases when economic conditions call for such a policy or an intention to encourage increases when conditions call for wage rises—supplementing such a general declaration with an attempt simply to make certain that union leaders and members understand the consequences of whatever they propose to do.

However reasonable such a policy, one might expect it to turn out to be quite inadequate. Its difficulties are twofold. It may be impossible to win the union's assent to the announced wage policy. And even if the union indicates its willingness to follow such a policy, it may in effect nullify it.

On the first point—for all the reasons given above for doubting the effectiveness of responsibility as a restraint on union policy—unions might be expected to oppose the subordination of union demands to announced government wage policy.

An announced government policy would, of course, focus whatever power lies in public opinion to stir doubts among union officials as to the reasonableness of their position or to persuade the rank and file that their officials are embarking on an unwise policy. But, although settlements often seem to be much influenced by pressure of public opinion, many strike settlements are made with apparent disregard of public sentiment.

Furthermore, we again run into the difficulty of establishing effective policy in the absence of acceptable criteria. Today, for example, it would be difficult for the government to win a skeptical union membership to the view that further wage increases were inflationary, since it is not unreasonable to suppose that, on the contrary, further wage increases are necessary to offset price increases which run ahead of wage increases. Lacking criteria—and consequently lacking any convincing evidence as to the consequences of various wage policies—government is reduced to suggestions that wage increases under some circumstances "might" endanger the stability of the economy. This is not the vigorous and definite kind of a statement which is needed to bring effective pressure to bear on union leadership.

As for the possibilities of an effective wage control where unions formally and explicitly accept the leadership of government in formulating wage policy, it is easy for wage increases to creep up around any general formula. During the war, the Little Steel Formula could be accepted by unions and yet in part nullified by wage increases won on fringe issues and special circumstances, such as those which any formula must always allow for.

If the issue were ordinarily starkly presented as an increase *versus* no increase at all, the possibilities of successful enforcement would be much improved. But wage rates should be allowed to rise gradually with productivity. As a consequence, the issue is usually over the size of a wage increase, it being assumed that some increase is justifiable. Thus it is easy for unions to push their wage demands to a degree which in effect ignores the government's announced policy. Yet these same unions intend to accept and genuinely believe that they in fact accept the leadership of government in formulating their policies.

3) Suggestions have recently been made that government can most successfully regulate union wage policy by committing itself in very certain terms to a policy of price level stability. The merit of the proposal is that it serves warning on union leadership that excessively high wage rates will not be compensated for by price increases but instead will produce unemployment. The belief is that this will inhibit union policy.

The difficulty of such a proposal is that it may be considered by union leadership to be a bluff. It is the kind of a pledge which if called as a bluff has to be abandoned, for presumably no administration in power will permit widespread unemployment to develop without taking steps to increase spending to remove it. A second difficulty is that union leadership will probably seriously overestimate the capacity of the economy to bear generally higher wage rates without producing unemployment. Once unemployment actually develops as a result of high wage policies, it will probably be taken by unionism to represent the result of other maladjustments in the economy. And the standard union remedy for general unemployment is maintenance of wage rates to maintain spending.

4) A further obstacle to this last or any other program of government leadership in wage policy is the strong possibility that the government will itself abandon its own wage policy in its concern to find a quick settlement to a major strike. Strong pressures drive government to find an expedient solution to a strike whenever the public interest is greatly affected, as in the case of the railroad strike which brought President Truman before Congress to propose special legislation. At crucial times industrial peace as a value itself emerges as the dominant value of the community. A settlement of some kind is important; the specific terms of the settlement are secondary and are easily compromised in the hope of finding a scheme to resume production. If government is interested both in industrial peace and in the enforcement of a general wage policy for the economy, in the circumstances of a major strike the latter must be subordinated to the former.

5) Voluntary arbitration is not an effective instrument of government wage policy, as is sometimes supposed. A union or a firm will offer to arbitrate a wage dispute only when they think they can win through arbitration roughly what they might win by continued dispute and possible strike, considering all their goals and values. When arbitration tribunals are committed to the enforcement of a general wage policy, unions desiring to go beyond what is permitted by such a policy will refuse to arbitrate. The possibilities of compulsory arbitration are another matter and will be considered below.

To encourage or permit unionism to develop the coordinated power which might potentially produce responsibility is to permit unionism the coordination of power which greatly increases its strength in the bargaining process and which specifically gives it enormously greater power to initiate general wage movements throughout the economy. What unionism can do through wage policy to cause instability in the economy is a function of its power and of its willingness to use its power for the interest of the union movement itself. If coordination is a method of developing broader responsibility and hence of inhibiting the use of union power in the interest of the union movement itself, it is also at the same time a method of greatly increasing the power which it can

exert if it so desires. Hence while it may be the only effective attack on
the wage problem, coordination is a dangerous policy and cannot be
predicted with great confidence to move in the right direction. It may
be our only hope, but at the same time it may turn out to be a disastrous
policy to follow.

The President's Council of Economic Advisers has indicated that it
believes stability can best be achieved by negotiations among a group
of highly coordinated economic blocs. One of their spokesmen, for example, has written: "The obvious remedy [for the wage problem] is
a long-range wage and price policy by arrangement with business and
labor." The problem begins where the statement ends. Aside from the
difficulty of establishing criteria satisfactory to the various interest
groups, the primary problem is to keep under control the vast aggregates
of power achieved by the coordination of labor and the coordination of
business.

In political terms the problem of union power is the problem of consensus. The members of a particular union represent a special interest
group so homogeneous that they do not sufficiently identify themselves
with the society as a whole. They do not need to ask themselves whether
their union policies are consistent with the public welfare because they
do not believe that the purpose of their union is the pursuit of the general public welfare.

Now it is supposed that by increasing the size of the union group
which is coordinated under one policy-making authority, the group becomes so large and embraces so many diverse interests that it comes to
identify itself with society as a whole. Policy-wise, the union movement
is thus encouraged to believe that no union policies are judicious in
terms of the union's special interests if these policies are not at the same
time in the public interest as well. Out of this identification of the union
with society a political consensus develops, that is, certain values come
to be agreed upon by union member and nonmember alike and by wage
earner and nonwage earner alike. General agreement develops, for
example, on the advantage of a stable price level and of full employment, from which follows general agreement on the desirability of limiting wage increases to those permitted by rises in productivity.

But coordination may in fact take quite another turn. It may simply
aggravate the already existing problems of "groupism" in economic and
political life. It may turn all political and economic issues into warfare
between three major power groups of organized industry, organized
agriculture, and organized labor. Coordination may develop consensus,
to be sure; but this consensus may be within the group only and it may
be marked by a kind of agreed antagonism to the other groups, among

whose members a similar antagonistic consensus develops. Under these circumstances the possibilities of developing wage policies consistent with stability are indeed remote; and, for that matter, the possibilities of maintaining a kind of economy outlined in the introductory chapters are likewise remote. Government through compromise among these major power groups may appear to be a hardheaded expedient; but few who advocate making the attempt to govern labor relations in this manner have taken the trouble systematically to inspect the kinds of economic and political policies likely to develop under the conditions of such an armed truce.

It is of course true that as a condition of survival these groups will have to find a compromise—some kind of working arrangement. But the compromise may be by mutual concessions of monopoly all the way around, which produce strong tendencies toward restricted output and unemployment not simply through wage policy but through industrial price and agricultural price policies. Of course these tendencies can be offset, but perhaps only at the price of a degree of inflation thought intolerable.

Government by the "balance" among these power groups—to use the terminology of the Council of Economic Advisers—may also substantially corrupt the democratic process, for it becomes incumbent upon governmental policy makers to balance off the interests of the various groups by treating each group (but not each individual) as equal in the number of favors it should be permitted, despite the great differences in the numbers of persons represented by the various groups.

Furthermore, public policy designed to balance the pressures or interests of these three major power groups comes to think of policy questions largely in terms of what is fair to the vested interest of each of the three groups concerned. This not only adds greater burdens to policy-making in terms of relatively clear goals involving the public interest as a whole but also influences policies strongly in the direction of preservation of the status quo from which these interests are derived. Public policy comes to be looked upon as a matter of finding compromises which are "fair" to the three major parties concerned without regard to the possibility that in a particular circumstance only one party may be proposing policies in the public interest and the others not. To some extent public policy is reduced to umpiring a game, the outcome of which is thought to be of little importance. The public is interested only in a fair fight.

IV. Finally, Some Policy Suggestions

So far we have attempted to assess union strength and have considered the possibilities that unionism will become responsible to the whole society. As has been suggested, it may turn out that unionism does no more than contribute to a mild chronic inflation in which prices rise so gradually year by year that no serious problem of public policy is presented. At the other extreme is the possibility that union pressure on wage rates may create a galloping inflation. This second possibility is extreme only in its consequences. It is not difficult to imagine these consequences as the probable or possible results of union power. For union wage pressure might be intensified if the cost of living rises year by year. A rising price level which is an escape from the inflationary consequences of rising wage costs may itself produce a consequent round of wage increases, with never-ending rounds of wage-induced price increases and price-induced wage increases. We have little assurance that this will not be the case.

As for policies to deal with this problem of uncertain magnitude, we have little ground for confidence in any. Policy oriented toward competitive labor markets seems out of the question; yet reliance on the alternatives, which are either the voluntary assumption of responsibility by unionism or an increased role for government in wage setting, is hardly warranted. Either or both of these alternatives may turn out to be capable of dealing with whatever wage-price problem arises, but both are gambles.

Yet there seems to be no way to proceed in the development of policy other than through these alternatives. The wisest course appears to be that of making the most of the best of a group of unsatisfactory policies. We propose, therefore, to consider further at this point the possibilities for government guidance in wage bargaining and union responsiveness to such guidance.

1. *The possibilities of consensus*

The major requirement for effective policy is consensus. Because we require a flexible policy to meet now unknown problems, it is necessary to win union leaders and members over to an appreciation of their great stake in the general welfare. We should not wish first to win unionists to any particular policy. Instead we want them to accept the value of *public* policy. We can then meet whatever problems develop.

Whether unionism is left to operate independently or whether it is brought under the influence of government, whether it has to be restrained slightly or severely, it is required that there develop in the union movement an identification of its interests with the interests of those outside the union movement and the conviction that union policy cannot ignore the consequences of union policy on the public welfare if union policy is to be successful.

What are the conditions in which responsibility may be had through such consensus?

Three major possibilities may be considered.

1) Unionists may be brought to realize that collective bargaining as a technique for redistribution of income and for securing status is inferior to legislative programs directed toward these same ends. The union member may be brought to believe that he has more to gain as a participating citizen through taxation, social security, public medical care, public housing, and other income and security programs than he has to gain as a union member through collective bargaining. If so, he may perhaps be induced to surrender his present rights to pursue income and security through the union by the offer of superior rights to income and security through the state.

2) The union movement may become politically so ambitious as to wish to develop a broad program of reform in the public interest as a condition of winning political support among the nonorganized working class and middle class. Either as a nucleus of the present Democratic party or as the nucleus of a new third party, organized labor could hope to win elections only by demonstrating its interest in programs of broad public appeal. Political parties cannot win elections so long as they behave as pressure groups. To win elections, therefore, organized labor would be compelled to drop many of its immediate group interests and identify itself with a potential majority of the population. This is of course a real possibility in view of the growing political participation of organized labor.

3) An economic catastrophe such as a runaway inflation or major depression could quite possibly force upon unionism a complete rethinking of its policy and commit unionism thereafter to a much broader public responsibility than it has so far considered.

Although disturbing to many people in the United States, the second possibility is perhaps the most promising of the three. The first offers possibilities of consensus which can best be developed in conjunction with the second. The third can be exploited to develop consensus but only in desperate circumstances in which we do not hope to find ourselves. It may seem far afield to suggest political realignment as a condition of establishing a successful income and employment stabilization policy for the economy. But given the power groups in our economy as they are now constituted, it may be that such a political development represents the only hope of coping with the problem.

Bearing these possibilities for consensus in mind, we can specify the kinds of policies which might well make the best of what is generally a discouraging situation. These specific policy suggestions are designed to make headway against the problem of union power without wholly disregarding the limits imposed by political feasibility.

1) Either through Congressional resolution or through loud and repeated pronouncements of highly placed government officials, it should be explicitly declared that the determination of the general level of wage rates in the economy is a matter of great public concern under all circumstances and cannot be left wholly in the hands of autonomous private groups.

2) For the time being, the President and his advisers and other officials of the national government engaged in conciliation of major disputes should use informal, persuasive influences and public pronouncements to bring pressure to bear upon employers and unions to settle wage disputes on terms consistent with an announced government wage-price policy. The difficulty with this proposal is, of course, that no agency of government is responsible for the determination and announcement of a government wage policy. Nor does this proposal suggest that such an agency be established. What is suggested in effect is merely a continuation of the devices by which government has in fact brought to bear in the case of major wage disputes—the opinion of the President and his advisers as to the desirability of inaugurating, continuing, or terminating rounds of wage increases. This is therefore a very crude policy suggestion, but it is necessary as a beginning for what may eventually develop into a more systematic set of public controls over collective bargaining.

3) At the same time it would be desirable to develop compulsory arbitration in the case of major disputes in railroads and certain other public utilities. For stabilization policy the purpose of this proposal is to take advantage of the current interest in eliminating strikes altogether in certain critical areas in order to develop governmental experience in the compulsory arbitration of disputes. This will provide opportunities for experimentation in the development and use of criteria for wage awards.

4) Either through Congressional resolution or through the pronouncements of government officials, it should be declared that general long-term wage movements should not outstrip the general long-term increase in productivity in the economy.

5) Consistent with the interest in wage movements tied to productivity, Congressional enactment should declare as a goal of public policy the maintenance of price stability and hence declare Congressional opposition to wage movements which necessitate inflationary price movements.

6) To win widespread acceptance for the long-term wage criterion suggested and for other more specific criteria income and security legislation ought to be held out to workers as an alternative to the accomplishment of these gains through unionism. It may turn out to be crucial to offer, in the form of negative income taxation or a social dividend, disposable cash income to low income groups as an alternative to a large expansion of free and subsidized public services. We have already mentioned the possibility that an income and employment stabilization program itself may reduce the insecurities which are presumably in part the motivation behind the drive for wage increases. But income stabilization programs may make no contribution at all to feelings of security among workers until the programs have had time to prove themselves. What is worse, it may turn out that they cannot prove themselves to be effective without first meeting whatever wage-price problems arise.

7) To win consent for the restrictions imposed upon union wage policy, public policy should refrain from the kind of ill-considered and unnecessary restraints on unionism which characterize much of the Taft-Hartley Act and which reflect bad faith rather than an honest attempt to improve industrial relations. If unionism is to be persuaded to become responsible, it is time that Congress drop its common subterfuge of attacking unionism through proposals alleged to regulate it. It is also desirable that public policy explicitly protect unions and union members through legislative endorsement of arrangements such as the union shop, arbitration of disputes over terms of contracts, grievance machinery, and the like. Such legislation could reduce insecurities and challenges to status, for the amelioration of which unionism must now be almost wholly responsible.

8) Likewise, union consent to these restrictions on its wage policies may require the imposition of new government controls over business. If organized labor is called upon to moderate its wage policies at the direction of government, it will no doubt call upon government to ask business enterprise to moderate its price policies. Organized labor can be expected to take the rational view that income and employment stability is dependent upon the policies of all the various economic blocs in the economy, from which it will easily draw the conclusion that the sacrifices imposed upon organized labor should be matched by commensurate sacrifices from other economic groups, such as agricul-

ture and business. In its focus on the possibility of a wage-induced inflation, the present chapter has been able to ignore the disruptive consequences of business monopoly and pegged prices in agriculture. But
stabilization policy requires that all of them be attacked.

And even if there were no justifiable complaints against business or
agricultural price and output practices, no doubt the unionist's feeling
of "fairness" would be outraged by restrictions on union wage policy not
matched by equivalent impositions on business and agriculture. Rationally or not, unionists and the public at large have come to look upon
labor-management relations as a kind of fight in which a government
acting as umpire should act impartially as between the two. Where the
public interest is at stake, as is the case in modern industrial relations,
such a concept of industrial relations is mistaken to the point of foolish-
ness. But however irrational such attitudes are they have to be taken
as given for the present; and public policy must meet the test of impar-
tiality imposed by them.

9) *If* despite these policies union wage rates continue to constitute
a serious inflationary pressure, it would appear that government wage
regulation, either through compulsory arbitration or through a government veto on private wage contracts, would become inevitable, even
if possibly unsuccessful in practice. It does not now seem politically
feasible to suggest such a program, even if we have the experience in
wage regulation to carry it off successfully, which we do not. But the
inflationary problem created by union wage pressures may constitute a
kind of emergency which will generate a consensus now lacking. New
and vigorous governmental action now impossible might then be taken.
There is at least an outside chance that, should government wage regulation be required, the public and the union public as well would accept
it. It is not sufficient that the nonunion public should favor government
wage regulation. The difficulties of enforcing awards upon unions and
workers suggest that wage control can be successful only when union
members themselves accept it as desirable.

10) As a last item on our list of possible policies—a last resort—permanent price control as well as wage control may at some point become
necessary. Wage control may fail to solve the problem of high wage
costs for several reasons: 1) Politically, it may be unacceptable to a
majority of the population or to a Congressional majority. 2) If enacted
into law it may fail in enforcement for lack of union acceptance of it.
3) Even with wholehearted consensus from all groups in the society, it
may flounder on the practical difficulty of regulating wage rates by so
crude a criterion as average productivity. For all the good intentions of

the regulatory commission and the assent of the population, the scheme may break down administratively.

If, however, a dangerous chronic inflation is present and wage control is not effective, then there seems to be no recourse but comprehensive price and wage controls such as characterized the economy during World War II. Price and wage controls of course do not provide a solution to the wage-price problem which is consistent with the goals of public policy outlined in the introductory chapters of this book. It is important therefore to understand, if it is not already clear, that *a major conclusion of this chapter is that it may turn out to be impossible to stabilize income with techniques of public control which meet the requirements of the introductory chapters of this book.*

Price control may come to be the only solution for an inflationary pressure generated by union power, not because price control affords any happy solution, but only because the economic disorganization caused by our possible inability to control wage rates may create overwhelming pressures to hold the lid down with price control. Price control is hardly an alternative to wage control. To be effective it requires wage control. But what it offers which wage control alone fails to offer is a method of legislating the inflation away by legally imposed maximum prices.

2. *Criteria for wage determination*

The above policy suggestions call for government to influence, guide, or formally regulate wage rates. We cannot propose them without facing up to the problem of suitable criteria for wage determination.

The common criteria of comparative wage rates, cost of living, ability to pay, and the like are too vague to serve as relatively objective criteria. Furthermore, they are not wholly consistent with income stability. A cost-of-living or ability-to-pay criterion, for example, can just as easily feed an inflation as stop it.

Should government regulation of the general level of wage rates and relative wage rates be attempted, it has sometimes been suggested that the general rules for pricing in a socialist price system might be followed. Under such a scheme, a governmentally determined wage rate would be set for each classification of worker in each labor market in the economy. Whenever a shortage of a particular kind of laborer in a particular market appears, the wage rate would be raised to eliminate the shortage. Whenever a surplus of a particular kind of laborer in a particular market appeared, the wage rate would be lowered to absorb such a surplus.

The practical difficulties in such a program are tremendous. The task of classification of workers and labor markets is great in itself. Beyond this the scheme runs into the difficulty that neither workers nor employers respond quickly to wage changes as a general rule. Nor do they respond even after a considerable lapse of time—as long as several years. Business firms "build up" a wage-price decision which at least in the short period commits the firm to the employment of a more or less fixed number of workers—unless the entire basic price-wage-production plan is reconsidered. Wage reduction will not therefore induce employers to increase hiring. Nor will wage increases result in layoffs. Likewise, workers are often not very responsive to wage changes because employment opportunities rather than wage rates are their primary interests. An assurance of employment is a more effective inducement to mobility than a wage increase in many cases.

For these and other reasons the mechanical rules of the socialist price system do not appear to offer practicable possibilities of government wage regulation in the foreseeable future.

The most promising criterion—mentioned several times—is productivity. The merit of the productivity criterion is simply that, if wage rates can somehow be tied roughly to productivity, wage costs will not rise and hence produce a wage-induced inflation. One of the difficulties of the criterion is that, while we can find a statistical index of productivity as a basis for influencing wage rates—the long-run average increase in national real output per man-hour, for example—any other measure of productivity is a crude statistical approximation.[4]

A more serious objection, however, is that the use of such a productivity index does not give much guidance to government policy in any immediate short-run situation or in any particular industry. In the short run, productivity and wage rates in fact display a tendency to move in opposite directions or in the same direction at quite different rates.[5] An attempt to influence wage rates in the short run in such a way as to bring the movement of productivity and wage rates close together would run counter to customs and expectations regarding wage rates held by both management and labor.[6]

Given a general commitment to long-term movements of wage rates in accordance with changes in productivity throughout the economy, the problem of what wage rates ought to be set at a particular time

4. See Solomon Fabricant, "Of Productivity Statistics: An Admonition," *Review of Economics and Statistics, 31* (November, 1949), 309–311.

5. Clark Kerr, "The Short-Run Behavior of Physical Productivity and Average Hourly Earnings," *Review of Economics and Statistics, 31* (November, 1949), 299.

6. See Clark Kerr's arguments on this point in his article, *ibid.,* p. 307.

must be viewed in the context of the issues pertaining to wage-price policy outlined in Chapter 3 (pp. 152 ff.); following the line of argument developed there, "we need to consider the impact of a wage increase . . . on the relation between consumption and income, on the level of business saving, and on the level of business investment."

The ways in which these variables are influenced by wage changes are many. Roughly speaking, wage rates which leave profits too large will reduce consumer spending, and wage rates which leave profits too small will reduce business spending. A lower limit to the range in which optimum wage rates are to be found is presumably set where further reductions would reduce consumer spending below the level desired for income and employment stability. The upper limit to the range is presumably set by wage rates which impose such high costs on employers as to reduce business spending by more than consumer spending increases.

To discover the optimum or the range of the optimum wage rate, we need to know more than we now do about the behavior of the variables involved, and we need more adequate and more precise statistics on these variables at any given time. But it would seem that we already know enough to conclude that no moderately simple criterion for wage changes can be seriously proposed. We can only hope that a relatively dispassionate inquiry into the relevant variables will, in a particular situation in which a decision must be made, give rise to some measure of agreement among investigators. To the limited extent that this is a possibility, government will be able to announce a wage policy and defend it. For all the different interpretations that may be put on the facts in any particular case, there is already a reasonably wide agreement on such useful policy propositions as, for example, that feasibility in policy requires respect for certain traditional differentials or, for another example, that expanding areas should have larger wage increases than other areas.

We shall probably have to abandon hope for establishing any effective control either through collective bargaining or through government wage regulation over *relative* wage rates, however. That is to say, the most we can hope for is control of the *general level* of wage rates sufficient to maintain economic stability. A more precise control of relative wage rates in order to maintain a reasonably efficient allocation of resources will be ours only by luck in collective bargaining, for we do not have at hand the political conditions or skills necessary to handle so detailed a regulation of wage rates.

Again it is clear that the problem of union power and the price of labor is much the same as the problem of the farm bloc and agricultural prices or the problem of business power and monopoly prices. With habits of thought and institutional arrangements suited to an atomized individualistic society, we are hard pressed to deal successfully with the political and economic problems forced on us by the dominant collectivities in our economy.

CHAPTER XII. *Full Employment versus Progress and Other Economic Goals*

BY PAUL A. SAMUELSON

I. INTRODUCTION

Full employment is an important goal; but it is not the only goal of modern economic society. We all wish for men to be employed rather than idle; but we also wish for them to be employed at useful tasks and under conditions of personal freedom. We wish for our parents to enjoy old-age security beyond that enjoyed by our grandparents; but we also profess to desire for our children a standard of living beyond any we have known. Attacks on the rights of property and on gross inequality in the distribution of wealth and income seem to elicit resonant responses in modern democracies; at the same time, our mixed system of private and public enterprise does require incentives to elicit human efforts and it does still depend upon pecuniary profits and losses to organize the bulk of economic activity.

Suppose economic science were more exact than it is, so that all experts could agree in prescribing a legislative package to abolish unemployment; and even suppose that good will among men were to overcome partisan and class differences, so that the American people, through Congress, were willing to buy this legislative package. Would a new Utopia on earth then follow? The answer is, obviously, no.

If anyone doubts this, he need only look at many countries of western Europe, such as Britain. In the postwar period such countries have had to worry about almost every conceivable economic problem except that of job shortages. They have been concerned with the low volume of imports that can be bought for their exports and with the virtual disappearance of their prewar investment income from abroad. They have been concerned with the problem of increasing the efficiency of manufacturing industry and with the need to increase their defensive strength. And this is only the beginning of a long list of basic economic difficulties other than those raised by depression unemployment.

I think it no exaggeration to say that for a dozen or more years following 1930 economists were obsessed with the problem of full employment. Probably this was only as it should have been. In time of plague one does not worry about sunburn nor even about senescence. But any single one note—whatever its quality and timbre—if held a long time becomes a little offensive to the ear. It was only to be expected, therefore, that many people should have begun to be a little bored with the continuous discussion of employment policy, particularly during the war and postwar years when the demand for labor seemed almost insatiable. And there is still another understandable reason for suspicion of full employment policies. For many years reform legislation of all kinds—social security, farm aid, etc.—has been advanced not only for its own sake but also in the name of full employment and as a device to bolster purchasing power. It is ironical that the argument used against the early New Deal—which asserted the opposition between reform and recovery—should in the end have been displaced by the opposite political allegation which tried to claim that reform was necessary for full employment.

The present chapter is concerned with one central theme: What are the relationships between employment stabilization policies and other goals of economic life? Does job security go hand in hand with technical progress, the one reinforcing the other? Or is the price of full employment some sacrifice in our rate of material progress? Does the twentieth-century democratic demand for so-called "greater equity" as between rich and poor subtract from, or contribute to, the growth of productivity? Will continued full employment strengthen us in case of war, or will it provide an extra obstacle to be overcome in some future political emergency? These are all complex issues that will become increasingly pressing as we succeed in maintaining high employment. To the extent that we fail in this goal, to the extent that mass unemployment prevails, these questions will be treated as academic and will be shelved in the face of an insistent political demand for governmental action.

II. Full Employment and Other Short-Run Goals

1. *Full employment, in itself, bad?*

The arguments against a full employment stabilization program are numerous and of varying quality. There are enough sound objections and enough real dilemmas of national policy to permit us to dismiss summarily a number of the more extreme and foolish viewpoints that have received expression in past years. Only in this way can we hope to clear the air for a consideration of the more thoughtful and rational doubts that have been expressed.

First we may dismiss the ascetic view that unemployment causing adversity and suffering is a good thing in itself. Such arguments carried considerable weight in nineteenth-century discussions of the poor laws, but they only injure the cause of those who advance them today. Congressional oratory, newspaper editorials, sermons and encyclicals, and the expressed votes of the electorate at poll after poll all clearly indicate that the American people are against unemployment. They apparently do not take seriously the argument that with plentiful job opportunities the family will be weakened, as women (and youths) are called out of the home. Just as the public is "agin sin" it is against unemployment.

2. *Effects on productivity*

There is a second, less crude, argument that deserves more consideration. Suppose that public policies do succeed in maintaining high employment levels so that any qualified person looking for a job can hope to find a reasonably good opening in not too long a time. What will happen to labor turnover and to factory discipline and productivity when workers no longer need fear being thrown into long-term unemployment and onto relief or worse?

In advancing the argument that unemployment is needed to police workers' willingness to do an honest day's work, extreme conservatives are often unknowingly repeating the thesis of communist critics of the capitalistic system. One of the central tenets of Marxism has always been the belief that a "reserve army of the unemployed" is absolutely necessary to the functioning of a profit system. As observers we may chuckle, but as analysts we cannot reject a view simply because of its bipolar sponsorship. The contention that unemployment may be good for productivity merits careful examination.

At the beginning we must be clear on one thing. This is not particularly an attack on government-created full employment. If valid it is an attack on full employment itself, and it scores a point against the desirability of a "new era" of spontaneous prosperity sustained by private enterprise just as much as it does against an era of publicly created prosperity. Again, this is not to deny the possible validity of the view under examination.

a. LABOR MOBILITY

On the face of it, I think it reasonable to expect higher voluntary labor turnover on the part of workers when they know the penalty of quitting a job is not likely to be long-time unemployment. And to some extent this is certainly an evil, an economic cost whose value must be measured in terms of lower realized national output. But labor mobility and turn-over is not an unmixed evil. One of the attributes of the good life is variety and change; when a worker changes jobs his pay is interrupted, but who is to say that (in moderation) this is not an acceptable way for him to spend his available income? More than that, we know from studies of geographical labor markets that much of labor turnover is among the very young; and it is by means of shopping around and by trial and error that the youthful entrants to the labor force finally settle down into their suitable niches.

Full employment is blamed for causing too high labor mobility. It is also blamed for causing too little! Thus an inventor who wishes to set up a factory to produce a new product is supposed to be unable in prosperous times to recruit a labor force for this worth-while purpose. Likewise the flexibility of the system in adjusting to changing tastes and conditions is believed to be impaired by full employment.

Implicit in all this is the hidden premise that high or full employment necessarily means a "seller's market" for labor. Must this always be so? When there is a high demand and supply for wheat, we do not regard it as impossible for a new baker to buy extra wheat for some new purpose. Of course his need (and his pecuniary ability) must be great enough to enable him to bid away wheat from other uses. Likewise, under conditions of full employment, any one enterprise should be able to draw labor from other uses, provided it can offer sufficiently attrac-tive working conditions and wages. It would be an uneconomic use of limited national resources to keep pools of manpower or equipment idle on the off-chance that some worthy innovator might like to use them in his experimental promotions. This would clearly involve a hidden subsidy to such activities, perhaps an excessive one in terms of eco-nomic cost and efficiency. If we do want to adopt a national policy of providing subsidies to pioneering activities, let us do so with our eyes wide open, knowing what costs we are incurring and not throwing the burden on the groups least able to afford them, namely, the families of the unemployed.[1] Policies designed to aid retraining and mobility of labor come to mind at once in this connection.

My preceding paragraphs do not meet squarely the contention that, while full employment policies do not *necessarily* mean a seller's market for labor (in which it becomes almost impossible for any one employer to expand his working force even if he has the money to meet an ex-

---

1. This raises the whole problem of our patent system, antitrust policies, regula-tion of capital flotations, Reconstruction Finance Corporation programs, and gen-eral credit and tax policies.

panded payroll), nonetheless full employment policies as pursued in many countries are in fact likely to lead to conditions of "repressed inflation." Indeed one leading exponent of such policies, Lord Beveridge, the author of *Full Employment in a Free Society*, has declared it as a goal of action that there be reached so high a level of monetary demand as to require direct price and output controls; and critics of European labor governments have sometimes alleged that there have been cases where factories have been completed only to find that no labor could be recruited for them.

I conclude that there is considerable force in the argument that we are here faced with something of a dilemma in our choice between 1) full employment and 2) price-wage stabilization. But this problem has been explored by other writers in this symposium and I shall for the most part neglect it in my discussion, interpreting my task to be that of appraising the costs of a successful two-sided stabilization program that guards against inflation as well as deflation.[2]

b. WORKER MORALE AND PRODUCTIVITY

Let me return to the problem of factory discipline and productivity. All of us are familiar with the more extreme examples of union featherbedding and make-work rules: limited-size paint brushes, stand-by musicians, etc. But it appears that even the experts in the field of labor economics cannot make up their minds on the *net* effects of unionization on productivity.[3] It is still harder to form an estimate of the relationship of full employment to productivity. Pretty clearly, some forms of work slowdowns grow out of a fear on the part of the workers that if they are "eager-beavers" they will quickly work themselves and their fellows out of a job. Good, plentiful employment opportunities can be expected, over time, to lessen this motive for such harmful practices; the growth of mass unemployment, on the other hand, can be expected to intensify such practices.

In the past workers were stimulated to put forth effort and skill by holding out wage incentives and by prodding them with the threat of discharge. From a hard-boiled production standpoint, no one has been able to work out the optimal combination of rewards and penalties, of carrots and kicks. Relaxed men may fall asleep; tense, frightened men may be equally poor producers. Psychologists and sociologists who have studied the modern factory place great emphasis—under present-

2. See Chapter 11 for discussion of the wage-price spiral problem.
3. See S. H. Slichter, *The Challenge of Industrial Relations* (Ithaca, Cornell University Press, 1947).

day conditions—upon factors of morale and teamwork and upon non-pecuniary aspects of the workers' environment.[4]

One further relationship between full employment and productivity deserves investigation. Unionization has grown in importance over the past years but it is still far short of covering all of American industry. Does full employment contribute to or work against the growth of this important but controversial institution? No pat answer can be given. Generally the historical record seems to show that expanding business conditions are good for the growth of unionization and depressions are bad. The two world wars, with their accompanying "overfull employment," represent high-water marks of organized labor; and in our more distant past depressions were associated with recessions in unions' strength and influence. Still, the prosperity era of the 1920's represents a major (and perhaps unrepeatable) exception; organized labor lost ground in those years. It is significant that in the years of expansion following 1932 organized labor, with the aid of new government attitudes, made its greatest peacetime advance; perhaps it is no less significant that the period 1933–36 was also one in which, although there was strong recovery from the depression trough, there still remained a sizable amount of unemployment.[5]

C. STABILIZATION AND GOOD MANAGEMENT

Labor productivity is in many ways a misleading concept. It tends to distract our attention from the important factors, other than personal attitudes and skills of workers, that are responsible for more or less efficient production. To the extent that continued high employment results in sellers' markets and protects business from the pinch of adversity, there may be a gradual relaxation of effort on the part of management and a slackening or slowing down of productivity improvements. Needless to say, such an outcome is not inevitable since, even with general demand being continuously maintained, there may still be such vigorous competition from rivals that productivity is kept up to par. Moreover, to the extent that costs rise and prices are held down by direct controls or other rigidities, there is a great incentive for management to introduce cost-saving methods. From the historical evidence we cannot be sure that there have been *any* significant differences in productivity growth during good and bad times.

Stabilization of business activity should carry with it some improve-

---

4. The pioneering work of Elton Mayo, Fritz J. Roethlisberger, and other Harvard Business School workers may be cited.

5. See Horace B. Davis, "The Theory of Union Growth," *Quarterly Journal of Economics*, 55 (August, 1941), 611–637.

ments in productivity even if management and worker attitudes are not particularly favorable. Stop and go production is expensive production. The fear of a decline in markets often prevents firms from using methods which would be extremely productive in turning out steady streams of output. This explains why many firms on their own initiative engaged in internal stabilization programs which guaranteed a certain continuity of employment and wages to their workers.[6] A quite similar favorable effect on productivity results from the fact that if borrowers and lenders did not have to fear sudden precipitous declines in business activity, the risks of capital formation would be greatly reduced, thereby making it possible for firms to use a more efficient amount of capital.

It should be noted that many of the points discussed in the last few paragraphs are more crucially affected by the stabilization of business activity than by the quantitative level of employment and output at which stabilization takes place. Thus, if we were to forego the target of full employment, replacing it instead by the goal of holding steadily to some 5 or 10% level of unemployment, many of the favorable effects on productivity would still take place. Too often stabilization of activity and maintenance of full employment are treated as if they were synonymous.

No final evaluation of the relationships between full employment and productivity can be attempted here. On balance I am inclined to the view that there are some net losses of potential productivity that must be charged against such a program and that perhaps these costs increase at an accelerated rate as we try to squeeze out the last little drop of extra employment from our system. Much research remains to be done in this area and other observers may, quite properly, read the record in the opposite way. Furthermore, the costs I have mentioned can perhaps be expected to become less important in the future and possibly even to reverse their net direction. Collective bargaining seems here to stay; when full employment has helped to unionize an industry it cannot unionize it again, and further full employment may help to make the unions "mature" and "responsible." In the future, gentle prods rather than the whiplash of chronic unemployment may be the better part of wisdom in handling the human animal.

Nor should we forget that man does not live by bread alone. High scores in productivity are not the sole ends of the good life. We do not

6. There is a voluminous literature on guaranteed annual wage plans of the Procter & Gamble or Hormel type. See *Guaranteed Wages,* Report to the President by the Advisory Board of the Office of War Mobilization and Reconversion, January 31, 1947, for references and discussion.

tell the American people they are wrong in taking out part of the historical increases in productivity in the form of shorter working weeks and more leisure. Similarly, we cannot say nay to the American worker if he wishes to give up something of material goods in exchange for working at a slower pace and enjoying greater independence and personal dignity on the job. The difficulty is to make sure that the worker is in fact getting something commensurate with his sacrificed output, and is not simply frustrating his instincts of craftsmanship in return for senseless bravado. Moreover, there may be dangers to traditional middle-class values in a worker-dominated society.

3. *Effects on total output*

Whatever the net effects are of a tight labor market on productivity of people on the job, they should not be confused with the changes in total output that will result from full employment. More people on the job should, other things being equal, result in larger total output available for current consumption or capital formation. Longer hours per week should have the same effect. In addition, there is the more subtle effect of upgrading of people into better jobs, this being the reverse effect of "disguised unemployment" that results from depressed levels of total effective demand. In prosperity marginal farm laborers leave the country for higher-productive city jobs. Door-to-door salesmen can give up the attempt to make a bare living at what is too often not very productive work by any criterion. And similarly with other examples of disguised unemployment.

Since increased employment may itself affect productivity, the percentage changes in output may be greater or less than the changes in employment. To the extent that the people brought into employment are qualitatively inferior, the resulting change in output may be expected to be less than proportional to the change in people or total man-hours. To the extent that short-run bottlenecks of full plant capacity are encountered short of the point of full employment, the law of diminishing returns may also be operative; and to the extent that natural resources are limited, this short-run effect may be carried over even into the indefinitely long run.

On the other hand, there is a possible countertendency in the form of increasing returns to scale: by "spreading overhead factors" and overcoming "indivisibilities" of productive organization, increased employment may actually result in increases rather than decreases in productivity. Again the statistical record is not clear. We cannot isolate the effects of employment changes from other concomitant variations. The statistical data, such as they are, do not seem to indicate any clear-cut tendency toward diminishing returns during upswings in the business cycle; if the recent wartime indexes of production could be taken seriously, the possibilities of the countertendency toward increasing returns would have to be taken seriously. Particularly must we recognize the "upgrading" that comes with expansions so that, even if productivity in each occupation were constant, average productivity for the community would rise because of shifts from low productivity jobs to high.

The existence of increasing returns can create some difficulties for the theoretical economists' vision of perfect competition—since it is often under these conditions that competition becomes "ruinous" and monopoly firms tend to drive out competitors. On the whole, depressions make this worse and full employment may help keep competition viable by so increasing the level of total demand as to permit a larger number of effective competitors to remain in the industry.

Our findings with respect to the problem of this section can be briefly summarized: *higher employment probably means higher output,* but not necessarily in the same degree. There is no conclusive evidence as to whether long-run returns of output would be in greater than or less than proportion to the increase in total man-hours worked. As to effects on progress, this will be discussed in the latter half of this chapter.

4. Full employment and our national security strength

We live in troubled times. Great interest attaches to the economic sinews of war. Would full employment increase or decrease our defensive and offensive strength in the next war years? The question of our *long-run* military strength—or economic war potential—is closely related to the question of our long-run rate of economic progress and may be deferred to a later section; but discussion of the short-run aspects belongs here.

An economist cannot pretend to give an expert opinion on some of the intangible political aspects of the question. Would mass unemployment help the growth of communism in America and lessen the fighting morale of our armed services and civilian labor force? Would it contribute to radical legislation having no immediate relation to recovery and that would be weakening to our productive system?

To some extent the answer to the first of these questions, I should suppose, must be yes. But it is probably *sudden* deterioration in people's economic position that causes them to be disappointed and to seek desperate solutions. If failure to achieve full employment were to mean that in the next few years we were to slip undramatically behind our true economic potential with the situation being glossed over by shorter hours and unemployment compensation of one form or another, the dangers to our democracy may perhaps have been exaggerated in the discussions of recent years. I question whether our democratic system is quite so fair-weather a flower as some have come to regard it. But undoubtedly failure to maintain high employment will involve important noneconomic costs of this character. Moreover, the rest of the world's opinion of us and of our way of life would be seriously blackened if we were to succumb to a great depression.

There is an opposing argument, according to which unemployment actually adds to the military potential of a nation. It used to be said that Hitler was fortunate to have come into power at the bottom of the depression, because this enabled him to syphon off the subsequent increase in German output almost entirely into war preparations. (Recent data made available by surveys of the German war effort show that consumption in Germany grew more after 1933 than it was fashionable for us then to believe, but this does not refute the point.) By the same token the war effort of the United States was considered to be helped after 1940 by the fact that we then still had eight million unemployed who could be moved into the war effort. This enabled us to have extra guns *and* extra butter; had employment been full, we should, according to this argument, have been forced to give up civilian goods for war products. A popular present-day extension of this type of reasoning leads to the conclusion that if war should break out in an atmosphere of full employment, such as prevailed in the early 1950's, consumption would have to be cut instantly and sharply.

On the factual side this last conclusion overlooks important hidden buffers of manpower in the American economy. These result from the fact that, as compared with other nations and with war conditions, we Americans work, even under full employment conditions, a small number of hours per week or year; and only a relatively small number of Americans of working age are normally in the working force. Simply by working longer hours and by having women, youths, and the aged return to the labor force, according to the pattern of World War II, we could substantially expand our military use of resources without cutting down on consumption. The further fact that consumers' and producers' durable goods are such an important part of the American economy makes possible an additional expansion in our war effort without any great reduction in *current* consumption of the *services* of those durable goods by final consumers or by producers.

Aside from being factually misleading, the view that unemployment actually improves our military potential is theoretically weak in the following respect. It is probably not easier or quicker to transfer an unemployed worker (say, in Detroit) from the relief rolls to war work than it is to transfer him from a peacetime job making automobiles to a wartime job making tanks. When employed, he has not evaporated away and been made unavailable for war purposes. Under modern conditions we must convert *whole enterprises* to military production; and it is perhaps easier to do this when people are attached to productive employment than when their skills are rotting in idleness. When total demand is depressed, it is employment in the durable goods trades that suffers most; and it is peculiarly these trades which, when they are in operation, can be regarded as stand-by military resources. The present argument is only strengthened when we add to these manpower considerations the fact that our plant capacities and inventories of goods and skills are likely to be more favorable for war purposes after a period of high rather than low employment. Undoubtedly our high levels of civilian production of steel and durables in the 1945–50 postwar period added to our strength to meet the post-Korean challenge.[7]

Starting out from full employment rather than depression, we are able to reach as high or higher a level of military strength (compatible with the same level of minimum civilian consumption). But in moving to this wartime position from a full employment starting point, it is indisputable that we appear to be giving up more of civilian consumption, investment, and governmental goods than if we were to move to that same position from a starting point of mass unemployment. In the latter cases we give up, so to speak, the goods we have been wasting in idleness.

People probably strive harder to maintain the consumption levels that they have already been enjoying than they do to reach levels they have never known. Here lies the essential truth in the view that unemployment makes it easier to run a war. Depression does not really add to our war potential, but it may put us in the frame of mind where we are more willing to make the civilian sacrifices necessary to reach that full potential.

For example, suppose that America and her allies need very heavy defensive military expenditures. If there should be heavy unemployment in the next few years, Congress and the people might be more willing to approve these necessary expenditures than they would if the civilian demand for goods is extremely brisk. Moreover, since need is a relative thing, this would be a rational decision, because the alternative needs

---

7. It should be admitted that high production does create problems in connection with the more rapid depletion of exhaustible resources such as copper, nickel, oil, etc.

for capital formation would be exercising a correspondingly smaller pull. Undoubtedly, high employment in western Europe complicates the problem of quickly building up effective defense programs.

Related to the problem of getting people to give up resources to a postulated war need, there is the problem of getting them to do so in a manner that will minimize inflation and the need for stringent price or fiscal controls. The problem of maintaining financial stability and preventing inflation will probably be more difficult if we start out our war program from a position of full employment. Having experienced rising prices recently, people are less likely to save voluntarily so large a fraction of their expanded money incomes; they probably will not respond so fully to patriotic drives to increase thrift and bond purchases; possibly the excess income which they cannot spend because of rationing and direct controls will not pile up so peacefully and harmlessly in the form of savings but instead will exert greater pressures on black markets and the enforceability of direct controls.

We may conclude that *full employment makes more difficult the problem of financing a war without inflation and undue controls,* and may increase the resistance of people within a democracy to endure austerity in the interests of the war effort. But these effects should not be confused, as they are in current discussions, with the view that depression unemployment actually boosts real war potential. The reverse is probably true, as we have seen.

5. *Full employment and proper use of all economic resources*

In my discussion up to this point, I have been able to take up the effects of stabilization policies in the abstract without having to go into the specific character of the public or private policies adopted to achieve full employment. To do justice to the question of whether such policies result in an inefficient pattern of labor and material resource use, our inquiry must become more specific: we must analyze the different effects of different possible employment programs on the wise allocation of economic resources.[8]

It is only too easy to imagine antidepression government program that do lead to a wasteful use of resources. Hiring people to dig holes and fill them up is a well-known example. During the worst years of depression and general despair, some people became so pessimistic as

8. There are of course many problems with which stabilization programs are not primarily concerned (e.g., monopoly, distressed areas, tariffs, quotas, etc.). It is remarkable how even these may be favorably affected by successful full employment programs (viz., our success during boom times in lowering tariffs, the almost miraculous impact of the war on distressed areas, etc.).

to think that governments had no other choice than to adopt such measures. They even defended such measures, arguing:

> Old-fashioned economists of the extreme "classical" persuasion have been talking palpable and patent nonsense for years. During the past century, when the world has gone through two score well-documented periods of boom and bust, these old fossils have been stubbornly denying that general overproduction is possible—that you can no more create or destroy purchasing power than you can create or destroy energy. This perverted form of the classical doctrine is not only logically erroneous but it is historically utter nonsense. Mass unemployment is a fact. The only cure is to "get purchasing power out" somehow; and for this purpose the government must find *by hook or crook* public work projects that will put people to work, and it must look for foreign markets upon which we can dump our exports and from whom we must stop buying goods. [So goes the argument.]

Of course this is a caricature of what may be called the *neomercantilist* doctrine—so named because it represents a return to the prenineteenth century views of the mercantilist writers who thought it important for people to work rather than to consume and to export goods rather than to import them. The neomercantilist view is as extreme and fallacious as the classical dogmas against which it is reacting. Careful students of economics are increasingly in agreement that our system is such as to permit us—by appropriate fiscal and monetary policies—to keep our resources from being wasted in mass unemployment, *and to do this in a great variety of alternative ways so as to yield almost any desired pattern of want fulfillment.*[9]

Specifically, we can make work by digging holes and filling them up, but why should we want to? We can pursue beggar-my-neighbor policies of foreign exchange depreciation and import controls. These may add to our total of domestic purchasing power; they may offer what appears to the worker to be useful work for his eager hands to do; they may even, from a narrow national viewpoint, seem preferable to a policy of do-nothing-at-all. But such policies—that get us nothing useful for our efforts and dollars—are demonstrably worse than alternatives that do have all the same favorable repercussions on total purchasing power and *also* give us useful public or private consumption and capital goods. There is nothing such despairing neomercantilist policies can do for us that an earthquake or a war catastrophe cannot do as well. If the people as a whole prefer private consumption goods to government public

9. See Chapters 5–9 for detailed discussion of alternative programs.

works, then we can fight mass unemployment by cutting taxes rather than by increasing public construction; we can improve the environment for venture capital; or we can expand welfare expenditure (such as social security, etc.), which will enlarge private consumption rather than government use of goods and services, if that is what is desired.

It took technical economists a decade to grasp this principle: *through a variety of such different actions, large-scale wastage of economic resources can be avoided, and the only sensible policy to be followed is that which yields the final pattern of production that a democratic people want.*

This may be called the neoclassical doctrine.[10] It, too, has been oversimplified in this exposition and should be qualified in a number of ways (e.g., there are problems of timing, of prediction, of wage-price spirals, of pressure groups, etc.). Within a framework of maintained high employment, the old and important classical problems of scarcity and economic cost and divergent group interests come into their own.

What does this rather optimistic viewpoint imply concerning the pattern of appropriate policies? The answer depends in part upon what the American people, as individuals and as interdependent citizens, really want. (To be sure none of us really knows his own mind completely, and we are all tempted to vote public projects whose true costs [11] to ourselves are not very apparent, since at the time we make our decision no down-payment may be exacted. On the other hand, we often neglect to carry out some public collective activities, which if we had them might seem worth while to most of us. A community can afford the governmental activities that it wants provided it is prepared to make the requisite sacrifices.)

The optimal policies also depend upon the choices open to us. For example, the desirable amount of public spending is a variable thing. If private investment opportunities happen to be very strong, so that many highly useful capital projects are crying to be done, most of us would consider it only prudent to contract the resources engaged in useful public activities. Correspondingly, when the pull of private capi-

10. By analogy with neomercantilism and not to be confused with the narrower neoclassical doctrine of pure theory. See my chapter in *Money, Trade, and Economic Growth: In Honor of John Henry Williams* (New York, Macmillan, 1951), entitled "Principles and Rules in Modern Fiscal Policy: A Neo-Classical Reformulation," for an elaboration of this neoclassical view. See also Chapter 8 of this book.

11. The exact nature of these costs cannot be expressed simply in terms of the tax dollars that one should raise in order to finance all or part of any given expenditure. We must also remember that no "neutral" tax system can ever be devised which will not "distort" production and consumption decisions; tax burdens of this kind must be considered as part of the cost of government outlay. See Chapter 6.

tal or consumption needs is relatively relaxed, the margin of desirable governmental use of resources should expand.[12] All this follows from the simple logic of rational choice and setting of priorities among alternatives.

The reader has missed the point of what I have called the neoclassical doctrine if he thinks that this boils down to the familiar notion that public works should be contracted in time of boom simply *in order to curb inflation* and expanded in depression simply *in order to stimulate purchasing power.* These are *not* the reasons for a countercyclical policy of government expenditure according to the neoclassical doctrine, since this already accepts it as axiomatic that deflation and inflation can be moderated by a variety of other devices. Except under highly special value standards, public works have no prior claim over other stabilization devices (such as variable tax collections and tax legislation). The only sound reason for justifying public works, or any other policies, is in terms of society's preference for the resulting pattern of output and resource use.

If this whole line of reasoning is acceptable—and I think it follows from traditional economic analysis—then we must raise our eyebrows at certain special prescriptions that have been popularized in recent years. I refer to the notion that while the total of the tax collections should vary anticyclically, the total of government expenditure should not be varied in this manner; and to the even more narrow dictum that *tax rates* should be kept constant over a long period of years, sole reliance for stabilization being placed on automatic variations in the taxes that will be collected out of varying national income. In principle, these are false guides to national policy—although occasionally there is something to be said for them on pragmatic grounds under special circumstances.[13]

12. If the reduction of private investment is due to "irrational" psychological expectations, there is a strong case for measures that expand private activity. Even if private investment is "genuinely" low, the gap it leaves should usually *not* be completely filled up by expansion of government expenditure, but rather by a mixture of extra private consumption and extra public expenditure.

13. The view that I am criticizing has been widely advocated in recent years. E.g., in the 1947 *Economic Report of the President* there is the statement (p. 40): ". . . we should attempt to stabilize public-works construction according to our long-term needs." Later this is qualified. See also Beardsley Ruml and H. C. Sonne, *Fiscal and Monetary Policy,* National Planning Association, Pamphlet No. 35 (1944) and *Taxes and the Budget: A Program for Prosperity in a Free Economy,* Committee on Economic Development (New York, 1948). In the following four-sentence quotation, the first two sentences are reasonably satisfactory, but the final two represent an illegitimate inference from the first two. ". . . government expenditures on goods and services . . . [should be determined] entirely on the basis of

6. *Some qualifications*

My optimistic account of the broad variety of paths to full employment must be realistically qualified. In a world subject to rapid unpredictable dynamic change, it would not be possible to act quickly
enough to offset all upward and downward movements in output and
prices, even if we should want to do so. Moreover, the repercussions of
any governmental program are themselves distributed over time in a
not completely predictable fashion, so that in trying to make a transient
situation better we may actually make it worse. It is more realistic,
therefore, to admit that short-run fluctuations of some amplitude are
to be expected even in the face of a successful stabilization program.
But mass unemployment and long-time deviations in one direction
should be capable of being largely avoided if we are agreed to do so.

A second warning may be needed lest my exposition be misunderstood. Although our arsenal of antidepression measures is a broad one,
it is not necessarily the case that in it are any weapons that achieve
their purpose *without costs.* Even when we have picked those which,
in terms of our set of ethical ends are least costly, there may still be an
irreducible minimum of costs. Therefore, full employment itself must
be regarded as one of many goals, and we must be prepared to pursue
it only to the extent that the gains outweigh the costs. This means that
the last ounce of high employment may be deemed not worth the sacrifices it would entail; and where high employment programs entail losses
in other directions—such as private autonomy, incentives, growth, etc.
—a calculation of alternative benefits is in order.

As a corollary of the above reminder, we must not reject any one
antidepression measure solely because it entails some disadvantages:
such a rejection would be rational only if there were a perfect alternative, and there is not. We must choose among the lesser of evils or
among the greater of goods. When we reject a measure like boondog-
gling on the ground that a better measure is possible, we must be sure

the community's desire, need, and willingness to pay for public services. Changes
in the level of expenditure should be made solely in response to alterations in the
relative value attached by the community to public services and private consumption. No attempt should be made to vary expenditure, either directly or inversely,
in response to cyclical fluctuations in business activity. Since the community's basic
objectives would presumably change only slowly—except in time of war or immediate threat of war—this policy would, with the same exception, lead to a relatively stable volume of expenditure on goods and services." M. Friedman, "A Monetary and Fiscal Framework for Economic Stability," *American Economic Review,*
38 (June, 1948), 246. See my previously cited essay for further elaborations and
also Chapter 8 of this volume.

that this better method is in fact being used and that the relevant political choice is not between a half-good measure and no action at all.

Most of the above qualifications refer to the problem of avoiding mass depression. Unfortunately the problem of inflation and the problem of deflation are not simple opposites: there is no simple algebraic 'flation problem. Inflation usually can be taken to mean generally rising prices; but deflation, in its most objectionable sense, is not simply a falling of prices but rather a general decline in output and employment.

Provided we can forestall a great slump from getting under way and cumulatively sending the system downward—and in my view this should be within our powers—the nature of the policies needed to fight general unemployment is fairly well understood. But our experiences in the last fifteen years suggest that the problem of maintaining reasonably steady prices is much more difficult than that of preventing mass unemployment. It is possible that whenever we attain enough steam in the purchasing power boiler to lead to high employment and to get rid of much disguised unemployment, we will encounter upward wage pushes on prices. Hence, under modern labor market conditions, perhaps we must choose between high employment and steady prices; perhaps we cannot have both.

This is the heart of the so-called wage-price problem and it presents us with a dilemma. If every upward thrust in wages, beyond improvements in real productivity, is accompanied by fiscal and monetary policies that enable full employment output to be sold at the new higher prices, then we may be able to keep full employment but with rising prices. Moreover, single unions and employers will then have every reason to continue the process. On the other hand, if we try to buck the upward pressure on prices from the supply side by fiscal and monetary policies that reduce demand or do not permit it to rise enough to absorb the full employment output at higher prices, then production and employment must fall. If we stubbornly insist on having average prices remain constant, and if trade unions stubbornly prescribe too high money wages, then the drop in employment may have to be very considerable.

Now it is possible that a very small degree of unemployment in the labor market might serve to persuade or to force unions from asking and getting increases in their money wages greater than productivity changes. If so, we are lucky and the wage-price dilemma does not exist. Unfortunately, our knowledge of the true empirical relations is necessarily scanty since nature has not performed the requisite controlled experiments for us. The price rise and course of events since 1935 is not inconsistent with the optimistic or pessimistic interpretation.

Much further investigation and observation are needed in this important realm.[14]

7. *Stabilization efforts and income distribution*

The first half of the present essay—that part dealing with current short-run effects of full employment policies as distinct from the effects on long-run trends—can be brought to a close after we have discussed one final issue. Do such stabilization programs fall in with the modern tendency—so dear to demagogues but also apparently so deeply rooted in our culture [15]—toward favoring a less unequal distribution of income? Do they tend to lead to soaking the rich and favoring the poor? If so, is this an inevitable consequence of such policies?

Among many early Keynesian writers there was, I think, the belief that America's problem in future years is more likely to be that of fighting deflation than inflation. There was also a belief that the rich have a much lower (marginal) propensity to spend their incomes than do the poor; so that aside from any intrinsic merits in heavily progressive income taxation, there was supposed to be an additional purchasing power argument in favor of such measures. More recent statistical studies of family spending habits have cast some doubts as to the quantitative leverage of redistribution of income on the total of American saving: the income of the very rich does not bulk large, and the spending habits of the rest of the income classes do not differ greatly in respect to *changes* in income. Also, it follows from the neoclassical viewpoint outlined above that if it were desirable on general ethical or other grounds to leave higher income in the hands of the wealthy, then means (other than income redistribution) can certainly be found to prevent unemployment. Hence, a move toward greater equality of income is never mandatory for stabilization purposes.

Nonetheless, any judicious person will have to admit that the existence of heavy unemployment has the effect, politically and economically, to reinforce any latent ethical and political tendencies favoring the adoption of policies designed to redistribute income in favor of the poor, especially since relief and other welfare programs are usually designed for the poor rather than the wealthy.

But by the same logic an honest person should admit that the reverse policies are indicated to the degree that our problem is one of inflation

14. See Chapter 11. Also see the essay by E. S. Mason cited in the Williams volume (n. 10, above) and the views expressed by John H. Clark, G. Haberler, Edward H. Chamberlin, and Milton Friedman in *The Impact of the Union* (New York, Harcourt, Brace, 1951), David McCord Wright, ed.

15. See Chapter 1.

rather than deflation, of too much rather than too little monetary demand. What is sauce for the goose is sauce for the gander, and many economists must feel a little uneasy advocating, during the inflationary cold-war period, tax increases that impinge most heavily on the more well-to-do.[16] Unfortunately, if one is really to fight inflation, some pressure has to be put upon consumption spending, unpalatable as such action may be.

On the whole, every large group stands to gain in the long run from stable prosperity, but it is the poor whose position deteriorates most in depression and improves relatively most in revival. The inequality of income (as measured by a so-called Lorenz curve or other statistical device) shows that inequality declines in prosperous times. Minority groups and those who stand at the bottom of the income pyramid—Negroes, marginal farmers, domestic servants—have the largest stake in a militant stabilization program. In short, the usual modern notions of so-called equity reinforce and are reinforced by full employment programs. And to the extent that you wish to give great weight to the well-being of the economically less fortunate groups, you should be all the more willing to push such programs, at the same time frankly recognizing the harm done to those with fixed money incomes.

III. Stability and Progress

The second half of this chapter is concerned with the problem of economic progress. For more than a century the American economic system has increased its productivity in each decade. Statistical measurements of real income show that—after corrections and adjustments have been made for changes in the purchasing power of the dollar—output per capita has increased, at the same time that the average hours each person works per week or year have gone down. Comparative statistics also

16. At least three valid loopholes to this criticism can be found. The past rise in prices had in effect raised the effective tax of the poorest classes beyond what was apparently considered "equitable," so that they were entitled to some relief. Also, the economists were almost alone in fighting for more taxes and they may have felt that it would not be possible politically to salvage a half-loaf of remedial action if one advocated more regressive taxation. In addition, perhaps one can make out a case that during boom periods the middle and wealthy classes are most likely to invest what they do not consume so that taxing them does reduce current total effective demand appreciably; this serves to damn the rich whether the winds are inflationary or deflationary and neglects favorable effects of capital on subsequent output. Finally, some government economists may have felt that there are worse things than mild inflation. It should be added that once we admit that investment incentives are affected by tax rates, we must admit the possibility that more unemployment could require lower taxes on the rich relative to the poor in order to stimulate private investment.

show that real wages are higher in the United States than anywhere else in the world. This increase in our standard of living is not something that can be taken simply for granted. There is nothing inevitable about material progress. There is no divine governor or thermostat that guarantees an increase in productivity of 2 or 3% per year. Historians and anthropologists record numerous examples of economic societies that have regressed from high to low standards of living. In our own annals the record of progress has not always been smooth or uniform.

Public policy must be concerned with dynamic economic development, and programs of stabilization must be scrutinized for their possible unfavorable or favorable effects upon the trend of productivity. Perhaps the booms and the busts of the last century were the inevitable costs of progress, the necessary price we must pay for vital growth. If such is the fact, let us face it unflinchingly and, facing it, decide whether the gains of progress are worth their social costs, or whether there is some golden mean involving neither a maximum of progress-*cum*-instability nor complete security-*cum*-decadence. On the other hand, it may turn out that certain types of stabilization programs are not so drastically opposed to economic growth but may even contribute toward healthy economic development. The problem is a thorny one to which no slick answer can be given. We must review and weigh the economic issues involved.

1. *The meaning of stabilization*

Of course, by stabilization we do not mean a state of suspended growth. Nor do we simply have in mind a dampening down of the roller coaster of business activity until the curve of total output is flattened into the shape of just any old trend. By stabilization we do mean 1) an absence of large fluctuations upward and downward in total employment, 2) absence of mass unemployment, overemployment, or "disguised unemployment," 3) the absence of excessive price inflation resulting from too-high effective demand and "overfull-employment" conditions. In short, the economic system is to hug relatively closely the line of its full *potential* (or producible) national output. The *task of progress is to further the growth of this "potential national product."*

The kind of over-all stabilization being discussed here has nothing to do with—and indeed is quite opposed to—stabilization of price or output in any particular market or industrial sector or geographical region. The needs and wants of consumers are constantly changing and so are the resources and technology of production. All this makes the numerical measurement of *potential output* difficult and approximate. It also implies that relative prices and outputs must be constantly varying and readjusting themselves; otherwise the optimal goal of full potential output cannot be achieved. It is only too clear, therefore, that some kinds of policies that have occasionally been associated with the name of stabilization—control agreements to stabilize output or price, legislation to protect the interests of particular workers or farmers—may be diametrically opposed to progress. They have, and should have, nothing to do with the full employment programs discussed in this volume.

Progress is an obstreperous and often cruel disturber of the *status quo*. It flings windfall gains to some and inflicts heavy economic penalties on others, often on groups and persons least able to afford them. Fear of change may breed more insecurity than its actual impact. People and institutions very naturally and understandably react to prevent or forestall adverse changes. And governments, feeling that there is a conflict or clash between progress and equity, take various actions designed to alleviate the losses of the afflicted. Some of these government actions can slow up economic progress, just as the steps taken by private trade unions or corporations to resist change may delay improvements in technology.

I cannot deal here with all such aspects of the problem. What I am concerned with is the effects of the successful maintenance of a high level of monetary demand upon such resistance to change. Surely the essence of the problem of, say, technological unemployment is not how to keep a man from losing his old job so much as to make sure that alternative jobs become available, at as high a wage as his revalued skill can command. The problem is similar in the case of displaced demand for the output of any particular plant or item of capital equipment. To the extent that people can be dissuaded from vetoing needed technological changes, a successful over-all stabilization program can be said to be favorable rather than opposed to a healthy rate of progress.

2. Inevitability of business cycles and growth trends

But are not most modern economists increasingly in agreement that technological change, innovation, and dynamic economic growth are the important causes of business cycles? [17] Are progress and the business cycle not inseparable? If governments had been successful in moderating the business cycle over the last century, would world productivity be as high as it now is? Could even a collectivized society succeed in

17. Continental writers such as Joseph A. Schumpeter or Arthur Spiethoff were most strongly associated with this view, but D. H. Robertson and (in more recent years) John M. Keynes, Alvin H. Hansen, and other Anglo-Saxon writers have increased their emphasis on such factors. See any work on business cycles, such as G. Haberler, *Prosperity and Depression.*

banishing the business cycle without at the same time killing off all progress? These questions have been widely discussed by economists.

Though progress may often have been the cause of the business cycle in the past, it does not follow that progress is the effect of the business cycle in the sense that when you abolish or moderate the cycle you will necessarily banish or lessen progress. A relatively small fluctuation in innovations may, unless something is done about it, set up a violently amplified oscillation in total business activity, since cumulative economic forces pile onto any upward or downward movement carrying it far beyond the initial push. In the train of genuinely important innovators are a host of imitators who, caught up with the boom fever, may carry the expansion to excess; when the crash comes the most inefficient firms may be eliminated, but there may follow a cumulative downward spiral which causes even the soundest firms and banks to become bankrupt or to curtail activity. Public policy designed to moderate the "secondary" excesses set up by primary fluctuations in investment opportunities can prevent much economic waste, while at the same time having little or no adverse influence on innovation and technological progress.

Granting that cycles of historically observed amplitude are not inevitable, we must critically examine a more recent notion that the rate of growth of an economy is foreordained by its rate of population growth and by the ratio of its capital stock to income. This secular aspect of the acceleration principle has been studied by Roy F. Harrod, Evsey D. Domar, and others. Moreover, it seems to lend weight to more intuitive notions of "balance," according to which there is during any period, such as the 1920's, some appropriate rate of capital formation which cannot be long exceeded without giving rise to depression. Now if we recognize all the rigidities in our system and if we set up a model of a laissez-faire system in which each investor's fears of future depression may be only too fully realized, then I have no doubt that high rates of capital formation for one period may be regarded as being at the expense of low rates later. Perhaps the great depression of the 1930's is to be explained partially in precisely these terms.

But if we revert to the optimistic neoclassical doctrines outlined above, and if we recognize that the amount of capital needed for any level of income is a variable depending upon the rate of interest and other factors, then I do not see why a well-run economy cannot have almost any rate of capital formation it wanted to. To show that there is nothing intrinsically in the technological nature of a system that limits its rate of growth, imagine a fully centralized and planned economy. It might be subject to many evils of arbitrary power and authority and of errors in judgments about particular investment projects, but I do not see why it could not make its capital grow at any desired yearly increase—at least up to the point where the net productivity of capital had been brought down practically to zero. This is because the parameters in the accelerator models must be regarded as variables rather than as constants.[18]

3. Stabilization and investment incentive

Stabilization policies may serve to further progress in two ways. First, the memory of a great speculative orgy such as 1929 may last so long as to discourage more investment in subsequent years than can be credited to the boom period itself. Hence in checking the excesses of the boom we may be advancing the average rate of economic growth. Second, and perhaps even more important, in offsetting slumps and preventing great declines in employment and incomes we are lessening their adverse influence on investment and risk-taking.

No more favorable environment could be imagined for venture capital and innovation than one in which businessmen could look forward to a steadily growing market not prone to sudden epidemics of general bankruptcy and insecurity. They could then scrutinize each bold new project on its merits without at the same time having to look into a crystal ball to foretell the course of general business conditions. While it is not yet within our power to provide such assurances, the favorable effects upon the trend of productivity of even partially successful stabilization programs seem hardly open to doubt. This of course assumes that the stabilization policies are not of the type which will give rise to grave ideological concern on the part of entrepreneurs.

There will not be smooth monotonous growth as a result of even the luckiest and most successful full employment policies. The true line of potential output can be expected to be subject to some ripples and accelerations. Inventions will not appear with perfect regularity and their promotion and economic introduction will show even greater clustering; but there need no longer be such great swings of investment once the

18. For a discussion of the nature of the business cycle in a planned economy, see the views of G. Haberler, Abram Bergson, and David McCord Wright in *Conference on Business Cycles*, held under the auspices of Universities–National Bureau Committee for Economic Research (New York, National Bureau of Economic Research, 1951). Note that the same jerkiness of progress, replacement waves, and backlogs might arise in a collectivist society as in our own: to the extent that these were not foreseen, we can make adverse ex post evaluations of the mistakes in planning; to the extent that they were foreseen and nonetheless rationally accepted as optimal programs, the shifting of resources occasioned by such jerkiness need not be regarded as wastes.

feedback effects of boom-bust pessimism, optimism, and money-market convulsions have been moderated. When change is proceeding at an especially rapid rate, layoffs and frictional unemployment will be at their peak; this is in part unavoidable if the advantages of progress are not to be indefinitely thwarted. But the measure of success of high employment programs will be the degree to which new productive job opportunities are found for those displaced and the degree to which cumulative slumps in jobs and sales can be avoided.

Some costs in terms of progress may have to be charged against stabilization programs. Historically, booms have often resulted from the creation of money and credit by the banking system at the behest of speculative investors. The result has often been inflation, with individuals being forced into lower consumption by shrinkage in the buying power of their wages and property income. This process of "forced savings" (forced doing without would be the better term, since the abstainers have no assets to show for their sacrificing) has been reinforced by the increase during inflationary boom periods in profits accruing to the more active speculators and risk-takers, who are just the people most ready to experiment with new products and processes. Especially for young developing countries, where investment opportunities always seem (at conventional interest rates) to be running beyond the full employment voluntary saving of the community, control over inflationary banking policies may slow down the rate of progress; and this possibility should be admitted.

On the other hand, if over the years the public authorities find themselves pursuing expansionary monetary and fiscal policies in order to offset incipient stagnation, then savings which would have been abortive may be brought into effective being. Under these circumstances full employment policy may be materially contributing to the rate of growth of industrial productivity. The degree to which this is true will depend upon the qualitative and quantitative composition of the program adopted.

4. *Factors underlying progress*

Before examining the different effects of various alternative government programs on the growth of productivity, we must catalogue some of the conditions necessary to improved levels of output. There is first the availability of resources, material and human. America has been singularly blessed in respect to land and mineral resources, and a significant fraction of our superiority can be attributed to this factor beyond our control. But the presence of resources in this land as of 1492 cannot explain our rising standard of living; and over the world as a whole the association between degrees of productivity and natural endowment of resources is by no means a close one.

From the standpoint of welfare rather than national power, we are probably more interested in per capita output than in total output. Therefore the type of growth to be explained is not that associated with mere increase in numbers of our population. A century ago population growth was a more significant cause of the total growth in our production than it will be in future years when our natural rate of increase will be smaller and when the flow of immigration into this country will be narrowly limited by law. Above and beyond the mere expansion in numbers, there has been a historical increase in output per capita, which requires all the more explanation since more workers means a dilution of the amount of God-given resources per worker.

The explanation may lie partially in the quality of our workers, the word "quality" having to be carefully limited in its meaning. Certainly few experts would attach great weight to any biological difference in our citizenry, since we are notoriously a nation of mixed ethnic, language, and anthropometric strains. Even if the difference cannot be traced to the germ cell, it is still true that the American worker by training and experience is often a more efficient agent of production than his counterpart abroad. He is not exerting greater physical efforts —usually much less; and even the mental and nervous strain of a week's work in an American factory is probably less instead of greater than prevails elsewhere. From birth the American grows up in a highly efficient, industrialized environment so that he unconsciously and easily acquires the skills and attitudes conducive to efficient production. He is no superman and, in any case, most of the credit is not his; nonetheless, no one who has tried to help less advanced nations improve their productivity is likely to underestimate the importance of the effective human skills available in the American labor force.

This is simply one reflection of the single most important reason for our productivity—namely, the advanced state of our technological know-how. The steady world-wide growth of fundamental scientific knowledge has been drawn upon by American engineers to further industrial productivity. The result has been dramatic new products and industries—electrical, chemical, etc. But equally important have been the almost unnoticed, undramatic steady improvements in machinery and methods. Not only has the level of technology been high within each plant, but in addition we have succeeded in building up a relatively large free-trade area in which an elaborate division of labor enables any one firm to purchase the precision instruments, raw materials, and parts it needs—a great advantage for which foreign producers greatly envy us.

All this has been built up largely through individual initiative and without active government direction. In fact some of our largest concerns, frowned on by the antitrust branch of the government, have often been focal points of most rapid technological progress. Perhaps as applied science becomes even more complex and costly, the advantages of size enjoyed by such large corporations in the research field may increase still more and their share in the growth of technology may swell. This may raise certain conflicts of social goals and certain dilemmas for government policy. Thus there may be a clash between our antipathy toward monopolistic concentrations of power and our desire for progress. On the one hand we are tempted to dangle before would-be innovators the promise of patent protection; on the other hand we deplore the influence of the dead hand of old patents upon competition, price, and output.[19]

All this takes us beyond stabilization policy. The important thing for our purposes is the emphasis on *effective technological knowledge* as the single, most important factor in economic progress. Closely related to technology is the role of *capital formation* in advancing productivity. The two cannot be entirely separated, but in earlier years economists put undue emphasis, I believe, on the mere accumulation of capital. Historically, it is true, as capital grew so did productivity. Any comparative cross-sectional view of different countries today will also show that those countries with the highest productivity also tend to have the most real capital per head. Abstract economic theory tells us, too, that as the interest rate is lowered, even without any new technical knowledge, processes which were previously unprofitable will now be adopted and the result will be greater output and labor productivity.

While the role of capital formation in progress is obviously an important one which no developing nation can afford to minimize, still it must be remembered that the historical association between capital abundance and high standards of life [20] is partly that of the latter making possible the former rather than vice versa. Also very much of capital formation consists of duplicative "widening" of existing, known facilities; a century later it will not matter whether there are one dozen or

19. See Chapter 10.

20. It may in part result from the way we measure capital. If labor's noncapitalizable share of the national income is somewhere around two-thirds of the total, and if property income is capitalized into wealth at an annual interest rate of between 5 and 10%, then the stock of capital will always appear to be about 4 to 7 years' national income *whatever* the *technological* relationship may be.

one thousand generators built in 1952, whereas the discovery of one fundamental principle today—which may be "free" capital—may change the face of the world forever. Thus I believe it is quite possible that, if the United States economy throughout its history had saved only one-twentieth of its income instead of roughly one-eighth and if a larger share of what was saved had gone into scientific research, pure and applied, into pilot-plant operations, and experimentation, we should today enjoy even larger levels of output than we now do. The significance of this for the future lies in the fact that less-advanced nations, simply by imitating the best known technological methods, can hope to improve their standards of living even with a minimum of available capital. Our Point Four program is based on this recognition. In some ways knowledge is the most important form of capital, and here as elsewhere in life it is often the best things that are free.

I must not underestimate the importance of capital formation. Even if a firm or nation could contrive to make progress just by replacing its old capital with better-designed new capital and without doing any "net" saving, its upward progress would presumably be even greater if new capital formation were also available. Resources used to produce such new capital processes must be taken away from the production of current consumption goods, once full employment is assured. Depending upon the people's habits of thrift and their expectations concerning the present and the future, people may voluntarily abstain from present consumption and channel their savings into investment assets. Historians such as Max Weber, Werner Sombart, and R. H. Tawney consider it no accident that the industrial revolution has been associated with the "Protestant ethic" and its emphasis on effort and thrift. Sometimes a country's capital needs are met by imports from outside; during the nineteenth century Britain made private development loans to Canada, Argentina, and the United States. Other countries such as Japan and Russia have, through choice or otherwise, been relatively self-reliant in their development. Japan is perhaps an example where a very unequal distribution of income between rich and poor has served the purpose of augmenting the savings available for capital development. In Russia the government through its successive five-year plans deliberately planned to hold down current consumption of the people in favor of industrialization and military expenditure.

5. *To save or not save?*

Let us turn to the policy aspects of the problem. It is doubtful that the government can by orthodox measures influence greatly the amount that people choose to consume out of their available disposable income.[21] Only by affecting the general environment of expected future prices can public policy do much about saving-consumption patterns. But questions may be asked—what *ought* we to wish for with respect to saving, and what problems will face the government as a result of different saving decisions?

The orthodox position with respect to saving used to be: the more the better; "a penny saved is a penny earned." While it is possible to be too miserly and to die too rich because one has not lived richly enough, the followers of Poor Richard would maintain that most people save too little and are insufficiently prudent and parsimonious. Moreover, in saving, the individual is thought to be not so much helping himself as aiding the laboring classes and society at large by providing new capital that will increase future real income. From the time of Adam Smith's bumbling definitions of "productive" and "unproductive" labor down through Pigou's emphasis on people's defective "telescopic faculty" that causes them to discount the future unduly, there has been a feeling that people if left alone tend to save too little. This feeling carries over into communistic and socialistic economies. Even those writers who think that people should be able under socialism to buy the goods they like better—apples rather than oranges if that is their choice—usually balk at letting people decide individually for themselves how much capital the present generation will pass on to the future generations; this, the state is to decide. The conservation movement reveals most clearly the latent notion that the present generation does not have the right to decide in terms of its own individual preferences how fast it shall use up exhaustible natural resources; instead the people set up their government as kind of a trustee to protect the interests of the as yet unborn.[22] Even within capitalistic countries a good deal of capital formation is governmentally and institutionally determined.

Against the orthodox glorification of saving there early grew up a whole school of critics who argued that excessive thrift might *reduce* rather than increase the rate of real capital formation. This was well expressed more than a century ago by the English economist, Malthus,

21. Corporate saving and investment is more amenable to the influence of changes in the tax structure. Also the government by its tax policy can affect the levels of disposable income that will prevail at full employment.

22. Since J. M. Keynes has in recent years been associated with the view that oversaving may be a problem, it is interesting to note his earlier statement in the *Economic Consequences of the Peace* (1919) that the middle classes have their *raison d'être* in the fact that they do save and not consume, and that post-World War I Europe might not quietly permit them to dis-save should they want to.

who far from being a radical agitator was an Anglican clergyman with the interests of the country gentry at heart. He said:

> No considerable and continued increase in wealth could possibly take place without that degree of frugality which occasions capital formation . . . and creates a balance of produce over consumption; but it is quite obvious . . . that the principle of saving, pushed to excess, would destroy the motive to production. . . . If consumption exceeds production, the capital of the country must be diminished, and its wealth must be gradually destroyed from its want of power to produce; if production be in great excess above consumption, the motive to accumulate and consume must cease from the want of will to consume. The two extremes are obvious; and it follows that there must be some intermediate point, though the resources of political economy may not be able to ascertain it, where taking into consideration both the power to produce and the will to consume, the encouragement to the increase of wealth is greatest.[23]

In England the followers of David Ricardo (particularly James Mill and J. R. McCulloch) made it a condition of membership in the economic profession to abjure such underconsumption heresy and to subscribe to the tenets of the so-called Say's law of markets which held that supply created its own demand and that overproduction or underconsumption were logically (and empirically?) impossible, so that excessive thrift could never be a problem. Nonetheless, the underconsumptionist view smoldered on both in England and on the Continent, until in our own day it burst forth in the new form of the modern theory of income determination.[24]

This analysis distinguishes sharply between the attempt to save and the amount of real saving and investment that society succeeds in making. The attempt by individuals to consume less of their income, if it is not translated into equivalent investment, will prove abortive: people will only succeed in reducing their own incomes to the point where they finally give up the attempt; or some people may succeed in adding to

23. T. R. Malthus, *Principles of Political Economy* (1820), pp. 6–7 of the London School of Economics reprint of the 1836 edition.

24. Associated in its beginning with Keynes, *General Theory of Employment, Interest, and Money* (London, Macmillan, 1936). But even prior to 1936 Harold G. Moulton and his associates at the Brookings Institute had insisted that an increase in the desire to consume might sometimes help rather than hinder capital formation.

their financial savings by forcing others to dissave. The situation may be even worse from the standpoint of increasing society's real capital formation and productivity: the fall in incomes resulting from attempts to save will make existing plants redundant and undermine confidence and the volume of capital formation.

This "paradox of thrift" needs a number of qualifications. If there is an "inflationary gap" with total spending tending to outrun the value of full employment output, then an increase in thriftiness may reduce the rate of inflation and lead to a stable full employment condition characterized by a high rate of capital formation. Even when there is some unemployment, an increase in thriftiness can be expected to lower interest rates via its downward impact on money incomes; this favorable lower-interest rate effect will oppose the unfavorable lower-income effect upon investment and, if thriftiness is not too great, the result may be increased capital formation.[25]

The neomercantilists were inclined to make much of this paradox of thrift. Claiming to desire more capital formation, they were able to advocate progressive taxes and other fiscal measures designed to redistribute income from rich to poor. Earlier I have mentioned that evidence from budget studies of different income groups' saving habits suggests that such redistribution has limited quantitative effects on total consumption and savings. (See p. 564 above.) Also we must not neglect any adverse effects upon investment resulting from the impact of high marginal rates of taxation (and inadequate loss offsets). There is the additional fact that the qualitative character of the saving done by the lower income groups—saving, accounts, insurance policies, etc.—may for institutional reasons be available primarily for gilt-edged bond investment rather than for equity capital.

If the proponents of the paradox of thrift overlooked its limitations, the critics of the doctrine were blind to its grain of truth. Thus when Alvin Hansen spoke in the 1930's of the need to make America a "high consumption economy," many interpreted this to mean a low investment economy, a deduction which would be tenable only if resources were always fully employed and if unemployment were not a variable in the problem. In my interpretation, by a high consumption economy Hansen

25. See O. Lange, "The Rate of Interest and the Optimum Propensity to Consume," in *Readings in Business Cycle Theory* (Philadelphia, Blakiston, 1944), ch. 8, and reprinted from *Economica*, New Series, 5 (1938). If prices and costs are flexible downward, the reduction in money income may not imply an equivalent loss of real income; also, the lower prices may increase the propensity to consume so that a smaller amount of *net* thriftiness finally ensues. This last so-called Pigou effect reinforces rather than negates the paradox of thrift.

meant one in which net capital formation would be absolutely high and even higher relative to income than in a depressed system.

6. *The optimal rate of saving*

How does our neoclassical doctrine stand on these matters? It will be recalled that earlier this was defined to mean that *high employment can be achieved by a wide variety of alternative programs so as to yield almost any pattern of resource use between the public and private sector* and—it now may be added—*between capital formation and present consumption goods.* If the policies described elsewhere in this volume are successful, then we need no longer fear thrift's possible damage to real income and capital formation. An effective stabilization program being assured, we can ask the purely classical question: How much of current national income ought to be saved, and how fast a rate of progress should be our goal?

The answer that we should save as large a percentage of income as possible and aim for the most rapid rate of progress makes little sense. Obviously it would be absurd to try to invest 100% of national income or to try to put everyone in the land into a scientific laboratory. Each increment of capital formation must be at the expense of current consumption; and while one can conceptually imagine a nation that uses *all* its machines and labor to produce more machines which will in turn make still more machines, no one would seriously set this up as a goal. To the extent that each new unit of capital will yield a net return (in terms of real output) over and above the depreciation costs for its ultimate replacement, we can think of each present sacrifice of consumption goods as making possible a perpetually higher flow of (real) income. But the more we invest, the more precious becomes each unit of the consumption that is left to us. The problem is how to strike the right balance.

Under certain heroic assumptions—such as the absence of any "time-preference" and the addition of independent utilities spread over all future time, etc.—some rather fine-spun theories as to the optimal rate of capital growth have been put forward.[26]

Moreover, the problem of saving is peculiarly one in which the actions

26. The Ramsey mathematical analysis of saving, made in 1928 by a brilliant short-lived philosopher-protégé of Keynes, is summarized in less technical terminology in J. E. Meade and C. J. Hitch, *An Introduction to Economic Analysis and Policy* (New York, Oxford University Press, 1938), Pt. IV, ch. 3. This theory assumes that society tries to maximize over all time the sum of "utilities," the latter being the same concave function of current consumption of each time period. Society should then do positive saving until either the "net productivity of capital" is zero or "bliss" has been attained with all goods free. The rate at which this

of people when left to themselves are widely regarded as not necessarily optimal. This view and its negation both involve ascientific ethical value judgments, and it is only in the role of a reporter and not as a special pleader that I call attention to this fact. An illustration of what I have in mind can be cited.

It is not at all impossible that the citizens of many countries of western Europe, living in the mid-century shadow of the atomic bomb, would if left to themselves dis-save on balance. Their "governments" will not let "them" do so. Is this good or bad? It all depends upon the philosophical viewpoint. The individuals who spend their patrimony may later regret it; to which some will reply that everyone is entitled to his own mistakes and having made one's bed. . . . On the other hand, even in the most individualistic society people are limited in the harm they can do themselves—especially if it is serious harm such as suicide. Also some will argue that there are military needs of society and a "right" for society to avoid its own economic suicide which should take precedence over the right of the individual to dissipate "his" property. Just as Louis XV is criticized for having said "après moi, le déluge," so a citizenry that has a net reproduction rate far below that necessary for group survival is often criticized, collectively and individually. To add to the paradox, the whole of the populace may give a vote of confidence to government's performing such "trustee" powers over capital formation, even though taken separately as individuals they distrust their own powers to resist excessive consumption. It is like the case where few will enlist in the army but all will vote to subject themselves to (risk of) the draft. However, the problem of insuring that government is responsive to our democratic collective wills is a more difficult one because of the quantitative nature of the investment process.

Leaving out the clash between present and future generations and between individuals and society, we must recognize a philosophical ambiguity in all decisions taking place over time that makes normative statements especially difficult. Our tastes change over time; the man who makes a decision today for tomorrow is different from tomorrow's man and also from the man who will reminisce the day after tomorrow.

---

happy state should be reached is determined by balancing the loss of present satisfaction from one more increment of present saving against the gain in future satisfaction involved in advancing the date that we reach bliss. This means that society should ultimately save a percentage of the national income almost equal to the percentage-income by which we fall short of bliss: e.g., if society now enjoys only three-fourths of the maximum producible income, it should save almost one-fourth of its current income. This is a rather fanciful prescription based on fanciful assumptions.

I may hate myself in the morning for what I do tonight; paradoxically, I may now know that I will be hating myself in the morning; and tomorrow, while hating myself, I may know perfectly well that given the same situation I would again behave in the same way. In technical parlance there are no invariant indifference curves over time, and where tastes are changing there is no frame of reference for normative decisions. This point has been strongly made by Professor M. Allais of Paris, who is otherwise a staunch advocate for free pricing.

It all adds up to this: there are no rules as to the optimum rate of progress. Richer societies are better able to save, but also they may have less reason to do so. Public policy, democratically arrived at, may be directed toward accelerating or holding down the rate of capital formation, or it may attempt to be neutral, letting people in some sense decide for themselves how much they will save. But since every decision about taxes, expenditures, and other economic matters impinges on the environment within which individuals make up their minds, the concept of neutrality would have to be given a very special meaning.

Fortunately, the sweeping neoclassical doctrine outlined in this chapter can sidestep the question of how much shall be saved. This is not the business of a stabilization program to decide. High employment can be achieved, theoretically, with almost any pattern of investment and consumption. If individuals are trying to save so much that their efforts threaten to become abortive through a fall in employment, this can be offset by policy and high employment can be maintained. If the resulting pattern of employment involves too little capital formation according to some prescribed standards, there exist other combinations of policy measures that will result in a more rapidly growing stock of capital. As an example, we could have full employment with money so cheap and plentiful as to be conducive to private capital formation, but with a federal budget strongly overbalanced to curb inflation; or, if we wish it, present consumption standards may be higher, with private investment expenditure being limited by a tight money market that rations out capital funds sparingly. Or we might have anything in between.

I do not wish to convey the impression that monetary policy, within the range of usually discussed changes in interest rates and credit availability, has the same potency as fiscal policy does within its usual range. Nor do I wish to imply that, by taking various mixtures of monetary and fiscal policy, you can bring about exactly the same kind of restriction of total demand: the effects of fiscal and monetary policy may be qualitatively and quantitatively different, and it is for this reason that we must choose the mixture best suited to prescribed ends.

In recent years it has become fashionable among technical economists to stress the possible effects on consumption and thriftiness of the real level of people's money and public debt holding. Price deflation is regarded as one way of bringing full employment saving into alignment with investment outlets. Such a view carries with it the empirical corollary that people do not possess deep invariant patterns of time preference and that they will be content to save much or little depending upon how we manipulate their financial wealth. This presents us with a three-way choice of a full employment program: 1) heavy reliance on fiscal policy; 2) heavy reliance on interest-rate monetary policy; 3) heavy reliance on price flexibility and so-called Pigou effects. But what mixture is optimal? Should every child be endowed with a nest egg of negotiable government bonds so as to overcome his feeling of insecurity? If the saving pattern changes greatly with the size of the nest eggs of these fictitious claims on wealth, which is the proper *natural* or *neutral* pattern of interest rates and asset structure? If we are willing to make heroic assumptions about the invariance of individuals' time preferences, and if we were given the ethical criteria by which we determine the proper "share" and deservingness of the born and unborn, a formal answer could be given.

In closing I must make one general qualification. Throughout this chapter I have been concerned with conflicts of ultimate goals at the high strategy level. I have not attempted to do anything like full justice to the tactical difficulties of achieving stabilization goals. I have been concerned with the problems we would face even after our stabilization policies were most successfully realized. This should not be interpreted as a belief that stabilization can be fully or easily attained; as the other chapters of this book show, the problems are many and difficult and go beyond the narrow confine of economics.

PART FOUR:

THE POLITICAL PROCESS

CHAPTER XIII. *The Political Framework of*
Stabilization Policy

BY VICTOR JONES

I. THE SOCIAL CONTEXT OF POLITICAL ECONOMY

Calvin Coolidge considered it to be the function of Congress to discover economic laws and to enact them. If this were the function of government, the problem of organizing ourselves for the task would be, although not simple, less complicated than that which actually faces the American people. Max Millikan has shown in Chapter 1 that noneconomic values compete with economic values for priority in our society, that economic action has noneconomic consequences, and vice versa, and that many of our cherished values can be realized or maintained only if we keep them constantly in mind as we formulate economic policy.

It is artificial to distinguish the political, the economic, and the social from each other, although it may be convenient as a division of attention or of labor. All politics and all economics (Robinson Crusoe excepted) are social; they deal with persons in some kind of relationship with other persons. What is known as the market is a more or less identifiable set of social relationships among individuals, families, firms, governments, and other groups. Government is likewise an institutionalized behavior of individuals in many kinds of groups, including the agencies of domestic government as well as those of the governments of other states.

I shall attempt in this section to do no more than recall to our attention the fact, well-known but often overlooked, that neither the market nor the government functions independently of society.[1] Any observer would include the size of the country, the plurality of interests, and the highly organized pressure groups among the major social factors

1. Many aspects of the social framework of stabilization policy are discussed by other contributors, e.g., Rostow on the structure of industry (Chapter 10) and Lindblom on labor policy (Chapter 11). The problem of communications as it effects stabilization policy is discussed by Lasswell (Chapter 14). Both Millikan (Chapter 1) and Coker (Chapter 2) are concerned with values and the rationalization of values.

which affect the formulation and execution of public policy in the United States. American society is big whether it is measured by its population of 156,000,000 people, by the continent on which they live, by the thousands of groups, in addition to the family, through which they function, by the technics which they use, or by the myriad constellations of values which they pursue. Its size and its pluralism must be taken into account in the formation of any public policy. The development, adoption, and administration of stabilization policies in Norway and the United States are problems of significantly different magnitude.

It is not necessary, however, to reason from the existence of these characteristics of American society to a deterministic theory of group politics.[2] Public policy is the "equilibrium reached at any moment in the struggle of contending coalitions" only if we ignore the possibility of using the major political parties to organize the "contending coalitions."

Closely associated with this theory of American politics is the theory that localism is so firmly and naturally a determinant of party and legislative behavior in a continental democracy that only the presidency can become a national (superlocal) symbol. American history is read as a constant swing between presidential (national) and Congressional (local-special interest) preeminence and power.[3]

There is no doubt of the force of the tradition and practice of localism in American government. The organization of the government on a federal basis provides for thousands of state and local elective officials, in addition to members of Congress, who are identified with a locality. Despite the increasing pressure toward a national orientation, political parties are organized most of the time on a similar basis and leave a member of Congress at the mercy of local pressures. Frequently, however, the so-called local pressures come from national groups locally organized.

There is danger that we may forget that groups consist of individual men and women. We have much to learn about the incidence of public policies upon personality. The only way to achieve a general sharing of respect, affection, well-being, enlightenment, rectitude, without which

2. See Earl Latham's propositions about the political process in "Giantism and Basing Points: A Political Analysis," *Yale Law Journal*, 58 (1949), 383, n. 1. These propositions are discussed and elaborated in Latham's *The Group Basis of Politics* (Ithaca, Cornell University Press, 1952), pp. 27–53.

3. For examples see W. E. Binkley, *President and Congress* (New York, Knopf, 1947) and Herbert Agar, *The Price of Union* (Boston, Houghton Mifflin, 1950).

policies aimed at a more general distribution of wealth, skill, and power will be ineffectual, is to develop "mature, reasonable people, free of guilts and inferiorities." [4]

We must also concern ourselves with personality from the manipulative point of view. We tend to recoil from the idea of deliberate manipulation of people as antithetical to individual dignity and to "genuine" public opinion. In a pluralistic society, however, it is necessary to develop and maintain a consensus among a majority of those empowered to act. It is also necessary to build up a consensus of support among people in the constituencies. Such manipulation is constantly going on even though we deny it a legitimate place in democratic theory.

We are too often content to explain political behavior in terms of local or pressure group interests. [5] The term "interest" is used freely as explanation, or as denigration, without defining the concept of interest. [6] The group itself consists of individuals with diverse personalities. The most important of these individuals are the leaders—formal and informal. How is the predisposition developed to favor one cluster of

4. G. B. Chisholm, "The Psychiatry of Enduring Peace and Social Progress," p. 17 (reprint from *Psychiatry*, 9, No. 1 [February, 1946]). Note Chisholm's remarks (p. 31) on full employment and happiness: "And so I think the time is going to come, if it hasn't come already, when we shall have to redefine a little our idea of employment. It may well be that within a few years, as atomic energy is made releasable and usable in industry, there won't be enough productive employment available for anything like all the people in the world. It may well be that this time can come within twenty years. What is education doing about that? Are we preparing our children to spend large parts of their lives denied the 'privilege' of working? Our children should be prepared to bring their children up so they won't have to work as a neurotic necessity. The necessity to work is a neurotic symptom. It is a crutch. It is an attempt to make oneself feel valuable even though there is no particular need for one's working. There are people who dig holes and fill them in just to 'busify' themselves. I think we need to look at this whole problem of employment in relation to man's enjoyment of living, not just with regard to his 'busification' which is something quite different."

5. The following remark of John R. Commons suggests why we perhaps unconsciously look upon group pressures as controllable only by equal and contrary group pressures: "By rhetorical analogy to the physical sciences, the word 'pressure' has been borrowed to mean collective action of 'pressure groups.'" *The Economics of Collective Action* (New York, Macmillan, 1950), p. 77.

6. Until the publication in 1951 of David B. Truman's, *The Governmental Process: Political Interests and Public Opinion* (New York, Knopf, 1951), the theory of interests had been little developed beyond the point at which A. F. Bentley left it in 1908 (*The Process of Government* [Chicago, University of Chicago Press]). For a critical evaluation of the theories see Avery Leiserson, *Administrative Regulation: A Study in Representation of Interests* (Chicago, University of Chicago Press, 1942).

values rather than another? How is it modified? How can congressmen be brought to support stabilization policies?

In this essay I shall emphasize the importance of governmental organization for the making of certain kinds of decisions. But organization involves more than procedures or the zoning of authority. The procedures are merely recognized ways in which the people involved are expected to behave with respect to the objectives of the organization. We need to understand, then, how the personalities of the people involved developed prior to involvement and how their personalities are affected by participating in the activities of groups, government agencies, and other institutions.

II. ECONOMIC POLICY WITHOUT POLITICS?

Another factor which affects the formulation of income stabilization policy is the attitudes of some economists and other people toward participation in politics. It is felt by some people that, even while participating in public policy formation, economists can and should avoid the "entanglement of politics." Others hold that the best way for an economist to influence public policy is to restrict his activities to the economic enlightenment of the public. These attitudes, I believe, are based upon incorrect assumptions and faulty analysis. Furthermore, ambiguous and loaded words, such as "politics," "political," "professional," "objective," and "scientific" are almost always used in expressing these attitudes.

The widespread interest of academic as well as government economists in issues of public policy is attested by the subjects discussed by economists in books and periodicals and at their professional meetings. Recent presidential addresses before the American Economic Association have been concerned with public policy or, in a few instances, they have been warnings to the profession to avoid steadfastly the diversions of the Sirens.

There are disagreements among economists over the proper role of government, the objectives of public policy, and the correct or desirable means of achieving given policies.[7] These disagreements appear to the political scientist not only as signs of health but as promises of usefulness in the give and take of policy formation.

The minority members of the Joint Committee on the Economic Report complained in 1949 that the President's Economic Report

7. In addition to the literature (including this volume), see the reports of the polls on public policies in the 1948 and 1949 *Proceedings* of the American Economic Association, *American Economic Review*, 38, No. 2 (May, 1948) and 39, No. 3 (May, 1949).

reads in many respects like a political argument. . . . The President's Economic Reports threaten to become political propaganda rather than scientific analysis. . . . When the [Joint] Committee was established, it was the hope of many that it would approach its task from a completely scientific and non-partisan position, relying on expert economic advisers, and would not be a piece of machinery representing those temporarily in control of Congress, and functioning only to approve and praise the Economic Report of the President.[8]

Senator Taft and his colleagues did not really object, despite their language, to the Council of Economic Advisers and the President presenting their interpretation of the economic condition of the country and their recommendations for dealing with those conditions. If the Republicans had been in power they would have presented the same type of report. Their particular recommendations might have differed from those of President Truman and the allocation of blame for the ills of the country would certainly have been different. Not being in the position, however, to write the Economic Report, they implied that the proper function of the council should be, to use the words of Harold G. Moulton in describing the objectives of the National Bureau of Economic Research, "to avoid controversial issues of public policy and to confine its activities chiefly to the assembling of relevant information." [9]

Some of the misunderstanding of the role of the council as a part of the government arises from a premise which no one would accept if explicitly stated. The argument proceeds as if the council were the only instrument for economic analysis which may affect policy. But the contact points between economists and policy formulators and policy makers are innumerable. The role of the council should neither be exaggerated nor underestimated. Nor should it be expected to duplicate the work of the National Bureau of Economic Research or of the Brookings Institution, nor should its reports to the President replace the publications of academic economists. One of the most fruitful ways of improving the public consideration of policies is for the minority party to establish its own council of economic advisers. If necessary it should be supported by public funds.

More significant than Senator Taft's complaint is the position of

8. Minority Views of the Joint Committee on the Economic Report on the January, 1949, *Economic Report of the President*, 81st Congress, 1st Session, Senate Report No. 88, Pt. 2, pp. 1, 3.

9. "Some Comments on Research Method," in *Economic Research and the Development of Economic Science and Public Policy* (New York, National Bureau of Economic Research, 1946), p. 37.

former Chairman Nourse and other economists that the Council of
Economic Advisers should be above, or outside, politics. Holbrook
Working, for instance, sees

> evidence of a weakness that could prove fatal unless vigilantly
> guarded against. Its [the first *Economic Report of the President*]
> recommendations seem to read a little too much like a political
> party platform. The report, it must be remembered, is that of a
> party leader as well as of the Chief Executive, and the Economic
> Advisers hold office at his pleasure. Exposure of the Council and
> of the Economic Report to the risk of use for partisan political ends,
> though probably necessary, is a major hazard to the success of the
> Employment Act. Every effort must be made to keep the economic
> report above party politics.[10]

Paul J. Strayer, Roy Blough, and Simeon Leland agree that the council is placed in a vulnerable though not untenable position.[11] It is certain to be shot at whether it is camouflaged in the Executive Office of
the President or steps forth in its own name. Blough's discussion of the
role of the council is particularly important since he has subsequently
been appointed to the council:

> Here, then, is the dilemma as I see it. A Council should be inde-
> pendent, but if it acts in a very independent manner, it can scarcely
> be recognized as an advisory body by the President, and if it is not
> so recognized, it loses much of its value as a body of independent
> economists. Likewise, the President may find it useful to have a
> Council which is sufficiently independent to have prestige in policy
> integration in the executive branch and in dealing with the Con-
> gress; yet he can hardly be expected to desire a Council which is so
> independent that it undermines his position with the Congress and
> the public. Here is a situation where both the Council and the
> President are benefited from the existence of what is at bottom an
> inconsistent position but where both run risks. The risk to the
> Council is that it will either lose its independence, or lose its posi-
> tion as Presidential adviser, or lose its neck. The risk to the Presi-
> dent is that he is better served by having an independent Council,
> but if it is too independent, his position is undermined. Obviously
> the incompatibility of the ideas of independence and of service to

10. Holbrook Working, "Reflections on the President's Economic Report," *American Economic Review*, 37 (1947), 386.

11. "Stabilizing the Economy: The Employment Act of 1946 in Operation,"
American Economic Review, 40 (May, 1950), 144–154, 165–178, 179–180, respectively.

the President is such that if they are carried to their logical conclusion the structure collapses.[12]

Both Leland and Nourse maintain that the members of the council
cannot retain their professional integrity if they do more than state "the
facts of the present economic health of the nation" and indicate "the
direction in which conditions seem to be moving." If it becomes involved in "the formulation or coordination of programs of specific action," Nourse says it becomes an economic attorney or a "kept" economist and Leland says it is reduced to the role of formulating "alibis for
past failures." [13]

The council has been divided over the "political" proprieties called
for by its relationship with the President and with Congress.[14] There is
no reason to suspect that any member of the council would accept as
his role the job of rationalizing or making respectable any program
handed to them by the President. But Leon H. Keyserling and John D.

12. *Ibid.*, p. 177. See, by the same author, *The Federal Taxing Process* (New
York, Prentice-Hall, 1952), pp. 125–145.

13. *Ibid.*, pp. 179–180, 186–190. Surely Leland had his tongue in his cheek
when he compared the relationship between the President and the Council of
Economic Advisers to that between a governor and a tax administrator. See Jacob
Viner's comments, "The President's Economic Program," Trade and Industry Law
Institute, Current Business Studies No. 3 (June, 1949), pp. 32 ff.

14. After his resignation from the council Nourse declared that President Truman
never discussed with the council its analyses and suggestions. "On no occasion did
the Council have so much as a single hour's time in which we could sit down with
the President to answer any question that arose in his mind, clarify data, or examine
alternative courses and probable consequences. We learned of his final policy
decisions through an assistant or an assistant to an assistant on the White House
staff. 'Armslength bargaining' has become a phrase of frustration in the business
world. Our position might be called 'armslength economic advising.' " *Collier's,*
February 18, 1950, p. 56.

But John D. Clark, a member of the council, suggested in testimony before a
Senate judiciary subcommittee on February 13, 1950, that Nourse did not know
how to exploit the interest of the President. He described the relationship between
the President and the council (after Nourse's resignation) in preparing the President's 1950 Economic Report to Congress: "The council's proposed draft was
studied by the President's personal staff . . . and then the council was called into
conference with Mr. Truman and his personal aides. This lasted from 3 p.m. until
2:15 a.m. . . . , with no time out for dinner.

"A revised draft of the report was then submitted to the President's staff. After
they studied it . . . a second conference, lasting two and a half hours, was held
with Mr. Truman.

"The President . . . read the revised draft 'word by word' to the council and
'the entire top group around the President' and requested comments. After the
draft was discussed the report was written in final form and submitted to Congress."
New York Times, February 14, 1950.

Clark do not consider it incompatible with their position as *economic*
advisers to testify before Congressional committees. Nourse, on the
other hand, took

> the position that if the precedent of such appearance is established,
> the time would come sooner or later when Council members would
> be asked to testify on matters on which the President has seen fit to
> take a position definitely contrary to their advice. This would pre-
> sent Council members with the alternative of arguing for the
> President's position regardless of their own professional convictions
> or, on the other hand, of arguing against a policy recommended by
> the President. The latter, in the chairman's judgment, would intro-
> duce an element of strain between the Council and the chief execu-
> tive, and impair the relationship under which the Council freely
> brings objective analyses of economic questions for his considera-
> tion prior to the determination of his position.[15]

Obviously, the term "politics" is being used here to refer to many
things. Senator Taft calls the recommendations of his opponents
politics. Working and Nourse are afraid that the council will be injured
by such charges, although the former admits that it is probably necessary to risk the use of the Economic Report for partisan political ends.
It is necessary to take this risk. Moreover, it is desirable that the President's report be recognized as political. It is oriented toward action and
many, if not all, of his proposals will be controversial. Furthermore, it is
addressed specifically to the Congress and indirectly to the public, both
of which consist of individuals and groups of individuals who will react
as partisans to the controversial proposals.

If it be said that the President and his advisers out of, and perhaps in,
the council are political when they take into account the influence of
his recommendations upon electoral response to his candidacy for re-
election, it must be emphasized that in a democracy the corollary of
defeating public officials who displease a majority of the voters is to return to office those who do please them.

Many people in and out of the government are timeservers; some are

15. Edwin G. Nourse and Bertram M. Gross, "The Role of the Council of Economic Advisers," *American Political Science Review*, 42 (April, 1948), 290. See
also Nourse, "Economics in the Public Service," *American Economic Review, Proceedings*, 37, No. 2 (1947), 21–30. For more emphatic statements of this position
see the *American Economic Review*, 40 (1950), 186–190, and "Why I Had to Step
Aside," *Collier's*, February 18, 1950, pp. 13, 51, 54–56 (reprinted in the *Congressional Record*, February 21, 1950, pp. A1331–A1335 by Senate Minority Leader
Wherry). The two associate members of the council appeared in February, 1949,
before the Joint Committee on the Economic Report.

venal, others are primarily interested in furthering their own interests or those of a particular group. There are demagogues in high and low places. Although they engage in politics we cannot reserve the terms "politicians" for these people nor "politics" for their activities. Politics is the entire process of formulating policies and organizing support to secure assent or dissent to, or overt approval or disapproval of, these policies. Many people participate in various parts of this process and few people, if any, are equally active in all its phases. Economists— whether they work in a government agency, or are members of the council or of its staff, or are temporary consultants, or are employed by pressure groups, or act as professors—can and do participate in this political process.

E. A. Goldenweiser warns economists against participating in the planning and execution of political strategy and tactics.[16] He does not say that the initial judgment of the economist should be his final judgment. Certainly economists as close to presidential policy as the President's Council of Economic Advisers may attempt to take all precautions to protect the *initial* economic judgments of themselves and their staff and at the same time participate in the process of synthesizing a presidential policy. Their function at this point does not differ from that of other men high in the government who advise that one policy be adopted or that another be rejected. The final decision often depends upon the form in which the advice is presented, its timing, and other tactical considerations.[17] As John R. Commons has put the matter:

> Although . . . the economist might tell *what* to do to prevent inflation and deflation, he did not tell the practical man entrusted with responsibility the other essentials he needed to know, just *when* to do it, *where, how much,* and with what *degree* of power

16. "There is danger for an economist in trying desperately to be practical, realistic, and to let political exigencies color his professional judgment. Much obscure thinking and one-sided interpretation has arisen from that source. When a policy-making individual or body consults an economist, he or it has a right to expect an economic not a political answer. Political expediency and compromise are the responsibility of the official, not of his consultant. . . . Intrusion of considerations of expediency is likely to throw his thinking out of gear, with the consequence that the answer he arrives at may be neither the best that he could reach as an economist nor the best that could be devised by a mind more expert in the game of politics. Modifications and compromises to meet political exigencies should be left for subsequent consideration and must not be permitted to cloud the economist's initial judgment." E. A. Goldenweiser, "Translating Facts into Policy," in *Economic Research and the Development of Economic Science and Public Policy,* pp. 57–58.

17. The desire of specialists and of particular clienteles to have their "politics" independent of general politics is discussed further in section XI.

to do it. . . . This control over human behavior depends on *doing* the "right" thing at the right *time,* the right *place,* with the right *degree of power* and *always in advance.*[18]

No economist who is concerned with what happens can afford to leave the politics of economics entirely to others and no politician is getting helpful advice from an economist who runs from his responsibilities.

The view that economists should not propose but only educate is based in part on the old piece of folklore that the people, if given light, will find their own way. The half-truth here is of the utmost importance. Some economists have paid us the great compliment of saying that the American people are becoming more literate in economics.[19] If so, the economists are directly responsible only in part. Their indirect responsibility is much greater. They have taught the politicians who have taught the people. Be this as it may, economists must make even greater efforts to communicate effectively as they participate in the debates over public policies. To impugn the motives of laymen may satisfy the ego of the specialist, but it does not bring back the lost chance to communicate one's reasoning, proposals, or criticism.[20] Economists, like all specialists when they wish to communicate with laymen (including political scientists and politicians), must take care not to use gobbledygook that will separate them from their communicants. Although much of the laughter at the use of technical and professional jargon comes from people who are too lazy to make the intellectual effort to understand the specialist, the stakes are too high for us to risk invoking laughter or disgust by using a strange language. I suspect that the following statement by A. H. Hansen failed, to say the least, to accomplish his purpose:

It would have been interesting to know how the Senate might have reacted to the following modified version of [an] amendment [to the Murray full employment bill of 1945]:

18. John R. Commons, *op. cit.,* p. 178.

19. Roy Blough is not so sanguine: "Political and Administrative Requisites for Achieving Economic Stability," *American Economic Review,* Supplement, *40* (May, 1950), 165–178.

20. See, for instance, the remarks of H. M. Groves in reviewing *Taxation for Prosperity* (New York, Bobbs-Merrill, 1947) by R. E. Paul in *American Economic Review,* 37 (1947), 689: "On many other matters, too, the Treasury seems to have had the weight of integrity and research on its side; its failure, if any, seems to have been in political artistry and imagination. One gets the impression of some such limitation when one reads of the reaction of a Congressional committeeman to the proposed spendings tax. 'It's just too complicated for an ordinary man like me to understand!' On the other hand what a difference if the Congressman had really wanted to understand!" See also E. D. Allen, "Treasury Tax Policies in 1943," *American Economic Review,* *34* (December, 1944), 707–733.

Provided that any program of Federal investment and expenditure, for the fiscal year 1948 or any subsequent fiscal year when the nation is at peace, shall be accompanied by a program of taxation over a period of years comprising the year in question and a reasonable number of years thereafter designed and calculated to prevent during that period any increase in the ratio of interest charges in the national debt to Gross National Product (interest on debt incurred for self-liquidating projects and other reimbursable expenditures not included) without interfering with the goal of full employment.[21]

At no other time or place has so much information been gathered and analyzed for its policy implications as in the first half of the twentieth century in the United States. Academic social scientists, pressure groups, foundations and research institutes, government agencies, presidential commissions, and Congressional committees are constantly bringing up policy questions, enlightening us about the social, economic, and political problems involved and suggesting solutions. The symposium in this book on *Income Stabilization for a Developing Democracy* is an example of such activity.

Some of these efforts have resulted in policy decisions and many others have created or helped to create a climate of opinion under which eventually a public policy was formed. But many of them seem to be academic exercises, contributing perhaps to knowledge and understanding but not to public policy. Policy decisions involve choices among alternatives even if the alternatives be simply action or no action. A complex policy is made up of many choices exercised by many people located in various parts of government and in other social institutions.[22] Such choices are not made simultaneously—certain ones must be made before others are possible or evident. The various decision makers are not all of one mind or of equally good will, nor do they hold the same values or the same institutional loyalties.

Neither the whole people nor any group of them will find their own way even if economists give them light unless the alternatives are presented in a form which enables them to make a choice. This can be done only through certain kinds of political organizations. Furthermore, the choice will be based not only upon knowledge and intellectual understanding but will be influenced by hopes, fears, desires, group identifications, and many other rational and irrational reactions.

21. A. H. Hansen, *Economic Policy and Full Employment* (New York, McGraw-Hill, 1947), p. 118.
22. See Paul H. Appleby, *Policy and Administration* (University, University of Alabama Press, 1949).

III. Significance of Governmental Organization for
Responsible Policy-Making

Public policy is a decision that government is going to do or not going to do something in certain ways and at certain times. Whoever makes these decisions, wherever he may be located in the government structure, makes public policy. The question before us is whether the political and governmental organization facilitates or impedes the making of decisions for which the makers can be held politically responsible. It is not denied in raising this question that policy decisions are made in the government as now organized. Decisions are inescapable—failure to make a particular policy and delay in making it are themselves policy decisions.

In the first year of the New Deal Mr. Justice McReynolds said: "In theory, at least, the legislature acts upon adequate knowledge after full consideration and through members who represent the entire public." [23] We have in this statement the four desirable elements of policy-making in a democracy: *action* by *responsible officials* based upon *adequate knowledge* and *consideration*. The concern of this paper is whether the government of the United States is organized to bring adequate information to responsible policy makers to enable them to give it full consideration, to make decisions, and to hold them responsible for their decisions.

My diagnosis is not new nor is my prescription. The American government as now organized permits the adoption of many particular policies, but makes it difficult to adopt comprehensive policies designed ahead of time to meet a foreseeable crisis when it arrives. This results from the lack of an integrative relationship between the President and Congress. This in turn results from the lack of a tradition and a mechanism of party *government*. Much of American consitutional and political theory is concerned with restraining government and ignores the problem of getting government to act when action is needed or desired. The political and governmental system we have inherited, despite the extension of the suffrage, the development of political parties, and the acceptance of new social, economic, and political values, is still dispersive.

23. *Southern Railroad Co.* v. *Virginia*, 290 U.S. 190, 197, 78 L. ed., 260, 266 (1933). From the qualifying words at the beginning of the statement it may be inferred that the Justice was not justifying legislative action but, to further his argument, attributing to the legislature characteristics which he did not see in the unallowable action of an administrator.

IV. GOVERNMENT BY PRESSURE GROUPS

Despite the frequency and righteousness with which Americans have condemned pressure groups, the "interests," lobbies, and "invisible government," the organization of Congress and of the administration invite and facilitate their activities. The dispersal of legislative leadership among many standing and special committees, and the further dispersal of leadership within committees to subcommittees has established a multitude of strategic points at which pressure and influence can be and are exerted. Clientele agencies, independent regulatory commissions, and government corporations present a similar opportunity in the administrative branch. There is no institutionalized leadership embracing the party, the executive, and the legislature to absorb the shock of inevitable pressures and protect public policy from the direct and collateral impact of special interests.

Coalitions are constantly being formed and reformed in order to organize a favorable majority in Congress or to secure favorable action elsewhere. Public officials in both the legislative and executive branches play a positive and creative role in pressure group government. "There are politicians in this town staying awake nights thinking about things for pressure groups that have never yet occurred to the groups themselves." [24] As E. S. Griffith wrote in 1939:

> One cannot live in Washington for long without being conscious that it has these whirlpools or centers of activity focusing on particular problems. The persons who are thus active—in agriculture, in power, in labor, in foreign trade, and the parts thereof—are variously composed. Some are civil servants, some are active members of the appropriate committees in the House and Senate, some are lobbyists, some are unofficial research authorities, connected perhaps with the Brookings Institution or with one of the universities, or even entirely private individuals. Perhaps special correspondents of newspapers are included. These people in their various permutations and combinations are continually meeting in each other's offices, at various clubs, lunching together, and participating in legislative hearings or serving on important but obscure committees set up within the department. [25]

The full employment bill of 1945 was born and matured into the Employment Act of 1946 in this manner. Because of its own significance, its

24. Jonathan Daniels, *Frontier on the Potomac* (New York, Macmillan, 1946), p. 154.

25. E. S. Griffith, *The Impasse of Democracy* (New York, Harrison-Hilton, 1939), p. 182.

importance to the makers of any subsequent stabilization policy, and as an illustration of how majorities are formed and destroyed in our present dispersive governmental system, all people concerned with policy-making should carefully consider the history of the Employment Act of 1946.

Before the war was over there developed a wide interest on the part of administrative agencies, members of Congress, pressure groups and academicians in postwar reconversion policies.[26] The Office of War Mobilization and Reconversion (the Baruch-Hancock report), the George committee in the Senate on Postwar Economic Policy and the Colmer counterpart in the House, the Murray War Contracts Subcommittee, and the Kilgore War Mobilization Subcommittee of the Senate Military Affairs Committee were all maneuvering during the war for position to control the development of reconversion policy. At the same time Louis Bean was bringing together interested men, in and out of government positions—such as Russell Smith of the National Farmers Union, Mordecai Ezekiel of the Bureau of Agricultural Economics, Geoffrey Shepard of the Committee for Economic Development and the Department of Commerce, and Gerhard Colm of the Division of Fiscal Analysis of the Bureau of the Budget—for bull-sessions on the problem.

In this atmosphere the Patton-Smith proposal of the National Farmers Union that the government underwrite a $40 billion annual investment was submitted in August, 1944, to Senator Murray's subcommittee. Agency comments were secured and Senator Murray decided to have a draft bill prepared. This was done late in 1944 by Bertram Gross, staff director of the War Contracts Subcommittee, with the assistance of Louis Bean, V. O. Key, and Gerhard Colm of the Bureau of the Budget, Emile Benoit-Smullyan of the Bureau of Labor Statistics, Walter Salant and James Early of the Office of Price Administration, James Maddox of the Bureau of Agricultural Economics, Russell Smith of the National Farmers Union, and Kurt Borchardt of the War Contracts Subcommittee staff.

Cosponsors in the Senate were secured as soon as the first session of the 79th Congress opened and the draft bill was revised by Gross and the sponsors. The revised draft was introduced by Murray on January 22, 1945, and as S. 380 referred to the Banking and Currency Committee. Gross was made head of an expanded committee staff and for fourteen months the staff planned the strategy of committee hearings, maintained liaison with favorable pressure groups, redrafted the bill, col-

26. In addition to the agencies and organizations mentioned here, one should note the activities of the National Planning Association, the Division of Fiscal Analysis of the Bureau of the Budget, and the National Resources Planning Board.

lected and analyzed data, and wrote speeches for senators and others. Particularly important was the work of the "continuations group," organized by Gross and Paul Sifton, of the Union for Democratic Action to arouse public interest, to lobby, and to develop indirect pressures on members of Congress. The early hesitancy of labor organizations was developed into full support of the bill. The bill received friendly hearings in the Senate Committee and passed the Senate on September 28, 1945, by a vote of 71–10.

In the House H.R. 2202 was introduced by Representative Patman on February 15, 1945, and referred to the unfriendly House Committee on Expenditures in the Executive Departments. Hearings began in September. Unlike the Senate hearings, there was an organized and intense opposition from "business" interests. After V-J Day President Truman became interested in the bill and designated OWMR Director John W. Snyder to organize the administrative pressures for passage. He was assisted by a Cabinet committee headed by Secretary of the Treasury Frederick M. Vinson and including Secretary of Commerce Henry A. Wallace, Secretary of Labor Edgar W. Schwellenbach, and Secretary of Agriculture Clinton P. Anderson. Administrative-legislative liaison was maintained by Ansel Luxford, special assistant to Vinson, Creekmore Path, special assistant to Snyder, and Thomas I. Emerson, general counsel of OWMR. Direct White House pressure was exerted on House committee members Carter Manasco, Richard Whittington, and Joseph Mansfield. In testifying before the committee, Snyder was critical of the Senate bill despite the President's support of the bill.[27]

After President Truman had castigated the House committee for its delay, the full committee voted not to report H.R. 2202. A subcommittee substitute, in which a Council of Economic Advisers first appears, was adopted by the committee and sent to the House under a rule from the Rules Committee insuring the committee substitute or nothing. Henry Wallace, at Vinson's request, persuaded the proponents of a "stronger" bill to accept the substitute and transfer their fight to the joint conference committee.

After the appointment of conference managers, Senator Robert F. Wagner became ill and was replaced as chairman by Senator Alben W. Barkley. President Truman wrote the conference leaders that only the Senate bill "can efficiently accomplish the purposes intended." This was

27. Snyder, as Secretary of the Treasury, again took a position contrary to that of the President when he informed the Senate Committee on Expenditures that he did not approve the provision of Reorganization Plan No. 1, which would place the Controller of the Currency under the supervision of the Secretary of the Treasury. *New York Times,* April 12, 1950.

followed by a radio address. Vinson prepared a substitute proposal which Snyder failed to transmit to the conference committee. After a lengthy discussion of the declaration of policy, the conference committee reported essentially the House version of the bill. Both the Senate and the House quickly accepted the conference report and the bill was signed by the President. Thus the full employment bill of 1945 became the Employment Act of 1946.

Stephen K. Bailey, who has reconstructed the complex story in detail but with a constant eye for its meaning as a case study of policy-making, is fully justified in saying: "In the absence of a widely recognized crisis, legislative policy-making tends to be fought out at the level of largely irresponsible personal and group stratagems and compromises based on temporary power coalitions of political, administrative, and non-governmental interests." [28]

Dispersive government by pressure groups, governmental, non-governmental, and mixed, results in inconsistent public policies. We can never achieve complete consistency but a successful stabilization policy requires that we organize ourselves to formulate and maintain policies as consistent as possible in a democratic society with many values, some of which are really and others apparently inconsistent with each other. More consistent policy as well as more responsible and informed government can be secured by replacing government by pressure groups with party government. [29]

This is not to suggest that pressure groups are either unnecessary or undesirable in a democracy. Pressures are the raw materials of politics and there is no convincing evidence that they are not active even in totalitarian governments. Certainly in the democratic countries with a parliamentary-cabinet form of government, pressure groups are an active force in the development and administration of public policy. [30]

28. Stephen K. Bailey, *Congress Makes a Law* (New York, Columbia University Press, 1950). For the basing point legislation of the 81st Congress see Earl Latham, *The Group Basis of Politics*. E. E. Schattschneider in *Politics, Pressures, and the Tariff* (New York, Prentice-Hall, 1935) has analyzed the committee hearings on the Hawley-Smoot Tariff Act of 1930. For less comprehensive coverage of any one statute but for an analysis of 90 different acts passed between 1882 and 1940 see L. H. Chamberlain, *The President, Congress and Legislation* (New York, Columbia University Press, 1946). See also the brief but revealing stories of the Wages and Hours, OPA, and Missouri Valley Authority bills by J. M. Burns, *Congress on Trial* (New York, Harper, 1949), pp. 67–97.

29. I say "more" consistent policies, because I am fully aware of inconsistencies in the policies of governments which are not dispersively organized.

30. Charles Aikin, "British Bureaucracy and Parliamentary Policy," *American Political Science Review, 33* (April, 1939), 231–232: "Within the House of Commons

To paraphrase Madison, then, we must conclude that the *causes* of pressure groups cannot be removed without destroying political freedom, and that relief is to be sought only in the means of controlling their *effects*.

V. CONTROLLING THE EFFECTS OF PRESSURE GROUPS

The activities of pressure groups have evoked proposals for controlling them which range from compulsory registration of lobbyists to Tugwell's proposal to establish a directive branch of the government, independent of the President and Congress and therefore, it is said, above politics.[31]

Diagnosis, prescription, and prognosis depend intimately upon one's conception of the respective roles of government and other social institutions in social control. Recently the theory of the 10th *Federalist* paper that society is divided into conflicting interest groups each of which, if it secured control of the government, will oppress the others and that popular despotism can be avoided only by fragmentizing and counterpoising the fragments of government, has been refurbished. Herbert Agar is one of the most recent defenders of the formulation of public policy through the struggle and manipulation of groups, with

---

are found representatives of all the major and of many minor pressure groups, including even the interests of some foreign nations. Ministers and civil servants act with the knowledge that these groups are capable of arousing a dormant public opinion. . . . There exist in London—contrary to what one often hears around Westminster—a considerable number of lobbies, many of which have headquarters in the neighborhood of Parliament. . . . Both the political and permanent authors of governmental policy must at least consider these groups, and may either discount them or, when it seems necessary, attempt to mollify them. It is indicative of the influence of the civil service that lobbies do not confine their activities to the Commons." See also Herman Finer, *Theory and Practice of Modern Government* (rev. ed., New York, Holt, 1949), pp. 462–469; W. Ivor Jennings, *Parliament* (Cambridge, Cambridge University Press, 1939), pp. 171–231.

31. "A power is needed which is longer-run, wider-minded, differently allied, than a reformed executive would be . . . a body useful to democracy but not farther removed from its rewards and penalties than would serve to resolve its worst paradoxes and to protect it from itself, . . . ought to be feasible. But it would have to be beyond and independent of the executive almost as certainly as the legislative.

". . . The directive has an advantage over the executive from not having to operate any organization, over the legislature from not representing any faction or region, and over the judicial from dealing with a volume of fact rather than a volume of precedent." R. G. Tugwell, "The Fourth Power," *Planning and Civic Comment,* 5 (April–June, 1939), 26, 30, 31. Tugwell was then chairman of the New York City Planning Commission.

government by and large limited to playing the role of umpire and rationalizer of the result.[32]

His book is a forceful (at times a tour de force) reading of American history to show that the American union was created, preserved, and can now be maintained only at the price of national policies which are a watering-down of "the selfish demands of regions, races, classes, business associations" and "which will alienate no major group and which will contain at least a small plum for everybody. This is the price of unity in a continent-wide federation."

Calhoun's theory of concurrent majorities is restated as an accurate description of the way the American federal system works and of the way it must operate if the federal union is to endure and if our liberties are to be protected. The concurrence of majorities is secured, not through a constitutional amendment as proposed by Calhoun, but through the American party system operating within the procedures of federalism, separation of powers, and checks and balances. ". . . a federal state must be an ever renewed compromise between 'the fractious negativism of minorities' and 'tyranny of numbers.'"[33]

It would be more descriptive of their theory if the latter-day Calhouns would call it the theory of concurrent minorities. Government is relegated to the role of establishing the rules for the conduct of the group struggle and of acting as an umpire. Earl Latham says that "a principle function of legislators is to referee the group struggle, to ratify the victories of successful coalitions, and to record the terms that define the compromises, surrenders and victories in statutes."[34] Agar

32. Herbert Agar, *op. cit.*, and his article, "How to Elect a Republican," *Harper's*, April, 1950, pp. 31–35. See also John Fischer, "Unwritten Rules of American Politics," *Harper's*, November, 1948, pp. 27–36; W. E. Binkley, *American Political Parties, Their Natural History* (New York, Knopf, 1943) and *President and Congress;* P. F. Drucker, "A Key to American Politics: Calhoun's Pluralism," *Review of Politics, 10* (October, 1948), 412–426; E. P. Herring, *Politics of Democracy* (New York, Rinehart, 1940) and *Presidential Leadership* (New York, Rinehart, 1940); Earl Latham, *The Group Basis of Politics;* Ernest S. Griffith, *Congress: Its Contemporary Role* (New York, New York University Press, 1951).

33. Agar, *The Price of Union*, p. 340.

34. Earl Latham, *Yale Law Journal*, 58 (1949), 383, n. 1. The quotation is the eighth of ten propositions he makes about the nature of the political process:

1. The principle social values of modern life are realized through group action.

2. Groups organize for security and advantage, to control the environment in which they exist, in order to make it predictable and safe.

3. Organization begets counter-organization.

4. Coalitions, constellations and combinations of groups struggle with each other for security and the advantage of their members.

5. The struggle takes place in the official as well as the private fields of controversy.

sees the function of parties as that of making "gentlemen's agreements (and committee rules) in Congress to prevent coalitions of enthusiasts from brushing aside minority protests."[35] Walter Lippmann in 1937 wrote that

> The temper of officialdom in a liberal society must be predominantly judicial: that holds not only for the judges themselves but for the legislators and executives as well, indeed for all who wish to serve the public interest. Except, of course, in emergencies when a community must temporarily renounce its freedom in order to defend itself against attack, upheaval, and disaster, the primary task of liberal statesmanship is to judge the claims of particular interests asking for a revision of laws, to endeavor amidst these conflicting claims to make equitable decisions.[36]

A summary criticism may do an injustice to the position of any one of the men we have been discussing. They seem to assume, however, that any important "interest" will protect or assert itself for "organization begets counterorganization." Stated thus baldly the proposition ignores the many instances in which organization does not beget counterorganization. It implies, furthermore, the tendency of people with similar "interests" to join the appropriate organization.[37] But the principal criticisms of the theories are that, first, they assume that dispersive politics are natural and inevitable and, therefore, desirable; second, they ignore the role of government as organizer of coalitions; and, finally, they assume that the three-way compromise among the conflicting coalitions and government officials and party leaders should be made in the legislature.

The principal conclusion of those who look upon government as the

---

6. The distinction between "official" and "private" is the social understanding that the first have the right to give known and knowable orders to the second.

7. In the struggle for security and advantage, private groups enlist the support of official groups in their behalf when the added leverage of official power is required.

9. Legislative votes tend to represent the composition of strength, i.e., the balance of power, among the contending coalitions at the moment of voting.

10. What may be called "public policy" is the equilibrium reached at any moment in the struggle of contending coalitions, an equilibrium which factions of groups constantly strive to weight in their favor.

35. Agar, *The Price of Union*, p. 334. He does, however, permit the President to participate as one of the antagonists in the struggle (p. 321).

36. Walter Lippmann, *Inquiry into the Principles of the Good Society* (Boston, Little, Brown, 1937), pp. 284–285.

37. For a criticism of this assumption see Robert E. Lane, "Notes on the Theory of the Lobby," *Western Political Quarterly*, 2 (March, 1949), 154–162.

umpire of the group struggle is that political parties cannot and should not organize their members in and out of government to adopt and execute a planned set of policies.[38] They look upon the government not as the advocate, developer, and executor of a positive program but rather as an agency to prevent a single interest group from developing such a program to the alleged detriment of others. There are undoubtedly times when interests are injured by governmental action, but it should be apparent to anyone who reads this book that a sensible income stabilization program will never emerge from the mere adjudication of disputes between interest groups.

VI. EXECUTIVE REORGANIZATION AND COORDINATION

Faced with the problems of world leadership, social welfare, and of economic stabilization, some people see our "only chance of successfully utilizing the expert knowledge and planning necessary to chart our way in the foul weather ahead" in a "presidential goverment operating through a nationalizing bureaucracy with Congress reduced to the role of a critic." [39] There are others who oppose what they call "presidential dictatorship" and urge a *restoration* of Congress as the maker of policy.[40] Both groups have urged that the respective branches of the government be reorganized to increase their efficiency and effectiveness. Before considering the role of the political party in formulating policies and in organizing a majority to support them, we should examine some of the proposals to reorganize the executive and the Congress. Attempts to coordinate the formulation and execution of public policies through the presidency are based upon the assumption that coordination can be achieved by improving the quality of program analysis and by facilitating communications among agencies and interests concerned, the President, and Congress.[41] The Hoover Commis-

---

38. See E. S. Griffith, *Congress: Its Contemporary Role* and Earl Latham, *The Group Basis of Politics.* Roy Blough discusses the formulation and adoption of tax policy without considering the role of political parties. "The attitude of congressional tax committees toward the Treasury, as well as the sense of responsibility of the Treasury would be improved if the fact were accepted that the Treasury is virtually the only group dealing with Congress that is in position to represent the whole public." *The Federal Taxing Process,* p. 477.

39. Norton E. Long, "Party Government and the United States," *Journal of Politics,* 13 (1951), 187–214. See also Louis Brownlow, *The President and the Presidency* (Chicago, Public Administration Service, 1949) and Don K. Price, as cited in n. 43 below.

40. See A. J. Zurcher, "The Presidency, Congress and Separation of Powers: A Reappraisal," *Western Political Quarterly,* 3 (March, 1950), 75–97.

41. S. K. Bailey, "The Coordination of Federal Economic Policies," mimeographed, April, 1949; see also Wayne Coy, "Federal Executive Reorganization Re-

sion recommends that the presidency be strengthened to prevent the executive branch from working "at cross purposes within itself." It finds that the "President and the heads of departments lack the tools to frame programs and policies and to supervise their execution." The additional "tools" recommended by the commission are increased staff aid "to give the President the greatest possible information on the activities of the Government as a whole, and to enable him to direct the policies of the departments and agencies"; [42] full responsibility of the department head to the President, and the delegation to the President of more responsibility for reorganization. According to Don Price, who assisted Mr. Hoover in the study of the Executive Office of the President:

> . . . the Commission rejected the logic that our system of checks and balances creates a fundamental conflict of interest between the President and Congress; accordingly, the Commission made recommendations that were designed to increase the ability of the Congress and the President to work together to make the executive branch into an integrated whole and to reduce the irresponsible power of individual bureaus and pressure groups.[43]

The recommendations of the Hoover Commission, however, will not "reduce the irresponsible power of individual bureaus and pressure groups" without a reorganization of the political relationships among bureaus, pressure groups, Congressional committees, and the President.[44] No one would deny the desirability and utility of improved economic analysis or of the easy and regular movement of information about demands, counterdemands, trouble points, presidential decisions, etc., up and down the executive branch of the government. "But," as Bailey has pointed out, "*except in so far as instruments of communication are in fact instruments of influence,* they do nothing but register existing agreements and disagreements."

examined: Basic Issues." *American Political Science Review*, 40 (December, 1946), 1133–1137, and Paul H. Appleby, *Big Democracy* (New York, Knopf, 1945), pp. 92–96.

42. Commission on Organization of the Executive Branch of the Government, *General Management of the Executive Branch* (1949), pp. 2, 14–15.

43. Don K. Price, "The Presidency: Its Burden and Its Promise," in *The Strengthening of American Political Institutions*, A. S. Mike Monroney and others (Ithaca, Cornell University Press, 1949), pp. 108–109; see also his article "Staffing the Presidency," *American Political Science Review*, 40 (December, 1946), 1154–1168.

44. See Norton E. Long, "Power and Administration," *Public Administration Review*, 9 (Autumn, 1949), 257–264 and H. A. Simon, Donald W. Smithburg and Victor A. Thompson, *Public Administration* (New York, Knopf, 1950), chs. 18 and 19.

The problems of coordination will be discussed in this volume by Professor Emerson. They are relevant to the discussion at this point, however, because coordination is a political process. Seymour Harris felt this when he recently urged, rather plaintively, that "as advisers of the President, the Council [of Economic Advisers] try to prevail upon government departments and Congress for as consistent policies as possible under our system." [45]

VII. CONGRESSIONAL REORGANIZATION

Another approach, offered as an antidote to pressure politics and as a prescription for the coordination of policy, is the reform of Congress. In the last decade congressmen, students, and publicists have been worried about the effectiveness of Congress as lawmaker and as watchdog of the administration. Many of them claim that Congress has lost its constitutional role of policy-making because it is "operating in the machine-age with horse-and-buggy tools." A few Congressional critics have urged a basic reorganization of Congress to enable it as a whole, under the guidance of genuine majority and minority leadership, to consider policy and its administration.

Most recommendations, however, have been directed toward making more effective the dispersive activities in which Congressional committees and individual congressmen are now engaged. The Joint Committee on the Organization of Congress, after extended hearings, reported the Monroney-LaFollette bill which was passed, with serious revisions by the House, in 1946. The act reduced the number of committees, authorized staff aides for the committees, increased salaries and expense accounts, required lobbyists to register, and provided that certain private claims be handled by administrative agencies and the courts. None of these reforms make any vital difference in the function of Congress. [46]

45. E. E. Schattschneider points out that "the essence of the governmental crisis consists of an inability to create, adopt and execute a comprehensive plan of action in advance of predictable emergencies in time to prevent or minimize them. The government suffers from a dangerous divorce of knowledge and power in which the specialists who foresee emergencies find it excessively difficult to make contact with public men who have the power to act, because no adequate focus of power exists." (Preliminary unpublished draft for discussion of an "Outline of a Proposed Program for Party Responsibility," 1949).

46. See the incisive criticisms of reform proposals and of the Monroney-LaFollette Act by Joseph P. Harris, "The Reorganization of Congress," *Public Administration Review,* 6 (1946), 267–282. His prognosis has stood the test of four sessions of Congress. See also J. M. Burns, *op. cit.,* pp. 132–143. Reluctant admission of doubts about the adequacy of the recent reforms, accompanied by reiteration of faith in further reforms of the same kind, is to be seen in the testimony before the

The Monroney-LaFollette Bill contained two germs that *might* have grown into effective ways of bringing order and responsibility into the formulation and adoption of public policies: the establishment of majority and minority policy committees and the creation of a joint budget committee to propose an over-all ceiling on expenditures.

The House leaders refused to establish party policy committees and they were subsequently created in the Senate by resolution. The Republicans appear to have used their party committee more successfully than the Democrats, perhaps because they have not had to face the question of supporting recommendations from a President of their own party. The principal difficulty with developing party policy committees into an effective group of legislative leaders is that there is no Congressional party to be led. The task is to develop parties to govern and to oppose the government. This cannot be done by designating a group of men, some of whom are not leaders in fact, as a party policy committee while Congress subcontracts its work to bipartisan committees and subcommittees.

> The basic trouble at present is not that there are no party leadership committees but that there are too many committees exercising various leadership functions. . . . The proliferation of leadership committees means that in neither house of Congress is there a body of party leaders who have the power of managing party affairs in Congress and who therefore can be held accountable for it. The result is that many things are left undone—or what is just as bad—are done in a dictatorial manner by individual party leaders. Also, too great a burden is thrown on the overworked Big Four and the Senate and House minority leaders.[47]

The short-lived requirement that an over-all legislative budget be adopted early in each session as a guide to the appropriation committees and to Congress represents an abortive attempt to consider the executive budget as a whole in its relation to general fiscal policy. The failure of this reform is usually ascribed to the unwieldy committee,[48] to the

---

Senate Committee on Expenditures in the Executive Departments, Legislative Reorganization Act of 1946, 80th Congress, 2d Session, 1948.

47. "Toward a More Responsible Two-Party System" (Report of the Committee on Political Parties of the American Political Science Association), *American Political Science Review*, Supplement, *44* (September, 1950), 59 (also published by the Dryden Press, New York, 1950).

48. The joint committee was composed of the members of the Senate and House Appropriations Committees, the House Ways and Means Committee, and the Senate Finance Committee. In the 80th Congress there were 102 members of the joint committee.

short time in which the committee had to make a decision, and to in-adequate staff.[49]

The basic reason for failure is that no attempt was made to integrate the scattered fragments of Congressional power as a support for an over-all budgetary policy. In 1950 a new device, the so-called omnibus appropriations bill, was tried and discarded in 1951. Its proponents claimed (before it was tried) that

> Appropriations will be more carefully processed; duplications, over-lapping and conflicts will be reconciled; legislative items will be eliminated; logrolling will be impracticable as all the cards will be on the table at one time and any attempted trades will be too ap-parent to withstand the light of publicity; the entire expenditures for the year will be submitted in one figure simultaneously with an authoritative estimate of the national income; deficit financing will be discouraged, as a last opportunity will be afforded for re-consideration in the subcommittees of the entire bill with a view of bringing annual expenditures within the annual revenues of the Government; the bill will have been passed and all annual appro-priations enacted before the end of the fiscal year, obviating the need for the usual continuing resolutions and permitting adjourn-ment of Congress much earlier than usual.[50]

It is already clear that these objectives of the procedure have not been realized. The bill was not approved by the President until early in September. The final vote was taken in the Senate on August 4, after four weeks of debate, and it was debated for an equally long time in the House. With unlimited debate in the Senate and with an open rule in the House, the bill was subject to all the logrolling of former sessions.[51]

Again, effective sponsorship of the substantive policies involved de-pends upon an organized working majority. A single appropriations bill should make it easier for congressmen and the public to keep more

49. See the testimony of Senator Taft (pp. 34–35), Robert Heller (pp. 37, 48–49), former Senator LaFollette (pp. 68–69), Representative Monroney (pp. 85–86), George Galloway (pp. 136–137, 152–153), George H. E. Smith (pp. 161–168, 183–184), Senator Millikin (pp. 215–216) before the Senate Committee on Expenditures in the Executive Departments, *op. cit.* (n. 46 above).

50. Clarence Cannon, "A Unique Opportunity—Improved Fiscal Control through Omnibus Appropriation Bill," *Tax Review* (February, 1950), reprinted in *Congressional Record,* March 3, 1950, pp. A1712–A1713.

51. See Professor Joseph P. Harris' forthcoming study of the procedures and politics of Congressional appropriations. In 1949 it was well into October before the last appropriation act was passed. See *Congressional Quarterly Almanac, 6* (1950), 104–153, for a detailed digest of Congressional action on appropriations.

clearly in mind the approximate total amount of appropriations. But congressmen, administrators, and pressure groups are also interested in appropriations for specific activities. As Dahl and Lindblom point out, in Chapter 8 above, "*a decision on the level of public expenditures is never made. Instead almost countless decisions are required.*" And yet the total amount appropriated will affect fiscal policies. At the least, these decisions should be made by the leaders of the majority party in each house. It would be better if they were made jointly by the majority party leaders in both houses, and better yet if the President's Budget Message were a statement of policy in the preparation of which Congressional party leaders participate.

The Joint Committee on the Economic Report is also assigned the function of developing policies on a broad front, but, without power to report bills itself, it is interposed between the President and the various legislative committees. During the Republican 80th Congress, Senator Taft, chairman of the Majority Policy Committee, served as chairman of the Joint Committee, but Senate majority leader White, Senate majority whip Wherry, Speaker Martin, and House majority leader Halleck were not on the committee. At the present time none of the majority and minority leaders of either house are on the committee.[52]

This is not to suggest that the public hearings on the President's Economic Report, the publication of reports by the majority and minority members of the committee, or the special investigations of the committee are not valuable contributions to public discussion of policies

52. "The seven Senate members of the Joint Committee have membership on ten standing committees. There are three members on Banking and Currency, two members on Interior and Insular Affairs, Labor and Public Welfare, and Public Works, respectively, and one member on Finance, Appropriations, Interstate and Foreign Commerce, and three other committees. Six committees have no cross-membership. The seven House members are represented on nine committees, including three on the Banking and Currency Committee, two on the Committee on Expenditures in the executive departments, and one each on four other committees. Thirteen committees have no cross-representation with the Joint Economic Committee and these include the Appropriations Committee and the Ways and Means Committee, which are the principal fiscal committees of the House. Since a good deal of the cross-representation is reflected in minority party membership which may have relatively little influence on current legislation, the net effect is perhaps even less than might be indicated by the statistics. Moreover, the educative effect of the work of the Joint Economic Committee on its own members is largely limited by their activity in the work of the Committee. It is the members who are present when the hearings are held and discussions take place who are able to go back to their standing committees with the knowledge and attitude needed to promote stabilization policies." Roy Blough, *op. cit., American Economic Review, 40* (May, 1950), 172, n. 7.

and useful sources of information to the legislative committees.[53] We should not, however, expect a committee so constituted and with such a tenuous relationship among its members, with other committee chairmen, and with official party leaders to coordinate the consideration of economic policy in Congress.

We know very little about the activities of the majority and minority policy committees in the Senate or of the steering and rules committees in the House. Some such institutionalization of the Congressional leadership as the title of these committees implies is necessary if we are to have party responsibility. As powerful as the Speaker of the House and the Majority Leader of the Senate may be, at times, it is unrealistic to try to develop a policy committee that excludes the important committee chairmen.[54]

There must be not only a liaison between the Congressional leaders and the President, but there must be active collaboration in executive-legislative policy-making and programing. President Truman is said to be "one of the few Presidents of this century who have faithfully maintained frequent and regular conferences with their legislative leaders." [55] We do not know to what extent policy is discussed along with strategy at these weekly presidential conferences with the Vice-President, the Speaker, and the House and Senate majority leaders.[56]

The consequences inherent in a system where a legislative leader could take advantage of the information about presidential plans which he would secure in a conference where policy is being formed have undoubtedly seemed too risky for most Presidents. Don Price asks us to

53. See E. A. Goldenweiser, "The Douglas Committee Report," *American Economic Review, 40* (June, 1950), 389–396.

54. This raises the old question of the selection of committee chairmen. It is well known that some committee chairmen in every session of Congress vote on the floor and conduct the affairs of their committees contrary to the general position of the party. Notice the low index of party regularity of the chairmen of the House and Senate committees of the 81st Congress. *Congressional Quarterly Almanac, 6* (1950), 59–61. "Party unity" is defined on p. 56. See the discussion of party responsibility for committee structure in the Report of the Committee on Political Parties of the American Political Science Association, "Toward a More Responsible Two-Party System," *op. cit.*, (n. 47 above), pp. 61–64; also, Robert A. Dahl, *Congress and Foreign Policy* (New York, Harcourt, Brace, 1950), pp. 145–150, 182–184.

55. Cabell Phillips, "The Men Around the President," *New York Times Magazine*, September 11, 1949, p. 72.

56. The President has not always informed his Congressional party leaders of his legislative plans. Senate Majority Leader Barkley thus described one such breakdown of communications: "It's like playing in a night ball game. I'm supposed to be the catcher and get the signals from the dugout. But I'm not only not getting the signals. Somebody sometimes even turns the lights out when the ball is tossed."

Consider the effect on the Presidency and on even our present degree of imperfect unity in the executive branch if each executive decision by the President were subject to the advice and consent —or even public discussion—by a congressional leadership which is under no binding obligations of party discipline, and which through independent committees can deal directly with the officials of subordinate bureaus and divisions.[57]

However, we must look to the institutionalization of the leadership of the majority party out of the collaboration of the President and the leaders of both houses of Congress for the effective development, adoption, and execution of any policy as broad and with as many ramifications, economic and noneconomic, as income stabilization. This cannot be done in the presidency alone or in Congress alone. The entire party must be reorganized to support such a structure of leadership. (See Chapter 16, p. 713, for a misunderstanding of the point of this paragraph.)

In any event, we should remember that the Presidential Big Four conferences have assumed their present form during the last decade. There is no reason to assume that this device has exhausted its organizational development in such a short time. It will be more profitable to concern ourselves with shaping this emergent institution into a genuine organ of majority party leadership than to consider proposals for an elaborate legislative-executive cabinet.[58]

If the objective be the making of consistent and comprehensive policy by public officials who can be held responsible for their action, neither the reorganization of the executive nor of the legislature will be sufficient without the development of political parties into instruments of government.

This is why the decision and opinions of the Supreme Court in the steel seizure case fail to settle the basic political issue. The court did not provide a means of responsible and effective political action when it said that "the founders of this nation entrusted the lawmaking power to the Congress alone in both good and bad times." Nor would the basic issue have been settled by a decision upholding the seizure by the President. The issue is not one of separation of powers. It is whether the President and the Congressional majority can collaborate in gov-

57. Don K. Price, "The Presidency: Its Burden and Its Promise," *The Strengthening American Political Institutions*, p. 94.

58. See, for instance, E. S. Corwin, *The President, Office and Powers* (3d ed., rev., New York, New York University Press, 1948), p. 361; T. K. Finletter, *Can Representative Government Do the Job?* (New York, Reynal & Hitchcock, 1945), p. 97; C. S. Hyneman, *Bureaucracy in a Democracy* (New York, Harper, 1950).

erning and whether the electorate can hold the majority party responsible for their decisions.

VIII. PARTY GOVERNMENT UNDER THE AMERICAN CONSTITUTIONAL AND
POLITICAL SYSTEM

American Constitutional theory can be and has been used to rationalize the dispersive governmental and political system.[59] While it was
recognized that government under the new Constitution was to govern,
the principal concern in the debate over its formation and ratification
was the efficacy of the system for restraining the government.

The alternative of making those who hold positions of high authority
responsible to the electorate is not favored by American constitutional
theory. The authors of the *Federalist* saw the problem in the following
terms:

> Ambition must be made to counteract ambition. The interests of
> the man must be connected with the constitutional rights of the
> place. It may be a reflection on human nature, that such devices
> should be necessary to control the abuses of government. But what
> is government itself, but the greatest of all reflections on human
> nature? If men were angels, no government would be necessary.
> If angels were to govern men, neither external nor internal controls
> would be necessary. In framing a government which is to be ad-
> ministered by men over men, the great difficulty lies in this: you
> must first enable the government to control the governed; and in
> the next place oblige it to control itself. A dependence of the people
> is, no doubt, the primary control on the government; but experience
> has taught mankind the necessity of auxiliary precautions.[60]

"The constitutional rights of the place" which are to provide ambition
"to counteract ambition" are a bicameral legislature, separation of powers modified and enforced by checks and balances, and federalism, all
ordained in a written constitution protected by judicial review.

The theory postulates that these "auxiliary precautions" are necessary
to make oppression difficult, to impede too hasty action, and to assure
sound policy.[61] (The term *necessary* is used in the strict sense as a syno-

59. A. N. Holcombe, *Our More Perfect Union* (Cambridge, Harvard University Press, 1950) is the most recent extended examination and, in large part, restatement of American Constitutional theory along these lines.

60. *The Federalist*, No. 51.

61. It is also maintained that the tripartite division of a government is a natural
division of labor. Cf. Carl J. Friedrich, *Constitutional Government and Democracy*
(rev. ed., Boston, Ginn, 1950), pp. 183–184, with Paul H. Appleby, *Policy and
Administration, passim.* See the comparison of the principle of separation of powers

nym for *indispensable.*) These are three different objectives. In operation constitutional restraints as institutionalized may or may not realize these objectives. Or one objective may be realized without achieving the others.

Despite the reiteration for the last 160 years of the doctrine that power can be controlled only by fragmentizing and counterpoising it, the most effective institutional restraint upon government in the United States, as well as in Great Britain, Canada, and Australia, has been the operation of the party system which includes a recognized and organized opposition. Furthermore, the most promising approach to the improvement of policy formulation in the United States is through the development of a more effective party government.

We shall have party government when the party in power mobilizes effectively the men they elect to office to formulate, adopt, and execute policies with respect to major issues. What changes in theory and practice are necessary to bring about party government in the United States? In the first place, party policy must be formulated jointly by the party leaders in Congress and in the executive. Secondly, the party leaders must draw the pressures to themselves and protect the individual congressman from the pressures of special and local interests. Thirdly, to protect congressmen, party leaders must go into the constituencies and take a hand in their nomination and election. Fourthly, candidates for office must pledge themselves to support the party policies, if they would continue to receive the endorsement of the party leadership.

And, finally, the opposition party must develop a vigorous and effective opposition. Even today, with our undeveloped party system, this is our principal check upon the arbitrary exercise of power. But the opposition does not present coherent criticism tied to a set of alternative policies upon which it seeks the power to govern.

It is obvious that the Congressional parties cannot be reorganized without corresponding changes in political behavior throughout the country to support them. The most hopeful development is the increasing recognition that the major problems requiring political action are no longer local or sectional but nation-wide in their impact.[62] This is particularly true of foreign policy and of income stabilization policies.

At the present time the national parties go to the voters for their suffrage on these issues once in four years. If the national parties gave

---

with the integration and ordering of "single autonomous individuals" in John Wild, *Introduction to Realistic Philosophy* (New York, Harper, 1948), p. 221.

62. For a description and evaluation of the political revolution of the last two decades, see Samuel Lubell, *The Future of American Politics* (New York, Harper, 1952).

the same attention to Congressional nominations and elections as they now give to the nomination and election of a President, nominees to Congress and incumbent congressmen would not be at the complete mercy of local interests and of national interests locally organized. As the Committee on Political Parties of the American Political Science Association says:

> As for party cohesion in Congress, the parties have done little to build up the kind of unity within the congressional party that is now so widely desired. Traditionally congressional candidates are treated as if they were the orphans of the political system, with no truly adequate party mechanism available for the conduct of their campaigns. Enjoying remarkably little national or local party support, congressional candidates have mostly been left to cope with the political hazards of their occupation on their own account. *A basis for party cohesion in Congress will be established as soon as the parties interest themselves sufficiently in their congressional candidates to set up strong and active campaign organizations in the constituencies.* Discipline is less a matter of what the parties do *to* their congressional candidates than what the parties do *for* them.[63]

Many nationally organized interest groups are far ahead of the national political parties in the interest taken in Congressional campaigns, in the registration of voters, and in getting them to vote for particular candidates.

If the party leaders determine to reorganize the Congressional party, and to establish a regular system of collaboration between Congress and the executive in the formulation of party policies, they can proceed without having to change the written Constitution. In time the Constitution may be amended to change, for instance, the terms of office of the President, representatives, and senators so that all federal elective officers will be returned to office or defeated together. There is nothing in the Constitution, however, to prevent a party from mobilizing and organizing its members in Congress and the executive to govern effectively.[64]

63. American Political Science Association, "Toward a More Responsible Two-Party System," *op. cit.* (n. 47 above), pp. 21–22. See pp. 37–56 for other specific proposals of the committee.

64. I hope it is clear that I do not believe that this can be done by saying, "Let there be party government." I do believe that deliberate and concerted action can be taken, as it has in the past, to modify political institutions—all within the limits of time, communication, and skill in the use of existing institutions. See the evaluation by the Committee on Political Parties of the American Political Science Associa-

This is not to say that Constitutional precedents and theories, rationalizing as they do many vested interests in dispersive government, will not affect the development of economic and social policies. As Churchill has said: "We shape our buildings and afterwards our buildings shape us."

The British cabinet system is usually proposed as the only alternative to the existing American system.[65] If this position be correct, then we should cease talking about an American form of party government. Fortunately, however, there is no reason to believe that the institutional ingenuity of man has been exhausted by the development, should we say perfection, of the British cabinet system and the American presidential system as they exist in 1952.[66]

IX. JUDICIAL REVIEW

If, as appears likely, the Supreme Court continues to find room for expanding governmental activities within the Constitution, the threat of judicial review to income stabilization policy may be dismissed. It is true, of course, that the court may again say that certain nongovernmental activities are immune to direct governmental regulation. Even so, judging from the past, any public policy that can be brought under the spending or fiscal powers appears to be safe.[67]

---

tion of the sources of support and leadership for party government, *ibid.*, pp. 85–91. These suggestions need to be refined and expanded into a full-fledged analysis of the politics of party government.

"The essential problem in securing coordinated legislative-executive leadership is to shift the nature of the risks that beset the legislator and bring them into somewhat closer conformity with those confronting the president. . . . If something approaching party government is to develop, therefore, it seems likely that it must form around selected lines of policy on which variations in local reaction are largely within rather than between constituencies." David Truman, *op. cit.*, pp. 532–533.

65. Woodrow Wilson, *Congressional Government* (Boston, Houghton Mifflin, 1885); Samuel W. McCall, *The Business of Congress* (New York, Lemcke & Buechner, 1911); William Macdonald, *A New Constitution for a New America* (New York, Viking Press, 1921); Henry Hazlitt, *A New Constitution Now* (New York, McGraw-Hill, 1942); W. Y. Elliott, *The Need for Constitutional Reform* (New York, McGraw-Hill, 1935); Thomas K. Finletter, *op. cit.*

66. Note the modification of parliamentary government in Canada and Australia. Contrary to the belief of some people in the United States that party government is incompatible with federalism and judicial review, all three are to be found in these two commonwealths.

67. If the court were again to declare a number of acts unconstitutional, it would not necessarily be for the reason suggested by C. B. Swisher, *The Growth of Constitutional Power in the United States* (Chicago, University of Chicago Press, 1946), p. 229: "Ultimately, perhaps, when the extension of governmental action reaches the approximate limits of the area to which the dominant sentiments of the people

The judiciary, however, is not to be read out of the government. Its influence on public policy through the construction of statutes and administrative regulations and orders is perhaps more extensive than ever. Furthermore, the court functions as a rationalizer of legislative and administrative actions of the federal and state governments. In the cases that come before it, the court adjusts symbolically the public policies involved with accepted constitutional theory. The present court, with its frequent dissents and separate concurrences, has brought this debate into the open for the people to hear and to use.[68]

X. Federalism

The American federal system affects the formulation and execution of national income stabilization policies in that 48 state governments and some 165,000 other units of government are legally independent, in large measure, to pursue contrary policies. Their independence is, of course, not absolute: they are forbidden by the Constitution to do certain things, e.g., to coin money, emit bills of credit, etc., and if Congress wishes it can forbid state action contrary or inconsistent with a federal regulatory act.

State and local policy makers are largely unaware of the consequences of their fiscal policies upon income stabilization. They are acutely conscious of the problem of balancing demands for services against inadequate revenue in the face of high prices and wages. But in all but perhaps a few of the larger states and cities, the relation of their day-to-day policy decisions to the fluctuations of the gross national product is not apparent to them.

It would be difficult in any event for state and local governments to plan and execute a fiscal policy designed to stabilize the economy. National policy is not the sum of 155,000 policies; nor is it the sum of 250 policies formulated and carried out independently by the 48 states and the larger units of local government.

There are several reasons why state and local governments are likely either to pursue fiscal policies that are contrary to national income stabilization policies or, given the desire to cooperate, will find it difficult to

---

would have it go, the Court may again resume the function of limiting the scope of governmental power by constitutional interpretation."

68. See Herman C. Pritchett, *The Roosevelt Court: A Study in Judicial Politics and Values, 1937–1947* (New York, Macmillan, 1948). The superior value often attached to a symbol as used by the Supreme Court is illustrated by C. L. Christenson's review of *The New Deal Collective Bargaining Policy* (Berkeley, University of California Press, 1951) by Irving Bernstein in *Journal of Political Economy*, 59 (April, 1951), 176–177.

do so.[69] In the first place, state and local revenue systems are more inflexible than the federal revenue system—some elements are quite rigid. Extensive reliance upon the property tax at the local level, constitutional and statutory limitations on tax rates and indebtedness, the dispersal of authority to levy taxes, assess property and incur indebtedness among a large number of governments, the fixed schedule of most debt payments, and other features do not allow the fiscal manipulation required by income stabilization policy.

Secondly, there is a widespread disparity between the need for particular services and the ability to pay for them. Likewise, in the areas of inadequate fiscal resources there will be a disparity between the need for compensatory spending and fiscal ability to finance the policy.

Thirdly, the demand and need for the principal state and local services do not vary with the cyclical fluctuations of the economy. This is particularly true in a period following a decade of depression and almost another decade of war and inflation. Governor after governor, mayor after mayor has declared that the replacement or expansion of school buildings, or highways, or hospitals, or institutions cannot wait. For these reasons, and probably others, state and local governments "have usually followed the swings of the business cycle, from crest to trough, spending and building in prosperity periods and contracting their activities in depression periods." [70]

Without doubt, in the next depression the federal government will have to step in to fill the gap in state and local revenues to enable these units of government to help fill the gap in the gross national product. Direct federal expenditures will be increased, but there will also be a substantial increase in the number and amount of grants-in-aid to state and local governments.[71] During and since the war Congress has authorized new programs in airport construction, tuberculosis control, venereal disease control, mental hygiene, hospital construction, school lunches, housing and urban redevelopment. President Truman in his Midyear Economic Report of July, 1949, urges an expansion and extension of grant-in-aid programs: "There are economic and social deficits that would be far more serious than a temporary deficit in the

69. See A. H. Hansen and H. S. Perloff, *State and Local Finance in the National Economy* (New York, Norton, 1944), and G. W. Mitchell, O. F. Litterer, and E. D. Domar "State and Local Finance," in *Public Finance and Full Employment,* Richard A. Musgrave, E. D. Domar, Roland I. Robinson, and others, Federal Reserve System, Postwar Economic Studies No. 3 (1945), pp. 101–130.

70. Hansen and Perloff, *op. cit.,* p. 49.

71. There are powerful pressure groups who favor particular grants and powerful groups who oppose them. Significantly, however, the Governors' Conference of 1949 refused to pass a resolution condemning federal grants to states.

Federal budget. . . . Could we be truly prosperous with gaping deficits in our education system or our housing or our health services or our programs for resource development?"

Many people, however, who are not opposed to federal aid in general or in particular, are critical of the piecemeal development of aid programs. This attitude is really one of all or nothing, and if pressed to a test there is no doubt that the answer would be nothing. This is not to depreciate the desirability of considering particular programs in the context of general policy objectives. It is now imperative, for instance, that these and many other policies be reconsidered in terms of their relations to income stabilization policies. The Division of Fiscal Analysis of the Bureau of the Budget has been concerned with this problem since before the war. In its first year the Council of Economic Advisers was asked by the President to undertake, in cooperation with the Bureau of the Budget and other federal agencies, "a study of federal grants to state and local governments to determine to what extent revised standards for the distribution of these grants may take into account more fully the needs for support that exist in various parts of the country." [72]

There are many other problems involved in the development and administration of grant-in-aid programs: problems of federal, state, and local organization and administration, problems of equalization, problems of timing. In fact, concern with these problems raises all the larger political and administrative questions of general and specific policy objectives and their implementation in our federal-state-local system of government. The establishment of a federal-state fiscal authority, as proposed by the Special Committee on Intergovernmental Fiscal Relations,[73] would by itself be insufficient to solve the problems of federalism.

The difficulty of separating "administrative" questions from policy is illustrated in the report of the Hoover Commission on federal-state relations. The commission did not print the task force report which was prepared by the Council of State Governments, an organization representing the "state" point of view. Dean Acheson and James Forrestal dissented from the truncated commission report on the grounds that "the report and the recommendations . . . are concerned chiefly with taxation, grants-in-aid, and other matters primarily in the realm of legislative policy."

72. See Chapter 8 of this volume, "Variation in Public Expenditure," by R. A. Dahl and C. E. Lindblom.

73. *Federal, State, and Local Government Fiscal Relations,* report submitted to the Secretary of the Treasury by a Special Committee designated to conduct study on Intergovernmental Fiscal Relations in United States, 78th Congress, 1st Session, Senate Document No. 69 (June 23, 1943).

The commission does not divulge its basic assumptions nor the analysis of present federal-state relations upon which it bases its recommendations. It does recommend the creation of a "continuing agency on federal-state relations" to develop, in cooperation with the Bureau of the Budget, "a unified system of budgeting and fiscal control over the operation of all grants-in-aid." The agency would advise Congress on "the problem as a whole, as well as the many and various divisions and parts thereof." And, finally, it should be concerned with all public policy. ". . . it should be an agency which, on a continuing basis, would appraise our public needs, our resources and ways and means for adjusting the one to the other in the interest of the American people." [74] On its face, this recommendation is that the agency duplicate, if not replace, the political responsibilities of the President, the heads of the executive agencies, and the Congress.[75]

This is not to say that a commission of inquiry should not be created to attempt to identify publicly the problems of governance in a developing federal system and to indicate their relationship with each other. The principal benefit of such an inquiry, and it would be invaluable, would be the identification of problems in terms of issues to be publicly debated, the collection and analysis of the mass of data now available, and the sponsorship of studies to fill the gaps in our knowledge and understanding of the federal system.[76]

The federal system is important not only because it divides authority to make policy decisions among the national, state, and local governments. This division of authority has conditioned the development of the major political parties. The parties themselves are decentralized; they are federalized. V. O. Key characterizes the national party as "a loose alliance of state and city leaders who work together most faithfully during a presidential campaign." As E. E. Schattschneider says, "Decentralization of power is by all odds the most important single characteristic of the American major party; more than anything else this

74. The Commission on Organization of the Executive Branch of the Government, *Overseas Administration; Federal-State Relations; Federal Research* (1949), pp. 25, 36–37.

75. On July 23, 1951, the Senate passed S. 1146 to create a temporary commission to study federal-state-local relations and on the next day requested the House to return the bills for further consideration.

76. Even a cursory examination of William Anderson's *Federalism and Intergovernmental Relations: A Budget of Suggestions for Research,* prepared on behalf of the Committee on Public Administration and the Committee on Government of the Social Science Research Council (Chicago, Public Administration Service, 1946), will show the many blind spots and unanswered questions that exist. "What is called for is a great work of diagnosis . . ."

trait distinguishes it from all others. Indeed, once this truth is understood, nearly everything else about American parties is greatly illuminated." [77]

We must concern ourselves, then, with federal-state-local relations in the parties as well as in the formal government. National party leaders, with few exceptions, take no part in the nomination and election of candidates for the House of Representatives and the Senate. It should not astonish us, therefore, that members of the national legislature should feel that they are ambassadors from local party organizations, from local pressure groups, or from pressure groups with strong or articulate local organizations. They are not indebted to the national party for their seat in Congress nor do they fear the national party when the chips are down for renomination.[78]

The third aspect of federalism relevant to the development of national income stabilization policies is that, like all institutions, federalism is a source of symbols for political debate. The battle cry of states' rights has been present throughout our history in the debates over whether government should do this or that or nothing at all. Issues are often debated almost wholly in terms of states' rights, with only scant attention to the economic, social, or political desirability of the proposed policy.

As used by some people the symbol has represented identification with local interests or institutions. Many others have used the symbol unconsciously to rationalize, or calculatingly to influence opinion on, their opposition to governmental action. As C. B. Swisher says:

> It behooves us, therefore, to take thought before drenching our handkerchiefs when the National Association of Manufacturers and the American Bar Association bewail the prostrate position of the states before the federal colossus. These mourners are not shedding tears over the lamentable condition of New Hampshire and North Carolina and Montana and Texas but over the enterprise caught in the grip of the Federal regulatory hand. Whether that enterprise merits our sympathy is at the moment not the question. The point is that the argument is hopelessly confused by the strategy of its use.[79]

77. V. O. Key, Jr., *Politics, Parties, and Pressure Groups* (2d ed., New York, Crowell, 1947), p. 290; E. E. Schattschneider, *Party Government* (New York, Rinehart, 1942), p. 129.

78. See J. M. Burns *op. cit.*, ch. 1, "The Congressman and His World." See also Edward A. Shils, "The Legislator and His Environment," *University of Chicago Law Review, 18* (Spring, 1951), 571–584.

79. C. B. Swisher, *op. cit.*, p. 33.

Terms such as the "national interest" are, of course, also used to rationalize or to further particular interests.

XI. SEPARATION OF POWERS

No one knows what our government would be like if it operated under pure separation of powers. We get no help from history and imagination is limited to the statement that each branch would tend to its own business. Separation of powers does not preclude effective collaboration among members of the majority party in the executive and legislative branches. The dispersive character of our government is the result of our failure to organize the majority party for the job of readjusting "existing forces into more effective patterns for action." [80] Little of the blame can be attributed to any provisions in the Constitution for a separation of powers.

Of course, the classical theory of separation of powers has had a significant influence upon the behavior of men who are members of the executive, the legislature, or the judiciary. Like federalism it has been an arsenal of symbols from which antagonists select their weapons. The most important effect, therefore, is the barrier to collaboration raised by the institutional identification of the members of the various branches or parts of the branches.[81] (Bicameralism is considered here as part of the system of separation of powers.)

Although congressmen are more likely to take their defense of prerogative onto the floor or directly to the press, there are many administrators who resent "political" interference. Andrew Johnson was not the only President to act on the premise that "your President is now the Tribune of the people and, thank God, I am, and intend to assert the power which the people have placed in me." [82]

The recognition of the effect of separation of powers on institutional identification should not, however, lead to the claim that the psychologi-

80. Herring, *Politics of Democracy*, p. 191.
81. Harold J. Laski has said that Congress' "own instinctive and inherent tendency is, under all circumstances, to be antipresidential. It may respect him; it may even fear him; it may give him a general if spasmodic support. But it is always looking for occasions to differ from him, and it never feels so really comfortable as when it has found such an occasion for difference. In doing so, it has the sense that it is affirming its own essence. It is more truly itself because it is exalting its own prestige. Some members, no doubt, act in this way because to fight the president is the highroad to notoriety. Others, the late Senator Borah, for example, are constitutionally uncomfortable if they support any president while he is in office." *The American Presidency* (New York, Harper, 1940), p. 123. See also Paul H. Appleby, *Big Democracy*, pp. 166–167.
82. Quoted in W. E. Binkley, *President and Congress*, p. 136.

cal reaction of men to the symbols of office would be eliminated if there were no formal separation of powers. We shall forever be faced with the problem of establishing and maintaining frames of reference to offset the tendency of individuals to evaluate "the several alternatives of choice in terms of their consequences for the specified group." [83] This is the problem of policy-making at a high level whether a budget, an appropriation act, a statute, or an executive order be the vehicle of policy.

The point to be emphasized here is that organization is an important means of accentuating or modifying institutional identifications. The reorganization of political parties along the lines being developed by the Committee on National Political Parties and Elections of the American Political Science Association would provide an institution inclusive of many interests and forming a working majority in the executive and the legislature. Such a reorganized party system, if it becomes a going concern, would also blunt the use by pressure groups of our current institutional symbols, whether taken from separation of powers or federalism, to set public official against public official.

No aspect of separation of powers has provoked more debate in recent years than the well-established practice of Congress to delegate to the President or directly to administrative agencies the contingent authority to act or the express or implied authority to develop a policy by the issuance of administrative rules and orders. Most of the literature on separation of powers is concerned with the constitutionality and the administration of delegated powers.

Such delegation is acceptable to the courts if the delegation be restricted by legislative standards. The problems of establishing "built-in-flexibility" in the tax structure or in the expenditure program are mainly those of politics, draftsmanship, and administration.[84] These problems are discussed by Dahl and Lindblom in Chapter 8.

How much control should the President have over agencies administering such delegated powers in the fields of taxation, public works, and credit control? Two of the reasons advanced for making an agency independent of the Chief Executive are that the administration of such policies should be nonpolitical and that if the objectives of the policies are to be achieved there must be a continuity of planning and operations.

83. H. A. Simon, *Administrative Behavior* (New York, Macmillan, 1947).

84. The original printed draft of the full employment bill provided for executive discretion in adjusting the rate of federal expenditures. "A Bill to Establish a National Policy and Program for Assuring Continuing Full Employment," Senate Committee on Military Affairs, Subcommittee Print No. 1, Sec. 6, 78th Congress, 2d Session, December 18, 1944.

While it is clear that these reasons are often advanced to cover opposition to the party in power, or more specifically to the President, we must face the dilemma posed by Barbara Wootton.

> The dilemma that we have to resolve . . . is that economic planning demands continuity, and political freedom appears to imply instability. Nothing can alter the fact that we cannot both make effective long-term plans, and continually exercise the right to change our minds about anything at any time.[85]

She suggests the further development in England of nonparliamentary boards, such as the London Transport Board, the Central Electricity Board, and the British Broadcasting Corporation, to administer those policies on which there is substantial agreement. They are able to plan and operate with requisite continuity and yet are sufficiently responsible to Parliament through provisions for periodical review when the budget is voted "for the Government department most closely concerned with the work of the Board in question."

If we apply the test of general agreement on a policy before assigning it to an independent agency or government corporation, then many policies so assigned in this country, and certainly the proposed fiscal controls, taxation, and compensatory spending schemes do not have behind them the requisite consensus for attempting to achieve continuity by this device.

The need for speedy action in the use of taxes, monetary controls, and expenditures to maintain economic stabilization is the principal reason for urging the Congressional delegation of these powers.[86] These are the areas of policy which most, and certainly the more powerful, pressure groups consider to be crucial to their interests. Congressmen responding to or leading these groups are not likely to relinquish in the near future the present method of enacting tax and expenditure programs. It is possible, however, that in the atmosphere of helplessness and frustration of a depression a majority in Congress could be mobilized to pass the buck to the executive. No one during the tariff revision of 1929–30 would have predicted the passage four years later of the Reciprocal Trade Act.[87]

85. Barbara Wootton, *Freedom under Planning* (London, George Allen & Unwin, 1945), p. 131.

86. W. W. Cooper, "Some Implications of a Program for Full Employment and Economic Stability," *Political Science Quarterly, 63* (June, 1948), 251–256.

87. See John D. Larkin, *The President's Control of the Tariff* (Cambridge, Harvard University Press, 1936), and *Trade Agreements* (New York, Columbia University Press, 1940), and E. E. Schattschneider, *Politics, Pressures and the Tariff*, p. 289.

Assuming the decision to delegate, there is a danger that Congress will disperse the delegation among many agencies accompanied by impediments to presidential coordination and control over policy. We are already faced with the problem, in the words of the Hoover Commission, of the "generally loose and casual . . . sometimes non-existent . . . coordination of policies pursued by [the] independent regulatory commissions with those of the executive branch as a whole." [88] Although there is some exaggeration in the unqualified language of the President's Committee on Administrative Management,[89] the independent commissions do "leave the President with responsibility without power." It is doubtful that the device proposed by the Hoover Commission will coordinate. This is to be accomplished by putting "machinery in the President's Office" and by suggesting that "the chairman of each commission effect liaison between their commissions and the rest of the Government."

No mention is made of the problem of coordinating the activities of these commissions with income stabilization policies. Specifically the commission recommends that certain "executive" or "operational" functions of the Federal Power Commission, the Maritime Commission, the Interstate Commerce Commission, and the Civil Aeronautics Board be transferred to the Departments of the Interior, Labor, and Commerce. Once this is done it believes that the area in which coordination is needed will be greatly minimized.

The only functions of the ICC which it recommends be transferred are those relating to equipment, car service, and safety inspection. Transportation rates and services are not insignificant items in the economy but the commission apparently considers the need for coordination between the ICC and other government agencies administering economic programs to be slight.[90] The experience of OPA with the

88. Commission on Organization of the Executive Branch of the Government, *Regulatory Commissions* (1949), pp. 4, 15.

89. President's Committee on Administrative Management, *Administrative Management in the Government of the United States* (1937), pp. 36–38: "They are in reality miniature independent governments set up to deal with the railroad problem, the banking problem, or the radio problem. They constitute a headless fourth branch of the Government, a haphazard deposit of irresponsible agencies and uncoordinated powers. . . . The evils resulting from this confusion of principles are insidious and far-reaching. . . . We speak of the 'independent' regulatory commissions. It would be more accurate to call them the 'irresponsible' regulatory commissions, for they are areas of unaccountability."

90. The Commission on Organization of the Executive Branch of the Government does say in its report on the *Department of Commerce* (1949), p. 15: "Moreover, since transportation is an element in the costs of practically every other industry, Government policies on transportation should be coordinated with Government policies toward industry in general."

ICC, and vice versa, during wartime should show that liaison alone will not result in coordination.

The Hoover Commission recommendations not only fail to reach the jugular vein but other recommendations, if adopted, would increase the independence of these agencies. It recommends, Commissioners Dean Acheson, Harold B. Rowe, and James Forrestal dissenting, that members of the Securities and Exchange Commission, the Federal Power Commission, and the Federal Communications Commission be removable only for cause and that a commissioner, upon the expiration of his term, remain in office until a successor has qualified. The latter recommendation would mean, as Commissioner Forrestal pointed out in a dissent, that senatorial failure to confirm a successor could frustrate a President's attempt to modify a commission's policies by appointing a man favorable to his own policies.[91]

XII. Conclusion

The American people cannot escape from politics nor from the complex and momentous issues about which decisions have to be made without allowing or seeking an authoritarian government to make our decisions for us. Fortunately the choice does not have to be between monism and a completely unorganized and uncontrolled pluralism. We are still individuals who take many of our most cherished values from face to face relations with other people. At the same time, our social, economic, and political values are now realizable and defendable only through big organizations claiming loyalty from millions of people spread over extensive areas. At the same time, again, there is a threat of oppression in each of the segments of the Great Society. The dilemma cannot be avoided or read out by the use of words.

We are faced with a task that has always faced mankind: that of organizing ourselves to give effective power to the men and women who govern us while holding them responsible for the purposes and manner in which they use that power. We no longer naively believe that such a reconstruction can or need be done as an intellectual tour de force based upon a calculus which ignores existing institutions or the multitude of interests of men and women. But a social institution is not, to use Schattschneider's figure, an oyster which develops subject to outside stimuli alone. It can be changed by the people who compose the institution, by taking thought and by taking action.

91. *Regulatory Commissions,* pp. 7–8. A wholly false and misleading impression of unanimity in the commission is given by the McGraw-Hill republication of the commission reports through the omission of dissenting and concurring opinions. Unfortunately, this one-sided version is the form in which the reports will be read by most people.

Our governmental and political system has been modified in this way. We are in the very center of such a process today. Among other struggles to reorganize ourselves there is a definite and recognizable struggle for party government. What the outcome will be no one knows, but an increasing number of people, including politicians as well as professors, believe that the development of party government is the most promising means of focusing power at strategic points and of controlling the men who are authorized and expected to govern. As Schattschneider has said:

> The major party is the only political organization in American life which is in a position to make a claim, upon any reasonable ground whatsoever, that it can measure up to the requirements of modern public policy. The party alone pretends to be interested in a general control of the government; only the party possesses the kind of power required to make the government work; it alone might reasonably be held responsible for the general state of public policy.[92]

Any reorganized party system in the United States will be indigenous in that it will be made by Americans. Furthermore, despite the fundamental difference it will make in American politics, it will not be drafted in a constitutional convention but will have to be developed while we are making policy decisions on civil rights, labor-management relations, the cold war, health insurance, and many other questions of the hour.

This means that economists must also participate in the struggle to develop more adequate and more responsible political means for making economic decisions. Men who are not economists will also participate. The most valuable participants, as Max Millikan has spelled it out for us, will be men and women, whether economists or not, who see clearly and feel deeply the need for developing and maintaining the dignity of man.

92. E. E. Schattschneider, *The Struggle for Party Government* (College Park, University of Maryland Press, 1948), pp. 10–11.

CHAPTER XIV. *Stabilization Technique and*
Patterns of Expectation

BY HAROLD D. LASSWELL

I. INTRODUCTION

1. *The problem*

Since economic decisions depend in some measure on expectations, the technique of stabilization calls for the influencing of the pattern of expectation in appropriate ways. In part this is a matter of utilizing the channels of communication. The aim of the present chapter is to inquire into the relations between policy and expectation, and to show how modern methods of research on public attitudes are being drawn into the service of stabilization programs and how these methods can be most effectively applied in the future. The members of the Council of Economic Advisers have the double task of arriving at trustworthy anticipations of the future and of acting upon the expectations of others in the interest of future stability at high levels of productive employment. Obviously the advisers have no Cyclopean eye placed above and beyond the economic process, capable of arriving at unblinking truth about the shape of things to be. What the advisers see darkly in the glass of the future must include some estimate of the impact of their own statements, or failure to make statements, upon the course of policy.

In general terms we recognize that a stable level of economic activity depends upon achieving an appropriate system of policy choices. Policies constitute a system when they act upon one another to maintain a given pattern of relationships, in this case a high level of productive employment. Choices operating to depress employment must be compensated by policy choices whose effect is to support employment. In the American economy the makers of policy are not concentrated at the apex of a huge monolithic edifice. On the contrary, the ebb and flow of business registers the outcome of choices made by millions of consumers, thousands of firms, and hundreds of regulators (the latter operating through government tribunals to affect business).

Certain patterns of expectation must be sustained if the necessary equilibrium is to be kept in being.[1] The fundamental principle as it relates to expectation can be stated in this way: choices conducive to good business depend upon the expectation that such choices will yield more net advantages to the chooser than choices leading to bad business. This is a special application of the basic postulate of choice, which is that choices are guided by the intention of maximizing gratification. In one sense this is a truism, particularly when it is understood to cover unconscious as well as conscious expectations. Undoubtedly it is one of the most serviceable truisms of common sense and science. Specific common-sense applications are: if consumers are to spend rather than to curtail their purchases, they must expect to be better off by spending; if managers are to enlarge output rather than cut back, they must expect by doing so to be in a better position.

How are the expectations determined upon which policies affecting employment are based? Expectations are the outcome of two sets of determining factors: whatever comes to the focus of attention during a given period; the predispositions with which these events are interpreted. What gets to the attention of consumers or business managers is partly a matter of primary contact with people and things. The executive is in regular touch with department heads and staff assistants. He sees a flow of paper originating in his own firm or specifically directed to it from outside. He comes in contact with the heads of other firms and their representatives. And these direct associations are supplemented by exposure to the mass media of communication, ranging from newspapers and broadcasts to private subscription dope sheets. Consumers, managers, workers, savers, investors all live the same bifocal existence, partly seeing people and objects at first hand and partly through long-range instrumentalities of communication.

When we consider stabilization technique in the United States we have in mind the alternatives open to public officials in sustaining high levels of productive employment. The problem occurs in two principal forms: the preventing of recession; recovery from recession. Policies designed to avoid inflation come in the first category, since it is probable that great busts follow great bursts. We think of the government in our economy as performing the functions of a governor on an electro-

1. Although the importance of expectations has long been part of economic theory, many recent developments have resulted in renewed emphasis upon such factors. The brilliant paragraphs by Keynes in the *General Theory* are often cited in this connection. A recent English treatise which proposes certain innovations is by G. L. S. Shackle, *Expectation in Economics* (Cambridge, Cambridge University Press, 1949). Shackle takes the degree of "surprise" as a measure of confidence that a specified event will occur at a designated future date.

turbine, where the role of the governing mechanism is to sustain the equilibrium of operation by setting off a compensating component in the system whenever the level of activity veers too much in any direction.[2] Given our mixed economy the problem is to devise institutions which keep the entire business picture under surveillance and stimulate compensating factors whenever the safe limits of the going equilibrium are in danger of being exceeded. When we construct an electrical generating plant, we can build into the setup circuits of adjustment which act whenever critical limits are reached. This "once and for all" solution is not now feasible for economic systems. We can take a step in the direction of "built-in" mechanisms, however, by setting up agencies whose special task is to keep the entire stream of economic life under observation.

Such an agency may gradually learn to perceive the cues in business and social life which signify that processes are beginning which, if unchecked, will presently upset the high employment level. Besides perceiving these cues the agency has the problem of discerning the courses of compensatory action which, if taken in time, would remove the danger of disequilibrium. Part of this problem is to discover the courses open to the agency for initiating needed adjustments. The nation has taken some steps toward developing a specialized mechanism of surveillance, of choice of compensation, and of choice of means for stimulating needed acts of compensation. But it is not possible at present to specify in advance and in detail the precise nature of the cues which if perceived will signalize danger, or identify the compensations capable of sustaining equilibrium, or identify the triggers adequate to bring the compensations to pass. It is, of course, a great advance to experiment with the President's Council of Economic Advisers. The point of the present symposium is how this sort of institution can evolve into a more perfect integrator of our total social process for the purpose of maintaining a high employment equilibrium in the economic process. To speak in the language of another discipline: we want to perfect the servomechanisms of our economy.

The official agencies which we have in mind must rely upon persuasion rather than coercion. Although the servomechanisms of the turbine do not themselves require much energy, they are built into the system in such a way that there is no denying response to their trigger action. The position of the President's council is very different. There is no inbuilt imperative constraining a President to adopt the views and

2. A generalization of the importance of servomechanisms is in Norbert Wiener, *Cybernetics, or Control and Communication in the Animal and the Machine* (New York, Wiley, 1948).

recommendations of the advisers. The council is weak or strong insofar as it carries conviction to the President directly, or to those who in turn influence the Chief Executive, or to other official or unofficial individuals who are able to get effective results irrespective of the President. The advisers lack authority of final decision or even of initiative, to say nothing of appointment and removal. If effective, therefore, they succeed by virtue of the impact of the communications which they direct to the President and to others. Obviously these communications must come to the focus of attention of those to be affected, and they must succeed in sustaining or modifying expectations according to the needs of economic equilibrium. If the level of national employment is to remain on the plateau sought by national policy, the expectations of policy makers must sustain choices which do in fact have the desired result.

Our proposition is, therefore, that stabilization technique is communication technique. True, it is not the exclusive technique. But an act of communication is an indispensable link between acts of choice. There is an endless chain—listening, choosing, saying, listening, choosing . . . In fact all social activities can conveniently be summed up in terms of communication and collaboration, since all social acts involve varying degrees of both. Some links between the advisers and significant acts of policy may be short and devoid of intermediaries, as when the advisers speak to the President, who promptly issues an executive order. However advisers and policy may be linked by many intermediaries, as when the reader of a report, after consultation with his own advisers, issues a broadside of news and editorial matter which influences the behavior of executives and consumers.

Our present purpose is to examine the nature of the process of communication and to consider how tools of communication can become effective implements in the hands of official agencies such as the President's Council of Economic Advisers. Most of the discussion will refer to the preventive rather than the recovery phase of stabilization policy.

2. The process of communication

When we consider the function performed by the process of communication in any community, three major roles can be distinguished.[3] There is the gathering and transmission of information about the world surrounding the community. There is the dissemination of ideas about what the community should do, if anything, to deal with the environment whose changes have been reported. And there is the transmitting

3. See Harold D. Lasswell, "The Structure and Function of Communication," in Lyman Bryson, ed., *The Communication of Ideas* (New York, Harper, 1948).

of the traditions acquired by the community in adapting its values to the threats and opportunities of history. For convenience we may speak of the task of the communication process as threefold: surveillance, correlation, transmission. It is *surveillance* of the environment which discloses the threats and opportunities affecting the value position of the community. It is *correlation* when the members of a community work out a common course of action in response to environmental threats and opportunities. It is *transmission* when children or strangers receive the social inheritance. Insofar as the economic equilibrium within the United States is affected by what goes on outside our geographical frontiers, the advisers are performing a surveillance function for the nation as a whole when they observe and interpret world trends. By making recommendations the advisers become part of the process by which the nation acts to maintain internal strength and to stabilize impacts upon the surrounding world. The advisers have as yet little to do with transmission.

The three categories of analysis apply to the communication process of any firm. One task of top management is to keep informed about developments in the environment which may affect the business. Hence a top executive keeps an eye on competitors, suppliers, customers, and regulators. It does not need to be demonstrated that the executive has a mighty role to perform in correlation and transmission within the firm.

The same analysis applies to any subgroup. For instance, top executives act to some extent as a distinct entity in relation to other elements in the firm and on the outside. In varying degree they share in surveillance, correlation, and transmission: they make and pool certain observations, and pass on traditional attitudes to newcomers.

It is not far-fetched to carry our categories to the study of specific individuals. Everyone spends part of his time receiving communications about his environment, making up his mind about how to respond, and remembering and recording experience for later use.

The various functions of communication are usually performed by specialized structures. The nation has agents abroad who observe and report (diplomats, correspondents, and spies, for instance). A large firm may have a contact man in Washington to supply information about legislative, administrative, or judicial action affecting the business. The correlation of national action calls for the dissemination of news and comment through the channels of communication and the impact of crystallized opinion upon government officials. A large firm may hire a lobbyist to deal with Congress, or to be present at administrative hearings or court proceedings. The transmission function is carried on for the nation by educational institutions at all levels from the nursery school to the university. Most businesses provide for the training of employees.

The structures of communication are specialized to various patterns of traffic. Press association traffic is largely one-way, but the prevailing pattern of a debating assembly is two-way (or, rather, multiples thereof). The staff of a trade association in Washington performs two-way functions, acting in part as an agency of surveillance for members and partly as a propagandist-lobby megaphone for the rank and file. Networks of communication are peripherally or centrally specialized. There are centers and subcenters at national, regional, state, and local headquarters.

The finer structure of the channels of communication is composed of links. A link is a place where content can be affected. Links are formed at breaks in the physical facilities for transmitting messages, as when electrical impulses are converted into typed messages, or one person addresses another. We have spoken of the link between the advisers and the President and of more complicated links like the following: advisers, report readers, consultants, editor and correspondent, and newspaper readers.

Depending upon the pattern of linkage, a communication center can bring about a very considerable modification of the messages that pass through it, much as the central nervous system integrates stimuli from several sources. At a great center like Washington or New York, the newspaper correspondents affect one another by constituting both formal and informal links among themselves. Financial correspondents read what other financial correspondents write, since they know that they are continually being compared by third parties. Besides, they have a craftsman's interest in seeing how another specialist handles a press release from the Treasury or an interview with the research director of the Federal Reserve Board. Correspondents who sit in the same press conference affect one another by manner as well as question. Mutual influencing goes on at the National Press Club (and elsewhere). Persons familiar with the press corps in Washington learn to identify the key men who set the tone reflected more or less unconsciously by other correspondents on certain questions.

When studying the function and structure of communication, it is often convenient to concentrate upon the several phases through which acts of communication may pass. In a completed sequence

someone says
something
somehow to

someone with
some result.
If we concern ourselves with "someone," we are studying the *control* phase of the act of communication and describe publishers, radio station owners, editors, regulators, and contributors. When we specialize upon the "something" said we engage in *content* analysis, classifying content as news comment or entertainment and evaluating statements as true or false or in good or bad taste (according to defined criteria). If stress is put upon "somehow," we inquire into the *media* by which content is transmitted. The media comprise the voice, print, film, and every psychophysical means of conveying a message. *Audience* analysis is the study of "someone," and seeks to discover who listens, sees, reads, or is otherwise exposed to media. *Effect* analysis ("result" analysis) is concerned with the impact of the message upon the audience and in principle takes everything into account from the smallest subjective twinge to the most complex overt deed.[4]

The task of the advisers is to relate themselves efficiently to the communication network of the country. The advisers obviously depend upon it as a source of information. Above all they need it as a means of affecting expectations.

3. Systems of policy and expectation

The expectations which influence individual choices are part of a total context of perspectives. These perspectives turn out on analysis to be more or less tightly knit expectations, demands, and identifications. It is obvious that long- and short-range expectations influence one another and also that wants are likely to affect expectations. The "demands" of

4. Some conception of the scope of modern research in communication can be obtained by examining *Propaganda, Communication and Public Opinion: A Comprehensive Reference Guide* by B. L. Smith, H. D. Lasswell, and R. D. Casey (Princeton, Princeton University Press, 1946). Journals include the *Public Opinion Quarterly* (Princeton) and the *International Journal of Opinion and Attitude Research* (Mexico City). A recent textbook covering much of the field is Leonard Doob, *Public Opinion and Propaganda* (New York, Holt, 1948). See also the numerous texts on social psychology which have been published since the war, especially by David Krech and R. S. Crutchfield, T. M. Newcomb, and M. Sherif and H. Cantril. An important contribution to the theory of communication has recently been made by mathematicians concerned with the psychophysical channels employed in transmitting the physical signs which mediate between the intentions of the communicator and the interpretation of the audience. See C. E. Shannon and Warren Weaver, *The Mathematical Theory of Communication* (Urbana, University of Illinois Press, 1949). The outstanding review of current research on *Language and Communication* is by George A. Miller (New York, McGraw-Hill, 1951).

an individual can be conveniently classified as values (categories of "desired events"). Besides economic values, it is customary to identify the political value (power) and the demand to be treated with respect. (Other value categories useful for analytic purposes are well-being, skill, affection, rectitude, and enlightenment.) In examining the perspective of any individual it is important to take his "identifications" into account. The identifications mark the boundaries of the self. The self is composed of symbols of reference to the family, friends, and others who are treated as an extension of the primary ego in certain situations.[5]

The many identifications which constitute the self are connected with more or less distinctive demands and expectations. It is traditional to think of profit as the main value sought by the self as businessman. The self as politician may include the ambition to achieve effective power as a big wheel on the state or national party committee. The principal value sought by the self as university trustee may be respect. The chief value sought by the self as family man may be affection given and received in the family circle.

We have a full understanding of an individual when we can successfully predict the choices he will make in future circumstances (or when we can retrospectively predict the choices he has made in the past). We often have accurate insight into specific persons, enabling us to make correct estimates of when they will save or spend, hoard or invest. Perhaps we can accurately forecast what they will do if they fail in business, or if they lose a job, or if some other deprivation abruptly impairs their value position. We may be able to foresee what will happen if business prospers, jobs get bigger, and other indulgences improve the value position of the individual. Most of us would admit, however, that some of the people we thought we knew best have occasionally taken us by surprise. We may have chosen a business partner who goes to pieces with success. Our treasurer may prove to be a crook. The junior executive, groomed and "heir apparent," may turn out to lack initiative, imagination, and self-confidence.

The truth is that we are often better able to foresee the behavior of "men in the mass" than particular persons. As members of American culture we share with millions of fellow citizens many of the same expectations, demands, and identifications. As members of the upper, middle, or lower class in terms of wealth, power, respect, or some other value, we share expectations, demands, and identifications with class members. Belonging to a generation that has lived through crises of depression

5. Concerning the value categories see H. D. Lasswell and Abraham Kaplan, *Power and Society* (New Haven, Yale University Press, 1950). See also the introductory chapter in the present volume.

and war, we share perspectives which set us apart from intercrisis generations. Finally, we share some perspectives with all who have the same basic form of personality.

The task confronting the advisers can now be more inclusively phrased. The problem is to use communication to arouse the predispositions that affect in appropriate ways the expectations upon which high employment depends. Since the communications that reach people during a given period are only part of what comes to their attention, the problem is to use communication so skilfully that the impact is not nullified by other factors in the environment.

II. THE STUDY OF EXPECTATION PATTERNS

1. *Improving the intelligence process*

One way to describe the task of the advisers is to say that they must maintain an intelligence process for themselves and others which is capable of facilitating the policies necessary to support economic equilibrium at high employment. The term "intelligence" refers to the stream of fact and comment upon which choices are based. (It is an old word in this sense, as the name of some early newspapers—*The Intelligencer,* for example—testifies. The term has dropped out of use in recent decades, save in military circles. We revive the word in order to characterize the communications important to policy.)

The first task is to set in motion an adequate intelligence mechanism for the advisers. In estimating outcomes the advisers must take account of all expectations which are significantly affecting employment (and influencing plans for the future). It is also essential to evaluate factors other than current expectations which enter into the equilibrium of the economy, since at some point nonexpectation factors will affect the structure of expectation. When the advisers evaluate the wisdom of measures to compensate against adverse tendencies, it is essential to estimate the probable course of expectations: How will a given policy influence expectations? What expectations must be influenced by the advisers if a certain policy is to be adopted?

Until recently economic expectations were not directly studied by systematic methods. Apparently the assumption was that economic behavior could be sufficiently well understood if more and more comprehensive indexes were gathered of prices and outputs. Recently, however, the procedures common to research on communication have been extended to some economic expectations.

2. Surveying trends by interviewing

The Board of Governors of the Federal Reserve System has been experimenting in recent years with direct interviewing as a means of surveying consumer finances.[6] Annual surveys are reported in the *Federal Reserve Bulletin* as the data are worked up. The results are also made available to writers for the press who are looking for article material. The business press (notably *Business Week*) has given frequent attention to the findings and so have the subscription services. The data have also been used by the business editors of weekly news magazines. The results have seeped through to many other mass media. The tone of the *Federal Reserve Bulletin* is factual and nonsensational; and the business press has handled the results in the same way. The growing demand for material of this kind is shown by the number of private agencies now making parallel surveys of their own, often with questions from the Federal Reserve Board list.

The objectives sought by the studies of consumer finances are to obtain data which show:

1) distribution of liquid asset holdings at the beginning of each year.

2) past and expected disposition of accumulated assets and factors affecting the disposition of assets.

3) past and expected rate of saving and factors affecting rates of saving.

4) plans for the purchase of consumer durable goods for the coming year and actual purchases during the past year.

5) expectations with regard to personal well-being and with regard to economy in general.

Between 3,000 and 4,000 interviews are made on a nation-wide sample. All metropolitan areas having over one million population are included in the sample. The rest of the nation is classified into 54 groups of counties having about the same proportion of the total population. These 54 groups are as homogenous as possible according to the variables which are known or suspected to be related to the factors under study in the survey. (In the statistical sense each group of counties is a stratum, and from each stratum one county is selected by using random numbers to represent it.)

6. The scientific work was done under the direction of Rensis Likert. Consult Likert, "The Sample Interview Survey as a Tool of Research and Policy Formation," in D. Lerner and H. D. Lasswell, eds., *The Policy Sciences* (Stanford, Stanford University Press, 1951), ch. 13; especially George Katona, *Psychological Analysis of Economic Behavior* (New York, McGraw-Hill, 1951), notably chs. 5, 6, 8, 13, and 15. This is the outstanding summary of theory and empirical studies.

Within the metropolitan areas and counties specific dwelling (consuming) units are designated. In cities the blocks are grouped into homogeneous groups according to census statistics and samples are picked by means of random numbers. Then by consulting maps that show all dwellings, specific dwellings are chosen at random for use in the sample. In rural areas the county is subdivided into small geographical units containing three to five farms. These are numbered so that when a random selection is made, the chosen units will be widely scattered through the county. Aerial photographs of the county are then obtained and the interviewers are instructed to interview the heads of all spending units in each dwelling located in the designated area. (No substitutions are permitted.)

The interview form is carefully tried out on representative persons in advance of final use. The questions are phrased in relation to problems which touch and concern the respondent. The form used on the consumer survey starts as follows:

1) Would you say *you* people are better off or worse off financially now than you were a year ago?

a) Why do you say so?

2) Are you making as much money now as you were a year ago, more or less?

a) Why is that?

3) How about a year from now—do you think that you will be making more money or less money than you are now, or will you be making about the same?

a) Why will that be?

4) Now considering the country as a whole, do you think we will have good times or bad times or what during the next 12 months or so?

a) Can you tell me a little more about what you see for (year)? Or: Just how do you think the good (bad) times will show up?

5) What do you think will happen to the prices of things you buy during (year)—do you think they will go up, or down, or stay about where they are now?

a) Why will they do that?

b) (If any change at all is mentioned) Do you think that prices in general will be a lot lower (higher) or only a little lower (higher) by the end of (the year)?

In training the interviewers care is taken to see that they understand the scope and importance of the survey. Interviewers are trained to introduce themselves in ways that explain the purpose of the government in terms that will be grasped by the respondent. In addressing an elderly woman who appears to be in poor circumstances, for example, the first words may be: "Nobody can tell whether we are going to have good times or poor times during the next year or so, and the government would like to get ready to do what it can to make sure we don't have another depression . . ."

Although it is not easy to arrive at definite conclusions on a matter of such subtlety, the data from the consumer surveys have probably had a stabilizing effect on estimates of the business future and on judgments of the policies needed to deal with pending problems. The "pay dirt" in the interview material relates to consumer durables, which for obvious reasons is a sensitive spot in the economy, deeply affecting inventory and manufacturing policies. In 1948 and early 1949 when there was great concern expressed in public and private over "inflationary pressures," the results of the consumer survey helped staff economists of the Federal Reserve Board to refrain from "going overboard" in appraising these pressures. The indications were that the consumers were in a less frantic mood to acquire durables than they had been a short while before. Hence the staff of the board did not share the judgment of those who urged upon the President the necessity of asking Congress for drastic authority to cope with pending inflation. Shortly after, the consumer data tended to put the economists on guard against the extreme pessimism current in many parts of the business community in mid-1949. I believe that the conclusion is warranted that a technically competent survey of consumer opinion provides a solid block of evidence which holds in check many of the more fanciful speculations about "what the public is thinking." Widely scattered over the nation, the private statements made by a sample of consumers are less subject to deliberate "editing" than many of the statements issued from the national headquarters of business or government.

Besides the information obtained by surveys of the consumer, some efforts have been made to use direct interviewing to find out about the plans for plant or equipment expansion made by firms in different industries. The important bearing of such plans upon the economic future is evident.[7]

3. Other possibilities (content analysis)

Another possible source of trend information is the content of media of communication. It is often noted that one sign of business pessimism is the increasing frequency with which discouraging forecasts are made in editorial columns or in reported speeches. For purposes of trend analysis it is important to take these statements as symptoms, not as testimony. Common sense tells us that optimistic and pessimistic state-

7. Referred to by Everett Hagen in Chapter 4.

ments may occur at the same time in different parts of the country, in various trade journals, in different papers in the same locality or line of business, or even in the same editorial or news release. If we summarize the frequency of statements about the future of business would we not have a useful series of data to add to the other series on which inferences are made about expected trends? [8]

It is not necessary to describe every one of the 1800 daily newspapers in the United States or the 10,500 weekly newspapers.[9] Only experience will disclose the most informative method of sampling, but several suggestions can be made now. We know that some newspapers have an opportunity for influence far beyond their circulation because of the reputation they have among other newspapers and the general public. (Stock examples are the *Times* and the *Herald-Tribune* in New York, the *Christian Science Monitor* in Boston, the *Sun* in Baltimore, and the *Post* in Washington.) From a circulation point of view, the country can be divided into a number of areas according to the circulation of newspapers originating outside the area. The papers from a metropolitan center are the most frequently read newspapers (from outside) in the towns immediately adjacent. As we go toward the next metropolis, we usually reach a zone where copies of the paper from the new metropolis are read with equal frequency. The circulation areas of the newspress do not entirely coincide with the listening areas of radio (or the other media) nor with the trading areas. Also, the zones of readership for a given paper or metropolis are not necessarily continuous. A Chicago newspaper which yields to other metropolitan papers in northern Iowa recovers its leading position in western Nebraska as the preferred outside publication, for instance.

We noted that one merit of interviewing consumers is that there are so many of them that they are not likely to be part of an organized plan to withhold or distort information. Statements issued by major firms or industrial headquarters are subject to public relations processing. It may be that small town papers and country weeklies will prove more useful indicators of the depth and scope of shifts in economic expectation than the sophisticated press. The plausibility of this is increased when we remember that it is important to consider other than explicit statements about the business outlook. It is well known to military intel-

8. On methods of content analysis the standard survey is Bernard Berelson, *Content Analysis in Communication Research* (Glencoe, Ill., Free Press, 1952). See also H. D. Lasswell, Nathan Leites, and associates, *Language of Politics: Studies in Quantitative Semantics* (New York, Stewart, 1948).

9. A concise collection of data about the mass media appears in the appendix to W. Schramm, ed., *Mass Communication* (Urbana, University of Illinois Press, 1949).

ligence experts that valuable indications can be obtained by observing how everyday activities are reflected in local journals.[10] It may be that the most sensitive indicators of the level of economic expectation are changes in the content of want ads or the personals in the local press.

With an eye to the potential repercussions in Congress and the White House of a changing economic outlook, it is wise to give particular attention to papers in balance of power areas (in terms of party and factional strength). Some states and Congressional districts have the reputation among party experts and voting analysts of going "as goes the nation." The shifting moods and expectations of such constituencies have a disproportionate impact at both ends of Pennsylvania Avenue. In some cases constituencies derive their importance from the fact that their representative or senator is the chairman of a potent committee in Congress, or occupies an important party or administrative post, or enjoys a special tie to the White House.

When publications are sampled in order to describe economic expectations, the many and diverse lines of activity in our economy must be taken into account. To some extent these differences are reflected in the daily press and can be disclosed by a properly selected newspaper sample. (Every circulation area is a somewhat distinctive pattern of agriculture, mining, lumbering, dairying, and heavy or light manufacturing.) The most useful samples may be the combined economic-political areas of the kind employed by Arthur N. Holcombe when he analyzed political party tendencies in the nation.[11]

The trade press lends itself to sampling by means of functional rather than territorial categories.[12] It is likely that over-all statements about business will be less indicative than the items of incidental intelligence appearing in the news columns of the trade journals.

Besides the general and the trade press it may be worth while to survey church publications. Churches are always engaged in fund-raising campaigns, often on a national scale. Indications of success or failure,

10. See Sherman Kent, *Strategic Intelligence: For American World Policy* (Princeton, Princeton University Press, 1949). Also Ithiel de Sola Pool et al., *The "Prestige Papers": A Survey of Editorials,* Hoover Institute Studies (Stanford, Stanford University Press, 1951).

11. *The Middle Classes in American Politics* (Cambridge, Harvard University Press, 1940). See also C. E. Merriam and H. F. Gosnell, *The American Party System: An Introduction to the Study of Political Parties* (4th ed., New York, Macmillan, 1949), chs. 5, 6.

12. In 1938 there were about 1,500 national and regional trade associations and perhaps 6,000 state and local ones. See C. A. Pearce, *Trade Association Survey,* Monograph 18, Temporary National Economic Committee, Washington, D.C. (1941). Publications ranged from elaborate periodicals to nothing.

ease or difficulty, can contribute useful hints about economic conditions. Since educational and charitable institutions also have their hands out most of the time, their press can be read with advantage.

Some professional journals touch, even though indirectly, upon the prevailing level of economic expectation among various groups in different parts of the country. Since social statistics are not always gathered in a satisfactory manner on a national scale, the best evidence of certain trends may be found in local or professional publications. Conduct in family and neighborhood life varies between good and bad times and trends are reflected in the records of social workers, personnel officers, physicians, and policemen. For instance, social workers testify that many women are aggressive in good times who in hard times are afraid to assert themselves against an undesirable husband. It is also observed that in times of prosperity the number of local festivities increases and children "of good family" get into scrapes which are reflected in scandals of sex, alcoholism, and other countermores activities.[13]

A systematic survey of national, regional, and local conventions held by trade associations and pressure groups may disclose drifts in the frequency with which bullish or bearish views are expressed about the economic outlook and significant problems come up for discussion or vote. Just before the war there were 400 pressure associations with national headquarters.[14] Presumably some of these associations are more indicative than others of salient trends. The associations of cooperatives (consumer, producer) are presumably more free of public relations than are the associations of "monopolistic competitors."

4. Panels of expert observers

The results obtained by interviewing or content analysis can be usefully supplemented by regular consultation with expert observers. Some individuals are reputed to be exceptionally detached and alert in describing the attitudes of others. During the war a "correspondence panel" of such experts performed an important function, and a similar group can be brought together in peace under nonpartisan auspices.[15]

13. Information about cyclical fluctuations and crime is in Thorstein Sellin, *Crime and the Depression*, Research Monograph (New York, Social Science Research Council, 1937).

14. See Donald Blaisdell, *Economic Power and Political Pressures*, Monograph 26, Temporary National Economic Committee, Washington, D.C. (1941).

15. Elizabeth G. Herzog, "Pending Perfection: A Qualitative Complement to Quantitative Methods," *International Journal of Opinion and Attitude Research*, September, 1947. See also A. W. Kornhauser, "Experience with a Poll of Experts: The Problems and Possibilities," *Public Opinion Quarterly, 12* (1948), 399–411.

5. The changing weight of factors

If the new indexes of expectation are to be generally accepted, the data brought together by interviewing and content analysis must fulfill one or both of the following criteria: a) provide better bases of prediction than goods and price data alone; b) when taken in conjunction with price and goods data, jointly provide a firmer basis of prediction.

There has been some reluctance in the past to experiment with other than price-goods indexes of expectation. Although several causal factors could be named, two appear to be sufficient to account for this attitude. One is the conviction that by improving the conventional indexes much better forecasting results can be obtained. The other factor is the early stage of development of the new indexes. Although systematic data about prices and goods have been available for decades, quantitative interview methods first came into general prominence during the middle thirties in connection with polls of opinion on political questions.[16] To this day there is no equally conspicuous application of content analysis, although there are many specific studies. If we apply the general theory of expectation to scientific work in this field, we can say that the successes achieved by accumulating past price-goods data confirmed the expectation of future net gain through improving such series, rather than by experimenting with methods which are as yet little known and but imperfectly developed.

Can future price-goods relationships be so well predicted on the basis of past price-goods data that there is no need of other supplementary indexes? This appears doubtful. When you look into the factors affecting price, information about price and goods is part of a larger context of relationships which comprehends not only other price-goods patterns but other factors as well. It is not appropriate here to make an exhaustive classification of the additional factors, but rather to cite a few representative items. Not only exposure to price quotations has some possible impact on policy but all statements about the future course of economic values and other values (including their interrelations). For example, statements concerning:

1) the over-all trend of business in the United States during the immediate and more remote future.

2) the probability of war and war scares affecting the United States.

16. The most important work on brief interviewing is by Samuel O. Stouffer, Carl O. Hovland, and associates in the four volumes of *Studies in Social Psychology in World War II* (Princeton, Princeton University Press, 1949). See Marie Jahoda, Morton Deutsch, and Stuart W. Cook, *Research Methods in Social Relations* (2 vols., New York, Dryden Press, 1951).

3) the likelihood of revolutionary and other internal transformations abroad affecting the United States.

4) the likelihood of legislative changes in the tax structure, or in other controls directly affecting business.

5) the probability of administrative action affecting business.

6) the likelihood of action by the courts affecting business.

7) the possibility of technological innovations affecting business.

It ought to be made explicit, perhaps, that such indexes are not wanted by economists who restrict themselves by definition to the study of relations between prices and goods. But if the scope of economic science is more broadly conceived, research will be directed to the discovery of all factors, whether prices are not, which modify price-goods patterns. If the scope of economic research were conceived in the most limited sense, it would be confined to propositions of the following type: "If the flexibility of the demand for x is so-and-so, y volume will be moved at the price z." Propositions of this kind are not enough to assist the advisers in predicting the future course of business. It is necessary to estimate the probability that y volume will, in fact, be offered at price z; and in making this estimate it will be unavoidable to take into account the probability that defense programs will remove supplies from the open market and that essential material and equipment will be inaccessible. Such a judgment depends upon estimating the severity of the defense crisis, including the legislative or administrative actions of government. In forecasting whether production will be expanded it is essential to consider the degree to which private businessmen will be influenced by the expectation that controls will be put upon prices and goods. Obviously political calculations enter at many points into the final determination.

In perfecting estimates of this nature we will learn more than we know today about the flexibility of expectation (and choice) on the part of consumers, business managers, and business regulators. For instance, how do they respond to various kinds of news? Experience and research unite in confirming the point that some changes in price and output act as triggers of further changes (often in other industries). It is generally held, for example, that the wage agreements of Big Steel have a strong bellwether impact upon wages. A problem for future research is whether the price and output changes that follow in the wake of such pivotal shifts invariably have the same magnitude (the "same" when defined as per cent of potential change). If there are differences, can they be accounted for solely by taking other price-goods relationships into consideration? Or is it truer (or simpler) to explain these differences by referring to the influence of other factors?

It is not necessary to describe in detail the methods which have been developed for interviewing and making analyses of content. The wide discussion of opinion polling during the last 15 years has spread knowledge of the problems of sampling, interviewer training, question choice, and other procedural matters involved in interviewing. Although less widely known, the methods of content analysis are in some respects simpler, quicker, and cheaper. The first step is to choose categories to be used in classifying statements. If it is desired to study the frequency of over-all statements about business conditions, for instance, the following may be selected: "General business conditions have been improving (getting worse; steady) in the last quarter." If it is desired to add refinements, five modes of describing business trends may be used: "much better, better, steady, worse, much worse." Opportunities may be given to characterize the trends for two quarters, three quarters, year, or longer.

Any one issue of a given medium of communication, like a newspaper, trade paper, or broadcast, can be described in several ways. Attention can be concentrated upon editorials or upon the leading articles on the financial page. Perhaps the entire contents of a "subscription service" may be read and summarized because of its brevity.

Another technical point is the unit to be used in making comparisons. Often the total number of articles or words per issue is taken, and the per cent of articles is noted in which a relevant statement occurs (or the per cent of words is recorded which are devoted to relevant statements).

If for any purpose it is desired to refine the method further, each statement can be characterized according to the degree of prominence given to it and the elaborateness of the devices which are used for the sake of emphasis. Special weight may be given to front page prominence, to size of headline, and to accompanying charts and pictures. (To describe such matters further would bog us down in minutiae.)

In a large-scale research project, readers are trained to apply the categories and procedures, and supervisors see that the rules, once fixed, are consistently and reliably followed.

6. The need of concerted attack

Perhaps it ought to be said in so many words that the best results are to be anticipated when all methods of research are focused upon the same communication situation.[17] Both interviewing and content pro-

17. An excellent example of the fruitfulness of studying a total situation through a given period is furnished by Paul Lazarsfeld, Bernard Berelson, and Hazel Gaudet, *The People's Choice* (2d ed., New York, Columbia University Press, 1948), a study of Erie County, Ohio, in the 1940 presidential campaign.

cedures can be applied to the study of effect, environment, or predisposition. (The "expectation effect" can be registered by means of an interview, or by the analysis of private or public statements. In locating the environing factors which explain the effect, we may use content analysis to describe either the media or nonmedia statements to which responders were exposed during a given period. Also interviews may be conducted to obtain testimony about what was seen or heard. Finally, if we push back to the predispositions with which an individual or group enters a situation, interviews can disclose the prevailing pattern of identifications, demands, and expectations. The content analysis of past statements can create a similar picture. Interviewing is limited to the recent past and the future. Content analysis, on the other hand, can describe any meaningful residue of the past. The method can be applied to mass media, correspondence files, minutes of meetings, document files, inscriptions, and all similar materials.)

As the expectation effect is more intensively studied, increasing attention will be given to social perception by scholars and scientists.[18] In a given field of attention, what is actually perceived by individuals and groups? We know how unstandardized results often are. Experts can inspect the same factory, interview the same loan applicants, and bargain with the same labor leaders and have quite different perceptions. One engineer may regard the equipment of a plant as obsolete but hold that other factors are compensatory, while another engineer is impressed by nothing save the antiquity of the machinery. One banker may be favorably struck by the readiness and candor of a loan applicant who, a colleague thinks, is "merely glib." One negotiator trusts a labor leader as a "straight shooter," while a colleague calls him "slippery." Eventually we may find it rewarding to study such situations in the hope of uncovering the factors that affect perception, even when the significant factors operate unconsciously.

7. Factors of culture, class, crisis, and personality

A concerted line of research on the interrelations of policy and expectations would try to disentangle the influence of several kinds of factors. Some predispositions are common to all who share American culture; others belong to a single class; some depend upon exposure to a common crisis (or intercrisis) period; and some depend upon type of personality.

18. See Jerome S. Bruner and Leo Postman, "An Approach to Social Perception," in Wayne Dennis and others, *Current Trends in Social Psychology* (Pittsburgh, University of Pittsburgh Press, 1948), pp. 71–118. Also Kurt Lewin, "Frontiers in Group Dynamics: Concept, Method, and Reality in Social Science, Social Equilibria, and Social Change," *Human Relations, 1* (1947), 5–41.

The controllers of the media of mass communication and the audience function within the framework provided by their common American culture.[19] It is true that American civilization is dynamic and that details are always changing. However, there are traits which alter during decades or generations rather than months or years. Though some traits are well understood, only careful study will disclose their full impact upon policy. Consider the well-known limitations upon the "propensity to consume." These are culturally imposed limitations on spending in order to hoard, save, or invest. Common experience teaches that some buyers defer purchases when the cash balance reaches some voluntarily imposed level. If thresholds of this kind are general—in relation to family or business expenditures—it will be worth studying the factors which determine chosen levels, particularly the determining elements in the stream of communication. Everyone is aware of the incessant attempt to stimulate consumer purchases through advertising. But what of the built-in checks on spending? Does our culture generate a state of jitters under conditions of high production and employment that is expressed in policies which provoke collapse by seizing upon unsettled world conditions as an excuse for "imposing discipline" through sacrificial taxes and controls?

On the other side of the ledger, it cannot be denied that there is much evidence that we are passing into a high consumption culture and that older norms of conduct—the early demands on the individual to save—are obsolete and obsolescing. But there are psychic costs of transition, especially when anxieties generated by guilt or shame or impotence feelings are awakened and suppressed.

Within the framework of patterns common to American civilization as a whole there are factors determined by class position within the culture.[20] We speak of class position in reference to the shaping and sharing of values such as economic security, political power, and respect. In general, values are unequally shared, and as a rule the mass media of communication are owned by top elite elements. If these groups follow the maximizing postulate, they select media content with a view to maintaining and improving their class position at the lowest cost. Our re-

19. Modern anthropology, psychiatry, and psychology have revived the study of "national character" as molded by different cultures. See especially the appraisal by Nathan Leites of "Psycho-Cultural Hypotheses about Political Acts," *World Politics, 1* (1948), 102–119; Margaret Mead, "The Study of National Character," in D. Lerner and H. D. Lasswell, eds., *op. cit.*, ch. 4.

20. The leading figure in empirical work on class structure is W. Lloyd Warner. Consult W. Lloyd Warner, Marchia Meeker, and Kenneth Eells, *Social Class in America: A Manual of Procedure for the Measurement of Social Status* (Chicago, Science Research Associates, 1948).

search problem is to discover which values, for which roles, with which the self is identified on the basis of what expectations will account for the news, editorials, and other features of the mass media which influence expectations affecting employment policies. Research results may show that the principal value being maximized by the owners of the media is not, after all, wealth. So far as impact upon economic policy is concerned, the research may demonstrate that mass media operate as exaggerators, stimulating judgments which are not countercyclical but hypercyclical. This may express not conscious purposes but ignorance and unconscious tendencies. Hence the tissue of contradictions: support for foreign aid "if we get something out of it," but opposition to imports; demands for education in thrift, but advertisements, stories, and other inducements to spend; encouragement of success through work versus success stories based on luck and charm disseminated in the mass media (and so on through the catalogue).

The study of class relations has already shown the operation of a great many factors of high importance to controllers and audiences alike. Economists are accustomed to describe variations in patterns of expenditure as a function of class position described in terms of income and wealth. Political analysts have described class differences in the strength of attitudes for and against government intervention in order to abolish mass unemployment. Studies have shown that the endorsement of free private enterprise varies according to upper, middle, and lower income position. Studies also reveal the prevailing level of "class consciousness."

Besides culture and class factors, the influence of crisis must be taken into account.[21] We expect that those who have lived through depressions or crop failures or invasions have developed special attitudes toward insecurity. For example, individuals whose lives are disrupted first by joblessness and then by war are not likely to be reluctant in demanding social security.

For many purposes it is helpful to include personality factors in addition to culture, class, and crisis determiners of response.[22] Sanguine, self-confident characters typically contrast with fearful, timid souls. Personality factors frequently loom large in official or unofficial agencies where the willingness to assume or evade responsibility is a matter of no little importance to policy.

21. Some of the relevant material on crisis can be found in Robin M. Williams, Jr., *The Reduction of Intergroup Tensions: A Survey of Research on Problems of Ethnic, Racial and Religious Group Tensions,* Bulletin 57 (New York, Social Science Research Council, 1947).

22. A guide to the voluminous literature is Gardner Murphy, *Personality, A Biosocial Approach to Origins and Structure* (New York, Harper, 1947).

8. A two-way intelligence process

We have been considering some of the "survey" methods available to the advisers for improving their intelligence function. Interlocking chains of personal contact are also an important feature of an intelligence setup. In this connection it is worth looking into the network which has gradually been evolved by one of the most comprehensive and best economic agencies of the national government. The reference is to the system of give and take among the policy makers who have some association with the Federal Reserve System.

Three major groups are involved in its work: directors, officials, and staffs.[23] By the use of meetings, seminars, bulletins, and reports the system provides for the interplay of academic and nonacademic opinion in the light of personal and also of quantified observations. Each director is the center of a considerable network of his own, which is composed of directors and owners of businesses and of managers and technical staffs. The estimates of the situation made by the members of this network influence the predispositions which he brings to the forums provided by the system; and experience in the system remolds the predispositions with which he returns to his private activities. Mutual appraisals are continually being made of the knowledge, imagination, and judgment of every participant. Supplementary lines of private communication are spontaneously constructed on the basis of congeniality and mutual usefulness. These subpublics are among the most influential channels for the interpretation of trends and possibilities in our society.

The connections of the Federal Reserve System ramify throughout the economy. Other branches of the federal government may be more intimately associated with special sectors of American economic life. For years the Department of Agriculture has been in personal and printed contact with persons, corporations, and associations representing many lines of agricultural production and processing. Through the county agent system and other devices the department reaches far down to the grass roots of county control. However, many of the groups who speak in the name of agriculture turn out to be credit institutions who hold land mortgages or crop liens and who are also represented in the forums of the Federal Reserve. The Department of Commerce has staff and committee connections with all branches of production and distribution. But the weight of the network is not as great as the Federal Reserve System. The Treasury has an enormous mechanism of contact with every

23. See Karl Richard Bopp and others, *Federal Reserve Policy*, Board of Governors of the Federal Reserve Board System, Post-War Economic Studies, No. 8.

corner of economic life. But the perspective of the Reserve System over the money markets provides a special frame of reference for the continuous study of the economy as a whole. Although the Bureau of the Budget is well-staffed, it lacks the top level committees and the traditions that might tie it into every phase of the economy. The Department of Defense has inherited prodigious connections with private industry, but the perspective is so slanted that employment maintenance is a tangential object.

Outside the national government, many important publics are composed of influential elements. The major investors and the large banks and industrial corporations are intertwined in a complex cobweb of subpublics. But the Federal Reserve System has the advantage of providing government authority and perspective as a supplement to the outlook of private business.

The advisers will be effective if they succeed over the years in becoming part of publics with no less scope than those already evolved in connection with the system.

III. The Intelligence Process and the Work of the Council of Economic Advisers

1. A potentially all-embracing process

The intelligence process is potentially all-embracing. In view of the tens, hundreds, thousands—even millions—of persons involved in the intricate process of estimating and reestimating the courses of action open to business and government, it is folly for any agency to try to cut itself off from the whole community and to concentrate upon "the policy makers." If our analysis has indicated anything, it is that the intelligence and policy process is multiple and pervasive. The individual or the committee that says "yes" or "no" to plans for more production or plant expansion is taking one step in an endless series. Those who vote are responding to a vast pattern of environing and predisposing factors, many of which operate outside the consciousness of those affected. We need not minimize the significance of the vote by adopting a metaphor and saying that the policy makers are corks bobbing up and down on a river which they cannot control. But this figure of speech would be closer to the facts than some of the exaggerated conceptions current about the "fifty rulers" of our society, or about the degree of independent control by government officials which is implied in many policy proposals.[24]

24. The study of power in the sense of decisions, or choices in which the expectation of coercion is involved, is in an unsatisfactory state, as is the study of all choices. On policy-making see: C. E. Merriam, *Systematic Politics* (Chicago, Uni-

In any case, the American way of life includes an imperative demand to "get in the act" whenever anybody feels like it. If there is the slightest whiff of conspiracy or secrecy, some part of the press, some element of the political opposition, some rival agency, some ambitious leader is likely to stir up a demand for disclosure. But the justification for planning to let everyone in on the process of discussion is more than a counsel of expediency. It is founded upon the goal values of our society, which affirm the principle of shared power, in the sense of participation in the making of important decisions.

The advisers are charged with giving public currency to their report, which brings unceasing pressure to meet the press and other articulate elements in the nation. The advisers are in the early stage of working out an effective routine for handling these initiatives.

2. The advisers are under surveillance

One of the many reasons why it is expedient as well as wise for the advisers to assume that intelligence is potentially universal is that the advisers are themselves in the spotlight.

The last thing a highly placed agency like the advisers has to worry about is whether anybody will listen. The agency cannot fail to be noticed by those who expect to be affected by what it does. (In general, people pay attention to whatever is expected to affect their value position.) So long as the advisers are expected to have some influence on the policy of the President and the Congress, and so long as private action is supposed to be modified by what is reported, the advisers will be the object of unremitting surveillance.

Officials and staff may not be aware of the amount of attention actually paid them, since much surveillance is done discreetly and with no trace. Some information-getters know how to "case the joint" without stirring up the occupants. Casual conversations with professional as-

versity of Chicago Press, 1945). Economists are enlarging the scope of their analyses of choice. For example: Duncan Black in the *Journal of Political Economy, 56* (1943), 23–34, *Econometrica, 16* (1948), 245–261, 262; and *Giornali degli economisti e annali di economia,* 1948, pp. 1–23. Further contributions are current in *Econometrica* on the decision process. The best-known work is doubtless that of J. A. Schumpeter, A. A. Berle, Jr., and Gardiner Means, C. I. Barnard, Robert A. Gordon, and J. G. Baker; and that of Elton Mayo and associates at Harvard. The point of view of class analysis is in Burleigh B. Gardner, *Human Relations in Industry* (Chicago, Irwin, 1945). Consult Kenneth J. Arrow, "Mathematical Models in the Social Sciences," in D. Lerner and H. D. Lasswell, eds., *op. cit.,* ch. 8. A theoretical model of a rational choice can be used to explore the rational and nonrational components of actual choices. The most stimulating rational theory is John von Neumann and Oskar Morgenstern, *Theory of Games and Economic Behavior* (2d ed. Princeton, Princeton University Press, 1947).

sociates and friends will build up a picture of what the agency is doing and how it goes about it. Former colleagues and friends will unwittingly contribute to the "dossier" by discussing the skills and biases of the official or staff member, adding something to the knowledge of predisposition.

Though covert rather than overt, this is not necessarily sinister. It is part of the predictable behavior of persons sensitized to whatever in the environment appears to affect their wealth, power, respect, and other values. As a matter of course the Washington staffs of big newspapers, magazines, and press associations inform themselves about public figures. This information may be made use of for other than editorial and news purposes, since owners, publishers, and editors are part of the upper influence group in the country and want information for use in all their capacities.

Information is also assembled by the Washington representatives of big investors and large corporations. Often the information which they obtain is for a fee paid privately to a newspaper man or a government official. Or no money may pass but favors can be done. Information about the financial status of individuals can be obtained from banks in the customary form of an interbank request (with no indication that there is any nonbanking purpose involved). Local information can be picked up by queries to local newspaper men, or trusted local lawyers, insurance agents, and bankers. Washington representatives are often lawyers.

Besides big investors and corporations, there are the pressure organizations whose staffs serve clients by providing information. In addition to the machinery of surveillance just mentioned, there are bureaus of special investigation, including detective agencies.

3. Prevent the formation of dangerous crowds

Another important ground for continuous and potentially universal sharing of intelligence on the part of the advisers is the need of forestalling the formation of crowds.

The wider the public the graver the danger to sound policy from the formation of crowds.[25] Some of the earliest useful work in analyzing the psychology of society was directed to the study of "the crowd mind."

25. Gustav Le Bon was the most widely quoted writer on this subject. Robert E. Park was the American sociologist who contributed most to clarifying the distinction between "crowds" and "publics." For a case study of crowd and panic, see Hadley Cantril, Hazel Gaudet, and Herta Herzog, *The Invasion from Mars, with the Broadcast Script of the War of the Worlds* (Princeton, Princeton University Press, 1940).

The crowds of the French Revolution are stock examples of the phenomenon, but speculative crazes whether in real estate or oil provide innumerable instances. Much remains to be known about crowds, but there is no transcending mystery about them. When a crowd turns into a roaring lynch mob, or wildly demands the sacrifice of a public figure for real or fancied wrong, we have to do with no supermind but with a special sort of interpersonal relationship. The essential fact about individual behavior in the crowd situation is that one acts regressively. The individual stops thinking or taking responsibility for himself. He returns to the attitude of an earlier phase of development when he was dependent upon outside care and suggestion. The functions of the critical, reflective ego are suspended and so are the autolimitation of conscience. Guidance and valuations are accepted from outside, since the person has abdicated his normal judgment and sense of responsibility. The exhilaration of belonging to a crowd comes from the thrill of being identified with a human aggregate enormously bigger and stronger than one's primary ego, an aggregate that absolves the individual from the stress and strain of self-control. Actually, the crowd response is not invariably malevolent and destructive. On the contrary, crowds may tremble in religious awe and ecstasy. They may march in serenity to certain death.

I need scarcely say that crowd states are full of danger in a world of instant communication when "psychic epidemics" can be spread over vast territories, and appalling damage can be done to the fabric of civilized life before balancing factors come into play. It is not necessary to assume that the menace arises only in connection with some deliberate manipulation of mass response. The propaganda element may be subordinate to spontaneous rumor.

The crowd response is not limited to huge audiences. "Little crowd states" can seize boards of directors, committee meetings, business conventions, and the exchanges. Men look back on the seizure with a sense of alienation, as though they were in trance. And it is true that the uncanny sense of the abnormal is part of the experience; justly so, since perceptions are distorted in much the same way in all regressive states. Investment programs have been approved or canceled, production plans have been endorsed or slapped down, officials have been hired or fired in a state of excitement bordering on full panic. When the hopes and fears connected with a business enterprise occur in a context in which the entire business community is involved, the little crowd states express the larger crowd.

And what are the preventives of the crowd response? The most important precaution is continuous scrutiny of developments and contingencies, so that events are fully discounted in advance. Hence the problem is to perfect the publics concerned with such vital policies as those touching upon employment.

4. The danger of public animosity

There is a more specific reason why the advisers have an interest in the continuity and universality of intelligence. There is some danger that the advisers will come to grief before they are taken for granted.

The way of the predictor is hard. The more prominent the forecaster's position, the more precarious his task. The predictor cannot be entirely certain of what he is talking about, because his talk is about the future which is both probable and contingent and therefore uncertain.

If ignorance were the only affliction of the forecaster his lot would be a happier one, since rational allowance can be made for the likelihood of error. But nonrational factors also affect the demands made upon predictors.

The President's advisers can suffer from the effects of the psychological mechanism of generalization.[26] Dominant sentiments tend to spread until they color the entire context in which they occur. When business goes badly, sentiments of disappointment and resentment are likely to incriminate the business forecaster regardless of his prediction. This is "guilt by association" in its most rudimentary form. Rage and resentment can permeate all perceptions in any way associated with the "syndrome" of adverse business conditions (not excluding those who merely speculated in advance about such conditions).

Of course, if the predictor fails to forewarn of approaching depression, his position is acutely vulnerable. But what if he calls the turn? It would be a mistake to imagine that all is well, since an undercurrent of animosity can give plausibility to opinions which detract from the predictor. May not the forecast have contributed to the debacle? Does not every word of a President's advisers have unusual weight? May not the report have been the straw that broke the camel's back? Might not the situation have righted itself if the advisers had taken a different line, or if they had been out of the picture altogether?

It is less perilous to fail to forecast good times than to fail in forecasting bad times. The mechanism of generalization works in favor of the predictor when times are good, and the euphoria induced by good business ensures some mitigation of failure.

The mechanism of generalization explains why it is essential for the advisers to avoid a glaring "error" during the first few years of their

26. Clark L. Hull, *Principles of Behavior: An Introduction to Behavior Theory* (New York, Appleton-Century, 1943), ch. 12.

existence as an institution of government. Once an institution is an accepted feature of the social landscape, not the institution as a whole but specific persons are likely to be attacked if things go badly.

The life of the predictor is complicated by the operation of another psychological mechanism. This is the quest for a scapegoat. Actually, two psychological factors are at work, the tendency to find a target for the discharge of the hostilities bred of disappointment and the tendency to reduce the misery of the self by using a target outside the self to bear the responsibility for failure.[27] The role of the first tendency is obvious on statement. The second tendency is more complex. People often defend themselves by blaming others for the disagreeable situations in which they find themselves. Youngsters alibi disobedience by claiming that "he did it first." And oldsters defend the "sacred ego" by projecting responsibility for failure on symbols ranging from Wall Street to the devil himself. The advisers of the President are eligible to play the role of scapegoat because they are conspicuous and also because the part that they play in shaping economic policy is not entirely clear and is therefore easy to stigmatize as dangerous.

The eligibility of the advisers as scapegoats is affected by some of the distinguishing traits of American civilization. Apparently the projection of blame is a universal mechanism present in varying degrees in everybody's mind. But there are enormous differences in the *degree* to which individuals who are reared in different cultures rely upon projection. It is also true that the importance of projecting blame changes from one period to another in the same civilization. At one time the dominant emphasis in American life was upon the responsibility of the individual for his economic success or failure. If John D. Rockefeller succeeded it was assumed that it was because he worked harder and saved more than his contemporaries. The maxims of *Poor Richard's Almanac* were part of the lore of the Americans who occupied a continent. "Strive and succeed" meant these simple rules: if you work, you will succeed; if you do not work, you will be responsible for failing; in general, what happens to you is your own affair, subject to the inscrutable will of God. There is evidence that in recent decades our culture has changed the patterns by which responsibility is assigned for economic success or failure. One pattern is "the conspiracy theory," which attributes bad business to plotting speculators and capitalists. But there are theories of a more impersonal sort which speak of "the system," either of a "capitalistic economy" or "the structure of our

27. Sigmund Freud has contributed most to our understanding of the mechanisms involved. See also Anna Freud, *The Ego and the Mechanisms of Defence* (New York, International Universities Press, 1946), ch. 4.

economy." Current formulations run the gamut from the early lore of America to the latest terminology of economists as spread by journalists, businessmen, trade unionists, party politicians, government officials, and other articulate elements. The trend is to select specific features of our institutional system and to stress the responsibility of top decision makers. The advisers are part of "the system."

Regardless of the niceties of constitutional law, a President is likely to be held responsible for bad times, since of all figures in America he is the most prominent and therefore most available for the projection of blame. But a President is somewhat protected from the scapegoat role by groups and individuals who recognize that they are likely to be fellow targets, or who feel sentimentally identified with a President's fate. In the first group—the fellow targets—are the members of a President's party insofar as they expect to benefit or suffer from prevailing estimates of a President. In the second group—the identified—are all persons who feel attached to a President on deeper grounds than conscious calculation of expedient advantage. These two groups are not exclusive, since many party leaders and rank and file members are warmly attached to a President, besides being dependent upon his popularity.

It is plain that the advisers are both protected and exposed by the relationship which they bear to a President. As appointees of the Chief Executive they are included within the presidential "self," which it is expedient for a President and his followers to defend. They are also covered by whatever sentiments of loyalty bind a President to the agency and its personnel. By the same token the advisers are fair game for the party out of power, whose tactical job is to discredit a President and his party and to win the next election.

The advisers can come to grief in either of two extreme positions. If the advisers "stick their necks out" and become unpopular with the leaders of American business, labor, agriculture, publishing, and other important elements, the holder of the presidency may disavow the council; this would end its existence. On the other hand, the council may take a position which though unpopular with a President is strongly supported by the opposing party and by disaffected factions within the President's party. If a President conflicts with his advisers, he may lose. But if the difference is understood to be partisan, the advisers will have endangered the position which they must establish if they are to guide economic expectations for the nation as a whole.

5. Relations to the organs of government

The advisers must rely for most of their incoming intelligence and for much expert criticism upon the organs of the executive branch of the government. And the agency cannot achieve the stature of a national rather than a party vehicle unless the more independent and able members of the Congress are convinced of the advisers' competence and concern for the great goal of stabilization.

The task of fitting the advisers into the previously existing machinery of the executive branch was far from simple. Every newcomer is on trial as a potential menace or ally of the established members of the official family. Would not the Bureau of the Budget fear that the voice of the budget director would be weakened? And what of the Treasury? Is not the scope of the Secretary diminished by the appearance on the scene of a top level agency like the advisers? In practice the first adjustments were made without serious friction. No doubt the caliber of the staff appointments made at the outset was reassuring, since some of the selections included economists who were personally and professionally accepted nearly everywhere in the community formed by top level civil servants. It is probably correct to say that the closest relations were with the Budget Bureau. Obviously, cooperation with the Treasury was essential, and for many purposes with the National Security Resources Board. But Agriculture, Commerce, Labor, and several other departments and agencies continually come into the picture. By 1949 a system of task forces composed of experts from all divisions of the executive was in use.

It is particularly important for national policy that the economists who serve as staff members of the advisers and the committees of Congress shall take a professional rather than a partisan view of their functions. No one can respect the claim to expertness or professional integrity of a skill group whose members act like party tacticians. It is suspicious when economic forecasts or statements of policy alternatives coincide with party lines, or split neatly as between the Chief Executive and the Congress.

Economists as a body of professionals have an obvious stake in keeping a vigilant eye upon the caliber of staff engaged at both ends of Pennsylvania Avenue. If the consensus is that the quality is low, this opinion should be made known where it will do the most good. Fortunately there are enough examples of excellent working relations among able experts to show that teamwork is possible in the national interest.

In dealing with Congress and the public the advisers cannot act as a rubber stamp for the Chief Executive and at the same time fulfill their obligations. On the other hand, there is no need of emphasizing divergences, save on issues of truly momentous importance for economic stabilization. It is appropriate for the advisers to "explain and amplify" the policy recommendations for which the President takes responsibility. But it is another matter to act as an "advocate," and to become a "lawyer-economist" on behalf of the proposals chosen by the Chief Executive. It need scarcely be said that the middle path in these relationships is more like a tightrope than a sidewalk.

The first chairman of the advisers refrained from testifying before Congressional committees in order to emphasize the responsibility of the advisers to the President, and at the same time to reduce the likelihood that a wedge would be publicly driven between the President and some or all of the members of the board. The general feeling in Congress was, I think, that it was rather artificial for the chairman to speak to practically any group of citizens in the country save the committees of the Congress.

Unless the advisers (whether they continue as a board or become a single official) can succeed in building a public image that gives them a considerable degree of independence, they will fail. The problem is to acquire something of the prestige that accepts the good faith of at least some persons who attempt to perform a trusteeship function. In this case the obligation of the trustee is to serve the continuing national interest in employment stabilization. To this end a firm yet modest role is indicated in predicting the future, stating alternatives of policy, and evaluating the alternatives in the light of the basic goal values of American life and the available stock of knowledge about trends and conditioning factors.

6. Lessons from past forecasters

Can we learn something useful by looking at institutions devoted to prediction which have become firmly entrenched?

Certain forecasting institutions can be discarded from our list. Some predictions are tolerated as part of American ritual, with no assumption that they will have an impact on policy. Consider the forecasts of victory issued by party chairmen, campaign managers, and candidates on the eve of election. Or the boasts of owners and managers of athletic teams.

Among the forecasts with an impact on policy are the crop predictions issued by the Department of Agriculture. Such forecasts are more likely to continue, despite inaccuracies, than the predictions made by the advisers, since it is generally admitted that a factor which as yet is largely beyond human control plays a big part: the weather. Another point is that enough commitments are involved to reduce the immediate impact of the prediction. Thousands of farmers and brokers have tied their hands in advance, and although future moves will be modified by the forecast the total situation is not liquid. Further, the crops, though a big factor in the economy, are a fraction of the whole. This diffuses responsibility for what happens to the whole beyond the forecaster of the part.

From what we know of governmental and private forecasting, it appears that every new group of clients goes through a process of education in the use of predictors. It is a mark of the inexperienced decision maker to throw out his forecaster when events fail to abide by the prediction. The more sophisticated policy-makers have learned what *not* to expect and refrain from projecting blame upon the technical expert for their own mistakes.

Part of the problem is to train the client to want "if, then" statements rather than unqualified statements. The disciplined decision maker recognizes the usefulness of being reminded of the factors upon which his profits depend. If the likelihood of the occurrence of a future event is given a number, this at least registers the intuition of a thoughtful expert who has subjected himself to the chastening influence of observing and projecting trends and reflecting upon the existing state of knowledge about the factors which affect business conditions. The experienced decision maker throws the dice and is willing to take full responsibility. As a means of disciplining his intuition, he hears predictions; but he supplies his own grain of salt and ultimate spin of a wrist. Ultimately he is alone with his God and his conscience and his urge to act; it is illusory to demand or to pretend to have more company.

In overcoming the tendency of every new group of clients to project blame upon the prediction makers, several devices have been used. A distinction can be drawn between a *prophecy* and a *prediction,* "prophecy" being an unqualified statement about future events, "prediction" being a qualified statement. Predictions are always "if" statements, and if they rest upon an explicit body of postulates, rules, and past observations they are truly scientific. Unsophisticated clients demand prophecies, or insist on turning predictions into prophetic utterances. By continually clarifying the difference, this demand may be diluted.

Another means of emphasizing the predictive nature of forecasts is to speak of odds or handicaps. From racing and other competitions it is generally recognized that odds or handicaps rest on at least two sets of inferences. One is the record of past wins and losses. The other is an estimate of the future which is based upon some "inside stuff" about a conditioning factor, or upon a hunch which uniquely relates to the coming race. In any case the final odds reflect several sorts of inference, relying to a considerable degree upon what can be called "subjective" as distinct from "objective" bases. (We might speak of objective inferences as those depending upon systematic extrapolation of the past.) Since most Americans have some familiarity with odds, this terminology can often be employed by the predictor to carry over the appropriate expectations toward his role in a new field. (The public opinion polls have suffered from lack of success in acquainting the public with the idea that polling forecasts are predictions rather than prophecies.)

7. *Maxims for advisers*

Common sense maxims can be laid down on the basis of experience for the guidance of the advisers and those in a similar position. (The numbering is for convenience only.)

1) Avoid flat statements about the future.
2) Make statements as predictions and not as prophecies.
3) Do not appear to hedge by multiplying qualifications.

Too many qualifying sentences, clauses, phrases, or words can undermine confidence in the competence or candor of the council. A crisp indication of the subjective state of the council hedges without parading indecisiveness.

4) Keep from overtechnicality.
5) Avoid extreme positions.
6) Do not limit too narrowly the range of policy alternatives.

Experience suggests that it is easy to get oversold on the importance of manipulating discount rates, or of some other detail of the total economic structure. Even when moves seem very necessary and comparatively easy to make, the council is not serving its own survival interest or the truth about the complexity of the economic system if it goes overboard for a narrow range of specific measures.

7) Do not limit the range of "causal" factors too narrowly.

This is another policy of caution. But it goes beyond the prudence born of the postulate that it is more important to survive than to perish. We are impressed by the number of "obvious" explanations accepted in the past which have been obviously wrong in the perspective of later knowledge.

8) Do not exaggerate in order to get immediate results.
9) Do not conceal either adverse or favorable factors.
10) Be rather short.
11) Maintain continuing private contact with leaders of all branches of American economic life.

The important point is continuity. The best way to avoid stampede effects is to keep the whole picture under survey at frequent intervals. (In private contacts, however, the only official commitment should be the last report to the President.)

No doubt this list could be extended. A number of points could be made about the verbal twists by which the maxims can be put into practice. But the upshot of such counsels of prudence are always unsatisfactory unless they are guided by an explicit theory of the whole process in which the advisers play a part.

The President's advisers use the channels of communication in order to affect expectations about the course of economic affairs, including the outcome of actions if any, which can be taken to affect employment policy. Unless the council has a progressively more adequate theory of the expectation process, the advisers are not likely to measure up to their heavy responsibilities for sustaining the equilibrium upon which a high employment economy depends. Limited to persuasion rather than command, the essential technique of stabilization is relevant communication.

CHAPTER XV. *Administration of*
Stabilization Policy

BY THOMAS I. EMERSON

INTRODUCTION

In the vast discussion of economic stabilization, remarkably little attention has been given to the problems of administration. The original full employment bill introduced in Congress in 1945, though the product of arduous drafting sessions attended by a talented group of experts, made virtually no provision for administration beyond the creation in Congress of a Joint Committee on the National Budget. In its passage through the legislature the emphasis in the bill shifted largely from substantive to procedural measures. This necessarily forced a greater consideration of administrative issues. Yet the final result, embodied in the Employment Act of 1946, added to the administrative process only the Council of Economic Advisers, possessing limited powers largely advisory in nature.

Subsequent legislative proposals for strengthening the Employment Act have virtually ignored issues of mechanics. The economists have given it scant attention and even the political scientists have never explored thoroughly the manifold and difficult questions involved in government administration of a comprehensive, positive program of economic stabilization.[1]

1. The most significant materials to date are: three symposia edited by Fritz Morstein Marx, published in the *American Political Science Review*, "Maintaining High-Level Production and Employment," 39 (1945), 1119–1179; "Federal Executive Reorganization Re-Examined," 40 (1946), 1124–1168, and 41 (1947), 48–84; "Formulating the Federal Government's Economic Program," 42 (1948), 272–336; Herman M. Somers, *Presidential Agency: Office of War Mobilization and Reconversion* (1950); the symposium on "The Executive Office of the President," *Public Administration Review*, 1 (1941), 101–140; John M. Millett, *The Process and Organization of Government Planning* (1947); the symposium, *New Horizons in Public Administration* (University of Alabama Press, 1945). The President's Committee on Administrative Management, reporting in 1937, and the Commission on Organization of the Executive Branch of the Government (Hoover Commission), reporting in 1949, dealt only with issues of administrative management, not with the broader problem of administering a coordinated policy of economic stabilization.

This lack of emphasis upon administrative issues is characteristic of American political thought. Americans have too often been content to pass a law and forget about its enforcement. The reason for this is undoubtedly to be found in our long adherence to doctrines of laissez faire. Since the government was not supposed to interfere in economic matters there was no reason to discuss how goverment regulation could best be administered. Even as the government came to take over more and more functions of economic control, we remained reluctant to face the fact. Rather than advancing with fanfare we have backed quietly into the operation of a modern service state. The inhibitions of laissez-faire theory, while not preventing this movement, have made us unwilling to proclaim it openly and hence have restrained public discussion of how to redesign government machinery to accomplish the task.

Yet the problems of administration are too pressing to be ignored. As anyone with experience in public service comes quickly to realize, the success of governmental operations depends as much, and in many cases more, upon effective administration as upon the substantive legislation. This is particularly true of a program for economic stabilization, where coordination of the functions of numerous government agencies becomes a central issue. Furthermore, successful solution of the outstanding problem of our times—how to expand governmental functions without endangering democratic freedoms—hinges to a substantial degree upon the development of new techniques of administration.

As a matter of fact we have made, almost unnoticed, great strides during the past two decades in the science and art of government administration. The expansion of government under the New Deal in the thirties was accompanied by a slow evolution of administrative policy and an increased managerial competence, the importance of which is difficult to overestimate. One has only to compare the fumbling of the early New Deal agencies, such as the National Recovery Administration, with the performance of later agencies, such as the Atomic Energy Commission, to sense the degree of progress. This movement was greatly accelerated by World War II. The management of the second world war was incomparably superior, under more trying circumstances, to that of the first. Important progress was made even in that most difficult of all areas—central planning and coordination.

Thus we have built up within recent years a significant accumulation of knowledge and experience. And we are in a much improved position to apply this information and understanding to the overriding commitment which the government has expressly undertaken—the guarantee of economic stabilization.

We are presently engaged in another great effort at mobilization for defense. In such a period the problems of administration are in many respects different from those prevailing in what may perhaps be termed "normal" times. More far-reaching types of government controls are imperative; the relations between the various branches of government—federal, state, and local—take on a different aspect; the attitude of private interest groups and the general public shows a marked change. No one can foresee what shape administrative developments will take as mobilization continues. Generally speaking the structure has followed the pattern developed in the last World War. Under the stimulus of that crisis, as will be sketched shortly, we were able to meet and solve tolerably well the problems forced upon us.

In the absence of a war crisis the solution of less pressing, but in many ways similar, problems of administration presents a more difficult issue. The present chapter, therefore, will be directed primarily at the administration of a stabilization program under conditions where the pressures of defense or war are not so immediate or compelling.

I. Nature of the Problem

Our point of departure, and our chief concern in this chapter, is the federal executive. Responsibility for administration of government policies and programs rests primarily with the executive branch. Furthermore, since the turn of the century the executive has assumed more and more the initiative in formulating basic policy and securing the approval of specific programs from the legislature. The issues are plainly national in scope. Hence the executive institutions of the federal government become the focal point for our consideration.

The nature of the problem depends, of course, upon the specific policies and programs that are to be administered. We take as the basis for discussion the substantive proposals outlined in previous chapters as necessary to stabilization in the absence of a war crisis. The suggestions there advanced do not involve any drastic shift in governmental functions such as to require radical reorganization of federal administrative machinery. Rather it is contemplated that economic stabilization can be achieved through the coordinated exercise of various limited, and in most cases commonly accepted, governmental powers. These concrete functions to be performed by government relate to such matters as taxation, monetary policy, public expenditures, expansion or contraction of private investment, antitrust policy, wage and price control, social security, and similar matters.

In large measure these powers are already being exercised by existing governmental agencies. To this extent the task of executing a program for economic stabilization does not differ essentially from the ordinary job of government administration. A detailed discussion of such matters is not possible within the compass of this chapter. But several features of a stabilization program do raise special issues, and these require particular consideration.

In the first place, responsibility for a stabilization program cannot be centralized in any one operating agency or any small group of operating agencies. On the contrary, normally we find that several agencies share responsibility for carrying out each of the functions essential to the program. Thus power in the field of monetary policy is vested in the Treasury Department, the Federal Reserve Board, the various loan agencies, and others. The collection of statistics—a function vital to adequate planning—is carried on by a score of agencies, including the Bureau of Labor Statistics, the Bureau of Foreign and Domestic Commerce, the Department of Agriculture, the Bureau of Internal Revenue, the Federal Reserve Board, the Securities and Exchange Commission, the Bureau of the Census, and the Federal Security Agency. And, as a matter of fact, the operations of virtually every agency have some significant bearing upon economic stabilization. Hence a basic task is that of over-all coordination.

On the other hand, while nearly every operating agency must thus be concerned with economic stabilization, rarely is any such agency concerned exclusively with stabilization. As has been pointed out in previous chapters, we do not want a public expenditures program operated only with an eye to stabilization. Even tax and monetary policy must be directed at other objectives as well. Thus the problem of coordination becomes a complex one. The conventional rules of administration, calling for a single clear line of authority, become difficult of application.

Another aspect of the administrative problem has also been stressed in the preceding chapters. This may be termed the problem of integration. While the executive branch of the federal government must carry primary responsibility for administration it does not function in a vacuum and cannot succeed unless its operations are integrated with those of other governmental and nongovernmental institutions. Most important in this connection is the relationship with the federal legislature. Also of significance are relations with state and local governments, political parties, private interest groups, and the general public.

Thus the major problems of administration emerge. They are the over-all coordination and direction of the stabilization program within the federal executive and the integration of its operations with other governmental and nongovernmental groups.

Before attempting to discuss these issues, however, certain general considerations must be briefly noted.

First of all, successful administration demands not only efficient operation, in the narrow sense, but maximum attainment of the democratic values outlined in the opening chapter. Thus bureaucratic effectiveness must be balanced against democratic participation in the decision-making process and against the possibility of unfairness to individuals and groups affected by those decisions. The achievement of this temper and balance in government administration, as has already been observed, is one of the central problems of the age.

Secondly, a favorable political climate is essential to the effective operation of any government program for economic stabilization in a democratic society. No matter how perfect the machinery devised for its administration—no matter how ingenious the organizational and procedural forms may be—such a program can succeed only if a majority of the electorate, the political party representing that majority, and both the executive and legislative branches of government genuinely and vigorously support it. The mechanics of administration, although important, are of secondary significance. Hitherto favorable political conditions have existed only during the emergency of depression or the emergency of war. A continuing program of stabilization cannot, however, await an emergency. Quite the contrary, its success requires the avoidance of an emergency. The American people and their representatives are thus confronted with the issue whether they *want* a program for full employment and production. Only when they are ready can any scheme of administration be workable.

We are not primarily concerned in this chapter with methods for obtaining adequate political driving power to assure successful administration of stabilization policy.[2] Nevertheless, no system of administration can fail to take into account the limitations and potentialities of the underlying structure within which it must operate. On pain of losing the path completely in a mass of details, we must constantly relate the mechanics of administration to the broader factors treated in other chapters. Moreover, it should be noted that the political atmosphere is itself affected by the very existence of a program and machinery for its administration. Thus, concrete proposals are essential in enlisting the support of the electorate, the political parties, and the various branches of government. So, also, the administrative apparatus can play a leading part in informing the public, demonstrating the feasibility of a planned economic program, and in general stimulating the basic sup-

2. For a discussion of some of these issues see Chapter 13.

port necessary for success. Hence the administrative detail is inevitably interlocked with over-all structure and policy.

Thirdly, it is unrealistic to undertake the preparation of an exact blueprint in advance of the event. Any plan of administration must necessarily depend upon numerous practical considerations impossible to foresee and unknown to those not intimately acquainted with the entire situation. A successful plan must take into account the qualifications of existing and available personnel, the effectiveness or shortcomings of agencies already functioning, the desirability of temporary arrangements, the need of continual adjustments, the current political atmosphere, and countless other factors not susceptible of abstract logical treatment. The fate of the plan for industrial mobilization on M day, prepared prior to World War II and found to be totally irrelevant to the actual situation that developed, warns us against projections of this nature. The establishment of satisfactory machinery must be a gradual and continuing process. The vital thing is to be conscious of the issues and to grasp the underlying direction in which progress is to be made.

Finally, the development of administrative procedures must take place within the framework of our existing institutions and traditions. The chief characteristic of American government has been the dispersion of power, the balance between contending forces, the resulting compromise. Partly this was deliberately built into the Constitution through such institutions as federalism, the separation of powers, and the whole system of checks and balances. But partly it is the natural growth of a healthy democratic process. Never monolithic, the government has become increasingly an arena in which the basic forces of the nation are represented and struggle toward partial agreement upon a course of action. This is as true of the executive branch as it is of the legislature. All these forces express their own views, often quarrel violently with each other, and are only with difficulty subject to a restraining or coordinating influence from the President or party leadership. At times this pluralism leads to clear inconsistencies in government policy and action.

Undoubtedly this dispersion of power frequently prevents effective action; a nice balance must be found between centralization and autonomy. But the basic tradition is a healthy one. Actually it constitutes a major source of strength in the democratic process—one of the principal advantages of democratic over totalitarian procedures. For it leaves room for free expression of ideas, for airing of grievances, for experimentation, for mutual adjustment. And it makes the bureaucracy far more responsive to popular desires and needs, more ready to adjust to individual and regional differences. One of the chief lessons of World War II is that, while all governments made serious mistakes, the Germans and Japanese persisted longer in their errors than we did in ours. Our ability to remain flexible and to improvise must be maintained and encouraged.

In any event we cannot now as a purely practical matter eliminate federalism, or the separation of powers, or checks and balances, even if we would. We must seek to perfect our present methods rather than start afresh. There is plenty of room for progress within the basic tradition. We have not yet begun to explore the possibilities of new techniques of government, particularly in connection with central planning and coordination. Our first task, therefore, is to undertake that exploration in an intensive and serious way. Only if we then fail will we be justified in turning to more drastic alternatives.

II. The Background of Executive Coordination and Integration

Federal responsibility for the initiation and administration of a positive program for economic stabilization has only recently been acknowledged. Throughout most of our history the executive branch has carried out its various specific functions on an *ad hoc* basis, with little thought to over-all coordination or integration. Nevertheless, as government operations gradually spread to wider areas there slowly emerged more intensive efforts to obtain greater effectiveness in the conduct of operating agencies, increased attention to central planning and coordination within the executive, and some attempt to improve relations between the executive and other institutions of society. These developments are worth tracing briefly as a background to discussion of the present situation and proposals for new machinery.

Prior to the first world war there was little progress toward executive coordination. Functions performed by the federal government were distributed among the Cabinet departments and, beginning with the Interstate Commerce Commission in 1887, a growing number of independent agencies. These operating units were subject to no central direction except that given by the President himself. Potentially the Cabinet might have constituted a coordinating mechanism. But actually, for reasons to be discussed later, it never functioned in that way. The only assistance available to the President in performing his centralizing function came from the various types of "kitchen cabinets" which grew up informally in virtually every administration.

Even the first world war produced little coordinating machinery. The United States was involved for only a relatively short period and its industry was never committed to the extent that made highly coordinated governmental controls necessary.

The first major step in executive coordination came with the passage of the Budget and Accounting Act of 1921. This legislation was the product of many years of effort to revamp the executive branch, extending back to the Taft administration. Previously authority to request appropriations from Congress, as well as full control over expenditures authorized, had rested in the heads of individual departments and agencies. The act placed in the President exclusive responsibility for submitting to Congress a single budget of executive expenditures and created a central agency of budgetary management in the new office of the Bureau of the Budget. This agency was also charged with responsibility for making a continuous study of the organization, operation, and efficiency of the executive branch and for advising the President with regard to changes. The new bureau was made a part of the Treasury Department but its director was directly responsible to the President.

Passage of the act marked an important advance. Authority over the fiscal life of executive agencies gave the President a powerful tool for centralized direction and the creation of a special staff in the Budget Bureau afforded him a significant institutional device for making that direction effective. For many years, however, the bureau's staff remained small—in 1937 it numbered only 45 employees—and its activities were confined largely to such control as was associated with the actual preparation of the annual budget.

The depression of 1929 and the mushrooming of the New Deal forced attention sharply upon the need for coordination of economic policy. As early as 1931 there had been created by the Employment Stabilization Act a Federal Employment Stabilization Board, composed of the Secretaries of the Treasury, Commerce, Agriculture, and Labor, to advise the President on economic trends and to cooperate with the federal construction agencies in planning a public works program. This statute was soon superseded by the New Deal legislation and the Stabilization Board merged into the New Deal agencies. The 1931 act, however, was relied upon as an important precedent in the discussions over the Employment Act of 1946.

Two developments of the New Deal period are of more lasting significance. One is the establishment of the Executive Office of the President; the other the creation and later abolition of the National Resources Planning Board.

Under the Reorganization Act of 1933 President Roosevelt had succeeded in regrouping some of the executive agencies. But basic problems remained unsolved and several Congressional committees continued to struggle with reorganization issues. In 1936 the President appointed a Committee on Administrative Management, composed of three eminent political scientists. The committee's report, filed in 1937, contained a number of proposals for "modernizing our governmental management." Most significant for our purposes were the recommendations that the hundred or more executive agencies be combined into 12 Cabinet departments; that the Bureau of the Budget take responsibility not only for preparation of the budget but for study of administrative management and assistance to the President in improving organization and procedure; that a permanent National Resources Board be established to formulate plans for use of national resources and to cooperate with other planning agencies; that the "managerial agencies" —the Bureau of the Budget, the National Resources Board, and the Civil Service Commission—be brought into the President's office and "developed as arms of the Chief Executive"; and that the White House staff be expanded through the addition of six presidential assistants. The suggestions of the committee, it will be noted, dealt with problems of administrative management in light of functions the federal government was then undertaking to perform. It did not consider measures necessary to operate a positive program for economic stabilization.

As a result of the committee's report and the ensuing agitation Congress finally passed the Reorganization Act of 1939. This legislation provided for the six presidential assistants recommended by the President's committee and authorized the President, within certain limitations, to promulgate reorganization plans subject to Congressional veto. In his first reorganization plan the President established the Executive Office of the President. Under this plan and a subsequent executive order the Executive Office of the President included the White House staff, the Bureau of the Budget, the National Resources Planning Board, the Office of Government Reports, a new Liaison Office for Personnel Management, and a new Office for Emergency Management. With the exception of the National Resources Planning Board the functions thus incorporated in the Executive Office of the President were basically those of administrative supervision and management rather than policy coordination and control.

The National Resources Planning Board was the successor of several agencies originally established in the Public Works Administration as planning and coordinating committees with purely advisory powers in the field of public works. Following its transfer to the Executive Office of the President the board continued primarily as a research and study group. Its activities resulted in a series of valuable reports on planning for the effective use of natural resources. It also served as a clearinghouse of information between federal, state, local, and private agencies concerned with planning. The board never functioned as an adviser to the President on short-term problems and never possessed any co-ordinating or directing power.

Despite its limited activity the National Resources Planning Board incurred the ire of conservative members of Congress and in 1943 was abolished by Congressional action. The board's unhappy fate illustrated dramatically the recurrent antagonism of the legislative branch to any kind of peacetime planning by the executive branch.

The pressures of World War II, however, did force the establishment of machinery designed affirmatively to coordinate and direct the war policies and programs of the operating agencies. Yet even here the development was slow.

With the outbreak of the war in Europe in 1939 American preparations for defense and for aid to Britain and France had begun to accelerate. Following the Nazi breakthrough in May, 1940, President Roosevelt took the first public and dramatic step to coordinate the program. Scrapping the Army-Navy Industrial Mobilization Plan the President appointed a National Defense Advisory Commission, under powers remaining from an unrepealed World War I statute. The commission was set up in the Executive Office of the President. It was mainly an advisory and review agency but it possessed both supervisory and operating powers in certain areas. Each of its seven members was assigned responsibility for a particular sector of the defense program.

Within a few months, as the problems in each field quickly multiplied, there began the process of breaking up the constituent elements of the commission into separate operating agencies. The first of these, the Office of Production Management, was established in January, 1941. It later became the War Production Board. OPM was followed by the Office of Price Administration and Civilian Supply (later the Office of Price Administration), the National Defense Mediation Board (later the National War Labor Board), the Office of Defense Transportation, the War Manpower Commission, the Office of Civilian Defense, and a number of others. Most of these agencies were technically part of the Office for Emergency Management in the Executive Office of the President. For a short period the OEM exercised a sporadic coordinating influence. As time went on, however, it functioned only as a housekeeping agency and the operating agencies were, for all practical purposes, independent.

The breakup into separate war agencies quickly generated serious problems of coordination. During brief periods the Supply, Priorities, and Allocation Board and the War Production Board, each composed of various agency heads dealing with defense measures, were assigned certain coordinating powers. The theory was to obtain cooperation through voluntary agreement by the operating agencies themselves, each represented on the central authority. But such arrangements soon proved abortive. After a long period of interagency bickering and public confusion the President, in October, 1942, created the Office of Economic Stabilization.

The OES was given authority to formulate "national economic policy," and to supervise and direct the operating agencies, on all matters relating to economic stabilization. The significance attached to the new office was attested by the resignation of Justice James F. Byrnes from the Supreme Court to become director. The OES soon demonstrated its worth. It succeeded in bringing some degree of consistency and harmony to the work of OPA in price control and consumer rationing, WPB in the allocation and control of scarce materials, the Department of Agriculture in price and allocation controls over farm products, and other agencies dealing with stabilization.

Yet a further difficulty in coordination remained, one that is inherent in peacetime as well as wartime stabilization controls. Stabilization of the economy is only one facet of a complex of interelated problems. Thus questions as to the allocation of resources between military and civilian needs were outside the scope of OES powers. As a final step, therefore, the President, in May, 1943, created the Office of War Mobilization with far-reaching powers to direct the whole war program on the economic front. Only military operations, foreign policy (except economic), and political strategy were excluded. Byrnes was shifted to director of OWM and Judge Fred M. Vinson left the Court of Appeals of the District of Columbia to become head of OES. The War Mobilization and Reconversion Act of October, 1944, placed the OWM on a statutory basis, changing its name to Office of War Mobilization and Reconversion and extending its powers to cover reconversion. Subsequent directors were Vinson, John W. Snyder, and John R. Steelman.

The OES, OWM, and OWMR were the first agencies ever created in the federal government with top broadscale power to direct and control operating agencies. The executive order establishing OWM set forth these functions in sweeping and unequivocal language:

It shall be the function of the Office of War Mobilization . . . subject to the direction and control of the President,

(a) To develop unified programs and to establish policies for the maximum use of the nation's natural and industrial resources for military and civilian needs, for the effective use of the national

manpower not in the armed forces, for the maintenance and stabilization of the civilian economy, and for the adjustment of such
economy to war needs and conditions;

(b) To unify the activities of Federal agencies and departments
engaged in or concerned with production, procurement, distribution or transportation of military or civilian supplies, materials, and
products and to resolve and determine controversies between such
agencies or departments . . .[3]

In order for OWM to make effective its control over the operating
agencies it was endowed (as was OES) with authority, in a somewhat
novel form, to issue "directives." This directive power was continued
by the War Mobilization and Reconversion Act which empowered the
director, subject to the President, to

issue such orders and regulations to executive agencies as may be
necessary to provide for the exercise of their powers in a manner
consistent with the plans formulated under this section or to coordinate the activities of executive agencies with respect to the
problems arising out of the transition from war to peace. Each
executive agency shall carry out the orders and regulations of the
Director expeditiously and, to the extent necessary to carry out such
orders and regulations, shall modify its operations and procedures
and issue regulations with respect thereto.[4]

The executive order and the statute creating OWM-OWMR also
attempted to deal with the problem of integrating the agency's operations with other governmental institutions and nongovernmental groups.
The executive order created a War Mobilization Committee, consisting
of the heads of the War and Navy Departments, the Munitions Assign-
ments Board, the WPB, and the OES. The purpose of this committee was
to "advise and consult" with the director of OWM. The act creating
OWMR required it to "consult and cooperate with State and local
governments, industry, labor, agriculture and other groups, both national and local, concerning the problems arising out of the transition
from war to peace." An Advisory Board of 12 members was created, of
which three were to have had "experience in business management,"
three in "matters relating to labor," and three in agriculture. Quarterly
reports to the President and Congress were required from the director.

3. Executive Order No. 9347, issued May 27, 1943, *Federal Register*, 8 (1943),
7207; the quotation is from Section 3.
4. Public Law 458, Title I, Section 101 (c) (2), 78th Congress, 2d Session, 1944,
U.S. Statutes, 58, 785.

The OWM-OWMR functioned somewhat differently, and with varying degrees of success, under different directors. Certain characteristics of the agency, however, were common to all directors. At all times, except possibly at the end of Steelman's regime, the director held, and was known to hold, the fullest personal confidence of the President. The director maintained his offices in the White House itself and was popularly regarded as the "assistant president." The staff, though differing at various times, was relatively small. The agency concerned itself almost exclusively with top policy issues, undertaking actual operating functions only in isolated instances for limited periods of time. Information was largely supplied by the subordinate agencies, not through original research. Most of the agency's effectiveness derived from personal contacts of the director in conferences and telephone conversations. The directive power was used sparingly.

Under Byrnes, the first director, the OWM-OWMR functioned on a highly personalized basis. The staff consisted of half a dozen assistants, whose primary duty was to prepare information for the director's use. Virtually all decisions were made personally by the director. In most cases contacts with subordinate agencies were made only with the heads of those agencies. Operations were normally carried on behind the scenes, OWMR not claiming public credit.

In this period OWMR was perhaps most successful in settling disputes between the operating agencies—a function in the nature of adjudication to which Byrnes by temperament and experience was best suited. Supervision of the operations of subordinate agencies was effective in certain instances, as in the reduction of the procurement plans of the military establishments in 1943, but was necessarily limited in scope by virtue of the methods employed. Over-all planning was scarcely feasible. OWMR did take the initiative in certain instances, as when it formulated the brownout and the ban on horse racing, but this was in a highly restricted area. Its other major accomplishment in planning at this time—the Baruch-Hancock report dealing mainly with contract settlement, surplus property disposal, and reemployment and retraining—was achieved through farming out the planning function to Baruch.

Beginning with Vinson, who served as director only three months, OWMR was gradualy transformed from a personal operation into an institutional operation. This was a shift of great significance. The staff was increased in size, reaching 80 in June, 1945, and nearly 150 at its peak in May, 1946, and organized into sections. As a result of these factors staff members came more in touch with the activity of subordinate agencies and were able to keep the director better informed of current and anticipated developments. Many decisions were now being made, or made subject to rather formal ratification, at levels below the director in OWMR. As the reliance upon the director's personal prestige decreased, more use was made of formal directives, not always with success. When reconversion problems became more acute the agency took a more positive lead in planning as well as direction.

The transformation of OWMR into an agency, in place of a personal operation, opened significant new possibilities but also created difficulties. Its effectiveness in settling disputes between operating agencies declined somewhat, partly because much of this work now was delegated to the staff, partly because the directors became progressively less able to compel agreement through resourceful compromise and personal force. The potential capacity of the agency to exercise an affirmative supervision over operating agencies increased enormously. But the practical ability to maintain control over agency resistance was not of a high order. Important planning operations were carried out, in many instances successfully, in specific fields. Examples are the work done in surplus property disposal, demobilization of the armed forces, and atomic energy legislation. But tentative efforts of the staff to develop comprehensive planning for the economy as a whole were discouraged by the directors and hence never seriously undertaken. The work of OWMR was never satisfactorily integrated with the functions of the Executive Office, particularly the Bureau of the Budget.

The relationship between OWMR and OES remained somewhat obscure. OWMR inevitably was concerned with stabilization and indeed had express jurisdiction over the field. OES in turn was forced to take into account the impact of its action upon the total picture. Actually the difficulty was resolved by informal arrangements under which OES operated very much as a subdivision of OWMR. The separate existence of OES was justifiable more as a convenient method for the delegation of authority, which relieved the director of OWMR from a substantial work load, than by reason of any logical division of jurisdiction. At a later stage the realities were recognized by the formal merger of OES into OWMR.

Noteworthy failures in the OWM-OWMR experiment were the War Mobilization Committee of OWM and the Advisory Board of OWMR. The committee, composed of agency heads frantically busy with their own problems, proved relatively useless and its meetings became more and more infrequent and futile. The Advisory Board, though it met regularly every two weeks, produced little of value. Its members were also busy in their own right and found it difficult to attend meetings in Washington consistently. As to most of the problems the board members could not have sufficient detailed information to reach an intelligent decision. By reason of the business-labor-agriculture representation the discussions of each group tended to become a mere restatement of official group-interest positions; since the board could only advise and not decide there was little or no incentive to compromise or modify points of view. Occasionally the board was useful in pressuring Congress in regard to matters on which its members were in agreement. But all in all the board was of small help on controversial issues and succeeded mainly in occupying the time of the chief OWMR staff members for two days every two weeks.

The lessons to be learned from these central planning and coordinating efforts made necessary by full mobilization for war are important ones. Although the experiment was made under the artificial conditions of a wartime atmosphere, it tends to demonstrate both the necessity and the feasibility of a top coordinating mechanism under the President's immediate direction. It sheds considerable light also upon such matters as the relation of stabilization issues to the broader decisions the government must make, the methods for bringing under control the activities of the operating agencies, and the difficulties in establishing satisfactory integration of the coordinating machinery with other government and private interests. The application of this wartime experience to comparable problems of peacetime will be considered in more detail hereafter.

Following the war the country was stirred for a time by the vision of transferring wartime techniques in planning and coordination to the problems of reconversion and permanent peace. In this spirit the full employment bill was drafted. As already noted, however, this proposed legislation was not primarily concerned with organizational matters. Surprisingly enough, in view of the previous attitude toward the National Resources Planning Board, several Congressional committees—principally the George and Colmer Committees—did give attention to these issues. The Colmer Committee went so far as to urge the retention of the wartime coordinating machinery for peacetime use. But in the reaction to war controls and the drive back to normalcy most of the war experiment was abandoned.

The Employment Act of 1946 did establish the Council of Economic Advisers. That act and the Legislative Reorganization Act of the same year also undertook to modernize Congressional procedures. In 1947 the National Security Act, designed to unify the armed services, was passed; two years later this act was strengthened by amendments. Early in 1949 the Hoover Commission filed its extensive report on reorganization of the federal government. Like the President's Committee on Administrative Management, however, the Hoover Commission limited its study to more effective methods of carrying on the traditional peacetime functions of the federal executive. It made no effort to mark the path toward creating machinery for more comprehensive government direction of the economic structure. In response to the Hoover Commission Report Congress passed the Reorganization Act of 1949, authorizing the President to consolidate and redistribute government functions. A number of reorganization plans were put into operation under this legislation.

These developments are considered in the following section, dealing with the existing machinery for peacetime coordination and integration.

In 1950 the country moved once again into semi-wartime conditions. Following the invasion of South Korea by the North Koreans in June, the immediate employment of United Nations military forces to resist this aggression, and the intervention of the Peoples Republic of China in November, the United States commenced a rapid and vast program of military mobilization. It was apparent from the start that the restoration of many of the wartime controls would be necessary. In September Congress passed the Defense Production Act of 1950, authorizing allocation, price, wage, credit and other controls, and in December President Truman issued a proclamation declaring the existence of a national emergency. The Defense Production Act was renewed, with amendments, in 1951 and again in 1952.

The machinery set up for administration of these controls paralleled closely the structure that eventually emerged in World War II. On the same day that he proclaimed a national emergency President Truman issued an executive order establishing an Office of Defense Mobilization, in the Executive Office of the President, as the top coordinating agency. The director of ODM was empowered, "on behalf of the President," to "direct, control, and coordinate all mobilization activities of the executive branch of the Government, including but not limited to production, procurement, manpower, stabilization, and transport activities." As in the case of OWMR the director was given authority to "issue such directives, consonant with law, on policy and operations to the Federal agencies and departments as may be necessary to carry out the programs developed, the policies established, and the decisions made by the Director." The pattern of operating agencies created to administer the mobilization program differed somewhat from that in World War II, but the system of coordination was essentially the same.

Thus the need for a central coordinating and directing mechanism in time of war has come to be accepted. No one can foresee how long the present mobilization effort will endure, or what imprint our further experience with wartime mobilization will leave on the structure of government. Yet the problem of administering a program of stabilization when the stimulation of large-scale mobilization is not present will eventually face us again. It is with this more difficult and ultimately more challenging problem that we are here primarily concerned.

III. Existing Machinery for Administration of a Peacetime Stabilization Policy

Our present governmental machinery for administration of a peacetime stabilization policy is the product of the developments just sketched. Except during the emergency of war we have never faced squarely the problem here presented—the administration of a comprehensive, positive program for economic stabilization. Nevertheless the existing machinery represents the basis from which any solution of that problem must proceed.

1. *Legislative machinery*

The difficulties arising out of the basic structure of our government —particularly the divisive forces in the legislature and the rivalry and frequent antagonisms between the legislative and executive branches— have often been described.[5] Little has happened within the past few years to change or ameliorate these conditions. Perhaps the only major development has been the growing willingness of Congress, compelled by circumstances, to delegate increased power to the executive. This has been partially balanced by an expansion of legislative investigatory and supervisory activities.

Not only the over-all structure of government but the structure of Congress itself presents grave obstacles to the operation of an economic program. These difficulties have also been discussed in prior chapters. The Federal legislature was not designed for the purpose of formulating or promulgating such a complex, swiftly moving, bafflingly difficult series of actions as is required in a program for economic stabilization. The existence of two houses, the whole system of formal debate and vote, the seniority tradition, the custom of annual appropriations, the unlimited debate in the Senate, the lack of staff assistance sufficient to aid in grasping the basic policy issues, and many other aspects of legislative organization and procedure do not lend themselves to detailed, rapid, flexible results. Nor does the dispersion of jurisdiction among numerous committees permit unified action.

Those minor reforms which have been attempted in recent years

5. See also Chapter 13.

have not substantially diminished these difficulties. As previously noted the Employment Act of 1946 created a Joint Committee on the Economic Report, composed of seven members of the Senate and seven of the House. The committee's function is to study issues of economic stabilization and to file a report of its findings and recommendations, the report to serve "as a guide to the several committees of Congress dealing with legislation relating to the Economic Report." But the device has had little effect thus far in clarifying the issues before Congress or crystallizing Congressional sentiment. The Legislative Reorganization Act attempted a mild streamlining of Congressional organization and procedure. But the major handicaps to efficient operation remain unchanged.

All in all small progress has been made in adapting our legislative institutions to the needs of a modern service state.

2. *The operating agencies*

The basic units of the federal executive are the operating agencies. Presently there are nine departments, represented in the Cabinet, and about 75 other agencies of various kinds. Of these, 30 to 35 are important. Some are of mammoth size, as the Post Office Department with over 500,000 employees and the Veterans Administration with nearly 200,000. Most are subdivided into bureaus, divisions, sections, and units—totaling in the thousands—some of which may act as operating agencies themselves. Many agencies and bureaus have regional offices, or a hierarchy of field offices, covering the country; only about 10% of the 2,500,000 federal employees work in Washington. To some extent the functions of these agencies or their subdivisions may overlap; at other points there may be serious gaps. As already indicated, practically all carry on functions which have a bearing upon economic stabilization.

These agencies are operating units in a very broad sense. They do far more than make the immediate decisions necessary in day-to-day operations. They collect and compile information, they prepare studies and reports, they plan programs, they recommend changes in their functions and authority, they maintain relations with other agencies and institutions of government, they consult and advise with private groups interested in their activities, they carry on campaigns to inform and educate the public, they service themselves through their own personnel, legal, fiscal, and similar staffs. An operating agency thus develops a complex life of its own. It evolves its own traditions, procedures, vested interests, and esprit de corps.

A principal characteristic of the operating agencies is their relative independence. Most of them tend to represent, and to derive their basic strength from, one or more of the interest groups that make up our society. This is obviously true of the Department of Agriculture, the Department of Labor, and the Department of Commerce. It is equally true of such agencies as the Department of Defense, the Railroad Retirement Board, the Interstate Commerce Commission, the Veterans Administration, the lending agencies, and many others. Similarly such agencies as the Securities and Exchange Commission, the Department of the Interior, and the Federal Security Agency have their own clientele.

Partly for this reason, partly for convenience, and partly as a matter of self-preservation, the operating agencies normally have their own lines of communication with the legislature. Close relationships are established with the Congressional committees that handle their legislation and appropriations, with Congressional blocs, and with individual congressmen.

Added to this is the natural inclination of large organizations to develop a keen sense of jurisdiction. The result is that the divisive tendencies in the federal executive are powerful.

Theoretically the President and his staff, principally the Bureau of the Budget, have substantial supervisory authority over the operating agencies. Major sources of this power are the legal authority of the President to make decisions, his right of appointment and removal, control over the amount and use of appropriations, and the personal and political prestige of the President or a representative enjoying his confidence.

In theory and in practice, however, the President's power over the operating agencies has serious limitations. Frequently legal authority to make decisions is conferred by Congress directly on the agency head or even on a subordinate within the agency. Particularly are the regulatory agencies beyond the President's sphere of direct control. The appointment and removal powers are restricted by political factors—factors deriving from the same political forces that buttress the operating agency. The removal of members of independent regulatory agencies is strictly limited by judicial application of the principle of separation of powers. Control over appropriations has the usual weaknesses of a negative sanction. Considerations of personal and political prestige are offset by similar factors operating in the contrary direction. Congressional powers over appropriations and the increasing use of Congressional power to investigate and supervise the operating agencies force the agencies to cultivate friends and appease enemies in the legislature.

And the frequent necessity for the agencies to operate with an eye to judicial review places further limitations on the supervisory authority of the Chief Executive.

Moreover, an experienced government employee does not lack devices to frustrate and nullify efforts at topside coordination. Information vital to an appraisal of the matter at issue, or essential to recognize even that a problem exists, may not be easy to extract from an operating agency. Decisions must frequently be based upon technical considerations not readily grasped by an outsider. Broad decisions on policy can be subverted in the process of detailed administration. A large and complex organization can absorb even precise commands without appreciable effect upon its actual operations. Resistance of this sort, particularly where the President himself is not personally involved, is more the tradition than the exception in the American government. The British concept of a civil service devoted to the effectuation of whatever policy the administration lays down—a tradition that has serious limits even in England—is not firmly embedded in the American system of government.

Nor can too much be expected from voluntary cooperation among the operating agencies. A great deal of such cooperation does, of course, take place. There are presently some 30 interdepartmental committees in the foreign field and a great many more in the domestic. But interdepartmental committees, or similar devices, have not been conspicuously successful. Where interests are in serious conflict voluntary settlement frequently cannot be obtained.

The foregoing is not necessarily a criticism of the institutions and practices described. It is intended only to point out some of the major difficulties in any attempt at coordination of the operating agencies.

3. *Machinery for coordination*

It is apparent from the above that the principal role of coordination of the federal executive must be played by the President. Only he has the authority and the prestige necessary to offset the centrifugal forces and compel the operating agencies to conform to some sort of uniform policy. The failure of Wilson Wyatt to put through his program as Housing Expediter after World War II illustrates the futility of any other basis for central coordination. Wyatt was granted sweeping powers to direct other government agencies to take all measures required for carrying his housing proposals into operation. Yet his program never got off the ground. In part this was because Wyatt was moving against the tide of postwar demobilization and decontrol. But a substantial factor was that Wyatt never received more than token support from the President —a fact quickly sensed by the operating agencies.

Similarly the failure of John Steelman to make the OWMR effective in its later stages was directly traceable to the well-founded understanding that Steelman was not then in the best of standing at the White House.

In tacit recognition of this situation such coordinating machinery as exists today centers around the President and his immediate office. The problem arises because the President obviously cannot do the job alone and unaided. There are too many operating agencies, too many issues, too much need of information, time, and energy for one man even to settle interagency disputes, quite apart from exercising affirmative supervision or undertaking any kind of advance planning. The need is to establish machinery tied in with the President that will enable the President to project his powers with sufficient competence and force to make an impression upon the undisciplined operating agencies.

That machinery is not provided by the Cabinet. The Cabinet has no existence apart from the occasions when its members meet together at the call of the President. Under President Truman, as under President Roosevelt, Cabinet meetings were normally held once a week. Generally they lasted about an hour. No advance preparations were made, except at times by individual members. Often there was discussion of broad issues affecting a number of departments, but rarely did there emerge a reasoned decision on policy or program. More often the meetings were used by the President to convey information or employed by department heads to discuss with the President matters of their own particular interest. Important decisions were almost invariably taken without advance consideration by the Cabinet as a whole. An outstanding example was President Roosevelt's launching of his famous plan for reorganization of the Supreme Court without notice to the Cabinet.

Nor does it seem likely that the Cabinet can be brought to life and made to function as a coordinating agency. Two major factors stand in the way. In the first place, the Cabinet members are heads of major operating agencies. As a result of any consolidation of agencies under reorganization plans they would take over even greater operating responsibilities. This means that the Cabinet members are busy men, normally snowed under with the work of their own agencies. They thus have limited time for other activities. The general failure of interdepartmental committees to function effectively demonstrates the unlikelihood that department heads would be able to take on the manifold duties of a central coordinating agency. Moreover, the position of Cabinet members as heads of operating agencies disqualifies them as coordinating officials. Their interests as operators would be inconsistent with their position as coordinators. The coordinating job must be performed by persons outside of, and superior to, the officials in charge of operations. The soundness of this principle is illustrated by the complete inability of the War Production Board, composed of operating heads, to exercise both functions during the early stages of the second world war.

In the second place, Cabinet members owe their positions in large measure to irrelevant political considerations. In forming his Cabinet the President undertakes to obtain a balanced representation of geographical and political interests. Hence the members of the Cabinet frequently do not possess that close relationship to the President—that personal loyalty and identity of interest—which wartime experience showed is essential to successful direction of the powerful operating units.

The Cabinet aside, the federal executive contains three major peacetime agencies capable of performing coordinating functions. These are the White House staff, the Bureau of the Budget, and the Council of Economic Advisers. All are part of the Executive Office of the President.

The White House staff includes the President's three secretaries (appointments, press, office manager), the assistant to the President, the special counsel to the President, the administrative assistants authorized by the Reorganization Act of 1939, the military, naval, and air force aides, and an executive clerk heading a clerical staff. Most of this group form a sort of inner council or kitchen cabinet. It was the custom of President Truman to hold an informal meeting of the group at 9 o'clock every morning. Sometimes the group also met at the close of the day. At these meetings current issues were discussed, plans for the day's activity made, and important decisions reached. The group was thus a powerful influence in presidential action.

In their individual capacities the staff members of chief importance for our purposes are the assistant to the President, the special counsel, and some of the administrative assistants. The two former, now aided by assistants, are used for personal liaison work; to prepare speeches, reports, and messages; and for various kinds of "trouble shooting." The administrative assistants are assigned to particular areas of operations, varying from time to time but normally including liaison with Congress, minority rights, labor problems, and personnel.

It is apparent that the White House staff is equipped primarily to accomplish the minimum necessary to keep the President's office operating. Apart from their participation in the kitchen cabinet the staff members function as individuals, largely on an ad hoc basis. The arrangement is not intended to provide planning or supervisory, or even adequate dispute-settling, machinery.

The Bureau of the Budget has expanded rapidly since 1937.[6] With a staff now totaling over 500 it has come to be the chief coordinating agency of the federal executive. The original, and still major, function of the bureau is the preparation of the annual budget and its supplements for submission by the President to Congress. Each year the bureau reviews the financial requests of every agency, determines in minute detail what funds may be sought and for what purpose, and submits to the President a proposed budget. Agencies may reverse the bureau only by going over its head to the President—action rarely taken and still more rarely successful. Preparation of the annual budget involves, of course, basic policy decisions as to total federal expenditures, the relationship of expenditures to receipts, the major areas of spending, and similar matters. It also places the bureau in a strategic position to influence, and to some extent control, the policies and activities of the operating agencies.

Capitalizing upon these sources of potential power, and under aggressive directorship, the Bureau of the Budget has extended its activities beyond the mere preparation of budget estimates. It plays an important part in the determination of over-all economic policy. Through its Division of Fiscal Analysis it prepares studies of basic economic conditions and, until the advent of the Council of Economic Advisers, was the only agency attempting over-all long range economic planning.

The Bureau of the Budget also engages in administrative supervision. Its control over budget estimates, as well as its power to make quarterly allotments of agency funds and to set up reserves, enable the bureau to maintain a close watch over the operations of all agencies. In addition the bureau has express authority to study the management of each agency and report to the President recommendations for change. Through its Division of Administrative Management the bureau makes continuous studies of agency management and is often effective in compelling improvements and influencing policy decisions.

The bureau also possesses certain powers to coordinate the administration's legislative program. Under existing executive orders legislation to be proposed by any agency must first be submitted to the bureau for determination that it accords with the President's program. Similarly any statement of agency position on pending legislation, as well as formal testimony before Congressional committees, is subject to clearance by the bureau. The bureau now also maintains a constant

6. For further discussion of the Bureau of the Budget see Chapter 5.

check on the status of various bills embodying the legislative program. All executive orders likewise must be approved by the bureau. In this area the bureau serves more as a clearing house for information and a method of reconciling interagency differences of opinion than as the initiator or supporter of legislative programs.

The bureau likewise has authority to clear all important statistical questionnaires which the agencies wish to use in obtaining information —a substantial, if limited, power to coordinate statistical activities.

In general the bureau performs effectively its task of preparing budget estimates. Its supervision of administrative management, although valuable, has been less significant. As coordinator of the legislative program the bureau has, at least in recent years, played a useful but far from major role. It has little or no share in the important decisions on legislative policy—it was not consulted on the Brannan farm plan—and it has never functioned as an active protagonist for the administration's legislative program. In long-range economic planning the bureau's role has been one of research and advice. It has never operated as an agency for affirmative control. It is to be noted that when wartime pressures for a coordinating agency became urgent it was not the Bureau of the Budget but new agencies—the OWMR and the ODM—that were assigned this task.

The Council of Economic Advisers, created by the Employment Act of 1946, is primarily a research and advisory group on economic policy. The powers conveyed by statute are "to gather timely and authoritative information concerning economic developments and economic trends"; to develop and recommend to the President national economic policies; to make studies and reports to the public on matters of national economic interest; to assist the President in the preparation of his annual Economic Report to the Congress and other reports; and to "appraise the various programs and activities of the Federal Government in light of the policy" of the act and to make recommendations thereon to the President.

The council's budget for staff salaries is limited by the act to $345,000. This provision restricts the size of its staff to about 30 professional employees and severely conditions all its operations. The council undertakes little or no original research, relying upon other agencies for its working data.

The chief activity of the council has been the preparation of an annual report and the drafting of the President's semiannual reports to Congress. These reports contain analyses of economic trends and recommendations for legislative and executive action. In addition the council has maintained a continuous study of the major areas of economic interest and has advised the President on important matters of economic policy.

The council possesses no authority over the operating agencies. The limitation in the size of its staff prevents it from following the activities of those agencies except in a general way. Nor does it participate in many major policy decisions. Thus it too had no advance knowledge of the announcement of the Brannan farm program.

Two other agencies in the Executive Office of the President are designed to coordinate matters relating to national security. The National Security Council, created by the National Security Act of 1947 (as amended in 1949), is composed of the President, the Vice-President, the Secretaries of State and Defense, and the Chairman of the National Security Resources Board. The President may add Cabinet members and certain others, subject to Senate confirmation. The council's function is to advise the President on the domestic, foreign, and military aspects of national security. The council has only a small staff and operates primarily as a top consulting group.

Prior to the mobilization crisis and the establishment of ODM major responsibility for planning the integration of the domestic economy with the military program was entrusted to the National Security Resources Board, likewise established by the National Security Act. This board consists of a chairman and the Secretaries of State, Treasury, Defense, Interior, Agriculture, Commerce, and Labor. Its purpose was to study and prepare plans for military, industrial, and civilian mobilization in the event of war, to establish policies for stock-piling, to work out programs for relocation of industry, and similar matters. The board membership, composed of busy heads of executive departments, does not function as an active body. But provision was made for a large staff, several times that of the Council of Economic Advisers, under the direction of the full-time chairman. Until the outbreak of the Korean crisis the staff devoted itself primarily to mobilization plans and stock-piling problems. As military preparations have accelerated the board's activities and influence have increased.

Apart from the Executive Office of the President other coordinating functions are performed by such agencies as the Civil Service Commission, the Department of Justice, and the General Accounting Office. These activities, however, are not directly related to economic stabilization.

4. Machinery for integration

One of the most seriously neglected aspects of federal administration has been the relations between the executive branch of government and other power groups, both governmental and nongovernmental. Liaison has been maintained at certain critical points but relatively little thought has been given to the stimulation or improvement of vital relationships.

By far the most important problem is the relation between the executive and Congress. The operating agencies, as has been pointed out, usually maintain close association with Congress, its committees, and key members. This is important and necessary but it frequently results in breaking down rather than building up the cohesion of the executive and its ability to carry out a disciplined program. At the top level, where close and harmonious relations are particularly significant, responsibility now rests primarily with the President and certain members of his personal staff. President Truman, in accordance with the example of his predecessor, followed the custom of meeting once a week, usually Monday morning, with the four principal administration leaders—the Vice-President and Majority Leader in the Senate and the Speaker and Majority Leader in the House. At these conferences broad issues of legislative policy and strategy were discussed. The President also spends a substantial proportion of his time in meeting, telephoning, or writing letters to key members of Congress. Presidential messages and broadcasts are likewise utilized to obtain support for the administration's program "on the hill." Presidential patronage has always been, and continues to be, an important source of political persuasion.

The follow-up is entrusted to various members of the White House staff. One of the administrative assistants represents the White House on detailed matters of legislative drafting and compromise. Another administrative assistant handles the political issues—patronage, election support, and similar matters. The special counsel and assistant to the President are available for special jobs. Under President Truman there also existed a close alliance with Leslie Biffle, Majority Secretary of the Senate, who wielded considerable influence with many members of that body.

The Bureau of the Budget, although it has responsibility for certain aspects of legislative coordination, does not participate in legislative lobbying. The Council of Economic Advisers has been divided over its function in connection with legislation. The first chairman consistently took the position that the council should refrain from active participation in pushing the President's legislative program through Congress. The other two members felt that the council should take affirmative responsibility in presenting testimony before Congressional committees and otherwise assisting in securing favorable action on presidential measures affecting economic stabilization. The second chairman, Leon H. Keyserling, followed this policy.[7]

Generally speaking there has been a serious lack of top planning and consistent direction in the executive's relations with Congress.

Party organization likewise has never been fully mobilized in support of the administration's program. President Truman's Monday conferences with his legislative leaders took up issues of party discipline in Congress. The President also met frequently with the chairman of the Democratic National Committee for discussion of patronage and other political problems. But party pressure upon the legislature has on the whole not been effectively implemented. And with rare exceptions there has been no real effort to call into action the party machinery as a means of marshaling public support.[8]

Our federal system of government makes relationships with state and local governments of vital significance. Many of the operating agencies maintain close contact with these groups. Thus one section of the Department of Justice participates with state representatives in drafting uniform state legislation and the agencies dispensing grants-in-aid are in constant touch with state and local agencies. Until recently, however no machinery has existed for liaison with the top levels of the federal executive. Some improvement has taken place since the passage of the Employment Act of 1946, authorizing the Council of Economic Advisers to consult with state and local governments. Yet the potentialities of federal-state-local cooperation have never been fully exploited.

The operating agencies maintain various kinds of relationships with private interest groups. The only regular procedures for such liaison with the top coordinating level are those that have been developed by the Council of Economic Advisers. The Employment Act provides that the council "may constitute such advisory committees and may consult with such representatives of industry, agriculture, labor, consumers . . . and other groups, as it deems advisable." The council has avoided the mistake of creating a single advisory committee along the lines of the OWMR Advisory Board. Rather it has followed the practice of meeting with representatives of particular interest groups separately. This procedure appears to be working successfully.

Effective operation of a complex program in a democracy also demands a two-way flow of information and education between the government and the general public. Various devices for facilitating such communication have developed within recent years, mostly from the

7. For a fuller discussion of the considerations involved see Chapter 13.
8. *Ibid.*

government to the public rather than in the reverse direction. All the operating agencies possess, within the limits of Congressional hostility, public relations staffs. For presentation of the over-all picture main reliance has been upon the President. His speeches, broadcasts, press conferences, messages, and reports constitute a most effective way of reaching the public. The Bureau of the Budget operates almost entirely without publicity. The Council of Economic Advisers, however, has taken as one of its major functions the presentation of economic data to the business world through its reports and studies. No central information service, apart from the World War II Office of War Information, has ever been established.

Most of the operating agencies collect statistical and other data, subject in part to the supervision of the Bureau of the Budget. Some of the agencies have experimented with new techniques for acquiring information not readily obtainable by the normal reporting methods.[9] Much of this data is utilized not only by the operating agencies but by the Bureau of the Budget and the Council of Economic Advisers.

5. *Inadequacies of existing machinery*

The shortcomings of our present peacetime machinery for administering economic policy are clear from the foregoing description. Briefly summarized they are:

1) Nowhere does there emerge from the labyrinth of government organization a clear-cut structure designed to take positive responsibility for the obligation assumed by the government in the Employment Act of 1946 to "use all practical means . . . to promote maximum employment, production and purchasing power."

2) Little has been done to overcome the difficulties arising out of the independence and hostility between legislative and executive branches of government, or to adapt the antiquated procedure of Congress to the complex issues of economic stabilization.

3) The central coordinating agencies now functioning are not authorized or equipped to perform the essential functions of planning and directing an affirmative economic program.

4) Relationships between the central coordinating agencies and other government and nongovernment groups have never been consciously stimulated on a scale necessary for effective operation.

Thus the federal government lacks both an adequate peacetime organization for formulating and administering a coordinated economic program and satisfactory machinery for integrating its operations with the various forces essential to carry out such a program.

9. See Chapter 14.

IV. Creating More Effective Machinery

The weaknesses in our present methods of administration deserve serious attention. Any attempt to prepare a detailed blueprint of administrative reform would, for reasons already made clear, be unrealistic and futile. Progress must be made, as it has been in the past, through a process of continuous experimentation and improvisation. Hence the proposals about to be discussed must be considered merely as illustrative of possible methods of improvement or as pointing the direction in which we should move.

1. Congress

Successful administration of a positive program of economic stabilization would require some modification in the functioning of Congress. The problems here involve both the relations of Congress with the executive and the internal operations of Congress itself.

First of all, there would undoubtedly be necessary an increased delegation of power by the legislature to the executive. The previous chapters have pointed out a number of areas in which greater delegation is essential or at least advantageous. Thus it has been suggested that the President be given authority to change the rate of public expenditures or certain aspects of the tax structure.[10] Other types of delegation may also be found imperative. All of this poses some troublesome problems.

The legal difficulties, arising out of the doctrine that the legislature may not delegate legislative power, can be met by adequate drafting. It appears unlikely that the Supreme Court will strike down a delegation of power for which a reasonable showing of necessity can be made so long as the conditions under which the power may be exercised are carefully defined.

But a more extensive delegation of authority to the executive does raise sharply the fundamental question of vesting excessive power in a single branch of government. The dangers should not be underestimated. But the need for effective government cannot be ignored either. We must search to find whether, in light of recent progress in the science of government, adequate procedures are available or can be devised to avoid undue concentration of authority or to mitigate its consequences.

Certain lines of approach are discernible. Clearly Congress should spell out with some precision the criteria or standards under which the executive is authorized to act. In the case of taxation, for instance, it would seem entirely feasible for Congress to set forth in advance under

10. See Chapters 5 and 6.

what set of economic conditions changes may be made by the executive, what increases or decreases in the rate or changes in exemptions are authorized, what new taxes at what rates may be evoked, and many other specific limitations of this kind. Working out the details of such a measure is a problem for the economists and lawyers. But it is one that with a little ingenuity is open to solution. The overriding requirement, as former Chief Justice Stone has pointed out, is that the criteria of action be "sufficiently definite and precise to enable Congress, the courts and the public to ascertain whether the Administration . . . has conformed to these standards." Where this is done effective opportunity for check on the executive remains.

Again, Congress should specify in some detail the procedures to be followed by the executive in exercising any newly acquired powers. Within recent years sweeping delegations of power to administrative agencies have normally been tempered by procedural provisions designed to safeguard against abuse in administration. Such procedures have included the requirement of notice, opportunity to be heard, a statement of findings and reasons, limited judicial review, and similar matters. The Emergency Price Control Act of 1942 contained a particularly complete arsenal of such devices. The necessary procedural requirements would vary with the circumstances. Thus the advisability of permitting judicial review would depend upon the particular issues at stake; under any circumstances a provision compelling compliance with executive action pending judicial review would probably be necessary. But the precise forms of procedure cannot be detailed here. The point is that, with the growth of the administrative process in the last two decades, many devices are available for keeping delegation of power within bounds. Congress is no longer in the position of issuing a blank check. It can devise means for a controlled delegation.

Another technique for limiting delegated power is the legislative veto. Under this procedure the executive issues a proposed order but the order does not become effective until it has been submitted to Congress and Congress has not, within a specified time, voted to annul the action. The procedure has been used in the various reorganization acts. It has been developed extensively, under different circumstances to be sure, in England. As a means of limiting executive power and narrowing the gap between executive and legislative branches this technique has great potential value.

Finally, Congress still possesses the power of lawmaking, control over appropriations, and an increasingly developed capacity for investigation. Delegated power is always subject to modification or revocation. The power of the purse and the power of inquisition are potent forces in the day-to-day life of every government administrator. So far there are no signs we have reached that point in delegation of authority at which the ultimate power of the legislature tends to wither away.

Thus it is entirely possible to invest the executive with sufficient authority to effectuate a program for stabilization and at the same time preserve adequate control over its actions. Congress, except in extreme emergencies, consistently and rather successfully challenges executive power. So does the judiciary, and at times private interest groups or even the general public. The dangers of a runaway executive appear far less portentous than the dangers of inaction.

Along with greater power to deal with substantive issues must go acceptance by Congress of fuller authority in the President to carry out his responsibilities. This was the central theme of the Hoover Commission reports and their principal contribution. Among the recommendations made by the commission were proposals for continuing presidential authority to submit reorganization plans, elimination of overdetailed legislation unduly restricting the organization of executive agencies, abandonment of the practice of conferring authority upon subordinate officials not subject to presidential control, and strengthening executive control over personnel and fiscal management. These are all applicable to our present problem and acceptance by Congress of such an approach would mark an appreciable advance.

Turning now to the internal structure and procedure of Congress itself, certain changes in the legislative process would appear essential. One of these involves the practice of annual appropriations. The difficulty of planning a program that relies heavily on public expenditures, where appropriations are limited to a period of one year, has been made clear by Gerhard Colm in a previous chapter. No legal obstacle stands in the way of making appropriations available over a number of years. The only Constitutional requirement is that no military appropriation shall be for a longer term than two years. Since Congress retains its amending and revoking power at all times it is difficult to see any valid objection to a more flexible use of the appropriating power, at least as concerns funds particularly crucial for a long-range stabilization program.

Another problem of legislative procedure relates to the coordination of activity within Congress, and especially coordination of the numerous committees which deal with various aspects of economic policy. The solution attempted in the Employment Act of 1946—creation of the Joint Committee on the Economic Report, composed of seven members from each house—has not proved effective. Even less successful has been the effort made in the Legislative Reorganization Act to combine the appropriations and revenue committees of each house into an over-all committee to guide action on the budget. A more satisfactory arrangement would probably be the establishment of a joint committee composed of the chairmen of the key committees in each house, a proposal incorporated in the full employment bill as originally drafted. Although the time available for work on such a joint committee would be severely limited, the members would be to some extent at least bound by its decisions and, equally important, in a strategic position to carry out policies agreed upon. Any real solution of the difficulty, however, would seem to depend upon the evolution of methods for tying together legislative and executive leadership and for intensification of party discipline. These matters are discussed subsequently.

Many other modifications in the internal organization and procedure of Congress have been proposed from time to time. These do not relate peculiarly to the administration of a stabilization program. They will, therefore, not be considered in detail. It is sufficient to observe that any improvement in the operation of Congress makes an important contribution to the success of economic stabilization. Thus the abolition of the seniority system in the appointment of committees, and the institution of a system based upon ability and responsibility to committee, Congress, and party, would go a long distance to make possible effective and coordinated operations. The same may be said of proposals to restore an effective caucus system, modification of the tradition of unlimited debate in the Senate, some expansion of staff assistance, improvement in appropriation procedures, substitution of electric voting for the half-hour roll call in the House, and many others. Sooner or later Congress will be forced to accept these changes, at peril of complete legislative stagnation and frustration.

2. *The operating agencies*

The operating agencies will, of course, continue to perform the varied specific operations that together constitute the program of economic stabilization contemplated in this symposium. Discussion of the detailed activities of these agencies is beyond the scope of this chapter. It is possible here merely to outline in generalized form the basic lines of development which should be pursued.

The responsibility of the operating agencies must include not only the making of immediate decisions within their sphere of activity but the collection of information, a large share in the planning function, the maximum degree of participation in the formulation of policy and program, the greatest leeway for experimentation. The objective should be to give them the widest possible scope of operation, subject only to the minimum supervision and direction essential for the conduct of a coordinated program.

Consolidation and simplification of the operating structure is essential. So also is reorganization within many of the agencies. As a result of the Hoover Commission report and subsequent reorganization legislation the path is open to a basic attack on these problems.

Beyond this the operating agencies should be guided and encouraged in the development of techniques to avoid the inherent tendencies of centralization toward rigidity and loss of initiative. Differences of opinion between agencies, and even within agencies, should be tolerated. Methods of decentralization—both functional and geographic—must be found. The OPA War Price and Rationing Boards and some of the plans for administration of additional river valley developments suggest some of the possibilities here. Careful thought should be given to improved relations with other government agencies, with Congress, its committees and subcommittees, with state and local governments, with political parties, with private interest groups, and with the general public. Underlying everything is the need for improved personnel policies in filling many key positions.

The success of the stabilization program—indeed the very preservation of democratic processes—will depend upon the courage, vision, and social understanding with which these problems are met in the operating agencies.

3. *Machinery for coordination*

An effective program for economic stabilization cannot be administered by the operating agencies left to themselves. The essence of the proposals outlined in the previous chapters is that each of the agencies charged with specific functions must direct its activities toward fulfillment of a planned program designed to maintain a stabilized economy. Thus the Treasury Department and the Federal Reserve Board must exercise their powers in the field of monetary policy with a view to achieving the same basic objectives. The Farm Credit Administration, the Home Loan Bank Board, the Federal Housing Administration, and the Reconstruction Finance Corporation must all pull together in the area of credit expansion and control. The manifold agencies handling public expenditures or dealing with wage-price policy must move in approximately the same direction at approximately the same time.

It follows that there must be some sort of central mechanism—some means of formulating a master plan and directing the operating agencies in its execution. Coordination by voluntary agreement—whether through interdepartmental committees, liaison arrangements between agencies, or infiltration of one agency by another—has not proved effective. Nor is central planning, without directive authority, sufficient. Moreover, since the operating agencies represent strong centrifugal forces any coordinating agency must be vested with presidential powers. Such a coordinating structure has been recognized as essential in periods of war or intensive war mobilization. It is no less vital for mobilization of the government's powers for peaceful objectives.

This central mechanism has three major functions to perform. First, it must be responsible for central planning. This involves the collection of information, its analysis, and the preparation of basic plans. Second, it must formulate a concrete program. This means consideration of proposed plans, consultation with interested agencies and groups, and the making of final decisions subject to presidential approval. Third, there must be supervision and direction of the agencies charged with execution of the program. This requires information as to what these agencies are doing, consultation and decision, and a follow-up to determine whether effective action is being taken.

In attempting to construct central coordinating machinery of this kind we are met at the outset with a fundamental issue involving the relationship of stabilization policy to general economic and social policy. Stabilization is only one aspect of the over-all picture. Other factors are equally important. Thus we must also be concerned with the allocation of resources between various possible uses, and with the maintenance of adequate standards of social welfare. Hence the planning and direction of a housing program requires not only consideration of the effect of such a program upon stabilization but a decision as to the proportion of total resources we wish to devote to housing, the various types of housing to be constructed, the methods to be employed, and other basic policy determinations. Similarly a lending program must take into account the value of encouraging small business or family-size farms. And a social security program must obviously weigh many factors other than its effect upon stabilization of income.

It must therefore be determined whether separate administrative machinery should be established for coordinating stabilization policy alone or whether machinery for this purpose should be devised as part of a broader plan for control of general economic and social policy. Important considerations point to the latter course.

The decisive factor is that these different aspects of general policy cannot readily be separated. As just stated, the formulation of an adequate housing program must necessarily give consideration to all the various aspects of housing policy. Furthermore, machinery created to decide questions of stabilization policy alone would in turn require coordination with the machinery for determination of other issues. Hence it would become necessary to establish a hierarchy of coordination agencies. The experience of the Office of Economic Stabilization during the second world war demonstrates the difficulties of isolating stabilization policy.

For these reasons it would appear that administrative machinery for formulating and directing the stabilization program must become merely one function of machinery established to coordinate general economic and social policy. Even then, this mechanism would have to be integrated with the administration of foreign policy and military policy, as well as other spheres of government operation.

Proceeding from these premises, first consideration should be given to the creation of a central coordinating mechanism out of existing institutions or agencies. Certainly the Cabinet as it has functioned in the past could not serve this purpose. It has been proposed, however, that the Cabinet be strengthened through the creation of a Secretariat. It would be the function of this Secretariat to prepare agenda for meetings, obtain information for Cabinet use, present issues at Cabinet meetings, and function generally as a professional staff of assistants. The British Cabinet relies heavily upon a Secretariat of this kind. The creation of such a staff, provided it remained under presidential direction, would undoubtedly add to the usefulness and importance of the Cabinet. But it would hardly serve to transform the Cabinet into an effective coordinating agency. For the reasons already outlined the Cabinet seems destined to remain largely an advisory council.

Nor does the Bureau of the Budget, in its present or a revised form, constitute a satisfactory central mechanism. The job is broader than the preparation of budget estimates or the technical supervision of administrative management. These are important functions, closely involved with the work of a central agency. They need to be performed by a unit located at some central point. But they are only part of the total operation.

Similarly the Council of Economic Advisers plays a vital but incomplete role in the work of a central coordinating agency. The council's authority is limited to research, study, planning, and reporting. It has no authority to formulate programs or direct the operating agencies in their execution. These latter functions must be performed by a related but separate administrative unit.

It is a fair conclusion, therefore, that some additional machinery of coordination is necessary. Two general lines of approach are possible. One is to supply the President with additional staff assistance assigned to coordinating work. The other is to create a formal coordinating agency, similar in structure and function to the Office of War Mobilization and Reconversion or the Office of Defense Mobilization.

The first approach would not require any drastic reorganization of the Executive Office of the President. The Council of Economic Advisers would remain in much its present form as the central agency for basic economic planning. The statutory limitation upon the size of its staff, however, should be removed. The Bureau of the Budget would continue with its functions of budget preparation, supervision of administrative management, and coordination of the administration's legislative program. The two latter functions should be accentuated, with the bureau taking more initiative than in the past. The task of over-all program formulation and program direction would be performed by the President himself, and for this he would need increased staff aid.

Such staff assistance would consist of an assistant to the President, or perhaps several assistants, each assigned to a particular sector. The assistant would be responsible for spotting issues that required presidential action, making sure that the necessary information was assembled and collated, participating with the President and the interested agency heads in formulating the decision, and to some extent following up the decision to assure its proper execution. Such an assistant might also be empowered to make decisions on certain matters himself, thus reducing the number of issues presented for presidential consideration. But he would in no sense cut across the channels of communication between the President and the Cabinet members, or between the President and the Council of Economic Advisers, or the Bureau of the Budget. He would operate informally as a sort of catalytic agent to facilitate presidential action.

Such an assistant to the President would have a staff of his own, but it would be a very small one. He would absorb some of the functions being performed by the present assistant to the President and the administrative assistants. His job would differ from theirs in that he would devote more conscious attention to coordination and would take more of the initiative in bringing up issues for the President's decision and in representing the President in the execution of policy. In order to accomplish his work effectively he would have to be a person of considerable ability, tact, and prestige.

A plan of this kind has a number of advantages. It would provide substantial aid to the President and encourage him to maintain a higher degree of coordination. It would not create in the Executive Office a powerful, semi-independent figure challenging the President's authority. It would retain unimpaired the lines of authority between the President and his agency heads. And it would cause the least disturbance in existing machinery.

Yet the crucial question is whether such an arrangement would be adequate for the job that needs to be done. Actual experience is the only sure guide. If the machinery of the President's office still did not function effectively then resort to the second approach—a well-staffed coordinating agency—might be desirable.

The creation of a new agency for coordination of economic and social policy leads us into relatively unchartered territory. It is possible only to sketch roughly and in broad outline some of the possibilities and some of the difficulties.

Under such a scheme the coordinating agency should be part of the Executive Office of the President. In it should be placed the three major functions outlined above—planning, formulation of program, and direction of program. It might perhaps be designated the Office of Economic Coordination.

The first question that arises is whether such an Office of Economic Coordination should be headed by a single individual or by a board or commission. On behalf of the multiple head it can be urged that a commission would allow various points of view to be represented; that the decision of a commission, reached after a full discussion among equals and embodying the adjustments necessary to obtain majority support, would be better reasoned and more carefully formulated; and that an impersonal body is in a more strategic position to resist pressures and force agency heads to comply with its decisions. Nevertheless there are important countervailing factors. The problems coming before the Office of Economic Coordination will be multitudinous and will demand prompt and decisive action. Most of the issues will not be of that quasi-judicial character where a multiple-headed tribunal makes its best contribution. More important, and perhaps most decisive, the head of the office must have a close, constant, and informal relationship with the President. This is scarcely feasible, as the experience of the National Resources Planning Board and the Council of Economic Advisers makes clear, when the contacts must be made by a commission rather than an individual. The same is true, to a lesser degree, of relations with agency heads and the legislature. Furthermore many of the advantages of the commission can be secured by creating that form at those places in the structure of the office where it is more suitable. All in all the case for a single head, or director, would seem persuasive.

The director would have to be an individual of national prestige possessing the intimate confidence of the President. He should be equipped with the symbols of power, such as an office in the White House itself. In order to give the President maximum control over his activities he should be removable at the President's discretion.

The Office of Economic Coordination should include two major divisions—planning, and program formulation and direction. The planning function should be entrusted to a Planning Commission. Here the opportunity for broader representation, wider discussion, and enhanced prestige all favor the commission form. The Planning Commission should be responsible for basic research and analysis, recommendation of immediate programs, and preparation of long-range plans. It should serve as a clearinghouse and depository of information. It would maintain close relations with the planning groups in the operating agencies, using their facilities and experience to the greatest extent possible and coordinating their efforts. Its public reports would be an important source of information, education, and persuasion. In these respects the commission would function somewhat as a combination of the National Resources Planning Board and the Council of Economic Advisers.

On the other hand, the commission would report to the director, not directly to the President or to Congress. The function of the commission would be to make expert recommendations rather than decisions on policy. Final policy determinations involve not only technical but political issues: a judgment as to the over-all situation; an estimation of legislative, executive, pressure group, and popular support; a calculation of the means available to carry a plan or program into execution. This task must be performed by the director and others in close association with the President. The President and director would in turn maintain liaison with the legislature, but the commission and its staff would serve as expert advisers to the director rather than to Congress.

The other major division of the Office of Economic Coordination would be responsible for program formulation and direction. Program formulation would be based upon studies made by the Planning Commission, recommendations of the operating agencies, and consultation with government and nongovernment groups. It would embrace both contemplated executive action and legislative recommendations. Such a program would not be confined to substantive matters but would include strategy and plans for carrying its substantive proposals into effect. All basic decisions would, of course, not only be subject to the President's approval but reached in consultation with him and, to the extent possible, in consultation with the Cabinet.

The public features of such a program, including the recommended budget, should be embodied in a presidential report and submitted to Congress at the beginning of each session. This report would replace both the present budget message and the Economic Report required by the Employment Act of 1946. Formulation of the program would be a continuous process, however, for it would need constant revision as conditions changed.

In general the Office of Economic Coordination should be responsible only for the formulation of major decisions. To the extent feasible, subsidiary issues and details should be left to the operating agencies. In the field of housing, for example, the office should include in its program only the broad outlines of housing development, such as the number and character of units to be constructed; it should be the function of the housing agencies to prepare detailed plans implementing the basic decision.

Program direction involves crucial but delicate issues. Generally speaking the Office of Economic Coordination would have to exercise this function affirmatively. A negative policy of merely awaiting events and settling disputes would not be sufficient. The director and his staff would have to take positive responsibility for supervising the execution of whatever program had been agreed upon. In order to accomplish this successfully at least three conditions are essential. In the first place, the director would have to have a constant stream of information coming to him at all times. He and his staff must be aware not only of current problems pending in the agencies but of anticipated developments. And sufficient data must be made available for the reaching of intelligent conclusions.

Secondly, the director should be formally empowered to settle particular issues and to promulgate directives on general policy. In this connection it should be noted that the directive power, while important, is not in itself sufficient. Unless a policy has been carefully worked out in discussion with the operating agencies, and if necessary cleared in advance with the President, the directive is likely to remain only a scrap of paper. The directive, in short, is essentially a device to formalize action, not a potent instrument in itself.

For this reason, and thirdly, the director and his staff would have to follow through to make certain that the program is being genuinely and effectively enforced. The real test of the director's success would come at this point.

Certain limitations upon the supervisory authority of the Office of Economic Coordination must, of course, be imposed. Thus, its powers with respect to the "quasi-judicial" agencies should not include the right to interfere in any specific adjudication of individual rights, difficult as this line is to draw. Again, the whole function of supervision must be exercised with the greatest restraint. Only major issues, or matters vital to the program, should be the concern of the coordinating agency. The drive at all times should be to avoid unnecessary detail, promote the greatest responsibility in the operating agencies, and use their facilities and knowledge to the maximum extent. A difficult balance must be struck between rigid controls on the one hand and isolation from the facts of life on the other.

The director and his office would also take a large measure of responsibility for the legislative features of the program. Again relying upon operating agencies as much as possible, the director must coordinate and direct the executive's efforts to assure favorable Congressional action. This involves supervision over the drafting of legislation, marshaling witnesses and presenting testimony at hearings, negotiating on compromises, and in general full mobilization of the executive lobby.[11]

Concededly, difficult problems of jurisdiction would arise. The line of authority between the Office of Economic Coordination and other parts of the executive branch would not easily be delineated. These issues would have to be resolved by presidential action. They would tend to diminish in volume and importance as jurisdictional fields were gradually mapped out.

Two areas that are particularly enmeshed with economic and social policy are national defense and foreign affairs. Clearly the military program must be closely integrated with the over-all economic and social program. At the same time the principle of civilian control over the military must be maintained. The best solution is probably to make the director a member of the National Security Council and to place the National Security Resources Board in the Office of Economic Coordination. This arrangement would also serve to coordinate economic and foreign policy.

If these proposals were put into effect, the present Council of Economic Advisers would be merged into the Planning Commission. The Bureau of the Budget would abandon its legislative functions and most of its activities in the area of general fiscal policy. Its responsibility would be confined to preparing budget estimates and to supervision of administrative management. The Bureau of the Budget could be placed within the Office of Economic Coordination, where the financial controls would be helpful in securing adherence to policy decisions. In the interests of avoiding overcentralization, however, the preferable solution might be to retain the bureau as an independent agency in the Executive

---

11. Vesting responsibility in the director, rather than the Planning Commission, would tend to resolve the dilemma of the Council of Economic Advisers' relations with Congress, discussed in Chapter 13.

Office of the President. If so, the bureau would have the same relationship to the director and his staff as the operating agencies have.

The White House staff would continue to operate as the President's personal staff. The daily meetings with the President would continue, the director of the Office of Economic Coordination becoming an additional member of this informal group.

Many of these suggested changes in machinery could be effectuated through the President's existing powers under the Reorganization Act. Nevertheless it might be desirable, as demonstrating the genuine intention of both branches of the government to institute an effective program, that the basic machinery be established by legislative action.

Certain persuasive objections can be advanced against the system of coordination here outlined. Most important, perhaps, is the argument that the President would be cut off from his Cabinet heads and other officials now directly responsible to him. At the same time, the director of the Office of Economic Coordination would become a sort of assistant president, possibly with presidential ambitions. As a result, it can be urged, the President would be relegated to the role of a symbolic chief of state with his major functions assumed by an American-type prime minister. On the other hand it might happen that the principle executive officials would refuse to accept the prime minister and the effect would be increased personal bickering and general chaos.

These dangers are real. But they could be avoided through the exercise of a moderate amount of statesmanship by those concerned. The scheme does not contemplate the isolation of Cabinet members from the President. On the contrary, close association in Cabinet meetings and otherwise would be essential. Where disagreement arose between the director and a Cabinet member the latter could always appeal to the President for final decision. The director's authority is based not upon absolute power but upon his standing with the President and upon the fact that, in practice, only major issues could be appealed. An arrangement of this sort has operated successfully for many years in the critical area of finances, where the director of the Bureau of the Budget has occupied the same position on budget policy as is suggested here for general economic and social policy. The experience of the Office of War Mobilization and Reconversion indicates also that the extension of such relationships to the economic and social program should not prove impracticable.

It is indeed likely that the arrangements here outlined would strengthen the President's position rather than weaken it. For the Office of Economic Coordination would serve as a buffer between the President and hundreds of calls upon his time. With this load taken off the President's shoulders he would be more free to concentrate upon the really important issues demanding his attention. As with any delegation of power properly controlled, the effectiveness of the delegator tends to increase rather than diminish.

In any event whatever risks there are might be risks that would have to be run. For there may be no satisfactory alternative. Obviously the President himself cannot do the whole job. Nor can the Cabinet. If other measures fail some institutional arrangement of the nature here suggested may be unavoidable.

A second major objection goes to the question of overcentralization. It is feared that any central mechanism would produce undue concentration of power, excessive rigidity, and all the abuses that follow. For the time being the fear would seem premature. Our present organization of government is more open to criticism as overweighted with checks and balances than as overcentralized. And this reflects the powerful disparate forces which, as previously described, underlie the governmental structure. Whether the dangers materialize in the future would seem to depend upon the exercise of wise statesmanship in avoiding them. Here again there may be no alternative to running the risk.

4. Machinery for integration

It has been stressed throughout these chapters that the administrative machinery of the executive branch does not function in a vacuum. Its activities must be geared not only to the legislature but to other institutions and groups that make or influence policy decisions.

Improvement in these relations, especially with the legislature, will depend very largely upon the extent to which the political party can be welded into a disciplined cohesive force. This development has been discussed by Victor Jones and is outside the scope of the present chapter. It is clear, however, that the President and his staff would have to play a major role in such a transformation of the political party. Presidential patronage, prestige, facilities, and leadership would be essential to its success. These relations with the party organization and the legislature should be handled by the President's personal staff, which would probably have to be materially strengthened for this purpose. The party organization itself would require extensive overhauling and expansion, particularly if it undertook to mobilize popular support for the administration's program through grass-roots activity.

As to state and local governments the coordinating machinery in the Executive Office of the President, whether it be an assistant to the President or an Office of Economic Coordination, should assume responsibility for development of closer liaison, except in the political or party sphere. Thus the coordination of grant-in-aid policy, mentioned by Dahl and Lindblom in Chapter 8, would fall within the scope of its activities. The coordinating office should also maintain a constant relationship with private interest groups on over-all economic and social policy. For reasons already stated, a single advisory council, including representation of all major groups, is often less effective than consultation with the groups separately.

The stimulation of public knowledge about economic trends and policies raises a difficult issue.[12] The American people, and Congress even more, have rightly been reluctant to sanction anything approaching a central propaganda agency. Most of the burden in this area should be borne by the separate operating agencies. Nevertheless there is an important role to be played by the President and his staff. Here also the coordinating machinery in the President's office must take the initiative on the broad issues of economic and social policy.

V. Conclusion

Our system of government is designed to make administration of government policy a difficult process. The formal structure of checks and balances, as well as many of our unwritten traditions, combine to put a series of hazards in the path of swift and efficient action. In addition the kind of administration we ask of our government has its own special difficulties. In many ways it would be simpler to administer a fully owned government enterprise than to administer regulatory controls imposed upon privately owned operations. Thus the task before us is not an easy one. Yet if we can show half the ingenuity and resourcefulness we have demonstrated in other fields we can be confident of success.

In his message transmitting to Congress the report of his Committee on Administrative Management President Roosevelt remarked:

> In striving together to make our Government more efficient, you and I are taking up in our generation the battle to preserve that freedom of self-government which our forefathers fought to establish and hand down to us. They struggled against tyranny, against nonrepresentative controls, against government by birth, wealth, or class, against sectionalism. Our struggle now is against confusion, against ineffectiveness, against waste, against inefficiency. This battle, too, must be won, unless it is to be said that in our generation national self-government broke down and was frittered away in bad management.

12. See Chapter 14.

Will it be said "Democracy was a great dream, but it could not do the job?" Or shall we here and now, without further delay, make it our business to see that our American democracy is made efficient so that it will do the job that is required of it by the events of our time?

I know your answer, and the answer of the Nation, because, after all, we are a practical people. We know good management in the home, on the farm, and in business, big and little. If any nation can find the way to effective government, it should be the American people through their own democratic institutions.

The issues have broadened somewhat and the difficulties intensified. But President Roosevelt's words still pose the challenge before us.

CHAPTER XVI. *A Cross Section of*
Views on Stabilization

REPORTED BY ROBERT F. LENHART

This chapter is an analysis of the reactions of a group of citizens to the proposals in this volume based on a round-table discussion held on December 8–9, 1950, in New Haven, Conn. The round table included three businessmen, a labor leader, a congressman, a banker, an editor of a business publication, a leader of women's groups, four members of the National Policy Committee of Yale University and the editor of the symposium.[1]

Members of the round table had been sent copies of the chapters to be considered well in advance of the meeting and they seemed to be well prepared to discuss many aspects of the complex problem of income stabilization. In terms of current events December, 1950, seemed an unfortunate time to discuss such a problem. The Chinese invasion of Korea had just begun, the defense mobilization of the nation was getting under way, price and wage controls were imminent, and direct allocation of some materials to industry had been started. The machinery of government and much of industry was being placed on a defense footing. The time had passed, at least in a political sense, when the measures proposed in this volume would be appropriate. The direct controls which the proposals on income stabilization were designed to obviate were becoming a part of our economy again. This process has, perhaps, not gone as fast since then as many expected it would. Then, too, a number of the

1. Mr. GEORGE BROOKS, Department of Research and Education, International Brotherhood of Pulp, Sulphite, and Paper Mill Workers; HONORABLE CLIFFORD CASE, U.S. Representative, Sixth District, New Jersey; MR. HENRY J. GUILD, Brightwater Paper Company; MR. HAROLD HODGKINSON, William Filene's Sons Company; MR. S. ABBOT SMITH, Thomas Strahan & Company; MISS ANNA LORD STRAUSS, League of Women Voters; MR. EDWIN THORNE, First National Bank of New York; MR. ROBERT F. LENHART, Rapporteur, Committee for Economic Development; PROFESSOR KENT HEALY, chairman, Department of Economics, Yale University; PROFESSOR V. O. KEY, Department of Political Science, Yale University; PROFESSOR JOHN PERRY MILLER, Department of Economics, Yale University; PROFESSOR MAX F. MILLIKAN, Department of Economics, Massachusetts Institute of Technology; PROFESSOR EUGENE V. ROSTOW, Yale University Law School.

proposals to curb inflation are pertinent to the current situation even though direct controls are invoked.

The chairman, noting the mobilization of the nation, asked that the discussion be in terms of more normal economic conditions than those currently prevailing. He requested members of the round table to look at the proposals for income stabilization as citizens and not as specialists. He pointed out that this volume was designed to cover a very broad area and that a number of disciplines besides economics were involved. He said that heretofore discussions of what the government should do about the economy had been discussions about measures the government could take with respect to inflation and depression without paying adequate attention to the impact of these measures on other objectives of the government. Also, he expressed the thought that income stabilization policy ought to be examined in a more practical context than that which economists frequently consider. Each of the measures considered is a measure which has to be administered by people in a particular institutional framework with particular pressures.

The discussion was informal and touched on ten of the chapters in this volume. Some chapters were covered very briefly while others were debated at some length.

In general the members of the round table approved of the idea of income stabilization as an objective. They asked some rather searching questions about the definition of income stabilization in the course of the discussion. Did it mean full employment at all times or was the stabilization concept one which allowed for some variation in unemployment and in prices and for an increase in productivity? Several members mentioned the value of some unemployment in keeping the economy healthy and said that they felt as much as 10 per cent would sometimes be desirable. In the symposium the economy is regarded as stable if unemployment does not exceed 5 per cent of the labor force and prices do not rise more than 5 per cent per year. The authors emphasize that stabilization must not interfere with increases in productivity and steadily growing output.

More questions were raised on the basic proposition that the government should be responsible for taking appropriate action in case of marked unemployment or inflation. All members of the round table somewhat grudgingly admitted, when pressed, that they thought the government had a responsibility to take action under these conditions. It was generally agreed, however, that the symposium had neglected the individual in discussing income stabilization in terms of government policy alone and that there should be a role for the individual to play in the stabilization process which had not been explored.

The editor explained the viewpoint of the authors, as expressed in the Introduction, namely, that the income stabilization policies proposed in the symposium were expressly designed to minimize direct government controls on the individual and to maintain a predominantly free price system. The authors felt that the economy would function more effectively if individuals were free to pursue their normal goals without adding another complex objective such as income stabilization, which would at times be in conflict with their primary aims. The function of the government would be to establish an environment in which the individual could pursue his normal course without interference. The authors were concerned throughout the volume with the problem of getting the individual and his political representatives to understand the concept of income stabilization as the basis for support of the required public measures for stabilization.

This explanation did not satisfy some members of the round table. They seemed to feel that the stabilization proposals, even though designed by the authors to have as little effect as possible on individual freedom, were top-heavy on the government side and would probably affect individual freedoms to some extent. The two authors present pointed out the effects of instability on individual freedom and human dignity and stated that they had considered the matter covered in their concept of stabilization in a democratic society. There was no real agreement between the authors and the round-table members on this issue. The gap between the two groups on this point is very wide and would seem to indicate the need for more discussion on the subject between various groups in the population and more education.

While not approving entirely the concept of government policy for stabilization the members of the round table were unanimous in stating their belief that there should be much wider public understanding of the stabilization policies and the economic reasoning behind them. They felt that an attempt should be made by the authors to simplify and shorten the material in the symposium so that it could be easily understood by a wide audience. One suggestion was made that the material in the symposium be cut down to a short pamphlet which could be widely distributed.

One of the round-table members stated:

Education is quite crucial. I could point out a large number of places in these papers where it is assumed that there is no bridge, there is no gap between the voter and the expert or that it can be bridged easily or, and this is the more frequent case, there is a plaintive statement that, of course, this depends a great deal upon understanding throughout the population. This is one of the primary problems. Just precisely to what extent is it possible to reconcile these broad democratic objectives with this necessary centralization without undertaking an educational program of a magnitude and of a kind never undertaken before.

Another member said that if an expert in simplification were put to work it should be possible to get an effective, simple statement expressing the major ideas in the symposium. Others agreed that such a pamphlet would be extremely useful if it could be written. There seemed to be considerable faith on the part of round-table members in the ability of the professional writer to present complex ideas simply and palatably to a wide audience.

The authors expressed doubt that such a simplification was possible. The editor pointed out that the authors attempted to write the symposium for an intelligent lay audience but that the technical complexity of the subject had made the task extremely difficult. He said the job of simplification would be a difficult undertaking in itself, which would require special talents and a great deal of effort to avoid distortions.

The round-table members felt that Chapter 3, "A Primer of National Income Analysis," was an effective piece of writing and would help further the objective of a general economic education. However, they thought it would be better if it were possible to make it shorter.

In Chapter 4, "The Role of Economic Forecasting in Income Stabilization," the author reaches essentially a negative conclusion. He says that absolute forecasting is not possible in the present state of our knowledge and that a very small margin of error in a forecast of employment makes the difference between deep depression and wild inflation. He does suggest, however, that conditional forecasting be done. This he defines as a process of analysis from which one can tell roughly the direction in which certain factors are likely to work.

The members of the round table were more optimistic than the author about the use of forecasts. One said that we did not need a razor to do the job but a grub-hoe and that in his opinion the results of this chapter were negative only to highly technical specialists in the field of forecasting. Other members cited their successful use of forecasts in business, in particular areas such as the durable consumers' goods field. The general conclusion of the members was that while forecasting may not be a precision instrument, it is an extremely useful device for showing directions and trends both in government and business.

The editor commented that it is easier to make reasonably useful forecasts of particular markets or segments of markets than it is of such global concepts as the gross national product, total employment, or national income because of the increased number of factors to be considered.

In Chapter 5, "Fiscal Policy and the Federal Budget," the author discussed the use of fiscal policy and the federal budget for stabilization purposes. The basic proposition stated in this chapter is that the budget ought to be considered as a tool of income stabilization policy. He states that in a period of depression it would be desirable to have an unbalanced budget and an increase in expenditures or a reduction in taxes or both, while in times of inflation it would be desirable to have a budget surplus and higher taxes. After some discussion of the limitations of fiscal policy, including the eighteen months' time lag between submitting budget estimates and the actual making of expenditures, and the relative inflexibility of a budget once appropriations are made, the round table agreed generally to the proposition stated above.

Chapter 6, "Taxation and Fiscal Policy," is an extremely technical chapter. Some parts of it were discussed by the round table, other parts received little or no discussion.

The section on the incentive effect of higher taxes—in which the author says that the higher taxes go the harder people will work to gain more disposable income—was disputed by members of the round table. It was their opinion that the first reaction of the wage earner would be to ask for a wage increase to offset the increased taxes withheld from his pay envelope. If this is true a tax increase may be directly inflationary because it induces a wage increase and subsequently a price increase, which is not brought about by an increase in demand.

There was considerable discussion of the effect of increased corporation taxes on the incentive of the managers but with little or no agreement among round-table members.

One member of the National Policy Committee said it was his impression that the management of corporations often takes satisfaction in reporting that they have earned as much per share in spite of paying a larger income tax. One of the round-table members said he was not sure that the adverse incentive impact of higher taxes was felt as quickly by corporations as by wage earners but that it was there nevertheless. Another observed that there were a number of corporation executives in Florida for the winter who did not think it worth while to stay home and work harder to earn an extra bonus because they would lose most of it in taxes. A third reaction was that the management of a corporation must work hard to maintain or increase its net earnings, otherwise the value of its stock would go down. Several members felt that there is a limit to the degree of freedom a corporation has to increase its profits. If it is operating efficiently, a tax increase would make no substantial difference in the incentive of management.

On the proposition of varying taxes in inflation and depression the round table seemed to feel that taxes should be cut in a depression and government expenditures should be cut in an inflation.

In general, members of the round table seemed to agree with the author on the use of taxes as a stabilization device but not with his hunches on the qualitative effects of taxation.

In Chapter 7, "Monetary Policy for Income Stabilization," the author outlines the place of monetary policy in an income stabilization program. This chapter covers a number of proposals for controlling generally the liquidity position of individuals and business firms, including limiting the instability of bank credit, which the author considers the principal function of monetary policy. He says monetary policy can not be operated countercyclically in any important way, but that it ought to be used to prevent the fluctuations of bank credit from acting as a destabilizer, which actually intensifies booms and depressions.

One of the members said that credit could be broken down into two major segments: first, consumer credit and, second, commercial credit. He said that consumer credit is highly inflationary while commercial credit is neutral. In his opinion there should be controls on consumer credit in times of inflation. On commercial credit, most of which, he said, goes into increased production, he would leave control to the judgment of the banks. Tight government control of all credit would tend to limit the amount of credit available over-all and would probably build up interest rates too high. This would inhibit the increase in production needed in times of inflation to meet the increased aggregate demand.

The author felt that credit controls affecting installment credits, stock exchange credits, mortgage credits, and other qualitative credit controls were a third choice. He is generally opposed to them because they have a special impact on particular groups of people whose behavior should be no more instable than the behavior of other groups which control cannot touch directly. He favors general control of all credit and would let all claimants for credit take their chances under general credit controls.

It was pointed out that the American Federation of Labor opposes qualitative credit controls on the basis that a great many wage earners can enjoy the fruits of our abundant economy only on a hand-to-mouth basis.

Most of the members favored consumer credit controls as an immediate means of cutting consumption of consumer durables and the construction of additional housing.

On the question of general credit restrictions which would tighten up private spending for plant and equipment in time of inflation, the members agreed that credit restriction was preferable to direct controls.

After discussion of the secondary reserve proposal to force banks to hold government bonds or an equivalent cash reserve, the Federal Reserve peg on interest rates, and other credit control devices, members of the round table agreed on indirect controls on credit as one part of the income stabilization program, although they did not agree on how this could best be done.

Chapter 8, "Variation in Public Expenditure," examines the use of public expenditures as a stabilization device, particularly on the depression side. The authors describe the ways in which public expenditures affect the level of income. They attempt to set up general criteria for public expenditure and come out with a formula. They say that expenditure ought to achieve economy, the maximum result from a minimum of expenditure, and that public expenditure always ought to be made in response to some clear public decision on the part of as wide a group of the electorate as possible. They point out that the over-all level of public expenditure from the standpoint of income stabilization should be examined and considered at the national level, but that fundamentally control should be maintained over expenditure at the local level in order to satisfy the democratic criterion.

The authors propose that in time of depression the federal government provide nonspecific allocation of funds in the form of grants-in-aid for local and state governments. The local government would receive the funds and spend them as it spends its own money, thus contributing to stabilization. This would mean that local governments would receive aid from the federal government to maintain its services, such as police, fire, etc., which it would not otherwise be able to maintain at appropriate levels when local revenues decline. The authors also provided some interesting figures on how long it takes to get public works started in order to get maximum employment.

A number of questions were raised by the round table about such grants-in-aid. One question involved the building up of vested interests with powerful support in Congress, so that once these grants-in-aid were started they could not be stopped when the need for them dropped. Other questions were raised about the wisdom with which the funds would be used by local governments and the size of the bureaucracy needed to administer such grants.

One of the members pointed out that Congress generally considers grants-in-aid on the basis of the merits of a particular project such as housing, school aid, highways, etc., rather than as a means of expanding or contracting the economy. He thought, however, that if the basis for the grants-in-aid was made clear to Congress it might be accepted for highway construction and other continuing programs which were already receiving federal help. He did not think Congress would make a grant of money to localities for ordinary operating expenses.

Another member said he thought that, on the whole, there was a good case for local spending as against national spending in time of depression because in that way there would be a wide decentralization of spending based on many local standards rather than one uniform set of standards imposed from the top. He did not feel, however, that this would necessarily meet the criterion of democracy the authors set up as the basis for local spending. He said it would merely transfer control over spending from one group of officials in the national government to the particular local officials in power at the time.

There seemed to be a lack of enthusiasm on the part of members of the round table to the proposals in this chapter, partly because they did not feel that it was politically feasible on account of the traditional attitude of Congress toward the grant-in-aid and because of the fear of building up powerful pressure groups to maintain the grants after the condition for which they were made had passed.

In the opinion of your rapporteur the proposals in this chapter are the kind of drastic measure which are not enacted until a crisis exists. Then and only then will such a proposal be considered and perhaps get the acceptance of a large number of people.

In Chapter 9, "Techniques for Influencing Private Investment," the author points out that the most important single source of fluctuations, in a quantitative sense, is the fluctuation in business and capital expenditure. He is concerned about stabilizing the level of private investment, particularly in keeping the level of investment up during a period of depression. He discusses the importance of the credit position, the availability of funds for investment, and the tax situation.

The members discussed this chapter briefly. Several suggestions were made. One was to lower the capital gains tax in time of depression so that a man would be encouraged to invest his funds and be able to realize a gain at a lower tax than presently prevails. Another was that faster depreciation be allowed on investments in time of depression, perhaps to be charged off at any time the investor chose. A further suggestion was to drop the tax imposed on common stock options. It was also mentioned that in time of depression the government, through guaranteeing mortgages with long maturities, low down payments, and low interest rates, might stimulate the construction of housing. It was suggested that this might also be done in other types of capital expansion.

While many ideas were expressed in the discussion no conclusions were reached on this problem.

In Chapter 11, "Labor Policy, Full Employment, and Inflation," the author states that government wage-price policy is not an effective instrument of business cycle control. His main thesis is that the gradually developing structure of the labor movement may be such as to thwart any effort to produce stability in the price and income level by other means because the resistances to wage advances are gradually disappearing. He cites the increase in the power of unions to force increases in wages where collective bargaining at the industry-wide level exists. Also, he points out that if employers know that all their competitors must face the same sort of wage boost resistance to the boost is much reduced. The author believes that perfectly genuine and proper objectives of labor unions and perfectly genuine and proper objectives of business firms are likely to lead, because of the change in the institutional structure, into a situation where there is continued repercussion between wages and prices which leads to an inflationary movement even in the absence of the pressure of spending in excess of the current level of potential output.

A member of the round table criticized this chapter sharply for skirting the issue of labor monopoly and for not acknowledging that the objectives of labor leadership are quite different institutionally from those of the rank and file. In his opinion the interests of the union membership are plainly on the side of stabilization while those of labor leadership may not be. He said that the author generalized too broadly about the methods of operation of labor unions and that there was wide variation in the scope of collective bargaining agreements which was not reflected in the analysis by the author. He suggested that more facts about the resistance of employers to wage raises would show that labor is relatively weak and that employer resistance has not been lowered significantly by institutional changes. This member of the round table said that unions have their own objectives and aspirations, which are not necessarily in the public interest any more than the objectives of any other organization.

The other members felt that this chapter should be more realistic about the attitude of labor. They suggested more careful study and consideration of the actual facts in collective bargaining before the author reaches a firm conclusion on the effect of labor union policies on income stabilization.

In the discussion of full employment in this chapter members of the round table felt that the author did not relate union strength or the strength of upward wage pressures to full employment particularly but more to changes in the structure of the labor movement. One member observed that he interprets full employment to mean full production and that in the effort to get full employment we increase the volume of credit and bring about pressure for wage increases, and the result is inflation—which is the opposite of what we want.

The editor agreed with this analysis and said that the objective of full employment may be wholly inconsistent with the objective of stable prices because full employment may produce forces which push prices up.

Another round-table member pointed out that full employment introduces significant changes into the internal economies of plants which has an extremely important effect on productivity. At times of full employment relatively inefficient workers are hired, of necessity, causing the efficiency of a plant to drop. When there is some unemployment these men can be dropped and better men hired. This can bring about sharp increases in productivity.

Members of the round table felt that this subject had not been adequately covered, although there was some agreement with the conclusions of the author.

In the discussion of Chapter 13, "The Political Framework of Stabilization Policy," the members of the round table strongly urged the need for objective economic information so that individuals would have a sound basis for making their own economic decisions. They pointed out that the only source of general economic analysis in the government is the Council of Economic Advisers, which is nonobjective, since it represents the viewpoint of the administration.

In this chapter it is recognized that the Council of Economic Advisers is not and cannot be wholly "nonpolitical" in the best sense of the word because it must advise the President on policy. The author suggests that a council of economic advisers be established for the minority party so that a balance of sorts might be achieved. The author also makes the point that economic policy is never economic policy alone but is also social and political policy as well because of the noneconomic impacts that exist in any policy.

After much discussion of the point some members of the round table seemed to agree with the author while others were of the opinion that an objective, nonpolitical economic analysis would be feasible and desirable. It was agreed by all members that there should be continuous pressure for the highest professional standards in the collection and analysis of data by the government and that in the reports of the Council of Economic Advisers there should be a factual part separate from the policy recommendations.

On the criticism of our present political party system and the recommendations for its reform members of the round table disagreed with the author. One said:

> I believe we have the best political system in the world, and that the reason why it is the best is that it is not a system in which our political parties are sharply divided on lines of program and policy. The drawing together of all kinds of people within both parties is perhaps the greatest value of our two-party system and anything which would tend to divide the parties along economic or social lines would be most undesirable. The first essential of any political system is to produce domestic tranquility and to preserve it. And our present political system does just that.
>
> An argument frequently made in support of a more "responsible" party system is that the "inefficiency" of our present system constantly leads to the assumption of more power by the President and a reduction in the importance of Congress. To me that argument is not too convincing. But at least one, and I think several, of the authors here urge that our political system be "reformed" so as to give the President *complete* power with respect to income stabilization. They want the President to be able to impose his decisions through party discipline, protecting members of congress from constituents who don't like those decisions, and punishing members who fail to go along.
>
> It seems to me highly doubtful that our present knowledge of economics and our present technical equipment are sufficiently developed to warrant real confidence that the best experts available will agree with any certainty on what measures should be taken, and when they should be taken, to maintain an agreed level of economic stability.[2] If our present economic knowledge and technical equipment are thus inadequate, it would seem unwise in itself that anyone should have such absolute control over our entire economic life and utterly wrong to destroy the great values of our present political system in order to place such power in the hands of the President. Is it not likely that when we have reached the stage where our economic wisdom and technical skills permit sufficiently accurate conclusions as to the kind and timing of measures necessary for this purpose that they will meet with such general public acceptance that we shall not need a dictator to apply them?

2. See Chapter 4, above.

CONCLUSIONS

The members of the round table agreed that the symposium was a very valuable document because it takes into account the pressures of various interests which operate in our society and the conflicts of objectives which exist in the policies of government and between levels of government. Even though they did not agree completely with the findings of this volume they felt that its findings should be widely disseminated in simplified form for educational purposes. This point was emphasized throughout the two-day meeting. To some extent it represented a high degree of faith in the ability of the professional writer to simplify complex economic reasoning to some degree. A feeling was evident that in a democracy economic and social concepts must be made simple so that the voters can comprehend them adequately.

A second point which came up again and again in the discussion was the importance of the individual. Members of the round table stated strongly that there should be a place in any stabilization program for the individual; they thought the authors turned to government for a program which seemed to exclude the individual. The authors pointed out the reason for the stabilization program was to maintain the freedoms of the individual and that freedom would be lost if the extreme fluctuations of our economy were not stabilized. No real meeting of minds between the members of the round table and the authors was achieved on this point.

A good summary of the reactions of most members of the round table to the symposium was given by one of them:

> This document has enormous value because it re-examines the concept of full employment at dozens of points throughout the volume. The volume notes that full employment conflicts with some other objective or may conflict and that if you want to pursue the objective of stabilization you've got to be prepared to do some rather tough thinking and perhaps make some real sacrifices of other objectives to achieve it. Finally, we have the hope that a great deal more individual initiative can be retained than do the authors. They seem to regard individual initiative as rather a vain hope in many fields. The members of the round table are closer together on this point than any of us are to the authors. I think they should emphasize rather sharply those points at which there will be restriction on individual action so that you will stimulate careful thinking on the part of readers.

Index